DATE DUE

FEB 2 0 2002	
MAR 1 9 2002	
FEB 0 5 2003	
FEB 2 7 2003	
SEP 3 0 2004	

BRODART   Cat. No. 23-221

MOOD DISORDERS ACROSS THE LIFE SPAN

MOOD DISORDERS ACROSS THE LIFE SPAN

Edited by

Kenneth I. Shulman
University of Toronto

Mauricio Tohen
Harvard Medical School

Stanley P. Kutcher
Dalhousie University

WILEY-LISS

A JOHN WILEY & SONS, INC., PUBLICATION

New York • Chichester • Brisbane • Toronto • Singapore

Library of Congress Cataloging in Publication Data:
Mood disorders across the life span / edited by Kenneth I. Shulman,
    Mauricio Tohen, Stanley P. Kutcher.
        p.   cm.
    Includes index.
    ISBN 0-471-10477-9 (cloth : alk. paper)
    1. Affective disorders. 2. Affective disorders—Age factors.
I. Shulman, Kenneth I., 1949–   . II. Tohen, Mauricio.
III. Kutcher, Stanley P.
RC537.M663   1996
616.89'5—dc20   96-15350

CONTENTS

THE NECESSITY OF A LIFELONG PERSPECTIVE ON BIPOLARITY

It is customary to divide our specialty by age into child and adolescent psychiatry, adult psychiatry, and geriatric psychiatry. When I trained in psychiatry in the late sixties, I was taught that manic–depressive illness is a disorder of adults; I was also taught that with few exceptions most childhood mental problems were transitory "adjustment" disorders which would disappear with the attainment of maturity. When I began my clinical research career in Memphis, I had the privilege to examine, in our mood clinic, a very large number of patients during their mild and grave episodes of illness as well as their "well intervals" over a period of two decades. This gave me the opportunity to observe their stormy lives and tragedies, their hopes and aspirations, their achievements, their loves and (multiple) marriages, and their families and children. While the episodic nature of these phenomena was the most apparent manifestation of their malady, it soon became obvious to me that what best defined these individuals was their special temperaments. Indeed, retrospectively, many could be described as dysthymic (melancholic), hyperthymic (sanguine), or cyclothymic (labile-choleric) for years before the onset of the florid illness. We defined temperaments, operationally, as subclinical or subaffective traits that characterized the habitual condition of the patient between clinical episodes. That the roots of these temperamental traits were to be found in childhood could be substantiated in the observation that many of the children of manic–depressive patients exhibited the very same temperamental traits. In the conventional language of child psychiatry, however, these traits were often considered manifestations of "conduct" or "externalizing" disorders. The utility of the temperamental descriptions we proposed resides in the continuity of subaffective and affective manifestations, thereby describing one morbid process as Kraepelin had originally envisioned.

Studies in child, adolescent, and adult psychiatry are now converging in support for such a unified perspective (as testified, for example, by a recent National Institute of Mental Health conference that brought together clinical scientists working on child, adolescent, and adult bipolarity). Although hypomanic and mixed manic children have been described, the preponderant childhood antecedents to adult bipolarity appear to be irritable–depressive or dysthymic; mania most characteristically—often explosively—appears post-pubertally. Puberty and adolescence also seem to herald the onset of cyclothymic moodiness which eventually crystallizes into a bipolar II pattern in early adulthood. The age of onset of hyperthymia has not been determined but, like the others, it appears to be in the juvenile years; this temperament too can evolve into adolescent mania or, more commonly, develop into major depressive episodes much later in life. Prospective data have further demonstrated the predictive power of labile-cyclothymic and energetic-hyperthymic temperaments in the switch from "unipolar" major depression to bipolar II during the mid-adult years. Such data testify to the continuous liability of the affective temperaments to develop clinical episodes of a cyclic nature.

The foregoing is a theoretical framework for understanding the continuity of the bipolar process between its childhood and adult expressions. As observed in contemporary psychiatric practice, the peak ages of onset for manic–depressive illness are in the teens, twenties, and thirties. Factors that may aggravate the course of bipolarity and bring on major episodes at a juvenile age (as some believe is happening) are not fully understood. They might include high genetic loading for manic–depressive illness which may in part be due to assortative mating between two affectively ill individuals; genetic anticipation (as proposed by the Johns Hopkins research team); substance abuse, especially stimulants and alcohol; teen pregnancy with post-partum episodes; ADHD or attention deficit hyperactivity disorder and so-called "borderline" personality disorder (although it is not clear to what extent these two disorders are distinct from the affective temperaments described earlier). Some—notably Koukopoulos—have even invoked the "high stimulation" that is characteristic of the current "media age" which, given the substrate of a vulnerable temperament, could lead to sleep deprivation and precipitation of major episodes. This style of reasoning also blames the excessive utilization of antidepressants which might provoke manic episodes earlier in the course of a cyclic depressive disorder. In the 1960s and 1970s when many psychotic adolescents and young adults were diagnosed as "schizophrenic," the prescription of neuroleptics, though not curative, may have paradoxically stabilized the course of the illness at least in the short term; in some cases tardive dyskinesia was no doubt the price of such stabilization. Thus, given the dangers of classical neuroleptics—and possibly that of many conventional antidepressants—for bipolar illness, early and accurate diagnosis and the institution of mood stabilizers as the mainstay of treatment for this long-term illness become paramount. Such a change, so crucial for secondary prevention, will not occur without adopting a lifelong perspective on manic–depressive illness.

Manic–depressive illness is a disorder with high mortality due to suicide, accidents, and possibly cardiovascular disease. Lithium is the only one of the mood stabilizers that has been used long enough to provide sufficient data for proper statistical analysis: data from mood clinics in this country and Europe converge in suggesting a major prophylactic effect against mortality, particularly suicide. Current practice patterns indicate that many, if not most, manic–depressive patients seen in tertiary care centers as well as in private practice are receiving multiple mood stabilizers, including carbamazepine and divalproex. Is this an indication that the illness has acquired a more malignant course? Or is this a function of post-DSM-III diagnostic practice which leads to the identification of the illness in its severest psychotic forms as well as complicated phases with alcohol and substance abuse comorbidity? I have already invoked the role of antidepressant prescriptions, which coupled with the current and understandable reluctance to utilize neuroleptics that followed their widespread use prior to 1980 may have contributed to the more severe and complex evolutive forms of the illness. This point of view is scientifically largely unproven, but clinically compelling. Clinicians must, in their day to day practice, come to grips with the timing, dosage (hopefully low), and duration (hopefully short) of antidepressants in the long-term course of this illness. Even the most "benign" antidepressants from a cycling standpoint (e.g., tranylcypromine, buproprion), can aggravate at times the course of bipolar disorder. Patients can be stuck in protracted mixed states or depressions that are punctuated with very brief hypomanic periods; ECT should be seriously considered in these patients (instead of an endless trial of antidepressants). The long-term course of bipolar disorder presents many challenges to the physician in charge of a large number of these patients; in the absence of the requisite science to help us meet these challenges, we often have to rely on what has been learned in clinical practice from the long-term course of other patients. Rational polypharmacy—including the short-term judicious use of classical and novel neuroleptics—often needed in the care of our patients can best be instituted in mood clinics that can weigh, for each patient, the advantages and disadvantages of these medications in combined use. Ideally, such clinics should not only take care of the patients requesting treatment, but their entire family, as well as their children, and be prepared to institute psychoeducation and other preventative measures.

Elderly bipolar patients present even greater challenges because of comorbidity of medical and neurologic disease. In some, the illness is a recurrence in their sixties or seventies of episodes experienced much earlier in life and which may have been mild and ignored. In others, with lesser genetic loading for affective illness, comorbid physical disease seems to play a precipitating role. It would be of interest, within the framework of the temperament–illness continuum presented here, whether subclinical temperamentality would serve as a predisposing factor in such late-onset cases. These elderly bipolars often respond well to the same interventions that are effective in younger bipolar patients, testifying indirectly to the neuropharmacologic and/or psychobiologic underpinnings which seem to characterize the lifelong nature of the illness.

For physicians in Greco-Roman times, the biology of the illness resided in the temperaments, hence the terms "melancholic" (black bile), "choleric" (yellow bile), and "sanguine" (excessive blood). Modern psychobiology is still in search of these humours and has invoked, respectively, norepinephrine, serotonin, and dopamine. Although the last neuro-humour is the least studied in manic–depressive illness, it would be a logical substrate in that form of the disorder that is characterized by comorbidity with ADHD and stimulant abuse. A "hot spot" on chromosome 5 may underlie such a bipolar subtype, as preliminary genetic analyses by my San Diego colleague, John Kelsoe, seem to indicate. I am signing off with this yet unproven example to further highlight the heuristic utility of a developmental approach to this grand and ageless illness.

HAGOP S. AKISKAL

Professor of Psychiatry
Director of the International Mood Clinic
University of California at San Diego

REFERENCES

Akiskal HS (1995): Developmental pathways to bipolarity: Are juvenile-onset depressions prebipolar? J Am Acad Child Adolesc Psychiatry 34:754–763.

Akiskal HS (1995): Toward a temperament-based approach to depression: Implications for neurobiologic research. Adv Biochem Psychopharmacol 49:99–112.

Akiskal HS, Maser JD, Zeller P, Endicott J, Coryell W, Keller M, Warshaw M, Clayton P, Goodwin FK (1995): Switching from "unipolar" to bipolar II: An 11-year prospective study of clinical and temperamental predictors in 559 patients. Arch Gen Psychiatry 52:114–123.

The idea for an academic treatise on the topic of mood disorders across the life span emerged from the unique clinical, research, and personal relationship among this book's three editors—Ken Shulman, Mauricio Tohen, and Stan Kutcher. Ken Shulman and Mauricio Tohen collaborated on a series of studies regarding mania in the geriatric population while working together at the McLean Hospital. Ken Shulman and Stan Kutcher collaborated on studies of pharmacotherapy and neuroendocrinology in geriatric depression while Stan was a "fellow" on Ken's geriatric service at Sunnybrook.

Each of the editors has furthermore developed an area of expertise that complements each others' interests. All are known for their research and clinical activities in the area of mood disorders—Stan Kutcher in children and adolescents, Mauricio Tohen in adults, and Ken Shulman in the elderly.

As recent colleagues at Sunnybrook Health Science Centre, University of Toronto, Stan Kutcher and Ken Shulman were able to compare ideas and experiences arising from their clinical and research activities. They recognized that combining their perspectives and understanding, derived primarily from work in their particular section of the life cycle, identified a number of important issues in the developmental aspects of mood disorder—mood disorders across the life span. Mauricio Tohen soon joined them in discussing and developing these issues further, following the collaborative work on geriatric mania.

These deliberations soon became organized into a number of distinct themes that were also beginning to emerge sporadically in the psychiatric literature. Epidemiology and diagnosis, clinical course, optimal acute and long-term treatment and outcome— their continuities and differences across the life cycle—became the focus of debate. As this process continued, it became apparent that each participant had much to learn from each others' perspectives and expertise. This learning intensified and broadened as various colleagues were brought into the discussions. Following from this, the three editors, along with Hagop Akiskal, Ross Baldessarini, Gabrielle Carlson, and Raymond DePaulo, presented a symposium at the American Psychiatric Association Meeting in Philadelphia in 1994 focusing on mania throughout the life span. They subsequently organized a symposium, which was presented at the Canadian Psychiatric Association Meeting in Ottawa in 1994, on the broader theme of mood disorders across the life span. The book was born somewhere along the way.

In this book, we have attempted to bring together a first-rate group of clinical researchers to focus on this life span approach. We divided the book into age-related sections for the reader who wants to review a particular age-specific area. Within each of these age-related sections, there are two subsections, depression and mania. Each of these subsections are divided into three chapters that cover the foci identified above: epidemiologic and diagnostic issues, course and outcome, and treatment. As each of these chapters occurs in each age-related section, the reader is able to pursue information and ideas across the life cycle, simply by reading each chapter in developmental sequence. We hope that this organization of the material will encourage both the growth of special age-related knowledge about mood disorders and at the same time provide a wider developmental perspective of these disorders across the life cycle.

We begin the book with a few chapters that provide the conceptual foundation for this life-cycle approach. These chapters deal with models of classification and genetics—both of which cut across the life cycle and yet are profoundly influenced by it (e.g., the concept of genetic anticipation). These chapters will provide the reader with a solid base for understanding the issues that arise in the remainder of the text.

Our hope is that each reader will enjoy this developmental understanding regarding mood disorders as much as we have done and continue to do. In putting together this volume, we have learned from each other and from our colleagues who have shared their knowledge and wisdom. We thank them for their valuable contributions. The strengths of this volume are theirs, the weaknesses rest with us. Additionally, we should like to thank Ginger Berman at John Wiley & Sons for her editorial direction and encouragement. We also thank Christine Punzo and Fiona Stevens for guiding the project to its completion. The staff and patients at the McLean Hospital and Sunnybrook Health Science Centre provided us support and raised our awareness of the limits of our knowledge. We would like this book to be in some way our appreciation for that as well.

KENNETH I. SHULMAN
MAURICIO TOHEN
STANLEY P. KUTCHER

CONTRIBUTORS

Hagop S. Akiskal, UCSD, 9500 Gilman Drive, La Jolla, California 92093-0603

Ross J. Baldessarini, Mailman Research Center 316, Harvard University, McLean Hospital, 115 Mill Street, Belmont, Massachusetts 02178-9106

Boris Birmaher, Western Psychiatric Institute and Clinic, University of Pittsburgh, Division of Child and Adolescent Psychiatry, 3811 O'Hara Street, Pittsburgh, Pennsylvania 15213

Robert J. Boland, Department of Psychiatry, Miriam Hospital, 164 Summit Avenue, Providence, Rhode Island 02906

Gabrielle A. Carlson, Department of Psychiatry and Behavioral Science, State University of New York at Stony Brook, Putnam Hall, South Campus, Stony Brook, New York 11974-8790

Martin G. Cole, Department of Psychiatry, St. Mary's Hospital, 3830 Lacombe Avenue, Montreal, Quebec, Canada, H3T 1M5

J. Raymond DePaulo, Department of Psychiatry and Behavioral Sciences, The Johns Hopkins Hospital, 600 North Wolfe Street, Baltimore, Maryland 21287-7279

Kelly L. Dunn, Department of Psychiatry, Sheppard and Enoch Pratt Hospital, 6501 North Charles Street, Baltimore, Maryland 21204

Carol R. Essom, Department of Psychiatry and Behavioral Sciences, Emory University School of Medicine, P.O. Box AF, Atlanta, Georgia 30322-4990

Gianni L. Faedda, Department of Psychiatry, Albert Einstein College of Medicine, and Research Division, Bronx Children's Psychiatry Center, Bronx, New York 10461

Alastair J. Flint, Department of Psychiatry, The Toronto Hospital (General Division), 8 Eaton North, Room 238, 200 Elizabeth Street, Toronto, Ontario, Canada, M5G 2C4

Barbara Geller, Department of Psychiatry, Washington University School of Medicine, 4940 Children's Place, St. Louis, Missouri 63110

Nathan Herrmann, Department of Psychiatry, Sunnybrook Health Science Centre, University of Toronto, 2075 Bayview Avenue, Toronto, Ontario, Canada, M4N 3M5

Paul E. Keck, Jr., Biological Psychiatry Program, Department of Psychiatry, University of Cincinnati, College of Medicine, P.O. Box 670559, 231 Bethesda Avenue, Cincinnati, Ohio 45267-0559

Martin B. Keller, Department of Psychiatry, Butler Hospital, 345 Blackstone Boulevard, Providence, Rhode Island 02906

Geri F. Kmetz, Department of Psychiatry, University of Cincinnati College of Medicine, P.O. Box 670559, 231 Bethesda Avenue, Cincinnati, Ohio 45267-0559

Stanley P. Kutcher, Department of Psychiatry, Dalhousie University, Camp Hill Medical Center, 1763 Robie Street, Halifax, Nova Scotia, Canada, B3H 3G2

Joan Luby, Department of Psychiatry, Washington University School of Medicine, 4940 Children's Place, St. Louis, Missouri 63110

Peter Marton, Department of Psychology, St. Joseph's Hospital, 50 Charlton Avenue East, Hamilton, Ontario, Canada, L8N 4A6

Susan L. McElroy, Biological Psychiatry Program, Department of Psychiatry, University of Cincinnati, College of Medicine, P.O. Box 670559, 231 Bethesda Avenue, Cincinnati, Ohio 45267-0559

Francis J. McMahon, Department of Psychiatry and Behavioral Sciences, The Johns Hopkins University School of Medicine, Meyer 3-181, 600 North Wolfe Street, Baltimore, Maryland 21287-7328

Charles B. Nemeroff, Department of Psychiatry and Behavioral Sciences, Emory University School of Medicine, P.O. Box AF, Atlanta, Georgia 30322-4990

George Papatheodorou, Department of Psychiatry, Sunnybrook Health Science Centre, University of Toronto, 2075 Bayview Avenue, Toronto, Ontario, Canada, M4N 3M5

Peter V. Rabins, The Johns Hopkins Hospital, Meyer 279, 600 North Wolfe Street, Baltimore, Maryland 21287-7279

Anthony J. Rothschild, Consolidated Department of Psychiatry at Harvard Medical School, McLean Hospital, 115 Mill Street, Belmont, Massachusetts 02178-9106

A. John Rush, Department of Psychiatry, Southwestern Medical Center, St. Paul Professional Building #1, 5959 Harry Hines Boulevard, Suite 600, University of Texas, Dallas, Texas 75235

Neal D. Ryan, Western Psychiatric Institute and Clinic, University of Pittsburgh, Division of Child and Adolescent Psychiatry, 3811 O'Hara Street, Pittsburgh, Pennsylvania 15213

Kenji W. Sax, Biological Psychiatry Program, Department of Psychiatry, University of Cincinnati, College of Medicine, P.O. Box 670559, 231 Bethesda Avenue, Cincinnati, Ohio 45267-0559

Kenneth I. Shulman, Department of Psychiatry, Sunnybrook Health Science Centre, University of Toronto, 2075 Bayview Avenue, Toronto, Ontario, Canada, M4N 3M5

Michael A. Strober, Neuropsychiatric Institute & Hospital, School of Medicine, University of California, Los Angeles, 760 Westwood Plaza, Los Angeles, California 90024-1759

Trisha Suppes, Department of Psychiatry, Southwestern Medical Center, St. Paul Professional Building #1, 5959 Harry Hines Boulevard, Suite 600, University of Texas, Dallas, Texas 75235

Richard Todd, Department of Psychiatry, Washington University School of Medicine, 4940 Children's Place, St. Louis, Missouri 63110

Leonardo Tondo, Department of Psychiatry, University of Cagliari and Lucio Bini Center for Mood Disorders Research, Cagliari, Sardinia, Italy

Mauricio Tohen, McLean Hospital, Harvard University, 115 Mill Street, Belmont, Massachusetts 02178-9106

Adele C. Viguera, Consolidated Department of Psychiatry at Harvard Medical School, McLean Hospital, 115 Mill Street, Belmont, Massachusetts 02178-9106

Douglas E. Williamson, Western Psychiatric Institute and Clinic, University of Pittsburgh, Division of Child and Adolescent Psychiatry, 3811 O'Hara Street, Pittsburgh, Pennsylvania 15213

Robert C. Young, The New York Hospital and Cornell Institute of Geriatric Psychiatry, Westchester Division, 21 Bloomingdale Road, White Plains, New York 10605

Carlos A. Zarate, Jr., McLean Hospital, Harvard University, 115 Mill Street, Belmont, Massachusetts 02178-9106

MOOD DISORDERS ACROSS THE LIFE SPAN

PART I

INTRODUCTION

CHAPTER 1

Evolving Clinical Characteristics or Distinct Disorders?

TRISHA SUPPES and A. JOHN RUSH

Department of Psychiatry, Southwestern Medical Center, University of Texas, Dallas, TX 75235

INTRODUCTION

Mania and melancholia are well described in ancient history. Efforts at classification of psychiatric illness date from Egypt (around 3000 B.C.), including Hippocrates' enlightened approach in conceptualizing mental disorders as due to natural versus supernatural causes (around 400 B.C.). The late 1700s and early 1800s are notable for a number of physicians advocating humane treatment of the mentally ill and their view of mental illnesses as due to physical causes. These early physicians paved the way for more contemporary researchers to develop differentiated nosologies of mental aberration (Rush, 1983).

Around the turn of the twentieth century, Kraepelin (1896, 1904) was one of the first to distinghish "manic–depressive insanity" from schizophrenia—distinguishing these illnesses by the presence of a deteriorating versus nondeteriorating course. During the early part of this century, psychodynamic conceptualizations of major mental illnesses were dominant. As more somatic treatments have become available, the field as a whole has turned to biologic explanations and understanding of these illnesses, and there has been a return to studying early pioneers such as Kraepelin (Faedda et al., 1995).

Despite greater understanding and ongoing debate on the boundaries of major mental illnesses, there continues to be significant uncertainty as to the boundaries between different groups of psychiatric conditions and specific conditions within each group, largely due to a lack of independent validity measures. Mood disorders have varied clinical presentations (e.g., major depressive disorder with "atypical" symptom features, rapid-cycling bipolar disorder). Whether different courses of illness or cross-sectional symptom features are varying manifestations of the same illness or reflect distinct disorders remains unresolved. For example, is cyclothymic disorder a variant of bipolar disorder? Is dysthymic disorder simply a course of illness variant of major depressive disorder?

Mood Disorders Across the Life Span, Edited by Shulman, Tohen, and Kutcher
ISBN 0-471-10477-9 © 1996 Wiley-Liss, Inc.

A second, related question is whether the same illness varies in its clinical presentation, physiology, treatment response, or in other ways over the course of the patient's life span or in relation to age at onset. For example, does onset in adolescence predict a different course of illness than onset in the middle adult years for major depressive or bipolar disorder? Are there specifics, such as organic factors, that predict the course of illness? If a depressive condition is responsive to a tricyclic agent in a 20-year-old patient, does this responsiveness persist when the same patient is 60 years of age?

This chapter discusses some of the conceptual issues relevant to the classification of mood disorders. Different perspectives (pathophysiology, genetics, course, and co-morbidity) provide dependent variables that can be used to evaluate the validity of various mood disorder groupings. We evaluate how an examination from these perspectives contributes to our conceptualization and classification of mood disorders. These perspectives also provide a conceptual framework for alternative study designs that may further our understanding of mood disorders, which we illustrate with available studies of bipolar and major depressive disorder.

TERMINOLOGY

The following discussion uses the *Diagnostic and Statistical Manual of Mental Disorders,* 4th edition (DSM-IV) (American Psychiatric Association, 1994) term *disorder* to refer to the mood syndrome (e.g., major depressive or bipolar I disorder). A particular syndrome typically has multiple etiologies and a shared pathophysiology. For example, nephrotic syndrome, congestive heart failure, or hypertension are each syndromes with multiple causes. On the other hand, for each syndrome grouping, there is sufficiently shared pathophysiology that the essential core clinical features of the syndrome are common to all etiologies. Similarly, in mood disorders, a major depressive episode may result from known and specifiable causes such as thyroid, other endocrinological or neurological conditions, intoxication or withdrawal from substances of abuse, from prescribed medications, or stressful precipitants (i.e., uncomplicated bereavement), or may be idiopathic such as dysthymic, major depressive, or bipolar disorders. These idiopathic and etiologically specific mood disorders share a final common pathway (Akiskal and McKinney, 1975) that is arrived at by various precipitants or causes and that, as a consequence, leads to a commonly shared cluster of signs and symptoms. We assume that major depressive disorder for instance, while coded as a single disorder in DSM-IV, is likely to be a syndrome with multiple, but as yet unspecified, etiologies.

The term *illness* refers to a syndrome for which a specific cause is known. For example, Cushing's disease is often associated with the clinical syndrome of a major depressive episode. Once Cushing's disease has been treated, the psychiatric symptomatology (i.e., the syndrome of major depression) remits. The cause is known, although the specifics of the pathophysiology may not be fully explicated, depending on the state of our knowledge at the time. We contend that a better understanding of the diverse, as yet unspecified, etiologies for the presently idiopathic mood disorders could be gleaned from studies that evaluate pathophysiology, course, familiality (genetics), and comorbidities (current and lifetime). Specifically, if we employ one of these four parameters to divide the idiopathic syndrome of major depression (or the group of idiopathic depressions), categories could be formed and tested for homogeneity with regard to the other three parameters. Ideally, a new entity would be drawn if all four parameters were to validate (i.e., distinguish) the new entity for the residual mood disorders. Obviously, this ideal has yet to be realized, perhaps because our ability to reliably measure key distinguishing parameters has not yet fully evolved.

AN APPROACH TO THE CONCEPTUALIZATION AND CLASSIFICATION OF AFFECTIVE ILLNESS

Cross-sectional symptom features, differential responses to antidepressant medications, pathophysiological findings, familial patterns, and current or lifetime psychiatric comorbidities have each been used to better circumscribe and characterize a particular mood disorder and to define its boundaries with other conditions. For example, it is entirely possible that a longer prior illness is associated with greater treatment resistance or at least with an evolving pattern of treatment nonresponse (Post, 1992). That is, the underlying biology of the disorder may evolve depending on the nature and number of prior episodes of illness.

Conversely, additional factors may independently either further improve differentiation offered by these perspectives or blur otherwise obvious distinctions. For example, age at onset may distinguish between juvenile and adult forms of the illness. Yet, age at onset may also be associated with a different prognosis (i.e., childhood onset may have a poorer prognosis), as well as a different range of causes (e.g., secondary mood disorders due to neurological events are more likely with geriatric onsets; greater familial loading and, therefore, greater genetic contribution is found with juvenile onsets). Thus, studies designed to determine whether mood disorders subgrouped by age at onset are distinct may, in fact, be comparing phenotypically similar but etiologically distinct syndromes. Age at onset, current age, and length of illness (time from the onset of the disorder to the present) are often inherently related in clinical populations. That is, if age at onset is identical, older patients with bipolar disorder typically have had more illness episodes than younger patients. Alternatively, if the length of illness is equivalent between these hypothetical older and younger patients, then the age at onset is different by definition. Consequently, when using age at onset to divide populations into juvenile and adult-onset forms, it may be necessary to control for such variables as treatment response, number of episodes, or total length of illness.

PATHOPHYSIOLOGY

The pathophysiology of a particular mood disorder has been viewed by some as the "gold standard" by which to delineate specific conditions within this disorder group, as well as to define the boundaries of the group. Pathophysiological abnormalities may be similar, whether genetic or environmental influences are primary etiologies. Thus, physiological and other biological manifestations may or may not distinguish different causes of particular mood disorders.

Substantial progress has been made toward understanding the physiology of mood disorders (Rush et al., 1991). However, whether these biological and physiological concomitants are causally related to the disorder is unclear. That is, if patients who are in a symptomatic episode differ from normal controls in regard to one or more biological measures, these abnormalities may be (1) simple concomitants of the illness episode (i.e., not present either prior to or following the episode), (2) scars caused by prior episodes or time spent in the present episode, or (3) true antecedents of the initial episode, which continue throughout the course of the illness. In addition, these abnormalities may be far removed or downstream effects from the actual cause (e.g., physiological adaptations to more etiologically primary abnormalities) or they may constitute both a necessary and sufficient cause (i.e., highly relevant to the etiology of the condition). Thus, while syndromes may reflect a final common pathway, multiple pathophysiological mechanisms can provide an explanation of, for example, differences in treatment response or in the course of illness.

Brain function is responsible for the mood shifts and other symptoms of mood disorders. Thus, the most basic understanding of these disorders must be at the cellular level with some degree of anatomical specificity. However, direct *in vivo* measurement of neuronal activity and function is not feasible in humans; therefore, we must rely upon indirect measures, such as an evaluation of central nervous system (CNS) function by electroencephalogram (EEG), evoked potentials, or dynamic imaging techniques such as single-photon emission computed tomography (SPECT), positron emission tomography (PET), magnetic resonance spectroscopy (MRS), or functional magnetic resonance imaging (FMRI). Some studies have relied on measures of peripheral cell function (e.g., platelets or leukocytes) with the notion that these peripheral cells will be representative of neurons (e.g., platelet imipramine binding sites). Earlier investigations have focused on an evaluation in blood, urine, or cerebrospinal fluid (CSF) of key CNS neurotransmitters, precursors, or metabolites. These peripheral measures have been used at rest or in response to provocation of CNS function. Provocation tests have included neuroendocrine challenges such as the thyrotropin-releasing hormone stimulation test (TRHST) (Loosen and Prange, 1980), the dexamethasone suppression test (DST) (Carroll et al., 1981), as well as changes in regional cerebral blood flow (rCBF) or the sleep EEG induced by agents that selectively act on specific neurotransmitter systems (e.g., arecoline and ipsapirone).

These efforts to clarify the biology of mood disorders provide methods to determine whether different clinical presentations or phenotypes share selected pathophysiological characteristics. For example, adolescent and geriatric onset major depressive disorders can be compared cross sectionally [e.g., is the incidence of reduced rapid eye movement (REM) latency or DST nonsuppression equivalent in these two groups?]. Alternatively, the effect of previous illness can be discerned by comparing the biological features of major depressive disorder in the first compared to subsequent major depressive episodes.

While these kinds of questions can be asked using current measurement methods, a major difficulty is interpreting the differences when they occur. For example, do differences imply a different disorder or are they simply consequences of more or less prior illness, prior treatment, current or past psychiatric comorbidities, or the biology of the disorder combined with distinct biologies inherent in different age groups?

GENETICS

In the future, it is likely that most illnesses will be defined at the most fundamental level of genetic material. However, we are presently limited to looking at the consequences of distinct genetic patterns by studies of the patterns of inheritance. Data support different patterns of inheritance across different mood disorders (e.g., Dunner, 1996). These observations support the notion that there are genetically distinct causes that result in a shared final common pathway leading to similarities in clinical symptomatology, while within each disorder group (e.g., bipolar I vs. bipolar II disorder) there may be identifiable and distinct inheritance patterns.

There are four approaches to the genetics of mood disorders—each providing a view of these conditions. They are: (1) familial loading studies (e.g., studies to compare patients with mood disorders from "loaded" pedigrees—familial depressive disease versus those with no familial loading vs. sporadic depressive disease); (2) studies that evaluate heritability (e.g., monozygotic vs. dizygotic twin studies); (3) studies of incidence in those at risk for, but not yet ill from, mood disorders to identify biological or psychological antecedents of these conditions; and (4) in theory, but not yet available, studies using specific genetic probes to determine which relatives and which phenotypes are associated with the genetic contributants to these conditions.

Familial loading studies have revealed a 12.2% risk for bipolar illness in first-degree relatives of probands with bipolar disorder. In addition, there is a 12.2% risk in first-degree relatives for recurrent major depressive disorder, and another 10–12% risk for dysthymic disorder and other not otherwise specified (NOS) mood disorders (e.g., depressive disorder, bipolar disorder). What remains unclear is which clinical presentations are accounted for by genetics.

We currently have little knowledge as to whether the milder forms of affective illness, for example, cyclothymic and dysthymic disorders, or the NOS groups are phenotypic variants. It is also unclear if early events or stressors play a critical role in the development of these disorders (e.g., traumatic loss, repetitive early trauma, or illicit drug use at an early age) (Nathan et al., 1995). Thus, the interplay between the environment and a genetic predisposition remains to be clarified.

COURSE OF ILLNESS

The phenomenological boundaries of mood disorders are central to considering the course of illness over time. For example, cyclothymic disorder, like bipolar disorder, is associated with mood lability, but little is known of its pathophysiology, and few studies document family history, comorbidity, or treatment responses for this patient group. Some studies suggest that over 30% of those with cyclothymic disorder will go on to develop a full-blown mood disorder—especially bipolar disorder (see Howland and Thase, 1996). This raises the question of whether cyclothymic disorder is, in fact, a prodrome for the development of later bipolar disorder. If cyclothymic disorder is a prodrome to bipolar disorder, then why the majority of patients do not show such an evolution is not clear.

A core issue is how to define the boundaries between conditions, especially among the milder variants (Angst, 1994). There may be a core disorder with different phenotypic variants, which implies a shared fundamental CNS pathophysiology. Other genetic or environmental factors may determine the phenotypic variants seen in the clinic. These different variants may be associated with different courses of illness, treatment responsivity, or comorbidities.

The course of illness can be described by the following elements: (1) age at onset of the first full illness episode; (2) presence or absence of a subsyndromal condition prior to the onset of the full mood disorder; (3) the length of the illness (e.g., current age minus age at onset of the full disorder or of the subsyndromal prodrome); (4) the number of full episodes; (5) the degree of interepisode recovery and residual symptoms; (6) the length of the current episode; (7) the frequency of episodes (i.e., episodes/

year); and (8) in some cases, the stereotyped episode sequence. For example, there seem to be differences that are consistent in bipolar disorder, depending on whether the onset of the illness is earlier or later in life, such as the likelihood of future episodes (Goodwin and Jamison, 1990). Additionally, those patients with bipolar or major depressive disorder who have poor interepisode recovery are more likely to have a more chronic subsequent course (Keller et al., 1992, 1993). Similarly, a rapid-cycling course may reflect the inability of the brain to sustain a stable mood state, which may occur across categories of affectiveness illness (e.g., bipolar I, bipolar II, recurrent brief depressive disorder, or premenstrual dysphoric disorder).

Mood disorders were classically viewed as recurring conditions with essentially well periods between episodes. More recently, it has been recognized that interepisode recovery may be incomplete in many patients. Even if psychiatric symptoms are minimized, substantial residual psychosocial dysfunction may remain in many patients (Mintz et al., 1992; Coryell et al., 1993). An additional consideration of interepisode functioning is whether patients with a disorder and incomplete interepisode recovery is descriptive of a different condition than those with full interepisode recovery (Alda et al., 1994; Grof et al., 1994). That is, full as compared to partial interepisode recovery may (1) define a different course of the same illness or (2) indicate different etiologies. It appears, however, that in general, patients with a history of poor interepisode recovery should expect only partial interepisode recovery in the future. For example, "double depressions" appear very likely to sustain recurrences if maintenance medication is discontinued even after one year (Kocsis, personal communication).

Age at onset may relate to subsequent course or etiology in a variety of ways, just as juvenile-onset diabetes or juvenile-onset obesity heralds a course and identifies a heritability of these conditions that is distinct from the adult-onset forms. Specifically, does an early age at onset of the illness predict a subsequently more severe, chronic, or recurrent illness during the individual's life span? In bipolar disorder, an early age at onset has been suggested to be associated with a higher percentage of symptoms consistent with mixed bipolar episodes. In adults, such mixed bipolar episodes have been shown to be associated with decreased interepisode symptom remission and an increased number of episodes (Keller et al., 1986; Prien et al., 1988; Post et al., 1989). If one is conducting an efficacy trial, usually a cross section in the life span of individuals with a lifetime illness is examined. Will the age at onset for a given individual be a predictive factor of the likelihood of treatment response?

Additional dimensions of age of onset would be an increased length of illness with the attendant risks such as developing general medical conditions with age. As with the general population, whether the development of general medical conditions is due primarily to poor health, patient behaviors, or other factors is not known. Additionally, with affective illness there are periods of altered judgment and impulsivity, both factors that could increase the likelihood of substance abuse or risky behavior, which could lead to inadvertent self-harm. In comparison to a youthful onset, with an onset of illness with no prior history, after 30, 40, 50, and 60 years, there is an increased likelihood of organic factors being precipitants of the disorder. Additionally, patients who are over 60 when they have their first episode of bipolar disorder are also more likely to have a second episode quickly and be poorly responsive to treatment (Goodwin and Jamison, 1990).

Little is understood regarding the impact of length of illness on pathophysiology. The illness itself may, over time, adversely affect CNS function such that more previous illness episodes may result in a more recurring or severe subsequent course (Post et al., 1992; Goodwin and Jamison, 1990). Whether treatment can ameliorate accumulated neuronal injury has been speculated (Post et al., 1992). In other words, is the length of illness distinct and separate from age at onset in affecting severity, chronicity, or treatment response? For example, if one develops the illness at age 15 versus age 35, after having the illness for 20 years how different will the presentation and treatment response be, given all other factors remain equal?

It is speculated that for bipolar disorder, a high number of episodes can lead to lithium nonresponsivity, which is an example of the putative profound interaction between length of illness and treatment response (Post et al., 1992). Does a history of multiple prior episodes lead to a more recurring subsequent course of illness? To a shift in treatment response? Is an earlier age at onset associated with more lifetime episodes? It will require studies designed specifically to separate out each element independent from one another to address these questions.

In spite of the suggestion that prior course could affect course of illness, few studies have evaluated the potential relationship between treatment response and course (Goodwin and Jamison, 1990). Treatment response may be affected by organic factors, history of illness, and phenomenological features of the illness such as the presence of depressive symptoms during a manic episode (Bowden et al., 1994). Certain syndromes in affective illness can be very difficult to distinguish between one another; for example, that of agitated depression or dysphoric mania (Secunda et al., 1985; McElroy et al., 1992; Swann et al., 1993). In some cases, psychiatrists may use treatment response to differentiate and to make a tentative diagnosis. Some have suggested that treatment response per se can be used to define different illnesses (Klein and Davis, 1969). This notion would, for example, suggest that monoamine oxidase inhibitor (MAOI) responsive depressions are distinct (either in etiology or pathobiology) from tricyclic antidepressant (TCA) responsive depression. In depressive disorders, pharmacological response has led to three suggested subgroups based on cross-sectional symptom features (atypical, psychotic, melancholic). There is associated biologic evidence to suggest, for example, that psychotic and nonpsychotic mood disorders are distinct, and that psychotic depressions are familial. Both findings suggest that this distinction may be useful in describing a separate type of mood disorder. We know of few systematic studies to validate or invalidate this approach.

An additional, newer consideration to evaluating the course of illness is whether repetitive medication discontinuation may lead to a more severe and persistent course of illness (Post et al., 1992). There is a current active debate on how to quantify retrospectively whether factors such as repetitive discontinuation could in fact contribute to a poorer prognosis. The first issue is whether multiple discontinuation of medications may, in and of itself, alter the course of the illness and affect treatment responsivity. A second related issue is whether the use of antidepressants can alter the long-term course of illness even after medication discontinuation (Kukopulos et al., 1980).

A final related element to consider is whether treatment modifies the impact of illness on the brain. Some treatments may mask the symptoms of the illness, while not affecting underlying pathophysiology dysfunction that could be additive (Suppes et al., 1991). Other medications may both mask symptoms and reduce the accumulated effect on CNS function as suggested by animal studies on the impact of anticonvulsants to block the development of kindling (Post et al., 1992).

COMORBIDITY

The term *comorbidity* has several related but different meanings. Epidemiologists use it to refer to the lifetime estimate of major diagnoses. Clinicians use it to refer to additional concurrent diagnoses. Those interested in the evolution of the phenomenology of the illness often use comorbidity to refer to conditions that precede the onset of the current mood disorder (e.g., a patient with bulimia in his or her 20s develops major depressive disorder without bulimia in his or her 40s). In recent work, the extent of comorbid conditions has begun to be recognized. In particular, there is a growing appreciation that significant comorbidity may be present even at the first episode of affective illness (Strakowski et al., 1992).

Comorbid diagnoses may (1) be causal of the mood disorder if they are present prior to or at least concurrent with the mood disorder (e.g., hypothyroidism); (2) be a common noncausal concomitant (e.g., generalized anxiety disorder plus major depressive disorder); (3) herald a mood disorder (e.g., dysthymia preceding major depressive disorder or panic disorder leading to subsequent major depressive disorder with or without panic disorder); or (4) represent the presence of two independent disorders.

Comorbidity may affect the course of illness and can have a number of dimensions, including medical, psychiatric, and neurological. The comorbid conditions pertinent to our understanding of mood disorders include other axis I disorders (e.g., anxiety or obsessive–compulsive disorder), general medical conditions (e.g., thyroid or adrenal conditions), neurological conditions, substance abuse, CNS trauma, or personality disorders. The presence of comorbid illness at the onset of illness may well carry implications for course of illness and treatment response. An example of this issue is a patient with no history of significant affective illness who experiences a closed-head injury and then develops bipolar disorder. Importantly, existing clinical data support a different treatment approach in this case (e.g., use of anticonvulsants instead of lithium).

Some axis I conditions (e.g., substance abuse) and axis II may modify the course of the mood disorder, compliance, or affect treatment response. Personality disorders (axis II) may lead to a more chronic course or affect the symptomatic presentation or the response to treatment. It appears that personality disorders can (1) predate the mood disorder or (2) develop in response to the debilitation and dependence resulting from the mood condition itself. In evaluating the dynamic nature of mood disorders, consideration of the comorbid illnesses before the onset of affective illness versus that which develops after the illness should be studied.

The interface between the biological and psychological consequences of early physical or sexual abuse is being actively studied. There is increasing interest focusing on neuroactive steroids and the effect these compounds may have on the developing nervous system. One hypothesis being studied is whether early abuse causes dysfunction or overactivity in the neuroactive steroid axis, which, in turn, increases later vulnerability to developing depression (Stout et al., 1995; Nathan et al., 1995). Consistent with these studies, recent imaging techniques show CNS biological differences following combat-related posttraumatic stress, which may be associated with the development of a specific disorder (Bremner et al., 1995).

It is important to conceptualize that recurrent mood disorders are lifelong illnesses. In the course of a lifetime, it is to be expected that the majority of patients will develop comorbid conditions, which may contribute or define what the future course of their psychiatric illness will be. Future studies will need to more carefully define comorbid conditions and evaluate more fully the impact of such conditions on the disorder being studied.

CLINICAL TRIAL DESIGN

In the first sections, we considered some issues relevant to the dynamic aspects of these illnesses over the patient's lifetime. A major difficulty in studying mood disorders is the interaction of a number of variables over an individual's life span. For example, as discussed earlier it is difficult to separate the interaction of age at onset and length of illness versus number of episodes in recurrent mood disorders.

In this section, we will focus on the implications for clinical trials of these dynamic aspects of affective illness throughout the life span. We will propose five different study designs, which could be used to address some of the questions raised. These study designs are not meant to be inclusive of all the possibilities but rather to illustrate approaches to the problem of resolving the relative impact of several dynamic and likely interacting factors as described above. We suggest potential clinical trial study designs for differentiating the relative impact of these elements on recurrent mood disorders over the life span. All trial designs will use the same variables: X_n is the variable held constant (e.g., current age), Y_n is a variable that varies (e.g., length of illness), and Z_n is the outcome variable (e.g., treatment response). Thus, we examine the impact of the Y variable on Z outcome variables.

Study Design 1

In order to evaluate the impact of length of illness per se, we propose the following study design. Using bipolar disorder as an example, a cohort of 35-year-old patients with bipolar I disorder would be stratified by age at onset. The stratification would be patients with onset of illness prior to age 21 (Y_1) and onset with the next 5 years (Y_2), the next 5 years, and so on. The variable to be held constant is the number of past episodes (X_1). All patients would be required to have two or fewer episodes (X_1), given the impression that greater than three episodes may herald an increase in the frequency of episodes (Goodwin and Jamison, 1990). Additionally, all of the patients would be required to have had a "good" treatment response (X_2) to a simple medication regime commonly used in bipolar disorder, such as lithium, lithium plus an anticonvulsant, or an anticonvulsant alone. Patients would be excluded who showed a history of multiple episodes, rapid cycling, going on and off their medications, or substance abuse. The domains to be examined in this cohort of 35-year olds would include psychosocial function (Z_1), residual symptoms (Z_2), and biological differences (Z_3). The goal of this study design is to predict the impact of the length of illness, with the null hypothesis being earlier onset leads to increased morbidity later.

While this is the simplest of designs, we are mindful of the difficulty of conducting this type of study and, in particular, in bipolar patients where additional considerations could potentially include the type of manic episode (e.g., euphoric or mixed). The critical element here is controlling for current age and then leaving other elements uncontrolled.

Study Design 2

One element of continuing debate is the relevant predictive and prognostic importance of family history. Some researchers assert that a positive family history can be both predictive of treatment response and course (Grof et al., 1994), while others, in more controlled trials, strongly assert that family history is not necessarily a pertinent variable when evaluating these factors (see Goodwin and Jamison, 1990).

One experimental design to evaluate these factors would be as follows. A cross section of bipolar patients whose current age is 30 would be entered into the study (X_1). Variables to be controlled would include the number of episodes being fewer than three (X_2). The groups would be stratified based on whether there was a positive history of affective illness in a first-degree relative (Y_1). In order to assure that the groups were comparable, an estimate of density of family illness would be made. Additional variables to covary for would include the level of dysfunction in the family of origin, socioeconomic status, and substance abuse. The outcome variables to be assessed would be treatment response (Z_1), social and functional impairment (Z_2), and course of illness (Z_3). In this study design, where age is held constant, we would first retrospectively and then prospectively examine the import of a positive family history of affective illness. The goal of this type of study design would be to evaluate the impact of a positive family history at a given age. This study could be extended with long-term follow-up to assess the predictive value of family history.

Study Design 3

The issue of whether repetitive episodes of an affective illness can, in and of themselves, cause cumulative effects in the brain has not been resolved. Suggestive evidence from the animal literature on sensitization and kindling might support that an affective illness in some sense mimics a seizure or damaging event in the CNS, either through excitatory amino acids, neuroactive steroids, or an as yet unspecified mechanism. This model would suggest that affective episodes would tend to lower the threshold for future episodes. Out of this body of work have come a number of speculations on the relative importance of using alternatives to lithium and, in particular, the anticonvulsants (Goodwin and Jamison, 1990; McElroy et al., 1992; Post et al., 1992). It has also been speculated that the anticonvulsants may not only inhibit the episodes but act to minimize the impact of damage from past episodes (Post et al., 1992).

One study design that could potentially address this issue would be to control for current age. A group of bipolar patients, all of whom are age 40 (X_1), would be randomized based on having had fewer than three episodes (Y_1) versus greater than three episodes over the last 15 years (Y_2). Onset of illness would be controlled, with onset required between ages 20 and 24 (X_2), thus controlling for length of illness. All patients would be required to be responsive to either lithium or lithium plus an anticonvulsant, but they would not require ongoing treatment with neuroleptics, thus controlling for treatment response (X_3). An additional exclusion would be patients with more than three episodes secondary to multiple discontinuation of medications. The group could be covaried for prior substance abuse and family history. Using such a design, it would be anticipated that the impact of repetitive episodes could be evaluated, including examining interepisode functioning (Z_1) and using biological measures such as activated imaging (Z_2), and so forth.

Evaluating the impact of repetitive episodes has clear clinical import. Recent observations by Post and colleagues (1992) support the notion that multiple discontinuations may lead to an increased likelihood of treatment resistance, but are not yet corroborated by whether repetitive episodes, in and of themselves, are indeed cumulative, and herald a significantly worse long-term prognosis. A study such as this could address this important research question.

Study Design 4

The three preceding cases share a commonality in that age is held constant. Rather than defining by symptomatic phenomenology, which is the approach of DSM-IV (American Psychiatric Association, 1994), it would be interesting to use the biological spectrum to define these illnesses. In large collected cohorts, such as those that exist in many clinical research centers, all patients would be entered who met criteria for an illness (e.g., major depressive disorder) (X). One would then take a biological test, which a majority of them have been subjected to, and this would define the study sample. One would then examine the biological test (Y) (e.g., macro- or micro-arthitectural sleep patterns) and define sets of patients by a particular pattern. A simple example of this would be those patients with onset of REM latency of 30, 60, or 90 minutes. The sample would then be evaluated to define specific domain(s) (Z) within subsets of the patient group. For example, one could look at such domains as family history, treatment response, clinical presentation, and course of illness to see if a pattern emerges.

An example in which this is routinely done in the opposite direction includes different metabolites in the CSF of those patients in a manic episode with more depressive features. Recent data support the notion that there may be a different CSF neurotransmitter metabolite profile in manic patients with depressive elements versus those with more classical euphoric or purely irritable mania (Swann et al., 1994). Such studies are examples of studying a group of patients defined by their clinical symptomatology, where one chooses a biological test to investigate whether or not there is a difference within these subsets. An alternative as proposed above would then be to take these samples of CSF and go the other direction in a blind fashion. A study conducted by Giles et al. (1987) where individual sleep patterns were evaluated in a large cohort of patients with major depression may contribute to our evaluation of the feasibility and appropriateness of this study design format. Historically studies have been limited by the numbers of patients receiving these interventions. However, there are a growing number of centers focusing on a given biologic measure of affective illness, and biological data from imaging, sleep studies, and so forth have become increasingly available.

Study Design 5

Another approach to studying affective illness would be to examine by length of illness. One very interesting prospective study would be to take a group of patients with onset between ages 14–18 versus 24–28 (Y). One would then follow each of the groups for 10 years (X). In this kind of study design, there would be many useful observations. These would include whether an earlier onset bipolar disorder is associated with more mixed features (Z_1), whether these younger patients have a higher rate of family history (Z_2), what the treatment response was between the two groups (Z_3), and so forth. Clearly, this kind of study design would also include significant samples with which to conduct biological studies.

There are a number of first-episode studies currently ongoing. Many of these should provide substantial and useful observations about the course of affective illness. Unfortunately, few of them control for treatment, nor necessarily see their patients on an ongoing basis or at frequent intervals. The utility of this type of study design, though, is well recognized by those interested in biological studies, in particular, those in which medications might obscure an essential finding such as in physiologic imaging.

IN CLOSING

In this chapter, we raised many more questions than we answered. Our hope is to present an approach to current questions in the field and to suggest clinical trial designs that will provide building blocks to better understand these complex syndromes. Currently, our understanding of the lifetime course of affective illness is limited. Diagnostic stability, spectrum of illness, and comorbidity, as well as issues delineated earlier (e.g., family history, repetitive episodes, etc.), remain unresolved. One impact of this uncertainty and interdependent overlapping variables is the difficulty in designing adequate clinical trials.

We have illustrated a few of the possibilities in designing clinical trials to study current issues of interest in affective disorders. The trial designs are simplified in an effort to provide data adequate to build more comprehensive studies in the future. Regardless of the study design chosen, it will be critical to make a clear delineation of what are the independent versus dependent variables. One complication is that the dependent variables as a group, which could be viewed as at least including pathophysiology, clinical presentation, treatment response, and illness prognosis either on or off medication can be quite variable. It is also reasonable to consider dependent variables as including family history (loading), prior course of illness, and comorbidity (past, current, or lifetime). It is crucial to establish specific boundaries defining populations of interest, for example, which characteristics will be included versus excluded and held constant.

The pathophysiology of the affective disorders is probably not due to a singular cause, even though the syndrome will appear very similar across a broad range of patients. Early pioneers recognized these factors and the range of presentation possible across these disorders. Current technology, scientific advances, and the broader array of disciplines now addressing these questions support that progress in our understanding will be made in the foreseeable future.

ACKNOWLEDGMENTS

Supported in part by NIMH Grant MH-01221 (T.S.), NIMH Center Grant MH-41115 (A.J.R.), Young Investigator Awards from the National Alliance for Research on Schizophrenia and Depression (NARSAD) (T.S.), the Lattner Foundation (T.S.), and by Texas State Legislature and Dallas County Hospital District funding to Mental Health Connections, a partnership between Dallas County Mental Health and Mental Retardation and the Department of Psychiatry, UT Southwestern. The authors appreciate the secretarial support of David Savage and Chris Claeson, and the administrative support of Kenneth Z. Altshuler, M.D., Stanton Sharp Distinguished Chair, Professor and Chairman, Department of Psychiatry.

REFERENCES

Akiskal HS, McKinney WT (1975): Overview of recent research in depression. Arch Gen Psych 32:285–305.

Alda M, Grof P, Grof E, Zvolsky P, Walsh M (1994): Mode of inheritance in families of patients with lithium-responsive affective disorders. Acta Psychiatr Scand 90:304–310.

American Psychiatric Association (1994): "Diagnostic and Statistical Manual of Mental Disorders," 4th ed. Washington, DC: American Psychiatric Press.

Angst J (1994): Bipolar disorder: epidemiology, comorbidity, premorbid personality (Presentation). First International Conference on Bipolar Disorder, Pittsburgh, Pennsylvania.

Bowden CL, Brugger AM, Swann AC, Calabrese, JR (1994): Efficacy of divalproex vs lithium and placebo in mania. JAMA, 271:918–924.

Bremner JD, Randall P, Scott TM, Bronen RA, Seibyl JP, Southwick SM, Delaney RC, McCarthy G, Charney DS, Innis RB (1995): MRI-based measurement of hippocampal volume in patients with combat-related posttraumatic stress disorder. Am J Psychiatry 152:973–981.

Carroll BJ, Feinberg M, Greden JF, Tarika J, Albala AA, Haskett RF, James NM, Kronfol Z, Lohr N, Steiner M, deVigne JP, Young EA (1981): Specific laboratory test for the diagnosis of melancholia. Arch Gen Psychiatry 38:15–22.

Coryell W, Scheftner W, Keller MB, Endicott J, Maser J, Klerman GL (1993): The enduring psychosocial consequences of mania and depression. Am J Psychiatry 150:720–727.

Dunner DL (1996): Bipolar depression with hypomania (Bipolar II). In Widiger TA, Frances AJ, Pincus HA, Ross R, First MB, Davis W (eds): "DSM-IV Sourcebook, Volume 2," Washington, DC: American Psychiatric Press.

Faedda GL, Baldessarini RJ, Suppes T, Tondo L, Becker I, Lipschitz DS (1995): Pediatric-onset bipolar disorder: A neglected clinical and public health problem." Harvard Rev Psychiatry 3:171–195.

Giles DE, Schlesser MA, Rush AJ, Orsulak PJ, Fulton CL, Roffwarg HP (1987): Polysomnographic findings and dexamethasone nonsuppression in unipolar depression: A replication and extension. Biol Psychiatry 22:872–882.

Goodwin FK, Jamison KR (1990): "Manic-Depressive Illness," New York: Oxford University Press.

Grof P, Alda M, Grof E, Zvolsky P, Walsh M (1994): Lithium response and genetics of affective disorders. J Affect Disord 32:85–95.

Howland RH, Thase ME (1996): Cyclothymic disorder. In Widiger TA, Frances AJ, Pincus HA, Ross R, First MB, Davis W (eds): "DSM-IV Sourcebook, Volume 2." Washington, DC: American Psychiatric Press.

Keller MB, Lavori PW, Coryell W, Endicott J, Mueller TI (1993): Bipolar I: A five-year prospective follow-up. J Nerv Ment Dis 181:238–245.

Keller MB, Lavori PW, Mueller TI, Endicott J, Coryell W, Hirschfield RMA, Shea T (1992): Time to recovery, chronicity, and levels of psychopathology in major depression: A 5-year prospective follow-up of 431 subjects. Arch Gen Psychiatry 49:809–816.

Keller MB, Lavori PW, Coryell W, Andreasen NC, Endicott J, Clayton PJ, Klerman GL, Hirschfeld RMA (1986): Differential outcome of pure manic, mixed/cycling, and pure depressive episodes in patients with bipolar illness. JAMA 255:3138–3142.

Klein DF, Davis JM (1969): "Diagnosis and Drug Treatment of Psychiatric Disorders." Baltimore: Williams and Wilkins.

Kraepelin E (1904): "Lectures on Clinical Psychiatry." London: Ballière, Tindall and Cox.

Kraepelin E (1896): "Psychiatrie. Ein Lehrburch für Studirende und Aerte." Leipzig: J.A. Barth.

Kukopulos A, Reginaldi D, Laddomada P, Floris G, Serra G, Tondo L (1980): Course of the manic-depressive cycle and changes caused by treatments. Pharmacopsychiatry 13:156–167.

Loosen P, Prange AJ Jr (1980): Thyrotropin releasing hormone (TRH): A useful tool for psycho-neuroendocrine investigation. Psychoneuroendocrinology 5:63–81.

McElroy SL, Keck PE Jr, Pope HG, Jr, Hudson JI, Faedda GL, Swann AC (1992): Clinical and research implications of the diagnosis of dysphoric or mixed mania or hypomania. Am J Psychiatry 149:1633–1644.

Mintz J, Mintz LI, Arruda MJ, Hwang SS (1992): Treatments of depression and the functional capacity to work. Arch Gen Psychiatry 49:761–768.

Nathan KI, Musselman DL, Schatzberg AF, Nemeroff CB (1995): Biology of mood disorders. In Schatzberg AF, Nemeroff CB (eds): "Textbook of Psychopharmacology." Washington, DC: APA Press, pp 439–477.

Post RM (1992): Transduction of psychosocial stress into the neurobiology of recurrent affective disorder. Am J Psychiatry 149:999–1010.

Post RM, Leverich GS, Altshuler L, Mikalauskas K (1992): Lithium-discontinuation-induced refractoriness: Preliminary observations. Am J Psychiatry 149:1727–1729.

Post RM, Rubinow DR, Uhde TW, Roy-Byrne PP, Linnoila M, Rosoff A, Cowdry R (1989): Dysphoric mania. Clinical and biological correlates. Arch Gen Psychiatry, 46:353–358.

Prien RF, Himmelhoch JM, Kupfer DJ (1988): Treatment of mixed mania. J Affect Disord 15:9–15.

Rush AJ (1983): "Beating Depression." New York: Facts on File.

Rush AJ, Cain JW, Raese J, Stewart RS, Waller DA, Debus JR (1991): Neurobiological bases for psychiatric disorders. In Rosenberg RN (ed): "Comprehensive Neurology." New York: Raven Press, pp 555–603.

Secunda SK, Katz MM, Swann AC, Koslow SH, Maas JW, Chuang S, Croughan J (1985): Mania. Diagnosis, state measurement and prediction of treatment response. J Affect Disord 8:113–121.

Stout SC, Kilts CD, Nemeroff CB (1995): Neuropeptides and stress: Preclinical findings and implications for pathophysiology. In Friedman M, Deutch AY, Charney DL (eds): "Neurobiological Consequences of Stress: From Normal Adaptation to Post-Traumatic Stress Disorders." New York: Raven Press, pp 103–123.

Strakowski SM, Tohen M, Stoll AL, Faedda GI, Goodwin DC (1992): Comorbidity in mania at first hospitalization. Am J Psychiatry 149:554–556.

Suppes T, Baldessarini RJ, Faedda GL, Tohen M (1991): Risk of recurrence following discontinuation of lithium treatment in bipolar disorder. Arch Gen Psychiatry 48:1082–1088.

Swann AC, Stokes PE, Secunda SK, Maas JW, Bowden CL, Berman N, Koslow SH (1994): Depressive mania versus agitated depression: Biogenic amine and hypothalamic–pituitary–adrenocortical function. Biol Psychiatry 35:803–813.

Swann AC, Secunda SK, Katz MM, Croughan J, Bowden CL, Koslow SH, Berman N, Stokes PE (1993): Specificity of mixed affective states: Clinical comparison of dysphoric mania and agitated depression. J Affect Disord 28:81–89.

CHAPTER 2

Epidemiology of Mood Disorders Throughout the Life Cycle

CARLOS A. ZARATE, Jr. and MAURICIO TOHEN

McLean Hospital, Harvard University, 115 Mill Street, Belmont, MA 02178-9016

INTRODUCTION

Epidemiology, the study of the distribution of physiological states and disease in time and space (Lilienfeld and Lilienfeld, 1980), can help to improve mental health services for children, adolescents, adults, and the elderly by increasing understanding of the causes, development, and course of psychiatric disorders (Costello et al., 1993). For the purpose of delivery of health care, epidemiologic research on psychopathology in different age groups can provide information on need, availability, and effectiveness of services. Epidemiology attempts to identify the factors that increase the likelihood of disease or impairment at each stage in this development process and intervene to reduce that risk, preferably to prevent a move to the next stage in the disease process. Information about prevalence and incidence is useful for planning primary, secondary, and tertiary prevention and treatment services. The epidemiologic study of depression and mania has a long history (Goodwin and Jamison, 1990). The community surveys of the 1950s and 1960s are relevant to our current understanding of mood disorders insofar as they adopted the methodology of direct interview in community, paid close attention to psychosocial variables, and recorded the levels of impairment due to psychiatric symptoms. However, most of these studies failed to establish rates of specific psychiatric disorders. Furthermore, most of the estimates on prevalence and incidence are based on adult populations with little emphasis placed on knowing more about other age groups. Moreover, the failure of most epidemiologic studies of mood disorder conducted prior to 1980 to use a structured instrument of diagnostic criteria made their results difficult to interpret. Difficulties in determining the prevalence or incidence of manic–depressive illness and depressive disorders in other age groups may be due to several factors, including how assessments are obtained, definition of age groups under study, presence of a comorbid diagnosis, and if subjects studied are from of a high-risk group. Any one of these factors may affect the estimates of the prevalence and incidence of psychiatric disorders. As a result of these problems, it is not unusual

Mood Disorders Across the Life Span, Edited by Shulman, Tohen, and Kutcher
ISBN 0-471-10477-9 © 1996 Wiley-Liss, Inc.

to extrapolate results obtained from studies in adults to other age groups. Thus, clinicians and researchers are possibly relying on data that is inaccurate and far from the truth.

In this chapter, we will review epidemiologic studies that used standardized interview instruments, operationalized diagnostic criteria, and reported data on widely agreed diagnostic categories, such as those in the *Diagnostic and Statistical Manual of Mental Disorders,* 3rd edition (DSM-III) (American Psychiatric Association, 1990). We will focus on two categories of affective disorder: major depression and mania in four age groups: children, adolescents, adults, and the elderly. The age groups are defined as ages 0–14 years for children, 5–17 years for adolescents, 18–63 years for adults, and 64 years or more for the elderly. The epidemiology of affective disorders in adults has received increased attention in the past two decades. The reader may wish to consult more extensive reviews on this topic (Horwath and Weissman, 1995; Tohen and Goodwin, 1994), as the focus of this chapter will be primarily on children and the elderly.

MAJOR DEPRESSION

Definition

The DSM-IV diagnosis of major depression requires a 2-week period of dysphoric mood or loss of interest or pleasure, and at least four other symptoms, which may include: (1) significant weight loss or gain, (2) appetite disturbance, (3) insomnia or hypersomnia, (4) psychomotor agitation or retardation, (5) fatigue or loss of energy, (6) feelings of worthlessness, (7) inappropriate guilt, (8) impaired concentration, and (9) recurrent suicidal ideas or a suicide attempt (American Psychiatric Association, 1994). DSM-IV in comparison to DSM-III-R adds a criterion C to ensure the clinical significance of the symptomatic presentation.

The core symptoms of a major depressive episode are the same for children, adults, and the elderly, although there are data that suggest that the prominence of characteristic symptoms may change with age. Certain symptoms such as somatic complaints, irritability, crying, and social withdrawal are particularly common in children, whereas psychomotor retardation, hypersomnia, and delusions are less common in prepuberty than in adolescence and adulthood (Strober et al., 1981; Friedman et al., 1983; Carlson and Kashani, 1988). In prepubertal children, major depressive episodes occur more frequently in conjunction with other mental disorders (especially disruptive behavior disorders, attention-deficit disorders, and anxiety disorders) than in isolation (Angold and Costello, 1993). In adolescents, major depressive episodes are frequently associated with disruptive behavior disorders, attention-deficit disorders, anxiety disorders, substance-related disorders, and eating disorders (Angold and Costello, 1993; Bird et al., 1993). The core symptoms of a major depressive episode are the same for the adult and the elderly, although there are data to suggest that the prominence of characteristic symptoms may change with age. In elderly adults, cognitive symptoms (e.g., disorientation, memory loss, and distractibility) may be particularly prominent. Downes et al. (1988) stressed the importance of somatic symptoms, especially hypochondriacal complaints, feelings of subjective slowing, and restriction of energy.

Prevalence of Major Depression in Children and Adolescents

Evidence that many psychiatric disorders frequently emerge in adolescence, perhaps even in childhood, has generated increasing interest in the early features of the illness.

An early evaluation of clinical features may reduce confounding factors such as secondary changes due to prolonged illness or effects of psychotropic medications. With a growing interest in epidemiology and development course of psychiatric disorders in children, considerable attention is being paid to the assessment methods in this population (Young et al., 1987). The contribution of both parents and children as informants with respect to child psychopathology is widely acknowledged. Fendrich and colleagues (1991) emphasize the importance of using multiple informants and longitudinal assessments in research on childhood psychiatric disorders. In their 2-year study, mother–child agreement with respect to a child's DSM-III lifetime diagnoses of major depression, based on Kiddie-Schedule for Affective Disorders and Schizophrenia for School-Age Children (K-SADS) interviews with children, were assessed for a sample of 59 children ages 6–16. A comparison of diagnoses based on mother and child reports with the psychiatrists' best estimate diagnoses of major depression suggested that children were more informative than mothers at the initial interview. However, at follow-up children were slightly less informative than the mothers (Fendrich et al., 1991).

Only a few epidemiological studies have been specifically concerned with children's depressive disorders and most of them look at clinical populations. Affective illness is less common in prepubertal children than in adolescents. The estimated prevalence of DSM-III major depressive disorders found in New Zealand by Kashani et al. (1983) was 1.8% with a sample of 9-year-old children. In contrast Anderson et al. (1987) found a prevalence of major depression of 0.5%. Fleming et al. (1989) reported that the prevalence of major depression was less than 3% of children. Polaino-Lorente and Domènech (1993) studied the prevalence of depressive disorders in 6,432 children aged 8–11 years, in four Spanish cities and two rural areas. The authors used the Children's Depression Inventory and found that 1.8% of children met DSM-III-R criteria for major depression. In summary, in prepuberty, the point prevalence of major depression has been estimated at 1.8–3.0%; "minor" forms of depression, including dysthymia, have been estimated at 2.5%.

Kashani et al. (1983) did not find a significant association between sex and depression in children 9 years of age. Depressive disorders were also found to be similar in girls and in boys (Velez et al., 1989; Fleming et al., 1989; Fleming and Offord, 1990). In contrast, Anderson et al. (1987) and Costello et al. (1988) found more boys depressed than girls. Polaino-Lorente and Domènech (1993) reported that the point prevalence of childhood depressive disorder (major depression plus dysthymic disorder) was similar in both sexes (4.3% for boys and 3.9% for girls). On the other hand, studies in adolescence indicated higher rates of depression in females (Fleming et al., 1989; Garrison et al., 1990; Domènech et al., 1992). In summary, depressive illness is equally common in males and females prior to puberty and more common in females during adolescence.

Similar to children of bipolar disorder, the incidence of depression in children may vary if parents are affectively ill, commonly referred to as high-risk studies. Welner et al. (1977) compared the incidence of depression in children ages 5–16 of individuals hospitalized for depression and the children of well individuals. Of 75 children of depressives, 5 met criteria for adult depression compared to none of the 152 children of well parents. Prospective studies such as those of Kovacs et al. (1984a,b) indicate that depressive episodes arising in childhood presage adolescent onset of manic illness in some 25% of cases. Certain features of adolescent depression predictive of the development of bipolar illness include: (1) a symptom cluster consisting of rapid onset, psychomotor retardation, and mood-congruent psychotic features; (2) family history of bipolar disorder and three generations of family members with affective illness; and (3) pharmacologically induced hypomania (Strober and Carlson, 1982).

Until recently, there have been no large epidemiological surveys of children examining rural–urban variation in depression. Zahner and colleagues (1993) reported on the results of two epidemiological surveys of 2,519 Connecticut children (preadolescent) to determine if there were rural–urban differences in childhood psychopathology. These two surveys were referred to as the New Haven Child Survey and the Eastern Connecticut Child Survey. Children's emotional and behavioral problems were assessed with the Child Behavior Checklist and Teacher's Report. The study showed no significant difference in depressed symptoms in urban children versus rural children (boys: 6.1 vs. 3.2%; girls: 6.4 vs. 4.3%).

Epidemiological studies of comorbidity in child and adolescent depression are rare. Psychiatric comorbidity, or the coexistence of two or more distinct psychiatric diagnoses in the same individual, has been reported both in clinically referred (Weinstein et al., 1990) and in community, nonreferred samples of children (McGee et al., 1990). Pfeffer and Plutchik (1989), in a study of comorbidity in child psychiatric patients, found that their patients with major depressive disorder ($n = 39$) were also given diagnoses of borderline personality disorder (46%), specific developmental disorder (38.5%), conduct disorder (28%), adjustment disorder (23%), anxiety disorder (20.5%), and attention-deficit disorder (13%). Only 7.6% of their patients were without a co-diagnosis. Another study using standardized interviews and DSM-III or DSM-III-R criteria showed that rates of conduct–oppositional disorders were between 3.5 and 9.5 times higher in depressed than in nondepressed children (Angold and Costello, 1993). The authors also report that the presence of depression in children or adolescents increases the likelihood of another disorder up to 100-fold.

Apart from age-specific increase in mood disorders, there appears to be a steady increase in mood disorders in adolescents and young adults over the years. There is evidence of a secular trend for both depression and suicide. Successive cohorts born after 1950 appear to have an increased risk for depression and suicide relative to earlier birth cohorts, based on both prospective and retrospective studies (Hagnell et al., 1982; Klerman et al., 1985; Shaffer et al., 1988; Ryan et al., 1992).

Longitudinal assessments of children and adolescents with mood disorders are becoming increasingly important as these disorders can become a chronic condition and recurrent in nature. Supporting the previous point are the results of one naturalistic study of depressed children aged 8–13 years; untreated major depression lasted an average of 7.2 months, whereas dysthymic disorder lasted an average of 50 months (Kovacs et al., 1984a). Subsequent follow-up of these children revealed that a cumulative probability of a recurrence of depression could be expected of 40% within 2 years, and 72% within 5 years (Kovacs et al., 1984b).

Prevalence of Major Depression in Adults

The Epidemiologic Catchment Area (ECA) and the National Comorbid Survey (NCS) studies showed that rates of major depression are considerably higher than bipolar disorder. The 1-month prevalence for a major depressive episode (cross-site mean 1.6%) range from 1.1% in Piedmont to 2.0% in Los Angeles and New Haven. The 6-month rate of major depression across five sites in the ECA study was 2.2%, ranging from 1.5% in Piedmont to 2.8% in New Haven. The 12-month prevalence in the ECA study across the five sites was 2.6%, with a range from 1.7% in Piedmont to 3.4% in

New Haven. The lifetime prevalence (cross-site mean 4.4%) ranges from 2.9% in Baltimore to 5.8% in New Haven (Weissman et al., 1988a). The 12-month and lifetime prevalence in the NCS of a major depressive episode was 10.3 and 17.1%, respectively. The 4.4% prevalence of at least one lifetime episode of major depression estimated by the ECA study appears conservative in light of the 17.1% prevalence recently detected by the NCS (Kessler et al, 1994). The lifetime prevalence of a major depressive episode in the NCS by age and sex is shown in Table 1.

With regards to incidence, the annual incidence of first-onset major depression was 1.6 per 100 across four sites (New Haven site was excluded) (Eaton et al., 1989). Clinical and epidemiological studies have consistently documented an increased risk for major depression in women (Weissman and Klerman, 1977, 1985; Blazer et al., 1994).

Prevalence of Depression in the Elderly

Demographic changes in industrialized countries have produced a steady increase in the proportion of the population aged 65 and over (Hauser, 1986). There has been a major interest in the characteristics of this age group, especially in its mental health problems, which are among the most important causes of disability in old age. Furthermore, considerable enthusiasm has been placed on studying the prevalence of depressive disorders in the elderly in the community (Newmann, 1989), reported to be the most common mental disorders in the population aged 65 and over (Blazer et al., 1987; Gurland and Toner, 1982).

The ECA studies found unexpectedly low rates of major depression in the elderly compared to younger adults. In the ECA studies, Regier et al. (1988) found a 1-month prevalence of 0.7% for DSM-III major depression in 5,702 persons aged 65 years and over, across five sites. Kay et al. (1985), who used a survey with a version of the Geriatric Mental State Examination, found a higher 1-month prevalence (6.3% in the 70–79 year age group, 15.5% in persons age 80 years and over) than the others. Perhaps the higher prevalence rate obtained was a result of the method of ascertainment used, definition of age groups used, or the type of population under study. The 6-month prevalence of a DSM-III major depressive episode without bereavement, employing the Diagnostic Interview Schedule in the over-65-year group in men ranged from as low as 0.1% in St. Louis to as high as 0.5% in New Haven. In women the 6-month prevalence ranged from 1.0% in St. Louis to 1.6% in New Haven (Myers et al., 1984). In the East Baltimore site, Kramer et al. (1985) reported the 6-month prevalence of DSM-III major depression to be 0.7% in those aged 65–74 years and 1.3% in those ≥ 75 years old. In the New Haven site, Weissman et al. (1985) found a 6-month

TABLE 1. Prevalence of Lifetime Major Depressive Episode by Sex and Age from the National Comorbidity Survey (N = 8,098)

Age (yr)	Male (%)	Female (%)	Total (%)
15–24	11.0	20.8	15.7
25–34	13.1	19.4	16.5
35–44	14.7	23.8	19.2
45–54	11.8	21.8	16.7
Total	12.7	21.3	17.1

prevalence of 1.1% (0.6% in men and 1.4% in women) for major depression (without bereavement) in persons aged 65 years and over. Blazer et al. (1987) reported a 6-month prevalence of 0.8% for major depression in a sample of 1,304 persons aged 60 years and over at the North Carolina site. Bland et al. (1988) found a 6-month prevalence of 1.2% for major depression in persons aged 65 years or more living in the community in Edmonton, Canada. In the ECA study, the 1-year prevalence for major depressive episodes in the 65+ age group (Weissman et al., 1988a) ranged in the five sites from as low as 0.1% in St. Louis and Piedmont to as high as 0.8% in New Haven in men. In women, 1-year prevalence rates vary from 0.6% in St. Louis to 1.8% in New Haven (women consistently showing higher rates than men for major depression in all age groups).

In a more recent epidemiological study, the point prevalence of depressive disorders in Canberra, Australia, was estimated in a sample of persons aged 70 years and over, which included those living in the community and in institutional settings. The point prevalence of depressive episodes for those between 70 and 79 years was 3.3 and 3.4% for those over 80 years as defined by ICD-10 diagnostic criteria. With DSM-III-R major depressive episodes, the point prevalence was 0.7% in the 70- to 79-year group and 1.8% in the 80+ year group (Henderson et al., 1993). Phillips and Henderson (1991) in a survey of Melbourne nursing homes found a point prevalence of 9.7 for DSM-III-R major depressive disorder. Using Draft ICD-10, they found rates of 6.7% for mild and moderate depression and 6.1% for severe depressive episodes. These last two studies illustrate how prevalence rates may vary (even in the same population under study) depending on the method of assessment used as well as on the setting in which it is determined. With regards to the incidence of major depression in the elderly, Eaton and colleagues (1989) showed that across four of the five sites in the ECA study, the rate of DSM-III major depression gradually declines in men 65 and older, and in women the annual incidence turns downward after the age of 45.

MANIA

Definition

The DSM-III-R diagnostic for manic episode are similar for children, adolescents, adults, and the elderly. DSM-III-R states that "because the essential features of Affective Disorders are the same in children and adults, there are no special categories corresponding to those disorders" (p. 27, American Psychiatric Association, 1990). A manic episode consists of a distinct period of elevated, expansive, or irritable mood accompanied by at least three (four, with irritability) of the following: (1) inflated self-esteem or grandiosity, (2) decreased need for sleep, (3) increased talkativeness, (4) flight of ideas, (5) distractibility, (6) increase in goal-directed activities or psychomotor agitation, and (7) increased involvement in pleasurable activities that have a high potential for painful consequence. There must also be marked impairment in functioning lasting a week or longer (American Psychiatric Association, 1990).

In bipolar children, affective disturbances are manifested more by irritability and crying than by a depressed or elated appearance. If depression or elation were present, children are more likely to be older (ages 9–12) at onset of illness (Carlson, 1980). The clinical presentation of early-onset illness differs from bipolar illness with later onset, as does the patient's experience of it. Diagnosis is difficult, and bipolar illness is frequently mistaken for conduct disorder, attention-deficit hyperactivity disorder, or schizophrenia. Strong evidence for the misdiagnosis of bipolar disorder in juvenile subjects comes from the study of Akiskal and colleagues (1985) who studied the offspring and juvenile kin of adult bipolar disorder patients. In this study, 68 subjects ages 6–24 years were seen within a year of the appearance of affective manifestations: prepubertal onset occurred in 10; adolescent onset in 41; and early adult onset in 17. Of these patients, 35% had major depression; 16% manic or mixed states; 18% dysthymia; 15% cyclothymia; and 16% presented with polysubstance abuse. The authors pointed out that none of the subjects were diagnosed correctly in prior episodes by a variety of clinicians, even though their clinical records were replete with affective symptoms (Akiskal et al., 1985). Bipolar disorder may be difficult to diagnose because its phenomenology overlaps with those of other disorders (e.g., attention-deficit hyperactivity disorder, conduct disorder, depression, schizophrenia, etc.) (Blacker and Tsuang, 1992).

Manic–depressive illness carries a high rate of relapse and recurrence. Because the vast majority of such manic episodes are recurring in nature and require psychiatric hospitalization, this illness has a major impact on the health care resources of the nation. In addition, the incidence and prevalence of any illness is of interest both for an understanding of the natural history of the disorder and for utilization of health services.

Incidence and Prevalence of Mania

In order to determine the incidence and prevalence of bipolar disorder, mania is the defining characteristic used, as depressive illness can also occur in a unipolar form. Accurate estimation of the incidence or prevalence of mania is difficult, as mania by definition results in admission to the hospital; thus, most incidence and prevalence estimates of mania correspond to "treated" mania (Tsuang et al., 1988).

Prevalence of Mania in Childhood

Many patients experience their first episode of manic–depressive illness before the age of 20 (Olsen, 1961). Although the occurrence of mania and depression in adolescence is well established, early childhood onset remains controversial. The onset of the manic phase of bipolar manic–depressive illness appears to be very rare prior to puberty. Reports of mania in prepubertal children have been primarily anecdotal. The requirement of stringent criteria that derived from the most typical features of adult patients and required the presence of family history of classic manic–depressive illness may make the diagnosis of bipolar disorder in children quite restrictive. Kraepelin in 1921 reported that in a sample of 900 manic–depressive patients, 0.4% had their first manic–depressive episode before the age of 10. He concluded that the greatest frequency of first attacks occurs between the ages of 15 and 20 years. Bleuler (1934) also observed that "individual cases" of manic–depressive illness may begin as early as in childhood. Gillispie's textbook (1939) discussed how other authors felt that manic–depressive illness in childhood was relatively uncommon. Later on, Winokur et al. (1969) concluded that manic–depressive disease could occur in childhood and probably begins before the onset of pubertal changes. Some authors suggest that the difficulties in identifying cases of childhood manic–depressive illness stem from the different definitions of the age group "children." Later investigators suggested that the designation be limited to those of 12 years and under (Bradley, 1937; Anthony and Scott, 1960; Winokur et al., 1969).

Anthony and Scott (1960) reviewed the psychiatric literature from 1884 to 1954 and identified only 28 cases of alleged manic episodes in young children. After applying systematic diagnostic criteria to these clinical reports, the authors felt that all of the cases had been erroneously diagnosed. Since this review, only a handful of cases have been described (Frommer, 1968; Feinstein and Wolpert, 1973; McKnew et al., 1974; Warneke, 1975; Weinburg and Brumback 1976; Davis, 1979). Weinburg and Brumback (1976) and Loranger and Levine (1978) have suggested that to identify cases of childhood mania, such children should have been followed up through adolescence and adulthood and then give evidence of bipolar affective illness. As of 1979, less than 100 cases of childhood manic–depressive illness have been described in the world literature (Coll and Bland, 1979). A later review of the literature by Carlson (1980) identified 19 additional cases of probable bipolar affective disorder in children age 12 or younger. The author reported the onset of first affective symptoms ranged from as early as 15 months of age to 12 years old, with a mean of 9 years. Following these reports, prepubertal manic–depressive illness continued to be reported as isolated case histories, including four cases of rapid-cycling beginning at age 11 or 12. Kron and colleagues (1982) argue that true bipolar illness, with its biphasic periodicity and elation, is "extremely rare" before the age of 12. In a recent review that included 898 patients, there were only 3 patients with manic–depressive illness under the age 10, compared to 24 patients in the 10 and 14 age group (Goodwin and Jamison, 1990).

The relative absence of bipolar affective illness in childhood has in part been hypothesized to be secondary to cognitive immaturity resulting in the lack of awareness of his or her mood state, a theory previously postulated to occur in childhood major psychoses. The theory postulates that true delusions and thought disorder cannot exist at such an early age because the lack of cognitive maturity prevents the use of deductive logic (Lester and LaRoche, 1978). Based on this theory, the incidence of mania increases from early childhood to adulthood. One retrospective chart review of 200 patients who met DSM-III criteria for mania found no case of treated mania prior to age 13, although five first became ill at that age (Loranger and Levine, 1978). This study also reported that in patients less than 14 years of age the cumulative percentage was 3% for first hospitalization, 4.5% for first treatment, and 8% of first symptoms. In agreement with the previous study, treatment data from affectively ill patients studied at the Lithium Clinic of New York State Psychiatric Institute revealed that only 5% of bipolar I patients had psychiatric treatment prior to the age of 15 years (Kuyler et al., 1980).

Rates of bipolar disorder in children may vary depending if the parents suffer from bipolar disorder. Weissman and colleagues (1988b) report a greatly increased rate (14-fold) in the onset of depression before age 13 in children of probands who had an onset before age 20.

In summary, it is estimated that the point prevalence of bipolar illness in prepuberty is uncommon and ranges from 0.2 to 0.4%.

Prevalence of Manic–Depressive Illness in Adolescence

Although the question of early childhood onset of manic–depressive disease remains to be answered, onset in adolescence seems established although uncommon (Coll and Bland, 1979). No cases of mania or hypomania were found in the studies of juvenile offspring (Greenhill and Shopsin, 1979; McKnew et al., 1979; O'Connell et al., 1979;

Kuyler et al., 1980). The affective symptoms in manic–depressive illness show a remark-able consistency between adolescents and adults (Carlson, 1980). The most common symptoms in the depressed phase were dysphoric mood, low self-esteem, fatigue, insomnia, anorexia, suicidal ruminations, and psychomotor retardation. In the manic phase the most common symptoms were euphoria, irritability, distractibility, grandios-ity, and insomnia. Psychotic symptoms during the depressed phase were, however, much more common in the adolescents. Goodwin and Jamison (1990) pooled data from 10 studies with a total of 1,304 patients and found that the most frequent age at onset was 20–30 years, with a second, smaller, peak in late adolescence (15–19 years). The National Institute of Mental Health Epidemiologic Catchment Area (ECA) study (Regier et al., 1988) found a median age at onset of 18. Estimates of the prevalence of mania in adolescents is difficult because of the often tumultuous nature of adoles-cence that confounds the problem of accurate diagnosis. Depression often is misdiag-nosed as a physical disease, and hypomania can be misdiagnosed as hyperactivity or antisocial personality disorders (Bowden and Sarabia, 1980). Most bipolar illness in young adolescents occurs as mixed state or a rapid-cycling disorder (Ryan and Puig-Antich, 1986). Mixed states in this age group can be confounded with a diagnosis of conduct disorder or depressed adolescents who are notably irritable. Another problem in the differential diagnosis of manic–depressive illness in adolescents results from the overdiagnosis of schizophrenia. Weiner and Del Gaudio (1976), in a study of 1,300 adolescent patients in Monroe County, New York, found that only 1 patient was diagnosed as manic–depressive; schizophrenia was diagnosed 40 times as frequently. Bipolar illness in adolescents also is commonly misdiagnosed as atypical psychosis (Hsu and Starzynski, 1986). Despite these difficulties in diagnosis, many studies make it clear that adolescent manic–depressive illness can be identified reliably through the use of standardized adult diagnostic criteria, such as the DSM-III-R. For adolescents, the point prevalence of bipolar disorder has been estimated at 1%, not much different than that of adults. In adolescents, bipolar disorder is of equal prevalence in both genders.

Prevalence and Incidence of Mania in Adults

The National Institute of Mental Health (NIMH) ECA (Regier et al. 1984, 1988; Robins et al., 1984) and more recently the Edmonton study (Fogarty et al. 1994) and the National Collaborative Study (NCS) (Kessler et al., 1994) provide rates for mania in the general population (Table 2). The ECA program collected data on bipolar disorder according to the DSM-III criteria with the use of the Diagnostic Interview Schedule (DIS) (Robins et al., 1981). With the exception of the study conducted by Weissman and Myers (1978), it is the first study in this country that has obtained prevalence rates for bipolar disorder utilizing structured diagnostic instruments. Using a probability sample, the ECA project obtained prevalence data for both bipolar I and specific manic symptoms (Weissman et al., 1991). The A criteria for a manic episode consisting of elevated, expansive, or irritable mood for at least one-week duration, had a lifetime prevalence of 2.7%. The most frequent manic symptom reported was hyperactivity (9.3%), followed by decreased need for sleep (7.5%), and distractibil-ity (7.2%). Not surprisingly, manic symptoms were more frequent in the age group 18–29, and also in men more than in women. The lifetime prevalence rate of manic episode was 0.8% (Robins et al., 1984). The age group with the highest lifetime preva-lence rate was 30–44, in contrast to manic symptoms where the highest prevalence

**TABLE 2. ECA and NCS Lifetime Prevalence *n* (%) of
Manic Episode by Age and Sex**

	ECA	Edmonton	NCS
Total	0.8	0.6	1.6
Age			
18–29	1.1		
30–44	1.4		
46–64	0.3		
65 +	0.1		
Sex			
Male	0.7	1.6	
Female	0.9	1.7	

was in the 18–29 group. There was also a difference for bipolar I across different sites with New Haven showing a 1.2% and St. Louis 1.0% in contrast to 0.6% for Baltimore and Los Angeles, and 3.4% for Durham. The rates for bipolar II disorder were also inconsistent across sites, ranging from 0.4% in Durham to 0.6% in Baltimore. The one-year prevalence of bipolar I disorder showed again only a difference in age, with the highest rate 1.2% in the age group 30–44.

One-month prevalence for manic episodes (Regier et al., 1988) ranged in the five sites from as low as 0.1% in Los Angeles to 0.6% in St. Louis. The highest prevalence for males concentrated in the 25–44 age group where it was 0.5%, and for females in the 18–24 age group, where it was 0.8%. Regier et al. (1993) recently estimated a one-year prevalence of 1.2%. Weissman et al. (1988a) reported that the mean age of onset of bipolar disorder in the ECA data was 21 years old. The mean age of onset across the five sites was 21.2 years, adjusting for the age distribution at each site. The range was 17.9 years for the Los Angeles site, compared to 26.3 years for the Baltimore site.

Egeland and Hostetter (1983) reported on their epidemiologic study of affective disorders among the Amish. It was a 6-year study of affective disorders among the Old Order Amish, with approximately 11,000 residents. The prevalence of bipolar I and II disorders in the population age 15 and over was 0.46%.

The National Comorbidity Survey (NCS) (Kessler et al., 1994) is based on a probability sample of individuals age 15–54 from noninstitutionalized individuals from 48 states. The NCS reported a lifetime prevalence of 1.6% for a manic episode compared to only 0.6% for nonaffective psychosis (schizophrenia, schizophreniform disorder, schizoaffective disorder, delusional disorder, and atypical psychosis). The one-year prevalence for a manic episode was 1.3% (Kessler et al., 1994). It is not clear why there was a higher prevalence rate in the NCS study compared to the ECA and Edmonton study. It is possible that the different diagnostic instrument used to arrive at a diagnosis of mania or the sampling strategy may account for this difference.

In addition to the ECA study, a number of population-based prevalent studies using structured diagnostic instruments and modern diagnostic criteria have been conducted outside the United States. We will describe some of those studies. In a community surveyed in Florence, Italy, by Faravelli et al. (1990), DSM-III one-year prevalence for bipolar I disorder was 1.86% for females and 0.65% for males. For bipolar II disorder, the overall prevalence was 0.2%. In a study in Taiwan, Hwu and collaborators (1989) utilized the DIS and found a prevalence for manic episode of

1.6% for Tapei, 0.7% for small towns, and 1.0% for rural villages. Another study that utilized DIS was conducted in Puerto Rico by Canino and collaborators (1987). The lifetime prevalence for manic episode was 0.7% for males and 0.4% for females. Bland et al. (1988) conducted a prevalence study in Alberta, Canada, utilizing the DIS and found the lifetime prevalence for manic episode was 0.7% for males and 0.4% for females. Another study conducted in the Netherlands (Hodiamont et al., 1987) utilized the Present State Examination (PSE) and found that for manic episodes, the prevalence was 0.1% for both genders. More recently, the Edmonton study reports a lifetime prevalence rate of 0.6% for both sexes combined (Fogarty et al., 1994).

Considerable variation in the incidence of bipolar disorder has been reported from 0.9 per 100,000 per year in Canada to 8.7 per 100,000 in the United Kingdom (Hunt et al., 1993). Boyd and Weissman (1981) have reported incidence data for bipolar disorders in Scandinavian countries. The annual incidence rate for bipolar disorders varied from 9.2 to 15.2 cases per 100,000 subjects in males and 7.4 to 32.5 cases per 100,000 in females. Leff and collaborators (1976), using the PSE, obtained first admission rates for patients hospitalized with mania in London, England, and Aarhus, Denmark. The prevalence rate was 2.6 per 100,000 individuals in both sites. The ECA project has also provided incidence data. In a recent publication, Regier et al. (1993) reported new cases during a one-year period (annual incidence rates). The project, known as Wave 2 of the ECA study, was conducted on approximately 20% of the initial population. This prospective follow-up permitted the estimation of new cases as well as of relapses. For bipolar disorder, the annual cumulative rate was 0.5 ± 0.1%.

Prevalence of Mania in the Elderly

The age of onset of bipolar illness in the United States generally fits a unimodal distribution. Manic–depressive patients have a mean age of onset of 30, whereas those with major depressive disorder first become ill between the ages of 40 and 50. Several investigators have reported that the incidence of manic–depressive illness rises until the age of 35 and then gradually declines (Faris and Dunham, 1939; Myers et al., 1984; Weissman et al., 1988a). Onsets of affective disorders generally are less frequent in the 65 and older age category (Myers et al., 1984; Weissman et al., 1988a). Spicer and associates (1973) found that the incidence of mania consistently increased with age and that half of the new cases occurred in those over the age of 50. Earlier, both Wertham (1929) and Roth (1955) presented data confirming the onset of mania after age 60. One study reported an incidence of 0.6% of mania of the total cases of affective disorder of a total of 472 patients admitted during the years 1934, 1936, 1948, and 1949 (Roth, 1955). Loranger and Levine (1978) reported that in patients more than 64 years old the cumulative percentages for first hospitalization was 98.5%, for first treatment 99%, and of first symptoms was 99.5%. The prevalence of DSM-III mania from the NIMH ECA study in the over-65 age group was reported to be 0.1%, similar to the 45- to 64-year-old age group and significantly lower than individuals aged 18–44 (Weissman et al., 1988a).

In the ECA study, the one-year prevalence for bipolar disorder in the 65+ age group (Weissman et al., 1988a) ranged in the five sites from as low as 0.0% in Baltimore and Los Angeles to as high as 0.4% in St. Louis. The 6-month prevalence of a DSM-III manic episode, employing the DIS in the over-65 year group in men and women was 0% for all three sites (Myers et al., 1984). The prevalence of manic syndromes are relatively common among elderly psychiatric patients. Mania or hypomania has been reported to range between 5 and 10% of the diagnoses of elderly patients (over 60 years old) referred for treatment of affective illness or admitted for psychiatric hospitalization (Roth, 1955; Post, 1965; Yassa et al., 1988a,b). In contrast, Kramer et al. (1985) did not detect a current manic syndrome in any of 923 ambulatory community residents aged at least 65 years for whom interview data were obtained as part of the ECA study. Some authors suggest that the risk of mania declines with aging (Wertham, 1929; Loranger and Levine, 1978; Clayton, 1981, 1986). In contrast, other authors suggest that the incidence of mania may be increasing (Spicer et al., 1973; Eagles and Whalley, 1985). Young and Klerman (1992) recently reviewed mania in late life with a focus on age at onset and concluded that the number of systematic studies of such patients is limited. Based on the literature available to date, it remains unclear whether the incidence of mania is changing with increased age. Many studies reported that late-onset mania was associated with neurological disorders (Krauthammer and Klerman, 1978; Shulman and Post, 1980; Stone, 1989). A recent study by Tohen and collaborators (1994) suggested that many first-episode bipolar cases in the elderly are associated with a comorbid cerebral-vascular disorder. One study found a higher mortality rate in elderly manic patients than in other elderly persons in a community sample (Dhingra and Rabins, 1991), whereas one study found this to be true only among men (Tohen et al., 1994). Finally, Krauthammer and Klerman (1978) point out that, with increasing age, the interval between episodes decreases and the length of episodes increases.

REFERENCES

Akiskal HS, Downs J, Jordan P, Watson S, Daugherty D, Pruitt DB (1985): Affective disorders in referred children and younger siblings of manic-depressives: Mode of onset and prospective course. Arch Gen Psychiatry 42:996–1003.

American Psychiatric Association (1994): "Diagnostic and Statistical Manual of Mental Disorders," 4th ed. Washington, DC: American Psychiatric Association.

American Psychiatric Association (1990): "Diagnostic and Statistical Manual of Mental Disorders," 3rd ed, revised. Washington, DC: American Psychiatric Association.

Anderson JC, Williams S, McGee R, Silva P (1987): DSM-III disorders in preadolescent children. Arch Gen Psychiatry 44:69–76.

Angold A, Costello EJ (1993): Depressive comorbidity in children and adolescents: Empirical, theoretical, and methodological issues. Am J Psychiatry 150:1779–1791.

Anthony EJ, Scott P (1960): Manic-depressive psychosis in childhood. J Child Psychol Psychiatry 1:53–72.

Bird HR, Gould MS, Staghezza BM (1993): Patterns of diagnostic comorbidity in a community sample of children aged 9 through 16 years. J Am Acad Child Adolesc Psychiatry 32(2):361–368.

Blacker D, Tsuang MT (1992): Diagnostic boundaries of bipolar disorder and the limits of categorical diagnosis in psychiatry. Am J Psychiatry 149:1473–1483.

Bland RC, Newmann SC, Orn H (1988): Prevalence of psychiatric disorders in the elderly in Edmonton. Acta Psychiatr Scand 77:57–63.

Blazer DG, Kessler RC, McGonagle KA, Swartz MS (1994): The prevalence and distribution of major depression in a national comorbidity sample: The national comorbidity survey. Am J Psychiatry 151:979–986.

Blazer DG, Hughes DC, George LK (1987): The epidemiology of depression in an elderly community population. Gerontologist 27:281–287.

Bleuler E (1934): "Textbook of Psychiatry." New York: The MacMillan Company.

Bowden CL, Sarabia F (1980): Diagnosing manic-depressive illness in adolescents. Compr Psychiatry 21:263–269.

Boyd JH, Weissman MM (1981): Epidemiology of affective disorders: A re-examination and future directions. Arch Gen Psychiatry 38:1039–1046.

Bradley C (1937): Definition of childhood in psychiatric literature. Am J Psychiatry 94:33–36.

Canino GJ, Bird HR, Shrout PE, Rubio-Stipec M, Bravo M, Sesman M, Geuvara LM (1987): Prevalence of specific psychiatric disorders in Puerto Rico. Arch Gen Psychiatry 44:727–735.

Carlson GA (1980): Manic-depressive illness and cognitive immaturity. In RH Belmaker, HM van Praag (eds): "Mania: An Evolving Concept." New York: Spectrum Books, pp 281–289.

Carlson GA, Kashani JH (1988): Phenomenology of major depression from childhood through adulthood: Analysis of three studies. Am J Psychiatry 145:1222–1225.

Clayton PJ (1986): Manic symptoms in the elderly. In Busse E (ed): "Aspects of Aging." Philadelphia: Smith Kline & French.

Clayton PJ (1981): The epidemiology of bipolar affective disorder. Compr Psychiatry 22:31–43.

Coll PG, Bland R (1979): Manic-depressive illness in adolescence and childhood: Review and case report. Can J Psychiatry 24:255–263.

Costello EJ, Burns BJ, Angold A, Leaf PJ (1993): How can epidemiology improve mental health service for children and adolescents? J Am Acad Child Adolesc Psychiatry 32:1106–1113.

Costello EJ, Edelbrock C, Bruns BJ, Dulcan MK, Brent D, Janiszewski S (1988): Psychiatric disorders in pediatric primary care. Arch Gen Psychiatry 45:1107–1116.

Davis R (1979): Manic-depressive variant syndrome of childhood: A preliminary report. Am J Psychiatry 136:702–705.

Dhingra U, Rabins PV (1991): Mania in the elderly: A five- to seven-year follow-up. J Am Geriatr Soc 39:581–583.

Domènech E, Canals J, Fernández J, Marti C (1992): Epidemiología de la depressió major a la pubertat; resultats de tres anys de seguiment. Revista de la Reial Acadèmia de Medicina de Barcelona 7(1):35–40.

Downes JJ, Davies ADM, Copeland JRM (1988): Organization of depressive symptoms in the elderly population: Hierarchical patterns and Guttman scales. Psychol Aging 3:367–374.

Eagles JM, Whalley LJ (1985): Aging and affective disorders: The age at first onset of affective disorders in Scotland, 1966–1978. Br J Psychiatry 147:180–187.

Eaton WW, Kramer M, Anthony JC, Dryman A, Shapiro S, Locke BZ (1989): The incidence of specific DIS/DSM-III mental disorders: Data from the NIMH Epidemiologic Catchment Area Program. Acta Psychiatr Scand 79:163–178.

Egeland JA, Hostetter AM (1983): Amish study I: Affective disorders among the Amish, 1976–1980. Am J Psychiatry 140(1):56–61.

Faravelli C, Degl'Innocenti BG, Aiazzi L, Incerpi G, Pallanti S (1990): Epidemiology of mood disorders: A community survey in Florence. J Affect Disord 20:135–141.

Faris REL, Dunham HW (1939): "Mental Disorders in Urban Areas: An Ecological Study of Schizophrenia and Other Psychoses." Chicago: University of Chicago Press.

Feinstein SC, Wolpert EA (1973): Juvenile manic-depressive illness: Clinical and therapeutic considerations. J Am Acad Child Psychiatry 12:123–136.

Fendrich M, Weissman MM, Warner V (1991): Longitudinal assessment of major depression and anxiety disorders in children. J Am Acad Child Adolesc Psychiatry 30:38–42.

Fleming JE, Offord DR (1990): Epidemiology of childhood depressive disorders: A critical review. J Am Acad Child and Adolesc Psychiatry 29:571–580.

Fleming JE, Offord DR, Boyle MH (1989): The Ontario Child Health Study: Prevalence of childhood and adolescent depression in the community. Br J Psychiatry 155:647–654.

Fogarty F, Russell JM, Newman SC, Bland RC (1994): Mania. Acta Psychiatr Scand Suppl 376:16–23.

Friedman RC, Hurt SW, Clarkin JF, Corn R, Arnoff MS (1983): Symptoms of depression among adolescents and young adults. J Affective Disord 5:37–43.

Frommer EA (1968): Depressive illness in childhood. In Coppen A, Walk A (eds): "Recent Developments in Affective Disorders." Br J Psychiatry. Special publication. No. 2. 117–136.

Garrison CZ, Jackson KL, Marsteller F, McKeown R, Addy C (1990): A longitudinal study of depressive symptomatology in young adolescents. J Am Acad Child and Adolescent Psychiatry 29:581–585.

Gillispie RD (1939): "A Survey of Child Psychiatry." London: Oxford University Press, p 65.

Goodwin FK, Jamison KR (1990): "Manic-Depressive Illness." New York: Oxford University Press.

Greenhill LL, Shopsin B (1979): Survey of mental disorders in the children of patients with affective disorders. In "Generic Aspects of Affective Illness." Mendlewicz J, Shopsin B (eds): New York: Spectrum Publications, pp 75–92.

Gurland BJ, Toner JA (1982): Depression in the elderly: A review of recently published studies. In Eiser C (ed): "Annual Review of Gerontology and Geriatrics," Volume 3. New York: Springer, pp 228–265.

Hagnell O, Lanke J, Rorsman B, Osjejo L (1982): Are we entering an age of melancholy? Depressive illness in a prospective epidemiological study of over 25 years: The Lundby Study, Sweden. Psychol Med 12:279–289.

Hauser PM (1986): Aging and increasing longevity of world population. In Hafner H, Moschel G, Sartorius N (eds): "Mental Health in the Elderly." Berlin: Springer-Verlag, pp 9–14.

Henderson AS, Jorm AF, Mackinnon A, Christensen H, Scott LR, Korten AE, Doyle C (1993): The prevalence of depressive disorders and the distribution of depressive symptoms in later life: A survey using Draft ICD-10 and DSM-III-R. Psychol Med 23:719–729.

Hodiamont P, Peer N, Syber N (1987): Epidemiological aspects of psychiatric disorder in a Dutch health area. Psychol Med 17:495–505.

Horwath E, Weissman MM (1995): Epidemiology of bipolar disorder. In Tsuang M, Tohen M, Zahner G (eds): "Textbook in Psychiatric Epidemiology." New York: John Wiley & Sons.

Hunt N, Adams S, Coxhead N, Sayer H, Murray C, Silverstone T (1993): The incidence of mania in two areas in the United Kingdom. Soc Psychiatry Psychiatr Epidemiol 28:281–284.

Hsu LKG, Starzynski JM (1986): Mania in adolescence. J Clin Psychiatry 47:596–599.

Hwu HG, Yeh EK, Chang LY (1989): Prevalence of psychiatric disorders in Taiwan defined by the Chinese Diagnostic Interview Schedule. Acta Psychiatr Scand 79:136–147.

Kashani J, McGee R, Clarkson S, Anderson J, Walton L, Williams S, Silva P, Robins A, Cyrtrin L, McKnew D (1983): Depression in a sample of 9-year-old children. Prevalence and associated characteristics. Arch Gen Psychiatry 40:1217–1223.

Kay DWK, Henderson AS, Scott R, Wilson J, Rickwood D, Grayson DA (1985): Dementia and depression among the elderly living in the Hobart community: The effect of the diagnostic criteria on the prevalence rates. Psychol Med 15:771–788.

Kessler RC, McGonagle KA, Zhao S, Nelson CB, Hughes M, Eshleman S, Wittchen HU, Kendler KS (1994): Lifetime and 12-month prevalence of DSM-III-R psychiatric disorders in the United States. Arch Gen Psychiatry 51:8–19.

Klerman GL, Lavori PW, Rice J, Reich T, Endicott J, Andreasen NC, Keller MB, Hirschfield RMA (1985): Birth-cohort trends in rates of major depressive disorder among relatives of patients with affective disorder. Arch Gen Psychiatry 42:689–693.

Kovacs M, Feinberg TL, Crouse-Novak MA, Paulauskas SL, Finkelstein R (1984a): Depressive disorders in childhood: I. A longitudinal prospective study of characteristics and recovery. Arch Gen Psychiatry 41:229–237.

Kovacs M, Feinberg TL, Crouse-Novak MA, Paulauskas SL, Pollock M, Finkelstein R (1984b): Depressive disorders in childhood: II. A longitudinal study of risk for a subsequent episode. Arch Gen Psychiatry 41:643–649.

Kramer M, German PS, Anthony JC, Von Korff M, Skinner EA (1985): Patterns of mental disorders among the elderly residents of eastern Baltimore. J Am Geriatr Soc 33:236–245.

Kraepelin E (1921): "Manic-Depressive Insanity and Paranoia," Barclay RM (trans). Edinburgh: E&S Livingston.

Krauthammer C, Klerman GL (1978): Secondary mania. Arch Gen Psychiatry 35:1333–1339.

Kron L, Decina P, Kestenbaum CJ, Farber S, Gargan M, Fieve R (1982): The offspring of bipolar manic-depressive: Clinical features. In Feinstein SC, Looney JG, Schwartzbert AZ (eds): "Adolescent Psychiatry," Vol 10: Chicago: University Press, pp 273–291.

Kuyler PL, Rosenthal L, Igel G, Dunner DL, Fieve RR (1980): Psychopathology among children of manic-depressive patients. Biol Psychiatry 15:589–597.

Leff JP, Fischer M, Bertelsen A (1976): A cross-national epidemiological study of mania. Br J Psychiatry 129:428–442.

Lester EP, LaRoche C (1978): Schizophreniform psychoses of childhood: Therapeutic considerations. Compr Psychiat 19:153–159.

Lilienfeld AM, Lilienfeld DE (1980): "Foundations of Epidemiology," 2nd ed. New York: Oxford University Press.

Loranger AW, Levine PM (1978): Age at onset of bipolar affective illness. Arch Gen Psychiatry 35:1345–1348.

McGee R, Feehan M, Williams S, Partridge F, Silva PA, Kelly J (1990): DSM-III disorders in a large sample of adolescents. J Am Acad Child Adolesc Psychiatry 29:611–619.

McKnew DH Jr, Cytryn L, Efron AM, Gershon ES, Bunney WE Jr (1979): Offspring of patients with affective disorders. Br J Psychiatry 134:148–152.

McKnew DH Jr, Cytryn L, White I (1974): Clinical and biochemical correlates of hypomania in a child. J Am Acad Child Psychiatry 13:576–585.

Myers JK, Weissman MM, Tischler GL, Holzer CE, Leaf PJ, Orvaschel H, Anthony JC, Boyd JH, Burke JD, Kramer M, Stoltzman R (1984): Six-month prevalence of psychiatric disorders in three communities: 1980 to 1982. Arch Gen Psychiatry 41:959–967.

Newmann JP (1989): Aging and depression. Psych. Aging 4:150–165.

O'Connell RA, Mayo JA, O'Brien JD, Misrsheidaie F (1979): Children of bipolar manic-depressives. In Mendlewicz J, Shopsin B (eds): "Genetic Aspects of Affective Illness." New York: SP Medical and Scientific Books, pp 55–68.

Olsen T (1961): Follow-up study of manic-depressive patients whose first attack occurred before the age of 19. Acta Psychiatr Scand 37 (Suppl 162):45–51.

Pfeffer CR, Plutchik R (1989): Co-occurrence of psychiatric disorders in child psychiatric patients and nonpatients: A circumplex model. Compr Psychiatry 30:275–282.

Phillips CJ, Henderson AS (1991): The prevalence of depression among Australian nursing-home residents: Results using draft ICD-10 and DSM-III-R criteria. Psychol Med 21:739–748.

Polaino-Lorente A, Domenèch E (1993): Prevalence of childhood depression: Results of the first study in Spain. J Child Psychol Psychiat 34(6):1007–1017.

Post F (1965): "The Clinical Psychiatry of Late Life." Oxford: Pegamon Press, pp 79–82.

Regier DA, Narrow WE, Rae DS, Manderscheid RW, Locke BZ, Goodwin FK (1993): The de Facto US Mental and Addictive Disorders Service System. Epidemiologic Catchment Area Prospective 1-Year Prevalence Rates of Disorders and Services. Arch Gen Psychiatry 50:85–94.

Regier DA, Boyd JH, Rae DS, Burke JD, Locke BZ, Myers JK, Kramer M, Robins LN, George LK, Karno M (1988): One-month prevalence of mental disorders in the United States: Based on five epidemiologic catchment area sites. Arch Gen Psychiatry 45:977–986.

Regier DA, Myers JK, Kramer M, Robins LN, Blazer DG, Hough RL, Eaton WW, Locke BZ (1984): The NIMH Epidemiologic Catchment Area (ECA) Program: Historical context, major objectives, and study population characteristics. Arch Gen Psychiatry 41:934–941.

Robins LN, Helzer JE, Weissman MM, Orvaschel H, Gruenberg E, Burke JD Jr, Regier DA (1984): Lifetime prevalence of specific psychiatric disorders in three sites. Arch Gen Psychiatry 41:949–958.

Robins LN, Helzer JE, Croughan J, Ratcliff KS (1981): National Institute of Mental Health Diagnostic Interview Schedule: Its history, characteristics, and validity. Arch Gen Psychiatry 38:381–389.

Roth M (1955): The natural history of mental disorder in old age. J Ment Sci 101:281–401.

Ryan ND, Puig-Antich J (1986): Affective illness in adolescence. In Hales RE, Frances AJ (eds): "American Psychiatric Association Annual Review," Vol. 5. Washington, DC: American Psychiatric Press, pp 420–450.

Ryan ND, Williamson DE, Iyengar S, Orvaschel H, Reich T, Dahl RE, Puig-Antich J (1992): A secular increase in child and adolescent onset affective disorder. J Am Acad Child Adolesc Psychiatry 31:4:600–605.

Shaffer D, Garland A, Gould M, Fisher P, Trautman P (1988): Preventing teenage suicide: A critical review. J Am Acad Child Adolesc Psychiatry 27(6):675–687.

Shulman KI, Post F (1980): Bipolar affective disorder in old age. Br J Psychiatry 136:26–32.

Spicer CC, Hare EH, Slater E (1973): Neurotic and psychotic forms of depressive illness: Evidence from age incidence in a national sample. Br J Psychiatry 123:535–541.

Stone K (1989): Mania in the elderly. Br J Psychiatry 155:220–224.

Strober M, Carlson G (1982): Bipolar illness in adolescents with major depression. Clinical, genetic, and psychopharmacologic predictors in a three- to four-year prospective follow-up investigation. Arch Gen Psychiatry 39:549–555.

Strober M, Green J, Carlson G (1981): Phenomenology and subtypes of major depressive disorder in adolescence. J Affective Disord 3:281–290.

Tohen M, Goodwin FK (1995): Epidemiology of bipolar disorder. In Tsuang M, Tohen M, Zahner G (eds): "Textbook in Psychiatric Epidemiology." John Wiley & Sons, New York.

Tohen M, Shulman KI, Satlin A (1994): First-episode mania in late life. Am J Psychiatry 151:130–132.

Tsuang MT, Tohen M, Murphy JM (1988): "Psychiatric Epidemiology" In: Nicholi AM (ed): the New Harvard Guide to Psychiatry. Cambridge, MA: Harvard University Press, pp 761–779.

Velez CN, Johnson J, Cohen P (1989): A longitudinal analysis of selected risk factors for childhood psychopathology. J Am Acad Child Adolesc Psychiatry 28:861–864.

Warneke L (1975): A case of manic depressive illness in childhood. Can Psychiatr Assoc J 20:195–200.

Weinburg WA, Brumback RA (1976): Mania in childhood: Case studies and literature review. Am J Diseases of Child 130:380–385.

Weiner IB, Del Gaudio AC (1976): Psychopathology in adolescence. Arch Gen Psychiatry 33:187–193.

Weinstein SR, Noam GG, Grimes K, Stone K, Schwab-Stone M (1990): Convergence of DSM-III diagnoses and self-reported symptoms in child and adolescent inpatients. J Am Acad Child Adolesc Psychiatry 29:627–634.

Weissman MM, Klerman GL (1985): Gender and depression. Trends Neurosci 8:416–420.

Weissman MM, Myers JK (1978): Affective disorders in a U.S. urban community: The use of Research Diagnostic Criteria in a epidemiologic survey. Arch Gen Psychiatry 35:1304–1311.

Weissman MM, Klerman GL (1977): Sex differences in the epidemiology of depression. Arch Gen Psychiatry 34:98–111.

Weissman MM, Bruce ML, Leaf PJ, Florio LP, Holzer C (1991): "Psychiatric disorders in America." In Robins L, Regier D (eds): Free Press: New York pp 53–81.

Weissman MM, Leaf PH, Tischler GL, Blazer DG, Karno M, Bruce ML, Florio LP (1988a): Affective disorders in five United States communities. Psychol Med 18:141–153.

Weissman MM, Warner V, Wickramaratne P, Prusoff BA (1988b): Early-onset major depression in parents and their children. J Affective Disord 15:269–277.

Weissman MM, Myers JK, Tischler GL, Holzer CE, Leaf PJ, Orvaschel H, Brody JA (1985): Psychiatric disorders (DSM-III) and cognitive impairment in the elderly in a U.S. urban community. Acta Psychiatr Scand 71:366–379.

Welner Z, Welner A, McCrary D, Leonard M (1977): Psychopathology in children of inpatients with depression: a controlled study. J Nerv Men Dis 164:408.

Wertham FI (1929): A group of benign psychoses: Prolonged manic excitements: With a statistical study of age, duration and frequency in 200 manic attacks. Am J Psychiatry 9:17–78.

Winokur G, Clayton PJ, Reich T (1969): "Manic Depressive Illness." St. Louis: CV Mosby.

Yassa R, Nair V, Nastase C, Camille Y, Belvile L (1988a): Prevalence of bipolar disorder in a psychogeriatric population. J Affective Disord 14:197–201.

Yassa R, Nair NPV, Iskandar H (1988b): Late-onset bipolar disorder. Psychiatr Clin North Am 11:117–131.

Young RC, Klerman GL (1992): Mania in late life: Focus on age at onset. Am J Psychiatry 149:867–876.

Young JG, O'Brien JD, Gutterman EM, Cohen P (1987): Research on the clincial interview. J Am Child Adolesc Psychiatry 26:613–620.

Zahner GEP, Jacobs JH, Freedman DH, Trainor KF (1993): Rural-urban child psychopathology in a Northeastern U.S. state: 1986–1989. J Am Acad Child Adolesc Psychiatry 32(2):378–387.

CHAPTER 3

Genetics and Age at Onset

FRANCIS J. McMAHON and J. RAYMOND DePAULO

Department of Psychiatry and Behavioral Sciences, The Johns Hopkins University School of Medicine, Baltimore, MD 21287-7321

Age at onset is a very important variable in understanding complex phenotypes such as mood disorders. Age at onset can play a key role in making the phenotypic distinctions important in the identification of disease genes or the interpretation of genetic mechanisms. For example, age at onset can serve as a marker of etiologic heterogeneity, separating genetic from sporadic cases of common illnesses, as seen in breast cancer. Age at onset can also serve as a marker of genetic heterogeneity, helping to separate cases of the same disorder caused by different genes, as in Alzheimer's disease, or different mutations in the same gene, as in Duchenne/Becker muscular dystrophy. Variable age at onset may be a sign of DNA instability, as occurs in the triplet repeat sequences in the gene causing Huntington's disease. However, while it can help illuminate complex genetic phenomena, age at onset is itself a highly complex biological event.

WHY SHOULD MOOD DISORDERS HAVE A DELAYED AGE AT ONSET?

Even though depression and mania can clearly occur in children, mood disorders are diagnosed primarily in adults and adolescents, and it is often taken for granted that mood disorders have a delayed age at onset. If age at onset is to have heuristic value beyond mere description, however, we must continually ask why the onset of a primarily genetic disease should be delayed. Cystic fibrosis, Down's syndrome, and testicular feminization are all manifest early in life, while Huntington's disease, breast cancer, and non-insulin-dependent diabetes mellitus (NIDDM) are not. This reflects, in part, the variable genetic contribution to diseases such as breast cancer and NIDDM. But the fact that some genetic diseases have a delayed onset while others do not raises more general questions about the genetic mechanisms of disease, the answers to which may ultimately help us to better understand the complex causes of mood disorders.

In this chapter we will discuss the age at onset of mood disorders as it relates to their genetic causes. While we recognize that not all mood disorders share a primary

Mood Disorders Across the Life Span, Edited by Shulman, Tohen, and Kutcher
ISBN 0-471-10477-9 © 1996 Wiley-Liss, Inc.

genetic etiology, the onset of nongenetic mood disorders has more to do with timing of their various causes than with the disorders themselves, so we will not address these in depth. We will begin with an attempt to define the concept of age at onset of mood disorders, including issues of operationalism, reliability, and validity. A brief review of the age-at-onset literature for mood disorders will follow. Next we will discuss current models to account for delayed onset of disease, focusing on degeneration, developmental failure, and "two-hit" theories. The rapidly advancing research into the genetic mechanisms of delayed onset will also be summarized. Finally, we will outline some future directions for age-at-onset research in mood disorders.

DEFINING AGE AT ONSET

As often occurs in psychiatry, concepts that seem obvious when applied to physical diseases (such as myocardial infarction, appendicitis, and stroke) can be particularly obscure and puzzling when applied to mental diseases. Age at onset is just such a concept. When does a mood disorder begin? Is the onset marked by the first treatment contact, the first clear episode, the first symptoms, or by some clinically occult process that bears no obvious relationship to symptoms?

Faced with these difficult questions, most investigators have made the reasonable accommodation of using landmarks that can be operationally defined and reliably identified. These include age at first hospitalization, age at first episode of major depression, and age at first identified impairment, among others. Such landmarks can be reliably judged by trained interviewers (Egeland et al., 1987) and seem clinically reasonable. However, it would be a mistake to assume that clinically evident landmarks accurately indicate the beginning of the disease process. If we considered blindness the onset of glaucoma, there would be little progress on preventive strategies or rational treatments.

Age-at-onset data is usually collected retrospectively, which carries certain distinct disadvantages. First, a subject may be biased in recalling the onset of illness. Some studies suggest that subjects often forget an episode of major depression they reported when interviewed 1.5–4 years earlier (Bromet et al., 1986; Prusoff et al., 1988). Such forgetting may lead to the so-called Little Bo-Peep effect, where the same subject reports a later age at onset as he or she ages; thus age at onset seems to follow along behind. Second, a subject may tend to report an onset that corresponds to when his doctor made the diagnosis or commenced treatment, even though the illness may have actually commenced years earlier. Third, subjects who die shortly after falling ill will not be represented in retrospective studies. For these reasons, the retrospective nature of most age-at-onset data should be carefully considered in the evaluation and review of age-at-onset studies.

Age-at-onset data also poses difficult analytic problems. Unlike height or IQ, age at onset is typically not normally distributed. Thus, statistical tools based on the assumption of normality, such as means, standard deviations, and t-tests, may give misleading results. For descriptive analyses, frequency distributions give a better representation of the data but are subject to distortion when inappropriate age intervals are selected (Schork and Schork, 1990). For hypothesis-testing analyses, so-called nonparametric statistics, which make no assumptions about the underlying distribution, are particularly useful but tend to be less powerful than traditional, parametric approaches. Computerized bootstrap methods avoid many of the problems inherent in traditional statistical approaches but require specialized software not usually in the possession of the average researcher (Efron and Tibshirani, 1991).

Another analytic problem follows directly from the fact that age at onset is an event in linear time, not merely an attribute of a disease or a patient. Onset may be preceded by events that preclude its occurrence, such as death from an unrelated cause, or onset may occur after the patient is examined, and thus go unobserved. Statistical techniques based on actuarial life tables or survival analysis handle this problem by correcting for deaths and age at examination. Commonly used survival analysis techniques include the Kaplan–Meier estimator (Kaplan and Meier, 1958) and the Cox Proportional Hazards model (Cox, 1972). These techniques represent a significant advance but are not perfect. They do not work well on small samples, and they do not allow prediction of age at onset for any particular individual (Chase et al., 1983). Nevertheless, survival analysis has become the standard statistical approach in age-at-onset studies.

Ascertainment biases can also significantly affect age-at-onset observations. Methods for dealing with this problem have recently been reviewed by Chen et al. (1992). When studying a series of independently ascertained probands, age at onset will be underestimated unless the age structure of the total population is taken into account (Heimbuch et al., 1980). This occurs because no onset of illness can be observed at an age exceeding that of the oldest person in the sample. When age at onset among family members is being studied, there are multiple potential biases related to the fact that a family is typically studied because one particular relative has fallen ill at a particular time. These biases have vexed genetic epidemiologists for decades and will be detailed later in the discussion on "anticipation."

Several epidemiologic studies have described earlier onset of unipolar or bipolar disorder among persons born after 1945 (Robins et al., 1984; Gershon et al., 1987; Weissman et al., 1984b). This so-called cohort effect is of mysterious origin but may result from several environmental and cultural phenomena, as well as recall bias (Klerman and Weissman, 1989; Giuffra and Risch, 1994). Whatever the cause, the cohort effect is too large to be ignored and must be controlled for in studies of age at onset in mood disorders.

LITERATURE REVIEW

Age-at-onset studies of mood disorders can be broken into two groups, or eras: those that occurred before the advent of modern diagnostic concepts (chiefly the bipolar/unipolar distinction) and those that occurred afterward. Although formulated without the benefit of operational diagnostic criteria, Kraepelin's (1921, pp. 167–168) classic account still gives a good description of age at onset for mood disorders:

> The greatest frequency of first attacks falls . . . in the period of development . . . between the fifteenth and the twentieth year. But in the next decade also the number of attacks is still very great, and only gradually decreases after the thirtieth year.

There is reasonably good agreement about age at onset in the modern literature, provided the methods of ascertainment are taken into account. The first episode of mania or major depression in bipolar I (BPI) disorder tends to occur in the early twenties. For nonbipolar cases, the first major depression occurs later, toward the early thirties. There is disagreement in the literature as to the onset of bipolar II (BPII) disorder. Some studies have suggested an age at onset intermediate between that of BPI and recurrent unipolar disorder (Ayuso-Gutierrez and Ramos Brieva, 1982; Gershon et al., 1982; Weissman et al., 1991). Other studies have suggested an age at onset for BPII that is very close if not identical to that of BPI (Endicott et al., 1985; Coryell et al., 1985; Egeland et al., 1987; McMahon et al., 1994). For example, in a sample of families ascertained through a treated bipolar proband, we showed that relatives and probands with BPI disorder and those with BPII disorder had essentially identical age-at-onset distributions (McMahon et al., 1994) (Figure 1).

Several other general conclusions can be drawn. There are no marked differences in age at onset between males and females, but females experience a slightly earlier onset in some studies (Loranger and Levine, 1978; McMahon et al., 1994). In both bipolar and unipolar disorders, there is a general tendency for age at onset to vary inversely with the proportion of affected relatives (Taylor and Abrams, 1981; Weissman et al., 1984a; James, 1977; Price et al., 1987). This interesting phenomenon has been interpreted as an indication of several genes, each of relatively small effect, contributing to the onset of illness. However, the phenomenon may also reflect a greater proportion of genetically caused cases among patients experiencing early onset of illness.

Several studies have attempted to further define clinical subtypes of affective disorder based on age at onset. In general, very little has emerged from these efforts. There is a remarkable clinical similarity between a first episode of mania occurring at the usual age of, say, 24 and one occurring at the distinctly unusual (but not rare) age of 64 (reviewed in Young and Klerman, 1992). The only clinical difference seen in several studies is a greater prominence of psychotic features (i.e., hallucinations or delusions) in cases of early-onset bipolar disorder (Rosen et al., 1983; McGlashan, 1988; Blumenthal et al., 1987). Similarly, most studies indicate that unipolar disorder first occurring in late life (archaically referred to as *involutional melancholia*) is phenomenologically indistinguishable from unipolar disorder occurring at other ages (Brodaty et al., 1991; Conwell et al., 1989; Nelson et al., 1989). This is not to say that older patients with major depression are identical to younger patients: some symptoms of depression, such as agitation and cognitive impairment, appear to be dependent on age but not age at onset (Brodaty et al., 1991; Garvey and Schaffer, 1994).

Many late-life illnesses play a direct etiologic role in mood disorders, even though these illnesses may not account for a large proportion of cases in unselected groups of elderly patients. Strokes (Robinson et al., 1983) and Parkinson's disease (reviewed by Ring and Trimble, 1991) are two well-known examples. Several studies have found that comorbid neurological disorders and/or abnormal brain magnetic resonance imaging (MRI) findings are more common in late-onset mania (e.g., Tohen et al., 1994). This again suggests that age at onset is of value in distinguishing idiopathic— presumably genetic—cases from secondary or organic cases. But the relationship between such organic insults and genetic vulnerability may be complex. Organic insults may interact with genetic vulnerability in an additive or multiplicative fashion. For example, ischemic brain injury may lead to changes in gene expression that unmask a genetic vulnerability to depression. A more complete discussion of gene expression is presented later in this chapter.

MODELS OF DELAYED ONSET

The scientific value of a disease model depends on its ability to account for established facts as well as its ability to generate specific hypotheses that can be tested experimen-

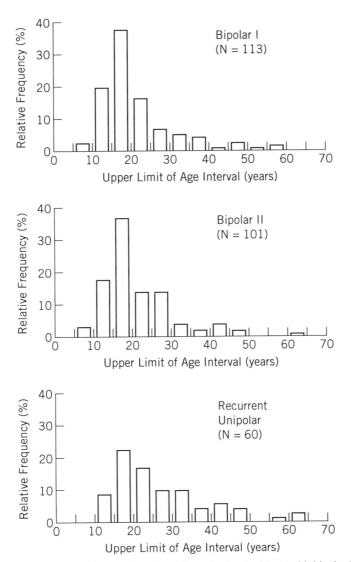

FIGURE 1. Age at first manic or major depressive episode of subjects with bipolar I, bipolar II, and recurrent unipolar disorders. From McMahon J, Stine OC, Chase GA, Meyers DA, Simpson SG, DePaulo JR (1994): Influence of clinical subtype, sex, and lineality on age at onset of major affective disorder in a family sample. Am J Psychiatry 151:210–215. Reprinted courtesy of the American Psychiatric Association.

tally. With this in mind, three models of delayed disease onset will be presented: degeneration, developmental failure, and the "two-hit" model. Degeneration refers to the gradual functional failure of an organ or body part over time, with symptoms becoming manifest when some biologic threshold is passed. Degenerative joint disease (DJD) is a concrete example of this. Cartilage and membranes in the large, weight-bearing joints gradually weaken and break down, leading to pain and functional impairment. While simple wear and tear on the joint is a major etiologic factor, different individuals have different liabilities to develop DJD under similar conditions of wear and tear. In this way, degenerative changes may interact with an individual's genetic endowment to bring about disease onset at a particular time.

Degeneration appears to be the best explanation for delayed onset in illnesses such as Alzheimer's disease (AD) and Parkinson's disease (PD). In AD, gradual loss of cholinergic neurons in the nucleus basalis correlates with the appearance of characteristic neuritic plaques and neurofibrillary tangles throughout the cortex (Whitehouse et al., 1982). In PD, clinical symptoms appear and progress in rough proportion to the loss of nigrostriatal dopaminergic neurons. There is currently no evidence of degenerative change contributing to the onset of most affective disorders. However, the affective disorders that complicate such degenerative conditions as PD and Huntington's disease probably arise as a direct result of the specific brain pathology (reviewed in McMahon and DePaulo, 1992).

Developmental failure refers to the onset of disease when a particular physiologic event fails to occur appropriately at the proper time in development. Many birth defects fit this model of onset, yet we lump these disorders together as "congenital" and do not think of them as having a delayed onset. The so-called developmental disorders of infancy and childhood, such as autism, may also be examples of this model, although it is unclear just what event or series of events is failing in this still mysterious illness.

The developmental model has, of course, been the leading model underlying psychodynamic theories of mood disorder (Freud, 1911). The developmental model offers an account, at least in general terms, for the fact that age-specific incidence for mood disorders peaks in late adolescence (Burke et al. 1990). However, the developmental changes of adolescence, both physiological and psychological, are numerous and complex. This makes the formulation and testing of specific etiologic hypotheses under a developmental model very difficult. Still, the developmental model holds considerable promise that may ultimately be fulfilled through further progress in developmental neurobiology (Greden, 1991).

Finally, there is the "two-hit" model of delayed onset. Compared to the first two models, this is a relatively young theory. It was first developed by Alfred Knudson in 1971 in his now-classic paper on the genetics of retinoblastoma (Knudson, 1971). Knudson proposed that some forms of cancer could arise from the unfortunate conjunction of two genetic mutations or "hits." He hypothesized that the same cancer may be caused by an inherited germinal mutation followed by a noninherited somatic mutation or by the chance occurrence of two somatic mutations. He illustrated the model with retinoblastoma. Bilateral cases of retinoblastoma are almost always familial, while most unilateral cases are not. Knudson observed an important difference in the age-specific incidences of bilateral and unilateral cases. The incidence of bilateral cases decreased linearly with age, while the incidence of unilateral cases decreased exponentially. Knudson showed that these age-specific incidence rates were consistent with his two-hit model, wherein bilateral cases result from a germinal followed by a somatic mutation, while most unilateral cases result from rare somatic mutations. A two-hit etiology has now been verified for several types of cancer. The two-hit model clearly exposes the false dichotomy of "genes versus environment," since, under this model, both genetic and environmental factors are essential.

The two-hit model deserves careful consideration in understanding the onset of mood disorders. The two-hit model offers one potential explanation for the apparent incomplete penetrance seen in families with mood disorders, that is, some persons who might be expected to inherit the disease genes never manifest the illness. Under the two-hit model, gene carriers would be expected to fall ill only after exposure to the second-hit event. The age-dependent penetrance of mood disorders is also consistent with a two-hit model. As noted, the age-specific incidence (an estimate of age-dependent penetrance) of BPI disorder rises abruptly in adolescence, peaks in late adolescence or early adulthood, then gradually falls. In contrast, the age-specific incidence of unipolar disorder rises gradually through the life span. This is precisely the predicted age-specific incidence if BPI cases were caused by an inherited mutation followed by a relatively common second hit, while unipolar cases arose from one (or more) nongenetic events occurring randomly over time.

If we broaden the concept of second hits to include nongenetic insults, such as adverse life events, the two-hit model can readily account for the apparent correlation between life events and illness onset in susceptible individuals. For example, Kennedy, et al. (1983) showed that patients admitted to hospital with mania experienced significantly more major life events before admission than after discharge, and also experienced more life events than matched controls. The list of other potential second-hit events might include exposure to substances of abuse, pregnancy, or viral infection.

GENETIC MECHANISMS OF DELAYED ONSET

Of the many genetic mechanisms posited to play a role in delayed onset disease, three will be highlighted herein: (1) triplet repeat expansion, (2) damage to mitochondrial DNA, and (3) age-specific changes in gene expression.

Triplet repeat expansion describes the increase in length of DNA sequences that consist of the same three nucleotides in a repeating pattern, for example, ---CAGCAG-CAGCAG---. This previously unsuspected form of mutation was first described in 1992, within the gene myotonin protein kinase, which causes myotonic dystrophy (Harley et al., 1992; Fu et al., 1992). Simultaneous with the discovery of the gene came the finding that age at onset correlated with the size of the triplet repeat expansion.

Myotonic dystrophy had puzzled geneticists and neurologists for decades, since it displayed highly variable age at onset and severity, and appeared to worsen in successive generations of a family. For example, an infant born with the severe, congenital form of the disease might have a mother with a mild, but unmistakable adult-onset form, and be found to have a grandfather with late onset of cataracts, frontal balding, and mild proximal muscle weakness, now known to represent the mildest phenotype.

This phenomenon of worsening of a genetic disease in successive generations is known as anticipation. Anticipation has a long and colorful history, starting with the pseudoscientific theories of nineteenth- and early-twentieth-century eugenicists ["degenerescence" (Morel, 1857)]. Anticipation was dismissed as an artifact of ascertainment after a classic paper was written on the subject by the great geneticist Lionel Penrose (Penrose, 1948). Penrose pointed out several selection biases that could create a false appearance of anticipation. These included: (1) a tendency to recognize disease in parents at the same time the diagnosis is made in offspring, (2) the tendency for those affected with certain severe diseases early in life to fail to reproduce (the "fertility bias"), and (3) the unlikelihood of observing parent–offspring pairs consisting of an early-onset case of disease in the parent and a late-onset case in the offspring, since the two onset events could span 60 or more years.

Penrose's biases probably do account for much of the apparent anticipation reported for mental illnesses. But the discovery of the molecular basis of anticipation in other diseases instantly rehabilitated anticipation as a legitimate object of study. Triplet repeat expansion has since been shown to underlie seven diseases, including Huntington's disease (Huntington's Disease Collaborative Research Group, 1993) and Fragile X Mental Retardation (Verkerk et al., 1991). Most show anticipation in terms of age at onset, severity, or both.

Anticipation in mood disorders was described by Mott in 1910, but his findings suffered from the diagnostic imprecision, statistical unsophistication, and cultural biases of the time (Mott, 1910). After the discovery of triplet repeats, several modern studies have revisited the question of anticipation in mood disorders. Our group studied a set of 32 families ascertained through probands with bipolar I or bipolar II disorder and selected for the presence of affected phenotypes in only one parental lineage (McInnis et al., 1993). We found that members of the probands' generation experienced an 8.9- to 13.5-year earlier onset of first mania or major depression and a 1.8- to 3.4-fold increased frequency of illness episodes compared to members of the parents' generation (Table 1).

In view of the nongenetic factors that can create the appearance of anticipation, several potential biases were evaluated. The difference in age at onset was too great to be explained by recall bias alone. By comparing aunts and uncles, who may have not reproduced, with the probands' sibs, we showed that the anticipation we observed was not simply due to a fertility bias. Furthermore, since families with affected phenotypes in both parental lines were excluded, potential additive effects of disease genes from both parents were minimized. Additional analyses demonstrated that different rates of mortality, substance abuse, and affective disorder between the generations did not account for our findings. Finally, while a cohort effect was observed, it did not wash out the anticipation findings in multivariate analyses. A subsequent study by another group has yielded similar results (Nylander et al., 1994).

TABLE 1. Pairwise Comparisons in Age at Onset and Episode Frequency Across Generations

	Sampling Scheme			
	I	II	III	IV
Median age at onset				
G1	30	35	30	30
G2	18	18	17	19
Median difference	12	12.5	13.5	8.9
Z^a	4.4	4.2	10.6	6.9
P	<.001	<.001	<.001	<.001
Median episode frequency				
G1	.17	.16	.20	.16
G2	.31	.31	.62	.55
Median difference	.15	.17	.32	.3
Z^a	3.3	2.84	6.76	5.88
P	<.001	<.001	<.001	<.001

[a] Wilcoxon matched-pairs test. G1: parents' generation; G2: probands' generation. See McInnis et al., 1993 for explanation of sampling schemes.
From McInnis MG, McMahon FG, Chase G, Simpson SG, Ross CA, DePaulo JR, Jr (1993): Anticipation in bipolar affective disorder. Am J Hum Genet 53:385–390. Courtesy of University of Chicago Press.

Damage to the mitochondrial DNA (mtDNA) is a well-described phenomenon that may underlie many age-dependent processes (Wallace, 1992). mtDNA consists of 16.5 kb circular molecules, which are physically separate from the DNA of the nucleus. mtDNA encodes a portion of the polypeptides essential in oxidative phosphorylation, as well as the transfer and ribosomal RNA involved in mtDNA expression. mtDNA damage is thought to be due primarily to oxygen radicals. mtDNA is more susceptible than the nuclear DNA to such damage, probably because it exists outside the nuclear envelope and lacks protective histones (Richter, 1988).

As reviewed by Wallace (1992), damage to the mtDNA decreases the efficiency of cellular respiration (oxidative phosphorylation). Tissues requiring a constant supply of oxidative energy, such as neurons, pancreatic islet cells, and myocardial muscle cells may not tolerate a significant loss in the efficiency of cellular respiration. These tissues in particular show signs of cellular ischemia as mtDNA damage accumulates. Neurons swell and lose myelin, islet cells stop producing insulin, and muscle cells lose contractility. At some point, a biologic threshold is crossed, and signs of disease appear, such as hyperglycemia, heart failure, and muscle weakness. Further, malfunctioning mitochondria accumulate oxygen radicals, leading to a vicious circle of additional mtDNA damage. Since cellular damage due to mitochondrial dysfunction adds to any existing cellular defects, mtDNA damage can play a role in age at onset even if mtDNA genes do not play a direct etiologic role in a disease.

mtDNA damage, in the form of small deletions and point mutations, has been found in postmortem brains (Corral-Debrinski et al., 1992). Interestingly, while the total proportion of damaged mtDNA increases with age, damaged mtDNA is not uniformly distributed throughout the brain (Figure 2). The cerebellum shows the smallest proportion of damaged mtDNA, while the highest proportions appear in the putamen. This regional variation in age-related mtDNA damage may reflect differences in the rates of glucose utilization and/or ischemia due to small vessel disease.

Studies of the mtDNA in persons with mood disorders are still in the beginning stages. Several case reports indicate that both unipolar and bipolar mood disorders can occur in persons with known mtDNA defects (Soumalainen et al., 1992; Stewart and Naylor, 1990; Suzuki et al., 1990; Wallace, 1970), but systematic studies are needed. One small study of mtDNA from the brains of deceased patients diagnosed with bipolar disorder and of suicide victims failed to find evidence of deletions, but no attempt was made to study multiple brain regions, and the assay could not have detected partial deletions if they occurred in less than 5% of total mitochondrial DNA (Stine et al., 1993).

Age-specific changes in gene expression constitute an exciting and burgeoning area of neuroscience. The importance of gene expression studies follows from one simple deduction: since all cells carry an identical endowment of DNA, tissue and age-specific variation in cellular function must arise from variation in the expression of specific genes. The existence of genetic mosaicism, that is, DNA variation between cells, does not diminish the fact that regulation of gene expression is a major source of the dynamic variation in cellular functioning in different tissues and at different ages. This section owes much to the review of Harrison and Pearson (1992).

Although still incompletely understood, gene expression is emerging as a complex process, with multiple steps that are subject to regulation or dysfunction. Genes are expressed through transcription into messenger RNA (mRNA), followed by modification, or *splicing,* of the mRNA transcript, and finally by translation of the spliced mRNA into the protein product. The splicing steps often vary between tissues. This

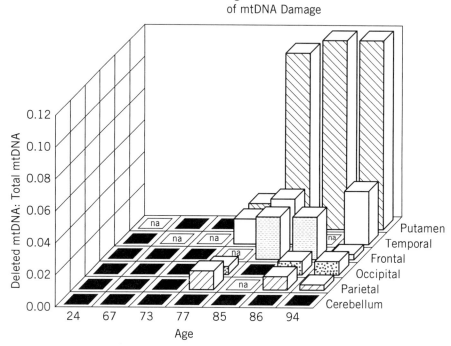

FIGURE 2. Regional distribution of mtDNA damage. Histogram showing the accumulation of the mtDNA[4977] deletion in six regions of the brains from seven individuals between ages 24 and 94. Deletion levels expressed as ratio of the mtDNA[4977] deletion to total mtDNA. na, Tissue not available for study. From Corral-Debrinski M, Horton T, Lott MT, Shoffner JM, Beal MF, Wallace DC (1992): Mitochondrial DNA deletions in human brain: Regional variability and increases with advanced age. Nat Genet 2:324–329. Courtesy of *Nature Genetics*.

alternative splicing enables one precursor mRNA to generate different mature mRNA species and, ultimately, different protein products. For example, the precursor mRNA transcript of the proopiomelanocortin gene is alternatively spliced to produce ACTH in the pituitary and β-endorphin in the brain.

Gene expression is regulated by multiple proteins, known as transcription factors. Transcription factors often contain a zinc-finger motif, a particular three-dimensional structure that is thought to enable transcription factors to "embrace" the DNA molecule during transcription (Parraga et al., 1990). Immediate early genes are an important class of transcription factors that are expressed in the central nervous system and other tissues. The immediate early genes c-fos, NGF, and jun, are induced by a wide variety of stimuli and physiological stressors, such as hormones, motor activity, and drugs (Sharp et al., 1993).

Age-dependent changes in gene expression are only beginning to be studied. The expression of the gene for the oxygen free-radical scavenger superoxide dismutase declines with age, a phenomenon that may play a significant role in normal aging (reviewed in Warner, 1994). Age-dependent changes in gene expression may also play a role in the pathogenesis of Alzheimer's disease. For example, nerve growth factor (NGF) is necessary for the health of the cholinergic neurons that die in AD, and NGF levels decline with age (Larkfors et al., 1987).

An appreciation of the role of gene expression changes in mood disorders awaits further study. Examination of mRNA in postmortem brain tissue is one approach but is limited by the availability of fresh specimens and by the retrospective nature of postmortem studies (Barton et al., 1995). Brain-imaging techniques, which allow *in vivo* visualization of changes in gene expression, particularly of immediate early genes, will provide essential data. It also seems plausible that ongoing genetic linkage studies of mood disorders will identify chromosomal regions containing transcription factors, thus directly implicating these genes in mood disorders.

Age at onset has been and will continue to be an important issue in the genetics of mood disorders. Ongoing and future research will likely transform age at onset from a primarily descriptive to a largely pathogenetic feature. Once this occurs, treatments that will indefinitely delay onset will become imaginable, bringing with them the promise of preventing the suffering and impairment mood disorders inflict.

REFERENCES

Ayuso-Gutierrez JL, Ramos-Brieva JA (1982): The course of manic-depressive illness: A comparative study of bipolar I and bipolar II patients. J Affective Disord 4:9–14.

Barton AJ, Pearson RC, Najlerahim A, Harrison PJ (1995): Pre- and postmortem influences on brain RNA. [Review]. J Neurochem 61:1–11.

Blumenthal RL, Egeland JA, Sharpe L, Nee J, Endicott J (1987): Age of onset in bipolar and unipolar illness with and without delusions or hallucinations. Comp Psychiatry 28:547–554.

Brodaty H, Peters K, Boyce P, Hickie I, Parker G, Mitchell P, Wilhelm K (1991): Age and depression. J Affective Disord 23:137–149.

Bromet EJ, Dunn LO, Connell MM, Dew MA, Schulberg HC (1986): Long-term reliability of diagnosing lifetime major depression in a community sample. Arch Gen Psychiatry 43:435–440.

Burke KC, Burke J, Regier DA, Rae DS (1990): Age at onset of selected mental disorders in five community populations. Arch Gen Psychiatry 47:511–518.

Chase GA, Folstein MF, Breitner JCS, Beaty TH, Self SG (1983): The use of life tables and survival analysis in testing genetic hypotheses, with an application to Alzheimer's disease. Am J Epidemiol 117:590–597.

Chen WJ, Faraone SV, Tsuang MT (1992): Estimating age at onset distributions: A review of methods and issues. Psychiatric Genet. 2:219–238.

Conwell Y, Nelson JC, Kim K, Mazure CM (1989): Depression in late life: Age of onset as marker of a subtype. J Affective Disord 17:189–195.

Corral-Debrinksi M, Horton T, Lott MT, Shoffner JM, Beal MF, Wallace DC (1992): Mitochondrial DNA deletions in human brain: Regional variability and increases with advanced age. Nat Genet 2:324–329.

Coryell W, Endicott J, Andreasen N, Keller M (1985): Bipolar I, bipolar II, and nonbipolar major depression among the relatives of affectively Ill probands. Am J Psychiatry 142:817–821.

Cox DR (1972): Regression models and life tables. J R Statist Soc 4:187–220.

Efron B, Tibshirani R (1991): Statistical data analysis in the computer age. Science 253:390–395.

Egeland JA, Blumenthal RL, Nee J, Sharpe L, Endicott J (1987): Reliability and relationship of various ages of onset criteria for major affective disorder. J Affective Disord 12:159–165.

Endicott J, Nee J, Andreason N, Clayton P, Keller M, Coryell W (1985): Bipolar II: Combine or keep separate? J Affective Disord 8:17–28.

Freud, S "Mourning and melancholia." In Strachey J (ed.) (1957): The Standard Edition of the Complete Psychological works of Sigmund Freud (Vol. 14) London: Hogarth Press, 243–258.

Fu YH, Pizzuti A, Fenwick RGJ, King J, Rajnarayan S, Dunne PW, Dubel J, Nasser GA, Ashizawa T, de Jong P, Wieringa B, Korneluk R, Perryman MB, Epstein HF, Caskey CT (1992): An unstable triplet repeat in a gene related to myotonic muscular dystrophy. Science 255:1256–1258.

Garvey M, Schaffer CB (1994): Are some symptoms of depression age dependent? J Affective Disord 32:247–251.

Gershon ES, Hamovit JH, Guroff JJ, Nurnberger JI (1987): Birth-cohort changes in manic and depressive disorders in relatives of bipolar and schizoaffective patients. Arch Gen Psychiatry 44:314–319.

Gershon ES, Hamovit J, Guroff JJ, Nurnberger JI, Goldin LR, Bunney WE (1982): A family study of schizoaffective, bipolar I, bipolar II, unipolar and normal control probands. Arch Gen Psychiatry 39:1157–1167.

Giuffra LA, Risch N (1994): Diminished recall and the cohort effect of major depression: A simulation study. Psychol Med 24:375–383.

Greden JF (1991): Annual meeting theme for 1992: Developmental neurobiology and clinical course. Biol Psychiatry 30:963–965.

Harley HG, Brook JD, Rundle SA, Crow S, Reardon W, Buckler AJ, Harper PS, Housman DE, Shaw DJ (1992): Expansion of an unstable DNA region and phenotypic variation in myotonic dystrophy. Nature 355:545–546.

Harrison PJ, Pearson RCA (1992): Gene expression and mental disease. Psychol Med 19:813–819.

Heimbuch RC, Matthysse S, Kidd KK (1980): Estimating age-of-onset distributions for disorders with variable onset. Am J Hum Genet 32:564–574.

Huntington's Disease Collaborative Research Group (1993): A novel gene containing a trinucleotide repeat that is expanded and unstable on Huntington's Disease chromosomes. Cell 72:971–983.

James NM (1977): Early- and late-onset bipolar affective disorder. A genetic study. Arch Gen Psychiatry 34:715–717.

Kaplan EL, Meier P (1958): Non-parametric estimation from incomplete observations. J Am Stat Assoc 53:457–481.

Kennedy S, Thompson R, Stancer HC, Roy A, Persad E (1983): Life events precipitating mania. Br J Psychiatry 142:398–403.

Klerman GL, Weissman MM (1989): Increasing rates of depression. JAMA 261:2229–2235.

Knudson AG (1971): Mutation and cancer: Statistical study of retinoblastoma. PNAS 68:820–823.

Kraepelin E (1921): "Manic-Depressive Insanity and Paranoia." Edinburgh: E & S Livingstone.

Larkfors L, Ebendal T, Whittemore SR, Persson H, Hoffer B, Olson L (1987): Decreased level of nerve growth factor and its messenger RNA in the aged rat brain. Mol Brain Res 3:55–60.

Loranger AW, Levine PM (1978): Age at onset of bipolar affective illness. Arch Gen Psychiatry 35:1345–1348.

McGlashan TH (1988): Adolescent versus adult onset of mania. Am J Psychiatry 145:221–223.

McInnis MG, McMahon FJ, Chase G, Simpson SG, Ross CA, DePaulo JR, Jr (1993): Anticipation in bipolar affective disorder. Am J Hum Genet 53:385–390.

McMahon FJ, DePaulo JR (1992): Clinical features of affective disorders and bereavement. Curr Opinion Psychiatry 5:580–584.

McMahon FJ, Stine OC, Chase GA, Meyers DA, Simpson SG, DePaulo JR (1994): Influence of clinical subtype, sex, and lineality on age at onset age of major affective disorder in a family sample. Am J Psychiatry 151:210–215.

Morel BA (1857): "Traite des Degenerescences." Paris: J.B. Bailliere.

Mott FW (1910): Hereditary aspects of nervous and mental diseases. Br Med J 2:1013–1020.

Nelson JC, Conwell Y, Kim K, Mazure C (1989): Age at onset in late-life delusional depression. Am J Psychiatry 146:785–785.

Nylander PO, Engstrom C, Chotai J, Wahlstrom J, Adolfsson R (1994): Anticipation in Swedish families with bipolar affective disorder. J Med Genet 31:686–689.

Parraga G, Horvath S, Hood L, Young ET, Klevit RE (1990): Spectroscopic studies of wild-type and mutant "zinc finger" peptides: Determinants of domain folding and structure. PNAS 87:137–141.

Penrose LS (1948): The problem of anticipation in pedigrees of dystrophia myotonica. Ann Eugenics 14:125–132.

Price RA, Kidd KK, Weissman MM (1987): Early onset (under age 30) and panic disorder as markers for etiologic homogeneity in major depression. Arch Gen Psychiatry 44:434–439.

Prusoff BA, Merikangas KR, Weissman MM (1988): Lifetime prevalence and age of onset of psychiatric disorders: Recall 4 years later. J Psychiatric Res 22:107–117.

Richter C, Park JW, Ames BN (1988): Normal oxidative damage to mitochondrial and nuclear DNA is extensive. PNAS 85:6465–6467.

Ring HA, Trimble MR (1991): Affective disturbance in Parkinson's disease. Int J Geriatric Psychiatry 6:385–393.

Robins LN, Helzer JE, Weissman MM, et al. (1984): Lifetime prevalence of specific psychiatric disorders in three sites. Arch Gen Psychiatry 41:949–958.

Robinson RG, Starr LB, Kubos KI (1983): A two year longitudinal study of post-stroke mood disorders: Findings during the initial evaluation. Stroke 14:736–741.

Rosen LN, Rosenthal N, Van Dusen PH, Dunner DL, Fieve RR (1983): Age at onset and number of psychotic symptoms in bipolar I and schizoaffective disorder. Am J Psychiatry 140:1523–1524.

Schork NJ, Schork MA (1990): Histograms: Multimodal or poorly constructed? Am J Hum Genet 46:396–397.

Sharp FR, Sagar SM, Swanson RA (1993): Metabolic mapping with cellular resolution: c-fos vs. 2-deoxyglucose. [Review]. Crit Rev Neurobiol 7:205–228.

Soumalainen A, Majander A, Haltia M, Somer H, Loenqvist J, Savontaus M, Peltonen L (1992): Multiple deletions of mitochondrial DNA in several tissues of a patient with severe retarded depression and familial progressive external opthalmoplegia. J Clin Invest 90:61–66.

Stewart JB, Naylor GJ (1990): Manic-depressive psychosis in a patient with mitochondrial myopathy—a case report. Med Sci Res 18:265–266.

Stine OC, Luu SU, Zito M, Casanova M (1993): The possible association between affective disorder and partially deleted mitochondrial DNA. Biol Psychiatry 33:141–142.

Suzuki T, Koizumi J, Shiraishi H, et al. (1990): Mitochondrial encephalomyopathy (MELAS) with mental disorder. Neuroradiol 32:74–76.

Taylor MA, Abrams R (1981): Early- and late-onset bipolar illness. Arch Gen Psychiatry 38:58–61.

Tohen M, Shulman KI, Satlin A (1994): First-episode mania in late life. Am J Psychiatry 151:130–132.

Verkerk AJ, Pieretti M, Sutcliffe JS, Fu YH, Kuhl DP, Pizzuti A, Reiner O, Richards S, Victoria MF, Zhang FP (1991): Identification of a gene (FMR-1) containing a CGG repeat coincident with a breakpoint cluster region exhibiting length variation in fragile X syndrome. Cell 65:905–914.

Wallace DC (1992): Mitochondrial genetics: A paradigm for aging and degenerative diseases? Science 256:628–632.

Wallace DC (1970): A new manifestation of Leber's disease and a new explanation for the agency responsible for its unusual pattern of inheritance. Brain 93:121–132.

Warner HR (1994): Superoxide dismutase, aging, and degenerative disease. Free Radic Biol Med 17:249–258.

Weissman MM, Bruce ML, Leaf PJ, Florio LP, and Holzer C (1991): Affective disorders. In Robins LN, Regier DA "Psychiatric Disorders in America: The Epidemiologic Catchment Area Study," New York: Free Press.

Weissman M, Gershon ES, Kidd KK, et al. (1984a): Psychiatric disorders in the relatives of probands with affective disorders. Arch Gen Psychiatry 41:13–21.

Weissman M, Wickramarante P, Merikangas KR, et al. (1984b): Onset of major depression in early adulthood. Increased familial loading and specificity. Arch Gen Psychiatry 41:1136–1143.

Whitehouse PJ, et al. (1982): Alzheimer's disease and senile dementia: Loss of neurones in the basal forebrain. Science 215:1237–1239.

Young RC, Klerman GL (1992): Mania in late life: focus on age at onset. [Review]. Am J Psychiatry 149:867–876.

PART II

CHILDHOOD AND ADOLESCENCE

CHAPTER 4

Depression in Children and Adolescents: Clinical Features and Pathogenesis

BORIS BIRMAHER, NEAL D. RYAN, and DOUGLAS E. WILLIAMSON

Western Psychiatric Institute and Clinic, University of Pittsburgh, Division of Child and Adolescent Psychiatry, Pittsburgh, PA 15213

Two decades ago, the existence of childhood and adolescent clinical depression was questioned. The features of depression were thought to be manifested by other nonspecific symptoms such as behavior problems, enuresis, and so forth, the so-called masked depression (Lesse, 1983; Carlson and Cantwell, 1980a). However, given the proper assessment and application of standardized diagnostic criteria, several investigations have shown that the symptoms of clinical depression in children and adolescents are similar to those manifested in depressed adults (e.g., Ryan et al., 1987). In addition, diverse nosology, epidemiology, course, family aggregation, and biological studies have established the validity of childhood and adolescent major depressive disorder (MDD) and dysthymic disorder. The rapid growth in the study of childhood depression was due, in part, to the development of valid and reliable structured and semistructured interviews, such as the Kiddie Schedule for Affective Disorders and Schizophrenia (K-SADS) (Chambers et al., 1985) and the Diagnostic Interview Schedule for Children (DISC) (Shaffer, 1989) for the assessment of mood symptoms in children and adolescents, and the use of diagnostic criteria such as the International Classification Diagnoses (World Health Organization, 1994), the Research Diagnostic Criteria (RDC) (Spitzer et al., 1978), and later, the Diagnostic Statistical Manual-IV (DSM) (American Psychiatric Association, 1994).

In this chapter, we will review the epidemiology, clinical features, and pathogenesis of MDD and dysthymic disorder. Other chapters in this book will address adolescent bipolar disorder and the course and treatment of clinical depression.

Mood Disorders Across the Life Span, Edited by Shulman, Tohen, and Kutcher
ISBN 0-471-10477-9 © 1996 Wiley-Liss, Inc.

EPIDEMIOLOGY

In a critical review of all community-based epidemiological studies of childhood and adolescent depressive disorders published until 1989, Fleming and Offord (1990) reported that MDD occurs in less than 3% of children (0.4–2.5%) and increases in adolescence (0.4–8.3%). The prevalence of both child and adolescent depression was lower when parents were the informants, suggesting a tendency for parents to underreport depression in their children. Recently, in a large prospective epidemiological study of high school adolescents, Lewinsohn et al. (1994) found a point prevalence for MDD of 2.9% and a lifetime prevalence of 20.4%. There was a substantial increase in the hazard rate for MDD onset between the ages of 13 and 19. These results are consistent with three large retrospective epidemiological studies of adult populations (Burke et al., 1991; Kessler et al., 1994; Lewinsohn et al., 1986), which reported a low prevalence of depression before age 9 and a rise from ages 9 to 19, especially in females. The rates of depression are higher in clinical samples ranging from 13 to 59% (e.g., Robbin et al., 1982; Kashani et al., 1982; Carlson and Cantwell, 1980b).

The few studies that have assessed dysthymic disorder reported a point prevalence from 0.6 to 1.7% in children, and 1.6 to 8.0% in adolescents (Lewinsohn, et al., 1993b).

Little information is available concerning preschool children. Kashani et al. (1986) reported 9 cases of MDD in a sample of 1,000 children aged 1–6 years old, consecutively referred to a child development unit. No community sample studies are available.

Childhood MDD occurs approximately at the same rate in girls and boys. In adolescents, the ratio changes to approximately 2 girls to 1 boy, similar to the ratio reported in adult MDD studies (Fleming and Offord, 1990; Lewinsohn et al., 1994). Although the reason for this bias is unknown, it has been speculated that genetic causes, biological changes associated with the sexual maturation, cognitive predisposition, and sociocultural factors may all contribute to females being more likely to experience a depressive disorder (Garber et al., 1994; Rutter, 1991).

Birth-Cohort Effect

Various independent epidemiological investigations have reported that individuals born in the latter part of the twentieth century are at greater risk for developing mood disorders and that these disorders are manifesting at a younger age (Hagnell et al., 1982; Klerman et al., 1985, Gershon et al., 1987; Lavori et al., 1987, Wickramaratne et al., 1989, Joyce et al., 1990, Lewinsohn et al., 1993a). The birth-cohort effect has also been reported in a large community sample of 14- to 18-year-old students (Lewinsohn et al., 1993b), a group of siblings of prepubertal normal and depressed children (Ryan et al., 1992a), and a clinically referred sample of school-age depressed children (Kovacs and Gatsonis, 1994). It has been speculated that the birth-cohort effect may be due to gene–environment interactions (Gershon et al., 1987; Klerman and Weissman 1988). Although it has not yet been proven, in successive birth-cohorts, susceptible individuals may have been exposed to more adverse environments (rapid social changes, unstable families, exposure to abuse or violence, etc.), and/or have less protective factors (e.g., support) at earlier ages. Additionally, the decrease in age at onset of mood disorder has been attributed to "genetic anticipation" (e.g., McInnis et al., 1993). It is also important to mention that in adults, the rate of melancholic or severe depressions seem to be stable across birth-cohorts, suggesting that the increase in lifetime prevalence of depression and early depressions may be due to an increase in secondary depressions (Ronald Kessler, personal communication; Hagnell et al., 1982).

CLINICAL CHARACTERISTICS

Childhood and adolescent MDD is characterized by depressed or irritable mood and markedly diminished interest or pleasure in all or almost all activities. Additional symptoms of MDD are: significant weight loss or gain, insomnia or hypersomnia, psychomotor agitation or retardation, fatigue or loss of energy, feelings of worthlessness or excessive guilt, lack of concentration, thoughts of death, and suicidal ideation or attempt. According to the DSM-IV classification (American Psychiatric Association, 1994), to be diagnosed as MDD, the child or adolescent needs to have at least five of the above symptoms for at least 2 weeks duration, and at least one of those symptoms must be either depressed mood, irritability, or loss of interest and pleasure. These symptoms must represent a change from previous functioning and produce psychosocial impairment and are not attributed to abuse of drugs, use of medications, or medical illnesses. Finally, these symptoms cannot be part of a bipolar mixed episode and are not accounted for by bereavement.

Dysthymia is characterized by significant depressive or irritable mood lasting most of the day, occurring more days than not, and present for at least one year. In addition, to be diagnosed as dysthymic, a child or an adolescent must have two or more of the following symptoms: poor appetite or overeating, insomnia or hypersomnia, low energy or fatigue, low self-esteem, poor concentration or difficulty making decisions, and feelings of hopelessness. The dysthymic disorder may not appear exclusively during episodes of schizophrenia, bipolar disorder, substance abuse, or medical illnesses, and no major depressive disorder is to have been present during the first year of the disturbance. However, a child can have an episode of major depression, fully remit, and develop dysthymia, or, after the first year of dysthymia, a child may also develop episodes of MDD warranting both diagnosis, the so-called double depression (Lewinsohn et al., 1991; Angst and Wicki, 1991; Keller et al., 1983).

The validity of childhood MDD and dysthymia as described in the DSM has been demonstrated by several nosologic studies. Chambers et al., (1985) demonstrated that children could be diagnosed as depressed using DSM or RDC "adult" criteria. Carlson and Cantwell (1979), using the DSM-III and RDC criteria for affective disorders, found that 27% of children and adolescents referred to an outpatient clinic met criteria for mood disorder. Symptoms of mood disorders were also found in children with other psychopathology. Strober et al. (1981) showed that the core symptoms of DSM-III major depression were present in 60–95% of a sample of depressed adolescents. Additionally, 30% had somatic concerns, 13% delusions, and 10% mood congruent hallucinations. Except for endogenous/melancholic subtype and severe impairment that were less frequently found in adolescents, the distribution of mood subtypes was similar to those found in adult populations. Friedman et al. (1982) reported that except for self-pity, there were no differences in the clinical picture of MDD between adults and adolescents. In a large sample of depressed children and adolescents, Ryan et al. (1987) showed that except for the frequency and severity of some symptoms, the clinical picture in children, adolescents, and adults with major depression was very similar. In comparison with the adolescents, however, children had more somatic complaints, psychomotor agitation, separation anxiety, phobias, and auditory hallucinations. Adolescents showed more hopelessness/helplessness, anhedonia, hypersomnia, weight changes, and lethality of suicidal attempt. No significant differences in the rate of RDC endogenous subtype were found between children and adolescents, but RDC psychotic depression was more frequently found before puberty.

The frequent occurrence of depressed appearance in younger children with MDD has been reported by others (Poznanski, 1982). In addition, the increased frequency of somatic complaints in children with MDD has been reported in other studies (e.g., Carlson and Cantwell, 1980b), suggesting that in this age group, depression can present with somatic complaints but proper symptom assessment may reveal the diagnosis of MDD. A principal components factor analysis of the sample studied by Ryan et al. (1987) showed five factors: endogenous, negative cognition, anxiety, appetite and weight changes, and disturbed conduct. These factors were similar for both the child and the adolescent groups. Suicidal ideation was a component of both negative cognitions factor and conduct factor. The endogenous and anxiety factors were similar to those found in adult studies (for a review, see Nelson and Charney, 1981) and one child study (Kolvin et al., 1991). Interestingly, the hallucinations factorized together with symptoms of anxiety, raising the question of whether they were actual hallucinations or other disturbances in perception sometimes found in anxious youths. Similar to the findings of Ryan and colleagues (1987), Carlson and Kashani (1988) found that depressed mood, decreased concentration, insomnia, and suicidal ideation occurred with equal frequency in all age groups, whereas symptoms such as anhedonia, diurnal mood variation, hopelessness, psychomotor retardation, and delusion increased with age. Symptoms such as low self-esteem, somatic complaints, and depressed appearance decreased with age. Mitchell et al. (1988) compared the RDC symptoms of MDD in a sample of depressed children, adolescents, and nondepressed psychiatric controls ages 7–17 years old. There were no significant differences between children and adolescents. In comparison with the adults, the adolescents had more suicide attemps, whereas the adults had more symptoms of melancholia.

In summary, the clinical picture of MDD in children, adolescents, and adults is similar. However, the relative frequency of the symptoms may be age related. In particular, adults appear to have more melancholic depressions (for further review, see Carlson and Kashani, 1988). These studies were carried out with clinical samples. Future studies using community samples are also needed.

Studies of childhood and adolescent dysthymic disorder are scarce. Recently, Kovacs et al. (1994) compared a group of school-age clinically referred children whose first depression was dysthymic disorder ($n = 55$) and a group of children whose first affective episode was MDD ($n = 60$). Dysthymic disorder was associated with earlier age at onset than MDD (mean 8.77 vs. 10.9 years). Similarly, Lewinsohn et al. (1991), in a community sample of adolescents, reported that dysthymia started 3 years earlier than MDD. Kovacs et al. (1994) found that dysthymia without MDD was manifested by gloomy and depressed mood, brooding about feeling unloved, irritability, anger, self-deprecation, somatic complaints, anxiety, disobedience, and other symptoms of affective dysregulation. As compared with MDD, dysthymia was characterized by the lower prevalence or absence of anhedonia, social withdrawal, guilt, morbid preoccupation, and impaired concentration. After controlling for multiple comparisons, the symptoms of anhedonia, social withdrawal, reduced sleep, reduced appetite, and fatigue were significantly more frequent in patients with MDD. In contrast with Kovac's findings, Fine et al. (1985), in a clinical sample of depressed adolescents, found no significant differences in symptoms between dysthymia and MDD. However, as Kovacs pointed out, Fine and colleagues included a small sample of patients, and it was unclear if patients with double depression were excluded.

COMORBIDITY

Studies of clinical populations have demonstrated that depression is often accompanied by other psychiatric disorders. Kovacs et al. (1984a,b) reported that 70% of children with MDD had another axis I disorder that predated the onset of MDD. Thirty-eight percent had dysthymia, 33% anxiety disorders, and 7% conduct disorder. Ryan et al. (1987) reported that 58% of the children and 37% of the adolescents had separation anxiety disorder (SAD) with functional impairment, 45% of the children and 27% of the adolescents had phobias with avoidant behavior, and 20% of both children and adolescents had overanxious disorder. Mild conduct problems were present in 38% of children and 25% of adolescents, but conduct disorder of sufficient severity to cause disturbances in psychosocial functioning was present only in 16% of children and 11% of adolescents. Other clinical studies have also reported high rates of comorbidity with anxiety and disruptive disorders (e.g., Carlson and Cantwell, 1979; Geller et al., 1985, Puig-Antich and Rabinovich, 1986).

Epidemiological studies have also shown a high degree of comorbidity in children and adolescents with MDD, with rates of comorbidity for anxiety disorders between 20 and 70%, disruptive disorders between 10 and 50%, and substance abuse in approximately 25%. At least 20–50% of depressed children and adolescents had two or more comorbid diagnoses (Anderson et al., 1987; Kashani et al., 1987; Bird et al., 1988). Recently, in a large community study of older adolescents ($n = 1{,}710$) and adults ($n = 2{,}060$), Rohde et al. (1991) showed that current and lifetime histories of depression in adolescents were highly comorbid with several other psychiatric disorders. The lifetime comorbidity for any psychiatric disorder was 42.9%, for anxiety disorders 21%, for disruptive disorder 12.1%, for substance abuse 19.9%, and for eating disorders 2.6%. Interestingly, adults had a lower degree of comorbidity than the adolescents. Similar to the clinical studies, with the exception of substance abuse, depression in both groups was more likely to occur after the onset of other disorders rather than to precede it. Comorbidity in adolescents was associated with greater frequency of suicidal behavior and treatment seeking.

Beginning with adolescence, alcohol and drug abuse are often comorbid with MDD. Lewinsohn et al. (1994), in a large community study of high school students, reported that depressed adolescents had a current and lifetime comorbidity with substance abuse of 14 and 19.9%, respectively. The current and lifetime comorbidity of substance abuse of nondepressed adolescents was 2.0 and 5.4%, respectively. Similarly, Kashani and Carlson (1987) and Kashani et al. (1987) reported that 25% of depressed adolescents had comorbidity with substance abuse.

As with MDD, dysthymia is often accompanied by other psychiatric disorders. In a study by Kovacs and colleagues (1994), 58% had a superimposed MDD. Forty-seven percent of the children with dysthymia had other pre-existing psychiatric disorders. Twenty-four percent were diagnosed with attention deficit hyperactive disorder (ADHD), 14.6% had enuresis or encopresis, 10.9% overanxious disorder, and 7.3% had SAD. Approximately 33% had one disorder, and 14.6% had two or more disorders.

The comorbidity of depression with personality disorders has been less well studied. Marton et al. (1989), in a sample of 35 adolescents with MDD or dysthymia, reported that 65% met criteria for personality disorders while depressed. The single most common diagnosis was borderline personality disorder, accounting for 30% of the personality disorders. Adolescents with concurrent personality disorders were less self-confident, had greater cognitive distortions, and had five times more suicide attempts than the depressive adolescents without personality diagnosis. Personality disorders, particularly cluster B type disorder, have been more commonly found in suicide victims than controls (Brent et al., 1993). Studies of personality disorders, however, have been carried out while the adolescents were acutely depressed. Therefore, it is not possible to determine whether the personality dysfunction is a state or a trait characteristic. A recent follow-up study (Marton et al., 1987) of depressed adolescents during 6–12 months after the acute phase of their illness and nondepressed controls suggested that most dysfunctional personality traits are state dependent.

Primary vs. Secondary Depression

The finding that a great majority of patients with MDD have comorbid psychiatric diagnosis has prompted the primary–secondary depression dichotomy. Primary depression refers to depressions present before the development of any other medical or psychiatric disorders, whereas secondary depression develops after other medical or psychiatric disorders. Cantwell and Carlson (1983) and Carlson (1984), in a sample of depressed children and adolescents, found no differences in core depressive symptoms between patients with primary or secondary depressions. Patients with secondary depression were more likely to have had the onset of their depression before puberty, were more likely to be males, and had more families with depressive spectrum disorders (as defined by Winokour, 1973). A noncontrolled 5-year follow-up of these patients showed that 89% were still symptomatic. Although the symptoms of depression remitted, they continued to manifest signs of their primary psychiatric disturbance. In contrast, patients with primary depression were more likely to have adolescent-onset depression, were more likely to be females, and have family histories of pure depression. At follow-up, only 38% of patients with primary depression were symptomatic.

In summary, both clinical and epidemiological studies have shown that the majority of depressed children and adolescents have comorbid disorders, the most common being anxiety disorders, followed by disruptive disorders. Except for substance abuse, the comorbid disorders tended to precede the development of both MDD and dysthymia.

The finding that the majority of depressed children and adolescents have comorbid disorders conveys nosological as well as clinical implications. For example, several studies have shown that depressed youth with comorbidity with other psychiatric disorders (e.g., anxiety, substance abuse, conduct disorder) are at higher risk for suicide (Brent et al., 1988; Lewinsohn et al., 1994), and depressed adolescents with comorbid anxiety disorders respond less well to psychotherapy (Brent et al., 1994). Furthermore, depressed patients with comorbid disruptive disorders had worse short-term outcome and a higher incidence of adult criminality (Harrington et al., 1991), significantly less family aggregation for mood disorders (Puig-Antich et al., 1989a), higher incidence of bipolar disorder (Kutcher et al., 1989), and higher levels of criticism (Asarnow et al., 1994) than patients without disruptive disorders, suggesting that depressive children with disruptive disorders may comprise a distinct etiologic subgroup.

Complications

One of the major complications of depression is suicide. Although it is beyond the scope of this chapter to review the literature on suicide, over 90% of adolescent suicides occur in the context of a psychiatric disorder, mainly depression (Brent et al., 1988; Shaffer and Fisher, 1981). Other factors such as being a white male, the severity and length of the depression (Brent et al., 1988), comorbidity with other psychiatric disorders (e.g., substance abuse, anxiety, disruptive, and personality disorders), history of previous suicidal behavior, family history of mood disorders or suicide, exposure to adverse life events (e.g., interpersonal, legal, familial), and availability of a lethal method have been widely recognized as predictors of suicide (Brent et al., 1987, 1988; Shaffer and Fisher, 1981; Ryan et al., 1987). The rates of adolescent suicides have also risen parallel to the increase of depression in successive birth cohorts (Frederick, 1978; Shaffer and Fisher, 1981), stressing the importance of accurate evaluation and preventive measures against suicide.

Depression may also be a risk factor for substance or alcohol abuse. For example, Deykin et al. (1987, 1992), examining college students ages 16–19 years old, found that the lifetime prevalence of alcohol abuse or dependence was 8.2%, of substance abuse or dependence was 9.4%, and of MDD was 6.8%. In this study, adolescents with MDD were 4.5 times more likely to abuse alcohol and 3.3 times more likely to abuse other substances than adolescents without a psychiatric disorder. They were also at increased risk compared to adolescents with other nonaffective psychiatric disorders. In general, the MDD preceded (by an average of 4.5 years) the onset of alcohol abuse. In half of the subjects with both alcohol abuse and MDD, the MDD preceded even the first exposure to alcohol. Similar findings were observed for MDD and substance abuse. In the Epidemiological Catchment Area Study (Eaton et al., 1989), mood or anxiety disorders during adolescence increased the lifetime risk for substance abuse during adulthood by 2–2.5 times.

Depression also compromises the child's family, social, and school functioning (Rutter et al., 1976; Asarnow and Ben-Meir 1987, 1988, 1990; Puig-Antich et al., 1985a,b, 1993; Hammen 1990). For example, Puig-Antich et al. (1985a) compared the psychosocial functioning in a group of children with MDD, nondepressive psychiatric disorders (mainly anxiety disorders), and a group of normal controls. In comparison with the normal controls, children with MDD had significant impairments in their school performance and in their relationships with parents, siblings, and teachers. Depressive children were also likely to have fewer special or "best" friendships, a lower ability to make and maintain positive peer relationships, and were more likely to be teased. When compared with the nondepressed psychiatric controls, depressive children had marked impairment in the mother–child relationship. However, most of the other psychosocial disturbances were also found in the nondepressed controls, questioning the specificity of these findings. Moreover, similar disturbances in psychosocial functioning have also been reported in children with disruptive disorders (e.g., Patterson, 1982). Additionally, poor family relationships appear to be a nonspecific risk factor for various psychiatric disorders (Fendrich et al., 1990). After recovery, depressed children show complete normalization of school functioning but only a partial improvement in the child's intrafamilial and extrafamilial relationships (Puig-Antich et al., 1985b).

Recently, Puig-Antich et al. (1993) compared the psychosocial functioning of a group of adolescents with MDD with a group of normal controls. As with depressed children, adolescents with MDD showed disturbances in all areas of psychosocial functioning. Similar results have been reported with clinical and community samples of adolescents (Kandel and Davis, 1982; Kaslow et al., 1984; Kovacs and Goldston, 1991; Kashani et al., 1988; Daniels and Moos, 1990). All of these studies, however, were completed after the depression developed, did not include psychiatric controls, and were made cross sectionally, making it impossible to determine if the psychosocial problems measured predated, co-occurred, or postdated the onset of the depressive disorder.

Recently, Rohde et al. (1994) evaluated a community sample of adolescents before and after they recovered from their first episode of major depression and a normal control group. Rohde and colleagues found that after recovery from the episode of depression, the adolescents continued to have subsyndromal symptoms of depression. In addition, they tended to smoke more cigarettes, had more major life events, were shy, anxious, and showed excessive reliance on others. Nolen-Hoeksema et al., (1992) in a prospective study also showed that pessimistic attribution style may be a residual effect of depression in children.

It is also important to mention that not only depression but other factors associated with the initiation, maintenance, and recurrence of depression, such as family psychopathology and other adverse stressors, may affect the psychosocial functioning of the individual (McCauley and Myers, 1992; Garber and Hilsman, 1992; Asarnow et al., 1994; Marton et al., 1989).

PATHOGENESIS

Familial aggregation, twin, and adoption studies have given evidence for genetic influences in the transmission of mood disorders (Reiss et al., 1991; McGuffin and Murray, 1991). Genetic factors account for at least 50% of the variance (e.g., Reiss et al., 1991). Therefore, other factors such as exposure to adverse life stressors, negative pattern of family interactions, lack of support, maladaptive coping, and cognitive style. The interaction of these features may be associated with the initiation, maintenance, or recurrence of clinical depression. In this section, we will briefly review the family aggregation, biological, life events, coping, and cognitive style studies in children and adolescents with clinical depression.

Family Aggregation Studies

Two methodological approaches have been used to study the family aggregation of mood disorders in children and adolescents. The so-called top–down approach examines the first-degree relatives (offspring or siblings) under 18 years of age of adult patients with mood disorders. The second, or bottom–up, approach ascertains lifetime psychiatric diagnoses of first- or second-degree relatives of child and adolescent probands with mood disorders.

Top–Down Studies—Children of Depressed Parents Initial investigations that examined the children of depressed parents did so primarily utilizing them for controlled comparisons with the children of schizophrenic persons. Generally, it was reported that the children of depressed parents exhibited similar behavioral and adjustment disturbances as did children of schizophrenic parents. Rooted in these early studies, research of early-onset psychopathology examined nonspecific symptoms of psychopathology rather than psychiatric diagnoses in children of depressed parents. Of these initial investigations, however, three presented rates of psychiatric diagnoses in children of parents with affective disorder (Orvaschel et al., 1981; McKnew et al., 1979; O'Connell et al., 1979). Orvashel et al. (1981) reported on 28 children (aged 6–17) of parents with various psychiatric disorders. Children were directly interviewed using the K-SADS, and diagnoses were made according to RDC and DSM-III (for disorders not covered in RDC). Forty-three percent of the children had a lifetime DSM-III psychiatric diagnosis. Due to the small sample size and the heterogeneity of psychiatric disorders, the authors did not attempt further analyses to examine specific transmission of disorders. McKnew et al. (1979), in a study of the offspring (aged 5–15 years) of 14 consecutive adult patients hosptialized at the National Institute of Mental Health (NIMH) with a diagnosis of bipolar and unipolar affective disorder, reported 77% of the children were depressed at the time of the initial assessment or at the 4-month follow-up interview. O'Connell and associates (1979) studied 22 offspring (aged 5–17 years) of adult patients being treated for manic-depressive illness. The diagnosis of bipolar disorder in the parents was made according to RDC criteria. Children were directly interviewed using the Children's Psychiatric Rating Scale (CPRS) (Children's ECDEU Battery, 1973). The authors report that 45% of the children were "symptomatic or moderately ill." Overall, the authors observed that anxiety and depression were the most predominant symptoms. Specific diagnoses were not reported, although it was reported that none of the offspring had the diagnosis of manic–depression.

Taken as a whole, these studies demonstrate that children of parents with affective disorder display both a high rate of behavioral disturbances and that offspring of parents with an affective disorder are at high risk for having an affective disorder.

Extending from these studies, other investigations have examined the effect of comorbidity in the depressed adult proband on lifetime rates of psychopathology in their offspring. In one study, the lifetime rates of DSM-III psychiatric disorders in children (aged 6–17 years) of depressed adult probands with and without comorbid anxiety disorders were compared with the children of adult probands without any lifetime psychopathology (Weissman et al., 1984a). Psychiatric morbidity in the children was assessed by family history method via reports from the mother and other relatives (children were not directly interviewed). Overall, the children of the depressed proband were at significantly greater risk for psychopathology (range from 15.6 to 42.1%) compared to the children of normal controls (8.1%). Compared to the children of depressed adults with no comorbid anxiety, children of adult depressed probands with comorbid panic disorder had the highest rates of separation anxiety disorder (36.8 vs. 0%) and major depression (26.3 vs. 10.5). While the rates appear to be significantly different, the authors did not report statistical significance tests. Based on the reported data, our analysis showed that the rates were not significantly different between the two groups for depression (Fisher's Exact Test, $P \leq .12$) but reached statistical significance for separation anxiety disorder (Fisher's Exact Test, $P \leq .0002$). Additionally, comorbid agoraphobia in the depressed adult proband was associated with higher rates of major depression (22.2%) and anxiety disorders (ranging from 5.6% for agoraphobia to 11.1% for separation anxiety disorder) in the children. From these data of the offspring of adult depressed probands with and without a comorbid anxiety disorder, depression and anxiety appear to be related and confer specific risks to their children. These results need to be interpreted with caution as one of the main limitations of this study was the reliability of reports of mothers and/or other relatives to ascertain diagnoses in the children. The pattern of findings may have been different had the children themselves been directly interviewed.

In a more recent study (Mufson et al., 1992), 220 children between the ages of 6 and 23 at high and low risk for major depression were studied. High-risk status was based on the presence of major depression in one or more parents (65 families) while the low-risk children were defined as having no parent with depression (26 families). Differing from their previous study (Weissman et al., 1984b), the authors directly interviewed the children using the Schedule for Affective Disorders and Schizophrenia for School-Aged Children, Epidemiologic Version (K-SADS-E) (Orvaschel et al., 1982). Both parents and children were directly interviewed about the child's lifetime psychopathology. Diagnoses were made based on a "best estimate" procedure (Leckman et al., 1982) in which a child psychiatrist and psychologist are blind to the parents' diagnostic status and assigned a DSM-III diagnoses for each child. Based on both parents' lifetime diagnoses, the families were split into four groups: (1) major depression with panic disorder, (2) major depression without panic disorder, (3) other psychiatric disorders, and (4) no psychiatric disorder. The results showed that children of depressed parents with panic disorder had increased lifetime rates of depression (32%), compared to the children of parents with other psychiatric disorders (9%). Interestingly, the results indicated that there was an ordered gradient for comorbid depression and anxiety in children, with the highest rates found in children of the depressed parents with panic disorder (21%) and the lowest rates were found in children of parents with no lifetime psychiatric disorders (5%). To compare the findings from their previous report (Weissman et al., 1984a), the authors analyzed the data limiting the sample to families of children between the ages of 6 and 17 years. Differing from the study by Weissman et al. (1984a), the results demonstrated that the rate of separation anxiety was 29.6% in the children of depressed parents with panic disorder, which was comparable to the children of parents with depression only (23.3%).

Biederman and colleagues (1991) examined the pattern of familial association between depressive and anxiety disorders in children (age 4–22 years) of parents with: (1) panic disorder and agoraphobia without comorbid depression ($n = 14$), (2) panic disorder and agoraphobia with comorbid depression ($n = 25$), (3) depression without comorbid panic disorder and agoraphobia ($n = 12$), (4) other psychiatric disorders ($n = 23$), and (5) normal controls ($n = 47$). The results indicated that children of panic disordered and agoraphobic probands, both with and without depression, had elevated rates of both depressive and anxiety disorders. However, children of probands with depression had elevated rates of depression but not anxiety. These results provide support for the hypotheses that depression without comorbid anxiety represents a distinct disorder from panic disorder and agoraphobia (with and without depression). The authors report further that the children of parents with panic disorder and agoraphobia with depression who had anxiety were not at greater risk for depression. This indicates that depression and anxiety did not cosegregate among the children of parents with panic disorder and agoraphobia, providing evidence that depression and panic with agoraphobia is not a distinct disorder separate from anxiety and depression. The findings from this study are limited as with the studies mentioned since the authors relied on mother's report to assess psychopathology in the children.

In summary, it appears that children of depressed parents have an elevated risk for depression as well as for other psychiatric disorders. Further, parental comorbid anxiety disorders seem to be differentially associated with risk for depression and anxiety in their offspring.

Bottom–Up Family Studies—Depressed Children   The familial aggregation of adult-onset affective disorders has been well documented. Family studies of adult-onset depressed proband have consistently reported a two- to threefold increase in the lifetime rates of depressive disorders in the relatives of depressed proband compared to normal controls (e.g., Weissman et al., 1982; Gershon et al., 1982; Weissman et al., 1984a,b; Tsuang et al., 1985).

An earlier investigation reported on the family histories of 12 children with a DSM-III anxiety disorder (8 with overanxious disorder and 4 with a separation anxiety disorder) and 11 with a DSM-III major depressive disorder (Livingston et al., 1985). Relatives assessed included both parents (mothers and fathers) and other relatives (aunts, uncles, and grandparents). Lifetime rates of psychopathology in the relatives were determined blind to the child probands' diagnoses and made according to the Family History Research Diagnostic Criteria (FH-RDC) (Endicott et al., 1975). Results indicated that 72% of the relatives of depressed children had an FH-RDC diagnosis, compared to 71% of the relatives of anxious children. Unipolar depression was equally common in the relatives of both groups with 29.3% of the depressed children's relatives having at least a possible lifetime depressive episode compared to 24.6% of the relatives of anxious children. The FH-RDC does not include criteria for anxiety disorders; therefore, all anxiety disorders were classified under the "other" psychiatric disorders category. The relatives of anxious children had 11.6% lifetime prevalence of "other" psychiatric disorders compared to 5.2% of the relatives of depressed children. Although not reported by the authors, our analysis showed that this was not statistically different (Fisher's Exact Test, $P \leq .18$). Based on the tables provided by the authors, analyses of the rates within parents revealed that the parents of both the anxious and depressed children had similar lifetime rates of all FH-RDC psychiatric disorders. Therefore, in this study, lifetime rates of psychopathology in relatives of depressed and anxious children appear to be the same.

In a study of depressed, schizophrenic, and conduct-disordered adolescents, Strober (1983) reported that the relatives of depressed adolescents were at significantly more risk for affective disorder (21.7%) compared to the relatives of schizophrenic (8.0%) and conduct-disordered (6.5%) adolescents. In a second report, Strober (1984) reported on the first- and second-degree relatives of depressed inpatient adolescents. Compared to epidemiologic data of adults, relatives of depressed adolescents had higher than expected lifetime rates of affective disorder and alcoholism. In another investigation (Mitchell et al., 1989), lifetime psychopathology in the parents of depressed and nonde-pressed children and adolescents were compared. Lifetime rates of depression were similar in the parents of the depressed and nondepressed youth for both mothers (56.3 vs. 53.3%) and fathers (34.1 vs. 22.9%). The authors did report finding that mothers of depressed children and adolescents had greater lifetime rates of anxiety disorders, substance abuse, and suicide attempts, and entered treatment earlier compared to the mothers of nondepressed subjects. A significantly greater number of depressed subjects had both mothers and fathers with depression compared to nondepressed subjects.

In a family study of prepubertal-onset depression (Puig-Antich et al., 1989a), the age-adjusted lifetime rate for depression in first-degree relatives was approximately twofold higher in the relatives of depressed probands (53%) compared to the first-degree relatives of nonaffective (anxiety) psychiatric controls (29%) and normal controls (28%). Among the second-degree relatives, the age unadjusted rate for depression was higher in the relatives of depressed proband (11%) compared to the relatives of normal controls (6%) but was the same for the nonaffective psychiatric controls (13%).

In a family study of adolescent-onset depressed patients (Kutcher and Marton, 1991), the age-unadjusted lifetime rates of unipolar depression were higher in the first-degree relatives of unipolar (20%) and bipolar (18.5%) adolescents compared to the relatives of normal controls (3.6%).

In a more recent report (Williamson et al., in press), the first-degree relatives of adolescents with MDD were reported to have significantly higher lifetime rates of MDD (25.0 vs. 13.1%) and "any" of the FH-RDC psychiatric disorders (53.1 vs. 35.5%) compared to the relatives of normal controls.

In summary, increased familial loading for affective disorder in the families of adult-onset and early-onset probands provides evidence for the validity of the diagnosis (Robins and Guze, 1970) and suggests that a familial/genetic component is important in the etiology of depression across the life span. Interestingly, it appears that there is an inverse relationship between age at onset and the density of familial aggregation of depression. Late-onset depression ($\geq$ 60 years) is associated with the least risk for depression in family members (Brodaty, et al., 1991; Maier et al., 1991) while early-onset ($\leq$ 20 years) seems to be associated with the greatest risk for depression in family members (Weissman et al., 1984b). The source of this inverse relationship deserves further research.

Biological Markers

Biological markers offer the potential to be informative about the psychobiologic continuity of major depression, which is syndromically relatively constant throughout the life span and yet which appears to possibly be less pharmacologically responsive during childhood and adolescence (see Chapter 3). In addition, such psychobiologic correlates of the disorder may give clues as to etiology.

Growth Hormone Studies

Growth hormone is a peptide hormone secreted by the anterior pituitary that is involved in controlling growth and metabolism throughout the body. While sleep is the time of greatest growth hormone secretion throughout the life span, with adolescence there is a relative increase in the total 24-hour growth hormone (GH) secretion, and this increase comes primarily from increased daytime secretion. Adults with either major depression or anxiety disorders tend to show a blunted release to a wide range of pharmacological challenges including dextroamphetamine, methyl-amphetamine, L-dopa, insulin, desipramine, and clonidine (Amsterdam and Maislin, 1990, 1991; Amsterdam et al., 1989; Ansseau et al., 1988; Brunswick et al., 1988; Calil et al., 1984; Casper et al., 1977; Charney et al., 1982; Checkley et al., 1981; Dinan and Barry, 1990; Gruen et al., 1975; Koslow et al., 1982; Langer et al., 1976; Matussek et al., 1980; Mueller et al., 1969; Sachar et al., 1971, 1973; Siever et al., 1992, 1982; Siever and Uhde, 1984).

In children with major depressive disorder, GH response to provocative stimuli has been found to be blunted after insulin-induced hypoglycemia compared to nondepressed psychiatric control children, and this finding appears to persist upon recovery (Puig-Antich et al., 1984a,b). Subsequently, four other studies have shown blunted GH in prepubertal MDD children compared to normal children after various stimuli including oral clonidine (Jensen and Garfinkel, 1990; Meyer et al., 1991), L-dopa (Jensen and Garfinkel, 1990) insulin-induced hypoglycemia (Puig-Antich 1984a,b; Ryan et al., 1994), and after intravenous growth hormone releasing hormone (Ryan et al.,

1994). In addition, we have demonstrated (Ryan et al., 1988) blunted growth hormone secretion in suicidal adolescent major depression in response to an intramuscular injection of desmethylimipramine. The finding of blunted GH may well be a *trait marker* for depression (present before, during, and after recovery) in both children (Ryan et al., 1994) and adults (Mitchell, et al., 1988).

The finding of blunted GH response to growth hormone releasing hormone (GHRH) (which acts directly at the pituitary) in combination with blunted GH response to agents acting at the level of the hypothalamus suggests that this finding may not reflect, as had earlier been hypothesized, purely a decreased α_2-adrenergic responsivity. It may also reflect (Ryan et al., 1994) the following possibilities: (1) increased somato-statin; (2) increased somatomedin C, which would increase somatostatin levels and have a direct negative feedback on the pituitary; (3) increased diurnal GH secretion with direct negative feedback on the hypothalamus and pituitary; and/or (4) increased nocturnal GH secretion with subsequent decrease in daytime pituitary GH reserve. Dysregulation of serotonergic systems that have a direct effect on control of somato-statin may account for this finding of blunted GH, but this hypothesis awaits further testing (Ryan et al., 1994).

While there is consistency in the finding of blunted GH after pharmacological stimuli associated with major depression, findings as to the control of nocturnal secretion of GH without stimulation are conflicting. Earlier studies of Puig-Antich et al. (1984c,d) and Kutcher et al. (1988, 1991) suggest that there may be a relative hypersection during sleep while more recent studies by our group (Dahl et al., unpublished data) have failed to replicate this finding and find no difference in the nocturnal GH secretion of depressed and normal children.

Serotonergic Studies   The blunting of the hormonal response of cortisol to seroton-ergic challenge agents has been repeatedly demonstrated in adults with major depres-sion and/or suicide when compared to normal adults. We have demonstrated entirely parallel findings in children with major depression examining the cortisol response to intravenous L-5-hydroxytryptophan (5HTP), a precursor of serotonin, which increases serotonin turnover after infusion (Ryan et al., 1992b). The MDD children secreted significantly less cortisol than did normal children. In addition, after the infusion with 5HTP, we found that the depressed females secreted more prolactin than did their normal counterparts (Ryan et al., 1992b).

Sleep Studies   While subjective sleep disturbances are common in children and adolescents with major depression (Ryan et al., 1987), objective measures show rela-tively low rates of adult-type sleep polysomnography changes with child depression and increasing rates with later adolescents and early adulthood. Of four sleep studies in prepubertal children, three (Puig-Antich et al., 1983; Young et al., 1982; Dahl et al., 1991a) found no evidence of sleep architecture differences and the other (Emslie et al., 1990) in an entirely inpatient sample found significantly reduced REM latency but not delta sleep differences and greater sleep continuity in depressed children. More recently, a small subgroup (8 of 36) of prepubertal depressed children in our sample have shown adult-type sleep disturbance (reduced REM and decreased delta sleep) (Dahl et al., 1991a), but overall the depressed children as a group did not differ from the normal control group.

In adolescents, sleep abnormalities appear to also occur less frequently than in adults with major depression. Goetz et al. (1987) found prolonged sleep latency but no other differences, and Lahmeyer et al. (1983) found reduced REM latency in a small group of late adolescents/young adults with major depression. Appleboon-Fondu et al. (1988) reported minor changes in sleep efficiency but no REM or delta sleep changes, and Kahn and Todd (1990) found no differences on sleep measures between depressed and normal adolescents. Dahl et al. (1990) found that a subgroup of MDDs, the inpatient/suicidal, tended to have short REM latencies. In comparison with a group of normal controls, Naylor et al. (1990) reported reduced REM latency in a small group of psychotically depressed adolescents. Kutcher et al. (1992) found significantly shortened REM latency and longer sleep latencies in a group of adolescents with endogenous MDD. Emslie et al. (1994) reported that a group of inpatient adolescents with MDD showed most of the sleep EEG disturbances found in symptomatic depressed adults.

Most recently, Rao et al. (in review) has followed up a cohort of adolescents who are now young adults and who participated in sleep studies during adolescence. Removing those initially depressed adolescents who became bipolar or who never experienced another depression and those initially normal adolescents who experienced one or more subsequent depression "cleaned up" the comparison between those normals who remained normal and depressives who went on to have recurrent unipolar major depression. In that comparison, at time of initial evaluation, the depressives, who subsequently developed further episodes, had significantly shorter REM latency than did those who were destined to remain normal. This suggests that eventual bipolarity and individuals with single episode of disorder may add "noise," making the between-group differences in sleep parameters in adolescents harder to detect. In addition, discrepant data in different studies of depressed children and adolescents may be accounted for by inpatient/outpatient status, suicidality, rates of melancholic/endogenous symptoms, and variations in methodology (Emslie et al., 1994; Dahl et al., 1990).

Hypothalamic–Pituitary Axis (HPA) Studies   A review of the validity of the dexamethasone suppression test (DST) in children showed that approximately 70% of the children with MDD and approximately 30% of children with other psychiatric disorders were nonsuppressors (Casat et al., 1989). The pooled DST sensitivity and specificity were both approximately 70%. However, as described in the adult literature (American Psychiatric Association, 1987), significantly more inpatient children with MDD were nonsuppressors (82%) than MDD outpatients (32%). Birmaher et al. (1992a) reported a study of 24-hour baseline cortisol and 24-hour cortisol plasma secretion after the administration of dexamethasone (DST) in a sample of predominantly outpatient children with major depressive disorder, nonaffective psychiatric controls, and normal controls. Baseline cortisol and cortisol secretion after the DST did not discriminate between the three groups. In addition, there were no significant between-group differences in the 24-hour serum dexamethasone concentrations. Puig-Antich et al. (1989b) also did not find statistically significant differences in 24-hour baseline cortisol secretion in a sample of outpatient depressed children and normal controls.

Casat et al. (1989) also reviewed the available studies on the use of the DST in adolescents with MDD. All DST studies in this age group reported data only with *inpatient samples*. Casat and colleagues (1989) showed that 47% of the adolescent inpatient subjects with MDD and 20% of the subjects with other psychiatric disorders were nonsuppressors. Recently, Birmaher et al. (1992b) in a large *outpatient* sample of depressed adolescents measured 16-hour cortisol levels following dexamethasone administration. In contrast with previous *inpatient* adolescent studies, the D‹ discriminate between MDD patients and normal controls. A study of 24-hou cortisol secretion with the same sample (Dahl et al., 1991b) and a study of .... cortisol secretion in another sample (Kutcher et al., 1991) also did not find significant differences between depressed and normal control groups.

Studies in adults with MDD have consistently shown blunted corticotropin hormone (ACTH) with normal cortisol plasma levels after the administration of corticotropin releasing hormone (CRH), particularly in inpatient and melancholic samples (for a review, see Birmaher et al. 1993). Birmaher and colleagues measured the cortisol and ACTH responses to an infusion of human CRH in prepubertal children with MDD and normal controls. Overall, there were no significant differences between the MDD and the normal controls in baseline or post-CRH stimulation values of either cortisol or ACTH. However, two subgroups, the inpatients and the melancholics, secreted significantly less total ACTH after CRH. There were no differences in the net ACTH secretion.

These results are consistent with a broad literature suggesting that the HPA abnormalities occur less frequently in early-onset depression than reported in adult studies. However, the pattern of results in the subgroups of inpatients and in melancholic children and adolescents suggest possible continuities with adult studies.

In summary, examination of GH measures and serotonergic probes in childhood depression suggest great continuity of these abnormalities associated with depression across the life span while examination of the HPA and sleep measures in childhood depression suggest there are developmental, age, severity, exposure to stress (i.e., hospitalization) effects on those two systems interacting with diagnosis. Nevertheless, in aggregate, the psychobiology of childhood depression appears more like than unlike that seen in adults. In addition to demonstrating these similarities and developmentally mediated changes, such studies have the potential to identify those at greatest risk for recurrence (as in the Rao study discussed earlier) or potentially to predict those who are not yet depressed who may become depressed in the future, permitting biologically targeted studies of primary prevention in this disorder.

Family Interactions

Studies of depressed adults recalling their early interactions, studies of offspring of depressed parents, and investigations of the family system in adolescents with depression, have shown that family interactions of depressed probands are characterized by more hostility, conflict, criticism, disengagement, rejection, problems with communication, less expression of affect, less support, and more abuse when compared with families of normal controls (e.g., Schwartz et al., 1990; Hammen, 1990; Kaufman, 1991; McCauly and Myers, 1992; Downey and Coyne, 1990; Rutter, 1990). Studies of infants of depressed mothers have shown that they are more insecure, have avoidant-attachment, express less positive affect, and less activity in comparison with infants of nondepressed mothers (Cohn and Tronick, 1989; Hammen, 1990). This pattern of behavior seems to persist when these infants interact with strangers (Forehand et al., 1988), suggesting that abnormal early relationships may affect the way that the infant continues to interact with other people. Interestingly, Dawson et al. 1992 reported that early maternal interactions caused alterations in electroencephalographic measures of frontal lobe arousal, also suggesting that early interactions may affect the development of the central nervous system.

Most of the above family interaction studies have investigated the relationships between mothers and their offspring and compared with mothers without psychiatric disorders. However, the few studies that have included other psychiatric control groups have questioned the specificity of these findings. When compared with families with normal parents, children of depressed parents have significantly more psychopathology (anxiety, depression, disruptive disorders) than children of normal parents. However, there were no significant differences when compared with children of parents with other psychiatric disorders but not depression (Downey and Coyne, 1990; Goodman and Brumley, 1990; Stubbe et al., 1993). Recently, Asarnow et al. (1994) reported that measurements of expressed emotion (critical and emotional overinvolvement family attitudes) were significantly higher in depressed children than in schizophrenic and normal controls. Within the depressed group, the presence of comorbidity with disruptive disorders was associated with higher levels of criticism. It is possible that expressed emotion was not causal because measurement occurred after the depression developed and also because it may reflect a coping strategy in which parents attempt to control the child's behavior.

Controversy exists regarding the mechanisms by which depression is transmitted to the offspring of depressed parents. Some studies conclude that offspring psychopathology is mainly due to parental psychiatric disorder while other studies conclude that offspring psychopathology is mainly due to family risk factors not associated with parent psychopathology (for a critical review see Rutter, 1990). Differences among these studies may be due to the use of small or heterogeneous samples and other methodological flaws. Current opinion suggests that both genetic and family/environmental mechanisms and their interactions are involved in the transmission of depression to the offspring of depressed parents. Thus, lack of affection or irritability expressed toward the child, diminished sensitivity or responsivity to child cues and needs, family or marital conflicts, the style of parenting before the development of the depressive disorder, and parents' comorbid diagnoses may also influence the offspring. In addition, factors such as mother's negative reaction in response to children's behavioral problems or depression, increased criticism, lack of parental supervision and disciplinary function, inappropriate use of children as a source of comfort, and adverse events that precipitated or maintained the depression in parents may be associated with childhood psychopathology. For example, Rutter and Quinton (1984) showed that parental discord and hostility directed toward the children and not the psychiatric disorder per se was associated with child psychopathology. Billing and Moos (1986) reported that children of depressed parents were at risk of developing depression, but levels of family distress and support independently contributed to the development of psychopathology in the child. High-risk children without psychopathology usually came from supportive families.

Abnormal early interactions between mother and child may also cause children to develop patterns of handling stress that predispose them to depression. Mothers may be teaching their children to "give up" when facing a stressful task and not modeling adaptive ways to regulate negative affect (Garber et al., 1991). It is also important to mention that not only are the mother's interactions with the children negative, but the children may also generate conflicts that will contribute to maintain their parents' and their own depression (Hammen et al., 1990).

As summarized by Rutter (1990), it seems that children of depressed parents are at less risk to develop mood disorders if parental disorder is mild, short, not recurrent, not associated with family conflict and disorganization, and if there is no impaired parenting and no family separation or divorce. Children may also have a better prognosis if they have good support, a better temperament, good relationship with at least one parent, relatives or peers, and, as discussed in the next section, good coping and problem-solving skills.

Finally, it is important to point out that the review of the literature presented here on the role of family environment in depressive conditions is at odds with recent behavior genetic studies. These findings suggest that environmental effects on most behavior traits arise almost entirely from environmental experiences that are *not shared* by members of the same sibship (e.g., Kendler et al., 1994; Plomin and Daniel, 1987).

Stressful Life Events

Stressful life events have been associated with depression onset and relapse (e.g., Brown and Harris 1978, 1989). Most of the adult MDD studies have reported that 70% of patients with their first episode of MDD had a major stressful life event 6 months prior to the onset of the depression. Among the various stressful life events, interpersonal life events characterized by loss, "exits" of significant others from the social network, and disappointments, in particular, appear to act as potent provoking agents for depression.

Paralleling studies of adults (e.g., see Paykel 1979a,b; Brown and Harris, 1989, for reviews) and some studies of depressed children and adolescents have established a significant relationship between stressful life events and depression (for a review, see Garber and Hilsman, 1992). Population studies, using self-report measures of depression and life events checklists have generally found a consistent positive correlation of approximately 0.3 between stressful life events and depressive symptoms (Johnson and McCutcheon, 1980; Swearingen and Cohen, 1985; Compas et al., 1986; Daniels and Moos, 1990; Goodyer et al., 1985, 1988; Nolen-Hoeksema et al., 1986). Several studies, but not all (Kutcher, 1993), of clinical populations (Garber et al., 1992) have also found an elevation of stressful life events in depressed youth compared to normal controls (for review, see Garber et al., 1992).

A major limitation for stressful life event research in early-onset depression is that much of the research has focused on cross-sectional correlational data obtained from self-report checklists, making it difficult to establish a causal relation.

The limitations of the checklist or respondent-based method of assessing life events have been widely reported. First, the checklist method does not provide for the assessment of accurate dating of event occurrence. The event is ticked by the subject but exact dating of when the event occurred is not coded. Second, life event checklists have generally been found to have low test–retest reliability with fall-off in reporting events approaching 5% per month (Cohen and Wills, 1985) which has been attributed to respondents not specifically being prompted to remember events (Jenkins et al., 1979). Third, life events checklists do not measure the dependence/independence of an event. In other words, whether the event is a consequence of the subject's involvement in the event is not delineated and therefore may be confounded with the depressive episode. Finally, checklists do not distinguish between different levels of severity within a particular stressor. For example, events such as birth of a sibling are included, but in the absence of the relevant contextual information (i.e., the meaning of the event for the adolescent) degree of stressful severity cannot be determined.

The studies by Goodyer and colleagues (1985, 1988) have circumvented the problems posed by checklists by using a life event interview. The authors specifically focused on whether events occurred prior to the onset of the illness symptoms and additionally identified the timing, duration, and context within which the event occurred. Additionally, events were rated on a five-point scale ranging from no negative impact to severe negative impact. Based on the interview methodology, the authors reported that between 60 and 70% of new cases of depression compared to 29% of the controls had a severely undesirable life event in the 12 months prior to onset (Goodyer et al., 1985, 1988). Subsequently, Goodyer and colleagues have found that specific contextual domains, both recent undesirable events and friendship difficulties, had independent effects for both depression and anxiety disorders (Goodyer et al., 1989). This finding suggests that friendship difficulties exert their influence through a separate pathway than do recent life events. Additional studies examining stressful life events partitioned into separate domains are warranted.

Thus far, while not causal in nature, few studies have examined the significance of stressful life events that occur during the depressive episode. Hammen (1991) reported on the findings from a one-year longitudinal study of depressed women that suggested that depressed women had higher rates of dependent (events in which the person was in part responsible for bringing about) stressful life events, predominantly interpersonal conflicts compared to women with bipolar disorder, women with a medical illness, and women who were not ill. A recent report of the offspring of these same women (Adrian and Hammen, 1993) found that the children of the depressed mothers had significantly more dependent stressful life events compared to children of mothers who had a medical illness or children of mothers without any lifetime psychopathology. Similar to their mothers, the children of the depressed women, who were not depressed themselves, were found to have significantly higher interpersonal conflict events (family and peer conflicts) compared to the control children. In a more recent investigation, depressed adolescents reported having more dependent (events they were most likely involved in) stressful life events during the depressive episode compared to normal controls. Interestingly, the depressed adolescents *with* dependent stressful life events appear to be less severely depressed than depressed adolescents *without* dependent stressful life events and loaded lower on symptom clusters reflecting "negative cognitions" and "anxiety" (Williamson et al., 1995a). Further work is needed that examines the role of stressful life events as they contribute to the onset, maintenance, remittance, and relapse of depression.

Few studies to date have examined the independent and combined effects of stressful life events and psychobiological measures for early-onset depression. In one recent investigation of the cellular immune system in depressed adolescents (Birmaher et al., 1994), stressful life events were positively correlated with natural killer cell activity. More recently, in a re-analysis of data from an earlier EEG sleep study (Goetz et al., 1987) stressful life events were found to be associated with decreased delta in both depressed and normal control adolescents and reduced REM latency only in the normal control groups (Williamson et al., 1995b). More studies are needed that examine the separate and combined effects of stressful life events and psychobiological measures and their combined effect on early-onset depression.

Cognitive Style

Although adverse life events have been associated with initiation, maintenance, and relapse of depression, not all subjects exposed to adverse events develop symptoms of clinical depression. Other factors such as subject's negative cognitive style and perception of stress have been implicated in the pathogenesis of depression.

According to the cognitive theory of depression (e.g., Beck 1967, 1987), depressed individuals usually have a negative view of themselves, the world, and the future. Characteristically, depressed individuals have low self-esteem, are very critical of themselves, and do not appreciate their abilities. Usually, they have a negative view of situations they encounter and their future. As Beck suggests, these individuals tend to distort or misinterpret new experiences according to their negative belief system instead of seeing the objective facts (for an excellent overview of the relationship between cognitive style, stress, and depression in children, see Garber and Hilsman, 1992). In the same line, investigations derived from the "learned helplessness" model of depression in animals (Seligman and Maier, 1967) have suggested that depressed individuals tend to attribute to themselves negative events, and they feel that they do not have any control over the so-called hopelessness model for depression (Abramson et al., 1980). This model proposes that individuals who have a depressogenic cognitive style and are exposed to significant adverse life events are at risk to develop clinical depression (Abramson et al., 1988).

Studies of community and clinical samples of depressed children and adolescents have been consistent with findings of adult studies (Garber and Hilsman, 1992). Depressed children and adolescents tend to have more cognitive distortions, negative attributions, hopelessness, tendency to attribute outcomes to external noncontrollable causes, and low self-esteem (for a review, see Hammen, 1990; Garber and Hilsman, 1992; Garber et al., 1993; Gotlib et al., 1993; Weisz et al., 1992). Cognitive distortions, however, are not universal for all clinically depressed adolescents, and they seem to be associated to more severe depressions (Marton and Kutcher, 1995).

Asarnow and Bates (1988) reported that inpatient children and adolescents with MDD had more cognitive distortions, more negative attributions, and lower self-esteem than nonaffective psychiatric controls and nonreferred and normal controls. Consistent with other investigations (Hamilton and Abramsom, 1983; Hammen et al., 1986a,b), Asarnow and Bates (1988) reported that after treatment there were no significant differences in any of the cognitive variables among the three groups. These findings suggest that the depressogenic cognitive style may be a state rather than a trait characteristic. In contrast, longitudinal investigations have shown that after remission, depressed children have lower self-esteem than nondepressed children and that low self-esteem predicts future episodes of depression (Jaenicke et al., 1987; Hammen, 1988; Gotlib et al., 1993). The lower self-esteem, however, could be a "scar" of the past depressive episode and not a trait. Investigations using patients at risk for depression (defined as high family aggregation for mood disorders) but who are not currently depressed may help to answer this question.

Although the way children and adolescents develop negative cognitive styles is not yet established, studies have suggested that certain factors such as modeling by significant others, perfectionistic standards, criticism, rejection, and experiences with uncontrollable adverse life events may play a role (Garber and Hilsman, 1992).

As described, current cognitive theories of depression have suggested that neither stress nor depressogenic cognitions alone, but their interactions, are associated with depression. Thus, the *cognitive-diathesis* model proposes that individuals who are exposed to adverse life events and who have negative ways to interpret and cope with the stress are at high risk to develop depressive symptoms. Cognitive-diathesis studies in adults and children have yielded mixed results (Garber and Hilsman, 1992). Most of these studies used different methodologies and were cross sectional. In children, recent studies have shown a moderately significant correlation between exposure to a stress, cognitive style, and depressive symptoms. Hammen et al. (1988) reported that low self-esteem and adverse life events predicted subsequent depression in children. However, the interaction of stress and attributional style did not predict depression. Nolen-Hoeksema et al. (1986) reported that the interaction between self-explanatory style and life events predicted future self-reported depressive symptoms. Turner and Cole (1994) reported that cognitive style moderated the relation between life events and self-reported depressive symptoms, but only in later childhood. In contrast, Garber et al. (1993) did not find an association between depressogenic thinking and age in a sample of seventh- through twelfth-grade adolescents.

Recently, prospective investigations in community and pediatric samples of children have given some support to the validity of the cognitive-diathesis model of depression. Garber and Hilsman (1992) investigated the development of depressive mood and symptoms in a large population of children before and after receiving the school report card. After controlling for initial levels of dysphoric mood and symptoms, Garber and colleagues showed that attributional style, perceived academic competence, and perception of control over academic achievement all interacted with the level of poor grades to predict dysphoric mood several days after the stressor. Among the children with poor grades, those with negative styles were more likely to maintain high levels of dysphoric mood than children without negative cognitive style. In another prospective study, Panak and Garber (cited in Garber and Hilsman, 1992) reported that children exposed to increased peer rejection after the grade transition had a transient increase in depressive symptoms. Consistent with a previous study (Metalsky et al. 1987), children exposed to peer rejection and who also had negative cognitive styles manifested dysphoric mood for a significantly longer period of time than children who did not have such cognitive styles. Finally, Walker et al. (1993) conducted a one-year propsective study to determine whether the interaction of high levels of negative life events and low perceived competence predicted emotional distress in a sample of pediatric patients referred for abdominal pain. After controlling for depressive symptoms at the initial evaluation and the medical diagnosis (type of abdominal pain), they found that both the high levels of stress and low levels of perceived academic competence significantly predicted high levels of depressive symptoms at the end of the study. These findings provide further evidence of the validity the *cognitive stress* model of depressive symptoms in community and pediatric samples of children. Most of these studies investigated the association between depressive symptoms and cognitive style. Future studies need to address the question whether clinical depression is associated with the cognitive stress model.

To summarize, genetic-biological, negative cognitive style, disturbed family interactions, and exposure to adverse life events may play a role in the pathogenesis of clinical depression. Other factors not reviewed in this chapter such as family and peer support may protect individuals against the development of depression. Many of the factors reviewed above, however, appear not to be specific to depression but are nonspecific correlates of child psychopathology (i.e., Kazdin et al., 1983, 1986). However, as Garber and Hollon (1991) have argued, "it is possible for a particular variable to be nonspecific yet still causal if the variable is part of a larger multivariable causal process." Finally, it is important to point out that depression is a heterogeneous disorder, and it is likely that different processes may operate in its pathogenesis. Longitudinal studies including all of these variables and using large samples of children and adolescents with depression, nonaffective psychiatric controls, children at risk to develop depression but who currently are asymptomatic, and healthy controls will improve our understanding of the pathogenesis of depression. These investigations will also serve to develop better treatments and preventive strategies.

REFERENCES

Abramson LY, Alloy LB, Metalsky GI (1988): The cognitive diathesis-stress theories of depression: toward an adequate evaluation of the theories validities. In Alloy LB (ed): "Cognitive Processes in Depression." New York: Guilford.

Abramson LY, Garber J, Seligman ME (1980): Learned helplessness: An attributional analysis. In Garber J, Seligman MEP (eds): "Human Helplessness: Theory and Applications." New York: Academic Press, pp 3–34.

Adrian C, Hammen C (1993): Stress exposure and stress generation in children of depressed mothers. J Consult Clin Psych 61(2):354–359.

American Psychiatric Association Committee on Nomenclature and Statistics (1994): "Diagnostic and Statistical Manual of Mental Disorders," 3rd ed. Washington, DC: American Psychiatric Association.

American Psychiatric Association Task Force on Laboratory Tests in Psychiatry (1987): The Dexamethasone Suppression Test: An overview of its current status in psychiatry. Am J Psychiatry, 144:1253–1262.

Amsterdam JD, Maislin G (1991): Hormonal responses during insulin-induced hypoglycemia in manic-depressed, unipolar depressed, and healthy control subjects. J Clin Endocrinol Metab, 73:541–548.

Amsterdam JD, Maislin G (1990): Comparison of growth hormone response after clonidine and insulin hypoglycemia in affective illness. Biol Psychiatry, 28:308–314.

Amersterdam JD, Maislin G, Skolnick B, Berwish N, Winokour A (1989): Multiple hormone responses to clonidine administration in depressed patients and healthy volunteers. Biol Psychiatry, 26:265–278.

Anderson JC, Williams S, McGee R, Silva PA (1987): DSM-III disorders in preadolescent children. Arch Gen Psych, 44:69–76.

Angst J, Wicki W (1991): The Zurich Study XI: Is dysthymia a separate form of depression? Results of the Zurich Cohor Study. Eur Arch Psychiatry Clin Neurosci, 240:349–354.

Ansseau M, Von-Frenckell R, Cerfontaine JL, Papart P, Franck G, Timsit-Berthier M, Geenen V (1988): Blunted response of growth hormone to clonidine and apomorphine in endogenous depression. Br J Psychiatry, 153:65–71.

Appleboon-Fondu J, Kerkofs M, Mendlewicz J (1988): Depression in adolescents and young adults—Polysomnographic and neuroendocrine aspects. J Affective Disorders, 14:35–40.

Asarnow JR, Ben-Meir S (1988): Children with schizophrenia spectrum and depressive disorders: A comparative study of premorbid adjustment, onset pattern and severity of impairment. J Child Psychol Psychiatry, 29:477–488.

Asarnow JR, Bates S (1988): Depression in child psychiatric inpatients: Cognitive and attributional patterns. J Ab Child Psych, 16:601–615.

Asarnow JR, Tompson M, Hamilton EB, Goldstein MJ, Guthrie D (1994): Family-expressed emotion, childhood-onset depression, and childhood-onset schizophrenia spectrum disorders: Is expressed emotion a nonspecific correlate of child psychopathology or a specific risk factor for depression? J Ab Child Psych 22(2):129–146.

Asarnow JR, Goldstein M, Marshall V, Weber E (1990): Mother-child dynamics in early onset depression and childhood schizophrenia spectrum disorders. Devel Psychopathology 2:71–84.

Asarnow JR, Carlson G, Guthrie D (1987): Coping strategies, self-perceptions, hopelessness, and perceived family environments in depressed and suicidal children. J Consult Clin Psychol, 55:361–366.

Beck AT (1987): Cognitive models of depression. J Cognitive Psychotherapy 1:537.

Beck AT (1967): "Depression: Clinical, Experimental, and Theoretical Aspects." New York: Harper & Row.

Biederman J, Rosenbaum JF, Bolduc EA, Faraone SV, Hirshfeld DR (1991): A high risk study of young children of parents with panic disorder and agoraphobia with and without comorbid depression. Psych Res, 37:333–348.

Billing AG, Moos RH (1986): Children of parents with unipolar depression: A controlled 1-year follow up. J Ab Child Psych 14:149–166.

Bird HR, Canino G, Rubio-Stipec M, Gould MS, Ribra J, Sesman M, Woodbury M, Huertas-Goldman S, Pagan A, Sanchez-Lacay A, Moscoso M (1988): Estimates of the prevalence of childhood maladjustment in a community survey in Puerto Rico: The use of combined measures. Arch Gen Psych, 45:1120–1126.

Birmaher B, Rabin BS, Garcia MR, Umesh J, Whiteside TL, Williamson DE, Al-Shabbout M, Nelson BC, Dahl RE, Ryan ND (1994): Cellular immunity in depressed conduct disorder and normal adolescents: Role of adverse life events. J Am Acad of Child Adoles Psych 33:671–678.

Birmaher B, Ryan N, Dahl R, Perel J, Williamson D, Nelson B, Nguyen N, Puig-Antich J (1993): Corticotropin Releasing Hormone Challenge Test in Children with Major Depression and Normal Controls 48th Annual Convention of the Society of Biological Psychiatry, San Francisco, California.

Birmaher B, Ryan ND, Dahl RE, Rabinovich H, Ambrosini PJ, Williamson D, Novacenco H, Nelson B, Puig-Antich J, Lo ES (1992a): Dexamethasone suppression test in children with major depressive disorder. J Am Acad Child Adol Psych 31:291–297.

Birmaher B, Dahl RE, Ryan ND, Rabinovich H, Ambrosini P, Al-Shabbout M, Novacenko H, Nelson B, Puig-Antich J (1992b): Dexamethasone suppression test in adolescents with major depressive disorder. Am J of Psych 149(8):1040–1045.

Brent DA, Birmaher B, Kolko D, Holder D (1994): CBT with suicidal youth. Child and Adolescent Depression Consortium, Omni Biltmore Hotel, Providence, Rhode Island, September.

Brent DA, Perper J, Johnson B, Connolly J, Bridge J, Bartle S, Rather C (1993): Personality disorder, personality traits, impulsive violence and completed suicide in adolescents. J Am Acad Child Adoles 32(1):69–75.

Brent DA, Perper JA, Goldstein CE (1988): Risk factor for adolescent suicide: A comparison of adolescent suicide victims with suicidal inpatients. Arch Gen Psych, 45:581–588.

Brent DA, Perper JA, Allman CJ (1987): Alcohol firearms and suicide among youth: Temporal trends in Allegheny county, Pennsylvania. J Am Med Assoc 257:3369–3372.

Brodaty H, Peters K, Boyce P, Hickie I, Parker G, Mitchell P, Wilhelm K (1991): Age and depression. J Affect Disorders 23:137–149.

Brown GW, Harris TO (1989): Life events and Illness. New York: Guilford Press.

Brown GW, Harris TO (1978): Social origins of depression: A study of psychiatric disorder in women. London: Tavistock.

Brunswick DJ, Frazer A, Koslow SH, Casper R, Stokes PE, Robins E, Davis JM (1988): Insulin-induced hypoglycaemic response and release of growth hormone in depressed patients and healthy controls. Psychol Med 18:79–91.

Burke KC, Burke JD, Rae DS, Regier DA (1991): Comparing age at onset of major depression and other psychiatric disorders by birth cohorts in five US community populations. Arch Gen Psychiatry 48:789–795.

Calil HM, Lesieur P, Gold PW, Brown GM, Zavadil A, Potter WZ (1984): Hormonal responses to zimelidine and desipramine in depressed patients. Psychiatry Res 13:231–242.

Cantwell DP, Carlson GA (1983): Issues in classification. In Cantwell DP, Carlson GA (eds): "Affective Disorders in Childhood and Adolescence." Jamaica, NY: Spectrum.

Carlson GA (1984): A comparison of early and late onset adolescent affective disorder. J Operational Psychiatry 15:46–49.

Carlson GA, Cantwell DP (1980a): Unmasking masked depression in children and adolescents. Am J Psych 137:445–449.

Carlson GA, Cantwell DP (1980b): A survey of depressive symptoms, syndrome, and disorder in a child psychiatric population. J Child Psych Psych 21:19–25.

Carlson GA, Cantwell DP (1979): A survey of depressive symptoms in a child and adolescent psychiatric population: Interview data. J Am Acad Child Psych 18:587–599.

Carlson GA, Kashani JH (1988): Phenomenology of major depression from childhood through adulthood: Analysis of three studies. Am J of Psych 30:144–150.

Casper RC, Davis JM, Pandey GN, Garver DL, Dekirmenjian H (1977): Neuroendocrine and amine studies in affective illness. Psychoneuroendocrinology 2:105–113.

Casat CD, Arana GD, Powel K (1989): The DST in children and adolescents with major depressive disorder. Am J Psychiatry 146:503–507.

Chambers WJ, Puig-Antich J, Hirsch M, Paez P, Ambrosini PJ, Tabrizi MA, Davies M (1985): The assessment of affective disorders in children and adolescents by semistructured interview: Test-retest reliability of the schedule for affective disorders and schizophrenia for school-age children present episode version. Arch Gen Psych 42:696–702.

Charney DS, Heninger GR, Sternberg DE, Hafstad KM, Giddings S, Landis DH (1982): Adrenergic receptor sensitivity in depression. Effects of clonidine in depressed patients and healthy subjects. Arch Gen Psychiatry 39:290–294.

Checkley SA, Slade AP, Shur E (1981): Growth hormone and other responses to clonidine in patients with endogenous depression. Br J Psychiatry 138:51–55.

Children's ECDEU Battery (1973): Psychopharmacology Bull, Special Issue, 196–239.

Cohn JF, Tronick E (1989): Specificity of infants' response to mother's affective behavior. J Am Acad Child Adolesc Psychiatry 28:242–248.

Cohen S, Wills TA (1985): Stress, social support and the buffering hypothesis. Psychological Bull 98:310–357.

Compas BE, Slavin LA, Wagner BM, Vannatta K (1986): Relationship of life events and social support with psychological dysfunction among adolescents. J Youth Adoles 15:205–221.

Dahl RE, Ryan ND, Birmaher B, Al-Shabbout M, Williamson DE, Neidig M, Nelson B, Puig-Antich J (1991a): EEG sleep measures in prepubertal depression. Psychiat Res 38:201–214.

Dahl RE, Ryan ND, Puig-Antich J, Nguyen NA, Al-Shabbout M, Meyer VA, Perel J (1991b): 24-hour cortisol measures in adolescents with major depression: A controlled study. Biol Psychiat 30:25–36.

Dahl RE, Puig-Antich J, Ryan NE, Cunningham S, Nelson B, Klepper T (1990): EEG sleep in adolescents with major depression: The role of suicidality and inpatient status. J Affec Disorders 19:63–75.

Daniels D, Moos R (1990): Assessing life stressors and social resources among adolescents: Applications to depressed youth. J Adolesc Res 5:268–289.

Dawson G, Klinger LG, Panagiotides H, Hill D, Spieker S (1992): Frontal lobe activity and affective behavior of infants of mothers with depressive symptoms. Child Development 63:725–737.

Deykin EY, Buka SL, Zeena TH (1992): Depressive illness among chemically dependent adolescents. Am J of Psych 149:1341–1347.

Deykin EY, Levy JC, Wells V (1987): Adolescent depression, alcohol and drug abuse. Am J Public Health 77:178–182.

Dinan TG, Barry S (1990): Responses of growth hormone to desipramine in endogenous and non-endogenous depression. Br J Psychiatry 156:680–684.

Downey G, Coyne JC (1990): Children of depressed parents: An integrative review. Psychol Bull, 108:50.

Eaton WW, Kramer M, Anthony JC, Dryman A, Shapiro S, Locke BZ (1989): The incidence of specific DIS/DSM-III mental disorders: Data from the NIMH Epidemiologic Catchment Area Program. Acta Psychiatr Scand 79:163–178.

Emslie GJ, Rush AJ, Weinberg WA, Rinteloran JW, Roffwarg HP (1994): Sleep EEG features of adolescents with major depression. Biol Psychiatry 36:573–581.

Emslie GJ, Rush AJ, Weinberg WA, Rintelmann JW, Roffwarg HP (1990): Children with major depression show reduced rapid eye movement latencies. Arch Psychiat 47:119–124.

Endicott J, Andreasen N, Spitzer RL (1975): "Family History—Research Diagnostic Criteria." New York: Biometrics Research, New York State Psychiatric Institute.

Fendrich M, Warner V, Weissman M (1990): Family risk factors, parental depression, and childhood psychopathology. Devel Psych 26:40–50.

Fine S, Moretti M, Haley G, Marriage K (1985): Affective disorders in children and adolescents: The dysthymic disorder dilemma. Can J Psychiatry 30:173–177.

Fleming JE, Offord DR (1990): Epidemiology of childhood depressive disorders: A critical review. J Am Acad Child Adolesc Psych 29(4):571–580.

Forehand R, Brody G, Slotkin J, Fauber R, McCombs A, Long N (1988): Young adolescent and maternal depression: assessment, interrelations, and family predictors. J Consult Clin Psycho 56:422.

Frederick C (1978): Current trends in suicidal behavior in the United States. Am J Psychotherapy 32:172–200.

Friedman RC, Clarkin JF, Corn R, Arnoff MS, Hurt SW, Murphy MC (1982): DSM-III and affective pathology in hospitalized adolescents. J Nervous Mental Dis 170:511–521.

Garber J, Hilsman R (1992): Cognition, stress, and depression in children and adolescents. In Lewis M, Cantwell DP (eds): "Child and Adolescent Psychiatric Clinics of North America: Mood Disorders." Philadelphia: W.B. Saunders.

Garber J, Hollon SD (1991): What can specificity designs say about causality in psychopathology research? Psychol Bull 110:129–136.

Garber J, Robinson NS, Little S, Hilsman, R (1994): Stress and Depression: Risk and Protective Factors in Girls versus Boys. Presented at AACAP Meeting, New York, November.

Garber J, Weiss B, Shanley N (1993): Cognition, depressive symptoms, and development in adolescents. J Ab Psych 102(1):47–57.

Garber J, Quiggle N, Schlundt D, (1991): Family Functioning and Interactions Among Depressed Mothers and Their Children. Presented at the Society for Research in Child Development, Seattle.

Geller B, Chesnut EC, Miller D, Price DT, Yates E (1985): Preliminary data on DSM-III associated features of major depressive disorder in childhood and adolescents. Am J Psychiatry 142:643–644.

Gershon ES, Hamovit JH, Guroff JJ, Nurnberger JI (1987): Birth-cohort changes in manic and depressive disorders in relatives of bipolar and schizoaffective patients. Arch Gen Psych 44:314–319.

Gershon EW, Hamovit J, Guroff JJ, Dibble E, Leckman JF, Sceery W, Targum SD, Nurnberger JI, Goldin LR, Bunney WE (1982): A family study of schizoaffective, bipolar I, bipolar II, unipolar, and normal control probands. Arch Gen Psych 39:157–167.

Geotz RR, Puig-Antich J, Ryan ND, Rabinovich H, Ambrosini PJ, Nelson B, Drawiec V (1987): Electroencephalographic sleep of adolescents with major depression and normal controls. Arch Gen Psychiat 44:61–68.

Goodman SH, Brumley HE (1990): Schizophrenic and depressed mothers: Relational deficits in parenting. Devel Psych 26:31–39.

Goodyer IM, Wright C, Altham PM (1989): Recent friendships in anxious and depressed school age children. Psychol Med 19:165–174.

Goodyer IM, Wright C, Altham PME (1988): Maternal adversity and recent stressful life events in anxious and depressed children. J Child Psychology Psychiatry 29:651–667.

Goodyer I, Kolvin I, Gatzanis S. (1985): Recent undesirable life events and psychiatric disorder in childhood and adolescence. Br J Psychiat 147:517–523.

Gotlib IH, Lewinsohn PM, Seeley JR, Rohde P, Redner JE (1993): Negative cognition and attributional style in depressed adolescents: An examination of stability and specificity. J Abnormal Psychology 102:607–615.

Gruen PH, Sachar IJ, Altman N, Sassin J (1975): Growth hormone response to hypoglycemia in postmenopausal depressed women. Arch Gen Psychiatry 32:31–33.

Hagnell O, Lanke J, Robman B, Ojesjo L (1982): Are we entering an age of melancholy? Depressive illnesses in a prospective epidemiological study over 25 years: The Lundby study. Sweden Psychological Med 12:279–289.

Hamilton EW, Abramson LY (1983): Cognitive patterns in major depressive disorder: A longitudinal study in a hospital setting. J Ab Psychol 92:173–184.

Hammen C (1991): Generation of stress in the course of unipolar depression. J Ab Psychol 100:555–561.

Hammen C (1990): Cognitive approaches to depression in children: Current findings and new directions. In Lahey B, Kazdin A (eds): "Advances in Clinical Child Psychology." New York: Plenum Press, pp 139–173.

Hammen C (1988): Self-cognition, stressful events, and the prediction of depression in children of depressed mother. J Ab Child Psychol 16:347–360.

Hammen C, Burge D, Stanbury K (1990): Relationship of mother and child variables to child outcomes in a high-risk sample: A casual modeling analysis. Devel Pysch 26:24–30.

Hammen C, Adrian C, Hiroto D, (1988): A longitudinal test of the attributional vulnerability model in children at risk for depression. Br J Clin Psychol 27:37–46.

Hammen C, Mayo A, DeMayo R, et al. (1986a): Initial symptoms levels and the life-event depression relationship. J Ab Psychol 95:114–122.

Hammen C, Miklowitz DH, Dyck, DG (1986b): Stability and severity parameters of depressive self-schema responding. J Social Clinical Psychol 4:23–45.

Harrington R, Fudge H, Rutter M, Pickles A, Hill J (1991): Adult outcome of childhood and adolescent depression. II. Links with antisocial disorders. J Am Acad Child Adoles Psychiatry 30:434–439.

Jaenicke C, Hammen C, Zupan B, et al. (1987): Cognitive vulnerability in children at risk for depression. J Ab Child Psychol 15:1559–572.

Jenkins CD, Hurst MW, Rose RM (1979): Life changes: Do people really remember? Arch Gen Psychiatry 36:379–384.

Jensen JB, Garfinkel BD (1990): Growth hormone dysregulation in children with major depressive disorder (see comments). J Am Acad Child Adolesc Psychiatry 29:295–301.

Johnson JH, McCutcheon SM (1980): Assessing life stress in older children and adolescents: Preliminary findings with the Life Events Checklist. Sarason IG, Spielberger CD (eds): "Stress and Anxiety." Washington, DC: Hemisphere.

Joyce PR, Oakley-Browne MA, Wells JE, Bushnell JA, Hornblow AR (1990): Birth cohort trends in major depression: Increasing rates and earlier onset in New Zeland. J Affec Disorders 18:83–89.

Kahn AU, Todd S (1990): Polysomnographic findings in adolescents with major depression. Psychiatry Res 33:313–320.

Kandel DB, Davies M (1982): Epidemiology of depressive mood in adolescents: An empirical study. Arch Gen Psych 39:1205–1212.

Kashani JH, Carlson GA (1987): Seriously depressed preschoolers. Am J Psychiatry 144:348–350.

Kashani J, Burback D, Rosenberg T (1988): Perceptions of family conflict resolution and depressive symptomatology in adolescents. J Am Acad Child Adolesc Psych 27:42–48.

Kashani JH, Beck NC, Hoeper EW, Fallahi C, Corcoran CM, McAllister JA, Rosenberg TK, Reid JC (1987): Psychiatric disorders in community sample of adolescents. Am J Psych 144:584–589.

Kashani JH, Holcomb WR, Orvaschel H (1986): Depression and depressive symptoms in preschool children from the general population. Am J Psychiatry 143:1138–1143.

Kashani JH, Cantwell DP, Shekim WO, Reid JC (1982): Major depressive disorder in children admitted to an inpatient community mental health center. Am J Psychiatry 139:671–672.

Kaslow N, Rehm L, Siegel A (1984): Social-cognitive and cognitive correlates of depression in children. J Ab Child Psychology 12:605–620.

Kaufman J (1991): Depressive disorders in maltreated children. J Acad Child Adolesc Psychiatry 30:257–265.

Kazdin AE, Colbus D, Rodgers A (1986): Assessment of depression and diagnosis of depressive disorders among psychiatrically disturbed children. J Ab Child Psychol 14:449–515.

Kazdin AE, French NH, Unis AS, Esveldt-Dawson K, Sherick RB (1983): Hopelessness, depression, and suicidal intent among psychiatrically disturbed inpatient children. J Consult Clin Psychol 55:504–510.

Keller MB, Lavori PW, Endicott J, Coryell W, Klerman GL (1983): Double depression: Two year follow-up. Am J Psychiatry 140:689–694.

Kendler KS, Walters EE, Truett KR, Keath AC, Neale MC, Martin NG, Eaves LJ (1994): Sources of individual differences in depressive symptoms: Analysis of two samples of twins and their families. Am J Psychiatry 151:1605–1614.

Kessler RC, McGonagle KA, Zhao S, Nelson CB, Hughes M, Eshelman S, Wittchen H, Kendler KS (1994): Lifetime and 12-month prevalence of DSM-III-R psychiatric disorders in the United States. Arch Gen Psychiatry 51:8–19.

Klerman GL, Weissman MM (1988): Increasing rates of depression. J Am Medication Assoc 261:2229–2235.

Klerman GL, Lavori PW, Rice J, Reich T, Endicott J, Andreasen NC, Keller MB, Hirschfeld R (1985): Birth cohort trends in rates of major depressive disorder among relatives of patients with affective disorder. Arch Gen Psych 42:689–693.

Kolvin I, Barrett ML, Berney TP, Famuyiwa OO, Fundudis T, Tryer S (1991): The Newcastle child depression project: diagnosis and classification of depression. Br J Psychiatry 159(11):25–28.

Koslow SH, Stokes PE, Mendels J, Ramsey A, Casper R (1982): Insulin tolerance test; human growth hormone response and insulin resistance in primary unipolar depressed, bipolar depressed and control subjects. Psychol Med 12:45–55.

Kovacs M, Gatsonis C (1994): Secular trends in age at onset of major depressive disorder in a clinical sample of children. J Psychiat Res 28:319–329.

Kovacs M, Goldston D (1991): Cognitive and social cognitive development of depressed children and adolescents. J Am Acad Child Adolesc Psychiatry 30:388–392.

Kovacs M, Akiskal S, Gatsonis C, Parrone PL (1994): Childhood-onset dysthymic disorder. Arch Gen Psychiatry 51:365–374.

Kovacs M, Feinberg TL, Crouse-Novak MA, Paulauskas SL, Finkelstein R (1984a): Depressive disorders in childhood. I. A longitudinal prospective study of characteristics and recovery. Arch Gen Psychiatry 41:229–237.

Kovacs M, Feinberg TL, Crouse-Novak M, Paulaskas SL, Pollock M, Finkelstein R (1984b): Depressive disorders in childhood. II. A longitudinal study of the risk for a subsequent major depression. Arch Gen Psych 41:643–649.

Kutcher SP (1993): Life Events and Depressed Youth: Findings, Issues, and Advances. Presented at the 40th Annual Meeting of the American Academy of Child and Adolescent Psychiatry, San Antonio, Texas.

Kutcher SP, Marton P (1991): Affective disorders in first-degree relatives of adolescent onset bipolar, unipolar and normal controls. J Am Acad Child Adoles Psychiatry 30:75–78.

Kutcher SP, Williamson P, Marton P, Szali J (1992): REM latency in endogenously depressed adolescents. Br J Psychiatry 161:399–402.

Kutcher SP, Malkin D, Silverberg J, Marton P, Williamson P, Malkin A, Szalai J, Katic M (1991): Nocturnal cortisol, thyroid stimulating hormone, and growth hormone secretory profiles in depressed adolescents [see comments]. J Am Acad Child Adoles Psychiatry 30:407–414.

Kutcher SP, Marton P, Koremblum M (1989): Relationship between psychiatric illness and conduct disorder in adolescents. Can J Psychiatry 34:526–529.

Kutcher SP, Williamson P, Silverberg J, Marton P, Malkin D, Malkin A (1988): Nocturnal growth hormone secretion in depressed older adolescents. J Am Acad Child Adoles Psychiatry 27:751–754.

Lahmeyer HW, Poznanski EO, Bellur SN (1983): EEG sleep in depressed adolescents. Am J Psychiatry 140:1150–1153.

Langer G, Heinze G, Reim B, Matussek N (1976): Reduced growth hormone responses to amphetamine in "endogenous" depressive patients: Studies in normal, "reactive" and "endogenous" depressive, schizophrenic, and chronic alcoholic subjects. Arch Gen Psychiatry 33:1471–1475.

Lavori PW, Klerman GL, Keller MB, Reich T, Rice J, Endicott J (1987): Age-period-cohort analysis of secular trends in onset of major depressions: Findings in siblings of patients with major affective disorder. J Psych Residency 21:23–35.

Leckman JF, Sholomskas D, Thompson WD, Belanger A, Weissman MM (1982): Best estimate of lifetime psychiatric diagnosis. Arch Gen Psych 39:879–883.

Lesse S (1983): Masked depression. Curr Psychiatr Ther 22:81–87.

Lewinsohn PM, Clarke GN, Seeley JR, Rohde P (1994): Major depression in community adolescents: Age at onset, episode duration, and time to recurrence. J Am Acad Child Adoles Psych 33(6):809–818.

Lewinsohn PM, Rohde P, Seeley JR, Fischer SA (1993a): Age-cohort changes in the lifetime occurrence of depression and other mental disorders. J Ab Psychol 102:110–120.

Lewinsohn PM, Hops H, Roberts RE, Seeley JR, Andrews JA (1993b): Adolescent psychopathology. I. Prevalence and incidence of depression and other DSM-III-R disorders in high school students. J Ab Psychol 102(1):113–144.

Lewinsohn PM, Rohde P, Seeley JR, Hops H (1991): Comorbidity of unipolar depression. I. Major depression with dysthymia. J Ab Psychol 100:205–213.

Lewinsohn PM, Duncan EM, Stanton AK, Hautzinger M (1986): Age at first onset of nonbipolar depression. J Ab Psychol 95(4):378–383.

Livingston R, Nugent H, Rader L, Smith GR (1985): Family histories of depressed and severely anxious children. Am J Psychiatry 142:1497–1499.

Maier W, Lichtermann D, Minges J, Heun R, Hallmayer J, Klingler T (1991): Unipolar depression in the aged: Determinants of familial aggregation. J Affec Disorders 23:53–61.

Marton P, Kutcher S (1995): The prevalence of cognitive distortion in depressed adolescents. J Neurosci Psychiatry. 20:33–38.

Marton P, Korenblum MP, Kutcher M, Stein S, Kennedy B, Pakes J (1989): Personality dysfunction in dysfunction in depressed adolescents. Canadian J Psychiatry 34:810–813.

Marton P, Koremblum M, Kutcher SP (1987): Personality Characteristics of Depressed Adolescent Outpatients—A Longitudinal Study. Presented at the Academy of Child and Adolescent Psychiatry, Seattle, Washington.

Matussek N, Ackenheil M, Hippius H, Muller F, Schroder HT, Schultes H, Wasilewski B (1980): Effect of clonidine on growth hormone release in psychiatric patients and controls. Psychiatry Res 2:25–36.

McCauley E, Myers K (1992): Family interactions in mood disordered youth. Child Adolesc Psych Clinics 1:111–127.

McGuffin P, Murray R (1991): "The New Genetics of Mental Illness." Oxford: Butterworth-Heinemann.

McInnis MG, McMahon FJ, Chase GA, Simpson SG, Ross CA, DePaulo JR (1993): Anticipation in bipolar affective disorder. Am J Human Gen 53(2):385–390.

McKnew DH Jr, Cytryn L, Efron AM, Gershon ES, Bunney WE Jr (1979): Offspring of patients with affective disorders. Br J Psychiatry 134:148–152.

Metalsky GI, Halberstadt LJ, Abramson LY (1987): Vulnerability to depressive mood reactions: Toward a more powerful test of the diathesis-stress and causal mediation components of the reformulated theory of depression. J Pers Soc Psychol 52:386–393.

Meyer W III, Richards GE, Cavallo A (1991): Depression and growth hormone (letter; comment). J Am Acad Child Adolesc Psychiatry 30:335.

Mitchell BP, Bearn JA, Corn TH, Checkley SA (1988): Growth hormone response to clonidine after recovery in patients with endogenous depression. Br J Psychiatry 152:34–38.

Mitchell J, McCauley E, Burke P, Calderon R, Schloredt K (1989): Psychopathology in parents of depressed children and adolescents. J Am Acad Child Adoles Psychiatry 28:352–357.

Mitchell J, McCauley E, Burle PM, Mass SJ (1988): Phenomenology of depression in children and adolescents. J Acad Child Adoles Psychiatry 1:12–20.

Mueller PS, Heninger GR, McDonald RK (1969): Insulin tolerance test in depression. Arch Gen Psych 21:587–594.

Mufson L, Weissman MM, Warner V (1992): Depression and anxiety in parents and children: A direct interview study. J Anx Disorders 6:1–13.

Naylor MW, Shain BN, Shipley JE (1990): REM latency in psychotically depressed adolescents. Biol Psychiatry 28:161–164.

Nelson JC, Charney DS (1981): The symptoms of major depressive illness. Am J Psych 138:1–13.

Nolen-Hoeksema S, Girgus JS, Seligman MEP (1992): Predictors and consequences of childhood depressive symptoms: A 4-year longitudinal study. J Ab Psychol 101:405–422.

Nolen-Hoeksema S, Girgus JS, Seligman ME (1986): Learned helplessness in children: A longitudinal study of depression, achievement, and explanatory style. J Pers Soc Psychol 51:435–442.

O'Connell RA, Mays JA, O'Brien JD, Misrsheidaie F (1979): Children of bipolar manic-depressives. In Mendlewicz J, Shopsin B (eds): Genetic Aspects of Affective Illness. New York: Spectrum Publications.

Orvaschel H, Puig-Antich J, Chambers W, Tabrizi MA, Johnson R (1982): Retrospective assessment of prepubertal major depression with the Kiddie-SADS-E. J Am Acad Child Psychiatry 21:392–397.

Orvaschel H, Weissman MM, Padian N, Lowe TL (1981): Assessing psychopathology in children of psychiatrically disturbed parents: A pilot study. J Am Acad Child Psychiatry 20:112–122.

Patterson G (1982): Coercive Family Process. Eugene, OR: Castalia.

Paykel E (1979a): Causal relationship between clinical depression and life events. In Barrett J (ed): Stress and Mental Disorder. New York: Raven Press, pp 71–86.

Paykel E (1979b): Recent life events in the development of the depressive disorders. In Depue R (ed): The psychobiology of the depressive disorders: Implications for the effects of stress. New York: Academic Press, pp 245–262.

Plomin R, Daniel D (1987): Why are children in the same family so different from each other? Behavior Brain Sci 10:44–54.

Pozanski EO (1982): The clinical phenomenology of childhood depression. Am J Orthopsychiatry 52:308–313.

Puig-Antich J, Rabinovitch H (1986): Relationship between affective and anxiety disorders in childhood. In Gittelman R (ed): Anxiety Disorders in Childhood. New York: Guildford.

Puig-Antich J, Kaufman J, Ryan ND, Williamson DE, Ronald BA, Dahl R, Lukens E, Todak G, Ambrosini P, Rabinovich H, Nelson B (1993): The psychosocial functioning and family environment of depressed adolescents. J Am Acad Child Adolesc Psych 32(2):244–251.

Puig-Antich J, Goetz D, Davies M, Kaplan T, Davis S, Ostrow L, Ashis L, Twomey J, Iyengar S, Ryan ND (1989a): A controlled family history study of prepubertal major depressive disorder. Arch Gen Psych 46:406–420.

Puig-Antich J, Dahl R, Ryan N, Novacenko H, Goetz D, Twomey J, Klepper T (1989b): Cortisol secretion in prepubertal children with major depressive disorder. Arch Gen Psych 46:801–809.

Puig-Antich J, Lukens E, Davies M, Goetz D, Brennan-Quattrock J, Todak G (1985a): Psychosocial functioning in prepubertal depressive disorders. I. Arch Gen Psych 42:500–507.

Puig-Antich J, Lukens E, Davies M, Goetz D, Brennan-Quattrock J, Todak G (1985b): Psychosocial functioning in prepuberal depressive disorders. II. Arch Gen Psych 42:511–517.

Puig-Antich J, Novacenko H, Davies M, Chambers WJ, Tabrizi MA, Weitzman ED (1984a): Growth hormone secretion in prepubertal children with major depression. I. Final report on response to insulin-induced hypoglycemia during a depressive episode. Arch Gen Psych 41:455–460.

Puig-Antich J, Novacenko H, Davies M, Tabrizi MA, Ambrosini P, Goetz R, Bianca J, Goetz D, Sachar EJ (1984b): Growth hormone secretion in prepubertal children with major depression. III. Response to insulin-induced hypoglycemia after recovery from a depressive episode and in a drug-free state. Arch Gen Psych 41:471–475.

Puig-Antich J, Goetz R, Davies M, Fein M, Hanlon C, Chambers WJ, Tabrizi MA, Sachar EJ, Weitzman ED (1984c): Growth hormone secretion in prepubertal children with major depression. II. Sleep-related plasma concentrations during a depressive episode. Arch Gen Psych 41:463–6.

Puig-Antich J, Goetz R, Davies M, Tabrizi MA, Novacenko H, Hanlon C, Sachar EJ, Weitzman ED (1984d): Growth hormone secretion in prepubertal children with major depression. IV. Sleep-related plasma concentrations in a drug-free, fully recovered clinical state. Arch Gen Psych 41:479–483.

Puig-Antich J, Goetz R, Hanlon C, Tabrizi MA, Davies M, Weitzman E (1983): Sleep architecture and REM sleep measures in prepubertal major depressives: Studies during recovery from a major depressive episode in a drug free state. Arch Gen Psych 40:187–192

Rao U, Ryan ND, Birmaher B, Dahl R, Williamson DE, Kaufman J, Rao R, Nelson (in review): Unipolar depression in adolescents: Clinical outcome in adulthood. J Am Acad Child Adolesc Psychiatry.

Reiss D, Plomin R, Hetherington EM, (1991): Genetics and psychiatry: An unheralded window on the environment. Am J Psych 148(3):283–291.

Robbin DR, Alessi NE, Cook SS, Poznanski ED, Yanchyshyn GW (1982): The use of the research diagnostic criteria (RDC) for depression in adolescent psychiatric inpatients. J Am Acad Child Adolesc Psychiatry 21:251–255.

Robins E, Guze SB (1970): Establishment of diagnostic validity in psychiatric illness: Its application to schizophrenia. Am J Psychiatry 126:107–111.

Rohde P, Lewisohn PM, Seeley JR (1994): Are adolescents changed by an episode of major depression? J Am Acad Child Adolesc Psychiatry 33(9):1289–1298.

Rohde P, Lewinsohn PM, Seeley JR (1991): Comorbidity of unipolar depression. II. Comorbidity with other mental disorders in adolescents and adults. J Ab Psychol 100:214–222.

Rutter M (1991): Age changes in depressive disorders: Some developmental considerations. In Garber J, Dodge KA (eds): "The Development of Emotion Regulation and Dysregulation." New York: Cambridge University Press.

Rutter M (1990): Commentary: Some focus and process considerations regarding effects of parental depression on children. Dev Psychol 26(1):60–67.

Rutter M, Quinton D (1984): Parental psychiatric disorder: Effects on children. Pyschol Med 14:853–880.

Rutter M, Tizard J, Yule W, Graham P, Whitmore K (1976): Research report: Isle of Wight studies 1964–1974. Psychol Med 6:313–332.

Ryan ND, Dahl RE, Birmaher B, Williamson DE, Iyengar S, Nelson B, Puig-Antich J, Perel JM (1994): Stimulatory tests of grown hormone secretion in prepubertal major depression: Depressed versus normal children. J Am Acad Child Adoles Psychiatry 33:824–833.

Ryan ND, Williamson DE, Iyengar S, Orvaschel H, Reich T, Dahl RE, Puig-Antich J (1992a): A secular increase in child and adolescent onset affective disorder. J Am Acad Child Adoles Psychiatry 31:600–605.

Ryan ND, Birmaher B, Perel JM, Dall ER, Meyer V, Al-Shabbout M, Iyengar S, Puig-Antich P (1992b): Neuroendocrine response to L-5-hydroxytryptophan challenge in prepubertal major depression. Depressed vs normal children. Arch Gen Psych 49:843–851.

Ryan ND, Puig-Antich J, Rabinovich H, Ambrosini P, Robinson D, Nelson B, Novaunko H (1988): Growth hormone response to desmethylimipramine in depressed and suicidal adolescents. J Affect Disord 15:323–337.

Ryan ND, Puig-Antich J, Ambrosini P, Rabinovich H, Robinson D, Nelson B, Iyengar S, Twomey J (1987): The clinical picture of major depression in children and adolescents. Arch Gen Psych 44:854–861.

Sachar EJ, Frantz AG, Altman N, Sassis J (1973): Growth hormone and prolactin in unipolar and bipolar depressed patients: Responses to hypoglycemia and L-dopa. Am J Psychiatry 130:1362–1367.

Sachar EJ, Finkelstein J, Hellman L (1971): Growth hormone responses in depressive illness. I. Response to insulin tolerance test. Arch Gen Psych 25:263–269.

Schwartz CE, Dorer DJ, Beardslee WR, Lavori PW, Keller MB (1990): Maternal expressed emotion and parental affective disorder: Risk for childhood depressive disorder, substance abuse, or conduct disorder. J Psych Res 24:231–250.

Seligman ME, Maier SF (1967): Failure to escape traumatic shock. J Exp Psychol [Gen] 74:1–9.

Shaffer D (1989): The Diagnostic Interview Schedule for Children (DISC-2): Its Development and Administration. Paper presented at the annual meeting of the American Academy of Child and Adolescent Psychiatry, New York.

Shaffer D, Fisher P (1981): The epidemiology of suicide in children and young adolescents. J Am Acad Child Psychiatry 20:545–561.

Siever LJ, Uhde TW (1984): New studies and perspectives on the noradrenergic receptor system in depression: Effects of the alpha 2-adrenergic agonist clonidine. Biol Psychiatry 19:131–156.

Siever LJ, Trestman RL, Coccaro EF, Bernstein D, Gabriel SM, Owen K, Moran M, Lawrence T, Rosenthal J, Horvath TB (1992): The growth hormone response to clonidine in acute and remitted depressed male patients. Neuropsychopharmacology 6:165–177.

Siever LJ, Uhde TW, Silberman EK, Jimerson DC, Aloi JA, Post RM, Murphy DL (1982): Growth hormone response to clonidine as a probe of noradrenergic receptor responsiveness in affective disorder patients and controls. Psychiatry Res 6:171–183.

Spitzer RL, Endicott J, Robins E (1978): Research diagnostic criteria: Rational and reliability. Arch Gen Psych 35:773–782.

Strober M (1984): Familial aspects of depressive disorders in early adolescence. In Weller EB, Well RA (eds): "Current Perspectives on Major Depression." Washington, DC: American Psychiatric Press.

Strober M (1983): Clinical and biological perspectives on depressive disorders in adolescence. In Cantwell DP, Carlson GA (eds): "Affective Disorders in Childhood and Adolescence: An Update." New York: Spectrum Publications.

Strober M, Green J, Carlson G. (1981): Phenomenology and subtypes of major depressive disorder in adolescence. J Affec Disord 3:281–290.

Stubbe DE, Zahner G, Goldstein MJ, Leckman JF (1993): Diagnostic specificity of a brief measure of expressed emotion: A community study of children. J Child Psychiatry 34:139–154.

Swearingen EM, Cohen LH (1985): Life events and psychological distress: A prospective study of young adolescents. Develop Psychology 21:1045–1054.

Tsuang MT, Faraone SV, Fleming JA (1985): Familial transmission of major affective disorders: Is there evidence supporting the distinction between unipolar and bipolar disorders? Br J Psychiatry 146:268–271.

Turner JE Jr, Cole, DA (1994): Developmental differences in cognitive diatheses for child depression. J Ab Child Psych 22(1):15–32.

Walker LS, Garber J, Greene JW (1993): Psychosocial correlates of recurrent childhood pain: A comparison of pediatric patients with recurrent abdominal pain, organic illness, and psychiatric disorders. J Ab Psychol 102(2):248–258.

Weissman MM, Leckman JF, Merikangas KR, Gammon RD, Prusoff BA (1984a): Depression and anxiety disorders in parents and children: Results from the Yale family study. Arch Gen Psych 41:845–852.

Weissman MM, Wickramaratne P, Merikangas KR, Leckman JF, Prusoff BA, Caruso KA, Kidd KK, Gammon GD (1984b): Onset of major depression in early adulthood: Increase in familial loading and specificity. Arch Gen Psych 41:1136–1143.

Weissman MM, Kidd KK, Prusoff BA (1982): Variability in rates of affective disorders in relatives of depressed and normal probands. Arch Gen Psych 39:1397–1403.

Weisz JR, Rudolph KD, Granger DA, Sweeney L (1992): Cognition, competence, and coping in child and adolescent depression: Research findings, developmental concerns, therapeutic implications. Develop Psychopathol 4:627–653.

World Health Organization (1994): International Classification Diagnoses (ICD-10).

Wickramaratne PJ, Weissman MM, Leaf PJ, Holford TR (1989): Age, period and cohort effects on the risk of major depression: Results from five United States communities. J Clinc Epidem 42:333–343.

Williamson DE, Ryan ND, Birmaher B, Dahl RE, Nelson B (in press): A family history study of adolescent-onset major depressive disorder. J Am Acad Child Adoles Psychiatry.

Williamson DE, Birmaher B, Anderson BP, Al-Shabbout M, Ryan ND (1995a): Stressful life events in depressed adolescents: The role of dependent events during the depressive episode. J Am Acad Child Adoles Psychiatry 34:591–598.

Williamson DE, Dahl RE, Birmaher B, Goetz RR, Ryan ND (1995b): Stressful life events and EEG sleep in depressed and normal control adolescents. Biol Psychiatry 37:854–865.

Winokour G (1973): The types of affective disorders. J Nerv Ment Dis 156:82–96.

Young W, Knowles JB, MacLean AW, Boag L, McCopnville BJ (1982): The sleep of childhood depressives: Comparison with age-matched controls. Biol Psychiatry 17:1163–1169.

CHAPTER 5

Outcome of Depressive Syndromes: Infancy to Adolescence

JOAN LUBY, RICHARD D. TODD, and BARBARA GELLER

Department of Psychiatry, Washington University School of Medicine, St. Louis, MO 63110

INTRODUCTION

Because of widespread clinical and public recognition that major depressive disorder (MDD) afflicts young children and adolescents, researchers and clinicians have attempted to better define and validate the formal diagnostic criteria for this disorder. Studies that have helped to clarify that childhood depression was diagnosable by adult criteria, as opposed to a "masked" phenomena, have catalyzed this effort (Carlson and Cantwell, 1980), and currently diagnostic classification similar to that of MDD in adults is widely accepted as applicable to the younger population as well. Validation of MDD as a diagnostic entity has furthermore entailed a plethora of studies into biological markers, genetics, treatment outcome, and long-term course of the disorder. This chapter will review current knowledge about the longitudinal course of MDD in children and adolescents.

The body of investigations cited in this chapter provide uniform evidence of the severe, chronic, and relapsing naturalistic course of childhood depression. Because these findings emerged from both community and clinical samples, referral bias from clinically identified populations does not fully account for the poor prognosis. High risks of suicide, relapse, and enduring psychosocial impairment have been reported. Further, retrospective data suggesting continuity of this disorder into adulthood have also been provided (Harrington et al., 1990).

In addition to these more recent publications, which focus on children and adolescents, there are earlier studies of *depressive manifestations* in infancy. The work of Spitz (1946), for example, pointed to the vulnerability of infants expressing disabling "depressed" mood states. These findings provided powerful contributions demonstrating that even infancy was not an age of protected innocence (Geller, 1993). Spitz described withdrawal, apathy, and developmental delay, including failure to thrive, in infants deprived of early nurturing within care-giving relationships. Spitz-labeled these phenomena *anaclitic depression*. Later systematic investigations of the infant offspring

Mood Disorders Across the Life Span, Edited by Shulman, Tohen, and Kutcher
ISBN 0-471-10477-9   © 1996 Wiley-Liss, Inc.

TABLE 1. Child and Adolescent MDD: Clinical Samples Longitudinal Course

Author	Criteria Diagnosis	N/Age	Instru/Setting	Outcome	Comments[a]
Poznanski et al. (1976)	"Clinical depressives"	Children	"Clinical interviews"	50% depressed at 4–11 yr follow-up	Broken homes, parental loss was not predictive of depression Poor prognosis for recovery.
Welner et al. (1979)	Feighner Unipolar	N = 19 Mean age = 16 yr	Clinical interview Inpatients	Follow-up after mean 9 yr 15/19 (94%) remained unipolar 4/19 (21%) became bipolar	Switch to BP findings similar to Strober et al. (1982)
Eastgate and Gilmore (1984)	Clinical "depress." Criteria of Brumback and Weinberg	N = 19 9–15 yr	Clinical criteria based on chart review	7–8 yr follow-up 8/19 (42%) experienced moderate to "severe" disability at follow-up Mean age at follow-up = 20 yr	High incidence of somatic sx (12/19) at the time of depressive dx was found
Kovacs et al. (1984a,b)	MDD or DD or ADDM DSM-III	N = 65 (mood disorders) N = 49 psych controls 8–13 yr	ISC Outpatients	MDD: 92% recovered at 18 months ADDM: 90% recovered at 9 months DD: 89% recovered at 6 yr Prob. of subsequent MDD: DD: 69% develop MDD within 5 yr MDD: 72% cumulative risk of relapse with 5 yr	Earlier age onset predicts more protracted recovery from MDD and DD. Episode length: ADDM: 25 (± 18) weeks DD: 3 yr (± 68 weeks) MDD: 32 (± 28) weeks
Arsanow et al. (1988)	MDD DD DSM-III	N = 20 MDD N = 8 DD N = 18 (Schizophrenia Spectrum Disorder) 7–13 yr	K-SADS E Inpatients	Follow-up over 1–6 yr 35% of patients with depressive disorders rehospitalized after 1 yr 45% rehospitalized after 2 yr	Rehospitalization rates greater in depressive disorders compared to SSDs. Rates highest for those with double depression. 15% of depressed group placed out of home within first year of discharge.

Garber et al. (1988)	MDD DD ADDM DSM-III	N = 11 N = 9 psych control 10–17 yr	DIS BDI HRS-D Inpatients	Follow-up after 8 yr 64% had ≥ 1 episode of recurrence over 8-yr period. All depressed subjects experienced some form of affective disorder during follow-up. Mean age = 22.8 yr	While higher rates of psych illness in 1st-degree relatives occurred in both groups; MDD group had more 1st-degree relatives with affect. illness. Study confirms continuity of affect. sx across adol. thru early adulthood.
Harrington et al. (1990)	"Depres. syndrome"	N = 52 MDD N = 52 controls	SADS-L at follow-up	40% developed RDC "adult" depression within 5 yr. 34% attempted suicide during follow-up period. Mean age at follow-up = 30.7 yr	Those with ≥ 1 episode of MDD after age 17 had 95% chance of another episode. Retrospective chart review to identify adults with childhood "depressive syndrome."
Strober et al. (1993)	MDD RDC	N = 58 13–16 yr	SADS LIFE Clin. adol inputs	6.9% recovered at 12 weeks 29.3% recovered at 20 weeks 90% recovered at 24 months	Time to recovery did not vary by RDC subtype.
McCauley et al. (1993)	MDD RDC	N = 65 MDD N = 25 psych controls 7–17 yr.	K-SADS Inpatients and outpatients	Follow-up over 3 yr 40% recovered at 6 months 80% recovered at 12 months 25% relapsed over 12 months 54% relapsed over 3 yr	Higher SES, longer initial episode and endogenicity associated with shorter time to relapse. Females had more severe disease and longer initial episodes. Mean duration of episode was 35.6 weeks (± 26)

[a] sx = symptom; dx = diagnosis.

of depressed mothers have provided further evidence of affective vulnerability in this early period. Findings from these more recent high-risk studies of infants of mothers with MDD underscore the need for the early identification, prevention, and treatment of this disorder.

OUTCOME IN CLINICAL SAMPLES

Over the last decade, multiple systematic longitudinal outcome studies have been conducted on clinical samples. Table 1 cites 11 studies, both retrospective and prospective, of clinically ascertained children with MDD. Although the earliest studies (Poznanski et al., 1976; Welner et al., 1979) did not have the benefit of structured diagnostic instruments, it is notable that the finding of continuity of affective symptomatology is uniform across all investigations to date. Although specific measures of outcome differed in each study, overall these studies all reported high rates of relapse for depressive episodes and/or chronicity of mood disturbance.

The work of Kovacs et al. (1984a, 1988, 1989, 1993) represents the longest prospective study of a clinically ascertained population of children. These investigations recruited prepubertal children (ages 8–13) with a spectrum of mood disorders: adjustment disorder with depressed mood (ADDM), dysthymic disorder (DD), and MDD assessed by structured interview. Specific findings pertaining to the longitudinal course of these disorders, rates of relapse and recovery, and the role of associated risk factors have been reported (see Table 1). Overall, Kovacs and co-workers reported a pattern of high rates of recovery from the initial episode of MDD followed by high rates of later relapse. This suggested that childhood-onset MDD is unlikely to manifest as a transient episode but rather is more likely to have a relapsing and chronic course. With regards to the effects of age of onset of illness on course, these data also suggested that earlier age of onset predicted a more protracted time to recovery. These findings suggest that children affected at a younger age may be at risk for a more severe form of the illness. Also important was the finding that the overwhelming majority (81%) of dysthymic children went on to develop MDD over a 9-year follow-up period in contrast to the group with ADDM who had minimal risk for later MDD. As Kovacs has noted, this would imply that DD is an early marker for later chronic MDD.

Poznanski et al. (1976) provided the first longitudinal follow-up of children with MDD. Despite the lack of standardized assessment tools and a small N (10 patients), this study made the valuable contribution of demonstrating stable depressive symptoms in approximately 50% of psychiatric inpatients 4–10 years after initial diagnosis. Furthermore, Poznanski and co-workers provided perhaps the first empirical evidence of specificity and continuity of childhood affective symptomatology. Welner et al. (1979) also provided early evidence of continuity of affective symptoms in a population of adolescent inpatients followed 8–10 years after discharge.

Longitudinal follow-up into adulthood in clinical samples suggests not only repeated MDD episodes but high risk for more severe outcomes such as later psychiatric hospitalization and suicide attempts (Harrington et al., 1990). Harrington et al. also showed that a substantial proportion of this child and adolescent population (40%) went on to manifest depression during early adulthood (Harrington et al., 1990).

Multiple studies have investigated possible risk factors associated with the development of future episodes of MDD following an initial childhood onset. One factor, length of initial episode of MDD, has been consistently identified in studies that, while differing in their methodologies, nevertheless arrived at similar findings. Rao et al. (1993), in a retrospective study of young adults with child- or adolescent-onset MDD, found that suicidal ideation, increased severity of the initial episode, shorter episode length, and later age of onset predicted higher risk of relapse in adulthood. McCauley et al. (1993) prospectively investigating children 7–17 with MDD over a 3-year period identified that longer initial episode length was associated with shorter time to relapse along with the additional factors of high socioeconomic status (SES) and endogenicity, while stressful family environment was associated with poorer overall outcome. As previously stated, Kovacs et al. provide the additional finding of more protracted illness in children with an earlier age of onset.

In addition to future depression episodes, children and adolescents with MDD are also at risk for mania. Table 2 shows the results of investigations on "switch" rates to bipolarity in two longitudinally assessed clinical samples. Strober and Carlson (1982), in a landmark study, reported a switch rate of 20% in a sample of inpatient adolescents with MDD. Psychotic symptoms, a rapid onset of the depressive episode, and tricyclic antidepressant medication use were associated with the onset of manic symptomatology. In a later investigation by Strober et al. (1982), a switch rate of 28% was found to occur in adolescents with psychotic depression. Geller (1994) reported that 32% of an outpatient group of prepubertal children with severe MDD developed bipolarity over a 2- to 5-year follow-up. Lower reported rates of switching in adult samples of 5–18% (Clayton et al., 1981) may reflect that adults are observed later in the period of the risk for developing bipolar disorder. That is, older populations of adults with MDD may have already developed bipolarity at an earlier age.

These studies, taken together, show that child- and adolescent-onset MDD is often the first onset of a chronic mood disorder. Depressions that first appear in children or teens predict future depressive episodes. Additionally, MDD in this young age group may also predict the development of bipolar illness. Thus, MDD in children and adolescents must be considered to be not only a serious acute disorder but also a signal for a long-term illness, which is known to have a significant impact on multiple aspects of functioning.

OUTCOME IN COMMUNITY SAMPLES

Table 3 summarizes the results of eight controlled longitudinal outcome studies of childhood MDD in epidemiological samples. These studies of community sample have focused primarily on adolescents. Similar to the clinical samples, the findings of significant relapse and chronicity across studies is again quite consistent. Lewinsohn et al. (1994) provide the largest and most recent community study, investigating time to onset, recovery, and recurrence in 1500 American high school students (14–18 years of age). With regard to course, these data showed a high rate of both recovery and later relapse. The additional findings of relatively brief depressive episodes (mean = 26.4 + 3.3 weeks) were also reported. Life table analyses of annual hazard rates revealed that the risk of developing the disorder increases with each year during the adolescent period studied. Suicidal ideation was found to be a predictor of longer episodes and shorter time to relapse. Similar to findings in studies of clinical samples, earlier age of onset was predictive of more protracted illness.

TABLE 2. Child and Adolescent MDD: Switching to Bipolarity

Author	DX	N/Age	Instru/Setting	Follow-up Period	Bipolar Outcome	Comments[a]
Strober et al. (1982)	MDD	N = 60 13–16 yr	SADS LIFE Clin. adol. inpts	3–4 yr	20%	Switching predicted by: (1) rapid sx onset, psychomotor retard., mood congruent, psychotic features; (2) family loading for affect. dis. and hx of BPD; (3) pharmacologic induction.
Geller et al. (1994)	MDD	N = 79 MDD N = 31 normal controls 6–12 yr	K-SADS-P-1986 K-SADS-E Outpatients	2–5 yr	32%	Mean age of switching was 11.2 yr and 80% were prepubertal

[a] sx = symptom; hx = history.

In a follow-up of an epidemiologic sample, Fleming et al. (1993) compared three groups of Canadian adolescents: those with depression, those with conduct disorder (CD), and subjects comorbid for both disorders. Specificity of affective symptoms was suggested by the increased risk of MDD and DD at follow-up in those adolescents who had been previously identified as exhibiting depressive symptoms. Further, one quarter of depressed adolescents went on to relapse during the 6-month period prior to follow-up 4 years later. These findings are similar to those reported in a New Zealand community sample of 9-year olds with MDD; one third were found to have persistent disease at 2- to 4-year follow-up (McGee and Williams, 1988).

Kashani et al. (1987) in a detailed diagnostic ascertainment study of a cohort of secondary school students ages 14–16 years reported a 4.7% prevalence of MDD and 3.3% prevalence of dysthymic disorder. Although rates are somewhat higher than those reported in preschool and latency age children in other samples (Kashani et al., 1983), they are consistent with findings of Lewinsohn and co-workers showing higher risk of this disorder with each year of age in adolescence. Furthermore, reporting a follow-up study of a nonreferred cohort of depressed adolescents, Keller et al. (1988) have demonstrated that not only do the episodes recur, but that prevalence rates of *double depression* (MDD and DD) approach those found in adults (about 25% of depressed adolescents) and that while most young people with MDD will recover, relapse rates are exceedingly high and probability of recovery decreases with the length of the index depression episode. Although psychosocial impairments were not specifically addressed in this study, Kandel and Davies (1986) have clearly demonstrated that depressive symptoms in adolescents are highly predictive of poor psychosocial functioning in adulthood.

Thus, epidemiologic studies of MDD in depressed children and adolescents show striking similarities across different countries and communities. Additionally, these studies describe a similar course and outcome of MDD and DD to that reported in clinical samples. Taken as a whole, these studies have identified the following: (1) MDD and DD in childhood and adolescence is predictive of a chronic mood disorder; (2) MDD and DD onsetting in early years is predictive of long-term psychosocial impairment and increased risk of suicide. The available literature clearly shows that MDD and DD when it occurs in children and adolescents is not a benign disorder with a limited time course. Rather, the disorder is a serious and significant long-term mental health issue.

OFFSPRING STUDIES

The available data from offspring studies also illustrate the continuity of childhood MDD into adulthood. Although the differential effect of direct genetic and environmental factors cannot be clarified by studies to date, the weight of current evidence shows that intergenerational effects on mood modulation do occur. A recent review of this field (Downey and Coyne, 1990) identifies that maternal depression in particular is associated with emotional and behavioral difficulties in their children. Although it is beyond the scope of this chapter to critically evaluate this area, Tables 4 and 5 are offered to provide examples of recent findings regarding parent–child interactions and outcomes in offspring of depressed parents.

Interactions between mothers and their infants may be affected by maternal mood—especially depression. Early findings by Cohn and Tronick (1983) of specific infant

TABLE 3. Child and Adolescent MDD: Community Samples Longitudinal Course[a]

Author	DX	N/Age	Instru/Setting	Outcome	Comments
Kandel and Davies (1986)	Depressive sxs	N = 162	SLC-90 New York City	Follow-up over 9 yr (at age 24–25). Depressed affect in adol. strongly predictive of depressive mood in adulthood.	Female adol. signif. more depressive sx than males.
Kashani et al. (1987)	MDD	N = 7 14–16 yr	DICS DICA-P Columbia, MO	High levels of comorbidity in MDD group (100% had other axis I dx). Anxiety disorder most freq.	Prevalence MDD higher than in adol. than Kashani studies of younger cohorts.
McGee and Williams (1988)	"Major + minor" depress. dis. RDC	N = 17 current depressive disorder N = 23 Hx depres. N = 81 Controls 9 year olds	KSADS-E New Zealand	Follow-up over 4 yr. Depression more persistent among boys than girls. Antisocial behavior associated with depression in boys.	MDD more common in boys aged 11–13 at a 5:1 ratio. Cohort born in one year in obstetric clinic
Keller et al. (1988)	MDD (current or past episode) DSM-III	N = 38 MDD 6–19 yr	DICA DICA-P Boston, MA	Follow-up over 2 yr Probability of remaining depressed at 1 yr = 21% 2 yr = 10%	Mean duration of episode longer for subjects with comorbid psychiatric disorder (32 vs. 9 weeks). Child chronicity after 1 yr about one-half the rate found in adults.
Garrison et al. (1990)	Depressive sxs	N = 550	CES-D South Carolina	Follow-up over 3 yrs. Higher levels of depressive sx assoc. with lower levels of family cohesion.	Females attain higher depress. scores than males. Blacks higher than whites. Scores decrease over time in males but not in females.
Nolen-Hocksema et al. (1992)	Depressive sxs	N = 508 3rd & 4th graders	CDI classroom-based New Jersey	Follow-up over 5 yr. Chronicity evident in 40% of population at 6 months.	Neg. life events signif. predicted later depression in younger children. "Explanatory style" was more predictive in older children.

Study	Diagnosis	Sample	Instrument / Location	Findings	Comments
Fleming et al. (1993)	MDD and/or Conduct Dis. "DSM-III-like"	N = 652 13–16 yr	CBCL Ontario, Canada	Follow-up over 4 yr 25% of depressed adol. relapsed within 6 months period preceding 4 yr evaluation	Adol. with MDD twice as likely to experience MDD at follow-up compared to CD group.
Lewinsohn et al. (1994)	MDD DMS-III-R	N = 362 14–18 yr	K-SADS K-SADS(E) K-SADS(P) Oregon	Follow-up over 1 yr 5% relapsed at 5 months 12% relapsed at 12 months 33% projected to relapse at 4 yr	Female gender, comorbid suicidal ideation associated with earlier onset. Relapse assoc. with SI, later age onset. Risk of MDD increases substantially in each year of adolescence.
Rao et al. (1993)	MDD RDC	N = 159 MDD N = 85 controls N = 37 anxiety disorder 6–17 yr	K-SADS K-SADS-E Outpatients	Follow-up over 5–13 yr Suicide rate = 4.4% after 10 yr	High rate of suicide in children with MDD. All suicide victims had MDD with prolonged course.
Kovacs et al. (1994b)	ADDM DSM-III	N = 30 N = 26 psych controls 8–13 yr	ISC Outpatients	Follow-up over 7–8 yr 97% recovered at 2 yr	Median epidose length was 7 months. ADDM has a very good short-term prognosis. Similar rates of dysfunction at follow-up for ADDM vs. controls.
Kovacs et al. (1994b)	Dysthmic Disorder (DD) DSM-III	N = 55 DD N = 60 MDD 8–13 yr	ISC Outpatients	Follow-up over 3–12 yr 81% DD will develop MDD in 9-yr period. (Cumulative time-dependent risk.)	DD in childhood assoc. with high risk for MDD. The first episode of MDD is "gateway" to further affective disorder.

a CES-D, Center for Epidemiology Studies Depression Scale; CDI, Child Depression Inventory; SADS, Schedule of Affective Disorders and Schizophrenia; DICA, Diagnostic Interview for Children & Adolescents; ISC, Interview Schedule for Children; DIS, Diagnostic Interview Schedule; BDI, Beck Depression Inventory; HRS-D, Hamilton Rating Scale for Depression.

TABLE 4. Selected Studies Maternal Depression—Infant Offspring

Author	N	Age of Infant/ Preschooler	Maternal DX Instrument	Comments
Fleming et al. (1988)	56	1 and 3 months old	BDI Multiple Affect Adject-Checklist Caroll Depression Scale	Mothers with postpartum depression exhibit fewer affectionate contacts toward infants.
Bettes et al. (1988)	36	3–4 months old	BDI	Depressed mothers slower to respond to infant vocalization and less likely to use exaggerated intonation.
Field et al. (1990)	48	3 months old	BDI	Depressed mothers and infants matched negative behavior states more often and positive behavior states less often.
Zahn-Waxler et al. (1990)	87	5–9 yr old	SADS-L	Patterns of guilt in children of depressed mothers was aberrant, distorted and unresolved according to semiprojective testing.
Rubin et al. (1991)	43	2 yr old	SADS-L	Higher rates of insecure attachment in offspring of affectively ill mothers.
Stein et al. (1991)	98	19 months old	MADRS PSE	Depressed mothers showed "reduced quality of interaction."
Murray (1992)	111	18 months old	SADS-L	Increased rates of insecure attachment patterns.
Campbell et al. (in press)	67 depressed 63 "normals"	5–9 yr old	SADS-L	Mother with postpartum depression > 6 months duration were less positive with their infants, and infants showed fewer positive responses as well.

TABLE 5. Child and Adolescent MDD: Selected High-Risk Offspring Studies

Author	N and Offspring Age	Parental Diagnosis	Child Assess Instrument	Outcome
Keller et al. (1986)	N = 72 6–19 yr	MDD	DICA DICA-P	Increased severity/chronicity in parents related to greater impairment in adaptive functioning in child. Maternal depression more strongly assoc. with child psychopathology than paternal.
Hammen et al. (1987)	N = 84 Offspring of: Unipolar (chronic) N = 19 Bipolar N = 12 Chronic med. illness N = 18 Normal control N = 35 8–16 yr	MDD Bipolar Medically Ill Normal controls	K-SADS	Increased rates of child affective disorder in offspring of affectively disordered parents vs. controls. No differences found when compared to medical records. Unipolar group had especially high rates of MDD in offspring.
Orvaschel et al. (1988)	N = 61 N = 46 controls 6–17 yr	Recurrent MDD vs. normal controls	K-SADS DSM-III	High-risk group offspring had greater prevalence of affective disorder and ADHD. 41% high risk children fit criteria for more than one psych. disorder compared to 15% in control group.
Weissman (1988)	N = 153 Normals = 67 6–23 yr	MDD Normal controls	K-SADS-E	Increased prevalence of MDD and increased rates of suicidal gestures or attempts in the children of depressed vs. normal control parents.
Beardslee et al. (1993)	N = 139 Ave. age = 18.5 yr	MDD	K-SADS-ER	Rates of MDD higher in children of parents with affective disorder (26%) compared to those who had no disorder (10%).

behavioral responses to simulated maternal depression, provided the first evidence that infants were sensitive and responsive to such mood states. A variety of studies of depressed mothers provide some evidence for compromised maternal responsivity in multiple caretaking domains (Stein et al., 1991; Bettes, 1988; Fleming et al., 1988) although the association of either maternal or child behaviors with maternal depression (and not other psychiatric disorders) cannot be determined from these reports. Tronick and colleagues [Tronick and Cohn, 1989; Weinberg and Tronick (in press)] hypothesized an impairment in the "mutual reciprocity" of these parent–infant relationships characterized in part by a failure of depressed mothers to be sensitive to their infants' emotional state.

Several authors have reported impairments in parent–infant relationships manifested by higher rates of insecure attachment in those dyads characterized by maternal depression (Murray, 1992; Rubin et al., 1991; Cummings and Cicchetti, 1990). A low prevalence of positive affective expression in infants of depressed mothers has also been reported (Campbell et al., 1995) and aberrant patterns of guilt and other forms of social adaptation have also been found in preschool offspring (Zahn-Waxler et al., 1990). Most of these studies, however, exhibit methodological difficulties that do not allow either for the determination of the direction or proportion of effect (i.e., what is the "weight" of the maternal depression contrasted to the "weight" of the temperamental style of the infant in producing the observed outcome) nor the specificity of effect (i.e., what aspects of the mother–child interactions are specific to depressed mothers and what may be observed in other maternal psychiatric illnesses). Nevertheless, they do identify that mood/behavior disturbances do arise as early as infancy in the offspring of depressed parents.

A number of studies investigating the older offspring of parents with MDD have shown high rates of psychopathology and social impairment in this group relative to normal controls (see Table 5). In particular, these children appeared to be at greater risk for the development of affective illnesses (Beardslee et al., 1983; Orvaschel et al., 1988; Hammen et al., 1987; Weissman, 1988). Epidemiologic studies indicated that children reared by depressed parents were two to three times more likely to suffer from depression (Weissman, 1987). In addition, the level of impairment in the child appears to be directly related to the severity of parental illness (Keller et al., 1986). While the relative contribution of genetic or environment factors cannot be ascertained from these studies, when taken together with the literature regarding mother–infant interactions described above, it is reasonable to hypothesize that both genetic and environmental effects may interact to contribute to the etiology of MDD and DD in children and adolescents.

In studies of adult children of mothers with MDD, both increased rates of affective illness (Weissman, 1987) and other psychiatric disorders (Beardslee et al., 1993) have been identified. This may suggest that the early and subtle impairments of mood and behavior as described above may be markers for later vulnerability to depressive disorder. While genetic heritability (Kendler, 1989) and exposure to suboptimal gestational factors (Zuckerman et al., 1990) are well accepted as components of risk for psychiatric disorders, the role of maternal infant interaction as described above may provide additional useful models for understanding the pathogenesis of depressive disorders in children and adolescents (Cohn et al., 1990, Cohn and Tronick 1983; Field 1984, Field et al., 1985, 1990).

IMPLICATIONS OF FAMILY HISTORY STUDIES ON THE OUTCOME OF CHILDHOOD ONSET MAJOR DEPRESSIVE DISORDER

As described by Robins and Guze (1970), family history information on the prevalence of psychiatric diagnoses in extended relatives may help predict the course, severity, and outcome of illness. For childhood-onset MDD there are only two studies that address the prevalence and pattern of psychiatric illness in extended relatives (Puig-Antich et al., 1989; Todd et al., 1993). In both studies there was a significant increase in the prevalence of a range of depressive spectrum disorders and alcoholism in first- and second-degree relatives. Moreover, Todd et al. (1993) found that this was true for first cousins (a type of third-degree relative) as well. Both studies also found an increased prevalence of bipolar affective disorder among relatives. Since these results in combination with the longitudinal studies described earlier in this chapter have important implications for treatment and outcome, these two family history studies will be described in some detail.

Puig-Antich et al. (1989) studied the first- and second-degree adult relatives of prepubertal children with major depression ($n = 48$), nonaffective psychiatric disorders ($n = 20$), and normal children ($n = 27$). A total of 195 first-degree and 785 second-degree adult relatives ages 17 years or older were assessed using the Family History–Research Diagnostic Criteria method (FH-RDC, Andreason et al., 1977). Age-corrected lifetime morbidity risks for major depressive disorder in the first-degree relatives of depressed, psychiatric control, and normal control children were 0.53, 0.29, and 0.28, respectively. Age-corrected lifetime morbidity risks for alcoholism in the first-degree relatives of the same three groups were 0.31, 0.15, and 0.15, respectively. The morbidity risk for mania was elevated in the relatives of depressed children but was not significantly greater than for the two other groups. Lifetime risks for alcoholism was also elevated for the second-degree relatives of depressed children. However, there were no significant differences in the risk for depression or mania among second-degree relatives of the three groups. As would be expected, major depressive disorder was more frequent in female relatives and alcoholism was more frequent in male relatives for all three groups. Interestingly, Puig-Antich and co-workers observed that the increased lifetime prevalence of depressive illness in the adult relatives of depressed children was most marked for children who had *no* comorbid conduct disorder and who had never had a concrete suicidal plan or act.

Todd et al. (1993) reported on family history data collected as part of a prospective, blindly rated, controlled study of prepubertal MDD (Geller et al., 1992, Geller, 1994). The probands included 76 nonadopted children with a diagnosis of major depressive disorder and 31 normal control children who had been matched for age, gender, and socioeconomic status. Family history data was obtained from the best informant parent using the FH-RDC (Andreason et al., 1977). Information was obtained on all relatives 15 years or older and was updated three times a year for 2–5 years prior to analysis. On 2- to 5-year follow-up of the probands, 8 non-adopted MDD children had changed diagnosis to bipolar I and 14 non-adopted MDD children had changed diagnosis to bipolar II. No children changed diagnosis in the normal control proband group. Family history information was analyzed on a total of 1,346 relatives. There were elevated rates of bipolar disorder and major depressive disorder in the first-, second-, and third-degree relatives of the depressive disorder child probands. The prevalence of alcoholism was also increased (Todd et al., in press). Mania and alcoholism were more common in male relatives while depression was more common in female relatives. Of particular note, however, when the major depressive disorder proband children were divided into those that had progressed to bipolar illness or not, there was a similar elevated prevalence of bipolar disorder in the relatives of both of these groups (compared to relatives of the normal control). In this study, the lifetime incidence of bipolar disorder and major depressive disorder in first-degree relatives of both the major depressive disorder and bipolar children were 10 and 35.5%, respectively. Relatives identified through children with bipolar disorder or MDD also had an increased frequency of suicide attempts. Segregation analysis of extended family data for bipolar and MDD child probands supported the presence of genetic factors in determining the liability for major affective disorder and bipolar disorder. Using logistic regression analysis of this same data, the authors have recently been able to show that in addition to affective disorder, paternal alcoholism *independently* increases the risk of affective disorders in offspring (Todd et al., in press).

The demonstration that there is an increased prevalence of both affective disorder and alcoholism among the adult relatives of families identified through children with major affective disorder has several important implications. First, the distribution of illness among adult relatives is most compatible with the presence of genetic factors that mediate the liability for developing an affective disorder. That is, these children have a genetic predisposition to developing serious affective disorders. Second, the lack of distinction of bipolar and MDD children based on family history suggest that these two forms of illness in children may have similar genetic bases. This is in keeping with the findings of Geller et al. (1994) that a high proportion of MDD children eventually develop bipolar affective disorder. It should be remembered, however, that the increased familiality of affective disorder in the Puig-Antich et al. (1989) study was in children who did *not* have comorbid conduct disorder. Hence, on a family history basis it appears likely that depression in the presence and absence of conduct disorder represents two distinct entities with different etiologies. Presumably, these forms of child MDD would respond differently to therapeutic interventions.

Since earlier age of onset of affective disorders has been associated with increased familiality and poor outcome in adults and adolescents (Rice et al., 1987; Strober et al., 1993), the similar observations in the family studies of Todd et al. (1993) would suggest that childhood onset illnesses should be chronic and poorly responsive to standard antidepressant treatment. As discussed above, this appears to be in keeping with both longitudinal and treatment studies of children with prepubescent onset of affective disorder (see e.g., Geller et al., 1992).

FUTURE STUDIES

The studies presented in this chapter contribute to our understanding of childhood depression as a chronic and disabling illness. A high risk of continuity into adulthood has been suggested by retrospective studies (Harrington et al., 1990). However, blind prospective investigations of depressed children into adulthood, with simultaneous follow-up of appropriate control groups, are still needed. Additionally, similar follow-up of infants with signs of risk into later childhood, in an attempt to establish early markers for the disorder, would facilitate efforts at primary prevention. Work to date on longitudinal outcome and familial genetic factors suggest that both genetic and psychosocial factors contribute to outcome.

ACKNOWLEDGMENT

This work was supported by National Institute of Mental Health grant R01 MH40273 to Dr. Geller.

REFERENCES

Andreason NC, Endicott J, Spitzer RL, Winokur G (1977): The family history method using diagnostic criteria. Arch Gen Psychiatry 34:1229–1235.

Asarnow JR, Goldstein MJ, Carlson GA, Perdue S, Bates S, Keller J (1988): Childhood-onset depressive disorders: A follow-up study of rates of re-hospitalization and out-of-home place-ment among child psychiatric inpatients. J Affect Dis 15:245–253.

Beardslee WB, Keller MB, Lavori PW, Staley J, Sacks N (1993): The impact of parental affective disorder on depression in offspring: A longitudinal follow-up in a non-referred sample. J Am Acad Child Adolesc Psychiatry 32(4):723–730.

Beardslee WR, Bemporad J, Keller MB, Klerman GL (1983): Children of parents with major affective disorder. A review. Am J Psychiatry 140:825–832.

Bettes BA (1988): Maternal depression and motherese. Child Dev 59:1089–1096.

Campbell SB, Cohn JF, Meyers T (1995): Depression in first-time mothers: Mother-infant interac-tion and depression chronicity. Dev Psychol 31:349–357.

Carlson GA, Cantwell DP (1980): Unmasking masked depression in children and adolescents. Am J Psychiatry 137:445–449.

Clayton P (1981): The epidemiology of bipolar affective disorder. Compr Psychiatry 22:31–43.

Cohn JF, Tronick EZ (1983): Three-month-old infants' reaction to simulated maternal depression. Child Dev 54:185–193.

Cohn JF, Campbell SB, Matias R, Hopkins J (1990): Face-to-face interactions of postpartum depressed and non-depressed mother-infant pairs at 2 months. Dev Psychol 26:15–23.

Cummings EM, Cicchetti D (1990): Toward a transactional model of relations between attachment and depression. In MT Greenberg, D Cicchetti, EM Cummings (eds): "Attachment in the Preschool Years: Theory, Research, and Intervention." Chicago: University of Chicago Press, pp 339–372.

Downey G, Coyne JC (1990): Children of depressed parents: An integrative review. Psychol Bull 108:50–76.

Eatsgate J, Gilmour L (1984): Long-term outcome of depressed children: A follow-up study. Dev Med Child Neuro 26(1):68–72.

Field TM (1984): Early interactions between infants and their postpartum depressed mothers. Infant Behav Dev 7:517–522.

Field T, Healy B, Goldstein S, Buthertz M (1990): Behavior-state matching and synchrony in mother-infant interactions of non-depressed versus depressed dyads. Dev Psychol 26:7–14.

Field T, Sandberg D, Garcaia R, Vega-Lahr N, Goldstein S, Guy L (1985): Pregnancy problems, postpartum depression, and early mother-infant interactions. Dev Psychol 21:1152–1156.

Fleming JE, Boyle MH, Offord DR (1993): The outcome of adolescent depression in the Ontario Child Health Study Follow-up. J Am Acad Child Adolesc Psychiatry 32:28–33.

Fleming AS, Ruble DN, Flett GL, Shaul DL (1988): Postpartum adjustment in first-time mothers: Relations between mood, maternal attitudes, and mother-infant interactions. Dev Psychol 24:71–81.

Garber J, Kriss MR, Koch M, Lindholm L (1988): Recurrent depression in adolescents: A follow-up study. J Am Acad Child Adolesc Psychiatry 27:49–54.

Garrison CZ, Jackson KL, Marsteller F, McKeown R, Addy C (1990): A longitudinal study of depressive symptomatology in young adolescents. J Am Acad Child Adolesc Psychiatry 29:581–585.

Geller B (1994): Rate and predictors of prepubertal bipolarity during follow-up of 6- to 12-year-old depressed children. J Am Acad Child Adolesc Psychiatry 33:461–468.

Geller B (1993): Longitudinal studies of depressive disorders in children. J Am Acad Child Adolesc Psychiatry 32:7.

Geller B, Cooper TV, Graham DL, Fetner HH, Marsteller FA, Wells JM (1992): Pharmacokinetically designed double-blind placebo-controlled study of nortriptyline in 6- to 12-year olds with major depressive disorder. J Am Acad Child Adolesc Psychiatry 31:34–44.

Hammen C, Gordon D, Burge D, Adrian C, Jaenicke C, Hiroto D (1987): Maternal affective disorders, illness, and stress: Risk for children's psychopathology. Am J Psychiatry 144:736–741.

Harrington R, Fudge H, Rutter M, Pickles A, Hill J (1990): Adult outcomes of childhood and adolescent depression. Arch Gen Psychiatry 47:465–473.

Kandel DB, Davies M (1986): Adult sequelae of adolescent depressive symptoms. Arch Gen Psychiatry 43:255–262.

Kashani JH, Carlson GA, Beck NC, Hoeper EW, Corcoran CM, McAllister JA, Fallahi C, Rosenberg TK, Reid JC (1987): Depression, depressive symptoms, and depressed mood among a community sample of adolescents. Am J Psychiatry 144:931–934.

Kashani JH, McGee RO, Clarkson SE, Anderson JC, Walton LA, Williams S, Silva PA, Robins AJ, Cytryn L, McKnew DH (1983): Depression in a sample of 9-year-old children. Arch Gen Psychiatry 40:1217–1223.

Keller MB, Beardslee W, Lavori PW, Wunder J, Drs DL, Samuelson H (1988): Course of major depression in non-referred adolescents: A retrospective study. J Affect Dis 15:235–243.

Keller MB, Beardslee WR, Dorer DH, Lavori PW, Samuelson H, Klerman GR (1986): Impact of severity and chronicity of parental affective illness on adaptive functioning and psychopathology in children. Arch Gen Psychiatry 43:930–937.

Kendler KS (1989): Limitations of the ratio of concordance rates in monozygotic and dizygotic twins (letter). Arch Gen Psychiatry 46:477–478.

Kovacs M, Akiskal HS, Gatsonis C, Parrone PL (1994a): Childhood-onset dysthymic disorder. Clinical features and prospective naturalistic outcome. Arch Gen Psychiatry 51:365–374.

Kovacs M, Gatsonis C, Pollock M, Parrone PL (1994b): A controlled prospective study of DSM-III adjustment disorder in childhood. Short-term prognosis and long-term predictive validity. Arch Gen Psychiatry 51:535–541.

Kovacs M, Goldston D, Gatsonis C (1993): Suicidal behaviors and childhood-onset depressive disorders: A longitudinal investigation. J Am Acad Child Adolesc Psychiatry 32:8–20.

Kovacs M, Gatsonis C, Paulauskas SL, Richard C (1989): Depressive disorders in childhood IV. A longitudinal study of co-morbidity with and risk for anxiety disorders. Arch Gen Psychiatry 46:776–782.

Kovacs M, Paulauskas S, Gatsonis C, Richards C (1988): Depressive disorders in childhood. III. A longitudinal study of co-morbidity with and risk for conduct disorders. J Affect Dis 15:205–217.

Kovacs M, Feinberg TL, Crouse-Novak M, Paulauskas SL, Pollock M, Finkelstein R (1984a): Depressive disorders in childhood. II. A longitudinal study of the risk for a subsequent major depression. Arch Gen Psychiatry 43:643–649.

Kovacs M, Feinberg TL, Crouse-Novak MA, Paulauskas SL, Finkelstein R (1984b): Depressive disorders in childhood. I. A longitudinal prospective study of characteristics and recovery. Arch Gen Psychiatry 41:229–237.

Lewinsohn PM, Clarke GN, Seeley JR, Rohde P (1994): Major depression in community adolescents: Age at onset, episode duration, and time to recurrence. J Am Acad Child Adolesc Psychiatry 33:809–818.

McCauley E, Myers K, Mitchell J, Calderon R, Schloredt K, Treder R (1993): Depression in young people: Initial presentation and clinical course. J Am Acad Child Adolesc Psychiatry 32:714–722.

McGee R, Williams S (1988): A longitudinal study of depression in nine-year-old children. J Am Acad Child Adolesc Psychiatry 27:342–348.

Murray L (1992): The impact of postnatal depression on infant development. J Child Psychol Psychiatry 33:543–561.

Nolen-Hoeksema S, Girgus JS, Seligman ME (1992): Predictors and consequences of childhood depressive symptoms: A 5-year longitudinal study. J Abnorm Psychology 101:405–422.

Orvaschel H, Wash-Allis G, Ye W (1988): Psychopathology in children in parents with recurrent depression. J Abnorm Child Psychology 16:17–28.

Poznanski EO, Krahenbuhl V, Zrull JP (1976): Childhood depression. J Am Acad Child Adolesc Psychiatry 15:491–501.

Puig-Antich J, Goetz D, Davies M, Kaplan T, Davies S, Ostrow L, Asnis L, Twomey J, Satish I, Ryan N, (1989): A controlled family history study of prepubertal major depressive disorder. Arch Gen Psychiatry 46:406–418.

Rao U, Weissman MM, Martin JA, Hammond RW (1993): Childhood depression and risk of suicide: A preliminary report of a longitudinal study. J Am Acad Child Adolesc Psychiatry 32:21–27.

Rice JP, Reich T, Andreasen NC, Endicott J, Van Eerdewegh M, Fishman R, Hirschfeld RMA, Klerman GL (1987): The familial transmission of bipolar illness. Arch Gen Psychiatry 44:441–447.

Robins E, Guze S (1970): Establishment of diagnostic validity in psychiatric illness; its application to schizophrenia. Am J Psychiatry, 126:7, 107–111.

Rubin KH, Both L, Zahm-Wazler C, Cummings EM, Wilkinson M (1991): Dyadic play behaviors of children of well and depressed mothers. Develop Psychopathol 3:243–251.

Spitz, R (1946): Anaclitic depression. Psychoanal Study Child 1:113–117.

Stein A, Gath DH, Bucher J, Bond A, Day A, Cooper PJ (1991): The relationship between postnatal depression and mother-child interaction. Brit J Psychiatry 158:46–52.

Strober M, Carlson G (1982): Bipolar illness in adolescents with major depression. Arch Gen Psychiatry 39:549–555.

Strober M, Lampert C, Schmidt S, Morrell W (1993): The course of major depressive disorder in adolescents: I. Recover and risk of manic switching in a follow-up psychotic and nonpsychotic subtypes. J Am Acad Child Adolesc Psychiatry 32:34–42.

Todd RD, Neuman R, Geller B, Fox L, Hickok J (1993): Genetic studies of affective disorders: should we be starting with childhood onset probands? J Am Acad Child Adolesc Psychiatry 32:6 1164–1171.

Todd RD, Geller B, Neuman R, Fox LW, Hickok J: Increased prevalence of alcoholism in relatives of depressed and bipolar children. JAACAP (in press).

Tronick EZ, Cohn JF (1989): Infant-mother fact-to-face interaction: Age and gender differences in coordination and the occurrence of miscoordination. Child Dev 60:85–92.

Weinberg MK, Tonick EZ (in press): Maternal depression and infant maladjustment: A failure of mutual regulation. In JD Osofsky (ed): "The Handbook of Child and Adolescent Psychiatry." New York: Wiley.

Weissman MM (1987): Advances in psychiatry epidemiology: Rates and risks for major depression. Am J Public Health 77:445–451.

Weissman MM (1988): Psychopathology in the children of depressed parents: Direct interview studies. In DL Dunner, ES Gershon, JE Barrett (eds): "Risk for Mental Disorder." New York: Raven Press, pp 143–159.

Welner A, Welner Z, Fishman R (1979): Psychiatric adolescent inpatients. Eight- to ten-year follow-up. Arch Gen Psychiatry 36:698–700.

Zahn-Waxler C, Kochanska G, Krupnick J, McKnew D (1990): Patterns of guilt in children of depressed and well mothers. Dev Psychol 26:51–59.

Zuckerman B, Bauchner H, Parker S, Cabral H (1990): Maternal depressive symptoms during pregnancy, and new born irritability. J Dev Behav Pediatrics 11:190–194.

CHAPTER 6

Treatment of Adolescent Depression

STANLEY P. KUTCHER and PETER MARTON

Department of Psychiatry, Dalhousie University, Halifax, Nova Scotia, Canada
B3H 3G2 (S.P.K.); Department of Psychology, St. Joseph's Hospital, Hamilton, Ontario,
Canada L8N 4A6 (P.M.)

Depressive disorders [major depressive disorder (MDD), dysthymic disorder (DYS)] commonly onset during the adolescent years (Kutcher and Marton, 1989a; Ryan and Puig-Antich, 1986; Fleming and Offord, 1990) with prevalance rates of MDD reaching "adult" levels of some 6–9% by late adolescence (McGee et al., 1990; Fleming and Offord, 1990). Adolescent-onset depressive disorders are characterized by prolonged course and repeated episodes (Strober, 1994; Garber et al., 1988; McCauley et al., 1988; Harrington et al., 1990) and are associated with poor academic performance, problematic social, interpersonal, and family functioning, and suicide (Marton et al., 1991; Puig-Antich et al., 1993; Brent, 1989). Major depressive disorder onsetting in adolescence is predictive of depressive episodes in adulthood (Harrington et al., 1990) and thus can be considered a chronic psychiatric disorder first manifesting itself relatively early on in the life cycle. Therefore, treatment of adolescent depression must be considered in both acute and long-term perspectives—to reduce morbidity of individual episodes, decrease rates of recurrence, and optimize long-term outcome. Additionally, treatment of adolescent onset depression must take into account not only the developmental issues of adolescence but also the multiple parameters of the disorder (symptoms, social, family, and academic functioning).

DIAGNOSIS

Whereas dysphoric or depressed mood is relatively common during the adolescent years and perhaps is best understood as a nonspecific symptom of psychological or physical distress, depressive disorders (clinical depression) as defined using the syndromal criteria for MDD or DYS [Diagnostic and Statistical Manual IV (DSM-IV) or Diagnostic and Statistical Manual III-Revised (DSM III-R)] are substantially less common (Kashani et al., 1987; Fleming and Offord, 1990; Fleming et al., 1989; Kandel and Davis, 1982; Kashani et al., 1989; McGee et al., 1990; Myers et al., 1984; Burke et al.,

Mood Disorders Across the Life Span, Edited by Shulman, Tohen, and Kutcher
ISBN 0-471-10477-9 © 1996 Wiley-Liss, Inc.

1990; Angold, 1987; Albert and Beck, 1975; Kutcher and Marton, 1989a; Garrison et al., 1991). Currently, although some age-associated differences in the relative frequency of symptoms making up the MDD syndrome have been described (Carlson and Ka-shani, 1988; Cantwell, 1985; Carlson and Garber, 1986), it is generally agreed that the core clinical criteria for diagnosis of MDD in adolescents is similar to that used in adults (Ryan et al., 1987). Nevertheless, constructs primarily derived from theories of adolescent development that lack empirical validation (such as *masked depression* or *normative adolescent mourning*) unfortunately continue to be used by some clinicians (Malmquist, 1971; Bemporad and Wilson, 1978; Bemporad, 1982; Kutcher et al., 1993).

Reliance on such unvalidated diagnostic practices may lead to overinclusive labeling of widely heterogeneous populations resulting in applications of treatments to patients who are not likely to benefit from them and who may be exposed to unnecessary adverse effects—physiologic, psychologic, or familial. Alternatively, such practices may lead to "normalization" of serious psychopathology or to diagnostic failure in which clear MDD or DYS is not identified. In these cases, potentially effective treatment may be withheld or ineffective or inappropriate treatments may be prescribed (Kutcher and Marton, 1990; Keller et al., 1991). Careful application of recognized diagnostic criteria as part of a comprehensive assessment in the adolescent with mood disturbance will improve diagnostic accuracy of both current and previous depressive episodes (Kutcher et al., 1985).

The use of assessment tools such as semistructured interviews in diagnosis is a valuable adjunct to clinical interviewing, and while these instruments cannot take the place of careful clinical assessment, they do provide a reliable method that allows for a comprehensive and thorough diagnosis (Rabkin and Klein, 1987). A number of clinically useful structured or semistructured diagnostic interview schedules are now available [Kiddie Schedule for Affective Disorders and Schizophrenia (K-SADS); Chambers et al., (1985); Diagnostic Interview for Children and Adolescents (DICA); Herjanic and Campbell, 1977; Child Assessment Schedule (CAS); Hodges et al., (1982)] and have been reviewed elsewhere (Orvaschel, 1985; Hanna, 1994).

All the above diagnostic interviews require separate administration to the adolescent and a parent or other appropriate adult. Final diagnostic ascertainment, however, must take into consideration both teen and parent reports as significant informant-based reporting; differences in symptom ascertainment are known to occur (Verhulst et al., 1985; Kendal et al., 1989; Gershon et al., 1985; Herjanic and Reich, 1982; Welner et al., 1987). Furthermore, to be clinically useful, these diagnostic schedules require both a sophisticated level of knowledge about adolescent depression and interviewer training before they can be appropriately used.

While no interview schedule has been shown to be clearly superior to any other, it is the opinion of the authors, following extensive use of various diagnostic interviews, that the Kiddie Schedule for Affective Disorders and Schizophrenia (K-SADS; Chambers et al., 1985) is arguably the most useful of the clinical interview schedules available. This is available in both present state (K-SADS-P) and lifetime (K-SADS-E; Orvaschel and Puig-Antich, 1987) versions and is currently being revised to accommodate DSM-IV criteria. The one available comparative study of interview schedules regarding diagnostic validity further supports this impression (Carlson, et al., 1987).

SYMPTOM MEASUREMENT

In addition to diagnostic interviews, symptom rating scales, which allow for measurement of symptom presence and severity, are of clinical importance—particularly as tools to evaluate treatment outcome (Rabkin and Klein, 1987; Petti, 1978, 1985). They are, however, *not clinically valid* diagnostic instruments and thus should not be used by themselves to make a diagnosis of a depressive syndrome in adolescents.

Two types of symptom rating scales are available: clinician rating and self-report. At this time, while self-report scales are generally considered to provide less valid information than clinician rating scales (Rabkin and Klein, 1987) no psychometrically well-validated clinician rating scales have been developed for use in assessing depressed mood in adolescents. While the Hamilton Depressing Rating Scale (HDRS; Hamilton, 1960) has been extensively used as an outcome measure of depression severity in psychopharmacologic treatment studies of adolescent depression, concerns have been raised regarding its applicability to assessing the full spectrum of symptoms and severity of depression in adolescents. Nevertheless, in anticipation of the development of an adolescent-specific clinician rating scale, the HDRS does in our experience demonstrate adequate clinical utility as a measure of symptom change. Additionally, an HDRS symptom severity score can be calculated from the K-SADS.

A variety of self-report measures are available for use with adolescents. These include the Depression Self-Rating Scale [DSRS (Birelson et al., 1987)]; Centre for Epidemiological Studies Depression Scale [CES-D (Weissman et al., 1980)]; Reynolds Adolescent Depression Scale [RADS (Reynolds and Coats, 1986)]; and the Beck Depression Inventory [BDI (Beck et al., 1961)].

At this time, the CES-D has not demonstrated clinical utility (Faulstich, et al., 1986) and the RADS has neither been updated to reflect advances in diagnostic developments nor has it received extensive clinical or research use (Reynolds and Coats, 1986; Kasdin, 1990). The BDI has been relatively well studied in depressed adolescents (Terri, 1982; Strober et al., 1981; Kutcher and Marton, 1989b; Marton et al., 1991) and has demonstrated clinical utility as a measure of symptom change in psychopharmacologic treatment of depressed teenageres (Kutcher et al., 1994). In both outpatient and inpatient settings, the BDI is easy to administer, well accepted by depressed teens, and provides a useful tool for evaluating clinical outcome in the treatment of depressed adolescents.

TREATMENT PROCESS

Treatment of adolescent depression can be considered as a three-phase process. The first phase includes diagnosis, symptom measurement, patient and family education about the disorder, evaluation of associated difficulties, and selection of specific treatment modalities. The second phase includes active treatments directed at symptom improvement and amelioration of associated difficulties. The third phase includes evaluation of progress to date and revisions to treatment or reformulation of new treatment goals.

PHASE ONE

Following appropriate diagnosis and symptom measurement, treatment of adolescent depression should begin with an educational approach that provides information about the disorder and the various available treatments. Ideally, this should be presented to both the adolescent and his or her family. The use of various printed materials regarding adolescent depression are a useful adjunct to clinician-initiated sessions. Appropriate educational materials regarding adolescent depression are easily available.

Although limited to information about medications (Bastiaens and Bastiaens, 1993), one such information package has received clinical evaluation with positive results (Bastiaens, 1992). However, more general material is most useful and some can be obtained from the American Academy of Child and Adolescent Psychiatry or the Depression Awareness, Recognition and Treatment (D/ART) Program (National Institute of Mental Health). Although not fully "field tested," an educational manual for teens is available from the Adolescent Division in the Department of Psychiatry at Sunnybrook Health Science Centre, Toronto, Canada, and a semistructured educational course for the families of depressed teenagers is currently in preparation at the Division of Child Psychiatry at the University of Pittsburgh, Pittsburgh, PA. In some cases, material originally designed for providing information regarding depression for adults (such as "Depression is a Treatable Illness: A Patient's Guide," U.S. Department of Health and Human Services) may be a reasonable starting point.

The importance of this initial education phase cannot be minimized, for in addition to providing a basic knowledge and understanding of the disorder, it provides an opportunity for the clinician to develop a positive therapeutic alliance with the teen and his or her family.

Additionally, prior to undertaking a specific treatment course, a careful evaluation of associated difficulties should be undertaken. This should include assessment of psychiatric, social, academic, and family functioning.

Associated psychiatric disorders must be identified during the first phase of treatment. Often these can be understood as comorbid psychiatric disorders. While it is beyond the scope of this chapter to discuss the issue of psychiatric comorbidity in adolescents, this has been recently reviewed elsewhere (Angold and Costello, 1992). Depressed adolescents are often found to exhibit comorbid psychiatric disorders, most commonly anxiety disorders such as obsessive–compulsive disorder, panic disorder, or generalized anxiety disorder (Kashani et al., 1987; Kutcher et al;, 1994; McGee et al., 1990; Strauss et al., 1988; Fleming and Offord, 1990; Boulos et al., 1992a; Puig-Antich and Rabinovitch, 1986; Geller et al., 1985; Hershberg et al., 1982). Comorbid attention-deficit disorder and conduct disorder may also frequently occur, especially in younger males (Chiles et al., 1980; Munir et al., 1987; Puig-Antich, 1982; Kutcher et al., 1989). If present, these disorders may require additional treatment strategies to those outlined below, or may complicate recovery from the depressive episode itself.

Additionally, specific symptoms not usually considered as core to the depressive syndrome may occur in association with depression and may require specific symptom-directed treatment strategies. Examples of these include school refusal and somatic complaints (Bernstein and Garfinkel, 1986; Pearce, 1977; Berney et al., 1981; Kolvin et al., 1984).

To complete the necessary evaluations prior to initiating a treatment course, systematic assessment of social, interpersonal, academic, and family functioning is indicated. Disturbances in these spheres of functioning are common in depressed adolescents and can be best understood as arising from the depressive episode. In some cases, functional difficulties may have preceded the depression, and in those teenagers interventions directed toward those problems may be undertaken as part of the overall treatment strategies (e.g., learning disability).

A variety of measures useful in the evaluation of social, interpersonal, academic, and family functioning are available. The Adolescent Autonomous Functioning Checklist

(Sigafoos et al., 1988), the Wide Range Achievement Test—Revised (Jastak and Wilkinson; 1984), and the Family Assessment Measure (Skinner, 1987) when taken together provide a useful battery of tests that are relatively well received by teens and their parents and that can identify ongoing difficulties and provide measures useful for evaluation purposes following treatment.

Medical Issues

Medical disorders presenting primarily as depression are uncommon in teenagers, although depression may complicate chronic medical illnesses (Kashani et al., 1981; Kashani and Hakami, 1982; Burke et al., 1989). Nevertheless, good clinical practice demands that a thorough medical history should be taken and appropriate follow-up investigations completed as indicated. There is, however, no evidence that exhaustive and expensive screening laboratory and neuroimaging tests are necessary in the absence of physical signs and symptoms of a medical illness.

Potential medication side effects, however, must be evaluated prior to initiating pharmacologic treatment. A medication-specific side effects scale should be used at baseline, prior to beginning pharmacologic treatment (see Figure 1 for an example), and this can be repeated at specific times during the second treatment phase and upon treatment completion. Using this tool, treatment-emergent side effects will rapidly become apparent and pre-existing somatic complaints, which may incorrectly be ascribed to medication effects when they occur in the context of pharmacologic treatment, are best differentiated from treatment-emergent side effects using this simple strategy.

Suicide Risk

Assessment of suicide risk is an essential component of evaluating the depressed adolescent. Similarly, clinician awareness of suicidal potential and addressing of this issue will continue to be important throughout the treatment process. Depression is the most frequent psychiatric disorder found in successful adolescent suicides (Crumley, 1979; Shaffer et al., 1988; Shaffi et al., 1985, 1988; Brent, 1989; Brent et al., 1988), and the suicide risk is increased in the presence of substance abuse (Allebeck and Allgulander, 1990; Crumley, 1990; Hoberman and Garfinkel, 1989; Levy and Denkin, 1989), behavioral disorders (Shaffi et al., 1988; Allebeck and Allgulander, 1990; Clark et al., 1990), a family history of suicide (Friedman et al., 1984; Roy, 1983), and the presence of firearms in the home (Brent, 1988; Boyd and Moscicki, 1986; Brent et al., 1987). Thus, these risk factors, in addition to assessment of suicidal ideation and intent, must be addressed. Specific strategies of value in decreasing adolescent suicide during treatment should be instituted during phase one. These include a strong therapeutic relationship with easy accessibility of the therapist by the teen, open discussion about suicide risk, antisuicide contracts, family education about warning signs of suicide, and removing firearms from easy accessibility.

Finally, prior to initiating specific treatment (phase two), both teen and parents should be informed about the estimated treatment length and the process of treatment reevaluation. As adolescent depression is known to respond slower to optimal psychological and biological treatments than adult depressions, it is imperative to clearly identify that 10–12 weeks of continuous treatment is necessary for symptomatic improvement. Associated disturbances such as school problems or social difficulties may take even longer to remit. Finally, in any discussion of treatment, the teen and parents

Subjective Side Effects	never		somewhat		constantly
trouble sleeping	0	1	2	3	4
heart racing	0	1	2	3	4
heart pounding	0	1	2	3	4
feeling dizzy	0	1	2	3	4
feeling the room spin	0	1	2	3	4
feeling tense inside	0	1	2	3	4
restlessness	0	1	2	3	4
numbness of hands or feet	0	1	2	3	4
tingling in hands or feet	0	1	2	3	4
trouble keeping balance	0	1	2	3	4
dry mouth	0	1	2	3	4
blurred vision	0	1	2	3	4
seeing double	0	1	2	3	4
constipation	0	1	2	3	4
diarrhea	0	1	2	3	4
delays in urinating	0	1	2	3	4
itchiness	0	1	2	3	4
light hurting eyes	0	1	2	3	4
nausea	0	1	2	3	4
vomiting	0	1	2	3	4
no appetite	0	1	2	3	4
stomach pains	0	1	2	3	4
drowsy	0	1	2	3	4
leg spasms at night	0	1	2	3	4
sweating	0	1	2	3	4
tremor	0	1	2	3	4
headache	0	1	2	3	4
other	0	1	2	3	4

Name: _____   Date: _____

wt. _____   BPsit _____   BPstand _____

Signature _____

FIGURE 1. Side effects of antidepressants.

should be made aware of the variety of potential treatments available, the rationale for selecting one or more of them, and the potential adverse effects of each treatment option. Informed decision making by teen and parents about treatment is an essential component of the therapeutic process. Furthermore, this type of process sets the treatment paradigm as a consensual partnership of therapist and patient with agreed-upon interventions, time lines, and goals.

PHASE TWO

While a number of treatment possibilities for adolescent depression (MDD and DYS) exist and are widely practiced, few have stood the test of empiric validation. This applies to psychological and biologic therapies alike. Thus, treatment for adolescent depression remains largely based on clinical lore and the application of treatment modalities currently known to be effective in adult depression. However, adolescents exhibit different cognitive, social, and biologic (central nervous system) milieus than those of adults, and simple extrapolation of adult treatments into the adolescent age group is not indicated (Kutcher et al., 1993; Arnold, 1993). At this time a number of well-controlled investigations into various biologic and psychologic treatments are under way. The following summary reviews biologic and psychologic treatments separately, although good clinical practice involves the conjoint administration of a somatic and psychological intervention concurrently.

Biological Treatment—Psychopharmacology

Tricyclics   Studies of tricyclic antidepressants, both open and controlled, have failed to establish the value of these compounds in the treatment of adolescent depression. Ryan et al. (1992) were not able to demonstrate effectiveness of imipramine in depressed adolescents, with less than half of their open-label sample showing symptomatic improvement. Other studies of imipramine (Strober et al., 1990; Strober, 1989) have also found similar results. Controlled studies of nortriptyline (Geller et al., 1989), desipramine (Boulos et al., 1992a), and amitryptyline (Kramer and Feigerine, 1981) have not shown efficacy of these compounds compared to placebo. Although these earlier studies have been criticized for employing small sample sizes, a recent double-blind, placebo-controlled study of desipramine (DMI) by Kutcher et al., (1994) of 66 teens with major depression failed to demonstrate the superiority of DMI over placebo. Furthermore, serum levels of DMI or its metabolite, 2-hydroxy-desipramine, were not associated with therapeutic response. The DMI-treated group, however, demonstrated considerably more side effects than the placebo group.

These data suggest that, unlike in depressed adults, tricyclic antidepressants may be ineffective in ameliorating depression in adolescents. While a number of hypotheses have been advanced to explain this difference (Ryan, 1992; Jensen et al., 1992; Kutcher et al., 1994), one possibility for which there is some empirical support (Ambrosini et al., preprint; Boulos, personal communication) is that treatment studies to date have failed to take into account the finding that depressive episodes in adolescents may be slower to respond to any treatment than similar episodes in adults (Strober, 1992); thus, available studies have been of too short a duration (4–6 weeks) to identify drug response. Alternatively, the length of depressive episode prior to treatment has been inversely correlated with treatment response in adult depressives (Nelson et al., 1994), and the extremely long length of the adolescent depressive episode prior to treatment (Geller et al., 1989; Kutcher et al., 1994) may have biased the available studies toward tricyclic nonresponse.

Nevertheless, given the negative response to tricyclics in all studies reported to date, the concerns, albeit controversial (Werry, 1994; Riddle et al., 1994; Ambrosini et al., 1994), regarding the exceedingly rare relationship between sudden death and desipramine use (Biederman, 1991; Popper and Elliot, 1990; Ryan, 1992) and the high rates of subjective side effects reported with these compounds, tricyclic antidepressants should not at this time be considered as first-line pharmacotherapy in depressed adolescents.

Serotonin-Specific Reuptake Inhibitors   Studies of serotonin-specific reuptake inhibitors (SSRI) have shown more promise, albeit in open clinical trials. Although a small controlled study by Simeon et al. (1990) did not demonstrate fluoxetine efficacy in treating adolescent depression, subsequent reports (Jain et al., 1992; Boulos et al., 1992b; Weiss, 1993) in adolescents with treatment-resistant major depression suggest that this compound may be of value in the pharmacologic treatment of depressed teens. Ongoing double-blind placebo-controlled studies of fluoxetine (Emslie, 1993) and placebo plus reference drug studies of paroxetine should provide definitive evidence regarding these compounds.

Side effects to fluoxetine in depressed adolescents have been generally found to be relatively uncommon and usually well tolerated (Boulos et al., 1992b; Strober, personal communication; Simeon et al., 1990; Jain et al., 1992; Emslie, personal communication). Although some concerns that fluoxetine may lead to increased suicidal behaviors in adults have been raised (Teicher et al., 1990) and self-destructive behaviors that were apparently treatment emergent with SSRIs in six young patients with obsessive–compulsive disorder have been described (King et al., 1993), the available evidence clearly demonstrates that fluoxetine use is associated with decreased suicidality (Stokes, 1993; Beasley et al., 1992), and extensive systematic assessment of suicidality in depressed adolescents treated with fluoxetine in our clinics did not find any increase in suicidal ideation, suicidal intent, self-harm behaviors, or suicide attempts with fluoxetine treatment.

The physician choosing to use fluoxetine should be aware, however, that in addition to the well-described potential side effects of nausea, headaches, and insomia (Cooper, 1988), a syndrome of restlessness, agitation, and nervous dysphoria can develop in some teens treated with fluoxetine. This appears to be dose related and thus treatment should be initiated at a maximal daily dose of 5 or 10 mg gradually increased to 20 mg and maintained for 8 to 10 weeks to determine potential efficacy.

Additionally, fluoxetine has been found to precipitate mania and hypomania in depressed teens (Rosenberg et al., 1992) and this presentation may be potentially confused with the agitation picture described above. If the clinician is uncertain as to differentiating these pictures in any one individual, prudent practice is to discontinue the medication and restart it using a lower dose following a 2-week "wash out."

While other SSRIs are available and are used for treating depressed adolescents in clinical practice, no systematic data on their efficacy or tolerability is available at this time. Clinical experience with these compounds in our population suggest that paroxetine, sertraline, and fluvoxamine (Grimsley and Jann, 1992) are all relatively well tolerated and demonstrate similar efficacy when used in amounts consistent with recommendations for adult daily dosage.

Monoamine Oxidase Inhibitors   Among other available compounds, monoamine oxidase inhibitors (MAOIs), although effective in adult depression, have received little investigation in depressed adolescents. Ryan et al. (1988b) have reported an open trial of an MAOI (phenalzine) in 23 previously tricyclic nonresponsive depressed adolescents. While about 60% were judged to exhibit a good clinical response to this treatment, a high rate of dietary noncompliance and frequent side effects, including two cases of significant hypertensive episodes, limited the widespread clinical use of this medication. Fleming et al. (1993) have reported on an ongoing trial of an MAOI comparing two doses of phenelzine (low, 30 mg daily; medium, 60 mg daily) against placebo. In the first 18 study completers, after 8 weeks, 50% of the placebo group were deemed treatment responders (by Clinical Global Impression Scale score) compared to 29% of the low-dose and 40% of the medium-dose groups. Although preliminary and comprised of a small sample size, these findings do not support a robust response of depressed teens to phenelzine.

In our adolescent outpatient clinics, an open clinical trial of trancylcypramine (parnate) was discontinued due to the high frequency of side effects, mostly orthostatic hypotension. Given the lack of demonstrated treatment response to the traditional MAOI compounds, concerns about their hypertensive potential and the well-known proclivity of adolescents for dietary adventure, there is little compelling evidence for the use of phenelzine or trancylcypramine in the first-line pharmacologic treatment of adolescent depression.

While the MAOI-A specific inhibitor moclobemide (Nair et al., 1993; Bakish et al., 1992) is now available in Canada as an antidepressant, no clinical trials in adolescents have to our knowledge been undertaken. Use of this compound in our clinic has shown promise with a favorable side effects profile and therapeutic response association with total doses of 600–900 mg daily; however, the potential utility of this compound in depressed teens awaits proper evaluation.

Other newer antidepressants such as the serotonin-specific $5HT_2$ receptor antagonist nefazodone or the azapirone buspirone have been reported effective in treating depressive episodes in adults (Fontaine, 1992; Schweizer et al., 1992; Rickels et al., 1991) but have not to our knowledge been specifically evaluated in adolescent populations. The clinical use of these and other promising novel compounds thus awaits the necessary reports of tolerability and efficacy in depressed teenagers.

Augmentation Studies

Although a variety of augmentation strategies for antidepressant nonresponsiveness have been employed in adult populations (Levitt et al., 1991), lithium carbonate (Henninger et al., 1983; deMontigny et al., 1983) and thyroid hormone (Joffe, 1993) have been perhaps the best validated. To date, no studies of thyroid hormone augmentation (triiodothyronine or thyroxine) have to our knowledge been reported in adolescent depressives. Two open studies of lithium augmentation in depressed teens, however, have shown promising results (Strober et al., 1990; Ryan et al., 1988a) suggesting that this may be a reasonable strategy to employ in the adolescent depressive unresponsive or partially responsive to antidepressant monotherapy. Finally, while combination therapies (i.e., SSRI and MAOI) are theoretically possible, few, if any, publications regarding this treatment for depressed adolescents are available. Kutcher and Boulos (submitted) have described successful combined paroxetine and moclobemide treatment in two severely ill, depressed adolescents with comorbid obsessive–compulsive disorder. At this time, such therapeutic interventions should only be used with full informed consent in specialized treatment centers experienced in treating refractory patients.

Other Somatic Treatments

Light therapy has been successfully applied to the treatment of seasonal affective disorder and other depressive states in adults (Lam et al., 1989). To our knowledge, no systematic information about the use of this potentially effective treatment modality is available for depressed adolescents. In our clinics, 10,000 lux of full-spectrum light delivered for 45 minutes twice daily has been used successfully in augmenting response to antidepressants, but this effect is most clearly seen in thymoleptic maintained bipolar teenagers with subsyndromal depressive "breakthrough" symptoms (Papatheodorou and Kutcher, submitted).

Electroconvulsive therapy (ECT) has been described in reports of small numbers of adolescent depressives (Bertagnoli and Borchardt, 1990; Guttmacher and Cretella, 1988; Schneckloth et al., 1993). Although recent reports regarding this treatment modality has suggested its safety and clinical efficacy (Fink, 1994; Kutcher and Robertson, 1994; Strober, 1994; Moise, 1994; Schneckloth et al., 1993), it is best used as an intervention for psychotic or catatonic depression if any of the following conditions apply:

1. Response to optimal pharmacologic treatment has been unsuccessful.
2. Severe side effects have limited medication use.
3. Clinical picture is complicated by catatonia.
4. Extreme agitation and aggressive suicidal or homicidal actions place the patient or others at serious risk.

In these cases, our experience (Kutcher and Robertson, 1994) has been to use bilateral, brief-pulse ECT delivered under appropriate anaesthesia at a dose of two treatments per week.

Seizure duration should be monitored routinely, and one report has suggested that prolonged seizures (greater than 100 seconds) may occur frequently, a finding not supported in other well-documented series (Kutcher and Robertson, 1994; Strober, 1994; Schneckloth et al., 1993) and most likely secondary to excessively high voltage selection (Fink, 1994). Although no significant long-term side effects of brief-pulse bilateral ECT delivered as above are known, no systematic study of this issue is to our knowledge available in the adolescent literature. Immediate posttreatment and short-term memory effects have been reported. However, these are generally found to remit over a few days to a few months. Disinhibition postically has also been described (Bertagnolli and Borchardt, 1990) as has headache and hypomanic-type symptoms (Kutcher and Robertson, 1994). Reviewing all objective (nursing observations) and subjective (patient complaints) reports of immediate post-ECT side effects of 166 adolescent ECT treatments, Kutcher and Robertson (1994) found a treatment-emergent side effects rate of 23%, the majority of which were transient headaches.

Informed patient and family consent and an independent psychiatric opinion from a consultant not involved in the case are essential prerequisites to ECT treatment. In our experience a course of 10–12 treatments should usually be sufficient, and this should be followed by maintenance pharmacotherapy—preferably with an SSRI.

Psychosocial Therapies

Psychosocial therapies for adolescent depression have been less extensively studied than somatic treatments. In addition to evidence of efficacy, important questions such as specificity of treatment, dose and duration, indications and contraindications, and toxic or antitherapeutic effects have not been addressed in the psychosocial therapy literature. Nevertheless, based more on tradition and theory than empirical evidence, psychotherapeutic approaches are often considered the treatment of choice for adolescent depression. The literature available on treatment outcome is reviewed below.

Depressive illness in adolescents is associated with morbidity in a variety of social, interpersonal, and vocational areas. Consequently effective treatment of acute depressive episodes and the prevention of relapses is vital. A variety of psychological therapies have been shown to be effective in the treatment of adult depression (Klerman et al., 1974, 1984; Baldessarini, 1983; Robinson et al., 1990). Initial attempts to evaluate psychological treatment of depression in adolescents has begun and has been reviewed by several authors (Harrington, 1992; Holmes and Wagner, 1992; Petersen et al., 1993). The predominant treatment strategy has been to adapt adult treatments to adolescent populations (Bemporad, 1988; Fine et al., 1989; Moreau et al., 1991; Wilkes and Rush, 1988). However, the extrapolation of "adult" treatments to adolescents is fraught with difficulties as there is a dearth of developmental data relevant to the modification of treatments for depression in adolescents (Weisz et al., 1992). Hence, psychotherapy modifications for adolescents are based mostly on clinical impression rather than on empirical data. This applies equally to psychodynamic, cognitive and behavioral modes of psychotherapy.

Psychologically, adolescents demonstrate different cognitive and emotional functioning than adults (Keating, 1980). The social milieu and support systems of the adolescent also differ significantly from those of adult (Coleman, 1980). Thus, psychological therapies designed for adults may not be directly applicable in the adolescent age group. Further, early pubertal teens may exhibit significant psychological differences from late pubertal teens, possibly necessitating different therapeutic approaches even within the adolescent age group. Therefore, developmentally sensitive therapies must be developed, and their efficacy demonstrated in adolescents of varying developmental stages—early, middle, and late. Treatments for adolescent depression must therefore arise out of studies in which the variables of age, pubertal stage, cognitive level, and social capabilities are addressed.

As with any treatment for a psychiatric disorder, psychotherapy for adolescent depression must meet specific criteria prior to general acceptance (Kasdin, 1986). First, it must be shown to be effective using carefully constructed and empirically validated studies using appropriate control groups and adequate sample sizes. Second, specific treatment factors that ameliorate the disorder must be identified and separated from more general or nonspecific treatment effects. Third, the relative efficacy of one treatment modality compared to another must be examined. This includes the evaluation of combined psychological and pharmacologic interventions. Fourth, predictors of treatment outcome must be identified. The available data for determining the efficacies of various psychotherapies in treating adolescent depression must be reviewed with these criteria in mind.

Psychological Therapies

Studies of psychotherapeutic approaches in adult depression have mostly evaluated cognitive, cognitive–behavioral, and interpersonal methods (Kasdin, 1986; Shea et al., 1988). In general, no one treatment approach has been shown to be superior to the others, although psychodynamically based long-term psychotherapy has not demonstrated efficacy in treating depression. These three psychotherapeutic approaches share a number of common features that may account—at least in part—for their effects: They are structured; they advocate a goal-oriented approach arising from collaboration between an active therapist and patient; and they all pay attention to issues ongoing in the patients' life—the here and now. A clear understanding of why psychotherapy is effective in treating adult depression, however, is not yet available.

A number of authors have adapted treatments for depressed adolescents that have initially been shown to be effective for depressed adults (Molick and Pinkson, 1982; Moreau et al., 1991; Schloss et al., 1984; Trautman and Rotheram-Borus, 1988; Wilkes and Rush, 1988; Wilkes et al., 1994). These have included cognitive techniques, cognitive–behavioral interventions, and interpersonal therapy.

In current practice, psychotherapy is the intervention most commonly recommended for the depressed adolescent during an acute episode. Unfortunately, the success rate in studies of clinical samples is modest. The use of a broad psychotherapeutic intervention with adolescents hospitalized with major depression in an open clinical trial found that only 47% responded (Robbins et al., 1989). Furthermore, studies that have followed clinical samples of depressed adolescents over more than the length of one episode report that depressed adolescents treated with various psychotherapies during the acute phase often demonstrate continued mood difficulties at follow-up (Garber et al., 1988; McCauley et al., 1988; DiNicola and Simeon, 1988). There are few outcome studies available on the efficacy of psychotherapy for adolescent depression. Those that are available are reviewed under the three main headings evaluated in the adult literature: cognitive therapy, cognitive–behavioral therapy, and dynamic psychotherapy.

Cognitive–Behavioral Approaches to Therapy

Reynolds and Coates (1986) compared a cognitive behavior therapy program with both a progressive muscle relaxation approach and a waiting list control group in subjects with depressive symptoms but who did not meet diagnostic criteria for a depressive disorder. Thirty students identified as depressed on the basis of scores above threshold on one of several depression scales were randomly assigned to one of the intervention groups. The two treatment groups underwent structured, goal-oriented interventions involving homework and face-to-face contact with an experienced school psychologist for ten, 1-hour sessions.

Six subjects dropped out of the active treatment groups (3 in each) leaving 14 treatment completers. Both treatments resulted statistically significant within group improvement on all depression ratings. However, when dropouts are considered, the success rate for the cognitive–behavioral therapy condition was only 55% and no significant between-group differences could be demonstrated. At one-month follow-up, improvement was maintained across both modalities.

Hains (1992) reported that group cognitive restructuring or anxiety management interventions produced greater reduction in depression ratings of a high school, volunteer group of adolescent boys than in a wait list control group. These benefits were maintained over an 11-week follow-up. Similar to the study of Reynolds and Coats (1986), however, there was no difference between the effectiveness of the cognitive or anxiety management interventions.

Clarke and colleagues (1993) applied a group prevention strategy to adolescents with mild to moderate depression but who scored below the clinical diagnostic threshold for major depression. These youngsters were given a trial of cognitive–behavior therapy. Compared to an untreated group, the prevention group was significantly less likely to develop a depressive disorder during an 18-month follow-up (14.5 vs. 25.7%).

Lewinsohn et al. (1990) assessed the efficacy of a 7-week course of cognitive-behavioral therapy, and adolescent adaptation of the Coping with Depression Course, in adolescent depression diagnosed by DSM-III and Research Diagnostic Criteria (RDC) using the K-SADS. In a group setting, the adolescents were taught skills for increasing pleasant activities, relaxation, controlling depressive thoughts, improving social interaction, communication, negotiation, and conflict resolution. Fifty-nine depressed teens were randomly assigned to three treatment conditions: a cognitive–behavioral group for the adolescent only, group cognitive–behavioral therapy for the adolescent plus parental involvement in a separate but complementary group, and a wait list condition. Forty-six percent of treated adolescents no longer met diagnostic criteria for depression compared with 5.3% of the wait list controls. Significant treatment effects were also found on self-report and parent report measures with no significant difference noted between type of treatment. Treatment gains were found to be maintained at follow-up for up to 2 years. These results require replication since there was substantial attrition at follow-up. Parental involvement was not found to significantly improve treatment response, above gains obtained through the adolescent group.

Fine and colleagues (1991) treated depressed outpatients with either a social skills group or a supportive psychotherapy group. Immediately after therapy, although both groups showed improvement, the support group improved significantly more than the social skills group. At a 9-month follow-up the social skills group caught up. Unfortunately, there was no placebo group for comparison and using absence of DSM-III-R diagnosed depression as the outcome criteria showed a response rate not dissimilar to the placebo rates reported in psychopharmacology studies of depressed teens.

These results suggest that cognitive–behavioral therapies may be useful in the treatment of adolescent depression. However, treatment outcomes with depressed adolescents have not been as strong (46–55% recovery rate) as in adults (65–85% recovery rate) (Clarke et al., 1992). Furthermore, Clarke et al. (1992) have reported that it is those adolescents with less severe depression and higher functioning at intake who tend to recover with cognitive treatment. Hence, studies with nonclinical groups may show treatment benefits that may not generalize directly to true clinical groups with more severe depression and less adequate functioning. Much further research remains to be done in this area before efficacy of cognitive therapy in this population is clearly established. Future studies should address symptom change as well as the effect of treatment on the concurrent features of depression, such as cognitive and attitudinal distortions, impaired social skills, and disturbed self-concept. In addition, the specificity of particular therapeutic techniques needs to be determined and isolated from general therapeutic effects. This is particularly important as available data from studies by Clarke et al. (1992) show that contrary to expectations, treatment response to cognitive therapy was not preferentially found in those depressed teens with cognitive distortions.

Similar issues arise in the ongoing study at the University of Pittsburgh, which compares the effect of cognitive behavior therapy (CBT) with systemic behavioral family therapy (SBFT) and nondirective supportive therapy (NST). Of the 56 subjects who have completed the study to date, the rate of remission shows no significant group differences, with the NST showing similar efficacy to both CBT and SBFT (Birmaher, 1994).

No evidence exists that depressed adolescents actually lack the skills being taught in the cognitive or cognitive–behavioral interventions. To date we only have evidence of impairment while the youngsters are dysphoric and thus the observed deficits may actually be state-dependent effects of the mood disorder itself. Given the lack of specificity of effects of interventions, this suggests that it may be the nonspecific psychotherapeutic aspects of the treatment that may be effective.

Psychodynamic Psychotherapy

The literature on traditional psychodynamic psychotherapy of adolescent depression generally describes models of depression and describes treatment derived from these assumptions (Anthony, 1970; Bemporad, 1988). Adolescent depression is assumed to result from the individual's failure to cope with normal adolescent developmental tasks or to relinquish childhood ideals of self (Holmes and Wagner, 1992). The state of the art in evaluating this form of adolescent psychotherapy has been reviewed by Shaffer (1984) and Kasdin (1986) and found to be lacking in conceptual and methodologic rigor. No new studies of this type of psychotherapy that meet acceptable scientific criteria are available. Thus, at this time, there is no empirical evidence to support the use of psychodynamic psychotherapies in treating adolescent depression.

Interpersonal Psychotherapy

The growth and interest in interpersonal psychotherapy and its more empirical base may signal a change toward evaluation in psychodynamic psychotherapy.

Interpersonal psychotherapy (IPT) is a brief, dynamically oriented therapy developed to alleviate depressive symptoms and improve interpersonal functioning. The patient is assisted in developing more effective strategies to deal with current interpersonal problems. In adults, controlled clinical trials have demonstrated the efficacy of IPT alone or in combination with antidepressant medication (Elkin et al., 1989).

To date, a number of attempts have been made to adopt and evaluate for adolescents the interpersonal psychotherapy model developed by Klerman et al. (1984). Moreau et al. (1991) have modified the IPT manual for use with adolescents. Treatment includes a psychoeducational component about depression, the exploration and clarification of feelings, improvement of communication skills, and cognitive–behavioral techniques. An open trial of IPT in a small number of depressed teens is currently underway, and early findings are promising (Mufson, 1994). This particular psychotherapy model is of interest because it addresses prominent areas of impairment and has clearly specified treatment procedures.

Similarly, a pilot, uncontrolled open clinical investigation of interpersonal psychotherapy combining family therapy, group therapy, and cognitive–behavioral therapy for adolescents with major depression found that 47% responded to this intervention (Robbins et al., 1989). The treatment did not use the current manual for adolescent IPT but was based on the investigator's familiarity with the procedure. A further limitation of this study is that a "kitchen sink" approach was used so that outcome could not be attributed solely to the IPT. Nevertheless, a clinical sample was used, and the results are encouraging of further more controlled trials.

Family Therapy

There is little empirical literature regarding the effectiveness of family therapy in treating adolescent depression, probably due to the lack of attention given by family therapists to diagnostic issues and the underdeveloped state of family therapy outcomes evaluation. Nevertheless, this is an important research area. The association of adolescent depression with dysfunctional family functioning has been documented by several investigators (King et al., 1993; Puig-Antich et al., 1993). Family therapists emphasize clear and potentially operationally defined techniques such as family sculpting, the use of genograms, and paradoxical interventions, which are amenable to outcome evaluation (Rutter, 1982; Coyne et al., 1987). Further, good studies of specific models of family intervention in adult schizophrenia (Kuipers and Babbington, 1988) and adult affective disorders (Clarkin et al., 1988; Epstein et al., 1985) may suggest possible treatment approaches that could be modified for use in adolescent depression.

The possibility of investigating family therapy with depressed adolescents is illustrated by a study examining whether there is "movement" in depression across the family members as predicted by systemic theory. Lantz (1986) demonstrated in an uncontrolled clinical trial that, as expected by systemic theory, reduction in adolescent depression in family therapy was initially associated with an increase in parental depression. This study is of heuristic interest only, but it serves as a model for further, more rigorous investigation. To date, however, the value of any kind of family therapy in treating depressed adolescents remains intuitively appealing but essentially unproven.

Combined Psychotherapy and Pharmacotherapy

In the adult literature there have been a number of studies comparing the combination of psychotherapies and antidepressant medication. Manning and colleagues (1992) reviewed this literature and found it methodologically weak but nevertheless were able to conclude that the combination of the modalities was at least as effective as either modality alone. No such comparisons are yet available for adolescents. This is a significant gap in the present literature.

Conclusions

Although adolescent depression is a relatively common psychiatric illness associated with serious morbidity, its psychologic treatment to date is often based on practitioner preference, unproven etiologic hypotheses, or uncritical applications of methods designed for adult patients. Well-conducted research studies of *all* types of psychologic treatment modalities in adolescent depression are urgently needed and should be a priority in the development of research programs in this age group.

None of the psychotherapy outcome studies with adolescents has yet demonstrated that the participants demonstrated deficits in the specific areas for which they were receiving treatment. Nor have they demonstrated improvement in these target areas as a function of treatment. Such a lack of empirical evidence will prevent the development of interventions that have specific as well as merely general effects. In the area of pathophysiology of adolescent depression, the field has yet to identify which symptoms of depression are actually precursors of the illness and not just correlates or consequences. Study is needed to determine whether cognitive and interpersonal deficits are correlates of depression or are actually stable traits of the depressed individuals. A further refinement would be to determine whether the cognitive or interpersonal deficits vary with developmental changes in the youngsters. Such information is necessary to develop psychotherapies in age groups that are developmentally sensitive.

In general, any of the psychotherapies that have been described above—cognitive, cognitive–behavioral, IPT—when administered by a practitioner who believes in the approach may be equally effective and can be expected to benefit one out of every two patients. Unfortunately, this is strikingly similar to placebo response rates in this population. With the advent of more refined investigations, it is hoped that the outlook will improve so that we can expect larger treatment effects and tailor treatments to the characteristics of the patient: developmental stage, severity of illness, and nature of the patients' psychosocial impairments.

PHASE THREE

The third phase of treating adolescent depression comprises the evaluation of outcome, modification of treatment, and further directions. At the designated time point, some 8–10 weeks following treatment onset, outcome should be evaluated. Ideally, this should take place outside of regularly scheduled therapy sessions and should include parent(s) as well as the patient. Measurement of symptoms and concurrent difficulties (such as social functioning), which were undertaken during phase one, should now be again completed and the pre–post differences in the scales determined. As treatment response is rarely global, one would expect to find that some areas had improved more than others. However, at the very least, significant symptomatic improvement should have occurred. This is usually considered to be demonstrated if the HDRS scale score has decreased by 50% from baseline or is 7 or below. Similarly, a self-report scale such as the BDI should show at least a 50% decrease. It is common to find that associated symptomatology such as school or social functioning may show a slower return to premorbid levels (Birmaher, 1994).

No change or worsening of the initial depression severity scores should lead to reevaluation of the diagnosis or further specialized consultation. Care should be taken to particularly review the evidence for or against a gradually onsetting psychotic illness or persistent substance abuse, which in some cases can be confused with treatment-resistant depressive illness (Gardner and Kutcher, 1993). Where ongoing substance abuse is suspected, appropriate serum and urine assay may be necessary to clarify the clinical picture. In this case, tetrahydrocannabis and dimenhydrinate levels should be included in the assay request.

A partial treatment response should lead to reevaluation of diagnosis and a review of treatments ongoing. Comorbid conditions impacting on outcome should be particularly reviewed and type, dose, and duration of treatment assessed. Compliance, particularly with pharmacotherapy or homework assignments in social–behavioral therapies should be scrutinized. A medication serum level, if available, may help address the issue of compliance with pharmacologic treatment but there is no evidence for "therapeutic levels" of any antidepressant compound in teenagers. If medications have not been part of the initial treatments prescribed, they should be added at this time as there is some evidence that antidepressants are most useful in those teens who have failed to respond to initial psychosocial treatment (Robbins et al., 1989).

In reviewing psychological treatments, particular care should be given to ensuring that a psychologic intervention that fits the needs of the patient and not the bias of the practitioner has been used. This is particularly important if a psychodynamic psychotherapy has been chosen as a primary treatment strategy, as proponents of these approaches usually anticipate an acute treatment course extending into 6 or 8 months or even longer. Unfortunately, although much has been written on specific methods and conceptual frameworks of psychoanalytic treatment for depressed teens (Toolan, 1978; Kestenbaum and Kron, 1987; Bemporod, 1982), there is no scientifically determined evidence to support the view that long-term psychodynamic psychotherapies are effective, either from a symptom relief, functional improvement, or cost–benefit perspective in treating adolescent depression. Clinical improvement of individual cases undergoing such treatment can often be explained by the natural remission of depressive episodes, which can be expected to occur in some cases even in the absence of any therapeutic intervention.

In reviewing pharmacologic treatment, in addition to issues of compliance, care must be taken to ensure that optimal dosage of medication has been obtained. Although published guidelines give minimal/maximal daily dose levels, individual differences in both pharmacokinetics and pharmacodynamic effects are considerable, and dose should be titrated to tolerability, using appropriate ancillary evaluations (i.e., electrocardiogram) as needed. In the face of partial response at optimal dosage, the next strategy should be lithium augmentation or a switch to another antidepressant. If the clinician opts for the latter choice, care must be taken to avoid potentially problematic drug–drug interactions, which can occur even weeks after discontinuance of a particular compound (especially fluoxetine).

In any case, partial response to treatment requires a modification of one or more treatment parameters and the setting of a new time for repeat evaluation. Care must be taken to allow sufficient time for treatment modifications to exert their potentially beneficial effects so as not to abandon an effective therapy prior to its onset of action. A further 8–10 weeks is a reasonable timeline.

Acceptable symptom remission signals the successful outcome of acute treatment and introduces the beginning of the maintenance treatment phase. Although no reports of maintenance therapy of any kind are available for depressed adolescents, the natural history of the disorder, the high rates of relapse, and the experience of treating adult depression (Altamura and Percerdani, 1993) all suggest that long-term treatment will be the rule rather than the exception. At this time the guidelines for long-term treatment found below are derived from clinical experience and will be modified as research data becomes available in the future.

Antidepressant treatment at the dose used to obtain symptomatic relief should be continued for at least 6–8 months to prevent relapse. Psychosocial treatments should be goal directed and tailored to issues of the "here and now" that are of importance to the adolescent patient. Crisis availability should be maintained and the frequency of therapeutic encounters should reflect patient need rather than therapist bias or scheduling ease. Treatments directed toward comorbid states (i.e., anxiety) or associated conditions (i.e., learning disorder) should be continued as needed. Education about the disorder, its natural course, avoidance of street drugs, and responsible use of alcohol should be offered.

After treatment is discontinued (following at least 6–8 symptom-free months and return to premorbid functioning), the patient should be advised that should the condition recur, early intervention with appropriate treatments is indicated to improve outcome and decrease morbidity. A signs and symptoms checklist, which can be kept at home by the patient, is a useful tool for evaluating potential relapse. If the teen is uncertain regarding relapse (i.e., has sustained a significant life stressor such as death of a friend with expected but prolonged dysphoria), a return consultation should be encouraged to allow for a more objective assessment of the teen's mood. In any case, prevention of repeat episodes becomes a lifelong treatment issue for the adolescent with a depressive illness.

ACKNOWLEDGMENTS

Support for S. Kutcher was provided in part by a Senior Research Fellowship from the Ontario Mental Health Foundation. Secretarial support was provided by Ms. Betty Rychlewski.

REFERENCES

Albert N, Beck AT (1975): The incidence of depression in early adolescence: A preliminary study. J Youth Adoles 4:301–307.

Allebeck P, Allgulander C (1990): Suicide among young men: Psychiatric illness, deviant behaviour and substance abuse. Acta Psychiatr Scand 81:565–570.

Altamura AC, Percudani M (1993): The use of antidepressants for long-term treatment of recurrent depression: Rationale, current methodologies, and future directions. J Clin Psychiatry 54(Suppl):29–38.

Ambrosini PJ, Bianchi MD, Metz C, Robinovich H (1994): The safety of desipramine. Reply. J Am Acad Child Adolesc Psychiatry 33:590.

Ambrosini P, Bianchi M, Metz C, Robinovich H (preprint). Response patterns of open nortriptyline pharmacologic therapy in adolescent major depression.

American Psychiatric Association (1990): Task Force on Electroconvulsive Therapy. The practice of ECT: recommendations for treatment, training and privileging. Convulsive Therapy 6(2):85–120.

Angold A, Costello EJ (1992): Co-morbidity in children and adolescents with depression. Child Adolesc Psychiatric Clinics N Am 1(1):31–51.

Angold A (1987): Childhood and adolescent depression. I. Epidemiological and netiological aspects. Br J Psychiatry 152:69–78.

Anthony E (1970): Two contrasting types of adolescent depression and their treatment. J Am Psychoanalytic Assoc 18:841–859.

Arnold EJ (1993): A comparative overview of treatment research methodology: Adult vs. child and adolescent psychopharmacologic vs. psychosocial treatments. Psychopharmacol Bull 29:5–17.

Bakish D, Bradwejn J, Nair N, McClure J, Remick R, Bulger L (1992): A comparison of moclobemide, amitriptyline and placebo in depression: A Canadian multi-centre study. Psychopharmacology 106:S98–S101.

Baldessarini R (1983): "Biomedical Aspects of Depression and Its Treatment." Washington, DC: American Psychiatric Press.

Bastiaens L, Bastiaens DK (1993): A manual of psychiatric medications for teenagers. J Child Adolesc Psychopharmacol 3:M1–M59.

Bastiaens L (1992): The impact of an intensive educational program on knowledge, attitudes and side effects of psychotropic medications among adolescent inpatients. J Child Adolesc Psychopharmacol 2:249–258.

Beasley C Jr, Dornseif BE, Bosanworth JC, Sayler ME (1992): Fluoxetine and suicide: A meta-analysis of controlled trial of treatment for depression. Int J Clin Psychopharm. Suppl 6:33–57.

Beck AT, Ward CH, Mendelson M, Mock JE, Erbaugh JK (1961): An inventory for measuring depression. Arch Gen Psychiatry 4:561–571.

Bemporad JR (1988): Psychodynamic treatment of depressed adolescents. J Clin Psychiatry 49:26–31.

Bemporad JR (1982): Management of childhood depressions: Developmental considerations. Psychosomatics 23:272–279.

Bemporad JR, Wilson A (1978): A developmental approach to depression in childhood and adolescence. J Am Acad Psychoanal 6:325–352.

Berney TP, Kolvin I, Bhate SR, Garside RF, Jeans J, Kay B, Scarth L (1981): School phobia: A therapeutic trial with clomipramine and short term outcome. Br J Psychiatry 138:110–118.

Bernstein GA, Garfinkel BD (1986): School phobia: The overlap of affective and anxiety disorders. J Am Acad Child Adolesc Psychiatry 25:235–244.

Bertagnoli MW, Borchardt CM (1990): A review of ECT for children and adolescents. J Am Acad Child Adolesc Psychiatry 29:302–307.

Biederman J (1991): Sudden death in children treated with a tricyclic antidepressant: A commentary. Biol Ther Psychiatry Newslett 14:1–4.

Birelson P, Hudson I, Buchanan DG, Wolff S (1987): Clinical evaluation of a self-rating scale for depressive disorder in childhood (Depression Self-Rating Scale) J Child Psychology & Psychiatry 28:43–60.

Birmaher B (1994): CBT with suicidal youth. 13th Annual Child and Adolescent Depression Consortium Meeting. Providence, R.I., September 18–20.

Boulos C, Kutcher S (1992): Antidepressant use in adolescents. Bull Canad Acad Child Psychiatry 1(4):52–56.

Boulos C, Kutcher SP, Marton P, Simeon J, Ferguson B, Roberts N (1992a): Response to desipramine treatment in adolescent major depression. Psychopharmacol Bull 27:59–65.

Boulos C, Kutcher S, Gardner D, Young E (1992b): An open naturalistic trial of fluoxetine in adolescents and young adults with treatment resistant major depression J Child Adolesc Psychopharmacology. 2:103–111.

Boyd J, Moscicki E (1986): Firearms and youth suicide. Am J Public Health 76:1240–1242.

Brent DA (1989): Suicide and suicidal behaviour in children and adolescents. Pediatr Rev 9:269–275.

Brent DA, Perper JA, Goldstein CE, Kolko D, Allan M, Allman C, Zelenak J (1988): Risk factors for adolescent suicide—A comparison of adolescent suicide victims with suicidal inpatients. Arch Gen Psychiatry. 45:581–588.

Brent D, Perper J, Allman C (1987): Alcohol, firearms and suicide among youth. J Am Med Assoc 257:3369–3372.

Burke KC, Burke JD Jr, Reigier DA, Ray DS (1990): Age at onset of selected mental disorders in five community populations. Arch Gen Psychiatry 47:511–518.

Burke P, Meyer V, Kocoshis S, Orenstein DM, Chandra R, Nord DJ, Sauer J, Cohen E (1989): Depression and anxiety in pediatric inflammatory bowel disease and cystic fibrosis. J Am Acad Child Adolesc Psychiatry 28:948–951.

Cantwell DP (1985): Depressive disorders in children. Psychiatr Clin N Am 8(4):779–792.

Carlson GA, Kashani JH (1988): Phenomenology of major depression from childhood through adulthood: Analysis of three studies. Am J Psychiatry 145:1222–1224.

Carlson GA, Kashani JH, DeFatima Thomas M, Vaidya A, Daniel AE (1987): Comparison of two structured interviews on a psychiatrically hospitalized population of children. J Am Acad Child Adolesc Psychiatry 26:645–648.

Carlson GA, Garber J (1986): Developmental issues in the classification of depression in children. In Rutter M, Izard CE, Read PP (eds): "Depression in Young People." New York: Guilford.

Carlson GA (1984): A comparison of early and late onset adolescent affective disorder. J Operat Psychiatry. 15:46–49.

Carlson GA Cantwell DP (1980): A survey of depressive symptoms, syndrome and disorder in a child psychiatric population. J Child Psychol Psychiatry 21:19–25.

Chambers WJ, Puig-Antich J, Hirsch M, Paez P, Ambrosini PJ, Tabrizi MA, Davies M (1985): The assessment of affective disorders in children and adolescents by semi-structured interview: Test-retest reliability of the schedule for affective disorders and schizophrenia for school age children, present episode version. Arch Gen Psychiatry 42:696–702.

Chiles JA, Miller ML, Cox GB (1980): Depression in an adolescent delinquent population. Arch Gen Psychiatry 37:1177–1184.

Clark DC, Sommerfeldt L, Schwartz M, et al. (1990): Physical recklessness in adolescence: Trait or by-product of depressive/suicidal states. J Nerv Ment Dis 178:423–433.

Clarke G, Hops H, Lewinsohn P, Andrews J, Seeley J, Williams J (1992): Cognitive-behavioural group treatment of adolescent depression: Prediction of Outcome. Behav Therapy 23:341–354.

Clarke G, Hawkings W, Murphy M, Sheeber L, Lewinsohn P, Seeley J (1993): Poster presented at the Annual Meeting of the American Academy of Child and Adolescent Psychiatry.

Clarkin J, Haas G, Glick I (1988): Inpatient family intervention. In Clarkin J, Haas G, Glick I (eds): "Affective Disorders and the Family. Assessment and Treatment." New York: Guilford Press, pp 134–152.

Coleman J (1980): Friendship and the peer group in adolescence. In Adelson J (ed): "Handbook of Adolescent Psychology." New York, Wiley.

Cooper GL (1988): The safety of fluoxetine: An update. Br J Psychiatry 153.3:77–86.

Coyne J, Kahn J, Gotlib I (1987): Depression. In Jacob T (ed): "Family Interaction and Psychopathology." New York: Plenum.

Crumley FE (1990): Substance abuse and adolescent suicidal behaviour. JAMA 263:3051–3056.

Crumley FE (1979): Adolescent suicide attempts. JAMA 241:2404–2407.

De Montigny C, Cournoyer G, Morissette R, Larglois R, Caille G (1983): Lithium carbonate addition in tricyclic antidepressant resistant unipolar depression. Arch Gen Psychiatry 40:1327–1334.

Department of Health and Human Services, Public Health Service, Agency for Health Care Policy and Research (1993): Depression is a treatable illness: A patient's guide. Pub. No. AHCPR 93-0553.

DiNicola V, Simeon J (1988): Managing adolescent depression: A follow-through study. Poster presentation at the Joint Meeting of the American Academy of Child and Adolescent Psychiatry, Seattle, October.

Elkin I, Shea T, Watkins J, Imber S, Sotsky M, Collins JF, Glass DR, Pilkonis PA, Leber WR, Docherty JP, Fiester SJ, Parloff, MB (1989): National institute of mental health treatment of depression collaborative program. General effectiveness of treatments. Arch Gen Psychiatry. 46:971–982.

Emslie G (1993): Fluoxetine treatment of adolescent depression: A double-blind, placebo-controlled study in progress. Child Depression Consortium Meeting, Toronto, Canada.

Epstein N, Miller I, Keitner G, Bishop D, Kabacoff R (1985): Family dysfunction in bipolar disorder: Description and pilot treatment study. Paper presented at the meeting of the American Psychiatric Association, Dallas.

Faulstich ME, Carey MP, Ruggiero L, Enyart P, Gresham F (1986): Assessment of depression in childhood and adolescence. Am J Psychiatry 143:1024–1027.

Fine S, Gilbert M, Schmidt L, Haley G (1989): Short-term group therapy with depressed adolescent outpatients. Can J Psychiatry. 34:97–102.

Fine S, Forth A, Gilbert M, Haley G (1991): Group therapy for adolescent depressive disorder: A comparison of social skills and therapeutic support. J Am Acad Child Adolesc Psychiatry 30:79–85.

Fink M (1994): ECT: Overview of indications and current thinking about efficacy. Child Depression Consortium, Providence, Rhode Island, Sept. 18–20.

Fleming JE, Atley S, Sanford MN, Steiner M, Streiner D (1993): Phenelzine in the treatment of adolescent major depressive disorder: Preliminary findings. Poster presentation at the Annual Meeting of the American Academy of Child and Adolescent Psychiatry, San Antonio, Texas, October.

Fleming JE, Offord DR (1990): Epidemiology of childhood depressive disorders: A critical review. J Am Acad Child Adolesc Psychiatry 29:571–580.

Fleming JE, Offord DR, Boyle MH (1989): Prevalance of childhood and adolescent depression in the community: Ontario Child Health Study. Br J Psychiatry 155:647–654.

Fontaine R (1992): Novel serotonergic mechanisms and clinical experience with nefazodone. Clin Neuropharm 15(51,pt A):99A.

Friedman RC, Corn R, Hart SW, et al. (1984): Family history of illness in the seriously suicidal adolescent: A life cycle approach. Am J Orthopsychiatry 547:390–397.

Garber J, Kriss MR, Kochin M, Lindholm L (1988): Recurrent depression in adolescents: A follow-up study. J Am Acad Child Adolesc Psychiatry 27:49–54.

Gardner D, Kutcher S. (1993): Dimenhydrinate abuse in adolescents. Can J Psychiatry 38(2):113–116.

Garrison CZ, Addy CL, Jackson KL, McKeown RE, et al. (1991): The CES-D, as a screen for depression and other psychiatric disorders in adolescents. J Am Acad Child Adolesc Psychiatry 30:636–641.

Geller B, Cooper TB, McCombs HG, Graham D, Wells J (1989): Double-blind, placebo-controlled study of nortriptyline in depressed children using a "fixed plasma level" design. Psychopharm Bull 25:101–108.

Geller B, Chestnut EC, Miller D, Price DT, Yates E (1985): Preliminary data on DSM III associated features of major depressive disorder in childhood and adolescents. Am J Psychiatry 142:643–644.

Gershon ES, McKnew D, Cytryn L, et al. (1985): Diagnoses in school-age children of bipolar affective patients and normal controls. J Affective Disord 8:283–291.

Grimsley SR, Jann MW (1992): Paroxetine, sertraline and fluvoxamine: New selective serotonin reuptake inhibitors. Clinical Pharmacy 11:930–957.

Guttmacher LB, Cretella H (1988): Electroconvulsive therapy in one child and three adolescents. J Clin Psychiatry 49:20–23.

Hains A (1992): Comparison of cognitive-behavioural stress management techniques with adolescent boys. J Counsel Develop 70:600–605.

Hamilton M (1960): A rating scale for depression. J Neurol Neurosur Psychiatry 23:56–62.

Hanna G (1994): Assessment of mood disorders. Child Adolesc Psych Clinics N Am 1(1):73–88.

Harrington R (1992): Annotation: The natural history and treatment of child and adolescent affective disorders. J Child Psychol Psychiatry Allied Disciplines 33:1287–1302.

Harrington R, Fudge H, Rutter M (1990): Adult outcomes of childhood and adolescent depression. Arch Gen Psychiatry 47:465–473.

Henninger GR, Charney DS, Sternberg DE (1983): Lithium carbonate augmentation of antidepressant treatment. Arch Gen Psychiatry 40:1336–1342.

Herjanic B, Reich W (1982): Development of a structured psychiatric interview for children: Agreement between child and parent on individual symptoms. J Abnorm Child Psychol 10:307–324.

Herjanic B, Campbell W (1977): Differentiating psychiatrically disturbed children on the basis of a structured interview. J Abnorm Child Psychol 5:127–134.

Hershberg SG, Carlson G, Cantwell DP, Strober M (1982): Anxiety and depressive disorders in psychiatrically disturbed children. J Clin Psychiatry 43:358–361.

Hoberman HM, Garfinkel BD (1989): Completed suicide in children and adolescents. J Am Acad Psychiatry 276:689–695.

Hodges K, Kline J, Stern L, et al. (1982): The development of a child assessment interview for research and clinical use. J Abnorm Child Psychol 10:173–189.

Holmes W, Wagner K (1992): Psychotherapy treatments for depression in children and adolescents. J Psychotherapy Practice Res 1:313–323.

Jain U, Birmaher B, Garcia M, Al-Shabbour M, Ryan N (1992): Fluoxetine in children and adolescents with mood disorders: A chart review of efficacy and adverse effects. J Child Adolesc Psychopharmacology 4:259–261.

Jastak S, Wilkinson GS (1984): "Wide Range Achievement Test—Revised." Wilmington, DE: Jastak Associates.

Jensen PS, Ryan ND, Prien R (1992): Psychopharmacology of child and adolescent major depression: Present status and future directions. J Child Adolesc Psychopharmacology 2:31–48.

Joffe RT, Levitt AJ, MacDonald C, Singer W (1993): A placebo-controlled comparison of lithium and triiodothyronine augmentation of tricyclic antidepressants in unipolar refractory depression. Arch Gen Psychiatry 50:387–393.

Kandel DB, Davies M (1982): Epidemiology of depressive mood in adolescents. Arch Gen Psychiatry 39:1205–1212.

Kasdin AE (1990): Child Depression. J Child Psychol Psychiatry 31:121–160.

Kasdin A (1986): The evaluation of psychotherapy: Research design and methodology. In Garfield S, Bergin A (eds): "Handbook of Psychotherapy and Behaviour Change: An Empirical Analysis." New York: Wiley.

Kashani JH, Orvaschel H, Rosenberg TK, et al. (1989): Psychopathology in a community sample of children and adolescents: A developmental perspective. J Am Acad Child Adolesc Psychiatry 28:701–706.

Kashani JH, Carlson GA, Beck NC, Hoeper EW, Corcoran CM, McAllister JA, Fallahi C, Rosenberg TK, Reid JC (1987): Depression, depressive symptoms and depressed mood among a community sample of adolescents. Am J Psychiatry 144:931–934.

Kashani JH, Hakami N (1982a): Depression in children and adolescent with malignancy. Can J Psychiatry 27:474–477.

Kashani JH, Lababidi Z, Jones RS (1982b): Depression in children and adolescents with cardiovascular symptomatology: The significance of chest pain. J Am Acad Child Psychiatry. 21:187–189.

Kashani JH, Barbero GJ, Bolande FD (1981): Depression in hospitalized pediatric patients. J Am Acad Child Psychiatry 20:123–134.

Keating D (1980): Thinking processes in adolescence. In Alderson J (ed): "Handbook of Adolescent Psychology." New York: Wiley.

Keller M, Lavori P, Beardslee W, Wunder J, Ryan N (1991): Depression in children and adolescents: New data on "undertreatment" and a literature review on the efficacy of available treatments. J Affective Disorders 21:163–171.

Kendel PC, Cantwell DP, Kazdin AE (1989): Depression in children and adolescents: Assessment issues and recommendations. Cognitive Therapy Res 13:109–146.

Kestenbaum CJ, Kron L. (1987): Psychoanalytic intervention with children and adolescents with affective disorders: A combined treatment approach. J Am Acad Psychonal 15:153–174.

King C, Segal H, Naylor M, Evans T (1993): Family functioning and suicidal behaviour in adolescent inpatients with mood disorders. J Am Acad Child Adolesc Psychiatry 32:1198–1206.

Klerman G, DiMascio A, Weissman M, Prusoff B, Paykel E (1974): Treatment of depression by drugs and psychotherapy. Am J Psychiatry 131:186–191.

Klerman G, Weissman M, Rounsaville B, Chevon E (1984): "Interpersonal Psychotherapy of Depression." New York: Wiley.

Kolvin I, Berney TP, Bhate SR (1984): Classification and diagnosis of depression in school phobia. Br J Psychiatry 145:347–357.

Kramer AD, Feigerine RJ (1981): Clinical effects of amitriptyline in adolescent depression. A pilot study. J Am Acad Child Adolesc Psychiatry 20:636–644.

Kuipers L, Babbington P (1988): Expressed emotion research in schizophrenia: Theoretical and clinical implications. Psychol Med 18:893–910.

Kutcher S, Robertson H. (1994): ECT treatment in bipolar adolescents: A review of the Sunnybrook Experience. Child Depression consortium. Providence, RI. September 18–20.

Kutcher S, Boulos C, Ward B, Narton P, Simeon J, Ferguson B, Szalai J, Katic M, Roberts N, Dubois C (1994): Response to desipramine treatment in adolescent depression: A fixed dose, placebo controlled trial. J Am Acad Child Adolesc Psychiatry 33:686–694.

Kutcher S, Marton P, Boulos C (1993): Adolescent depression—Update and review. In Cappeliez P, Flynn R (eds): "Depression and the Social Environment: Research and Intervention with Neglected Populations," Vol. 3. Montreal: McGill-Queen's University Press. pp 73–92.

Kutcher S, Marton P (1991): Affective disorders in first degree relatives of adolescent onset bipolars, unipolars and normal controls. J Am Acad Child Adolesc Psychiatry 30:75–78.

Kutcher S, Marton P (1990): Adolescent depression: A treatment review. In J. Simeon and B. Ferguson (eds). Advances in the Treatment of Child Psychiatry Disorders. New York: Plenum Press.

Kutcher S, Marton P (1989a): Parameters of adolescent depression: A review. Psych Clinics N Am 12:895–918.

Kutcher S, Marton P (1989b): The utility of the Beck Depression Inventory with psychiatrically disturbed adolescent outpatients. Can J Psych 30:107–109.

Kutcher S, Marton P, Korenblum M (1989): Relationship between psychiatric illness and conduct disorder in adolescents. Can J Psych 34:526–530.

Kutcher S, Yanchyshyn G, Cohen C (1985): Diagnosing affective disorders in adolescents: The use of the Schedule for Affective Disorders and Schizophrenia. Can J Psych 30:605–608.

Lam RW, Kripke DF, Gillin JC (1989): Phototherapy for depressive disorders: A review. Can J Psych 34:140–147.

Lantz J (1986): Depression movement in family therapy with depressed adolescents. Child Adoles Social Work 3:123–128.

Levitt AJ, Joffe RT, Kennedy SH (1991): Bright light augmentation in antidepressant nonresponders. J Clin Psychiatry 52:336–337.

Levy JC, Denkin EY. (1989): Suicidality, depression and substance abuse in adolescence. Am J Psychiatry 146:1462–1469.

Lewisohn P, Clarke G, Hops H, Andrews J (1990): Cognitive-behavioural treatment for depressed adolescents. Behav Therapy 21:385–401.

Malmquist C. (1971): Depressions in childhood and adolescence. N Engl J Med 284:887–892.

Manning D, Markowitz J, Frances A (1992): A review of combined psychotherapy and pharmacotherapy in the treatment of depression. J Psychotherapy Practice Res 1:103–116.

Marton P, Maharaj S (1993): Family factors in adolescent unipolar depression. Can J Psych 30(6):373–382.

Marton P, Churchard M, Kutcher S, Korenblum M (1991): The diagnostic utility of the Beck Depression Inventory with depressed adolescent outpatients and inpatients. Can J Psych 36:428–431.

McCauley E, Mitchell J, Burke P, Myers LC, Calderon R, Schloredt B (1988): Clinical course of depression in young people: A three year prospective study. Abstract, (54). Am Acad Child Adolescent Psychiatry Annual Meeting, Seattle.

McGee R, Feehan M, Williams S, Partridge F, Silva P, Kelly J (1990): DMS-III disorders in a large sample of adolescents. J Am Acad Child Adolesc Psychiatry 29:611–619.

Moise F (1994): ECT in adolescents—the SUNY Stony Brook Experience. Child Depression Consortium, Providence, RI, September 18–20.

Molick R, Pinkston E (1982): Using behavioural analyses to develop adaptive social behaviour in a depressed adolescent girl. In E. Pinkston, J. Levitt, G. Green, et al. (eds): "Effective Social Work Practice." San Francisco: Jossey-Bass.

Moreau D, Mufson L, Weissman M, Klerman G (1991): Interpersonal psychotherapy for adolescent depression: Description of modification and preliminary application. J Am Acad Child Adolesc Psychiatry 30:642–651.

Mufson L (1994): Interpersonal Therapy—Adolescence. Presented at the 13th Annual Child and Adolescent Depression Consortium Meeting, Providence, Rhode Island, Sept. 18–20.

Munir K, Biederman J, Knee D (1987): Psychiatry comorbidity in patients with attention deficit disorder: A controlled study. J Am Acad Child Adolesc Psychiatry 26:844–848.

Myers JK, Weissman MM, Tischler GL, et al. (1984): Six month prevalance of psychiatric disorders in three communities, 1980 to 1982. Arch Gen Psych 41:959–967.

Nair NPV, Ahmed SK, Ng Ying Kin NMK (1993): Biochemistry and pharmacology of reversible inhibitors of MAO-A agents: Focus on moclobemide. J Psychiatr Neurosci 18:214–225.

Nelson JC, Mazure C, Jatlow PI (1994): Characteristics of desipramine-refractory depression. J Clin Psychiatry 55:12–19.

Orvaschel H, Puig-Antich J. (1987): Schedule for Affective Disorder and Schizophrenia for School-Age Children. Epidemiologic version (K-SADS-E), version 4. Western Psychiatric Institute and Clinic, Pittsburgh, PA.

Orvaschel H. (1985): Psychiatric interviews suitable for use in research with children and adolescents. Psychopharmacol Bull 21:737–745.

Papatheodorou G, Kutcher S (in press): Light therapy in the treatment of adolescent onset bipolar depression. J Psych Neurosci.

Pearce J (1977): Depressive disorder in childhood. J Child Psychol Psychiatry 18:79–82.

Pearlman C (1991): Electroconvulsive therapy: Current concepts. General Hospital Psychiatry 13:128–137.

Petersen A, Compas B, Brooks-Gunn J, Stemmler M, Ey S, Grant K (1993): Depression in adolescence. Am Psychol 48:155–168.

Petti TA (1985): Scales of potential use in the psychopharmacologic treatment of depressed children and adolescents. Psychopharmacol Bull 21:951–955.

Petti TA (1978): Depression in hospitalized child psychiatry patients: Approaches to measuring depression. J Am Acad Child Adolesc Psychiatry 17:49–59.

Popper CW, Elliott GR (1990): Sudden death and tricyclic antidepressants: Clinical considerations for children. J Child Adol Psychopharmacol 1:125–132.

Puig-Antich J, Kaufman J, Ryan ND, Williamson DE, Dahl RE, Lukens E, Todak G, Ambrosini P, Robinovich H, Nelson B (1993): The psychosocial functioning and family environment of depressed adolescents. J Am Acad Child Adolesc Psychiatry 32(2):244–253.

Puig-Antich J, Rabinovitch H (1986): Relationship between affective and anxiety disorders in childhood. In Gittleman R (ed): "Anxiety Disorders of Childhood." New York: Guilford.

Puig-Antich J (1982): Major depression and conduct disorder in prepuberty. J Am Acad Child Psychiatry 21:118–128.

Rabkin JG, Klein DF (1987): The clinical measurement of depressive disorders. In Marsella AJ, Hirschfeld RMA, Katz MN (eds): "The Measurement of Depression." New York: Guilford Press, pp 30–83.

Reynolds WM, Coats KI (1986): A comparison of cognitive-behaviour therapy and relaxation training for the treatment of depression in adolescents. J Consult Clin Psychol 54:653–660.

Rickels K, Amsterdam J, Clary C, Puzzuoli G, Schweizer E (1991): Buspirone in major depression: A controlled study. J Clin Psychiatry 52:34–38.

Riddle MA, Geller B, Ryan N (1994): Letter to Editor. J Am Acad Child Adolesc Psychiatry 33:589–590.

Robbins DR, Alessi NE, Colfer MV (1989): Treatment of adolescents with major depression: Implications of the DST and the melancholic clinical subtype. J Affective Disorders 17:99–104.

Robinson L, Berman J, Neimeyer R (1990): Psychotherapy for the treatment of depression: A comprehensive review of controlled outcome research. Psychol Bull 108:30–44.

Rosenberg DR, Johnson K, Sahl R (1992): Evolving mania in an adolescent with low-dose fluoxetine. J Child Adolesc Psychopharmacol 2:299–306.

Roy A (1983): Family history of suicide. Arch Gen Psychiatry 40:971–974.

Rutter M (1982): Family and social influences: Meanings, mechanisms and implications. In Nichol A (ed): "Practical Lessons from Longitudinal Studies." Chicester: Wiley.

Ryan ND, Meyer V, Dachille S, Mazzie D, Puig-Antich J (1988a): Lithium augmentation in TCA-refractory depression in adolescents. J Am Acad Child Adolesc Psychiatry 27:371–376.

Ryan ND, Puig-Antich J, Rabinovich H, Fried J, Ambrosini P, Meyer V, Torres D, Dachille S, Mazzie D (1988b): MAOI's in adolescent major depression unresponsive to tricyclic antidepressants. J Am Acad Child Adolesc Psychiatry 27:755–758.

Ryan ND, Puig-Antich J, Ambrosini P, Rabinovich H, Robinson D, Nelson B, Tyengar S, Twomey J (1987): The clinical picture of major depression in children and adolescents. Arch Gen Psychiatry 44(10):854–861.

Ryan ND (1992): The pharmacologic treatment of child and adolescent depression. Psychiatry Clinics N Am 15(1):29–40.

Ryan N, Puig-Antich J (1986): Affective illness in adolescence. In Francis A, Hales R (eds): "American Psychiatry Association Annual Review," Volume 5. Washington DC: American Psychiatric Press.

Schloss P, Schloss C, Harris L (1984): A multiple baseline analysis of an interpersonal skills training program for depressed youth. Behav Disorders 9:182–188.

Schneckloth TD, Rummans TA, Logan KM (1993): Electroconvulsive therapy in adolescents. Convulsive Therapy 9(3):158–166.

Schweizer E, Clary C, Weise C, et al. (1992): A placebo-controlled trial of nefazodone versus imipramine for treatment of major depression. ACNP Dec. 14–18.

Shaffer D (1984): Notes on psychotherapy research among children and adolescents. J Am Acad Child Adolesc Psychiatry 23:552–561.

Shaffer D, Garland A, Gould M, Fisher P, Trautman P (1988): Preventing teenage suicide. A critical review. J Am Acad Child Adolesc Psychiatry 27:675–687.

Shafii M, Steltz-Lenarsky J, McCue Derrick A, et al. (1988): Co-morbidity of mental disorders in the post mortem diagnosis of completed suicide in children and adolescents. J Affective Disord 15:227–233.

Shafii M, Carrigen S, Whittinghill JR, Derrick A (1985): Psychological autopsy of completed suicide in children and adolescents. Am J Psychiatry 142:1061–1064.

Shea M, Elkin I, Hirschfeld R (1988): Psychotherapeutic treatment of depression. In Francis A, Hales R (eds): "Review of Psychiatry," Vol. 7. Washington, DC: Am Psych Press.

Sigafoos AD, Feinstein CB, Damond M, Reiss D (1988): The measurement of behavioral autonomy in adolescence: The autonomous functioning checklist. Adolesc Psychiatry 15:432–462.

Simeon JG, Ferguson HB, DiNicola VF, Coppiag W (1990): Adolescent depression: A placebo-controlled fluoxetine treatment study and follow-up. Progress Neuropsychopharm Biolog Psych 14:791–795.

Skinner H (1987): Self-report instrument for family assessment. In T Jacob (ed): "Family Interaction and Psychopathology." New York: Plenum Publishing, pp 427–452.

Stokes PE (1993): Fluoxetine: A five year review. Clin Therap 15:216–243.

Strauss CC, Last CC, Herzen M, Kazdin AE (1988): Association between anxiety and depression in children and adolescents with anxiety disorders. J Abnorm Child Psychol 16:57–68.

Strober M (1994): ECT in adolescents: The UCLA experience. Child Depression Consortium, Providence, RI, September 18–20.

Strober M, Freeman R, Rigali J, Schmidt S, Diamond R (1992): The pharmacotherapy of depressive illness in adolescence. II. Effects of lithium augmentation in nonresponders to imipramine. J Am Acad Child Adolesc Psychiatry. 31:16–20.

Strober M. (1992): The pharmacotherapy of depressive illness in adolescence. III. Diagnostic and conceptual issues in the study of tricyclic antidepressants. J Child Adolesc Psychopharm 2:23–29.

Strober M, Freeman R, Rigal J (1990): The pharmacotherapy of depressive illness in adolescence. Psychopharmacol Bull 26:80–84.

Strober M (1989): Effects of imipramine, lithium and fluoxetine in the treatment of adolescent major depression. N.I.M.H., New Clinical Drug Evaluation Unit (NCDEU) Annual Meeting, Key Biscayne, Florida, June 4–6.

Strober M, Green J, Carlson G (1981): Utility of the Beck Depression Inventory with psychiatrically hospitalized adolescents. J Consult Clin Psychol. 49:482–483.

Teicher MH, Glod C, Cole JO (1990): Emergence of intense suicidal preoccupation during fluoxetine treatment. Am J Psychiatry 147:207–210.

Teri L (1982): The use of the Beck Depression Inventory with adolescents. J Abnorm Child Psychol 10:277–284.

Toolan JM (1978): Therapy of depressed and suicidal children. Am J Psychotherapy 32:243–251.

Trautmann P, Rotheram-Borus MJ (1988): Cognitive therapy with children and adolescents. In Frances A, Hales R (eds): "Review of Psychiatry," vol. 7. Washington, DC: American Psychiatric Press.

Verhulst FC, Berden GF, Sanders-Wondstra JAR (1985): Mental health in Dutch children. II. The prevalence of psychiatric disorder and relationship between measures. Acta Psychiatr Scand 72(Suppl. 324):1–45.

Weiss M (1993): Fluoxetine treatment of adolescent depression. Child Depression Consortium Meeting, Toronto, Canada. Sept. 16–18.

Weissman MM, Orvaschel H, Padin N. (1980): Children's symptoms and social functioning self-report scales. J Nerv Ment Dis 168:736–740.

Weisz J, Rudolph K, Granger D, Sweeney L (1992): Cognition, competence and coping in child and adolescent depression: Research findings, developmental concerns, therapeutic implications. Develop Psychopath 4:627–653.

Welner Z, Reich W, Herjanic B, Jung KG (1987): Reliability, validity and parent-child agreement studies of the Diagnostic Interview for Children and Adolescents (DICA). J Am Acad Child Adolesc Psychiatry 26:649–653.

Werry JS (1994): Letter to Editor. J Am Acad Child Adolesc Psychiatry 33:588–589.

Wilkes TCR, Belsher G, Rush AJ, Frank E, Beck AT, Brent G, Emslie GJ, Lerner MS, Nowels A, Weinberg WA (1994): Cognitive therapy for depressed adolescents. New York: Guilford Press.

Wilkes T, Rush J (1988): Adaptations of cognitive therapy for depressed adolescents. J Am Acad Child Adolesc Psychiatry 27:381–386.

CHAPTER 7

Clinical Features and Pathogenesis of Child and Adolescent Mania

GABRIELLE A. CARLSON

Department of Psychiatry and Behavioral Science, State University of New York at Stony Brook, Stony Brook, NY 11974-8790

WHAT IS UNIQUE TO YOUTH

The recent interest in bipolar disorder in youth accrues from acknowledgment that the disorder begins in youth and young adulthood (Goodwin and Jamison, 1990; Lish et al., 1994), that there is a familial-genetic component that presupposes the possible existence of clinical markers of risk status (Strober, 1992), that age of onset of mood disorders seems to be declining (Burke et al., 1991), and that there are psychopharmacological interventions that might control or at least modify the disorder (Goodwin and Jamison, 1990). Although the full-fledged, classically defined disorder is uncommon prior to adolesence, there are a number of case reports (see Carlson, 1983, for review: Poznanski et al., 1984; Tomasson and Kuperman, 1990) as well as discussions about reasons for misdiagnosis in this age group (Casat, 1982; Weller et al., 1986) attesting to its existence. One concludes from these reports that the major diagnostic issues in this age group have to do with distinguishing manic behavior from the more common externalizing disorders (attention-deficit hyperactivity disorder and its fellow travelers, oppositional defiant disorder and conduct disorder), and the observation that early episodes of the disorder may not be clearly affective in nature. For instance, the point at which character traits in children are, in fact, "soft" bipolar signs that may be predictive of future frank bipolar I disorder (Akiskal, 1995; Carlson, 1995) or are behavioral variants without specific diagnostic significance needs more research.

The specific criteria overlap between attention-deficit hyperactivity disorder (ADHD) and oppositional conduct disorder (ODD) and mania/hypomania is considerable. If the chief distinction between hypomania and mania is level of impairment, then ADHD/ODD children are *manic* rather than *hypomanic* because they are, by definition, seriously impaired.

Even symptoms "unique" to mania (decreased need for sleep and poor judgment and impulsivity that go along with "excessive involvement in activities with high

Mood Disorders Across the Life Span, Edited by Shulman, Tohen, and Kutcher
ISBN 0-471-10477-9   © 1996 Wiley-Liss, Inc.

potential for painful consequences," mood lability) are associated symptoms of ADHD (see Table 1). The distinction between the silly, intrusive, "class clown" behavior of ADHD children and euphoria is not always easy to make. This leaves racing thoughts/flight of ideas and true grandiosity as the most distinguishing features. We have discussed elsewhere (Carlson, 1990) the boundary problems between externalizing disorders and mania. The question is not whether children in general with externalizing disorder have *masked bipolar disorder*. There is no indication from genetic and follow-up studies to suggest they do. What needs clarification is whether a subpopulation (e.g., those at genetic risk) have a mood disorder that looks like ADHD or has co-occurring ADHD.

The major feature that should distinguish mania from the externalizing disorders is that mania is supposed to be episodic since the symptoms represent a change from previous behavior. If a manic episode is superimposed on prior psychopathology, especially symptoms and behaviors that include dysphoric symptoms, it will be more difficult to determine confidently if the acceleration in symptoms represents the onset of an exacerbation in difficulties prompted by the natural history of the other disorder or supervening environmental circumstances, or if it represents an autonomous, episodic disorder (e.g., Jemerin et al., 1988; Carlson, 1993).

Peripubertally, manic and depressive episodes become somewhat easier to distinguish, although there is still considerable inaccuracy in making the diagnosis. The diagnostic complications in this age group merge with a different set of comorbidities, that is, drug and alcohol abuse, and with the fact that serious psychosis begins to increase in frequency and poses a different type of confusion.

IMPLICATIONS OF CRITERIA CHANGES IN DSM NOSOLOGY (see Table 2)

It is perhaps worth examining at this point how the "minor adjustments" in criteria over the past 15 years have shaped and will continue to shape who we identify as having bipolar disorder. While the *symptom* criteria have changed little since Kraepelin (1921) described them, and over the past iterations of the *Diagnostic and Statistical Manual* (DSM) (American Psychiatric Association, 1980; 1987; 1994) (only hyperactivity was modified between DSM III and subsequent renditions to read "increase in

TABLE 1   Comparison of DSM-IV Mania and ADHD/ODD Criteria

Mania	ODD and ADHD
Elevated, expansive mood	Often loses temper; touchy, easily annoyed
Irritable mood	Often runs about; often leaves seat; often on the go; has difficulty awaiting turn
Increase in goal-directed activity or psychomotor agitation	Often talks excessively
More talkative than usual; pressured speech	Is often distracted by extraneous stimuli
Distractibility	
Excessive involvement in activities with high potential for painful consequences	
Decreased need for sleep	
Inflated self-esteem	
Flight of ideas/racing thoughts	

goal directed activity or psychomotor agitation"), definition of an *episode* has changed. The *distinct period* was defined in DSM-III as requiring a week or be serious enough to require hospitalization. In DSM-III-R the duration criterion was dropped, only to be re-adopted in DSM-IV. Recognition of the level of psychosis has changed as well so that *mood incongruent* features were disallowed in DSM-III but were subsequently allowed in DSM-III-R. In DSM-IV, there are fifth-digit specifiers for the level and mood congruence of psychotic features. There has been, therefore, a gradual recognition of how severe a manic episode can be. Formal acknowledgement of a "mixed" episode was introduced in DSM-III-R and maintained with DSM-IV. In this case, the distinct period fits a manic episode; the syndromic features must include full criteria for mania and depression. Distinguishing a youngster with severe ADHD with depressive symptoms or disorder from someone with a mixed episode will be impossible if the criterion of episode is ignored, if the onset of the mixed episode is very early, and if the course is chronic (Wozniak et al., 1995).

Hypomania has evolved considerably over the various DSMs. An episode of hypomania did not exist in DSM-III. Hypomania was seen with dysthymia as being part of cyclothymia. The descriptors emphasized both a milder form of mania and a somewhat more euphoric ("inappropriate laughing, punning or joking; extreme gregariousness; overoptimism"), cognitive (sharpened thinking), and productive (increased productivity) form. In DSM-III-R, both dysthymia and hypomania were redesigned to be the same as a major depressive disorder (MDD) and mania, distinguished only by course and, possibly, severity. Without the previous descriptors, the approximation of childhood externalizing disorders and mania/hypomania became more difficult to distinguish. No duration criteria were specified in DSM-III-R; in DSM-IV, a 4-day duration, observable by others, during which "an unequivocal change in functioning uncharacteristic of the person when not symptomatic" is demanded. This, of course is perhaps easy enough to recognize if the premorbid and intermorbid level of functioning is either completely normal or clearly depressed. Superimposed on other psychopathology, it again becomes more difficult to distinguish.

In DSM-III-R, cyclothymia was defined as the "presence of numerous hypomanic *episodes*," and numerous periods "with depressed mood or loss of interest or pleasure that did not meet criterion A of Major Depressive Episode," that is, not even a full dysthymic syndrome was required. In DSM-IV, cyclothymia no longer consists of hypomanic episodes and depressive symptoms but rather *hypomanic symptoms* (perhaps only elevated, expansive, or irritable mood without any particular duration or other symptoms) and *depressive symptoms* (perhaps only sad or irritable mood without duration or other symptoms). At that rate, it will be easy to reclassify all sorts of children with cyclothymia since "expansive, irritable, or elated mood" and "depressed, irritable, sad mood" for no particular duration is much more common (Carlson and Kashani, 1988). Whether the family studies that showed relationships between cyclothymia and bipolar disorder in times past will hold with these criteria changes remains to be seen.

While there is no evidence that unequivocal cases of uncomplicated mania and bipolar disorder as they occur in youth, or even mentally retarded (and thus cognitively immature) adults, are phenomenologically different from adult cases (Carlson, 1979, 1994), there may be some distinctions worth noting. For instance, longitudinal studies of adolescent onset bipolar cohorts have determined that depression is commonly found as the first mood disturbance and about 70% of bipolar teens experience a major depressive episode prior to the first manic episode (Kutcher and Robertson, 1994).

TABLE 2 Comparisons of DSM-III, DSM-III-R and DSM-IV—Mania and Hypomania

	Mania	
DSM-III	DSM-III-R	DSM-IV
Distinct period of predominantly elevated, expansive or irritable mood, prominent and persistent for at least a week (or hosp)	Distinct period of abnormally + persistently elevated, expansive or irritable mood Of sufficient severity to cause marked impairment	Mood predominantly elevated, expansive, irritable or suspicious—definitely abnormal for person; mood prominent, sustained for at least a week (less if hosp.)
Three of following symptoms (4 if mood irritable)	Same	Same
Increase in activity (either socially, at work or sexually) or physical restlessness	Increase in goal-directed activity or psychomotor agitation	Same
More talkative than usual or pressure to keep talking	Same	Same
Flight of ideas; racing thoughts	Same	Same
Less need for sleep	Same	Same
Inflated self-esteem (grandiosity which may be delusional)	Same	Same
Distractibility—attention too easily drawn to irrelevant details	Same	Difficulty concentrating or distractibility
Excess involvement in activities with high potential for painful consequences, which are unrecognized (spending, hypersexuality, reckless driving)	Same	Behavior that is foolhardy or reckless and whose risks the subject does not recognize
		Marked sexual energy or sexual indiscretions
No mood incongruent psychosis or bizarre behavior	Mood incongruent psychotic features allowed	No schizophrenia or schizoaffective disorder

	Hypomania	
Period of elevated, expansive, or irritable mood + 3 of following:	Period of elevated, expansive, or irritable mood + 3 of following:	Definitely abnormal elevated or irritable mood lasting more than 2 days on end:
Less need for sleep	Decreased need for sleep	Same criteria as mania
More energy than usual	Increase in goal-directed activity or psychomotor agitation	May lead to interference with work or social activity, but not to the extent that social rejection or severe work disruption occurs
Inflated self-esteem	Inflated self-esteem	Episode associated with unequivocal change in functioning uncharacteristic of person when not symptomatic
Increased productivity	Distractibility	Observable by others
Sharpened thinking	Excess involvement in activities with high potential for painful consequences	
Extreme gregariousness	More talkative than usual or pressure to keep talking	
Hypersexuality	Flight of ideas/racing thoughts	
Excess pleasurable activities		
Physical restlessness		
More talkative		
Overoptimism		
Inappropriate laughing or punning or joking		
No psychosis or OBS	No psychosis	No psychosis
	No marked impairment	Not due to effects of a substance or general medical condition

The average age of onset for a first depression was 14, while mania onset was about age 17. Furthermore, Strober et al. (1995) have found that early-onset bipolar disorder is characterized by protracted episodes of depression and mania compared to adult probands even in the presence of optimal treatments. Finally, manic episodes are often of the rapid cycling or mixed type such that clear periodicity is difficult to distinguish.

Without a "gold standard," and with our changing framework of what constitutes mania/hypomania, extrapolation of adult research to children becomes more problematic. In addition, there are a number of limitations that hamper our ability to collect more definitive data on the subject of bipolar disorder in youth. For instance, Bowring and Kovacs (1992) and Carlson (1994) note the following: (1) Because there is symptom overlap with other psychiatric disorders presenting in childhood described earlier, one must be familiar with the whole range of developmental psychopathology, not just disorders that occur in adults. (2) Furthermore, knowledge of "normal" child development is necessary. Adult psychiatrists may thus apply criteria willy-nilly because they do not recognize other psychiatric disorders in children or the developmental appropriateness of certain symptoms. Knowing how much "grandiosity" is part of the normal, egocentric nature and/or imagination of a young child and the degree of difference from a true delusion requires considerable experience. (3) We are limited in our ability to study the disorder because of its low base rate, that is "classical mania" in children is uncommon. Thus, while those working primarily with adults have knowledge deficiencies, clinicians working only with children and young adolescents may not have had adequate exposure to mania and may misidentify it. Although the DSM criteria help to operationalize the clinical picture, they do not begin to substitute for seeing patients with the disorder. Unlike Kraepelin (1921), we did not evolve a clinical picture of juvenile bipolar disorder from hundreds of cases followed longitudinally. On one hand, we may be at risk of needlessly restricting ourselves to criteria that were developed for adults or being unnecessarily conservative. For instance, Anthony and Scott (1960) required, in addition to the recognizable clinical picture, the presence of a positive family history of mania, a premorbid cyclothymic personality, episodes of both depression and mania, and evidence of inpatient treatment with "heavy sedation or ECT." While these criteria are very specific, they are not particularly sensitive. On the other hand, there may be an equal risk to misapplying criteria to a population where the criteria may mean something different than they do in adults (Carlson, 1995).

IS MANIA RARE AND WHY

The relative rarity of youth-onset mania may appear to be in stark contrast to the observation that up to one third of adults state their disorder began in childhood or adolescence (see Goodwin and Jamison, 1990 for review; Lish et al., 1994). However, that conclusion has usually been drawn some years after the disorder has become clear, at which point symptoms are identified with the vision of hindsight. Two studies, one from the Old Order Amish (Blumenthal et al., 1987) and another from McGlashan (1988) report a considerable time lapse from first noticeable symptoms (usually in midadolescence) to first time hospitalized (early to mid-20s). This 5- to 10-year lag time is longer than it is for adult-onset patients suggesting both that *fully symptomatic* bipolar disorder may be less common in youth and the time lag to full symptoms in early-onset patients is longer than for those with later onset (Carlson, 1994). A conclusion drawn by Goodwin and Jamison (1990, p. 160) from a completely different database is that cycle length shortens with later age of onset.

PHENOMENOLOGY

Additional "complications" that are not unique to youth, but seem to be more prominent for that age group, have to do with severity and boundary issues. Identifying an episode of severe psychosis as manic (Carlson et al., 1994) or sorting out bipolar symptomatology from the collection of other comorbid symptoms and disorders that occur at all ages may happen relatively often in youth because "classic" cases seem to be less frequent.

Severity

The phenomenon of misdiagnosing severe, psychotic episodes in youth is worldwide (e.g., Ballenger et al., 1982; Carlson and Strober, 1978; Hassanyeh and Davison, 1980; Joyce, 1984; Rosen et al., 1983; Stanton and Joyce, 1993; Verdoux and Bourgeois, 1993; Werry et al., 1991). In the past, schizophrenia was the most frequent diagnosis made. For instance, Joyce (1984) found that 72% of young manics (onset prior to age 20) versus only 24% of older manics (onset after age 30) were called schizophrenic. Similarly, Werry et al. (1991), who followed up 61 young, psychiatrically hospitalized youth with a variety of "psychoses" found over half of those with bipolar diagnoses at follow-up had initially been given schizophrenia diagnoses.

Although a significant percentage of adolescents with a future bipolar course will present with an acute, severe, psychotic, and psychomotor retarded depression, and will have a family history of bipolar or major depressive disorder (Strober and Carlson, 1982), other presentations occur that still allow for misdiagnosis. In fact, Carlson et al. (1994) reported that bipolar disorder in youth is still underdiagnosed as compared to this disorder in adults. This was demonstrated by the finding that the *research* consensus diagnosis of bipolar disorder at 6-month follow-up (based on strict criteria, structured interview, multiple sources of information) was similar for youth and adults. However, the low sensitivity (0.31) of bipolar diagnoses *made by community clinicians* on the same cases was specific only to 15- to 20-year old subjects. Furthermore, data demonstrated that short-term (between intake and 6 month re-interview) diagnostic stability did not differ because of age. It was not, therefore, the change in symptoms over time that accounted for the difference between research and clinical diagnosis. Interestingly, most of these early onset bipolars (71%) had a more complicated initial presentation. That is, young people admitted with a psychotic mania were more likely to have past or concurrent other psychopathology than adult-onset patients (at least as quantified by academic difficulties, adolescent drug use, and other comorbidity). This may have made the manic presentation less clear. Although bipolar disorder was underdiagnosed in youthful patients admitted to the community and state hospitals, frank schizophrenia was no longer the major misdiagnosis. Rather, a range of DSM-III-R alternatives reflective of various kinds of acute psychosis not otherwise specified [i.e., psychosis (NOS), schizophreniform, brief reactive, etc.] was given. The increased stringency of the schizophrenia criteria partly account for this change. Now, the misdiagnosis problem appears to result from *misinterpreting* symptoms that meet criteria for mania and from the fact that early presentations of bipolar disorder may, in fact, be less obvious.

In addition to the confusing clinical picture presented by acute psychosis, there is some suggestion that "mixed states" may occur more frequently in young people (Himmelhock and Garfinkel, 1986; Ryan and Puig-Antich, 1986). According to McElroy et al. (1992), a mixed state may be broadly defined as mania/hypomania with any depressive symptom, or narrowly defined, as in DSM-III-R and IV as a clear episode distinct from the person's normal functioning with both mania and full syndromic depression. Data from Kutcher's (1994) longitudinal study of bipolar adolescents reveals that 75% of the sample showed either mixed or rapid cycling in the first manic episode with "classic" euphoria being seen in less than 10% of the adolescents. Of further interest is that when the various dimensions of mood are disordered during an episode of adolescent mania, the picture that emerges is one of a disturbance in amplitude, frequency, and cohesion of mood states. Thus, irritability, dysphoria, depression, euphoria, lability, grandiosity, and anger seem to oscillate widely and relatively independently of each other. Successful resolution of the manic episode is characterized not only by a decrease in amplitude and frequency of mood swings, but also in increased coherence of the various mood states.

Case 1

Jessica, a 14-year-old girl, was referred for outpatient evaluation because of increasing depression. A previously good student, she had failed three courses in the second semester of ninth grade. According to her father's history (mother had essentially abandoned father and Jessica 7 years earlier), her progressive social withdrawal and disinterest became especially noticeable at Christmas in that she was not her usual excited self about decorating the house, buying the tree, and going to parties. By spring, Jessica had actually come to her father for help with her depression. She was seen for a while by the school social worker and then referred to the psychiatric clinic. Regarding other parent observations, father was unaware of sleep or appetite changes. He did remark that during the school year, she had more of an "attitude" (i.e., she was irritable) and that her previously neat room had become uncared for and disorganized. With such a background, one would have expected to see a subdued and depressed adolescent.

Jessica presented as a well groomed, pretty girl, physically remarkable only for bright purple lipstick (which father said she always wore). Mental status was compatible with mania rather than depression. Jessica had pressured speech, was overtalkative; her thoughts and speech were so disorganized she virtually could not give any meaningful responses to questions asked of her about her mood, thought process, or other psychiatric symptoms. One culled from her disjointed responses, however, that she felt depressed rather than euphoric. However, her affect was more euphoric than depressed. On the other hand, Jessica's motor behavior was neither agitated, hyperactive, nor depressed. Her manner was not irritable (in fact, her father said subsequently that her attitude had "improved" in recent weeks). Interpersonally, it appeared that she was trying hard to relate and was quite personable. She described her thoughts as blocked rather than racing. She was not up all night. In fact, she went to bed at 8 p.m. (rather early for a teenager). She may have experienced hallucinations (she referred to "voices" in her pressured ramblings but could not clarify this other than to say these were "aspects of her being"). She was not grandiose or delusional in any way. She denied any drug or medication use and there were no signs of organicity. She was oriented, could do serial 3s from 20 and serial 7s to 62 (instead of 72), and realized it was too hard to concentrate.

When his daughter's thought disorder was brought to his attention, Jessica's father indicated that he had noticed "she hadn't been making much sense lately," and dated the onset of that to 2 months earlier. Given that level of observation and reporting, it is difficult to interpret the absence of other history or family history (which was reportedly negative for any psychiatric disorder). As the assessment was initiated over the summer, it was not possible to obtain information from school staff.

Initially, and for the next 2 weeks, Jessica did not meet criteria for anything. Her history and presentation were most compatible with an affective disorder. She may have been presenting with a *mixed state*, that is, she had a thought disorder that was compatible with mania but had no other symptoms of that syndrome. She had recently experienced what sounded like an episode of major depression. Kraepelin (1921) described both "manic stupor" and "depression with flight of ideas" (pp. 106–107). She could have been in the early stages of schizophrenia, before the appearance of negative symptoms or evidence of other psychotic symptoms. There were no other clues to help the diagnosis along possibly because the historians were poor. She received a diagnosis of psychosis NOS. Father refused treatment for his daughter. Subsequently, Jessica became more depressed, withdrawn (refusing to go to school and sitting and staring out her bedroom window all day), suicidal, and paranoid. She was afraid her body was rotting and that she was becoming "The Fly" (i.e., the horror movie subject). She was brought to the emergency room by a friend and hospitalized with a major depressive episode, psychotic subtype, and is at high risk for a future bipolar course.

A systematic, comparative study of a representative sample of patients with a first episode of mania, or psychotic depression followed by mania, in adolescence and adulthood is needed to clarify the question of (1) whether psychotic symptoms occur more frequently in youth, (2) whether other issues specific to adolescence obfuscate what is otherwise a clear picture, or (3) whether early episodes of bipolar disorder, regardless of the age at which they occur, are more atypical and thus more perplexing.

Comorbidity

As was noted earlier, if identifying manic symptoms from a cross-sectional clinical picture of severe psychosis is sometimes difficult, sorting them from their co-occurrence with other nonpsychotic disorders may also be troublesome. Carlson (1983) first noted that children with bipolar disorder identified before age 8 usually had another psychiatric problem as well. Strober et al. (1988) found that 20% of his adolescent-onset patients had preadolescent psychiatric disorder and that these teenagers were more frequently treatment resistant and had very high rates of affective disorder in their first- and second-degree relatives. As with depression, then, other psychiatric disorders seem to co-occur with a high degree of frequency in prepubertal and young-adolescent bipolar patients (Geller et al., 1994; Kovacs and Pollack, 1995; Kutcher et al., 1989, 1990). Carlson has discussed elsewhere (1990) the possible interpretations of behavior disorders that co-exist with bipolar disorder in youth. These include: (1) that complicated mania represents, in its early onset, a particularly virulent form of the disorder; (2) that it may represent a secondary affective disorder with the implication that the prior psychopathology usually confirms greater treatment resistance; (3) that it may represent secondary mania where the primary disorder is of medical/neurological (organic) etiology, which is also more difficult to treat; (4) that the behavior disorders reflect nonspecific effects of growing up in a family with major mental illness (Lee and Gotlib, 1989).

The issue of comorbidity with *childhood disorders* is particularly relevant in adults where bipolar disorder frequently co-exists with substance abuse (see Goodwin and Jamison, 1990, for review), personality disorder (McGlashan, 1983; Akiskal et al., 1983) and anxiety (Savino et al., 1993; Young et al., 1993). The relationship of these findings to studies of complicated bipolar disorder in youth is difficult to address definitively, however. Although most of these reports use structured interviews to make diagnoses, except for mood disorder, none of these instruments enquire about childhood psychopathology. In addition, a condition such as substance abuse requires a considerable lapse of time of drug *use* before criteria for *abuse* or dependence is made. Thus, the temporal relationship of two conditions becomes difficult to disentangle.

Case 2

George is a good example of the aforementioned diagnostic situation. He presented to the psychiatric emergency room at age 9 with a suicide attempt. He had given away his Nintendo game and fish tank and tried to choke himself with his suspenders during school. Interview with the K-SADS (Orvaschel et al., 1982) revealed that he met criteria for major depressive disorder for at least the past month and had probably been dysthymic at least a year earlier. He had multiple, severe psychosocial stressors, including paternal physical abuse and drug abuse, extreme parental discord, a sister recently psychiatrically hospitalized with Tourette syndrome and behavior problems, and change of school. Early history revealed prior criteria met for oppositional defiant disorder since age 4, attention-deficit hyperactivity disorder since age 5 (and treated since with either methylphenidate or pemoline), separation anxiety disorder starting at age 5, and possible phobias also starting at age 5. His disruptive behavior prompted referral to Special Education at age 8. During the first hospitalization, his pressured speech, emotionally labile behavior, insomnia, intrusiveness, silliness, and irritability warranted a diagnosis of mixed mania. He was treated variously with lithium, neuroleptics, methylphenidate, desipramine, and combinations of these. None of these regimens significantly impacted his behavior, and when he was discharged, somewhat less hyperverbal and hyperactive, his depression was better, but his oppositional, explosive behavior was only mildly improved.

George was followed in a day treatment program for the next 1.5 years. Severe family strife continued unabated. Reattempts to control his behavior with lithium and carbamazepine were unsuccessful. By the time of his second psychiatric hospitalization, he had become increasingly physically aggressive, destructive of property, and had begun stealing from home. Lying had been present for years. He thus graduated from oppositional–defiant disorder to conduct disorder. He now met criteria for overanxious disorder and was probably having spontaneous panic attacks (some of his tantrums were described as starting with a terrified look, complaining of shortness of breath, shaking, and palpitations). His attention-deficit symptoms continued as did his pressured, hyperverbal speech, racing thoughts, intense irritability, poor judgement, and severe insomnia. His dysthymia also continued.

His third admission, at age 12, was prompted by physical violence toward his sister. Conduct disorder problems had increased; ADHD and dysthymic symptoms continued. He refused to take responsibility for his behavior, and his projection of blame onto others had almost a paranoid flavor. However, he was no longer found to meet criteria for various anxiety disorders, and his explosive, aggressive behavior was not felt to be manic in origin. He was treated with dexedrine and thorazine, the latter because his mother insisted it was the only thing that helped his aggression.

Between age 12 and 16, he remained in day treatment programs. His medication noncompliance precluded systematic treatment. At age 13, he was caught selling his dexedrine. Alcohol use began at age 14. The fact that he could have periods of time (once as long as 6 weeks) during which his behavior was less explosive and he could be quite charming (or manipulative depending on how one wishes to view this), invariably reinstituted the question of whether he really had a severe episodic affective disorder. During these "better" times, he remained somewhat impulsive, easily agitated and mildly paranoid, aggressive, irritable, cocky, and defiant but was less hyperactive. He was also far behind academically. Group home placement was finally allowed by mother, though he was withdrawn from this within a few months.

Family history was positive for paternal antisocial behavior with violent temper outbursts and severe alcohol abuse, Tourette syndrome, and late-onset paranoia in George's maternal grandmother. Mother, the chief provider of this information, denied psychiatric disorder, but she was felt to be as erratic as her son.

George did not yet meet criteria for drug abuse or alcohol abuse at last contact, though it was clear he was using both. Unlike mood disorders, symptoms for which usually co-occur at the same time, substance abuse/dependence takes time to develop. Like conduct disorder, the behavior accumulates over time. Thus, dating its "onset" at the point at which it is out of control may allow one to establish "caseness," but it is not "onset" from the standpoint of when the problem started.

George also presents with longstanding depressive, anxiety, and attention deficit/hyperactivity symptoms as well as symptoms that meet criteria for mania and highlights the observation that there is a frequent co-occurrence of symptoms of depression, anxiety, and explosive aggression/irritability in patients. In adult studies of major psychopathology one often sees overlap in manic symptoms, externalizing disorders (substance/alcohol abuse being the one studied with axis I directed structured interviews) and anxiety symptoms (see Carlson, 1993, for a similar history in an adult). For instance, Young et al. (1993) describe anxious and nonanxious bipolar disorder (those with anxiety symptoms had more suicidal behavior, alcohol abuse, cyclothymia, and possibly lithium nonresponsiveness). Savino et al. (1993) explored affective psychopathology in 140 outpatients with panic disorder and found comorbidity with mania (2.1%), hypomania (5%), cyclothymia (6.4%), and hyperthymic temperament (34.3%). The relationship between substance/alcohol abuse and bipolar disorder has been amply demonstrated (see Goodwin and Jamison, 1990, pp. 210–226, for review). Specific relevance to youth is noted in a study by Roy et al. (1991). They described a population of 339 patients who met Research Diagnostic Criteria (Spitzer et al., 1978) for alcoholism and found that those with a history of early onset (before age 20) of heavy drinking had significantly higher rates compared to older onset alcoholics of drug abuse (42 vs. 19%), hypomania (9 vs. 3%), bipolar disorder (9 vs. 2%), panic disorder (15 vs. 6%), antisocial behaviors as assessed on the Schedule for Affective Disorders and Schizophrenia—Lifetime version (SADS-L) (Spitzer and Endicott, 1978), and suicide attempts.

In studies of youth, one sees the relationship between anxiety, depression, behavior disorder, and manic symptoms at all levels of clincial interface. For example, in a study of 150 nonreferred 14- to 16-year olds, Carlson and Kashani (1988) found that the 13% of adolescents who endorsed manic symptoms on structured interview (Diagnostic

Interview for Children and Adolescents, Herjanic and Reich, 1982) had significantly higher rates of DSM-III attention-deficit disorder, conduct disorder, depressive disorders, anxiety disorders, and psychoticlike symptoms compared to those without manic symptoms. Also found were higher rates of anxiety and hostility, poor impulse control and lower rates of introversion, and respectfulness. Lewinsohn et al. (1995) confirmed these findings in a much larger study of nonpsychiatrically referred adolescents (n = 1,709) ages 14–18. They also used a different structured interview (Schedule for Affective Disorders and Schizophrenia for Children (K-SADS-E, Orvaschel et al., 1982). They found that the 5.7% of adolescents who had only mood symptoms of mania (i.e., elated, irritable, or expansive mood without meeting other criteria for mania) had significantly higher rates of DSM-III-R separation anxiety, overanxious, panic and obsessive–compulsive disorders, higher rates of ADHD, ODD/CD, higher rates of drug and alcohol use, and eating disorder than teens without these manic symptoms. This wide range of psychopathology was also true for the 1% of subjects who actually met criteria for mania/hypomania. The point is that endorsement on structured interview of elated/irritable/expansive mood seems also to bring endorsements for many other psychiatric disorders. It is worth noting that in both studies, the level of impairment for these youth with manic symptoms was significantly worse than those without; so the symptom is not trivial.

A number of studies have described co-occurring conduct disorder and bipolar disorder (Carlson et al., 1992; Issac, 1991; Kutcher et al., 1989). Prospective studies of depressed children who developed mania/hypomania by mid to late adolescence as elicited on structured interview also demonstrate a relationship. Of the 26 children who developed a manic/hypomanic episode that were gleaned from the original depressed 8- to 13-year olds in her study, Kovacs and Pollack (1995) found a 69% lifetime rate of comorbid conduct disorder. Only 3 of the 26, in fact, had uncomplicated bipolar disorder. Geller et al. (1994) found that 31.7 of 79 children with MDD assessed by K-SADS-E prospectively every 4 months developed a manic/hypomanic episode at follow-up. 68% had a "mixed" episode. Although her latest paper with the expanded sample does not discuss specific rates of anxiety and conduct disorder co-morbidity, 84% of the original sample of 50 had separation anxiety, 18% had conduct disorder (Geller et al., 1994). Only the presence of a loaded family history predicted a bipolar course, but one assumes that anxiety and behavior disorder symptoms were occurring in the youth who "switched." In addition, 74% of the original sample had a family history of alcoholism as well as affective disorder.

In a prospective longitudinal study of offspring at risk for bipolar disorder compared to normal controls, Carlson and Weintraub (1993) found that the bipolar risk offspring had significantly higher rates of attentional and behavioral psychopathology as children, lower adaptive functioning scores as young adults, and higher rates of psychiatric disorders as adults. These subjects were also compared to offspring of parents hospitalized with other psychopathology and differed from these as young adults only in their higher scores on a "bipolarity" rating scale and the fact that the attention and behavior problems in childhood predicted both an affective disorder and other psychopathology (mostly drug/alcohol problems) outcome. In the offspring of the other two groups, childhood behavior/attention problems predicted only other young adult psychopathology. While this might seem to provide a definitive relationship between externalizing disorders and affective disorders in those at risk, the Stony Brook High Risk Study, from which these data were taken, was done at a time (1972–1982) when comorbidity in parents was not measured, psychopathology in the nonhospitalized spouse was not controlled for, and comorbidity in the subjects at risk was not specifically delineated. Thus, a young man with bipolar II disorder and alcohol abuse was coded as having had an affective disorder outcome whereas a subject with alcohol abuse alone was classified as having "other psychopathology."

Wozniak and colleagues (1995) recently reported that 43 of 262 (16%) youths referred to an outpatient psychopharmacology clinic met criteria for prepubertal mania based on the K-SADS-E (Orvaschel et al., 1982). Of these youngsters, 98% met criteria for ADHD, 88% for oppositional–defiant disorder, 86% for major depressive disorder, 56% had multiple anxiety disorders, 37% had conduct disorder, and 16% had psychotic symptoms. These were obviously very seriously disturbed youths whose psychopathology was felt to be far worse than a comparison group of children with ADHD alone. Interestingly, only 16% were found to have an episodic course and 2% a biphasic course. In other words, most met criteria for a manic syndrome but lacked the "A" criterion for episode.

To explore the relationship, if any, between manic symptoms, depression, anxiety symptoms and behavior problems in inpatients, I compared a hospitalized sample of 277 youths aged 5–12 years on whom we have gathered K-SADS-E diagnoses, and ratings of mania [Mania Rating Scale (MRS); Young et al., 1978], depression [Children's Depression Rating Scale (CDRS-R)-Revised, Poznanski et al., 1984], and self-rated measures of depression [Children's Depression Inventory; Kovacs, 1981]. Fifty-four children with high scores on the MRS (scores between 22 and 45) were compared with those with MRS scores between 1 and 5. Because the ratings of depression and mania are completed by the child's primary nurse after the first 7–10 days of admission blind to diagnosis, they are cross-sectional measures of a manic syndrome rather than measures of actual diagnosis, which requires longitudinal history as well as observation. Results are seen in Table 3.

These data suggest that in a very disturbed population of children with maniclike symptoms, high rates of internalizing and externalizing psychopathology occur. Like Wozniak's sample, they were the most disturbed children on the inpatient unit, frequently requiring seclusion and restraint for high levels of aggression. Not surprisingly, there are more cases of pure anxiety/depression in the low MRS group. While depression (CDRS-R) scores are higher in the high MRS group, this is mostly because of

TABLE 3 Mania Rating Scale Scores and Accompanying Diagnoses

Item	MRS Scores 22–45	MRS Scores 1–5	Significance
n	54	56	
Diagnostic group: behavior disorder only	44% (24)	19.6% (11)	$X^2 = 7.79$
Comorbid affective/ behavior disorder	24% (13)	25% (14)	X^2 ns
Affective disorder of anxiety/affective disorder only	2% (1)	21% (12)	$X^2 = 10.1$
Psychosis or pervasive developmental disorder	25% (14)	8.9% (5)	$X^2 = 8.38$
CDRS score (mean)	41.2	37.2	$t = 1.2, p = 0.03$
CDI score (mean)	19.9	15.8	$t = 2.1, p = 0.02$

high ratings of irritability. Children feel depressed and anxious in both groups. One again concludes that the presence of elated or irritable mood carries with it a high likelihood of serious psychopathology that crosses a variety of diagnostic domains. (Although 12 children have, in fact, met criteria for bipolar disorder, they have been found at all levels on the MRS, depending on what phase of their disorder they were in at hospitalization).

CONCEPT OF BIPOLAR SPECTRUM

One way to explain the overlap of affective and other psychopathology is to conceive of any disorder in which symptoms of mania occur as part of a *bipolar spectrum.* Others have described in adults (e.g., Blacker and Tsuang, 1992), and I have noted elsewhere (Carlson, 1990), there are no clear demarcations between emotional lability, hyperthymic temperament (Akiskal et al., 1979), cyclothymia, bipolar II disorder, bipolar I disorder, and schizoaffective disorder. The spectrum concept has certainly existed to explain childhood variants for a number of years (Davis, 1979; Kestenbaum, 1979). It is relevant that a similar dialectic has transpired for schizophrenia. However, over the past 70 years, the definition of schizophrenia has *narrowed* in an effort to define a more homogeneous group. As this has occurred, the "leftovers," which were defined out of the disorder (schizotypal personality disorder, paranoid personality disorder, atypical psychosis, brief reactive psychosis, schizophreniform psychosis, schizoaffective psychosis, delusional disorder), have themselves been refined and studied. It is apparent that there is some genetic relationship with the main disorder (Kendler and Diehl, 1993), though the relationship is neither unequivocal, clear, nor are there therapeutic implications. Kendler and Diehl even make the startling statement that "the correlation in the liability from the recent methodologically strong family studies (around +0.35) is about half of the aggregate estimate of heritability obtained from twin studies. These conclusions, which apply to general populations of individuals with schizophrenia, and not to individual cases, are *not* inconsistent with the hypothesis that in some individuals, schizophrenia is largely environmental in origin, while in others, the disorder is caused largely by genetic factors" (p. 266).

High-Risk Studies

The implications of family genetic studies in bipolar disorder are discussed elsewhere in this volume. However, one strategy that enables us to examine both the development of psychopathology and the question of risk factors is the "high-risk" paradigm. A variety of methodological problems in early studies resulted in findings that were often contradictory. Some studies found no differences compared to controls, and others found higher rates of either general psychiatric disorder or depressive disorder (Lee and Gotlib, 1989). Two recent studies that have paid close attention to diagnoses in parents and prospective follow-up of offspring continue to produce divergent findings. Studies by both Radke-Yarrow et al. (1992) and Hammen et al. (1990) examine offspring of mothers with unipolar depression, bipolar disorder, and controls without psychiatric disorder. (Hammen's study also included a medically ill comparison group). At 2-year follow-up, Hammen's sample of 8- to 16-year olds appeared to have very few differences in either rates of psychiatric disorder or psychosocial outcomes between bipolar offspring and normal control offspring. By contrast, children of unipolar mothers were more troubled and impaired. While the Radke-Yarrow study is more developmentally oriented, and tracks two groups of sibling pairs over 3 years so there are data on children between the ages of 1½ and 11, offspring of bipolars (by age 11) show rates of internalizing, externalizing, and comorbid disorder at significantly higher rates, and were similar to offspring of unipolar depressed mothers. Interestingly, a careful scruitiny of the samples reveals that all of Hammen's proband mothers were hospitalized with bipolar disorder. Radke-Yarrow's sample was obtained from the community and 17 of the 22 *were diagnosed with bipolar II disorder and were more likely therefore impaired by chronic depression rather than mania.* Radke-Yarrow also noted (personal communication) that they had high rates of comorbid personality disorder. It is possible, therefore, that the problems in the offspring arise from the comorbidity or chronic depression rather than the more intermittent if more flagrant episodes of bipolar I disorder.

Longitudinal Studies

Although findings from longitudinal studies of patients with bipolar disorder should clarify the implications of having a "spectrum" disorder, results are often confusing. For instance, criteria for bipolar II disorder vary depending on whether inpatient or outpatient samples are used (Akiskal et al., 1983), whether patients with comorbidity are included or excluded (Cassano et al., 1992; Coryell et al. 1989; Endicott et al., 1985), or whether the population studied is selected for studies of lineality (Simpson et al., 1993; McInnis et al., 1994). In a recent review, Cassano and colleagues (1992) enumerate the studies that demonstrate a relationship between bipolar I and bipolar II disorder. There appears to be some consensus on genetic overlap, though it is not clear whether bipolar "breeds true," and absence of consensus on whether bipolar II disorder has an earlier or later age of onset than bipolar I or II, or has a more chronic and treatment refractory course or not. In the study Cassano et al. (1992) subsequently describe, the continuity between unipolar depression and hyperthymia, bipolar II disorder and bipolar I disorder, are contrasted to pure unipolar disorder; they found relatively low rates of chronic course in the bipolar II's (13.3 vs. 11.4% in bipolar I's), rates of 10.6% bipolar disorder in first-degree relatives (vs. 22.9% in bipolar I's), and rates of suicide attempts (18.1%) in bipolar II's compared to 25.7% in bipolar I's. They conclude that bipolar II is a milder variant than bipolar I. Endicott et al. (1985) found that bipolar II disorder is distinct from bipolar I because it remains consistent over time, genetically "breeds true," and has more other mental disorders and "types of chronic symptoms that have been found to be predictive of a less satisfactory response to the usual treatments for major affective disorder." The most important distinction between their findings and those of Cassano et al. (1992) is that the latter *systematically excluded patients with anxiety and substance abuse comorbidity.* The implications, of course, are that the comorbid disorders are affecting much of the phenomenology and course of bipolar disorder.

Another example of relevance of comorbidity to interpreting bipolar behavior comes from the Collaborative Depression Study. In this study, 19.6% of the bipolar II's and 23.7% of the bipolar I's reported "hyperactivity" as children (Endicott et al., 1985). Furthermore, rates of hyperactivity are significantly higher in the bipolar relatives compared to the unipolar depressed relatives (Winokur et al., 1993). If these rates are present mostly in the comorbid bipolar patients, they may be more suggestive of anlage of the comorbidity than "formes fruste" of the bipolar disorder. As noted in the Carlson and Weintraub (1993) study, this is an important distinction to make.

Up to now, this chapter has avoided the discussion of personality disorder as part of the affective spectrum. For many years, cyclothymia was considered a "personality type" and only in DSM III was it classified as a disorder. However, the personality most often linked with bipolar disorder is "borderline personality disorder." An examination of the criteria for borderline personality disorder will attest to the reasons why this might occur. Of the nine criteria, five reflect behaviors that have been considered the domain of bipolar disorder. These include impulsivity in at least two areas that are potentially self-damaging; recurrent suicidal behavior, gestures, or threats; affective instability due to a marked reactivity of mood (e.g., intense episodic dysphoria, irritability, or anxiety usually lasting a few hours and only rarely more than a few days); inappropriate, intense anger or difficulty controlling anger (e.g., frequent displays of temper, constant anger, recurrent physical fights); transient, stress-related paranoid ideation. While there is certainly no agreement about what borderline personality disorder is, and there are many who feel there is a strong association between this and bipolar disorder (Akiskal, 1994), the nature of that association has yet to be clarified. The construct certainly combines features of both internalizing and externalizing disorder, appears to be enduring, of early onset, and not easily amenable to conventional treatment. Those observations certainly fit the youth described with mania comorbid with other disorders.

If, as Kendall (1989) states, outcome is "the most important and the most widely applicable criterion of validity available to the clinician, "what does our knowledge of outcome tell us about comorbidity of child/adolescent mania? If the comorbidity were a developmental manifestation that disappeared with age, one would expect young-onset bipolars to "straighten out" as they got older. If the manifestations of all co-occurring disorders persist, one might expect that the association of behavior and mood psychopathology was inextricably intertwined. Finally, if the mood problems were incidental to the behavior problems, one might expect the mood disorder psychopathology to become less prominent with time.

With regard to "typical" adult-onset bipolar disorder, Coryell and Winokur's (1982) review can be summarized as follows: Of 414 patients with bipolar disorder described in studies from 1942 to 1974, 15–53% (average about 32%) were considered chronically disabled. Of the 92 manic patients studied and followed after 40 years in the Iowa 500 study, the suicide rate was 11.1%, with excess mortality greatest in the first decade (Tsuang, 1978). Carlson et al. (1977) found that bipolar adults (with uncomplicated mania) who reported symptom onset in adolescents had an outcome similar to those adults who were older at age of onset. McGlashan (1988) reported similar findings.

A follow-up study by Welner et al. (1980) found a very high suicide rate in adolescents who were hospitalized with bipolar disorder. These young people had very stormy histories and were chronically ill (Welner, personal communication). Preliminary findings from the Suffolk County Mental Health Project suggest that those with an adolescent onset of manic psychosis requiring hospitalization are significantly more impaired than their older age counterparts (Carlson et al., 1994) insofar as they have much higher rates of co-occurring behavior disorder and special education. What may be most important to note in the question of adolescent onset of disorder, then, is the level of severity with which it onsets. Thus, while many subjects might say they experienced their first episode in youth (e.g., Lish et al., 1994; Carlson et al., 1977), those who are disturbed enough to require hospitalization during their teens may be a more severely affected group. The co-occurrence of other psychopathology is a manifestation of this. Their follow-up suggests that the course does not attenuate with age.

In studies of the relationship of conduct disorder and mood disorder, the conduct disorder pathology has been more predictive of outcome than the mood disorder (Harrington et al., 1991; Robins and Price, 1991). Even the prediction of a new onset of a major depressive disorder in adults who had never been depressed was best accomplished when there was a preexisting substance abuse or anxiety disorder (Coryell et al., 1992). In these studies, then, the mood disorder appears to be a secondary phenomenon. Studies of adult attention deficit disorder find substantial numbers of people with emotional lability (Wender, 1987, p. 123). A recent follow-up of adolescents with disruptive behavior disorders found that significant numbers met criteria for borderline personality disorder as young adults (Rey, 1994). These studies all suggest that the "comorbidity" persists and that the behavior problems are not simply an early manifestation of mood disorder in children that disappears with age.

CONCLUSION

Our understanding of bipolar disorder youth has evolved over the past several decades and continues to evolve. There are, in fact, parallels with other disorders. For instance, for theoretical reasons, childhood depression was not felt to exist, though on closer inspection of the literature, it appears that "endogenous" depression was the type of depression being described. There is now an abundance of data to confirm that major depressive disorder occurs in both children and adolescents. Interestingly, however, non-comorbid depression in preadolescents is distinctly less common (Carlson, 1994). Similarly, manic–depressive illness was considered rare in youth. Once it is disentangled from schizophrenia and other psychoses, bipolar disorder may be, in fact, the most common of the psychoses in adolescence. On the other hand, strictly defined manic–depressive illness, as described by Anthony and Scott (1960), remains uncommon, at least in prepuberty. The manic syndrome, however, is much more frequently observed. Those children who have the symptoms of mania have wide-ranging psychopathology. Their problems are not trivial and frequently require hospitalization.

The next step in our understanding of bipolar disorder is determining the implications of the manic syndrome when it occurs with other disorders. Whether it is the primary disorder to which other symptoms are complications, a signal of emotional dysregulation that has some relationship to bipolar disorder, or a phenotype that has no diagnostic implications remains to be clarified. This will have both genetic and treatment relevance.

REFERENCES

Akiskal HS (1995): Developmental pathways to bipolarity: Are juvenile-onset depressions pre-bipolar? J Am Acad Child Adolesc Psychiatry 34:754–763.

Akiskal HS, Hirshfeld RMA, Yerevanian BI (1983): The relationship of personality to affective disorders: A critical review. Arch Gen Psychiatry 40:801–810.

Akiskal HS, Khani MK, Scott-Strauss A (1979): Cyclothymic temperamental disorders. Psychiatric Clinics of North America 2:527–554.

Akiskal HS (1994): The temperamental borders of affective disorders. Acta Psychiatric Scandinavica, Supplementum 379:32–37.

American Psychiatric Association (1980; 1987; 1994): Diagnostic and Statistical Manual for Psychiatric Disorders III, III R, IV. Washington, DC: American Psychiatric Association.

Alpert JE, Maddocks A, Rosenbaum JF, Fava M (1994): Childhood psychopathology retrospectively assessed among adults with early onset major depression. J Affect Dis 31:165–171.

Anthony EJ, Scott P (1960): Manic depressive psychosis in childhood. J Child Psychol Psych 1:53–72.

Ballenger JC, Reus VI, Post RM (1982): The "atypical" presentation of adolescent mania. Am J Psychiatry 139:602–606.

Blacker D, Tsuang MT (1992): Contested boundaries of bipolar disorders and the limits of categorical diagnosis in psychiatry. Am J Psychiatry 149:1473–1483.

Blumenthal RL, Egeland JA, Sharp L, Nee J, Endicott J (1987): Age onset in bipolar and unipolar illness with and without delusions and hallucinations. Comprehensive Psychiatry 28:547–554.

Bowring MA, Kovacs M (1992): Difficulties in diagnosing manic disorders among children and adolescents. J Am Acad Child Adolesc Psychiatry 31:611–614.

Burke KC, Burke JD Jr, Rae DS, Regier DA (1991): Comparing age at onset of major depression and other psychiatric disorders by birth cohorts in five U.S. community populations. Arch Gen Psychiatry 48:789–795.

Carlson GA (1995): Identifying prepubertal mania. J Am Acad Child Adolesc Psychiatry 34:750–753.

Carlson GA (1994): Adolescent bipolar disorder. In Reynolds WM, Johnson F (eds): "Handbook of Depression in Children and Adolescents." New York: Plenum Press.

Carlson GA (1993): Can we validate child psychiatric disorders in adults? Am J Psychiatry 150:1763–1766.

Carlson GA (1990): Annotation: Child and adolescent mania—Diagnostic considerations. J Child Psych Psych 31:331–341.

Carlson GA (1983): Bipolar affective disorders in childhood and adolescence. In Cantwell DP, Carlson GA (eds): "Affective Disorders in Childhood and Adolescence–An Update." New York: Spectrum Publications, pp 61–84.

Carlson GA (1979): Affective psychosis in mental retardates. Psychiatric Clin N Am 2:449–510.

Carlson GA, Davenport YB, Jamison KR (1977): A comparison of outcome in adolescent and late onset bipolar manic– depressive illness. Am J Psychiatry 134:919–922.

Carlson GA, Strober M (1978): Manic depressive illness in early adolescence: A study of clinical and diagnostic characteristics in six cases. J Am Acad Child Psychiatry. 17:138–153.

Carlson GA, Weintraub S (1993): Childhood behavior problems and bipolar disorder— relationship or coincidence? J Affect Dis 28:143–153.

Carlson GA, Fennig S, Bromet ET (1994): The confusion between bipolar disorder and schizophrenia in youth: Where does it stand in the 1990's? J Am Acad Child Adolesc Psychiatry 33:453–460.

Carlson GA, Kashani JH (1988): Manic symptoms in nonreferred adolescent population. J of Affective Disorders 15:219–226.

Carlson GA, Rapport MD, Pataki CS, Kelly KL (1992): Lithium in hospitalized children at 4 and 8 weeks: Mood, behavior, and cognitive effects. J of Psychology and Psychiatry 33:411–425.

Casat CD (1982): The Under- and Over-Diagnosis of Mania in Children and Adolescents. Comprehensive Psychiatry 23:552–559.

Cassano GB, Akiskal HS, Savrino M, Musetti L, Perugi G (1992): Proposed subtypes of bipolar II and related disorders: With hypomanic episodes (or cyclothmia) and with hyperthymic temperament. J Affect Dis 26:127–140.

Coryell W, Endicott J, Keller M (1992): Major depression in a non clinical sample: Demographic and clinical risk factors for first onset. Arch Gen Psychiatry 49:117–125.

Coryell W, Winokur G (1982): Cause and outcome. In Paykel ES (ed): "Handbook of Affective Disorders." New York: Guilford Press, pp 93–108.

Coryell W, Keller M, Endicott J, Andreasen N, Clayton P, Hirshfeld R (1989): Bipolar II illness: course and outcome over a five year period. Psychol Med 19:129–141.

Davis RE (1979): Manic depressive variant syndrome of childhood: A preliminary report. Am J Psychiatry 136:702–706.

Endicott J, Nee J, Andreasen N, Clayton P, Keller M, Coryell W (1985): Bipolar II—Combine or keep separate? J Affect Dis 8:17–28.

Geller B, Fox LW, Clark KA (1994): Rate and predictors of prepubertal bipolarity during follow-up of 6–12 year old depressed children. J Am Acad Child Adolesc Psychiatry 33:461–468.

Goodwin FK, Jaminson KR (1990). Manic Depressive Illness. New York: Oxford University Press.

Hammen C, Burge D, Burney E, Adrian C (1990): Longitudinal study of diagnosis in children of women with unipolar and bipolar affective disorder. Arch Gen Psychiatry 47:1112–1117.

Harrington R, Fudge H, Rutter M (1991): Adult outcome of childhood and adolescent depression—11 links with antisocial behavior. J Am Acad Child Adolesc Psychiatry 30:434–439.

Hassanyeh F, Davison K (1980): Bipolar affective psychosis with onset before age 16, report of 10 cases. Br J Psychiatry 137:530–539.

Herjanic B, Reich W (1982): Development of a structured psychiatric interview for children: Agreement between child and parent on individual symptoms. J Abnor Child Psychology 10:307–324.

Himmelhoch JM, Garfinkel ME (1986): Sources of lithium resistance in mixed mania. Psychopharm Bull 22:613–620.

Issac G (1991): Bipolar disorder in prepubertal children in a special educational setting: Is it rare? J Clin Psychiatry 52:165–168.

Jemerin JM, Roebrick K, Philips I (1988): Bipolar disorder in a six year old boy: A diagnosis by proxy. J Am Acad Child Adolesc Psychiatry 27:133–137.

Joyce PR (1984): Age of onset in bipolar affective disorder and misdiagnosis as schizophrenia. Psychol Med 14:145–149.

Kendell RE (1989): Clinical validity. Psychol Med 19:45–55.

Kendler KS, Diehl SR (1993): The genetics of schizophrenia: A current genetic-epedemiologic perspective. Schizoph Bull 19:261–284.

Kestenbaum CJ (1979): Children at risk for manic-depressive illness: Possible predictors. Am J Psychiatry 13:1206–1208.

Kovacs M (1981): Rating scales to assess depression in school aged children. Acta Paedopsychiatrica 46:305–315.

Kovacs M, Pollock M (1995): Bipolar disorder and conduct disorder in childhood and adolescence. J Am Acad Child Adolesc Psychiatry 34:715–723.

Kraepelin E (1921): "Manic Depressive Insanity and Paranoia." Edenburgh: Livingstone.

Kutcher SP (1994): Mania through the life span—Adolescent mania. Symposium presented at the American Psychiatric Association Annual Meeting, Philadelphia, PA, May 17–21.

Kutcher SP and Robertson H (1994): Outcomes in unipolar and bipolar disorder. Symposium presented at the American Academy of Child and Adolescent Psychiatry Annual Meeting, New York, October 25–30.

Kutcher SP, Marton P, Korenblum M (1990): Adolescent bipolar illness and personality disorder. J Am Acad Child Adolesc Psychiatry 29:355–358.

Kutcher SP, Marton P, Korenblum M (1989): Relationship between psychiatric illness and conduct disorder in adolescents. Can J Psychiatry 34:526–529.

Lee CM, Gotlib IH (1989): Maternal depression and child adjustment: A longitudinal analysis. J Abnor Psych 98:78–85.

Lewinsohn PM, Klein DN, Seeley JR (1995): Bipolar disorder in a community sample of older adolescents: Prevalence, phenomenology, comorbidity and course. J Am Acad Child Adolesc Psychiatry 34:454–463.

Lish JD, Dime MS, Whybrow PC, Price RA, Hirshfeld RMA (1994): The National Depressive and Manic-depressive Association (DMDA) survey of bipolar members. J Affect Dis 31:281–294.

McElroy SL, Kick PE, Jr, Pope HG, Jr, Hudson JI, Faedda GL, Swann AC (1992): Clinical and research implications of the diagnosis of dysphonic or mixed mania or hypomania. Am J Psychiatry 149:1633–1644.

McGlashan TH (1983): The borderline syndrome. II. Is it a variant of schizophrenia or affective disorder? Arch Gen Psychiatry 40:1319–1323.

McGlashan TM (1988): Adolescent vs adult onset mania. Am J Psychiatry 145:221–224.

McInnis MG, McMahon FJ, Chase GA, Simpson SG, Ross CA, DePaulo JR, Jr (1993): Anticipation in bipolar affective disorder. Am J Human Genetics 53:385–390.

Orvaschel H, Puig-Antich J, Chambers W, Tabrizi MA, Johnson RA (1982): Retrospective assessment of child psychopathology with the Kiddie-SADS-E. J Am Acad Child Psychiatry 21:392–397.

Poznanski EO, Grossman JA, Buchsbaum Y (1984): Preliminary studies of the reliability and validity of the Childrens Depression Rating Scale. J Am Acad Child Psychiatry 23:191–197.

Radke-Yarrow M, Nottelman E, Martinez P, Fox MB, Belmont B (1992): Young children of affectively ill parents: A longitudinal study of psychosocial development. J Am Acad Child Adolesc Psychiatry 31:68–77.

Rey JM (1994): Adolescent diagnosis and adult personality disorder. Presented at the American Academy of Child and Adolescent Psychiatry Meetings, New York, Oct. 25–29.

Robins LN, Price RK (1991): Adult disorders predicted by childhood conduct problems: Results from the NIMH Epidemiologic Catchment Area Project. Psychiatry 54:116–132.

Rosen LN, Rosenthal NE, Van Dusen PH, Dunner DL, Fieve RR (1983): Age at onset and number of psychotic symptoms in bipolar I and schizo-affective disorder. Am J Psychiatry 140:1523–1524.

Roy A, DeJong J, Lamparski D, Adenoff B, George T, Moore V, Garrett D, Kerich M, Linnoila M (1991): Mental disorders among alcoholics. Relationship to age of onset and cerebraspinal neuropeptides. Arch Gen Psychiatry 48:423–427.

Ryan ND, Puig-Antich J (1986). Affective illness in adolescence. In Halet RE, Frances AJ (eds): "American Psychiatric Association Annual Review," Vol. 5. Washinton, DC: American Psychiatric Press, pp 420–450.

Savino M, Perugi G, Simonini E, Soriani A, Cassano GB, Akiskal HS (1993): Affective comorbidity in panic disorder: Is there a bipolar connection? J Affect Dis 28:155–163.

Simonsen E, Rosenberg R, Birket-Smith M (1994): Final discussion (Borderline Personality Disorder). Acta Psychiatricia Scand 89(Supplement 379):73–75.

Simpson SG, Folstein SE, Meyers DA, McMahon FJ, Brusco DM, DePaulo JR, Jr. (1993): Bipolar II: The most common bipolar phenotype? Am J Psychiatry 150:901–903.

Spitzer RL, Endicott J (1978): Schedule for Affective Disorders and Schizophrenia. NY Biometrics Research, Evaluation Section, NY State Psychiatric Institute.

Spitzer RL, Endicott J, Robins E (1978): Research diagnostic criteria: Rationale and reliability. Arch Gen Psychiatry 35:773–782.

Stanton MW, Joyce PR (1993): The stability of psychiatric diagnosis in New Zealand psychiatric hospitals. Australian New Zealand J Psychiatry 27:2–8.

Strober M (1992): Relevance of early age-of-onset in genetics studies of bipolar affective disorder. J Am Acad Child Adolesc Psychiatry 31:606–610.

Strober M, Carlson GA (1982): Bipolar illness in adolescents with major depression: Clincial, genetic and psychopharmacologic predictors. Arch Gen Psychiatry 39:549–555.

Strober M, Schmidt-Lackner S, Freeman R, Bower S, Lampert C, De Antonio M (1995): Recovery and relapse in adolescents with bipolar affective illness. J Am Acad Child Adolesc Psychiatry 34:724–731.

Strober M, Morrell W, Burroughs J, Lampert C, Danforth H, Freeman R (1988): A family study of bipolar I in adolescence: Early-onset of symptoms linked to increased familial loading and lithium resistance. J Affect Dis 15:255–268.

Tomasson K, Kuperman S (1990): Bipolar disorder in a prepubescent child. J Am Acad Child Adolesc Psychiatry. 29:308–310.

Tsuang MT (1978): Suicide in schizophrenics, manics, depressives and surgical controls. Arch Gen Psychiatry. 35:153–155.

Verdoux H, Bourgiois M (1993): A comparison of manic patients subgroups. J Affect Dis 27:267–272.

Weller RA, Weller EB, Tucker SG, Fristad MA (1986): Mania in prepubertal children: Has it been under diagnosed? J Affect Dis 11:151–154.

Welner A, Welner Z, Fishman R (1980): Psychiatric adolescent inpatients 8 to 10 year follow-up. Arch Gen Psychiatry. 36:698–700.

Wender P (1987): "The Hyperactive Child, Adolescent, Adult-Attention Deficit Disorder Throughout the Lifespan." New York: Oxford University Press.

Werry JS, McClellan JM, Chard L (1991): Childhood and adolescent schizophrenic, bipolar and schizo-affective disorders: A clinical and outcome study. J Am Acad Child Adolesc Psychiatry 30:457–465.

Winokur G, Coryell W, Endicott J, Akiskal HS (1993): Further distinctions between manic-depressive illness (Bipolar Disorder) and Primary Depressive Disorder (Unipolar Depression). Am J Psychiatry 150:1176–1181.

Wozniak J, Biederman J, Kiely K, Ablon JS, Faraone SV, Warburton R (1995): Manic-like symptoms in referred prepubertal children suggestive of bipolar disorder. J Amer Acad Child Adolescent Psychiatry 34:867–876.

Young LT, Cooke RG, Robb JC, Levitt AJ, Jaffe RT (1993): Anxious and non-anxious bipolar disorder. J Affect Dis 29:49–52.

Young RC, Biggs JT, Ziegler VE, Meyer DA (1978): A rating scale for mania: Reliability, validity, and sensitivity. Br J Psychiatry 133:429–435.

CHAPTER 8

Outcome Studies of Mania in Children and Adolescents

MICHAEL A. STROBER

Neuropsychiatric Institute & Hospital, School of Medicine, University of California, Los Angeles, CA 90024-1759

INTRODUCTION

Bipolar illness is nearly always characterized by recurrence (Winokur et al., 1994). In some who are afflicted, the disease assumes an even more debilitating form over time as evidenced by accelerating cycle frequencies, persistence of subsyndromal symptoms between major episodes, and spontaneous treatment refractoriness (Kraepelin, 1921; Post et al., 1994). There is also growing evidence (see Post, 1992) that a wide array of neurochemical, anatomic, genetic, and psychosocial events associated with recurrent attacks can be examined for their heuristic relevance to the distinctive patterns of recurrence, progression, and chronicity observed among patients, as well as differential efficacy and specificity of treatment interventions at early and later stages of illness.

In a similar vein, developmental psychopathologists would assert that any assumption of uniformities in the course and outcome of juvenile and adult onsets of psychiatric illness may be premature; rather, the unfolding of life-course patterns of psychopathologic conditions may conceivably bear the imprint of developmentally important social, behavioral, and biological reorganizations that are temporally concurrent with onset of disease. If such contextual influences play at least some role in the triggering of symptomaticity, or have implications for differences in how underlying psychobiological processes restore health and stability across the life span, then outcome studies of juvenile bipolar patients will have a special importance to achieving a fuller understanding of causal mechanisms and pathogenesis and to efforts at identifying patients entering longitudinal pathways distinguished by heightened morbidity and seriousness of psychopathology.

HISTORICAL OBSERVATIONS

Unfortunately, real-time prospective studies of childhood psychiatric disorders are sparse; for this reason, our knowledge of the course and outcome of juvenile bipolar

Mood Disorders Across the Life Span, Edited by Shulman, Tohen, and Kutcher
ISBN 0-471-10477-9 © 1996 Wiley-Liss, Inc.

illness remains fragmentary. Even so, the evidence is substantial that bipolar illness presents as a clearly identifiable syndrome in adolescence. Kraepelin's (1921) observation that puberty heralded the period of the greatest frequency fo first onsets of the disease is generally supported by subsequent studies of age of onset (Baron et al., 1983; Egeland et al., 1987; Loranger and Levine, 1978; Olsen, 1961; Perris, 1968; Wertham, 1929; Winokur et al., 1969), which indicate that upward of 25% of bipolars suffer their first full-blown attack prior to age 20. However, relatively little information can be gleaned from the early literature on course and outcome in the subset of patients with documented juvenile age of onset. According to Pollock's (1931) study of 1,700 patients, some 22% of patients whose first hospitalization for bipolar illness occurred before age 20 had multiple prior episodes of illness. The results of Landolt (1957) of a 5- to 25-year follow-up of 60 bipolar patients first hospitalized between 15 and 22 years of age complement Pollock's (1931) observation, observing a relapsing course in 90% of the cohort. A variety of small case series published during the 1930s and 1940s (Barrett, 1931; Kasanin, 1930; Olkon, 1945; Rice, 1944) are also noteworthy for their description of recurring, circular episodes of severe depression and elation in children and adolescents running their course over several years and typically associated with heavy familial loading of affective disease.

COMPARATIVE STUDIES OF EARLY- VERSUS LATE-ONSET SUBGROUPS

Only two studies have directly compared patients with juvenile- versus adult-onset of illness with respect to clinical outcome. Carlson et al. (1977) reported that patients with onsets prior to age 20 differed little from those with onset after age 45 in gender, polarity of illness at onset, number of episodes per year, educational level, rate of divorce, or overall psychosocial adjustment. In a follow-up examination averaging 15 years after discharge from Chestnut Lodge, McGlashan (1988) reported that 35 adolescent-onset manics were indistinguishable from 31 adult-onset manics with respect to marital and parental status, number and length of hospitalizations, number and intensity of symptoms, and global adjustment, while displaying significantly better outcome in the domains of social and heterosexual contacts. Other reports (Coryell and Norten, 1980; Taylor and Abrams, 1981; Winokur et al., 1969) likewise suggest little meaningful difference between early- and late-onset subgroups in overall outcome or prognosis; however, the precise relevance of these reports to juvenile bipolar is unclear, insofar as the stratification of subgroups is at age 30 and the proportion of patients with onsets prior to age 20 is not mentioned.

AGE OF ONSET AS A COURSE MODIFIER

There is also the question of the degree to which age of onset of illness is predictive of certain qualitative aspects of course in bipolar illness. The findings to date have been conflicting. A number of studies suggest that early age of onset is associated with more frequent recurrence of illness or a preponderance of manic episodes (Angst, 1978; Lish et al., 1994; Mendlewicz et al., 1972; Okuma and Shimoyama, 1972; Winokur and Kadrmas, 1989), while others find no differences in course attributable to age of onset (Carlson et al., 1977; Roy-Byrne et al., 1985; Taylor and Abrams, 1973; Winokur et al., 1993, 1994), or a predominantly depressive or mixed course in the early stages of the illness (Lish et al., 1994).

Also unclear is whether or not age of onset independently predicts cyclicity of the disease process in bipolar illness. Zis et al. (1979) noted a prolongation of the interval between the first and second episode of illness in a series of 105 patients, with age and age of onset each predicting relapse. Thus, for example, whereas roughly 20% of patients with onset of illness in the teens or twenties have a relapse within 24 months, the probability is substantially higher (50%) among patients whose illness begins in the thirties. On the other hand, neither Dunner et al. (1979) nor Roy-Byrne et al. (1985) observed a significant effect of age of onset on the initial cycle length.

Age of Onset and Psychotic Symptoms

Far more certain is evidence relating juvenile onset to symptom phenomenology, specifically an increased susceptibility to psychotic states, at least in the initial unfolding of episodes. Thus, in cross-sectional comparisons, more florid psychotic states, increased number of psychotic symptoms, and schizoaffective presentations have each been noted to occur more frequently in juvenile- versus adult-age bipolars (Ballenger et al., 1982; McGlashan, 1988; Rosen et al., 1983; Rosenthal et al., 1983), consistent with other literature linking earlier average age of onset to more atypical, or mood-incongruent, psychotic features in patients with affective disease (Angst, 1986; Rennie, 1942; Tsuang et al., 1977).

FOLLOW-UP STUDIES OF JUVENILE SAMPLES

Course and Outcome of Manic Illness

The author is familiar with three studies that provide descriptive information on course and outcome in adolescents with well-documented manic illness. A study by Welner et al. (1979) described the course of 28 adolescents 10 years after their index hospitalization for either primary depression or bipolar illness. Of the 16 nonbipolar depressives, 11 exhibited an episodic course and the remaining 5 recovered from their index illness and remained well. The course was decidedly more grim among the 12 bipolars; 3 committed suicide and the remaining 9 had continuous cycling of episodes with extremely poor social and occupational functioning. However, Werry et al. (1991) employed more comprehensive and objective instruments of evaluation to assess the outcome of 30 schizophrenic and 23 bipolar adolescents after a mean interval of 5 years from their index hospitalization and found a more favorable course in the bipolar group. Bipolars had a shorter median time to recovery from the acute phase of illness than schizophrenic patients, and half were rated as recovered from the index episode at the time of discharge, as compared to 20% of schizophrenics; in contrast, there were no significant differences in age of onset, number of episodes prior to index hospitalization, or the proportion with psychosis at the time of presentation. At outcome, adolescents with bipolar illness were less likely than schizophrenics to have a chronic course (83% in remission) and had significantly better functioning in the social (80% in independent or semi-independent living as compared to 20% of schizophrenics) and occupational domains (50% in full-time employment or schooling as compared to 17% of schizophrenics).

Only one study exists that makes use of real-time longitudinal, prospective assessments of adolescents with bipolar I illness (Strober et al., 1995). Among the unique features of this study were uniform application diagnostic criteria for patient selection; stratification of patients by episode polarity at time of presentation; and repeated assessments of symptom levels, psychosocial adjustment, and treatment exposure at fixed time intervals through 5 years of follow-up. A total of 54 patients were entered into the study, and all but two recovered from the index. Time to recovery, defined as a minimum of 8 weeks with no more than one or two symptoms of mild severity (Shapiro and Keller, 1981) was, however, influenced significantly by episode polarity, with patients entering in a pure manic, mixed, or cycling state recovering at substantially faster rates compared to those with pure depression at entry. Median times to recovery in weeks were 9, 11, 15, and 26 in manic, mixed, cycling, and depressed patients, respectively. Relapse into a new episode was not uncommon, observed in 44% of the cohort over the 5 years, with 21% of patients exhibiting at least two relapses following recovery from the index episode, this propensity for multiple relapses being greatest among patients whose index episodes were cycling or mixed. These patterns show points of convergence and dissimilarity when compared alongside the picture seen in a recent longitudinal, prospective study of adults with bipolar I illness (Keller et al., 1993). Here, the median time to recovery was 6 weeks after entry for patients with pure mania, 17 weeks for patients with mixed/cycling episodes, and 11 weeks for patients with pure depression at entry. Other recent studies would also suggest that older patients are at greater risk for relapse over a 4- to 5-year period, with relapse probabilities on the order of 0.65–0.90 (Keller et al., 1993; Tohen et al., 1990a,b).

Switches in Polarity in Outcome Studies of Depressed Children and Adolescents

The natural histories of juvenile depressives are of great interest because of the potential to illuminate predictors of later manic illness, which may then ultimately guide rational clinical and psychopharmacologic interventions. A number of studies, whose original intent was mainly to establish through use of either retrospective or prospective longitudinal strategies the degree to which childhood depressives disorders have continuity with affective illness in adulthood, provide data on the probability of manic switching over time. The study of Strober and Carlson (1982) is noteworthy because it represents one of the first investigations of the follow-up course of primary depressive disorders using standardized measures of diagnostic outcome. They found that 20% of their sample of 60 adolescents hospitalized at UCLA Neuropsychiatric Institute for nonbipolar major depression followed over a 3- to 4-year period developed mania. A comparison of the bipolar and unipolar outcome groups on symptom ratings obtained at the time of index hospitalization showed that adolescents with manic outcomes were more likely to display rapid onset of illness, psychomotor slowing, and delusions of a mood-congruent nature. This triad was present in 8 of the 12 (67%) patients with manic outcome compared with only 2 of 48 (4%) with nonbipolar outcome, a highly significant difference with high specificity and predictive value. The adolescents with manic outcome were also shown to have inheritance patterns suggesting greater genetic deviance in the form of loaded, multigenerational, and bipolar positive pedigrees. A subsequent investigation by Akiskal et al. (1983) found this same configuration of symptom-based and family-genetic variables to be a strong predictor of manic outcome in a prospective follow-up of depressed adolescents. Adding to these findings, Strober et al. (1993) have recently reported strong evidence for an increased likelihood of manic switching during the follow-up course of delusional depression in adolescents. These results were based on the 24-month follow-up of 58 adolescents entered into a 5-year prospective, longitudinal study of recovery and relapse after receiving a diagnosis of nonbipolar major depression; 18 of the 58 patients fulfilled Research Diagnostic Criteria (Spitzer et al., 1978) for delusional depression at the time of this index hospitalization. After discharge, information on level of psychopathologic disturbance, psychosocial functioning, and treatment exposure was obtained every 6 months using structured interviews designed to quantitate outcome within these domains. By 24 months, 5 of the 18 adolescents (28%) with delusional subtype of major depression at intake had switches in polarity, whereas manic switching was nonexistent among the 40 nondelusional patients; an analysis of the outcome through 5 years is now in progress, but preliminary results show that adolescents who were delusional during their index hsopitalization have as much as a fivefold greater risk of manic switching through 5 years of follow-up than adolescents with nondelusional major depression.

The few other studies that have examined the developmental course of juvenile depression give contradictory findings concerning risk for later onsets of manic illness. In the first large-scale naturalistic prospective follow-up study to assess the outcome of prepubertal children with dysthymia or major depression into adolescent and young adult, Kovacs and Gatsonis (1989) examined a total of 104 subjects, including 46 cases with major depression, 23 with dysthymia, 16 with major depression superimposed on dysthymia, and 19 with adjustment disorder with depressed mood. Using Kaplan-Meier estimators of the time-dependent probability of an outcome since onset of the index episode, the cumulative probability of developing bipolar I or II illness was 0.17 by 30 months in subjects with major depression and 0.29 by 81 months in those with dysthymia; in marked contrast, no case of bipolar illness was observed during the follow-up of subjects with adjustment disorder. A subsequent report, based on an analysis of course data over a 3- to 12-year interval (Kovacs et al., 1994) on an expanded sample of 55 subjects with dysthymia and 60 subjects with major depression, showed nearly equal proportions displaying manic outcomes—13 and 15%, respectively. Geller et al. (1993) presented data on the rates of onset of bipolar I, bipolar II, and hypomania in a 2- to 3-year follow-up of fifty-four 6- to 12-year-old children with major depression who had previously participated in a randomized, double-blind placebo-controlled study of nortriptyline. Based on Kaplan-Meier estimators of survival, there was no difference in the cumulative probability of developing some form of bipolar illness between subjects who had a history of receiving tricyclic drugs and those who did not—0.34 and 0.32, respectively; however, full manic syndromes occurred only in subjects with a history of tricyclic pharmacotherapy. Within the group receiving tricyclic drugs, duration of treatment exceeding 25 weeks increased the risk of mania twofold; bipolarity was unrelated to sex, age, age of onset of major depression, family history of bipolar illness, mean daily dose of drug, comorbidity with dysthymia, or individual metabolism of nortriptyline. However, McCauley et al. (1993) observed only a single case of full mania, and four cases of hypomania, in a 3-year prospective follow-up of sixty-five 10- to 16-year-old children with major depression. Likewise, only 5 cases of bipolar I or bipolar II illness were documented in the adult psychiatric follow-up examination of fifty-two 6- to 16-year-old children who attended the Maudsley Hospital in London during the late 1960s and early 1970s and who fulfilled operationally defined criteria for a depressive syndrome (Harrington et al., 1990). By contrast, the cumulative probability of developing a major or minor depression in adulthood in the childhood depressed group was 0.6, but only 0.27 in controls. Moreover, all 5 of the bipolar outcomes were observed among subjects who had reached pubertal status at the time of their index Maudsley admission. Only one case of bipolar illness was found at follow-up among 52 matched control subjects with initial Maudsley diagnoses of nonaffective disorder.

CONCLUSION

Mounting evidence points in the direction of greater genetic loading underlying juvenile onset of bipolar illness (see Strober, 1992). However, the existing literature presents a somewhat inconsistent picture of how the familiality of bipolar illness may impact on course or outcome—whether it confers a heightened risk for multiple recurrences over time (Winokur et al., 1993) or actually offsets such risk by predicting a more favorable response to lithium maintenance therapy (see Goodwin and Jamison, 1990). While these findings would seem to have obvious relevance to longitudinal studies of young patients, few efforts have been undertaken to chart the developmental course of large, representative samples of juvenile bipolars as they move through adolescence and into adulthood, and to compare these course trajectories with adult-onset cohorts followed prospectively using similar methods of prospective evaluation and observed under similar naturalistic conditions. It is because of this paucity of data that we are left with only the most tentative and sketchy of statements concerning developmental trends.

The results of the 5-year prospective study of bipolar I adolescents by Strober et al. (1995) suggests that recovery from episodes is the rule; but the temporal pattern of recovery depends importantly on polarity of illness at the time of initial observation, with the most rapid stabilization occurring in episodes of pure mania and unexpectedly protracted courses of illness in the average patient with pure depression upon entry. Recent reports from the National Institute of Mental Health (NIMH) Collaborative Study of the Psychobiology of Depression (Keller et al., 1993) suggest points of similarity, but impressive differences as well in course patterns; thus, in both the juvenile sample studied by Strober et al. and the NIMH adult sample, recovery is most rapid in pure manics, and a propensity for multiple recurrences is particularly characteristic of patients with mixed or cycling episodes. On the other hand, index episodes of pure depression appear to herald a considerably poorer outcome for younger patients as evidenced by the decidedly longer median time to recovery compared to that reported for adults in the Keller et al. (1993) study (26 weeks vs. 11 weeks, respectively). Likewise, the two studies suggest rather different patterns of recovery from the acute episode in patients with mixed episodes at entry, the adults showing slower time to recovery as compared to the adolescents.

Younger patients followed in the study by Strober et al. (1995) appear to be slower to relapse than adult bipolars over the same period of time, at least judging from data on adult cohorts (Keller et al., 1993; Tohen et al., 1990a,b), and consistent with evidence presented by Zis et al. (1979) on the association between early age of onset and increased duration of the initial cycle length. These differences are not explicable in terms of treatment exposure, as the pharmacotherapy received by adolescents in the Strober et al. (1995) study was aggressive by conventional standards. Thus, a plausible, though admittedly still tentative hypothesis, is that age of onset in its broadest sense may indeed be a modifier of illness course whose effects operate via any number of interacting genetic, biological, and experiential mechanisms, thereby accounting for discontinuities in illness course across age groups or developmental stages. Of course, only through longer term follow-ups of juvenile samples will it be possible to gauge the strength and persistence of these predictive associations and their developmental discontinuities; to the extent that such differences exist, their nature and source clearly warrant further attention.

The findings summarized here also suggest that childhood depressive illness has continuity with adolescent and young adulthood risk for manic illness, although risk estimates per se seem to vary appreciably across different samples. One interpretation of these differences is that life-course patterns documented in longitudinal studies will inevitably reflect attributes of the sample itself—specifically, the degree to which selection factors skew the sample toward more severe or familial forms of depression, which may represent part of the broader spectrum of bipolar illness. Even so, the rate of switching to bipolarity in these juvenile depressives is impressive, generally surpassing the rate of unipolar to bipolar switches found in longitudinal follow-up studies of adult depressives (Angst, 1985; Bronisch et al., 1985; Dunner et al., 1976; Winokur et al., 1982; Winokur and Wesner, 1987). At the same time, the results of work by Strober and colleagues (Strober and Carlson, 1982; Strober et al., 1993), suggesting that risk of later manic switching is particular to adolescents with severe melancholia, corroborates and extends other research showing that switch to bipolarity is especially characteristic of depressives with earlier age of onset, more severe endogenous symptoms and psychotic features, and history of multiple episodes of illness (Endicott et al., 1986; Winokur and Wesner, 1987), and with family-genetic studies, which link delusional depression in probands to increased transmissibility of bipolar illness in relatives (Weissman et al., 1984; 1988). Thus, here again, a comparison of juvenile and adult follow-up studies points up substantial heterogeneity in outcome within the depressive disorders per se, and the need to attend to similarities and differences in prospective associations, as well as differential effects of predictors, across juvenile and adult age groups.

REFERENCES

Akiskal HS, Walker P, Puzantian VR, King D, Rosenthal TL, Dranon M (1983): Bipolar outcome in the course of depressive disorders: Phenomenologic, familial, and pharmacologic predictors. J Affective Dis 5:115–128.

Angst J (1986): The course of major depression, atypical bipolar disorder, and bipolar disorder. In Hippius H, Klerman GL, Matussek N (eds): "New Results in Depression Research," Berlin: Springer-Verlag, pp 26–35.

Angst J (1985): Switch from depression to mania: A record study over decades between 1920 and 1982. Psychopathology 18:140–154.

Angst J (1978): The course of affective disorders: II. Typology of bipolar manic–depressive illness. Arch Psychiatr Nervenkr 226:65–73.

Ballenger JC, Reus VI, Post RM (1982): The "atypical" picture of adolescent mania. Am J Psychiatry 139:602–606.

Baron M, Risch N, Mendlewicz J (1983): Age at onset in bipolar-related major affective illness: Clinical and genetic implications. J Psychiatr Res 17:5–18.

Barrett AM (1931): Manic–depressive psychosis in childhood. International Clin 3:205–211.

Bronisch T, Wittchen HU, Krieg C, Rupp HU, von Zerssen D (1985): Depressive neurosis: A long-term prospective and retrospective follow-up study of former inpatients. Acta Psychiatr Scand 71:237–248.

Carlson GA, Davenport YB, Jamison KR (1977): A comparison of outcome in adolescent- and late-onset bipolar manic–depressive illness. Am J Psychiatry 134:134–139.

Coryell W, Norten SG (1980): Mania during adolescence: The pathoplastic significance of age. J Nerve Ment Dis 168:611–613.

Dunner DL, Murphy D, Stallone F, Fieve RR (1979): Episode frequency prior to lithium treatment in bipolar manic–depressive patients. Compr Psychiatry 20:511–515.

Dunner DL, Fleiss JL, Fieve RR (1976): The course of development of mania in patients with recurrent depression. Am J Psychiatry 133:905–908.

Egeland JA, Blumenthal RL, Nee J, Sharpe L, Endicott J (1987): Reliability and relationship of various ages of onset criteria for major affective disorder. J Affective Dis 12:159–165.

Endicott J, Nee J, Coryell W, Keller M, Andreasen N, Croughan J (1986): Schizoaffective, psychotic, and nonpsychotic depression: Differential familial association. Compr Psychiatry 27:1–13.

Geller B, Fox LW, Fletcher M (1993): Effect of tricyclic antidepressants on switching to mania and on the onset of bipolarity in depressed 6- to 12-year-olds. J Am Acd Child Adolesc Psychiatry 32:43–50.

Goodwin FK, Jamison KR (1990): "Manic–Depressive Illness." New York: Oxford University press.

Harrington RC, Fudge H, Rutter M, Pickles A, Hill J (1990): Adult outcome of childhood and adolescent depression: I. Psychiatric status. Arch Gen Psychiatry 47:465–473.

Kasanin J (1930): The affective psychoses in children. Am J Psychiatry 10:897–926.

Keller MB, Lavori PW, Coryell W, Endicott J, Mueller TI (1993): Bipolar I: A five-year prospective follow-up. J Nerve Ment Dis 181:238–245.

Kovacs M, Gatsonis C (1989): Stability and change in childhood-onset depressive disorders: Longitudinal course as a diagnostic validator. In Robins LN, Barrett JE (eds): "The Validity of Psychiatric Diagnosis." New York: Raven Press, pp 57–75.

Kovacs M, Akiskal HS, Gatsonis C, Parrone PL (1994): Childhood-onset dysthymic disorder: Clinical features and prospective naturalistic outcome. Arch Gen Psychiatry 51:365–374.

Kraepelin E (1921): "Manic–Depression Insanity and Paranoia." Edinburgh: E&S Livingstone.

Landolt AB (1957): Follow-up studies on circular manic–depressive reactions occurring in the young. Bull NY Acad Sciences 33:65–73.

Lish JD, Dime-Meenan S, Whybrow PC, Price RA, Hirschfeld PMA (1994): The National Depressive and Manic-depressive Association (DMDA) survey of bipolar members. J Affective Dis 31:281–294.

Loranger AW, Levine PW (1978): Age of onset of bipolar illness. Arch Gen Psychiatry 35:1345–1348.

McCauley E, Myers K, Mitchell J, Calderon R, Schloredt K, Treder R (1993): Depression in young people: Initial presentation and clinical course. J Am Acad Ch Adolesc Psychiatry 32:714–722.

McGlashan TH (1988): Adolescent versus adult onset mania. Am J Psychiatry 145:221–223.

Mendlewicz J, Fieve RR, Rainer J, Fleiss JL (1972): Manic-Depressive illness: A comparative study of patients with and without a family history. Br J Psychiatry 120:523–530.

Olkon DM (1945): "Essentials of Neuropsychiatry." Philadelphia: Lea & Fabiger.

Olsen T (1961): Follow-up study of manic–depression patients whose first attack occurred before the age 19. Acta Psychiatr Scand (Suppl) 162:45–51.

Okuma T, Shimoyama N (1972): Course of endogenous manic–depressive psychosis, precipitating factors and premorbid personality—A statistical study. Folia Psychiatr Neurol Japonica 26:19–33.

Perris C (1968): The course of depressive psychosis. Acta Psychiatr Scand 44:238–248.

Pollock HM (1931): Recurrence of attacks in manic–depressive psychoses. Am J Psychiatry 11:568–573.

Post RM (1992): Transduction of psychosocial stress into the neurobiology of recurrent affective disorder. Am J Psychiatry 149:999–1010.

Post RM, George MS, Ketter TA, Denicoff K, Leverich GS, Mikalauskas K (1994): Mechanisms underlying recurrence and cycle acceleration in affective disorders: implications for long-term treatment: In Montgomery S (ed): "Psychopharmacology of Depression." New York: Oxford University Press.

Rennie TAC (1942): Prognosis in manic–depressive psychoses. Am J Psychiatry 98:801–814.

Rice KK (1944): Regular 40 to 50 day cycle of psychotic behavior in a 14 year old boy. Arch Neurol Psychiatry 51:478–483.

Rosen LN, Rosenthal NE, VanDusen PH, Dunner DL, Fieve RR (1983): Age at onset and number of psychotic symptoms in bipolar I and schizoaffective disorder. Am J Psychiatry 140:1523–1524.

Rosenthal NE, Rosenthal LN, Stallone F, Dunner DL, Fieve RR (1983): Toward the validation of RDC schizoaffective disorder. Arch Gen Psychiatry 37:804–810.

Roy-Byrne P, Post RM, Uhde TW, Porcu T, Davis D (1985): The longitudinal course of recurrent affective illness: Life chart data from research patients at NIMH. Acta Psychiatr Scand 71 (Suppl 317):1–34.

Shapiro RW, Keller MB (1981): Initial six-month follow-up of patients with major depressive disorder: A preliminary report from the NIMH Collaborative Study of the Psychobiology of Depression. J Affective Dis 3: 205–220.

Spitzer RL, Endicott J, Robins E (1978): Research Diagnostic Criteria: Rationale and reliability. Arch Gen Psychiatry 35:773–782.

Strober M (1992): Relevance of early age-of-onset in genetic studies of bipolar affective disorder. J Am Acad Ch Adolesc Psychiatry 31:606–610.

Strober M, Carlson G (1982): Bipolar illness in adolescents with major depression: Clinical, genetic, and psychopharmacologic predictors in a three- to four-year prospective follow-up investigation. Arch Gen Psychiatry 39:549–555.

Strober M, Schmidt-Lackner S, Freeman R, Bower S, Lampert C, DeAntonio M (1995): Recovery and relapse in adolescents with bipolar affective illness: A five-year naturalistic, prospective follow-up. J Am Acad Ch Adolesc Psychiatry 34:724–731.

Strober M, Lampert C, Schmidt S, Morrell W: (1993): The course of major depressive disorder in adolescents: I. Recovery and risk of manic switching in a follow-up of psychotic and nonpsychotic subtypes. J Am Acad Ch Adolesc Psychiatry 32:34–42.

Taylor MA, Abrams R (1981): Early- and late-onset bipolar illness. Arch Gen Psychiatry 38:58–61.

Taylor MA, Abrams R (1973): Manic states: A genetic study of early and late onset affective disorders. Arch Gen Psychiatry 28:656–658.

Tohen M, Waternaux CM, Tsuang MT (1990a): Outcome in mania: A 4-year follow-up of 75 patients utilizing survival analysis. Arch Gen Psychiatry 47;1106–1111.

Tohen M, Waternaux CM, Tsuang MT, Hunt AT (1990b): Four-year follow-up of twenty-four first-episode manic patients. J Affective Dis 19:79–86.

Tsuang MT, Dempsey GM, Dvoredsky A, Struss A (1977): A family history study of schizoaffective disorder. Biol Psychiatry 12:331–338.

Weissman MM, Warner V, John K, Prusoff BA, Merikangas KR Wickramaratne P, Gammon GD (1988): Delusional depression and bipolar spectrum: Evidence for a possible association from a family study of children. Neuropsychopharmacology 1:257–264.

Weissman MM, Prusoff BA, Merikangas KR (1984): Is delusional depression related to bipolar disorder? Am J Psychiatry 141:892–893.

Welner A, Welner Z, Fishman R (1979): Psychiatric adolescent inpatients: A 10-year follow-up. Arch Gen Psychiatry 36:698–700.

Werry JS, McClellan JM, Chard L (1991): Childhood and adolescent shizophrenic, bipolar, and schizoaffective disorders: A clinical and outcome study. J Am Acad Ch Adolesc Psychiatry 30:457–466.

Wertham FI (1929): A group of benign psychoses: Prolonged manic excitements: With a statistical study of age, duration, and frequency in 2000 manic attacks. Am J Psychiatry 9:17–78.

Winokur G, Kadrmas (1989): A polyepisodic course in bipolar illness: Possible clinical relationships. Compr Psychiatry 30:121–127.

Winokur G, Wesner R (1987): From unipolar depression to bipolar illness: 29 who changed. Acta Psychiatr Scand 76:59–63.

Winokur G, Coryell W, Akiskal HS, Endicott J, Keller M, Mueller T (1994): Manic-depressive (bipolar) disorder: The course in the light of a prospective ten-year follow-up of 131 patients. Acta Psychiatr Scand 89:102–110.

Winokur G, Coryell W, Keller M, Endicott J, Akiskal H (1993): A prospective follow-up of patients with bipolar and primary unipolar affective disorder. Arch Gen Psychiatry 50:457–466.

Winokur G, Tsuang M, Crow R (1982): The Iowa 500: Affective disorder in relatives of manic and depressed patients. Am J Psychiatry 139:209–212.

Winokur G Clayton PJ, Reich T (1969): "Manic Depressive Illness". St. Louis: CV Mosby.

Zis AP, Grof P, Goodwin FK (1979): The natural course of affective disorders: Implications for lithium prophylaxis. In TB Cooper, S Gershon, NS Kline, M Schou (eds): "Lithium: Unresolved Controversies." Amsterdam: Excerpta Medica, pp 381–398.

CHAPTER 9

Treatment of Bipolar Disorder in Adolescents

GEORGE PAPATHEODOROU and STANLEY P. KUTCHER

Department of Psychiatry, Sunnybrook Health Science Centre, University of Toronto, Toronto, Ontario, Canada, M4N 3M5 (G.P.); Department of Psychiatry, Dalhousie University, Halifax, Nova Scotia, Canada, B3H 3G2 (S.P.K.)

INTRODUCTION

Bipolar disorders often onset during the adolescent years (Kraepelin, 1921; Goodwin and Jamison, 1990), and retrospective studies of adult bipolar patients have identified some 30–40% as experiencing their first manic episode in adolescence (Winokur et al., 1969; Perris, 1968; Loranger and Levine, 1978; Baron et al., 1983; Lish et al., 1994). If the first depressive episode is used as a retrospective *marker,* however, the estimation of onset during adolescence could be much higher since studies of adolescent-onset bipolar cohorts find that up to 70% of bipolar teens experience a major depression as the initial presentation of the disorder (Robertson et al., 1994). Diagnosis of bipolar disorder in adolescents, however, remains problematic with manic presentations in this age group often misdiagnosed as schizophrenia or personality disorder (Carlson, 1996; Ballenger et al., 1982; Hassanyeh and Davison, 1980; Joyce, 1984; Rosen et al., 1983; Stanton and Joyce, 1993; Verdoux and Bourgeois, 1993; Werry et al., 1991).

Mania in adolescence often presents in "atypical" form with mixed affective states, rapid mood cycling, and irritability of mood as prominent features (Kutcher, 1994, 1993; Geller et al., 1993; Himmelhoch and Garfinkel, 1986; Bashir et al., 1987; Bowden and Sarabra, 1980; Ryan and Puig-Antich, 1986). Although careful history and mental status evaluation should identify the bipolar disorder, a clinician evaluating a teen who presents with mood lability, psychotic symptoms, or a behavioral disturbance of recent onset should consider the possibility of a mood disorder. Careful application of standardized diagnostic criteria in these cases will improve diagnostic ascertainment of the disorder.

Adolescent-onset bipolar disorder may be more severe due to its early age of onset (Kutcher, 1994; Carlson et al., 1994), and both the depressive and manic phases of the

Mood Disorders Across the Life Span, Edited by Shulman, Tohen, and Kutcher
ISBN 0-471-10477-9 © 1996 Wiley-Liss, Inc.

illness are reported to remit more slowly in adolescents than adults (Strober et al., 1993; Strober, 1994). Even with optimal pharmacologic and psychosocial treatments, bipolar adolescents show high rates of relapse of both depressive and manic episodes. Robertson et al. (1994) reported that in their longitudinal study of 20 adolescent-onset bipolars, patients had a mean of 2.6 hospitalizations for depressive episodes and 1.6 hospitalizations for manic episodes, over a mean follow-up period of 4.2 years.

Additionally, the long-term psychosocial outcome of bipolar patients may be worse if the initial manic presentation occurs in the adolescent years, possibly related to the effect of multiple affective episodes on normative growth and development. Adolescent-onset bipolar disorder is a serious, chronic psychiatric illness that may be associated with disturbed interpersonal functioning, decreased academic/vocational attainment, disordered family relationships, legal difficulties, substance abuse, problematic sexual behaviors (promiscuity, venereal diseases), multiple hospitalizations, and a high rate of mortality often because of suicide (Goodman and Jamison, 1990; Strober and Carlson, 1982; Akiskal et al., 1985; Carlson et al., 1974, 1977; McGlashan, 1988; Strober et al., 1989). Effective treatments are needed to shorten the length and decrease the severity of affective episodes, provide prophylaxis against the onset of further affective episodes, and optimize social, interpersonal, and academic/vocational functioning. Treatment is complicated by the unique and changing biological, psychological, cognitive, and social aspects of adolescent development. Therefore, models of pharmacologic and psychosocial interventions developed for use in adult populations cannot be a priori assumed to apply equally well to teenagers who may require either modifications of "adult" treatments or treatment strategies not applicable to adult populations.

Although a small number of reports regarding the use of pharmacotherapy in acute adolescent mania are available, placebo-controlled studies of large cohorts are lacking. Reviewing this literature, however, indicates that about 50–60% of adolescents show a response to lithium treatment. More recently, two reports have identified the utility of valproic acid in the treatment of acute mania in adolescents (Papatheodorou and Kutcher, 1993; Papatheodorou et al., 1995).

Psychosocial therapies are considered to be an integral part of the treatment of bipolar disorder. Unfortunately, no rigorous study of any one specific type of psychosocial intervention in this population is, to our knowledge, available. However, Robertson et al. (1994) in an ongoing follow-up study of bipolar adolescents report that when asked to identify those psychosocial treatments the adolescent found most helpful to him or her during the course of the illness, education directed to understanding the illness and treatment with medications was rated most highly as "very much helpful" (see Figure 1).

In the absence of scientifically valid data regarding optimal treatments, experience derived from many years of clinically treating and studying teens with bipolar disorder can provide useful guidelines that can be modified when properly controlled studies are available. Generally, pharmacologic treatment is directed to both control acute episodes of mood dysfunction and to provide protection against relapse. Psychosocial therapies should be designed to deal with specific functional problems encountered by the adolescent. Thus, if social functioning is problematic, attempts are made to minimize this using a variety of social and cognitive behavioral interventions. Similarly, academic, vocational, family, interpersonal, and psychological (such as self-esteem) functioning remain valid targets for active treatment.

This review of the treatment of bipolar disorder in adolescents draws on currently available research literature and on the combined experience of the authors in the

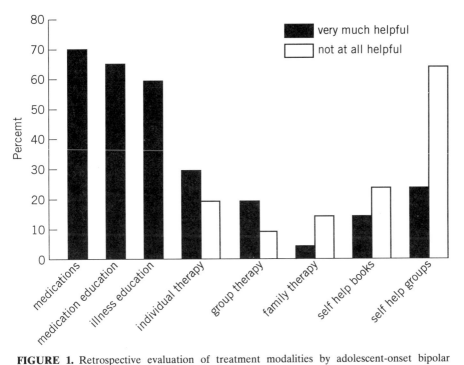

FIGURE 1. Retrospective evaluation of treatment modalities by adolescent-onset bipolar patients.

acute and long-term treatment and study of teens with bipolar disorder. It is divided into four sections, which approximate the temporal sequence of interventions:

1. Initiation of treatment
2. Thymoleptic treatment
3. Alternative and augmentation strategies
4. Maintenance treatment

The following three main sections deal with the acute phase. Although they are discussed separately, good clinical practice integrates these various components into a coherent whole.

INITIATION OF TREATMENT

The initiation of any treatment (Figure 2) in the manic phase will often require hospitalization particularly if the patient's behavior is such that serious negative, social, or personal consequences can arise if supportive containment is not implemented. Acute pharmacologic therapy is designed to provide behavioral control and to improve symptoms. Psychosocial management is directed toward providing a safe and expected environment with appropriate reality testing and consistent monitoring of the patient's

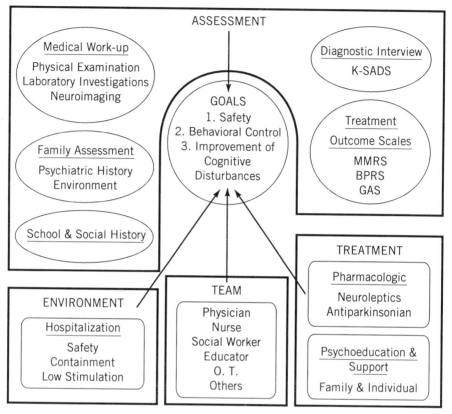

FIGURE 2. Initiation of treatment.

medical condition and mental status. During this phase, a complete psychiatric diagnostic evaluation and medical assessment is undertaken. Concurrently, psychoeducation regarding the disorder and its treatment and the provision of support for the patient and the family are begun.

Safe Environment and Baseline Evaluation

The first imperative in treating the manic adolescent is the provision of patient safety. With any teenager experiencing a full-blown manic episode, outpatient treatment is generally extremely difficult and probably should not be attempted. In addition to impaired judgment and risk taking associated with these episodes, manic adolescents may be likely to engage in deliberate self-harm behaviors either as a result of delusions or because of the rapid onset of severe, short-lived depressions and dysphoric symptoms commonly found in adolescent mania. Furthermore, impaired social judgment and sexual or interpersonal disinhibitions often lead to behaviors that, even if not physically harmful, may cause consequent long-lasting social or interpersonal difficulties as illustrated in the following case.

Case Example   A.J. was an 18-year-old male who presented accompanied by his parents to the emergency room of a large urban hospital in a manic state of some 6 days duration. Although he was seriously ill, he refused hospitalization and was not legally committable. He agreed to pharmacologic treatment and was referred to an outpatient clinic but did not attend his appointment scheduled for the next day. When next seen, 2 days later, he was brought to the emergency room by police officers who had arrested him for causing a disturbance. Believing that he was sexually irresistible, he had stripped off his clothing and was running up and down his street demanding that the neighbors have sex with him. He was committed to hospital and, following successful treatment with full resolution of his manic symptoms, A.J. returned home where he felt exceedingly embarrassed about his previous behavior. Although he made a point of visiting his neighbors and explaining his behavior to them, he continued to feel uncomfortable for years following this incident.

Apart from safety and containment, the hospital ward can provide a low stimulation environment, which in our experience is essential in the stabilization of mood and the minimization of the use of chemical restrains to control severe behavioral disturbance.

Baseline Assessment

A complete baseline assessment includes psychiatric, medical, family, and psychosocial evaluations. While the primarily utilized diagnostic tool is the psychiatric interview, recent findings continue to support previous literature regarding the misdiagnosis of adolescent mania (Carlson, et al., 1994). The diagnostic process can be greatly enhanced by the routine use of a semistructured diagnostic interview, and this type of misdiagnosis can be limited. In the experience of the authors, the Kiddie Schedule for Affective Disorders and Schizophrenia [K-SADS (Chambers et al., 1985)] provides an excellent diagnostic tool for adolescent mania. Although other semistructured interviews are available and have been reviewed elsewhere (Orvaschel, 1985; Hanna, 1992; Journal of the American Academy of Child and Adolescent Psychiatry, 1987) routine use of the K-SADS in the diagnostic evaluation of an adolescent presenting with mood, cognitive, and behavioral disturbance is to be highly recommended. While the optimal use of this instrument requires interviewer training, once a clinician becomes proficient in its use, the entire diagnostic assessment process will become more time efficient and valid. The K-SADS is available in two versions: the present episode (K-SADS-P), which evaluates current psychopathology, and the epidemiologic (or lifetime) version (K-SADS-E), which evaluates past psychiatric diagnoses. Thus, the clinician can determine not only the presence or absence of a current bipolar episode but also will be able to detail past difficulties and comorbid states as well.

An additional advantage of using the K-SADS-P is that each symptom is assessed along a severity continuum. Thus, treatment progress can be evaluated over time, not only in terms of the syndrome as a whole but for each particular symptom as well.

Baseline assessment must also provide a rating of illness severity. For this purpose, standardized symptom rating scales are useful. These can be specific for the manic episode such as the Modified Mania Rating Scale (MMRS) or of a more general type useful in the evaluation of multiple features of a psychotic episode such as the Brief Psychiatric Rating Scale (BPRS).

The MMRS (Blackburn et al., 1977) was specifically developed for the assessment of manic symptoms and provides a useful tool for the measure of manic severity and the determination of treatment outcome. It is a clinician-rated scale and is scored from information that the clinician obtains from interviewing the patient and discussing the patient's clinical condition with other informed raters such as nursing staff. This scale has been successfully applied in pharmacologic studies of treatment outcome in bipolar adolescents and takes about 5–10 minutes to complete following the assessment interview.

The BPRS (Overall and Gorham, 1962) provides a well-validated and commonly used symptom identification and severity measurement scale. It has the additional advantage of being able to be analyzed using a variety of subscales, which can provide for more detailed evaluation of treatment outcome. The BPRS has been successfully used in studies of the pharmacologic treatment of mania in adolescents and provides the standard symptom evaluation and outcome measure on the adolescent inpatient services of the authors. When utilized on an inpatient unit, to continuously monitor treatment outcome, these scales are best applied weekly. Graphing the results in the patient's hospital record provides an easily understandable visual demonstration of the patient's progress to date. This allows the treatment team to carefully monitor the outcome of treatment as it progresses and quickly identifies plateaus in improvement or fluctuations in symptoms that may indicate a need for immediate alterations in the treatment plan.

The Global Assessment Scale (GAS) ("Rating Scales," 1985) can be used to evaluate the outcome of acute treatment but can be particularly useful in following the functioning of adolescents over the long-term course of their disorder.

Additionally, a necessary evaluation is the baseline determination of anticipated side effects prior to the initiation of pharmacologic treatments whenever possible. Use of a standardized side effects scale, specifically developed to identify those side effects most likely to emerge with treatment by a specific medication, is most useful. It has been our clinical and research experience that manic adolescents tend to report multiple "somatic symptoms" prior to the initiation of pharmacologic treatments. As they improve, they report somatic symptoms but are more reliable in their reporting. A demonstration of a baseline level of physical complaints will thus allow the clinician and treatment team to properly identify true treatment emergent side effects when they do occur. This will allow for a more rational and optimal use of pharmacologic therapies throughout the course of the patient's illness (Figure 3).

A complete baseline medical assessment is also necessary. This should consist of a detailed medical history, which will need to be taken from the patient with additional information coming from the parent or other responsible adult. Baseline laboratory investigations may include electrolytes, glucose, blood urea, creatinine, liver enzymes, complete blood cell count and differential, electrocardiogram, urine analysis, thyroid function tests, and a serum pregnancy test in females. A drug screen is also most useful but should be obtained (both serum and urine) at the time of evaluation in the emergency room or immediately upon admission to hospital.

The use of other laboratory and ancillary investigations should be based on the findings from physical examination and medical history. Routine laboratory screening for all possible medical causes of affective psychosis in adolescents is not to be encouraged. The possibility that an occult medical disorder (one showing no signs and symptoms of the disorder) will present in adolescents with its only manifestation being an affective psychosis is exceedingly rare. Thus, screening tests can be expected to provide more false positives than true positives, leading to intensive and unnecessary further costly investigations of the patient.

SES VALPROIC ACID SIDE EFFECTS				

Study Day ☐   Date | | | | |

DO   MM   YY

Subjective SE	Never		Somewhat		Constantly
Tremor	0	1	2	3	4
Drowsy	0	1	2	3	4
Unsteady gait	0	1	2	3	4
Headache	0	1	2	3	4
Dizziness	0	1	2	3	4
Double vision	0	1	2	3	4
Numbness of hands or feet	0	1	2	3	4
Tingling of hands or feet	0	1	2	3	4
Muscle weakness	0	1	2	3	4
Nausea	0	1	2	3	4
Vomiting	0	1	2	3	4
Decreased appetite	0	1	2	3	4
Stomach pains	0	1	2	3	4
Heartburn	0	1	2	3	4
Diarrhea	0	1	2	3	4
Constipation	0	1	2	3	4
Weight gain	0	1	2	3	4
Change in taste	0	1	2	3	4
Hair loss	0	1	2	3	4
Bruising	0	1	2	3	4
Rash	0	1	2	3	4
Irregularity of periods	0	1	2	3	4
Swelling of hands or feet	0	1	2	3	4
Bloated abdomen	0	1	2	3	4
Other	0	1	2	3	4

Objective SE   0 = none,   1 = mild,   2 = moderate,   3 = severe

Alternating movements . . . . . . ☐

Truncal ataxia . . . . ☐   Bilateral grip strength . . . . . . ☐

Balance   Rt foot. . . . . ☐   Nystagmus on lateral gaze . . . ☐

           Lt foot. . . . . ☐   Dysarthria . . . . ☐

FIGURE 3. Valproic acid side effects scale (VA-SES).

Routine neuroimaging screening is expensive and generally not productive of clinically significant findings. In a recent review of over 100 cases of first-onset adolescent psychosis, Adams et al. (1994) were unable to identify any reported result from routine neuroimaging screening [including computerized axial tomography (CAT) scan and electroencephalogram (EEG)] that was of clinical utility in the diagnosis or psychiatric management of the patient. Certainly, if a space occupying lesion or other central nervous system disorder is suspected on the basis of history or physical examination, then the appropriate neuroimaging investigations must be obtained.

The family assessment should be directed toward understanding various parameters of family functioning and the possible effect of the child's illness on these parameters. It must be kept in mind that even well-functioning families may experience state-dependent dysfunction in the presence of an acute psychiatric illness of a family member. Thus, labeling families as "dysfunctional" during the acute phase of the illness is much less helpful than attempting to determine a good overview of family function prior to the illness onset and to come to an understanding of how the disorder has affected the way in which the family interacts.

Of particular importance, however, is the determination of a psychiatric history for every member of the family. Studies of first-degree relatives of bipolar adolescents have shown high rates of bipolarity, depression, alcoholism, and other psychiatric disorders in the first-degree relatives of adolescent bipolars (Strober et al., 1988; Kutcher and Marton, 1991). If these disorders have been unrecognized or untreated, they may impact negatively on the treatment outcome of the manic adolescent. Thus, optimal acute phase treatment for the teenager involves not only an understanding of family functioning but also identification and treatment of family members suffering from a psychiatric illness themselves. Finally, as part of the family assessment, the understanding that the family has about the illness and the family's views regarding treatment should be ascertained. Knowledge of any specific cultural or religious perspectives that may impact on treatment also need to be determined. These factors are often important in obtaining optimal psychosocial and pharmacologic treatments for adolescents with bipolar disorder since, unlike many adults, they are still heavily dependent on their families for advice, guidance, and financial support.

Behavioral Control

Following the determination of a diagnosis and the comprehensive medical history, which includes the review of known medication allergies and recent drug use, a physical examination and laboratory investigations directed toward pharmacological treatment should be initiated. In all cases, consent to treatment must be obtained and in those cases where the patient is unable to provide consent, substitute consent to treatment should be given by a parent or legally constituted authority. As part of this process, the patient must be instructed as to the purpose, expected adverse effects, and anticipated outcome of treatment with medications. Although oral medications are preferred, in some cases intramuscular medication may be necessary. Should this occur, it is imperative that the treating physician not neglect to inform the manic adolescent as to why the medication is being given and what the medicine is expected to do. Providing clear information about pharmacologic interventions in the context of a supportive mileau is not only ethically and legally necessary but is part of the therapeutic contract between physician and patient.

The primary goals of initial medication treatments are to provide behavorial control, improve cognitive disturbances such as delusions or hallucinations, and restore the patient to more appropriate physiological functioning (sleeping and eating). Because the therapeutic action of thymoleptics is usually delayed (for up to one week or more depending on the thymoleptic chosen), initial treatment is often begun with neuroleptics, which will provide adequate pharmacologic management for the disturbances described. Low-potency neuroleptics, particularly chlorpromazine, are preferred because of the increased incidence of extrapyramidal side effects obtained with the use of high-potency neuroleptics.

The dose of neuroleptic medication should be titrated to the target symptoms of behavior and restoration of physiologic functioning as these are the features most likely to show rapid improvement. Nursing care during the acute phase should be directed toward reality testing and the maintenance of a secure and nonstimulating environment. Some patients will be able to tolerate an open milieu setting and others will need safer, quieter accommodations. It is imperative that ongoing staff contact be maintained at all times with the severely ill manic adolescent. Some adolescents may be so disturbed and agitated that constant nursing care is necessary to prevent severe self-injury or suicide.

Although the use of benzodiazepines has been reported in the treatment of adult mania (Modell et al., 1985; Chouinard, 1987; Chouinard et al., 1983), in our experience these benzodiazepines, such as lorazepam or clonazepam, should generally be avoided as a significant percentage (greater than 40%) of acutely manic adolescents are likely to exhibit behavioral toxicity—particularly disinhibition states. This can then be incorrectly interpreted as the worsening of the manic state and then inappropriately treated by increasing the dose of the benzodiazepine.

Invariably, the concurrent administration of an antiparkinsonian agent is necessary during the initiation of neuroleptic treatment in adolescents. The first 2–3 weeks of such treatment, even with low-potency neuroleptics, is the highest risk period for acute dystonic reactions. The first few months is the period at which highest risk for rigidity and tremors occurs. Significant extrapyramidal symptoms are extremely distressing to the patient and increase the likelihood of noncompliance with pharmacotherapy. Our antiparkinsonian agent of choice is procyclidine as it seems to have fewer cognitive side effects than other agents such as benztropine. Divided doses of 5–20 mg per day are well tolerated and should be titrated to the presence of breakthrough extrapyramidal side effects. The antiparkinsonian medications can be gradually discontinued at a later date, and this is usually done some 4–6 weeks following the initiation of neuroleptic interventions.

Akathisia provides a special pharmacologic management problem in the manic adolescent. It can be misdiagnosed as a worsening of the clinical condition and if neuroleptics are being used, the dose of these compounds can be inadvertently raised, thus worsening the akathisia. Akathisia in this age group can be best treated by lowering the dose of neuroleptics. If this is not feasible, then the addition of a small amount of benzodiazepine, 0.25 mg twice a day of clonazepam for example, is useful. This amount of benzodiazepine is unlikely to lead to a dysinhibition state and has been shown to be successful in ameliorating neuroleptic induced akathisia in psychotic adolescents (Kutcher et al., 1989). Alternatively, beta blockers may be used. The latter strategy is of value in those cases in which lithium treatment accompanies neuroleptic interventions and lithium-induced tremor presents as a side effect.

Psychoeducation and Support

The psychosocial needs of the patient and family must be considered at the very onset of treatment. Both the patient and family are in need of therapeutic support. In our experience it is common that many adolescents who are experiencing the first manic episode may have had a period of subsyndromal symptoms during which they may have been assessed by mental health professionals, and various types of psychosocial or pharmacologic treatments may have been attempted, usually without success and sometimes with exacerbation of symptomatology. In some cases, extensive psychotherapeutic attempts at changing family functioning or providing behavioral interventions designed to ameliorate the teenager's difficulties, coupled with possible previous failed pharmacologic trials, have led to family frustration and skepticism about mental health treatment.

If a diagnosis of bipolar disorder is made, the patient and the family also face the traumatic situation of understanding and dealing with a diagnosis that predicts a serious chronic, psychiatric illness. In many cases, there may be a family history of mood disorders, and the interpersonal and family difficulties around issues arising from the family member with that illness will appear. In some families, an awareness of the genetic implications of their child's disorder may raise family guilt or worries about their other children. Thus, therapeutic support and education about the illness and its management are necessary to begin at the time of diagnosis and to continue thereafter.

THYMOLEPTIC TREATMENT PHASE

The thymoleptic treatment phase (Figure 4) should involve the continuation of individual and family support and psychoeducation as outlined above. The goals of this phase of treatment should be to attain control of mood disorder symptoms, improve cognitive functioning (specifically controlling delusions and hallucinations and increasing attention span), and social reintegration while continuing to provide safety, behavioral control, and monitoring of physiologic functions. This section will focus on pharmacologic interventions to control mood symptoms and is divided into three subsections to allow for the discussion of choices for three possible presentations: bipolar-manic episodes; bipolar-depressive episodes; and unipolar major depression predictive of bipolar outcome.

Bipolar-Manic Episode

This section will deal with the use of the more "traditional" thymoleptic medications: lithium and anticonvulsants. Discussion of alternatives will be reserved for later in this chapter.

Treatment with thymoleptics should be initiated within 3 days of presentation, which should allow for completion of the baseline assessment as noted above. It is important to keep in mind the expected time frame for symptomatic improvement once thymoleptics are begun. This is necessary both to educate the patient and family as to the expected outcome over time and also to be used by the physician and treatment team as a method of monitoring expected outcome, as significant deviations from this time frame indicate a need to reassess and perhaps change treatments. Thus, initial symptom improvements should occur within 7–10 days of beginning thymoleptics with moderate symptom changes (30–50% reduction in baseline symptomatology) noted in 3–4 weeks. Patients should be approaching significant symptom improvement (70% and greater change from baseline) within 6–8 weeks. The graphing of symptom assessment scales on a weekly basis in the patient chart as mentioned above provides an excellent visual guide for the clinician. In Figure 5 we have provided a representative graph of the weekly mean scores on these scales for illustrative purposes.

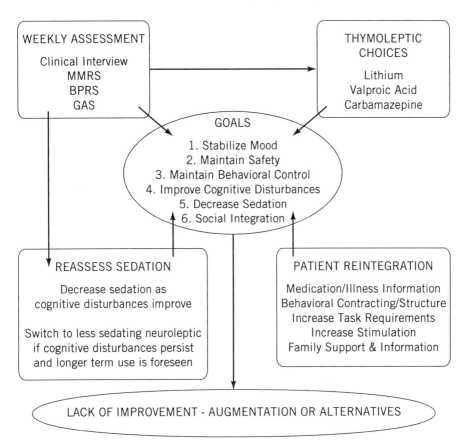

FIGURE 4. Thymoleptic treatment phase.

Lithium Lithium has established efficacy in the treatment of acute adult mania and prophylaxis of mood episodes, although it is perhaps more effective in prophylaxis against mania than depression. Traditionally, it has been used as a first-line thymoleptic treatment in the adult population. Although lithium has not been extensively studied in adolescents, a number of reports of lithium response in mania in this population have been published and are reviewed elsewhere (Strober et al., 1989; Youngerman and Canino, 1978; Alessi et al., 1994). Youngerman and Canino (1978) have reported the most extensive review, which included 211 cases of children and adolescents treated with lithium. Of these, 46 cases gave detailed descriptions and 30 had responded to lithium. Eleven of the 30 responders had histories consistent with typical bipolar disorder. Delong and Aldershot (1987) similarly reported a 66% response rate to lithium in 59 children diagnosed with bipolar disorder. Delong and Nieman (1983) reported on significant improvements in behavior in 11 manic children in a double-blind placebo-controlled trial of 3 weeks of lithium. Additionally, lithium has been reported to have had varying degrees of success in treating other adolescent disorders that may be related to the core manic syndrome such as cyclical behavioral disturbances,

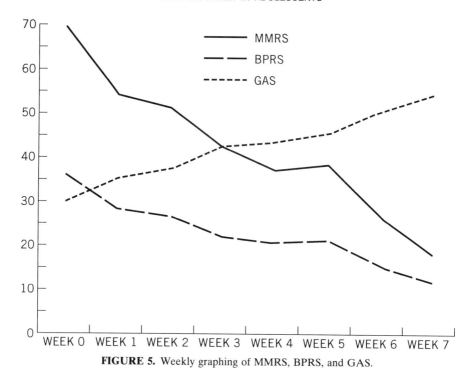

FIGURE 5. Weekly graphing of MMRS, BPRS, and GAS.

cyclothymia, aggressivity, and nonspecific psychiatric disturbances in the children of lithium-responding parents (reviewed in Alessi et al., 1994).

Taken as a whole, the literature suggests that lithium may be potentially effective in adolescent mania, but the rate of response seems to be between 50 and 66%. This relatively low rate of response is confirmed by our own clinical experience and may be due to the specific type of manic presentation commonly found in adolescents. As identified elsewhere (Kutcher, 1993, 1994; Himmelhoch and Garfinkel, 1986; Ryan and Puig-Antich, 1986), adolescent mania often presents with atypical and mixed mood states. These are the clinical features that have been identified as predictive of poor response to lithium in adult mania and in adolescents as being associated with relative lithium resistance (Strober et al., 1988; Hsu, 1986).

However, while the evidence for the efficacy of lithium in adolescent mania is not overwhelming, it still remains a reasonable first medication choice. This may be particularly the case if there is clear evidence that a family member with bipolar disorder or other associated psychiatric disturbance has demonstrated a clear response to lithium. Additionally, the information available on the use of lithium as a medication for a bipolar disorder is quite extensive particularly when compared with what is known about other potentially useful thymoleptics. Thus, the clinician is faced with much less uncertainty in the description of potential treatment emergent side effects. This is of particular importance as the long-term effects of lithium have now been relatively well studied, while the long-term effects of treatment with other thymoleptics such as valproate and carbamazepine have not yet been fully evaluated even in adult populations.

If the physician considers using lithium as the thymoleptic of choice, a number of initial considerations must be kept in mind. In terms of contraindications, lithium should not be administered to patients with significant renal disease, severe dehydration, or sodium depletion because these conditions predispose to lithium toxicity. While initial reports may have overestimated the risk, lithium administration to a pregnant adolescent during the first trimester may lead to cardiac anomalies in the fetus, particularly Epstein's anomaly. Although lithium can be administered to patients with concurrent thyroid illnesses, they should be carefully monitored, and thyroid supplementation should be considered if laboratory parameters indicate clinically significant thyroid dysfunction. In such cases, conjoint management with an endocrinologist is preferred.

Prior to the initiation of lithium treatment, a number of baseline investigations specific to its pharmacologic actions should be conducted.

1. Serum electrolytes should be measured as hyponatremia decreases lithium excretion and may lead to lithium toxicity. Hypokalemia increases the risk of cardiac and neurologic side effects.

2. Blood urea nitrogen and serum creatinine should be measured as lithium is preliminarily eliminated by renal clearance. Although uncommon in adolescents, in cases of suspected renal disease, a 24-hour urine collection for volume and creatinine clearance should be undertaken.

3. Pregnancy testing should be undertaken in females as lithium has been reported to be associated with increases in cardiac anomalies when administered during the first trimester.

4. Complete blood count with a differential is important as lithium is associated with a benign reversible leucocytosis.

5. A baseline electrocardiogram is justified as lithium is associated with benign T-wave flattening and inversion. Conduction abnormalities [atrioventricular (AV) block, changes in sinus rhythm, arrhythmias] are rarely seen as benign effects of lithium but are more commonly associated with lithium toxicity. These effects may be exacerbated by concurrent hypokalemia. If specific conduction abnormalities are noted on the cardiogram prior to lithium administration, a cardiac consultation may be obtained.

6. Baseline thyroid functioning, especially thyroid-stimulating hormone (TSH) determination is essential as lithium use is associated with the development of euthyroid goitre, hypothyroidism, and other changes in peripheral measures of thyroid functioning. A thyrotropin-releasing hormone (TRH) stimulation test, however, is not necessary unless clinically indicated.

7. Measurement of serum thyroid immunoglobulins (antimitochondrial and antithyroglobulin) is useful as their presence alerts the clinician to a patient with preexisting thyroid gland damage who may be at subsequent increased risk for lithium-induced thyroid dysfunction.

8. The evaluation of baseline calcium and phosphorous levels, although not essential, may be of interest as long-term lithium use is reported to be associated with hypercalcemia and hypophosphatemia. Although it is known that lithium can replace calcium in developing bones and has been associated with an inhibitory effect on bone development in animal models, the long-term effect of this on bone formation in adolescents is not known.

Knowledge of the pharmacokinetics of lithium is important in terms of determining dosage. The primary route of lithium elimination is renal clearance and children may thus require higher dose–body weight ratios to acquire therapeutic plasma lithium levels than adults because they have a significantly higher renal clearance of lithium. Adolescents may metabolize lithium more like adults, although there is quite a marked interindividual variation in the total daily lithium dose needed to attain acute phase therapeutic serum levels of 1.0–1.2 mEq/L.

Initiation of lithium treatment should begin with a modest dose as this will minimize gastric irritation. Doses of 900–2400 mg given in two or three divided amounts will be required to reach therapeutic levels of 1.0–1.2 mEq/L. The attainment of this serum level should be targeted to be reached over a 2-week period from the initiation of lithium treatment. Lithium levels require about 4–5 days to reach steady state following the last dosage change, and thus the initial lithium serum level should be assessed about 1 week after lithium therapy has been stabilized at a dose of 900 mg daily. Alterations in lithium dose should then be made depending on the serum level obtained after the first week with "fine tuning" occurring after 2 weeks of lithium treatment. Additionally, it may be necessary to engage in further fine tuning of lithium dosage as the manic episode improves. It has been our clinical experience that a number of manic adolescents will require slightly less lithium to maintain a serum level within the therapeutic range of 1.0–1.2 mEq/L as their mania comes under pharmacologic control. Thus, in a hospital setting for acute treatment it is reasonable to monitor lithium levels on a weekly basis.

Maintenance therapy with lithium requires serum levels in the range of 0.8–1.2 mEq/L and once a steady state has been clearly determined, levels can be checked every 2–4 months. Of course, should any complications arise, unforeseen or unexpected side effects occur, or medical disorders that may effect lithium levels (such as gastroenteritis), serum lithium monitoring will need to be more frequent.

The most common side effects of lithium are nausea, abdominal discomfort, diarrhea, fine tremor of the hand, weight gain, polyuria, polydipsia, exacerbation of dermatologic disorders (including acne and psoriasis), confusion, memory impairment, and concentration problems. Less common are euthyroid goiter, hypothyroidism, benign reversible leucocytosis, and cardiac conduction abnormalities. The evidence for significant renal damage with long-term use of lithium is equivocal. In adolescents, the most common side effects of acute lithium treatment tend to be nausea, weight gain (up to 30lb), polydipsia, polyuria, and acne. In particular, the weight gain and acne are most distressing because of the importance of body image issues at this phase of the life cycle, and in our experience many adolescents choose not to use lithium as their thymoleptic treatment because of concerns about these side effects.

The early signs of lithium toxicity include ataxia, course tremors, confusion, drowsiness, slurred speech, muscle fasiculation, and hyperreflexia. When a patient presents with these symptoms the lithium should be stopped and a serum lithium level obtained. Temporary withholding of lithium until the level has returned to normal range—usually 2–4 days—is usually a sufficient treatment. Adjustments to the total daily lithium dose should then be made.

When serum lithium levels approach 2.0–4.0 mEq/L, the patient may present with hyperreflexia, muscle tremors, decreased urine output, coma, hypertension, pulse irregularities, cardiac arrhythmias, and seizures. Deaths have been reported. Treatment at this stage includes hospitalization and intravenous fluids to restore volume and correct hyponatremia. An emetic should be administered in the case of an overdose if the patient is alert. At moderate serum levels, osmotic diuresis and alkalization of the urine with sodium lactate is of benefit. Severe toxicity (serum levels greater than 4.0 mEq/L) may require hemodialysis, even if the patient appears to be clinically stable.

The low therapeutic index of lithium requires very careful management in the adolescent patient. The risk of suicide in the young bipolar patient is known to be high, and lithium is a compound with a potential high fatality risk. Thus, when choosing a thymoleptic, the clinician should consider both personal aspects (suicidal risk status) and environmental aspects (is there appropriate monitoring and support or is the environment apt to be toxic and create situations where the impulsive adolescent will respond by overdosing) of every case where overdose is a significant risk.

Anticonvulsants   The use of anticonvulsants in the treatment of mania has undergone systematic assessment in the treatment of adult bipolar patients where a number of compounds have been reported to be effective in the amelioration of the symptoms of acute mania. At this time, however, anticonvulsants have not been systematically studied in the adolescent population, except for two publications from our group, which will be discussed below (Papatheodorou and Kutcher, 1993; Papatheodorou et al., 1995). Of particular interest for adolescent mania is the reported efficacy of anticonvulsants in atypical presentations of mania such as mixed states and rapid cycling. This may be an important consideration in adolescents, where available information suggests that there is a poorer response to lithium in patients with this clinical picture and that atypical presentations in adolescents are common.

Although the etiology of bipolar disorder is unknown, recent hypotheses suggest that a central nervous system kindling mechanism may be involved (Post et al., 1984). Some anticonvulsants may be effective partly through their ability to modify this process. The two most commonly used anticonvulsants in treating mania are carbamazepine and valproic acid, both of which have been extensively used in the treatment of seizure disorders in children and adolescents.

In studies of adult mania, carbamazepine has been reported as a useful thymoleptic in monotherapy or in combination with lithium or neuroleptics and can be used in the treatment of the acute phase or in prophylactic treatment of mania (Keck et al., 1992). Its ability to prevent depressive episodes is less well established however. It has been reported to be particularly useful in lithium-resistant mania and in rapid cycling mania (Post et al., 1987).

The current literature on psychiatric applications of anticonvulsants in teenagers is limited to reviews of epileptic children that have shown improvement of aggressive behavior and dysphoric mood treated with carbamazepine, a number of reports of the treatment of behavioral disorders accompanied with fluctuations in mood with carbamazepine, and a few case reports of the use of carbamazepine in manic adolescents with good results. However, to date, there have not been properly conducted studies of this compound in adolescent mania.

In terms of common side effects, carbamazepine is associated with dizziness, drowsiness, ataxia, nausea, blurred vision, weight gain, and tremors. Slow-release preparations may limit some of these side effects. The neurotoxic potential of carbamazepine may increase with concomitant use of neuroleptic medication, thus limiting its use in the acute phase of treatment for manic teenagers in whom low-potency neuroleptics are often required to provide early behavioral control and restoration of physiologic functioning.

Carbamazepine dosing should be initiated slowly, beginning with 100 mg daily and increasing by 200–400 mg weekly, until a therapeutic level of 17–50 mol/L is achieved. It is known to produce liver enzyme induction and, as a result, stimulates its own metabolism as well as that of other medications metabolized by the liver. Due to this autoinduction metabolism, an upward adjustment of the dosage may be required a few weeks after the initiation of treatment. Additionally, it has the potential to be involved in serious multiple drug–drug interactions; thus great care must be taken when concomitant medications are used.

As carbamazepine is associated with hematologic suppression (aplastic anemia, transitory leukopenia, eosinophilia, thrombocytopenia, purpura, and agranulocytosis), complete blood counts must be conducted at regular intervals. Hepatocellular and cholestatic jaundice has been reported and require liver enzyme monitoring.

Valproic acid (valproate sodium, divalproex sodium) has also been used in treatment of acute mania in adults. Early case reports and open clinical trials of sodium valproate in acute adult mania (Calabrese and Delucchi, 1989; McElroy et al., 1987, 1988, 1989) were followed by a double-blind placebo-controlled trial that showed a significant improvement in 36 adult acute manic, lithium nonresponding patients (Pope et al., 1991). In the above reports, sodium valproate was also shown to be reasonably well tolerated, and some evidence has suggested that it may be particularly helpful in the "atypical," "mixed," or rapid cycling manic patient (Post et al., 1985; Clothier et al., 1992; Calabrese and Delucchi, 1989). More recently, valproate has been compared to lithium and placebo where it has shown similar therapeutic efficacy combined with a more benign side effects profile than lithium (Bowden et al., 1994).

The systematic study of valproic acid in adolescent mania has only recently been reported. We have undertaken a 7-week open clinical trial of divalproex sodium in adolescents with a diagnosis of acute mania. Of the 15 cases in this study, 8 showed marked improvement, 4 showed moderate improvement, 1 showed minimal improvement, 1 patient was withdrawn early due to lack of improvement, and 1 dropped out due to subjectively intolerable side effects (Papatheodorou et al., 1995). Overall, divalproex sodium appeared to be effective and relatively well tolerated, but confirmation of these results using larger samples and comparative treatments are necessary.

Valproic acid is associated with common treatment emergent side effects of sedation, nausea, queasiness, tremor, dizziness, rash, and mild hair loss. In our clinical and research experience, the major side effects reported have been drowsiness, tremors, weight gain, and transient hair loss. Transient benign elevations in liver enzymes are common, but liver failure is rare and has only been reported in the neurologic literature as occurring in children under the age of 10, who have been treated with combined multiple anticonvulsant administration or who have had a concurrent physical illness. Hematologic suppression is less common with valproic acid than has been reported with carbamazepine and may be dose related, although clinically insignificant thrombocytopenia is common. Endocrinologic dysfunctions (hypothyroidism and hypocortisolemia), although rare, have been reported, and the literature regarding these has been recently reviewed (Papatheodorou et al., 1995).

The dosing of divalproex sodium should be initiated at a level of 500 mg per day and increased to a range of 1000–1750 mg per day over 2 days to 1 week for acute mania with serum levels being obtained weekly during initiation of treatment for a target serum level of 400–700 mmol/L. There is recent evidence of rapid improvement in manic symptoms with minimal side effects in adult patients treated for acute mania with oral "loading" of valproate. In this study, valproate was initiated and maintained at a dose of 20 mg/kg/day, and improvement was seen within 3 days (McElroy and Keck, 1993). Liver enzyme levels and complete blood counts should be checked initially weekly and every 2–6 months during maintenance therapy. Although no clear evidence exists, our experience indicates that the required maintenance dosage may be slightly lower than that required for acute treatment, and this may minimize side effects.

Bipolar Depression Episode

The treatment of depression in adolescents is under active investigation, but the efficacy of a variety of therapeutic interventions have not yet been convincingly demonstrated (Kutcher and Marton, 1989; Ryan and Puig-Antich, 1986; Kutcher and Marton, 1996). Controlled psychotherapy studies are essentially lacking and psychopharmacologic studies have failed to show clear-cut superiority of tricyclic antidepressants over placebo in adolescent major depressive disorder (MDD) (Kutcher et al., 1994). Concurrently, concern has been raised about the sensitivity of adolescents to the side effects of tricyclic antidepressants and monoamine oxidase inhibitors (MAOI) (Boulos et al., 1991; Puig-Antich et al., 1987; Geller et al., 1990; Kramer and Feiguine, 1981; Ryan et al., 1988; Kutcher et al., 1994). Studies specifically examining the treatment of the depression cycles of adolescent bipolar patients have not, to our knowledge, been published. Therefore, the treatment of depression breakthrough in adolescent bipolar patients presents a difficult therapeutic challenge and little guidance is offered by the presently available literature.

The lack of information on the optimal treatment of bipolar depression in adolescents is accentuated by the paucity of rigorously obtained information on the treatment of adults with bipolar depression. The risk of "flipping" depressed bipolar adult patients into mania with the use of antidepressant medication has been described (Bunney et al., 1972, a, b, c) and has been extensively reviewed elsewhere (Goodwin and Jamison, 1990). This same concern has been voiced for adolescents as well (Jain et al., 1992; Boulos et al., 1992). Although current clinical practice in adult psychiatry continues to be that of treating bipolar depression with the addition of antidepressants, recent reviews have revealed a limited basis upon which this recommendation can be made to patients, and concerns have been raised about possibly altering the nature of the disorder toward a more malignant course (Solomon and Bauer, 1993; Prien and Potter, 1990). The adult literature also indicates that prophylaxis of depressed mood by thymoleptic medication is generally less effective than the prophylaxis of mania or hypomania (Prien, 1983; Prien, et al., 1984), and concerns about the possible adverse effects of antidepressant treatment need to be balanced with the necessity of treating bipolar patients suffering from a depressive episode.

Although adult data should not uncritically be extrapolated to teenagers, a recent complete review of the treatment of adult acute bipolar depression may provide some guidelines (Goodwin and Jamison, 1990). Thymoleptic medications have been shown to have some antidepressant effects. Lithium has been the most studied of these medications, showing about an 80% efficacy in bipolar depressed patients, although there is evidence that the lithium antidepressant effect may not become evident until the third or fourth treatment week (Goodwin and Jamison, 1990). In our experience, many patients admitted to hospital for depressive relapse often present with thymoleptic levels that are lower than our advised lithium maintenance levels of 0.8–1.0 mg/L, either due to noncompliance or due to the outpatient physicians lowering dosages to control side effects or to target presumed lower maintenance levels such as 0.4–

0.6 mg/L. The first step in the treatment of a mild to moderate acute bipolar depression should be to maximize the antidepressant effect of thymoleptics by increasing dosing to obtain maximal therapeutic levels (lithium 1.0–1.2 mg/L; valproic acid 600–700 mmol/L; carbamazepine 35–50 μmol/L) as long as side effects remain tolerable. If lithium is being used, our recommendation is to allow a period of up to 3–4 weeks to evaluate the potential antidepressant effects of this strategy.

Following an adequate but unsuccessful trial of thymoleptic treatment in mild to moderately severe bipolar depression, there are two alternatives: antidepressants or light therapy. The literature on antidepressant use in adolescents is reviewed in Chapter 6 and will not be repeated here. Presently, the only promising antidepressants appear to be the selective serotonin reuptake inhibitors (SSRI) with two retrospective chart reviews showing evidence of treatment response (Boulos et al., 1992; Jain et al., 1992) in depressed teenagers. Although these medications are generally well tolerated, induction of manic or hypomanic states with their use has been reported.

The possible efficacy of light therapy in treating the breakthrough depression of bipolar disorders, however, remains relatively unexplored. Following an early case report of the use of light therapy to treat a bipolar patient with seasonal cycles (Lewy et al., 1982), a number of other case reports using this modality in adult patients have appeared. Most of these reports have included only patients who were unmedicated and who more appropriately met the diagnosis of seasonal affective disorder (SAD) bipolar rather than non-SAD bipolar, or who were bipolar II (Stinson and Thompson, 1990; Kripke et al., 1992; Delito et al., 1991). However, it has been reported that nonseasonal depressed bipolar patients also may respond to light therapy (Kripke et al., 1992) and that bipolar or bipolar II depressed patients may respond more readily to light therapy than unipolar depressed patients (Kripke et al., 1992; Delito et al., 1991).

There have only been two reports that we are aware of regarding the use of light therapy to treat depressed bipolar patients concurrently with thymoleptic medication. Bauer (1993) reported three cases of bipolar adults, presenting in a depressed state while on thymoleptic medications, treated with light therapy during the summer months. Bauer followed his patients for seven weeks and noted response after 1–3 weeks of treatment with 2,500 lux for 2 hours in the morning. Our group (Papatheodorou and Kutcher, 1995) recently attempted light treatment of seven bipolar adolescents and young adults (age range 16–22 years) with subsyndromal (i.e, not meeting DSM-III-R criteria for major depressive episode) breakthrough depressive symptoms, while concurrently receiving thymoleptic medications. Five of the seven had a marked or moderate symptomatic response ($\geq$ 40% change from baseline), and the Beck Depression Inventory and Symptoms Checklist—58 scores for the seven patients showed a significant improvement after one week of 10,000 lux cool-white fluorescent light (Medic Light) administered continuously for 45–60 minutes between 7:00 and 9:00 o'clock every morning, and for 45–60 minutes between 7:00 and 9:00 o'clock every evening.

Light therapy thus may be a potentially useful treatment of breakthrough depressive symptoms in bipolar disorder in adolescence and may avoid both the "manic switch" and the negative subjective side effects associated with antidepressant medication. None of our patients reported any adverse events during their treatment with light therapy, but there have been reports of light therapy precipitating hypomanic or manic episodes in adult patients (Schwitzer et al. 1990; Kantor et al., 1991; Kripke et al., 1992), and concerns regarding possible ocular damage by bright-light therapy have also been raised, particularly when used in combination with some psychopharmacologic agents, including tricyclics, tetracyclics, and lithium (Terman et al., 1990).

The two protocols that have been used with effect in medicated bipolar depressed patients are: (1) 2,500 lux for 2 hours in the morning (Bauer, 1993) and (2) 10,000 lux for 45 minutes in the morning and 45 minutes in the evening (Papatheodorou and Kutcher, 1995). There is insufficient information to be able to recommend which protocol would provide optimal efficacy while minimizing side effects, although the study by Papatheodorou and Kutcher (1995) suggests that early aggressive intervention with light therapy may be effective in both ameliorating depressive symptoms and preventing the onset of a more severe depressive episode.

If a patient presents with a severe depression, the use of an antidepressant may be considered (Figure 6). The major issue at this point would be whether the patient is suffering from concurrent psychotic symptoms, which is often the case in bipolar adolescents presenting with severe depression. The concurrent administration of a neuroleptic is necessary for patients with psychotic symptoms, and pharmacotherapy may become quite complex as various compounds are added.

Electroconlusive therapy (ECT) should be considered in adolescents with severe bipolar psychotic depression who meet the following conditions: (a) an adequate trial of thymoleptic, antidepressant, and antipsychotic has not been successful; (b) extreme agitation, suicidal ideation, or homicidal ideation put the patient or others at risk; (c) the patient is unable to adequately nourish or hydrate himself or herself and is at imminent danger of serious physiological consequences; (d) severe side effects are significantly limiting the use of medication. The clincial use of ECT will be discussed in a later section of this chapter.

Unipolar Major Depression Potentially Predictive of Bipolar Outcome

The appropriate treatment of an adolescent presenting with a unipolar depression is found in Chapter 6. In this section, we will focus on treatment considerations for the adolescent presenting with a pattern potentially predictive of a bipolar outcome. It is necessary to be cognizant of this possibility in the assessment of all adolescent depres-

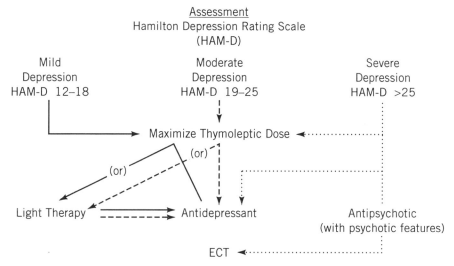

FIGURE 6. The treatment of bipolar depression episodes in adolescents.

sions in order to ensure that the appropriate questions are asked, and the patient and the family are fully informed of this possibility before therapeutic choices are made.

A long-term follow-up study of depressed adolescents has identified a number of potential risk factors for the onset of future bipolarity (Strober and Carlson, 1982). These include:

1. Pharmacologically induced hypomania
2. Symptom cluster of acute onset of symptoms, mood-congruent psychotic features, and psychomotor retardation
3. Family history of
   a. Bipolar illness in family pedigree
   b. Affective disorder in three successive generations
   c. Loaded pedigree

Given this information our clinical recommendations are that thymoleptic coverage prior to antidepressant trials be given to:

1. Any patient with a prior history of a pharmacologically induced mania/hypomania
2. Any patient with a presentation of acute onset psychotic depression with psychomotor retardation and a family history of bipolar illness

Furthermore, strong recommendations for thymoleptic coverage and clear explanation of the risk of the use of antidepressants are give to:

1. Any patient with a presentation of acute onset psychotic depression with psychomotor retardation
2. Any patient with a history of bipolar illness in the family pedigree

AUGMENTATION STRATEGIES

There have only been a few case reports of the use of anticonvulsants for augmentation of lithium treatment in adolescents (Hsu, 1986; Hsu and Starzynski, 1986). The combination of thymoleptics may be attempted in acute mania after a lack of response following 4 weeks of treatment on maximal dosing with one thymoleptic. In prophylactic treatment, recurrent episodes despite maximal tolerated dosage with lithium should result in the combination of two thymoleptics. The use of lithium and carbamazepine together in rapid cycling disorders is well documented, and some authors feel this should be a first-line approach, although we would favor the use of valproic acid. The combination of two anticonvulsants should be avoided due to the potential increases in liver toxicity. The combination of lithium with anticonvulsants may result in an increase in action tremors and other neurotoxic side effects (i.e., drowsiness, dizziness, headaches, and ataxia), and careful patient monitoring is indicated.

ALTERNATIVES

The major alternative treatment to thymoleptic use in severe acute mania is ECT. This very effective treatment is probably one of the most underutilized and underinvestigated form of treatments in adolescent bipolar disorder. The reasons are multiple and may be related to the negative public image of this treatment modality. This makes consideration of ECT use by families and the patients extremely difficult as they often initially oppose any suggestions regarding use of this mode of treatment. A clinical team that is knowledgeable about the usefulness of this treatment can often be instrumental in helping the family and the patient in this decision-making process with informed psychoeducation and support.

The use of ECT in adults with mania dates back to the 1940s. During these initial trials, about 65% of patients treated with ECT for mania responded (Mukherjee et al., 1994). Following this early interest, there were no further reports of the use of ECT in mania for about two decades, as studies of psychopharmacologic interventions took precedence. Since the 1970s, there have been a series of well-designed prospective and retrospective studies, with adult manic patients, whose results indicate that 75–100% of patients respond when ECT is used as the initial treatment and 60–70% respond when ECT is used for treatment-resistant mania (Mukherjee et al., 1994). The anticonvulsant properties of ECT are currently proposed as the mechanism of action (Keck et al., 1992; Mukherjee et al., 1994) of this modality.

In adolescents, one specific study reported that in 10 adolescents with bipolar disorder (9 in an episode of psychotic depression and 1 in an episode of psychotic mania) treated with ECT 9 of 10 improved (8/9 of the depressed and 1/1 of the manic) (Campbell, 1952). Since then the published literature has generally included reviews of series of case reports (Schneekloth et al., 1993; Bertagnoli and Borchardt, 1990). Guttmacher and Cretella (1988) published a report on the use of ECT in four patients (none of which were bipolar) and suggested that adolescents were predisposed to prolonged seizures (3/4 of their patients had seizures lasting longer than 4 minutes) and were refractory to ECT (2/4 of their patients required increased voltage settings during the series of ECT treatments and only 1/4 showed improvement). A recent review of a group of 20 mixed-diagnosis adolescents treated with ECT showed efficacy of this form of treatment and did not confirm the finding of predisposition of adolescents to prolonged seizures (Schneekloth et al., 1993).

Recently, a chart review conducted in our unit revealed that ECT was suggested as an intervention for treatment-resistant bipolar adolescents on 22 different occasions. It was accepted 16 times and refused on 6 occasions. Although all patients eventually improved and discharge outcome measures showed no significant differences between those accepting ECT treatment and those choosing to continue with optimal pharmacologic interventions, the mean length of stay in hospital of the patients who accepted was less than half of the patients who refused ECT treatment (Kutcher and Robertson, 1994). There was no evidence of prolonged seizures, with the average seizure duration of about 50.6 seconds and reported side effects were found in about 30% of cases, with headaches being the most common complaint (54%).

Our protocol for ECT in the treatment of our adolescents would consider any adolescent who has not responded to an adequate 4 to 6-week trial of thymoleptic treatment, in combination with neuroleptics, as a candidate for ECT. Following laboratory evalution, including a complete blood count and differential, electrolytes, renal functions, and electrocardiogram, the adolescent is assessed by two psychiatrists, one of which is a specialist in ECT treatment, for independent second opinions. The patient and the family are fully informed about ECT with meetings with our unit staff, direct discussions with the physician in charge, appropriate readings supplied by the staff for the patients and family, and, when possible, a meeting with parents of adolescents who have previously undergone ECT in our program. After the appropriate consent has been signed by the patient and the parent or legal guardian, a target list of symptoms are identified and severity rating scales are entered in the chart. Bilateral ECT treatment occurs twice weekly and these symptoms are reviewed weekly by the treatment team. At the end of 6 treatments, the symptoms list is compared to pretreatment values, and at that time a decision is made as to whether to continue to 10 treatments. A course of 10–12 treatments is usually sufficient for symptom resolution and is followed by maintenance therapy with a thymoleptic.

MAINTENANCE PHASE

Following the acute episode, a gradual decrease to maintenance thymoleptic dosing may be considered. This would largely be guided by side effects in the case of anticonvulsants, since a clear distinction between acute phase and maintenance phase blood levels has not been established. In the case of lithium, a gradual decrease from the acute phase levels of 1.0–1.2 mEq/L to maintenance phase levels of 0.8–1.0 mEq/L could be attempted in symptom-free patients, especially if side effects are an issue. Our recommendation, however, is that if side effects are not a problem, the same thymoleptic serum levels used to obtain remission in the acute state be used for prophylaxis. The use of lithium requires periodic serum lithium and thyroid function monitoring. The use of anticonvulsants requires periodic medication serum levels, cell counts with differential, and liver function tests. Regular outpatient follow-up should be arranged after hospital discharge with graded reintegration into the patient's usual social environment. It should be noted that exceeding rapid reintegration may be associated with a worsening of the clinical condition.

In the only report on long-term pharmacologic prophylaxis in adolescent bipolar disorder, Strober et al. (1990) reported a three times higher rate of relapse in patients who discontinued their lithium soon after stabilization (92.3%) as compared to patients who completed an 18-month follow-up protocol on a set lithium dose (37.5%). This is consistent with our clinical experience and the findings of a study by Kutcher (unpublished data) in which bipolar patients were used as their own controls. Of a variety of social, family, and psychological measures, only the serum lithium level (significantly lower prior to relapse) differentiated their relapse period compared to a time of euthymia.

TREATMENT TEAM

The importance of a multidisciplinary team that is committed to working with adolescents with major psychiatric disorders is essential for optimal treatment of bipolar disorder. Besides the physician, who heads the team and is responsible for prescribing the appropriate medical management and assuring that the agreed-upon treatment plan is effectively, efficiently, and expeditiously delivered, a number of key persons are essential for both inpatient and outpatient care.

For the hospitalized patient, nursing care in assessing and monitoring the patient and assuring his or her safety is an important component of acute treatment. At first, maintaining a low stimulation environment, to permit the patient a period of initial recovery, is necessary. Later, contracting with the patient about his or her activities and responsibilities becomes a central role. Contracting is a mutually (patient and staff) agreed-upon list of goals and objectives to be achieved each week and successful completion gains the patient increased privileges. At first the goals are basic and relatively easy to achieve (i.e., hygiene) and later increase in difficulty (i.e., completing medication education assignments and organizing discharge planning). The process of contracting provides a measure of the patient's ability to follow structures and problem solve. It can also be used in assessing recovery and provides the patient with a sense of mastery over tasks during a period when they may feel devastated by this illness. Nursing input is essential in monitoring the patient's ability to take on new tasks and responsibilities.

In our center, the majority of individual psychotherapy is conducted by our nursing staff. This follws an interpersonal, problem-solving model with a strong emphasis on education about the illness, its effects, and its treatments. Also, therapy groups that focus on psychoeducation, medication education, illness management, goal setting, lifestyle, activities of daily living, and social skills are led by nurses with the assistance of other team members including a pharmacist, occupational therapist, recreational therapist, and academic consultant.

The social workers on our team have the primary role of family assessment and support. Their successful work with the families of bipolar teens depends on their accurate and up-to-date knowledge about this disorder. They are also keenly aware of the impact of this illness on family functioning and equilibrium. The information that they gather regarding the family history and the patient's premorbid functioning is essential for optimal diagnosis and treatment. They play a central role in family psychoeducation regarding the illness and its treatment, and this is pivotal in increasing treatment compliance and long-term outcome. They must also support the family in crisis and thus are available on a daily basis to assist families with issues that arise. Additionally, they provide regularly scheduled meetings for longer and more detailed family discussions. The illness may have also caused significant changes in interpersonal relationships within the family, and readjustment of functioning may be required to appropriately handle the return of the patient to home following discharge. A good summary of the role of social workers working with bipolar patients is provided by Sands (1985).

Our academic consultants deal with any illness related to schooling issues including decreased concentration, difficulty in subjects requiring sustained attention, delays or inabilities in recovering previous levels of academic functioning, social problems, decreased self-esteem, and increased negative thinking. These are complicated by side effects of medications that may interfere with school performance including drowsiness, blurred vision, hand tremors, nausea, dry mouth, and motor rigidity. Other side effects such as weight gain, acne, and transient hair loss may have an impact on social activities and self-esteem. The academic consultant often must advocate for these patients in the school system and acts as a liaison between the hospital and the school. Some helpful strategies for school reintegration include: reduced course loads, reduced academic level, classroom time-outs (to handle akathisia/restlessness), time extensions and homework done in small blocks (for patients with concentration and sustained attention difficulties), oral exams instead of written (helpful for patients with significant tremors or muscle rigidity), tutors, and magnifying glasses (for patients with blurred vision). A central role often is that of helping the patient and family develop reasonable expectations for academic achievement given the realities of the illness.

CONCLUSION

Pharmacologic treatment, in combination with appropriate psychosocial support, of adolescent mania is necessary for the optimal management of this disorder. The guidelines used for treatment in adult bipolar disorder can be largely applied in this population for the short term, although this is not ideal. Hopefully, the growing body of literature on adolescent mania will soon provide more developmentally sensitive, specific, and validated treatment guidelines.

ACKNOWLEDGMENTS

Support for Dr. Kutcher was provided in part by a Senior Research Fellowship from the Ontario Mental Health Foundation. Secretarial support was provided by Ms. Betty Rychlewski, and helpful input regarding specific aspects of nursing, education, and social work interventions were provided by Diane Sarin, Peter Chaban, Doug Quackenbush, and Lori Tanzer.

REFERENCES

Adams M, Kutcher S, Bird D, Antoniew E (1994): The utility of screening tests in the diagnosis of first episode psychotic adolescents. Canadian Academy of Child Psychiatry, Annual Meeting, September.

Akiskal HS, Downs J, Jordan P, Watson S, Daugherty D, Pruitt DB (1985): Affective disorders in referred children and younger siblings of manic–depressives: Mode of onset and prospective course. Arch Gen Psychiatry 42:996–1003.

Alessi N, Naylor MW, Ghaziuddin M, Zubieta JK (1994): Update on lithium carbonate therapy in children and adolescents. J Am Acad Child Adolesc Psychiatry 33:291–304.

Bashir M, Russel J, Johnson G (1987): Bipolar affective disorder in adolescence: A 10-year study. Aust NZ J Psychiatry 21:36–43.

Ballenger JC, Reus VI, Post RM (1982): The atypical clinical picture of adolescent mania. Am J Psychiatry 139:602–606.

Baron M, Risch N, Mendlewicz J. Age at onset in bipolar-related major affective illness: Clinical and genetic implications. J Psychiat Res 17:5–18.

Bauer MS (1993): Summertime bright-light treatment of bipolar major depressive episodes. Biol Psychiatry 33:663–665.

Bertagnoli MW, Borchardt CM (1990): A review of ECT for children and adolescents. J Am Acad Child Adolesc Psychiatry 29:302–307.

Blackburn IM, London JB, Ashworth OM (1977): A new scale for measuring mania. Psycho Med 7:453–458.

Boulos C, Kutcher S, Gardner D, Young E (1992): An open naturalistic trial of fluoxetine in adolescents and young adults with treatment-resistant major depression. J Child Adolesc Psychopharmacol 2:103–111.

Boulos C, Kutcher S, Marton P, Simeon J, Ferguson B, Roberts N (1991): Response to Desipramine Treatment in Adolescent Major Depression. Psychopharmacol Bull 27:59–65.

Bowden CL, Sarabia F (1980): Diagnosing manic–depressive illness in adolescents. Compr Psychiatry 21:263–269.

Bowden CL, Brigger AM, Swann AC, Calabrese JR, Janicak PG, Petty F, Dilsaver SC, Davis JM, Rush AJ, Small JG, Garza-Trevino ES, Risch SC, Goodnick PJ, Morris DD (1994): Efficacy of divalproex vs. lithium and placebo in the treatment of mania. JAMA 271:918–924.

Bunney WE, Murphy DL, Goodwin FK, Borge GF (1972a): The "switch process" in manic-depressive illness: A systematic study of sequential behavioural changes. Arch Gen Psychiatry 27:295–302.

Bunney WE, Goodwin FK, Murphy DL, House KM, Gordon EK (1972b): The "switch process" in manic–depressive illness: Relationship to catecholamines, REM sleep, and drugs. Arch Gen Psychiatry 27:304–309.

Bunney WE, Goodwin FK, Murphy DL (1972c): The "switch process" in manic–depressive illness: Theoretical implications. Arch Gen Psychiatry 27:312–317.

Calabrese JR, Delucchi GA (1989): Phenomenology of rapid cycling manic depression and its treatment with valproate. J Clin Psychiatry 50(3, Suppl):30–34.

Campbell JD (1952): Manic–depressive psychosis in children: Report of 18 cases. J Nerv Ment Dis 116:424–439.

Carlson GA (1996): Clinical features and pathogenesis of child and adolescent mania. In "Mood Disorders Across the Life Span," Shulman K, Tohen M, Kutcher SP (eds): New York: Wiley.

Carlson G, Strober M (1979): Affective Disorders in Adolescents. Psychiat Clin North Am 2:511–526.

Carlson GA, Fennig S, Bromet EJ (1994): The confusion between bipolar disorder and schizophrenia in youth: Where does it stand in the 1990's? J Am Acad Child Adolesc Psychiatry 33(4):453–460.

Carlson GA, Davenport YB, Jamison K (1977): A comparison of outcome in adolescent-and late-onset bipolar manic–depressive illness. Am J Psychiatry 134:919–922.

Carlson GA, Kotin J, Davenport YB, Adland M (1974): Follow-up of 52 bipolar manic–depressive patients. Br J Psychiatry 124:134–139.

Chambers WJ, Puig-Antich J, Hirsch M, Paez P, Ambrosini PJ, Tabrizi MA, Davies M (1985): The assessment of affective disorders in children and adolescents by semi-structured interview: Test-retest reliability of K-SAD-P. Arch Gen Psychiatry 42:696–702.

Chouinard G (1987): Clonazepam in acute and maintenance treatment of bipolar affective disorder. J Clin Psychiatry 48(Suppl):29–36.

Chouinard G, Young SN, Annable L (1983): Antimanic effect of clonazepam. Biol Psychiatry 18:451–466.

Clothier J, Swann AC, Freeman T (1992): Dysphoric mania. J Clin Psychopharmacol 12(1, Suppl.):13S–16S.

Delong GR, Aldershot AL (1987): Long-term experience with lithium treatment in children: Correlation with clinical diagnosis. J Am Acad Child Adolesc Psychiatry 26:389–394.

Delong GR, Nieman GW (1983): Lithium induced changes in children with symptoms suggesting manic–depressive illness. Psychopharm Bull 19:258–265.

Deltito JA, Moline M, Pollak C, Martin LY, Maremmani I (1991): Effects of phototherapy on non-seasonal unipolar and bipolar depressive spectrum disorders. J Affective Disord 23:231–237.

Geller B, Fox LW, Fletcher M (1993): Effect of tricyclic antidepressants on switching to mania and on the onset of bipolarity in depressed 6 to 12 year olds. J Am Acad Child Adol Psychiatry 32(1):43–50.

Geller B, Cooper TB, Graham DL, Marsfeller FA, Bryant DM (1990): Double-blind placebo-controlled study of nortriptyline in depressed adolescents using a "fixed plasma level" design. Psychopharmacol Bull 26:85–90.

Goodwin FK and Jamison KR (1990): "Manic–Depressive Illness." New York: Oxford University Press.

Guttmacher LB, Cretella H (1988): Electroconvulsive therapy in one child and three adolescents. J Clin Psychiatry 49:20–23.

Hanna G (1992): Assessment of mood disorders. Child Adolesc Psychiatr Clin North Am 1:73–88.

Hassanyeh F, Davison K (1980): Bipolar affective psychosis with onset before age 16 years: Report of 10 cases. Br J Psych 137:530–539.

Himmelhoch JM, Garfinkel ME (1986): Sources of lithium resistance in mixed mania. Psychopharmacol Bull 22(3):613–620.

Hsu LKG (1986): Lithium-resistant adolescent mania. J Am Acad Child Psychiatry 25:280–283.

Hsu LKG, Starzynski JM (1986): Mania in adolescence. J Clin Psychiatry 47:596–599.

Jain U, Birmaher B, Garcia M, Al-Shabbout M, Ryan N (1992): Fluoxetine in children and adolescents with mood disorders: A chart review of efficacy and adverse effects. J Child Adolesc Psychopharmacol 2:259–265.

Journal of the American Academy of Child and Adolescent Psychiatry (1987): 26:611–675.

Joyce PR (1984): Age of onset in bipolar affective disorder and misdiagnosis as schizophrenia. Psychol Med 14(1):145–149.

Kantor DA, Browne M, Ravindran A, Horn E (1991): Manic-like response to phototherapy. Can J Psychiatry 36:697–698.

Keck PE, McElroy SL, Nemeroff CB (1992): Anticonvulsants in the treatment of bipolar disorder. J Neuropsychiatry Clin Neurosci 4:395–405.

Kraepelin E (1921): "Manic Depressive Insanity and Paranoia," Barclay RM (trans) Robertson GM (ed). Edinburgh: E&S Livingstone.

Kramer AD, Feiguine RJ (1981): Clinical effects of amitriptyline in adolescent depression. J Am Acad Child Psychiatry 20:636–644.

Kripke DF, Mullaney DJ, Klauber MR, Risch SC, Gillin JC (1992): Controlled trial of bright light for nonseasonal depressive disorders. Biological Psychiatry 31:119–134.

Kutcher SP (1994): Bipolar disorder in adolescence. Mania Through the Life-Cycle. Symposium, American Psych Association, Philadelphia, May.

Kutcher SP (1993): Rapid cycling and mixed mania in adolescent bipolar illness. Am Acad Child Adolesc Psychiatry, Annual Meeting, San Antonio, Texas, October.

Kutcher SP, Marton P (1996): Treatment of adolescent depression. In Shulman K, Tohen M, Kutcher SP (eds): "Mood Disorders Across the Life Span." New York: Wiley.

Kutcher SP, Marton P (1991): Affective disorders in first degree relatives of adolescent onset bipolars, unipolars and normal controls. J Am Acad Child Adolesc Psychiatry 30:75–78.

Kutcher SP, Marton P (1989): Parameters of adolescent depression: A review. Psychiat Clin North Am 12:895–918.

Kutcher SP, Robertson H (1994): ECT treatment in adolescents: A review of the Sunnybrook experience. 13th Annual Child & Adolescent Depression Consortium Meeting, Providence, RI, September.

Kutcher SP, Boulos C, Ward B, Marton P, Simeon J, Ferguson B, Szalai J, Katic M, Roberts N, Dubois C (1994): Response to desipramine treatment in adolescent depression: A fixed dose, placebo controlled trial. J Am Acad Child Adolesc Psychiatry 33(5):686–694.

Kutcher SP, Williamson P, MacKenzie S, Marton P, Ehrlich M (1989): Successful clonazepam treatment of neuroleptic induced akathisia in older adolescents: A double blind placebo controlled study. J Clin Psychopharmacol 9:403–406.

Lewy AJ, Kern HE, Rosenthal NE, Wehr TA (1982): Bright artificial light treatment of a manic-depressive patient with seasonal mood cycle. Am J Psychiatry 139:1496–1498.

Lish JD, Dime-Meenan S, Whybrow PC, Price RA, Hirschfeld RMA (1994): The National Depressive and Manic-Depressive Association (DMDA) Survey of Bipolar Members. J Affect Dis 31:281–294.

Loranger AW, Levine PM (1978): Age at onset of bipolar affective illness. Arch Gen Psychiatry 35:1345–1348.

McElroy SL, Keck PE (1993): Treatment guidelines for valproate in bipolar and schizoaffective disorders. Can J Psychiatry 38(Suppl.2):S62–S66.

McElroy SL, Keck PE, Pope HG, Hudson JI (1989): Valproate in psychiatric disorders: Literature review and clinical guidelines. J Clin Psychiatry 50(3, Suppl.):23–29.

McElroy SL, Keck PE, Pope HG, Hudson JI (1988): Valproate in the treatment of rapid-cycling bipolar disorder. J Clin Psychophramcol 8:275–279.

McElroy SL, Keck PE, Pope HG (1987): Sodium valproate: Its use in primary psychiatric disorders. J Clin Psychopharmacol 7:16–24.

McGlashan TH (1988): Adolescent versus adult onset of mania. Am J Psychiatry 145:221–223.

Modell JG, Lenox RH, Weiner S (1985): Inpatient clinical trial of lorazepam for the management of manic agitation. J Clin Psychopharmacol 5:109–113.

Mukherjee S, Sackeim HA, Schnur DB (1994): Electroconvulsive therapy of acute manic episodes: A review of 50 years' experience. Am J Psychiatry 151:169–176.

Orvaschel H (1985): Psychiatric interviews suitable for use in research with children and adolescents. Psychopharmacol Bull 21:737–745.

Overall JE, Gorham DR (1962): The Brief Psychiatric Rating Scale. Psychol Rep 10:799–812.

Papatheodorou G, Kutcher SP (1995): The effects of adjunctive light therapy on ameliorating breakthrough depressive symptoms in adolescent onset bipolar disorder. J Psychiatry Neurosci 20:226–232.

Papatheodorou G, Kutcher SP (1993): Divalproex sodium treatment in late adolescent and young adult acute mania. Psychopharmacol Bull 29:213–219.

Papatheodorou G, Kutcher SP, Katic M, Szalai JP (1995): The efficacy and safety of divalproex sodium in the treatment of acute mania in adolescents and young adults: An open clinical trial. J Clin Psychopharmacol 15:110–116.

Perris C (1968): The course of depressive psychosis. Acta Psychiatr Scand 44:238–248.

Pope HG, McElroy SL, Keck PE, Hudson JI (1991): Valproate in the treatment of acute mania: A placebo-controlled study. Arch Gen Psychiatry 48:62–68.

Post RM, Uhde TW, Roy-Byrne PP, Joffe RT (1987): Correlates of antimanic response to carbamazepine. Psychiatry Res 21:71–83.

Post RM, Uhde TW, Joffe RT, Roy-Byrne PP, Kellner C (1985): Anticonvulsant drugs in psychiatric illness: New treatment alternatives and theoretical implications. In Trimble MR (ed): "The Psychopharmacology of Epilepsy." New York: Wiley, pp 141–171.

Post RM, Rubinow DR, Ballenger JC (1984): Conditioning, sensitization, and kindling: Implications for the course of affective illness. In Post RM, Ballenger JC (eds): "Neurobiology of Mood Disorders." Baltimore: Williams and Williams, pp 432–466.

Prien RF (1983): Long-term prophylactic treatment of bipolar illness. In Grinspoon L (ed): "Psychiatry Update: The American Psychiatric Association Annual Review," Vol. 2. Washington, DC: American Psychiatric Press, pp 303–318.

Prien RF, Potter WZ (1990): NIMH workshop report on treatment of bipolar disorder. Psychopharmacol Bull 26:409–427.

Prien RF, Kupfer DJ, Mansky PA, Small JG, Tuason VB, Voss CB, Johnston WE (1984): Drug therapy in the prevention of recurrences in unipolar and bipolar affective disorders. Arch Gen Psychiatry 41:1096–1104.

Puig-Antich J, Perel JM, Lupatkin W, Chambers WJ, Tabrizi MA, King J, Goetz R, Davies M, Stiller RL (1987): Imipramine in prepubertal major depressive disorders. Arch Gen Psychiatry 44:81–89.

Rating scales and assessment instruments for use in pediatric psychopharmacology research. Psychopharmacology Bull 21(4):714–1124.

Robertson HA, Kutcher SP, Antoniew E, Bird D, Newton S, Shott P, Ward V (1994): Adolescent bipolar I outcome study. Paper presented at the American Academy of Child and Adolescent Psychiatry, 41st Annual Meeting, New York City, October.

Rosen LN, Rosenthal NE, Dusen PH, Dunner DL, Fieve RR (1983): Age at onset and number of psychotic symptoms in bipolar I and schizoaffective disorders. Am J Psych 140(11):1523–1524.

Ryan ND, Puig-Antich J (1986): Affective illness in adolescence. In France AJ, Hales RE (eds): "Psychiatry Update: American Psychiatric Association Annual Review," Vol 5. Washington DC: American Psychiatric Press, pp 420–450.

Ryan ND, Puig-Antich J, Rabinovich H, Fried J, Ambrosini P, Meyer V, Torres D, Dachille S, Mazzie D (1988): MAOI's in adolescent major depression unresponsive to tricyclic antidepressants. J Am Acad Child Adolesc Psychiatry 27:755–758.

Sands RG (1985): Bipolar disorder and social work practice. Social Work Health Care 10:91–105.

Schneekloth TD, Rummans TA, Logan KM (1993): Electroconvulsive therapy in adolescents. Convulsive Therapy 9:158–166.

Schwitzer J, Neudorfer C, Blecha HG, Fleischhacker WW (1990): Mania as a side effect of phototherapy. Biol Psychiatry 28:532–534.

Solomon DA, Bauer MS (1993): Continuation and maintenance pharmacotherapy for unipolar and bipolar mood disorders. Psychiat Clin North Am 16:515–540.

Stanton MW, Joyce PR (1993): Stability of psychiatric diagnoses in New Zealand psychiatric hospitals. Australian New Zealand J Psychiatry 27(1):2–8.

Stinson D, Thompson C (1990): Clinical experience with phototherapy. J Affective Disord 18:129–135.

Strober M (1994): Juvenile bipolar illness: Course and treatment response. Child Psychiatry Day, University of Toronto.

Strober M, Carlson G (1982): Bipolar illness in adolescents with major depression: Clinical, genetic and psychopharmacologic predictors in a three-to four-year prospective follow-up investigation. Arch Gen Psychiatry 39:549–555.

Strober M, Lampert C, Schmidt S, Morrell W (1993): The course of major depressive disorder in adolescents: I. Recovery and risk of manic switching in a follow-up of psychotic and nonpsychotic subtypes. J Am Acad Child Adol Psychiatry 32(1):34–42.

Strober M, Hanna G, McCracken J (1989): Biploar disorders. In Last CG, Hersen M (eds): "Handbook of Child Psychiatric Diagnosis." New York: Wiley.

Strober M, Morrell W, Lampert C, Burroughs J (1990): Relapse following discontinuation of lithium maintenance therapy in adolescents with bipolar I illness: A naturalistic study. Am J Psychiatry 147:457–461.

Strober M, Morrell W, Burroughs J, Lampert C, Danforth H, Freeman R (1988): A family study of bipolar I disorder in adolescents: Early onset of symptoms linked to increased familial loading and lithium resistance. J Affective Disord 15:255–268.

Terman M, Reme CE, Rafferty B, Gallin PF, Terman JS (1990): Bright light therapy for winter depression: Potential ocular effects and theoretical implications. Photochem Photobiol 51:781–792.

Verdoux H, Bourgeois M (1993): A comparison of manic patient subgroups. J Affective Dis 27(4):267–272.

Werry JS, McClellan JM, Chard L (1991): Childhood and adolescent schizophrenia, bipolar, and schizoaffective disorders: A clinical and outcome study. J Am Acad Child Adolesc Psychiatry 30:457–465.

Winokur G, Clayton PJ, Reich T (1969): "Manic Depressive Illness." St. Louis: CV Mosby.

Youngerman J, Canino IA (1978): Lithium carbonate use in children and adolescents: A survey of the literature. Arch Gen Psychiatry 35:216–224.

PART III

ADULTHOOD

CHAPTER 10

Depression: Clinical Features and Pathogenesis

ADELE C. VIGUERA and ANTHONY J. ROTHSCHILD

Consolidated Department of Psychiatry at Harvard Medical School, McLean Hospital, Belmont, MA 02178–9106

INTRODUCTION

Current evidence suggests that depression is not a single entity but a heterogenous group of disorders characterized by a broad spectrum of symptom type, severity, and course of illness. Depression is a rather vague descriptive term with a broad and varied meaning ranging from normal sadness and disappointment to severe incapacitating psychiatric illness. William Styron in his book *Darkness Visible* aptly describes the unsatisfactory descriptive nature of the term *depression:* "a noun with bland tonality and lacking any magisterial presence, used indifferently to describe an economic decline or rut in the ground, a true wimp of a word for such a major illness" (Styron, pg. 37, 1990).

For clinicians, diagnosing depression can be challenging given the variability of its presentation. A patient may present with prominent feelings of self-reproach and tearfulness while another patient will present with multiple physical complaints. Or a patient may present with classic neurovegetative signs and symptoms of depression while another patient presents with "reverse" neurovegetative symptoms. Moreover, diagnosing depression in patients with medical illness can also be challenging since many of the symptoms and signs of depression, such as weight loss, apathy, insomnia, and low energy, may be due to the medical condition itself or to a complication of medical treatment. Despite its clinical variability, depression carries a similar and significant morbidity and mortality for the sufferer. This chapter will discuss the clinical features of depression, specifically focusing on the major subtypes as described in DSM-IV (melancholia, atypical, seasonal, postpartum onset, and psychotic) as well as briefly review various biological theories regarding the pathogenesis of the disorder, focusing on recent developments.

There have been only minor modifications to the criteria of major depression from DSM-III-R to DSM-IV (American Psychiatric Association, 1994). In DSM-IV, major

Mood Disorders Across the Life Span, Edited by Shulman, Tohen, and Kutcher
ISBN 0-471-10477-9 © 1996 Wiley-Liss, Inc.

depression is now known as major depressive disorder in an effort to emphasize that it is a syndrome that includes both psychological and somatic symptoms (Hales et al., 1994). As in DSM-III-R, DSM-IV continues to emphasize the duration of symptoms as at least 2 weeks. There has also been no change in criteria regarding the neurovegetative symptoms of depression. According to the DSM-IV, five out of the following nine symptoms must be met for the diagnosis to be made: (1) depressed mood most of the day, nearly every day; (2) markedly diminished interest or pleasure in all activities most of the day, nearly every day; (3) decrease or increase in appetite nearly every day or significant weight loss when not dieting or weight gain; (4) insomnia or hypersomnia; (5) psychomotor agitation or retardation; (6) fatigue or loss of energy nearly every day; (7) feelings of worthlessness or excessive or inappropriate guilt; (8) diminished ability to think or concentrate, indecisiveness; (9) recurrent thoughts of death, recurrent suicidal ideation, or suicide attempt (American Psychiatric Association, 1994). At least one of the five symptoms needed to make the diagnosis is either (1) depressed mood, or (2) loss of interest or pleasure. The diagnostic criteria include four general categories: (1) *disturbances in mood:* sad, blue, depressed, hopeless, "blah," irritable, "down in the dumps," worried; (2) *disturbances in cognition:* loss of interest, difficulty concentrating, low self-esteem, negative thoughts, indecisiveness, guilt, suicidal ideation, delusions, hallucinations; (3) *behavior:* social withdrawal, psychomotor retardation; (4) *somatic:* fatigue, sleep disturbance, appetite, weight loss, or gain (Hales et al., 1994).

In an effort to avoid a functional versus organic dichotomy, the DSM-IV Task Force has transferred two diagnostic categories—mood disorder due to a general medical condition and substance-induced mood disorder—from the organic mental disorders section in DSM-III-R (American Psychiatric Association, 1987) to the general category of mood disorders in DSM-IV (American Psychiatric Association, 1994). The essential feature of this diagnostic category is determining whether the mood disturbance is etiologically related to the general medical condition or substance abuse through a physiological mechanism. An important consideration in guiding the diagnosis is the presence of a temporal association between the onset, exacerbation, or remission of the general medical condition (or substance abuse) and that of the mood disturbance.

A final catch-all category, depressive disorder NOS (not otherwise specified), incorporates the following conditions: (1) premenstrual dysphoria disorder; (2) minor depressive disorder; (3) recurrent brief depressive disorder; (4) postpsychotic depression of schizophrenia; and (5) a major depressive episode superimposed on delusional disorder, psychotic disorder not otherwise specified, or the active phase of schizophrenia.

There has been significant debate in the literature regarding the potential shortcomings of an overreliance on categorizing disorders primarily by their presenting symptoms. Some have argued that treatment response should also be included as a key variable in categorizing psychiatric disorders (Fink 1993; Schatzberg and Rothschild, 1992). While the recent Diagnostic and Statistical Manuals have assiduously avoided using specific treatment response as a criteria for categorization, there are data to support differential treatment response of specific disorders such as catatonia (Rosebush et al., 1990; Fink and Taylor, 1991) and delusional depression (Schatzberg and Rothschild, 1992). This trend is evident in the current DSM-IV (American Psychiatric Association, 1994), which uses specifiers to describe the most recent mood disorder. These include: (1) with psychotic features, (2) with catatonic features, (3) with melancholic features, (4) with atypical features, (5) with postpartum onset, (6) with seasonal pattern.

DEPRESSIVE SUBTYPES

Currently, there are numerous treatment strategies for the treatment of a major depressive disorder. It has also become increasingly clear that not all major depressive episodes respond to a given treatment strategy (Schatzberg and Rothschild, 1992; Rosebush et al., 1990; Quiktin et al., 1993). Among the reasons for this is that the category of major depression appears to encompass a heterogeneous group of disorders with distinct pathophysiologies and treatment response. However, the decision of which somatic intervention to choose may rest in part on the subtype of the major depressive episode (i.e., presence of atypical features, catatonia or psychotic features, and postpartum onset). For the purposes of this review we will focus on six of the major subtypes: melancholia, atypical, seasonal, postpartum, psychotic, and catatonic.

Melancholic Features

The essential feature of the specifier with melancholic features is loss of interest or pleasure in all, or almost all, activities or a lack of reactivity to usually pleasurable stimuli (American Psychiatric Association, 1994). In addition, the patient's depressed mood does not improve when something good happens. These criteria are reminiscent of the older term *endogenous*. At least three of the following symptoms also need to be present to meet criteria for melancholia: (1) a distinct quality of the depressed mood, (2) depression that is regularly worse in the morning, (3) early morning awakening, (4) psychomotor retardation or agitation, (5) significant anorexia or weight loss, or (6) excessive or inappropriate guilt. A diagnosis of major depression with melancholia is associated not only with greater overall syndrome severity, but also with greater severity of nonmelancholic symptoms (Zimmerman et al., 1986). Controversy exists as to whether melancholic features in depression reflect a distinct phenomenological subtype or merely a gradient along a continuum of severity (Klerman et al., 1987). Although characteristic of a major depression with psychotic features (see below), marked psychomotor disturbance has also been described as a hallmark of melancholic depression (Nelson et al., 1981). The subtyping of major depression with melancholic features does allow for a more homogeneous group of patients, in whom biological studies can be undertaken, than the major depressive category as a whole. Thus, melancholic features are more frequently associated with abnormal laboratory findings such as dexamethasone nonsuppression, hyperadrenocorticism, reduced rapid eye movement (REM) latency, abnormal tyramine challenge test, and an abnormal asymmetry on dichotic listening tasks (American Psychiatric Association, 1994).

Atypical Features

The term *atypical depression* has been used for many years by clinicians to refer to a patient with any *nonendogenous* depression who responded well to monoamine oxidase inhibitor (MAOI) antidepressants. Numerous research groups have used different criteria for this diagnosis, making it difficult to interpret studies of outcome (West and Dally, 1959; Sargant, 1960; Paykel et al., 1983; Davidson et al., 1988). Over the past two decades, the Columbia group (Quitkin et al., 1993) has been refining operational criteria for atypical depression, which is enumerated in DSM-IV. These criteria only apply when the patient makes criteria for DSM-IV major depressive disorder. These criteria include mood reactivity and two (or more) of the following features:

(1) hypersomnia, (2) significant weight gain or increase in appetite, (3) leaden paralysis, i.e., heavy leaden feeling in arms or legs, and (4) a long-standing pattern of interpersonal rejection sensitivity that results in significant social or occupational impairment (American Psychiatric Association 1994; Quitkin et al., 1991, 1990, 1989; Liebowitz et al., 1988). Using these criteria, the Columbia group has been able to demonstrate in several placebo-controlled double-blind studies that patients exhibiting these atypical features respond preferentially to MAOIs as compared to tricyclic antidepressants (TCAs) (Liebowitz et al., 1984, 1988). Approximately 50% of patients with atypical depression can be expected to improve on imipramine compared to approximately 80% on MAOIs (Liebowitz et al, 1984; Quitkin et al., 1993).

Seasonal Pattern

In DSM-IV, the course specifier, seasonal pattern, may be applied to the onset and remission of any affective disorder (bipolar or unipolar depression) at characteristic times of the year. In making the diagnosis of cyclical or recurrent depression, it is important to try to discriminate between a seasonal versus a bipolar component (Blehar and Lewy, 1990). In unipolar disorders, this represents a subtype of depression in which episodes generally begin in fall or winter and remit in spring (Rosenthal et al., 1984, 1985). This pattern must be consistent over the last 2 years prior to diagnosis. Major depressive episodes that occur in a seasonal pattern are often characterized by reverse neurovegetative symptoms including anergia, hyperphagia, and hypersomnia. In the spring, some patients may experience a remission in their symptoms or some may experience a hypomanic or manic episode. Patients with a seasonal pattern to their depression may respond well to phototherapy (Rosenthal et al., 1984, 1985). There are limited data, however, on the long-term treatment with phototherapy, and it is generally reserved for patients with less severe and well-defined winter depressions.

Postpartum Onset

The postpartum onset specifier is a new addition to DSM-IV and has important implications for both prognosis and treatment. Postpartum onset may be applied to either manic or major depressive episodes in bipolar disorder, major depressive disorder, or brief psychotic disorder. In general, the symptoms that characterize a postpartum depression do not differ from symptoms in a nonpostpartum episode. Typically, symptom onset occurs within 4 weeks postpartum (Dean and Kendall, 1981; Meltzer and Kumar, 1985). Symptoms may include psychotic features such as delusions that the newborn is possessed by the devil or will be doomed to a terrible fate (American Psychiatric Association, 1994). Psychotic features appear from 1 in 500 to 1 in 1000 deliveries and are typically more common in primiparous women (Kendell et al., 1987). The risk for psychotic features is generally greater in women with a prior history of postpartum psychosis (Dean and Kendall, 1981; Davidson and Robertson, 1985; Kendell et al., 1987). There are data to suggest that postpartum psychotic depressive episodes may herald an ultimate bipolar disorder (type I) or precipitate an already established underlying bipolar disorder (Pugh et al., 1963; Davidson and Robertson, 1985). In both the psychotic and nonpsychotic presentations, there may be associated suicidal ideation, obsessional thoughts regarding violence to the child, insomnia (i.e., early morning awakening), spontaneous crying long after the usual duration of "baby blues" (i.e., 3–7 days postpartum), panic attacks, and disinterest in the infant (American

Psychiatric Association, 1994; Davidson and Robertson, 1985; Meltzer and Kumar, 1985; Platz and Kendall, 1988, Dean and Kendall, 1981).

Psychotic (Delusional) Depression

Schatzberg and Rothschild (1992) have argued that there are sufficient data and clinical reasons to designate major depression with psychotic features—a disorder with considerable morbidity and mortality—as a distinct depressive syndrome in DSM-IV. However, in DSM-IV, psychotic features is a specifier that indicates the presence of either delusions or hallucinations (which are typically auditory). Generally, the content of the delusions or hallucinations is consistent with the depressive themes. Such mood-congruent psychotic features include delusions of guilt, delusions of deserved punishment, nihilistic delusions, somatic delusions, or delusions of poverty. Less commonly, the content of the hallucinations or delusions has no apparent relationship to depressive themes. Such mood-incongruent psychotic features include persecutory delusions, delusions of thought insertion, delusions of thought broadcasting, and delusions of control.

Unfortunately, unlike patients with other psychotic disorders, such as schizophrenia or mania, patients with psychotic depression (PD) are often able to keep their unusual thoughts and feelings to themselves. Because the detection of delusions and hallucinations is often difficult in patients with PD, a number of investigators have attempted to study whether there are other characteristics that may help distinguish between PD and nonpsychotic depressed patients. Several groups have reported that patients with PD demonstrate a more frequent and severe psychomotor disturbance (either retardation or agitation) than do patients with nonpsychotic depression (NPD) (Charney and Nelson, 1981; Coryell et al., 1984b; Frances et al., 1981; Glassman and Roose, 1981; Lykouras et al., 1986; Nelson and Bowers, 1978). Psychotically depressed patients have also been reported to exhibit more pronounced paranoid symptoms (Frances et al., 1981; Lykouras et al., 1986), cognitive impairment (Rothschild et al., 1989), hopelessness (Frances et al., 1981), hypochondriasis (Coryell et al., 1984b; Glassman and Roose, 1981), anxiety (Charney and Nelson, 1981; Glassman and Roose, 1981), early insomnia (Frances et al., 1981; Lykouras et al., 1986), middle insomnia (Lykouras et al., 1986), and constipation (Parker et al., 1991) than NPD patients. PD patients have also failed to show a diurnal variation in mood compared with endogenous depressed NPD patients (Parker et al., 1991).

Patients with PD have much greater short-term morbidity and mortality in the acute episode than do NPD patients. The risk of suicide has been reported to be greater among hospitalized patients with PD than among their NPD counterparts (Roose et al., 1983). Suicidal ideation itself (without acts) has also been reported to be significantly greater among patients with PD than NPD (Nelson et al., 1984). However, other studies that compared the two groups on suicidal ideation or suicide attempts failed to find statistically significant differences between them (Charney and Nelson, 1981; Feighner et al., 1972; Frances et al., 1981; Glassman and Roose, 1981; Lykouras et al., 1986; Nelson and Bowers, 1978). In general, patients with PD have longer recovery times than patients with NPD (Coryell et al., 1984a; Robinson and Spiker, 1985). Some studies have suggested that PD patients have residual social impairment but not depression or psychosis at 1 year (Rothschild et al., 1993a) and 5 years (Coryell et al., 1990) after the initial index episode. In general, PD patients make good recoveries from their illness, although at a much slower rate than NPD patients.

Before antidepressant medications became available, it was less important than it is now to distinguish between psychotic and nonpsychotic depression. At that time, most severely depressed patients received electroconvulsive therapy (ECT), which is effective for both types. Today it is more important to make the distinction because PD usually responds poorly to antidepressant drugs alone (Spiker et al., 1985; Schatzberg and Rothschild, 1992) but better to a combination of a tricyclic antidepressant and neuroleptic or amoxapine (Spiker et al., 1985; Schatzberg and Rothschild, 1992). Selective serotonin reuptake inhibitors in combination with neuroleptics are less well studied but may be effective as well (Rothschild et al. 1993b; Wolfersdorf et al., 1995). For some patients, especially those with a history of mania, it may be helpful to add lithium to the antidepressant/neuroleptic combination (Price et al., 1983).

Catatonic Features

Similar to the debate in the literature on whether psychotic depression should be considered a distinct syndrome in DSM-IV (American Psychiatric Association, 1994), Fink and others have argued that catatonia be designated as a distinct syndrome in part because of its unique responsivity to ECT rather than to neuroleptics (Fink, 1993; Schatzberg and Rothschild, 1993; Gelenberg, 1976; Rosebush et al., 1990; Fink and Taylor, 1991). DSM-III-R maintained a very narrow definition of catatonia as a subtype of schizophrenia, which derives from Kahlbaum's original description of the syndrome. In his 1874 monograph (Levi and Pridan, trans., 1973) Kahlbaum was the first to use the term *catatonia* to describe a group of patients with a disease pattern characterized by cycles of depression and mania accompanied by a wide range of somatic components including immobility, withdrawal and refusal to eat, posturing, grimacing, rigidity, vegeturism, mutism, staring, stereotypies, waxy flexibility, echolalia, and echopraxia (Rosebush, et al. 1990; Levi et al., 1973). In addition to the above findings, Kahlbaum noted that psychosis was also frequently present. However, he classified catatonia primarily as a form of schizophrenia despite his detailed description of a disorder with frequent disturbances of mood. This narrow definition of catatonia persisted over several decades until the recent publication of DSM-IV, which endorsed the separate classification of catatonia to improve the therapeutic and prognostic consideration of patients.

Catatonia has been designated as a distinct syndrome (i.e., catatonic disorder due to a general medical condition) in part because of its unique treatment responsivity. The literature supports the preferential response of patients with catatonia to ECT and benzodiazepines (i.e., lorazepam) rather than to neuroleptics (Fricchione et al., 1983; Rosebush et al., 1990; Fink and Taylor, 1991; Schatzberg and Rothschild, 1993; Gelenberg, 1976; Vinogrado and Reiss, 1986; Greenfield et al., 1987). Catatonic disorder is generally diagnosed when the presence of catatonia is judged to be due to the direct physiological effects of a general medical condition such as hypercalcemia, neoplasm, head trauma, cerebrovascular disease, encephalitis, and hepatic encephalopathy (American Psychiatric Association, 1994).

ANIMAL MODELS OF DEPRESSION

Animal models of depression have been useful to further understanding of the physiological basis of depressive symptomatology in humans. These models have also shown that changes in neurotransmitters and regulatory systems can be corrected in animals by the medications that are used in humans as antidepressants or mood-stabilizing drugs. In humans, depression consists essentially of two types of symptoms: (1) disturbances of mood and feelings, which cannot be tested in animals, and (2) vegetative symptoms and alterations in observable behaviors, including sleep, activity, sexual interest and activity, appetite and weight, and ability to concentrate. Animals subjected to specific stressors exhibit weight loss, sleep difficulties, loss of sexual activity, inability to learn, and decreased motor activity, [which closely resembles the clinical signs of endogenous depressions (Weiss et al., 1976)], and alterations in immune and hormonal functioning (Bartrop et al., 1977; Schleifer et al., 1984). Animal models of depression have been useful to further understanding of the physiological basis of depressive symptomatology in humans, the mechanisms of antidepressant and mood-stabilizing drugs, and the development of new medications for the treatment of mood disorders.

Separation and Loss Models

Animal models have demonstrated that specific stressors such as separation and loss can alter the effect of brain biogenic amine systems and immune and endocrine parameters. Infant monkeys separated from their mothers or from groups of peers develop symptoms characterized by agitation, sleeplessness, distress calls, and screaming, followed after 1–2 days by "depression," characterized by a decrease in activity, appetite, play and social interaction, and the development of a "sad" facial expression (Hinde et al., 1978; Kaufman and Rosenblum, 1967; McKinney and Bunney, 1969; Reite et al., 1981; Suomi et al., 1970, 1976; Bowden and McKinney, 1972; Kraemer and McKinney, 1979). Treatment with antidepressants modifies the development of these symptoms following the separation (Hrdina et al., 1979). Moreover, data on juvenile and adolescent monkeys reared with peers instead of their mothers demonstrate that they are more sensitive to the depressant effects of inhibition of norepinephrine (NE) and dopamine (DA) synthesis than are monkeys reared with their mothers (Kraemer and McKinney, 1979). In addition, rhesus monkey infants deprived of maternal interaction have lower levels of cerebrospinal fluid (CSF) NE than infant monkeys who were reared by their mother (Kraemer et al., 1989). The infants deprived of maternal interaction also showed instability in their neurotransmitter levels and metabolites in the CSF. In addition, there were changes in cerebrospinal fluid NE levels associated with social separation and social group formation. Thus, the brain NE system appears to be sensitive to changes in the social environment. Its level of activity, as reflected in levels of NE in CSF, appears to depend on both the prevailing social environment and the prior rearing environment (Kraemer et al., 1989).

There is also data to support alterations in immune function (i.e., lymphocyte proliferation, macrophage responses) to premature maternal separation or psychosocial stress (Coe et al., 1985; Irwin, 1995). Evidence is also available to suggest that these effects of maternal separation on immune function persist into adulthood leading to possible increased vulnerability to infectious disease (Laundenslager et al., 1985; Irwin, 1995).

There is also a decrease in cellular immune response in monkeys that are subject to a chronic social stressor such as having a changing social group (Irwin, 1995). This reaction may be attenuated by the social behavior of the animal at the time of the stressor. Those animals who showed affiliative behaviors while undergoing social stress did not suffer as great a decrement in lymphocytes as compared to less affiliative animals. Social behaviors that are affiliative appear to protect animals from immunosuppressive effects of chronic social stress (Irwin, 1995).

Studies of the hypothalamic–pituitary–adrenal (HPA) axis in separated monkeys provides further evidence for the biological sequelae of loss. Separation in monkeys is accompanied during the protest phase by a rise in plasma cortisol concentrations (Smotherman et al., 1979), and the size of this elevation has been found to predict the intensity of the depressive response during the despair phase (Higley et al., 1982). As in endogenously depressed humans, some separated monkeys also failed to suppress plasma cortisol concentrations in response to dexamethasone challenge (Kalin et al., 1982).

In addition to animal models of separation and loss, learned helplessness and behavioral despair models provide interesting data on the pathogenesis of depression. The term *learned helplessness* describes a paradigm in which exposure to any uncontrollable stress produces performance deficits in subsequent learning tasks that are not seen in subjects who are able to control the stressor. This phenomenon was first described by Seligman and co-workers in dogs and subsequently extended to a large number of other species, including humans (Garber et al., 1979; Maier and Seligman, 1976; Miller et al., 1977; Seligman, 1975). In the original experiment, dogs were subjected to electric shocks, which some animals could escape but others could not. Approximately two-thirds of animals exposed to inescapable shock eventually accepted the shock passively but failed to learn how to make a successful escape response. It is assumed in the learned helplessness model that during exposure to inescapable shock, the animals learned that nothing they could do would possibly be effective and they became helpless. Learned helpless animals show a variety of symptoms and behavioral changes that have obvious similarities to the syndrome of major depression. Helpless animals show decreased locomotor activity (Wagner et al., 1977), less motivation to eat (Anderson et al., 1968; Rosellini, 1978; Rosellini and DeCola, 1981; Zacharko et al., 1982), decreased aggression (Maier et al., 1972), early awakening (Weiss et al., 1984), and loss of appetite and weight (Weiss, 1968). Although there is considerable variability in how long the helplessness effects last, in some studies the effects have been reported to last for periods of up to several months (Hannum et al., 1976).

Another example of an animal model of helplessness and behavioral despair is if mice or rats are forced to swim in a confined space. They will initially make a considerable attempt to escape but then will soon give up and assume an immobile posture. On subsequent immersion, the onset of immobility is much more rapid. This onset of immobility in the swimming test is delayed by pretreatment with a wide variety of antidepressants (Willner, 1985). In addition, there is a significant correlation between clinical potency of antidepressants in humans and the medication's ability to prevent behavioral despair in animals (Willner, 1985). In humans, exposure to uncontrollable stress such as loud noise has also been found to induce subsequent performance deficits (Garber and Seligman 1980; Garber et al., 1979; Miller et al., 1977). Inescapable shock leads to depletion of brain catecholamines similar to pharmacological treatments that impair catecholaminergic neurotransmission (Anisman et al., 1979). The behavioral manifestations of learned helplessness can be reversed by treatment with tricyclic antidepressants, monoamine oxidase inhibitors, and other antidepressants (Anisman et al., 1979). The effect appears to be relatively specific to antidepressants, since neuroleptics, benzodiazepines, and sedatives were ineffective (Anisman et al., 1979).

Summary

In summary, animal models of depression have provided clues to understanding the pathophysiology of mood disorders. They also have added to our understanding of the relationships among psychosocial stressors, genetics, changes in brain neurochemistry, and immune and endocrine function. Animal models provide evidence that brain biochemistry and behavior is a two-way street; namely, what an organism experiences can affect its neurochemistry and, likewise, changes in the neurochemistry can affect the organism's behavior.

NEUROTRANSMITTER AND RELATED HYPOTHESES

Norepinephrine (NE)

In the late 1950s several investigators proposed that catecholamines might be involved in the pathophysiology of depression (Everett and Tolman, 1959; Jacobsen, 1964; Rosenblatt et al., 1960). At that time it was clear that reserpine and tetrabenzamine could cause depression as a side effect (Lingjaerde, 1963). Both these medications were known to cause profound depletion of NE in various tissues, including the brain, by interfering with the binding of NE by storage granules. This caused the NE to diffuse freely within the cell where it was exposed to monoamine oxidase (MAO) and degraded (Carlsson, 1961; Shore, 1962). Shortly thereafter, inhibitors of MAO (the first effective antidepressants) were shown to elevate NE levels and, at high doses, produce behavioral excitation in experimental animals (Spector et al., 1963). Moreover, pretreatment of the animals with MAOIs prevented the sedative and NE-depleting effects of reserpine (Carlsson, 1961). It was soon established that tricyclic antidepressants, such as imipramine, worked by blocking the reuptake mechanism and prolonging the synaptic effects of NE in the brain (Glowinski and Axelrod, 1964; Hertting et al., 1961). Furthermore, amphetamines, which had been used as antidepressants prior to the discovery of tricyclics and MAOIs, were shown to potentiate the effects of NE by promoting its release and inhibiting its reuptake (Iversen, 1964). Urine studies of the NE metabolite 3-methoxy-4-hydroxyphenylglycol (MHPG) also indicated that depressed patients had low levels of this metabolite when compared to normal controls (Schildkraut, 1965). The accumulating evidence for a biological basis of depression gave rise to the original catecholamine (NE) hypotheses of major depression, which stated that this disorder resulted from a functional deficit of NE at critical effector sights in the central nervous system (Bunney and Davis, 1965; Schildkraut, 1965).

Norepinephrine has become one of the most intensively studied neurotransmitters in the brain. One of the principal sights of NE synthesis, the locus coerulus in the midpons, sends a dense network of fibers to terminal fields in such disparate areas as the hypothalamus and hippocampus and throughout the cerebral cortex (Moore and Bloom, 1979). The location and functional effects of NE were appropriate for a neurotransmitter thought to be involved in an illness like major depression.

Initial studies by fluorometric assays of the NE metabolite MHPG showed generally decreased levels in the CSF, plasma, and urine in patients with major depression (Schildkraut, 1965; Bunney and Davis, 1965; Schildkraut, 1978). These studies were originally interpreted as supporting the original catecholamine depletion hypotheses of major depression. More recent studies, employing the direct assay of NE itself and the mass-spectroscopic assay of MHPG, support the conclusion that the NE system in the locus ceruleus is activated in patients with major depression (Siever et al., 1984). These studies report normal or increased levels of cerebrospinal fluid NE (Post et al., 1984; Christensen et al., 1980), increased plasma NE (Wyatt et al., 1971; Esler et al., 1982; Lake et al., 1982; Siever et al., 1984; Roy et al., 1985), and increased CSF and urinary MHPG in patients with major depression (Koslow et al., 1983). These clinical data are consistent with laboratory data that indicates that MAOIs and tricyclic antidepressants decrease the firing rate of neurons in the locus ceruleus (Nyback et al., 1975, Campbell et al., 1979; Murphy et al., 1986) and reduce the level of NE metabolites in the brain (Nielsen and Braestrup, 1977). In addition, the tricyclic antidepressants downregulate the cortical beta receptors (Sulser, 1978, 1983; Sulser et al., 1978), which are thought to mediate the arousal-producing effects of NE.

The data supporting the catecholamine hypotheses of depression have at times been paradoxical. While some investigators have proposed that there exists a relative deficiency of catecholamines in central synapses in depression (Baldessarini, 1975; Waldmeier, 1981), others have suggested that net catecholaminergic activity might be increased in depression (Koslow et al., 1983; Lake et al., 1982). The present data do not consistently support either of the formulations; however, there is too much evidence implicating abnormalities of the NE system to dismiss its importance in the pathogenesis of depression (Siever and Davis, 1985). A reformulation of the catecholamine hypothesis was proposed by Siever and Davis (1985) to help clarify the inconsistencies in previous studies. This *dysregulation hypothesis* (Siever and Davis, 1985) is grounded in the appreciation of the dynamic properties of neurotransmitter systems; mainly, their time-dependent and stimulus-dependent regulation (Foote et al., 1983) mediated by multiple control mechanisms (Langer, 1980). These hypotheses attempt to avoid the old arguments that patients have too little or too much catecholaminergic activity and instead view depression as a failure of the regulation of these systems (Siever and Davis, 1985). The model proposes that noradrenergic activity in depression is altered whereby noradrenergic neuronal firing is increased and erratic, while the NE released per nerve impulse in decreased, which reduces the overall responsiveness of the system to specific stimuli. The model is consistent both with animal models of uncontrollable shock-induced behavioral depression and with the clinical phenomenology and course of affective disorders (Siever and Davis, 1985).

Indoleamine Hypothesis

Coppen and colleagues (1972) hypothesized that indoleamines play a role in the pathogenesis of depression. Several studies have demonstrated that there is a reduction in CSF concentrations of 5-hydroxyindolaceticacid (5-HIAA), the principle metabolite of serotonin, in some depressed patients (Asberg et al., 1976a,b; Gibbons and Davis, 1986; Roy et al., 1989). Asberg and colleagues (1976a) reported that low concentrations of 5-HIAA may be a marker for suicidal behavior and for suicide risk in depressed patients. The initial observations of Asberg have been replicated in subsequent studies (Banki et al., 1984; Brown et al., 1982; Traskman et al., 1981). However, since low levels of 5-HIAA have also been observed in patients with aggression or poor impulse control (Linnoila et al., 1983; Virkkunen et al., 1987), it is conceivable that low 5-HIAA levels may be a marker for violent or impulsive behavior in general. Other major lines of evidence that serotonin is important in depressive disorders include: (1) virtually all known antidepressant agents regardless of their receptor-specific properties have been shown to increase the efficacy of central nervous system (CNS) serotonergic transmission; (2) decreased CSF concentrations of the major serotonin (5-HT) metabolite, 5-HIAA in postmortem brains of suicide victims (Stanley and Mann, 1983); (3) decreased 5-HT reuptake in the platelets of depressed patients (Tuomisto and Tukiainen, 1976), (4) depletion of plasma tryptophan precursors may reverse antidepressant-induced remissions (Delgado et al., 1990); and (5) *p*-chlorophenylalamine (PCPA), which decreases 5-HT synthesis, reverses the clinical efficacy of antidepressants (Shopsin et al., 1976). The introduction of the selective serotonin reuptake inhibitors (SSRIs) into clinical practice in 1988 has led to a considerable increase in research into the role of serotonin in the pathophysiology of major depression.

Acetylcholine

Data on the cholinergic nervous system suggests that acetylcholine alone or acting in concert with other neurotransmitters may play an important role in the regulation of mood. Janowsky et al. (1972) proposed a role for monoaminergic–cholinergic balance in the pathogenesis of mood disorders in which a relative increase in cholinergic activity, in comparison to central norepinephrine production, is thought to play a role in the pathogenesis of depression. Conversely, a decrease in cholinergic activity relative to central noradrenergic activity is thought to play a role in producing mania.

Research findings from both animal and human studies suggest that central muscarinic and possibly nicotinic mechanisms may play a role in the psychophysiology of affective disorders. Preclinical animal behavioral models of depression (as discussed in the previous section) have demonstrated that, if centrally acting cholinomimetic agents are given to these animals, there is enhanced learned helplessness and behavioral despair (Janowsky et al., 1972). Probably the most convincing evidence that acetylcholine is involved in the regulation of affective disorders is the observation that centrally active cholinomimetic drugs such as insecticides rapidly induce depressed moods (Janowsky and Overstreet, 1995). There is also evidence that antidepressants including ECT treatment: (1) decrease brain acetylcholine levels and (2) increase choline acetyltransferase activity (Kapur and Mann, 1993). Spectroscopic studies have also provided evidence to support a role for increased acetylcholine in depression. Using magnetic resonance imaging (MRI), Charles and colleagues (1994) have observed that patients with major depression when compared to normal controls have higher levels of brain choline.

There is also evidence that nicotinic cholinergic mechanisms may also be linked to depression. A high rate of cigarette smoking is associated with major depression (Glassman, 1993). It is unclear whether the depression results from a direct interaction of nicotine on the postsynaptic nicotine receptor or is due to an indirect interaction with presynaptic nicotine receptors leading to stimulation of the release of acetylcholine onto muscarinic receptors (Glassman, 1993).

Dopamine (DA)

Dopamine (DA) was ignored for many years as a possible cause of depression because tricyclic antidepressants were relatively ineffective as blockers of DA reuptake when compared to their effects on NE reuptake (Carlsson 1970). However, much of the evidence that supports the role of NE in depression also implicates DA. For example, both NE and DA are metabolized by MAO (Molinoff and Axelrod, 1971) and have their destruction hastened by reserpine (Carlsson, 1961). Moreover, the stimulant effects of amphetamines appear to be mediated by DA rather than NE (Kelly et al., 1975). Clinically, some depressed patients show decreases in CSF concentrations of homovanillic acid (HVA), the major DA metabolite in humans (Goodwin et al., 1973), and several conditions in which DA function is depleted such as Parkinson's disease, neuroleptic treatment, and withdrawal from chronic amphetamines are also associated with depression (Randrup et al., 1975). Kapur and Mann (1993) recently reviewed the role of dopamine in depressive disorders. In addition to the examples cited above for dopamine's role in depression, they also included the following evidence: (1) an increased incidence of depression in patients receiving dopamine depleting or antagonistic agents; (2) the antidepressant effect of agents that enhance dopamine transmission such as psychostimulants (methylphenidate, dextroamphetamine), which are particularly efficacious in the treatment of mood disorders due to a general medical condition (Kaufmann et al., 1982; Katon and Rasking, 1980; Woods, 1986; Fernandez et al., 1988; Chiarello and Cole, 1987; Masand et al., 1991a,b); and (3) the ability for various classes of antidepressants and electroconvulsive therapy to enhance dopamine effects in animal models.

Gamma-Aminobutyric Acid

Gamma-aminobutyricacid (GABA), the principle inhibitory agent in the mammalian brain, restrains the firing of the locus coerulus (Foote et al., 1980; Aston-Jones et al., 1984). Cerebrospinal fluid and plasma GABA levels tend to be low in depressed patients (Gerner and Hare, 1981; Berrettini et al., 1982; Gold et al., 1980; Petty and Schlesser, 1981; Morselli et al., 1980) and progabide, a GABA agonist, has been shown in a preliminary study to have antidepressant effects (Morselli et al., 1980).

RECEPTOR AND SECOND-MESSENGER SYSTEMS

Receptors for neurotransmitters are often regarded as the locks to which the transmitter is the key (Willner, 1985). Generally, receptors function homeostatically: "down-regulating" when their input increases, and "up-regulating" when their input decreases. It is believed that specific receptors for DA as well as alpha- and beta-receptors for NE exist. These adrenergic receptors are similar to those in the peripheral sympathetic nervous system (Baldessarini, 1983). Several studies have demonstrated altered receptor function in depressed patients. Growth hormone, heart rate, and plasma MHPG responses to the alpha-2-receptor agonist clonidine are blunted (Charney et al., 1982; Checkley et al., 1988; Matussek et al., 1980; Siever et al., 1984), and lymphocyte beta-2-receptors are down-regulated (Extein et al., 1979; Pandey et al., 1979) in depressed patients. Chronic treatment with antidepressants (2–3 weeks) has been shown to reduce the physiological sensitivity of central beta-receptors, as assessed by the ability of NE to stimulate cyclic adenosine monophosphate (cAMP) (Vetulani and Sulser, 1975); this form of treatment also reduced the actual number of beta-receptors (Banerjee et al., 1977). The ability to reduce beta-receptor function is a property of all effective antidepressant treatments (Vetulani and Sulser, 1975). These observations lead to the formulation of new hypotheses that "down-regulation" of beta-receptors was a mechanism of antidepressant action (Sulser, 1978).

As in the peripheral autonomic noradrenergic nervous system, there is also evidence of presynaptic autoreceptors for DA and NE (Baldessarini, 1983), which are sensitive to their own transmitter. In general, autoreceptors appear to mediate inhibitory functions and to serve as negative feedback systems (Usdin and Bunney, 1975). Some antidepressant medications down-regulate the inhibitory autoreceptors, which tends to increase NE function overall. This may also be one of the mechanisms for the therapeutic effects of antidepressant medications (Baldessarini, 1983).

More recently, investigators have studied second-messenger systems (i.e., receptor–ligand binding relationships) in order to study intraneuronal events stimulated by this interaction. Evidence suggests (Wachtel, 1990) that the adenylate–cyclase and phosphoinositol second-messenger systems are involved in the pathogenesis of depression. Wachtel (1990) has proposed that a functional disturbance in intraneuronal signal amplification systems distal to the neurotransmitter receptor are a possible cause of mood disorders.

NEUROIMAGING

With the advent of advances in neuroimaging such as computed tomography (CT), magnetic resonance imaging (MRI), single photon emission tomography (SPECT), and photon emission tomography (PET) more attention is now being focused on the structural and functional basis of depression. However, neuroimaging studies in mood disorders have been difficult to interpret due to complicating factors such as: (1) heterogeneity of the disorder; (2) small sample sizes; (3) episodic nature of the illness and whether underlying neuroimaging abnormalities are detectable only during periods of illness or whether they are independent of clinical status; and (4) differences in imaging methodology, which makes comparing results from various studies difficult.

The structural abnormalities initially thought to be specific to schizophrenia have now been reported in mood disorders. Specifically, patients with major depression were found to have increased ventricle-to-brain ratios (VBRs) (Teste et al., 1988). Other abnormalities noted: (1) sulcal widening (Dolan et al., 1986) and (2) atrophy of the cerebellum (Weinberger et al., 1982; Nasrallah et al., 1982).

One of the most consistent findings with regard to structural abnormalities specific for mood disorders are abnormalities in the subcortical white matter and basal ganglia. Findings in the basal ganglia include: (1) increased radiodensity of the head of the caudate in depressed elderly patients (Beats et al., 1991), and (2) smaller volumes of caudate and putamen nuclei as demonstrated by MRI (Krishnan et al., 1992; Husain et al., 1991). The lesions on MRI have been called various names such as leukoencephalopathy, subcortical hyperintensities, or unidentified bright objects (UBOs). Studies have found high rates of UBOs in depressed patients in middle and late life (Rabins et al., 1991; Krishnan, 1990, 1988; Coffey et al., 1988, 1989; Deicken et al., 1991).

Functional abnormalities have been assessed using SPECT and PET as techniques for measuring cerebral blood flow and metabolic rate. Although findings are inconsistent, studies have shown abnormal metabolic activity and blood flow in regions of the frontal cortex in depressed patients (Hurwitz et al., 1990; Mayberg et al., 1990; Martinot et al., 1990). There is evidence that with treatment patients who originally hypoperfused their prefrontal cortex may then show relative hyperperfusion in parts of the limbic system (Ebert et al., 1991).

PSYCHONEUROIMMUNOLOGY

Several centers have reported immunological abnormalities in depressed patients. Animal models of the effect of stress on cellular and humoral responses have provided insight for the study of immune dysfunction in mood disorders in humans. In animals, administration of aversive stressors such as tail shock or social status change have been found to significantly alter cellular immune functions such as lymphocyte responses and natural killer (NK) cell activity as well as humoral immune function, specifically suppression of IgG antibody response to an antigen (Irwin, 1995). Investigators have also demonstrated that stress may alter accessory cells of the immune system such as macrophages (Irwin, 1995). Moreover, other data suggests that stress may also play an important role in altering immune cell second-messenger systems. For example, initial studies have begun to investigate whether the effects of stress on lymphocyte function are mediated by alterations in calcium mobilization or calcium-dependent biochemical measures (Irwin, 1995). Acute and chronic stress have been found to suppress mitogen-stimulated increases in calcium, suggesting that stress induces an inhibition of calcium mobilization in lymphocytes and interferes with this obligatory signal for certain signal transduction pathways (Irwin, 1995).

Life stressors such as bereavement, marital separation, and academic examinations have all been shown to have effects on immune function (Bartrop et al., 1977; Schleifer et al., 1983, 1984, Glaser et al., 1990). Individuals undergoing bereavement show alterations of cellular immunity including reduction of NK cell activity suppression of lymphocyte responses to antigen stimulation and alteration of T-cell subpopulations (Bartrop et al., 1977; Schleifer et al., 1983, 1984). Psychological stress during relatively minor aversive events such as academic examinations are also temporarily associated with higher white blood cell counts, an increased absolute lymphocyte count, a reduction of lymphocyte proliferation and NK activity, and alterations in regulation of interleukin-2 (IL-2) and IL-2 receptor in perpherial blood lymphocytes (Glaser et al., 1990). Chronic stressors that last over periods of several years increase the risk for depression and altered immune function. Glaser and colleagues (1990) have shown that family caregivers of Alzheimer's patients as compared to controls are more likely to be psychologically distressed and to have significantly reduced percentages of total T-lymphocytes and T-helper cells (Kiecolt-Glaser et al., 1991). Finally, in a recent study by Evans and colleagues (1992) depressed subjects exhibited reductions in the number and activity of NK cell activity.

NEUROENDOCRINE HYPOTHESES

The major biological manifestations of depression consist of alterations in the hypothalamic centers that govern food intake, libido, and circadian rhythms. Patients with depression typically have anorexia, decreased sexual interest, early morning awakening, diurnal variation of mood, and endocrine abnormalities such as hypercortisolism (Gold et al., 1988a,b; Sachar et al., 1970; Carroll et al., 1976a,b). Data in experimental animals have suggested that neurohormones modulate the influence of conventional neurotransmitters and can coordinate complex behavioral and physiologic processes relevant to survival (Gold et al., 1988a,b).

Various neuroendocrine abnormalities have been associated with depression including blunted growth hormone and prolactin responses (Checkley et al., 1988), blunted thyrotropin-stimulating hormone (TSH) response to thyrotropin-releasing hormone (TRH) (Prange et al., 1972; Kastin et al., 1972), as well as reduced luteinizing hormone secretion and disturbances in B-endorphin, vasopressin, and calcitonin. However, the most extensively studied neuroendocrine abnormalities in depression are of the hypo-thalamic–pituitary–adrenal (HPA) axis. In the 1930s Cannon and colleagues (Cannon, 1929, 1939) showed that the adrenal glands were involved in the body's response to stress. This observation prompted other investigators to examine the effects of the pituitary–adrenal axis on emotional and biologic disease states (Friedman et al., 1963; Price et al., 1957). Hyperactivity of the HPA axis is one of the most robust and reproducible findings in patients with major depression (Sachar et al., 1970; Stokes et al., 1984; Linkowski et al., 1985; Carroll, 1982), especially in those with melancholia or psychotic features. These abnormalities of HPA axis dysfunction include: (1) increased secretion of cortisol particularly in the evening and night (Fukushima and Gallager, 1970); (2) increased 24-hour urinary excretion of cortisol (Carroll et al., 1976a,b); (3) resistance to suppression of cortisol, B-endorphin, and ACTH (adrenocorticop-tropin) by dexamethasone; and (4) hypersecretion of corticotrophin-releasing factor (CRF) as evidenced by increased concentration of CRF in cerebrospinal fluid (Nemer-off and Evans, 1984; Risch et al., 1992). Other studies have demonstrated a reduced number of CRF binding sites in the frontal cortex of suicide victims (Nemeroff et al., 1988), which may be secondary to CRF receptor down-regulation as a result of CRF hypersecretion.

The dexamethasone suppression test (DST) was originally developed as a diagnostic aid to evaluate dysfunction of the HPA axis in endocrine disease. However, since the observation that DST results are frequently abnormal in patients with major depression (Carroll et al., 1976a,b; Schlesser et al., 1980; Stokes et al., 1975), the DST has been extensively studied in depressive disorders. Although its use in the clinical setting has decreased, the test may have utility in certain situations such as predicting clinical outcome. Several studies have reported that patients who fail to convert to normal suppression on the DST even after an apparently adequate response to treatment may be at increased risk for relapse (Greden et al., 1980; Rothschild and Schatzberg, 1982; Nemeroff and Evans, 1984; Ribeiro et al., 1993). Our group has reported on the relationships between one-year cortisol measures and outcome at one year in depressed patients (Rothschild et al., 1993a). We observed significant correlations between mea-sures of cortisol activity [DST, urinary free cortisol (UFC)] at one year and measures of social and occupational functioning at one year. Depressed patients with UFC values great than 100 μg/24 hours at one year had significantly poorer functioning as measured by the Social Adjustment Scale–Self-Report (SAS–SR) (Weissman et al., 1978) total score at one year than did patients with UFC values less than 100 μg/24 hours. A similar relationship was observed between DST nonsuppressor status at one year and poorer social and occupational functioning at one year (Rothschild et al., 1993a). The relationship between higher cortisol levels at one year and poor overall functioning at one year was observed in both psychotic and nonpsychotic depressed patients and appeared even stronger statistically when degree of depression [as measured by total Hamilton Depression Rating Scale (HDRS) score] was partialled out. We have hypoth-esized that the association between higher levels of cortisol at one year and poorer social/occupational functioning is secondary to subtle cognitive deficits caused by higher cortisol levels seen in depressed patients (Rothschild et al., 1993a). Our hypothesis is based on observations that increased HPA axis activity in depressed patients is associ-ated with larger ventricle-to-brain ratios (VBRs) (Kellner et al., 1983; Rothschild et al., 1989; Rao et al., 1989) and cognitive disturbances (Rothschild et al., 1989; Reus, 1982; Rubinow et al., 1984; Wolkowitz et al., 1990; Brown and Qualls, 1981; Demeter et al., 1986; Winokur et al., 1987; Sikes et al., 1989). These studies suggest possible associations among cognitive disturbances, cortisol hypersecretion, and enlarged ventricles.

Studies in animals also provide supporting evidence for the dysregulation of the HPA axis in depression. Exposure to uncontrollable stress and a disruption of attachment bonds alters the regulation of the HPA system (Kalin and Takahashi, 1988). Although one exposure to an uncontrollable shock schedule does not result in differential release of adrenocorticotrophic hormone (ACTH) between animals receiving escapable or inescapable shock, repeated exposure to uncontrollable shock enhances the secretion of ACTH (Kalin and Takahashi, 1988). In addition, prolonged separation results in increased cerebrospinal fluid ACTH concentrations suggesting that activation of brain ACTH neurons occurs in the despair response (Kalin and Takahashi, 1988). Furthermore, the intracerebral ventricular administration of CRF produces many of the pathophysiologic changes classically associated with depression (Gold et al., 1988a,b).

Complex relationships exist between the neuroendocrine and monoamine systems in the central nervous system. *In vitro* secretion of CRF from rat hypothalami is stimulated by NE and acetylcholine and inhibited by GABA (Gold et al., 1988b). The stimulatory effect of NE (Holsboer et al., 1983) is of great interest because when CRF is applied locally to neurons in the locus coerulus of awake animals, the firing of the locus coerulus increases markedly (Valentino et al., 1983), presumably because of binding to the dense network of receptors for CRF within the locus coerulus (Gold et al., 1988b). The levels of CRF in the CSF of patients with major depression correlate positively with indexes of locus coerulus activation such as cerebrospinal fluid NE and MHPG, which supports the theory of a functional connection between the activities of the locus coerulus, NE, and CRF systems (Roy et al., 1987).

The regulation of CRF release from *in vivo* and *in vitro* studies have provided evidence for direct dopaminergic, noradrenergic, and/or adrenergic control of CRF release (Owens and Nemeroff, 1992). Other studies have implicated serotonin, acetylcholine, other monoamines, and neuropeptides. CRF has been shown to exert excitatory action in a variety of brain areas including the locus coerulus, hippocampus, cerebral cortex, and parts of the hypothalamus (Owens and Nemeroff, 1992). It is unclear at the present time whether a hyperfunctioning CRF system is a result of alterations in monoaminergic systems in depression or whether changes in monoaminergic circuits are secondary to CRF hypersecretion. However, it appears that CRF and the locus coerulus–NE systems are the principal biological effectors of the generalized stress response. Gold and colleagues (1988b) have speculated that melancholic depression arises from an acute generalized stress response coupled with a dysregulation of the CRF and locus coerulus–NE systems.

CONCLUSION

In summary, research over the past three decades has led to more precise diagnostic criteria and a better understanding of the biologic basis of depression. As with most diseases in medicine, there is no single type of depression nor a single cause. The hope for the future is that with further refinements in our ability to subtype depressions combined with advances in the fields of neurochemistry, neuroendocrinology, molecular genetics, and brain imaging, the clinician will be better equipped to characterize and rapidly treat patients suffering from depression.

REFERENCES

American Psychiatric Association (1994): Diagnostic and Statistical Manual of Mental Disorders, 4th ed. Washington, DC: American Psychiatric Association.

American Psychiatric Association (1987): Diagnostic and Statistical Manual of Mental Disorders, 3rd ed, revised. Washington, DC: American Psychiatric Association.

Anderson DC, Cole J, McVaugh W (1968): Variations in unsignalled inescapable preshock as determinants of responses to punishment. J Comp Physiol Psychol 65: (Monog. Suppl.):1–17.

Anisman H, Remington G, Sklar LS (1979): Effects of inescapable shock on subsequent escape performance: Catecholaminergic and cholinergic mediation of response initiation and maintenance. Psychopharmacology 61:107–124.

Asberg M, Thoren P, Traskman L, Bertilsson L, Ringberger V (1976a): Serotonin depression—a biochemical subgroup within the affective disorders? Science 191:478–483.

Asberg M, Traskman L, Thoren P (1976b): 5-HIAA in the cerebrospinal fluid: A biochemical suicide predictor? Arch Gen Psychiatry 33:1193–1197.

Aston-Jones G, Foote SL, Bloom FE (1984): Anatomy and physiology of locus coerules neurons: Functional implications. In Ziegler MG, Lake CR (eds): "Norepinephrine." Baltimore: Williams and Williams, pp 92–116.

Baldessarini RJ (1983): "Biomedical Aspects of Depression." Washington: American Psychiatric Press.

Baldessarini RJ (1975): The basis for amine hypotheses in affective disorders: A critical evaluation. Arch Gen Psychiatry 32:1087–1093.

Banerjee SP, Kung LS, Riggi SJ, Chanda SK (1977): Development of beta-adrenergic subsensitivity by antidepressants. Nature 268: 455–456.

Banki CM, Arato M, Papp Z, Kurcz M (1984): Biochemical markers in suicidal patients: Investigations with cerebrospinal fluid amine metabolites and neuroendocrine tests. J Affect Disord 6:341–350.

Bartrop RW, Luckhurst E, Lazarus L, Kiloh LG, Penny R (1977): Depressed lymphocyte function after bereavement. Lancet 83:834–836.

Beats B, Levy R, Forstl H (1991): Ventricular enlargement and caudate hyperdensity in elderly depressives. Biol Psychiatry 30:452–458.

Berrettini WH, Nurnberger JI, Jr, Hare TA, Gershon ES, Post RM (1982): Plasma and CSF GABA in affective illness. Br J Psychiatry 141:483–487.

Blehar MC, Lewy AJ (1990): Seasonal mood disorders: Consensus and controversy. Psychopharmacol Bull 26:465–494.

Bowden DM, McKinney WT (1972): Behavioral effects of peer separation, isolation, and reunion on adolescent male rhesus monkeys. Dev Psychobil 5: 353–362.

Brown GL, Ebert MH, Goyer PF, Jimerson DC, Klein WJ, Bunney WE, Goodwin FK (1982): Aggression, suicide, and serotonin: Relationships to CSF amine metabolites. Am J Psychiatry 139:741–746.

Brown WA, Qualls CB (1991): Pituitary-adrenal disinhibition in depression: Marker of a subtype with characteristic clinical features and response to treatment? Psychiatry Res 4:115–128.

Bunney WE, Davis JM (1965): Norepinephrine in depressive reactions. Arch Gen Psychiatry 13:483–494.

Campbell IC, Murphy DC, Gallager DW, Tallman JF, Marshall EF (1979): Neurotransmitter-related adaptation in the central nervous system following chronic monoamine oxidase inhibition. In Singer TP, Von Korff RW, Murphy DL (eds): "Monoamine Oxidase: Structure, Function, and Altered Functions." New York: Academic Press, pp 517–530.

Cannon WB (1939): The Wisdom of the Body." New York: WW Norton.

Cannon WB (1929): "Bodily Changes in Pain, Hunger, Fear, and Rage." New York: Appelton-Century-Croft.

Carlsson A (1970): Effects of drugs on amine storage mechanisms. In Schumann HJ, Kroneberg G (eds): "New Aspects of Storage and Release Mechanisms of Catecholamines. Heidelberg: Springer, pp 223–233.

Carlsson A (1961): Brain monoamines and psychotropic drugs. Neuropsychopharmacol 2:417–421.

Carroll BJ (1982): The dexamethasone suppression test for melancholia. Br J Psychiatry 140:292–304.

Carroll BJ, Curtis GC, Mendels J (1976a): Neuroendocrine regulation in depression. I: Limbic system-adrenocortical dysfunction. Arch Gen Phychiatry 33:1039–1044.

Carroll BJ, Curtis GC, Mendels J (1976b): Neuroendocrine regulation in depression II: Discrimination of depressed from nondepressed patients. Arch Gen Psychiatry 33:1051–1058.

Charles HC, Lazeyras F, Krishnan KKR, Boyko OB, Payne M, Moore D (1994): Brain choline in depression: In vivo detection of potential pharmacodynamic effects of antidepressant therapy using hydrogen localized spectroscopy. Prog Neuro Psychopharmacol Bio Psychiatry. 18(7):1121–1127.

Charney DS, Nelson JC (1981): Delusional and nondelusional unipolar depression: Further evidence for distinct subtypes. Am J Psychiatry 138:328–333.

Charney DS, Heninger GR, Sternberg DE (1982): Adrenergic receptor sensitivity in depression: Effects of clonidine in depressed patients and healthy controls. Arch Gen Psychiatry 39:290–294.

Checkley, SA, Slade AP, Shur P (1988): Growth hormone and other responses to clonidine in patients with endogenous depression. Br J Psychiatry 138:51–55.

Chiarello RJ, Cole JO (1987): The use of psychostimulants in general psychiatry: A reconsideration. Arch Gen Psychiatry 44:286–295.

Christensen NJ, Vestergaard P, Sorensen T, Rafaelson OJ (1980): Cerebrospinal fluid adrenaline and noradrenaline in depressed patients. Acta Psychiatr Scand 61:178–182.

Coe CL, Rosenberg LT, Levine S (1985): Immunological consequences of psychological disturbance and maternal loss in infancy. In Rove E, Collier C, Lipsitt LP (eds): "Advances in Infancy Research." Norwood, OH: Ablex Publishing, pp 98–136.

Coffey CE, Figiel GS, Djang WT, Saunders WB, Weiner R (1989): White matter hyperintensity on magnetic resonance imaging: Clinical and neuroanatomic correlates in the depressed elderly. J Neuropsychiatry Clin Neurosci 1:135–144.

Coffey CE, Figiel GS, Djang WT, Cress M, Saunders WB, Weiner RD (1988): Leukoencephalopathy in elderly depressed patients referred to ECT. Biol Psychiatry 24:143–161.

Coppen A, Prange AJ, Jr, Whybrow PC, Noguera R (1972): Abnormalities of indoleamines in affective disorders. Arch Gen Psychiatry 26:474–478.

Coryell W, Keller M, Lavori P, Endicott J (1990). Affective syndromes, psychotic features and prognosis. I: Depression. Arch Gen Psychiatry 47:651–657.

Coryell W, Lavori P, Endicott J, Keller M, VanEerdewegh M (1984a): Outcome in schizoaffective, psychotic, and nonpsychotic depression. Arch Gen Psychiatry 41:787–791.

Coryell W, Pfohl B, Zimmerman M (1984b): The clinical and neuroendocrine features of psychotic depression. J Nerv Ment Dis 172:521–528.

Davidson J, Robertson E (1985): A follow-up study of postpartum illness. Acta Psychiatr Scand 71:451.

Davidson JRT, Giller EL, Zisook S, Overall JE (1988): An efficacy study of isocarboxazid and placebo in depression, and its relationship to depressive nosology. Arch Gen Psychiatry 45:120–127.

Dean C, Kendell RE (1981): The symptomatology of postpartum illness. Br J Psychiatry 139:128.

Deicken RF, Reus VI, Manfredi L, Wolkowitz O (1991): MRI deep white matter hyperintensity in a psychiatric population. Biol Psychiatry 29:918–922.

Delgado PL, Charney DS, Price LH, Landis H, Heininger GR (1990): Neuroendocrine and behavioral effects of dietary tryptophan restriction in healthy subjects. Life Sci 45:2323–2332.

Demeter E, Rihmer Z, Arato M, Frecska E (1986): Association performance and the DST [Letter]. Psychiatry Res 18:289–290.

Dolan R, Calloway S, Thacker P, Mann A (1986): The cerebral cortical appearance in depressed subjects. Psychol Med 16:775–779.

Ebert D, Feistel H, Barocka A (1991): Effects of sleep deprivation on the limbic system and the frontal lobes in affective disorders: A study with Tc-99m-HMPAO SPECT. Psychiatry Res 40:247–251.

Esler M, Turbott J, Schwarz R, Leonard P, Bobik A, Skews H, Jackman G (1982): The peripheral kinetics of norepinephrine in depressive illness. Arch Gen Psychiatry 39:295–300.

Evans DL, Folds JD, Petitto JM, Golden RN, Pedersen CA, Corrigan M, Gilmore JH, Silva SG, Quade D, Ozer H (1992): Circulating natural killer cell phenotypes in men and women with major depression. Arch Gen Psychiatry 49:388–394.

Event GM, Tolman JEP (1959): Mode of action of Rauwolfia alkaloids and motor sensitivity. In Masserman J (ed): "Biological Psychiatry." New York: Grune & Stratton, pp 75–81.

Extein I, Tallman J, Smith CC (1979): Changes in lymphocyte beta-adrenergic receptors in depression and mania. Psychiatry Res 1:191–197.

Feighner JP, Robins E, Guze SB, Woodruff RA, Winokur G, Munoz R (1972): Diagnostic criteria for use in psychiatric research. Arch Gen Psychiatry 26:57–73.

Fernandez F, Adams F, Levy JK, Holmes V, Neidhart M, Mansell P (1988): Cognitive impairment due to AIDS-related complex and its response to psychostimulants. Psychosomatics 29:38–46.

Fink M (1993): Catatonia and psychotic (delusional) depression: Distinct Syndromes in DSM-IV [Letter]. Am J Psychiatry 150:1130.

Fink M, Taylor MA (1991): Catatonia: A separate category for DSM-IV? Integrative Psychiatry 7:2–10.

Foote SL, Bloom FE, Aston-Jones G (1983): Nucleus locus coeruleus: New evidence of anatomical and physiological specificity. Physiol Rev 63:844–914.

Foote SL, Aston-Jones G, Bloom FE (1980): Impulse activity of locus coeruleus neurosis in awake rats and monkeys is a function of sensory stimulation and arousal. Proc Natl Acad Sci USA 77:3033–3037.

Frances A, Brown RP, Kocsis JH, Mann JJ (1981): Psychotic depression: A separate entity? Am J Psychiatry 138:831–833.

Fricchione GL, Cassem NH, Hooberman D, Hobson D (1983): Intravenous lorazepam in neuroleptic induced catatonia. J Clin Psychopharmacol 3:338–342.

Friedman SB, Mason JW, Hamburg DA (1963): Urinary 17-hydroxycorticosteroid levels in parents of children with neoplastic disease. Psychosom Med 25:364–376.

Fukushima DK, Gallagher RF (1970): Disrupted 24-hour patterns of cortisol secretion in psychotic depression Arch Gen Psychiatry 28:289–298.

Garber J, Seligman MEP (1980): "Human Helplessness: Theory and Application." New York: Academic.

Garber J, Miller WR, Seaman SF (1979): Learned helplessness, stress and the depressive disorders. In Depue RA (ed): "The Psychobiology of the Depressive Disorders: Implications for the Effects of Stress." New York: Academic, pp 335–363.

Gelenberg AJ (1976): The catatonic syndrome. Lancet 1:1339–1341.

Gerner RH, Hare TA (1981): CSF GABA in normal subjects and patients with depression, schizophrenia, mania, and anorexia nervosa. Am J Psychiatry 138:1098–1101.

Gibbons RD, Davis JM (1986): Consistent evidence for a biological subtype of depression characterized by low CSF monoamine levels. Acta Psychiatr Scand 74:8–12.

Glaser R, Kennedy S, Lafuse WP, Bonneau RH, Speicher C, Hillhouse J, Kiecolt-Glaser JK (1990): Psychological stress induced modulation of interleukin-2 receptor gene expression and interleukin-2 production in peripheral blood leukocytes. Arch Gene Psychiatry 47:707–712.

Glassman AH (1993): Cigarette smoking: Implications for psychiatric illness. Am J Psychiatry 150:546–553.

Glassman AH, Roose SP (1981): Delusional depression: A distinct clinical entity? Arch Gen Psychiatry 38:424–427.

Glowinski J, Axelrod J (1964): Inhibition of uptake of tritiated noradrenalin in the intact rat brain by imipramine and structurally related compounds. Nature 204:1318–1319.

Gold PW, Goodwin FK, Chrousos EP (1988a): Clinical and biochemical manifestations of depression: Relation to the neurobiology of stress (first of two parts). NEJM 319:348–353.

Gold PW, Goodwin FK, Chrousos EP (1988b): Clinical and biochemical manifestations of depression: Relation to the neurobiology of stress (second of two parts). NEJM 319:413–420.

Gold BI, Bowers MG, Jr, Roth RH, Sweeney DW (1980): GABA levels in CSF of patients with psychiatric disorders. Am J Psychiatry 137:362–364.

Goodwin FK, Post RM, Dunner DL, Gordon EK (1973): Cerebrospinal fluid amine metabolites in affective illness: The probenecid technique. Am J Psychiatry 130:73–79.

Greden JF, Albala AA, Haskett RF, James NM, Goodman L, Steiner M, Carroll BJ (1980): Normalization of dexamethasone suppression test: A laboratory index of recovery from endogenous depression. Biol Psychiatry 15:449–458.

Greenfield D, Conrad C, Kincare P, Bowers MB (1987): Treatment of catatonia with low-dose lorazepam. Am J Psychiatry 144:1224–1225.

Hales RE, Yudofsky SC, Talbott JA (1994): "Textbook of Psychiatry," 2nd ed. Washington, DC: American Psychiatric Press, pp 465–494.

Hannum RD, Rosellini RA, Seligman MEP (1976): Retention and immunization of learned helplessness from weaning to adulthood. Dev Psychol 12:449–454.

Hertting G, Axelrod J, Whitby LG (1961): Effect of drug on the uptake and metabolism of ^{3}H-norepinephrine. J Pharmacol Exp Ther 134:146–153.

Higley JD, Suomi SJ, Scanlon JM, McKinney WT (1982): Plasma cortisol as a predictor of individual depressive behavior in rhesus monkeys (Macca Mulatta). Soc Neurosci Abstr 8:461.

Hinde RA, Leighton-Shapiro ME, McGinnis L (1978): Effects of various types of separation experience on rhesus monkeys 5 months later. J Child Psychol Psychiatry 19:199–211.

Holsboer F, Steiger A, Maier W (1983): Four cases of reversion to abnormal dexamethasone suppression test response as indicator of clinical relapse: A preliminary report. Biol Psychiatry 18:911–916.

Hrdina PD, Von Kulmiz P, Stretch R (1979): Pharmacological modifications of experimental depression in infant macaques. Psychopharmacology 64:89–93.

Hurwitz TA, Clark C, Murphy E, Klonoff H, Martin WR, Pate BD (1990): Regional cerebral glucose metabolism in major depressive disorder. Can J Psychiatry 35:684–688.

Husain M, McDonald W, Doraiiswamy P, Figiel GS, Na C, Escalona R, Boyko O, Nemeroff C, Krishnan R (1991): A magnetic resonance imaging study of putamen nuclei in major depression. Psychiatry Res 40:95–99.

Irwin M (1995): Psychoneuroimmunology of depression. In Bloom FE, Kupfer DJ (eds): "Psychopharmacology—The Fourth Generation of Progress." New York: Raven Press, pp 983–998.

Iversen LL (1964): Inhibition of noradrenaline uptake by sympathomemetic amines. J Pharm Pharmacol 16:435–437.

Jacobsen E (1964): The theoretical basis of the chemotherapy of depression. In Davis EB (ed): "Depression: Proceedings of the Symposium Held at Cambridge, September, 1959." New York: Cambridge University Press, pp 208–213.

Janowsky DS, Overstreet DH (1995): The role of acetylcholine mechanisms in mood disorders. In Bloom FE, Kupfer DJ (eds): "Psychopharmacology—The Fourth Generation of Progress." New York: Raven Press, pp 945–956.

Janowsky DS, El-Yousef MK, Davis KM, Sekerke HJ (1972): A cholinergic-adrenergic hypothesis of mania and depression. Lancet 2:632–635.

Jeste DV, Lohr JB, Goodwin FK (1988): Neuroanatomical studies of major affective disorders: A review and suggestions for further research. Br J Psychiatry 153:444–459.

Kahlbaum KL (1874) trans. Levi Y and Pridan T (1973): "Catatonia." Baltimore: Johns Hopkins University Press.

Kalin NH, Sherman ME, Takahashi LK (1988): Antagonism of endogenous CRH systems attenuates stress-induced freezing behavior in rats. Brain Res 457:130–135.

Kalin NH, Weiler SJ, McKinney WT, Kraemer GW, Shelton SE (1982): Where is the "lesion" in patients who fail to suppress plasma cortisol concentrations with dexamethasone? Psychopharm Bull 18:219–220.

Kapur S, Mann JJ (1993): Antidepressant action and the neurobiologic effects of ECT: Human studies. In Coffey CE (ed): "The Clinical Science of Electroconvulsive Therapy." Washington, DC: American Psychiatric Press, pp 235–250.

Kastin AJ, Schalch DS, Ehrensing RH, Anderson MS (1972): Improvement in mental depression with decreased thyrotropin response after administration of thyrotropin-releasing hormone. Lancet 2:740–742.

Kaufman IC, Rosenblum LA (1967): The reaction to separation in infant monkeys: Anaclitic depression and conservation-withdrawal. Psychosom Med 29:648–675.

Kaufmann MW, Murray GB, Cassem NH (1982): Use of psychostimulants in medically ill depressed patients. Psychosomatics 23:817–819.

Katon W, Raskind M (1980): Treatment of depression in the medically ill elderly with methylphenidate. Am J Psychiatry 137:963–965.

Kellner CH, Rubinow DR, Gold PW, Post RM (1983): Relationship of cortisol hypersecretion to brain CT scan alternations in depressed patients. Psychiatry Res 8:191–197.

Kelly PH, Seviour PW, Iversen SD (1975): Amphetamine and apomorphine responses in the rat following 6-OHDA lesions of the nucleus accumbens septi and corpus striatum. Brain Res 94:507–522.

Kendell RE, Charlmers JC, Platz C (1987): Epidemiology of puerperal psychoses. Br J Psychiatry 150:662–673.

Kiecolt-Glaser JK, Dura JR, Speicher CE, Trask OJ, Glaser R (1991): Spousal caregivers of dementia victims: Longitudinal changes in immunity and health. Psychosom Med 53:345–362.

Klerman GL, Hirschfeld RMA, Andreasen NC, Coryell W, Endicott J, Fawcett J, Keller M, Scheftner W (1987): Major depression and related affective disorders. In Tischler GL (ed): "Diagnosis and Classification in Psychiatry: A Critical Appraisal of DSM-III." Cambridge, England: Cambridge University Press.

Koslow JH, Maas JW, Bowden CL, Davis JM, Hanin I, Javaid J (1983): CSF and urinary biogenic amines and metabolites in depression and mania: A controlled, univariate analysis. Arch Gen Psychiatry 40:999–1010.

Kraemer GW, McKinney WT (1979): Interactions of pharmacological agents which alter biogenic amine metabolism and depression. J Affect Dis 1:33–54.

Kraemer GW, Ebert MH, Schmidt DE, McKinney WT (1989): A longitudinal study of the effect of different social rearing conditions on cerebrospinal fluid norepinephrine and biogenic amine metabolites in rhesus monkeys. Neuropsychopharmacology 2:175–189.

Krishnan KRR (1990): Organic bases of depression in the elderly. Ann Rev Med 42:261–266.

Krishnan K, McDonald W, Escalona R, Doraiswamy PM, Na C, Husain MM, Figiel GS, Boyko OB, Ellinwood E, Nemeroff CB (1992): Magnetic resonance imaging of the caudate nuclei in depression: Preliminary observations. Arch Gen Psychiatry 49:553–557.

Krishnan KRR, Goli V, Ellinwood, France RD, Blazer DG, Nemeroff CB (1988): Leukoencephalopathy in patients diagnosed as major depressive. Biol Psychiatry 23:519–522.

Kendell RE, Chalmers JC, Platz C (1987): Epidemiology of puerperal psychoses. Br J Psychiatry 150:662–673.

Lake CR, Pickar D, Ziegler M, Lipper S, Slater S, Murphy DL (1982): High plasma norepinephrine levels in patients with major affective disorder. Am J Psychiatry 139:1315–1318.

Langer SZ (1980): Modern concepts of adrenergic transmission. In Legg N (ed): "Neurotransmitter Systems and Their Clinical Disorders." London: Academic Press.

Laudenslager M, Capitanio JP, Reite M (1985): Possible effects of early separation experiences on subsequent immune function in adult macaque monkeys. Am J Psychiatry 142:862–864.

Liebowitz MR, Quitkin FM, Stewart JW, McGrath PJ, Harrison W, Markowitz JS, Rabkin J, Tricamo E, Goetz D, Klein DF (1988): Antidepressant specificity in atypical depression. Arch Gen Psychiatry 45:129–137.

Liebowitz MR, Quitkin FM, Stewart JW, McGrath PJ, Harrison W, Rabkin J, Tricamo E, Markowitz JS, Klein DF (1984): Phenelzine and imipramine in atypical depression: A preliminary report. Arch Gen Psychiatry 41:669–677.

Lingjaerde O (1963): Tetrabenazine (Nitoman) in the treatment of psychoses. Acta Psychiatr Scand 39(Suppl. 170):1–109.

Linkowski P, Mendlewicz J, LeClercq R, Brasseur M, Hubain P, Goldstein J, Copinschi G, Van Cauter E (1985): The 24-hour profile of ACTH and cortisol in major depressive illness. J Clin Endocrinol Metab 61:429–438.

Linnoila M, Virkkunen M, Scheinin M, Nuutila A, Rimon R, Goodwin FK (1983): Low cerebrospinal fluid 5-hydroxyindoleacetic acid concentration differentiates impulsive from nonimpulsive violent behavior. Life Sci 33:2609–2614.

Lykouras E, Malliaras D, Christodoulou GN, Papakostas Y, Voulgari A, Tzonou A, Stefanis C (1986): Delusional depression: Phenomenology and response to treatment: A prospective study. Acta Psychiatr Scand 73:324–329.

Maier SF, Seligman MEP (1976): Learned helplessness: Theory and evidence. J Exp Psychol 1:3–46.

Maier SF, Anderson C, Lieberman DA (1972): Influence of control of shock on subsequent shock-aggression. J Comp Physiol Psychology 81:94–100.

Martinot J, Hardy P, Feline A, Huret JD, Mazoyer B, Attar-Levy D, Pappata S, Syrota A (1990): Left prefrontal glucose hypometabolism in the depressed state: A confirmation. Am J Psychiatry 147:1313–1317.

Masand P, Murray GB, Pickett P (1991a): Psychostimulants in post-stroke depression. J Neuropsychiatry 3:23–27.

Masand P, Pickett P, Murray GB (1991b): Psychostimulants for secondary depression in medical illness. Psychosomatics 32:203–208.

Matussek N, Ackenheil AH, Hippius H (1980): Effect of clonidine on growth hormone release in psychiatric patients and controls. Psychiatry Res 2:25–36.

Mayberg HS, Starkstein SE, Sadzot B, Preziosi T, Andrezejewski P, Dannals R, Wagner H, Robinson RG (1990): Selective hypometabolism in the inferior frontal lobe in depressed patients with Parkinson's disease. Ann Neurol 28:57–64.

McKinney WT, Bunney WE (1969): Animal model of depression: Review of evidence and implications for research. Arch Gen Psychiatry 21:240–248.

Meltzer ES, Kumar R (1985): Puerperal mental illness, clinical features and classification: A study of 142 mother-and-baby admissions. Br J Psychiatry 147:647.

Miller WR, Rosellini RA, Seligman MEP (1977): Learned helplessness and depression. In Maser JD, Seligman MEP (eds): "Psychopathology: Experimental Models." San Francisco: Freeman, pp 104–130.

Molinoff PB, Axelrod J (1971): Biochemistry of catecholamines. Ann Rev Biochem 40:465–500.

Moore RY, Bloom FE (1979): Central catecholamine neuron systems: Anatomy and physiology of the norepinephrine and epinephrine systems. Annu Rev Neurosci 2:113–168.

Morselli PL, Bossi L, Henry JF, Zarifian E, Bartholini G (1980): On the therapeutic action of SL 76 002, a new GABA-mimetic agent: Preliminary observations in neuropsychiatric disorders. Brain Res Bull 5(Suppl 2):411–414.

Murphy DL, Aulukh C, Garrick N (1986): How antidepressants work: Some continuing conclusions based on clinical and laboratory studies of the longer-term consequences of antidepressant drug treatment. In Murphy DL (ed): "Antidepressant and Receptor Functions." Chichester: Wiley, pp 106–125.

Nasrallah H, McCalley-Whitters M, Jacoby C (1982): Corticol atrophy in schizophrenia and mania: A comparative CT study. J Clin Psychiatry 43:439–441.

Nelson JC, Bowers MB (1978): Delusional unipolar depression. Arch Gen Psychiatry 35:1321–1328.

Nelson WH, Khan A, Orr WW (1984): Delusional depression, phenomenology, neuroendocrine function and tricyclic antidepressant response. J Affect Disord 6:297–306

Nelson JC, Charney DS, Quinlan DM (1981): Evaluation of the DSM-III criteria for melancholia. Arch Gen Psychiatry 38:555–559.

Nemeroff CB, Evans DL (1984). Correlation between the dexamethasone suppression test in depressed patients and clinical response. Am J Psychiatry 141:247–249.

Nemeroff CB, Owens MJ, Bissette G, Andorn AC, Stanley M (1988): Reduced corticotropin-releasing factor binding sites in the frontal cortex of suicides. Arch Gen Psychiatry 45:577–579.

Nielsen M, Braestrup C (1977): Chronic treatment with desipramine causes a sustained decrease of 3, 4-dihydroxyphenylglycol-sulphate and total 3-methoxy-4-hydroxyphenylglycol in the rat brain. Naunyn Schmiedebergs Arch Pharmacol 300:87–92.

Nyback HV, Walters JR, Aghajanian GK, Roth RH (1975): Tricyclic antidepressants: Effects on the firing rate of brain noradrenergic neurons. Eur J Pharmacol 32:302–312.

Owens MJ, Nemeroff CB (1992): The physiology and pharmacology of corticotropin releasing factor. Pharmacol Rev 43:425–473.

Pandey GN, Dysken MW, Garver DL, Davis JM (1979): Beta-adrenergic receptor function in affective illness. Am J Psychiatry 136:675–678.

Parker G, Hadzi-Pavlovic D, Hickie I, Boyce P, Mitchell P, Wilhelm K, Brodaty H (1991): Distinguishing psychotic and nonpsychotic melancholia. J Affect Disord 22:135–148.

Paykel ES, Rowan PR, Rao B, Bhat A (1983): Atypical depression: Nosology and response to antidepressants. In Clayton P, Barrett J (eds): "Treatment of Depression: Old Controversies and New Approaches." New York: Raven Press, pp 237–251.

Petty F, Schlesser MA (1981): Plasma GABA in affective illness: A preliminary investigation. J Affective Disord 3:339–343.

Platz C, Kendell RE (1988): A matched control follow-up and family study of "puerperal psychoses." Br J Psychiatry 153:90.

Post RM, Jimerson DC, Ballenger JC, Lake CR, Uhde TW, Goodwin FK (1984): Cerebrospinal fluid norepinephrine and its metabolites in manic-depressive illness. In Post RM, Ballenger JC (eds): "Neurobiology of Mood Disorders." Baltimore: Williams and Wilkins, pp 539–553.

Prange AJ, Wilson IC, Lara PP, Alltop LB, Breese GR (1972): Effects of thyrotropin-releasing hormone in depression. Lancet 1:999–1002.

Price LH, Conwell Y, Nelson JC (1983): Lithium augmentation of combined neuroleptic-tricyclic treatment in delusional depression. Am J Psychiatry 140:318–322.

Price DB, Thaler M, Mason JW (1957): Preoperative emotional states and adrenal cortical activity: Studies on cardiac and pulmonary surgery patients. Arch Neurol Psychiatry 77:646–656.

Pugh TF, Jerath BK, Schmidt WM, Reed RB (1963): Rates of mental disease related to childbearing. N Engl J Med 268:1224.

Quitkin FM, Stewart JW, McGrath PJ, Tricamo E, Rabkin J, Ocepek-Welikson K, Nunes E, Harrison W, Klein DF (1993): Columbia atypical depression. Br J Psychiatry 163(Suppl):30–34.

Quitkin FM, Harrison W, Stewart JW, McGrath PJ, Tricamo E, Ocepek-Welikson K, Rabkin J, Wager SG, Nunes E, Klein DF (1991): Response to phenelzine and imipramine in placebo nonresponders with atypical depression: A new application of the crossover design. Arch Gen Psychiatry 48:318–323.

Quitkin FM, McGrath PJ, Stewart JW, Harrison W, Tricamo E, Wager SG, Ocepek-Welikson K, Nunes E, Rabkin J, Klein DF (1990): Atypical depression, panic attacks and response to imipramine and phenelzine. Arch Gen Psychiatry 47:935–941.

Quitkin FM, McGrath PJ, Stewart JW, Harrison W, Wager SG, Nunes E, Rabkin JG, Tricamo E, Markowitz J, Klein DF (1989): Phenelzine and imipramine in mood reactive depressives: Further delineation of the syndrome of atypical depression. Arch Gen Psychiatry 46:787–793.

Rabins P, Pearlson G, Aylward E, Kumar A, Dowell K (1991): Cortical magnetic resonance imaging changes in elderly inpatients with major depression. Am J Psychiatry 148:617–620.

Randrup A, Munkvad J, Fog R (1975): Mania, depression, and brain dopamine. In Essman WB, Valzelli L (eds): "Current Developments in Psychopharmacology, Vol. 2." New York: Spectrum, pp 206–248.

Rao VP, Krishnan KRR, Goli V, Saunders WB, Ellinwood E, Blazer DG, Nemeroff CB (1989): Neuroanatomical changes and hypothalamic-pituitary-adrenal axis abnormalities. Biol Psychiatry 26:729–732.

Reite M, Short R, Seiler C, Pauley JD (1981): Attachment, loss and depression. J Child Psychol Psychiatry 22:141–169.

Reus VI (1982): Pituitary-adrenal disinhibition as the independent variable in the assessment of behavioral symptoms. Biol Psychiatry 17:317–325.

Ribeiro SCM, Tandon R, Grunhaus L, Greden JF (1993): The DST as a predictor of outcome in depression: A meta-analysis. Am J Psychiatry 150:1618–1629.

Risch SC, Lewine RJ, Kalin NH, Jewart R, Risby E, Caudle J, Stipetic M, Turner J, Eccard M, Pollard W (1992): Limbic-hypothalamic-pituitary-adrenal axis activity and ventricular-to-brain ratio studies in affective illness and schizophrenia. Neuropsychopharmacology 6(2):95–100.

Robinson DG, Spiker DG (1985): Delusional depression: A one year follow-up. J Affect Disord 9:79–83.

Roose SP, Glassman AH, Walsh BJ (1983): Depression, delusions, and suicide. Am J Psychiatry 140:1159–1162.

Rosebush PI, Hildebrand AM, Furlong BG, Mazurek MF (1990): Catatonic syndrome in a general psychiatric inpatient population: Frequency, clinical presentation and response to lorazepam. J Clin Psychiatry 51:357–362.

Rosellini RA (1978): Inescapable shock interferes with the acquisition of a free appetitive operant. Anim Learn Behav 6:155–159.

Rosellini RA, DeCola JP (1981): Inescapable shock interferes with the acquisition of low-activity response in an appetitive context. Anim Learn Behav 9:487–490.

Rosenblatt S, Chanley JD, Sobotka H, Kaufman MR (1960): Interrelationships between electroshock, the blood-brain barrier, and catecholamines. J Neurochem 5:172–176.

Rosenthal NE, Sack DA, Carpenter CJ, Parry BL, Mendelson WB, Wehr TA (1985): Antidepressant effects of light in seasonal affective disorder. Am J Psychiatry 142:163–170.

Rosenthal NE, Sack DA, Gillin JC, Lewy AJ, Goodwin FK, Davenport Y, Mueller PS, Newsome DA, Wehr TA (1984): Seasonal affective disorder: A description of the syndrome and preliminary findings with light treatment. Arch Gen Psychiatry 41:72–80.

Rothschild AJ, Samson JA, Bessette MP, Carter-Campbell J (1993a): Efficacy of the combination of fluoxetine and perphenazine in the treatment of psychotic depression. J Clin Psychiatry 54:338–342.

Rothschild AJ, Samson JA, Bond TC, Luciana MM, Schildkraut JJ, Schatzberg AF (1993b): Hypothalamic-pituitary-adrenal axis activity and one-year outcome in depression. Biol Psychiatry 34:392–400.

Rothschild AJ, Benes F, Hebben N, Woods B, Luciana M, Bakanas E, Samson J, Schatzberg A (1989): Relationships between brain CT scan findings and cortisol in psychotic and nonpsychotic depressed patients. Biol Psychiatry 26:565–575.

Rothschild AJ, Schatzberg AF (1982): Fluctuating cortisol levels in a patient with melancholia. Am J Psychiatry 139:129–130.

Roy A, De Jong J, Linnoila M (1989): Cerebrospinal fluid monoamine metabolites and suicidal behavior in depressed patients. Arch Gen Psychiatry 46:609–612.

Roy A, Pickar D, Linnoila M, Chrousos GP, Gold PW (1987): Cerebrospinal fluid corticotropin-releasing hormone in depression: Relationship to noradrenergic function. Psychiatry Res 20:229–237.

Roy A, Pickar D, Linnoila M, Potter WZ (1985): Plasma norepinephrine level in affective disorders: Relationship to melancholia. Arch Gen Psychiatry 42:1181–1185.

Rubinow DR, Post RM, Savard R, Gold PW (1984): Cortisol hypersecretion and cognitive impairment in depression. Arch Gen Psychiatry 41:279–283.

Sachar EJ, Hellman L, Fukushima DK, Gallager RF (1970): Cortisol production in depressive illness. Arch Gen Psychiatry 23:289–298.

Sargant W (1960): Some newer drugs in the treatment of depression and their relation to other somatic treatments. Psychosomatics 1:14–17.

Schatzberg AF, Rothschild AJ (1993): Letter to the Editor (Reply to Fink, M): Am J Psychiatry 150:1131.

Schatzberg AF, Rothschild AJ (1992): Psychotic (delusional) major depression: Should it be included as a distinct syndrome in DSM-IV? Am J Psychiatry 149:733–745.

Schildkraut JJ (1978): The catecholamine hypothesis of affective disorders: A review of supporting evidence. Am J Psychiatry 122:509–522.

Schildkraut JJ (1965): Current status of the catecholamine hypothesis of affective disorders. In Lipton MA, DiMascio A, Killam KF (eds): "Psychopharmacology: A Generation of Progress." New York: Raven Press, pp 1223–1234.

Schleifer SJ, Keller SE, Meyerson AT, Raskin MJ, Davis KL, Stein M (1984): Lymphocyte function in major depressive disorder. Arch Gen Psychiatry 41:484–486.

Schleifer SJ, Keller SE, Camerino M, Thornton JC, Stein M (1983): Suppression of lymphocyte stimulation following bereavement. JAMA 250(3):374–377.

Schlesser MA, Winokur G, Sherman BM (1980): Hypothalamic-pituitary-adrenal axis activity in depressive illness: Its relationship to classification. Arch Gen Psychiatry 37:737–743.

Seligman MEP (1975): "Helplessness: On Depression, Development, and Death." San Francisco: Freeman.

Shopsin B, Freedman E, Gershon S (1976): PCPA reversal of tranylcypromine effects in depressed patients. Arch Gen Psychiatry 33:811–819.

Shore PA (1962): Release of serotonin and catecholamines by drugs. Pharmacol Rev 14:531–550.

Siever LJ, Davis KL (1985): Overview: Toward a dysregulation hypothesis of depression. Am J Psychiatry 142:1017–1031.

Siever LJ, Uhde TW, Jimerson DC, Lake CR, Silberman ER, Post RM, Murphy DL (1984): Differential inhibitory noradrenergic responses to clonidine in 25 depressed patients and 25 normal control subjects. Am J Psychiatry 141:733–741.

Sikes CR, Stokes PE, Lasley BJ (1989): Cognitive sequelae of hypothalamic-pituitary-adrenal (HPA) dysregulation in depression (abstract). Biol Psychiatry 25(7A):148A–149A.

Smotherman WP, Hunt LE, McGinnis LM, Levine S (1979): Mother-infant separation in group-living rhesus macques: A hormonal analysis. Dev Psychobiol 12:211–217.

Spector S, Hirsch CW, Brodie BB (1963): Association of behavioral effects of pargyline, a non-hydrazide MAO inhibitor with increase in brain norepinephrine. Int J Neuropharmacol 2:81–93.

Spiker DG, Weiss JC, Dealy RS, Griffin SJ, Hanin I, Neil JF, Perel JM, Rossi AJ, Soloff PH (1985): The pharmacological treatment of delusional depression. Am J Psychiatry 142:430–436.

Stanley M, Mann JJ (1983): Increased serotonin-2 binding sites in frontal cortex of suicide victims. Lancet i:214–216.

Stokes PE, Stoll PM, Koslow SH, Maas JW, Davis JM, Swann AC, Robins E (1984): Pretreatment DST and hypothalamic-pituitary-adrenocortical function in depressed patients and comparison groups. Arch Gen Psychiatry 41:257–267.

Stokes PE, Pick GR, Stoll PM, Nunn WD (1975): Pituitary-adrenal function in depressed patients: Resistance to dexamethasone suppression. J Psychiatr Res 12:271–281.

Styron W (1990): "Darkness Visible." New York: Random House.

Sulser F (1983): Deamplification of noradrenergic signal transfer by antidepressants: A unified catecholamine-serotonin hypothesis of affective disorders. Psychopharmacol Bull 19:300–304.

Sulser F (1978): New perspectives on the mode of action of antidepressant drugs. Trends Pharmacol Sci 1:92–94.

Sulser F, Ventulani J, Mobley PL (1978): Mode of action of antidepressant drugs. Biochem Pharmacol 27:257–261.

Suomi SJ, Collins ML, Harlow HF (1976): Effects of maternal and peer separations of young monkeys. J Child Psychol Psychiatry 17:101–112.

Suomi SJ, Harlow HF, Domek CJ (1970): Effects of repetitive infant-infant separation of young monkeys. J Abnorm Psychology 76:161–172.

Traskman L, Asberg M, Bertilsson L (1981): Monoamine metabolites in CSF and suicidal behavior. Arch Gen Psychiatry 10:253–261.

Tuomisto J, Tukiainen E (1976): Decreased uptake of 5-hydroxytryptamine in blood platelets from depressed patients. Nature 262:596–598.

Usdin E, Bunney WE (eds) (1975): "Pre- and Postsynaptic Receptors." New York: Dekker.

Valentino RJ, Foote SL, Aston-Jones G (1983): Corticotropin-releasing hormone activates noradrenergic neurons of the locus coeruleus. Brain Res 270:363–367.

Vetulani J, Sulser F (1975): Action of various antidepressant treatments reduces reactivity of noradrenergic cyclic AMP generating system in limbic forebrain. Nature 257:495–496.

Vinogradov S, Reiss AL (1986): Use of lorazepam in treatment-resistant catatonia. J Clin Psychopharmacol 6:323–324.

Virkkunen M, Nuutila A, Goodwin FK, Linnoila M (1987): Cerebrospinal fluid monoamine metabolite levels in male arsonists. Arch Gen Psychiatry 44:241–247.

Wachtel H (1990): The second messenger: Dysbalance hypothesis of affective disorders. Pharmacopsychiatry 23:27–32.

Wagner HR, Hall TL, Cote IL (1977): The applicability of inescapable shock as a source of animal depression. J Gen Psychol 96:313–318.

Waldmeier PC (1981): Noradrenergic transmission in depression: Under or overfunction? Pharmacopsychiatry 14:3–9.

Weinberger D, DeLisi L, Perman G, Targum S, Wyatt R (1982): Computed tomography in schizophreniform disorder and other acute psychiatric disorders. Arch Gen Psychiatry 39:778–783.

Weiss JM (1968): Effects of coping responses on stress. J Comp Physiol Psychol 65:251–260.

Weiss JM, Goodman PA, Ambrose MJ, Webster A, Hoffman LJ (1984): Neurochemical basis of behavioral depression. In Katkin E, Manack (eds): "Advances in Behavioral Medicine, Vol. I." Greenwich, CT: JAI Press.

Weiss JM, Glazer HI, Pohorecky LA (1976): Coping behavior and neurochemical changes: An alternative explanation for the original "learned helplessness" experiments. In Serban G, Kling A (eds): "Animal Models in Human Psychobiology." New York: Plenum, pp 141–173.

Weissman MM, Prusoff BA, Thompson WD (1978): Social adjustment by self-report in a community sample and in psychiatric outpatients. J Nerv Ment Dis 166:317–326.

West ED, Dally PJ (1959): Effects of iproniazid in depressive syndromes. Br Med J i:1491–1494.

Willner P (1985): "Depression: A Psychobiological Synthesis." New York: Wiley.

Winokur G, Black DW, Nasrallah A (1987): DST nonsuppressor status: Relationship to specific aspects of the depressive syndrome. Biol Psychiatry 22:360–368.

Wolfersdorf M, Barg TH, Konig F, Leibfarth M, Grunewald I (1995): Paroxetine as antidepressant in combined antidressant-neuroleptic therapy in delusional depression: Observation of clinical use. Pharmacopsychiat 28:56–60.

Wolkowitz OM, Reus VI, Weingartner H, Thompson K, Breier A, Doran A, Rubinow D, Pickar D (1990): Cognitive effects of corticosteroids. Am J Psychiatry 147:1297–1303.

Woods SW (1986): Psychostimulant treatment of depressive disorders secondary to medical illness. J Clin Psychiatry 47:12–15.

Wyatt RJ, Portnoy B, Kupfer DJ, Snyder F, Engelman K (1971): Resting plasma catecholamine concentrations in patients with depression and anxiety. Arch Gen Psychiatry 24:65–70.

Zacharko RM, Bowers WJ, Kokkinidis L, Anisman H (1982): Alterations of intracranial self-stimulation in mice following inescapable stress. Soc Neurosci Abstr 8:898.

Zimmerman M, Coryell WH, Pfohl B (1986): Melancholic subtyping: A qualitative or quantitative distinction? Am J Psychiatry 143:98–100.

CHAPTER 11

Outcome Studies of Depression in Adulthood

ROBERT J. BOLAND and MARTIN B. KELLER

Department of Psychiatry, Miriam Hospital (R.J.B); Department of Psychiatry, Butler Hospital (M.B.K), Providence, RI, 02906

INTRODUCTION

Although Kraepelin described recurrent depression among his patients, it has been common to view depression as a discrete illness with a self-limiting course. In the last two decades, however, long-term studies have become available that have changed our view of depression; we are beginning to see it as a lifelong disease with periods of relapse and recurrence. Many individuals may never return to a state of "normalcy" but instead achieve only partial recovery to a state of chronic minor depression or dysthymia.

In this chapter, we will review the studies that have changed our view of depression. We will first define the "change points" in depression and then consider studies that elucidate aspects of those change points. Some studies of particular interest will be first listed separately with a summary of their methodology. Though most longitudinal studies of depression have concentrated on symptomatology, a few have looked at other outcomes, such as work and social functioning; these are considered separately. The search for biological correlates of depressive course will be briefly reviewed, with examples of different possible biochemical and physiologic markers of course. Finally, several specific course modifiers are examined, including double depression, other comorbid illnesses, and the role of treatment in modifying the course of depression.

DEFINITION OF COURSE CHANGE POINTS

Investigations of the outcome of depression have been hampered by conceptual differences over what are the pertinent change points in depression. In their review of studies on unipolar depression, Prien and colleagues (1991) found no consistency in the use of terms to define such change points. Variations in the particular terms used,

Mood Disorders Across the Life Span, Edited by Shulman, Tohen, and Kutcher
ISBN 0-471-10477-9   © 1996 Wiley-Liss, Inc.

as well as different definitions of specific terms, made comparability between studies difficult if not impossible. For example, some studies would alternately use the terms *remission* or *recovery* to define the end of an episode. While the terms *relapse* and *recurrence* were generally thought to define separate phenomena, most studies differed as to the distinction between the two, and some used them interchangeably. The issue of treatment further clouded the matter: Could a person be said to have recovered from an illness if that person was still in treatment or was the illness ongoing albeit "masked" by the treatment?

In response to this confusion, a task force commissioned by the MacArthur Foundation Research Network on the Psychobiology of Depression (Frank et al., 1991) recommended using only five terms to define the various change points in the course of unipolar depressive illness: *episode, remission, recovery, relapse,* and *recurrence* (*partial remission,* if considered separately from *response* would constitute a sixth term). They defined these terms purely on phenomenological—hence observable and measurable—grounds. Both symptomatic and temporal criteria would be included. Furthermore, the observation of these phenomena would not be affected by the status of treatment. Their definitions were conceptual rather than specific—that is, they did not recommend what symptom or temporal criteria should be used but rather provided a theoretical framework for incorporating these criteria.

The five terms were defined as follows:

Episode   To define the phases of an illness, one must first be able to define what constitutes an episode of the illness. Here, an episode is defined as having (at least) a certain number of symptomatic criteria for (at least) a certain number of days.

Partial Remission and Response   Partial remission is a period of time in which an individual no longer meets full symptomatic criteria for the disorder but evidences more than minimal symptoms. Treatment is not necessary for partial remission, and it can be spontaneous.

Response is defined as the point at which partial remission begins. Unlike partial remission, response implies that the individual is being treated. Theoretically, the term *response* implies that we know why the individual's condition has changed (i.e., what the individual is responding to). Clearly, this assumption may be incorrect.

Full Remission   Full remission is defined as a period of time in which the individual no longer meets criteria for the disorder and has no more than minimal symptoms. It is relatively brief: greater than a defined minimal period and less than the period defined by recovery. As with partial remission, treatment is not required for full remission.

Recovery   This term implies recovery from the episode defined, not the illness per se. Recovery is defined as a full remission that lasts for a defined period (at least). Again, treatment is not required.

Relapse   A relapse is defined as a return of symptoms sufficient to satisfy the full criteria of an episode. A relapse occurs in that period before a recovery would be defined. The implication is that a relapse represents a return of symptoms from the ongoing episode, not a new episode of the disease.

Recurrence   The term *recurrence* implies a new episode of the disorder. It would, thus, require full symptom criteria to be met. To distinguish it from a relapse, it must occur during the period defined as a recovery.

Thus, the MacArthur Foundation task force provided a conceptual framework for the change points in the course of a depressive episode. The advantage of such a system is that each maximal and minimal point mentioned above, be it symptomatic or temporal, can be precisely defined. The disadvantage of such a system is that one must give up the hope of absolute distinctions in favor of statistical ones: For example, one must "draw a line" between relapse and recurrence based on a probabilistic understanding of the average length of a depressive episode. Undoubtedly, the hope for such absolute distinctions was neither possible nor adaptable to research designs.

The task force did not suggest specific criteria. As some of the major studies are reviewed in this chapter, the different criteria they chose will be discussed.

SPECIFIC STUDIES

Some specific studies, notable for their longitudinal designs, adherence to strict methodologies, and sizable study populations, will be referred to frequently in this chapter. A summary of each study follows:

The National Institutes of Mental Health—Clinical Research Branch Collaborative Program on the Psychobiology of Depression—Clinical Studies

The Collaborative Depression Study (CDS) was designed as a prospective long-term naturalistic study of the psychopathology, treatment, and psychosocial functioning of a group of depressed subjects (Katz and Klerman, 1979). Subjects were recruited from those seeking psychiatric treatment at one of several sites (university or teaching hospitals in Boston, Chicago, Iowa City, New York, and St. Louis). Of the 955 subjects that entered the study, 431 were in an episode of major depressive disorder. These depressed subjects did not have a comorbid history of schizoaffective disorder, hypomania, or dysthymia. The median duration of the index episode was 30 weeks. All were white and English speaking, with median family incomes between $10,000 and $16,000 (in 1979). They were examined at 6-month intervals for 5 years and then annually for a minimum of 13 years (as of 1994, with plans to increase the follow-up to at least 17 years).

Initial assessment was done with the Schedule for Affective Disorders and Schizophrenia (SADS) (Spitzer and Endicott, 1979), Research Diagnostic Criteria (RDC) (which requires five depressive symptoms for a minimum of 2 weeks) (Spitzer et al., 1985), and the Personal History of Depressive Disorders (a questionnaire designed to elicit demographic information). Subsequent follow-up used the Longitudinal Interval Follow-up Evaluation (LIFE-II) (Keller et al., 1987). Changes in psychopathology, measured to the week, were determined on a time line using the Psychiatric Status Rating (PSR), which provides a means of quantifying the severity of symptoms on a six-point scale (Keller et al., 1992).

Recovery was defined as a PSR of 1 or 2 (indicating no to mild symptoms) for 8 weeks.

National Institute of Mental Health Treatment of Depression Collaborative Research Program (TDCRP)

This multicenter (George Washington University, University of Pittsburgh, and University of Oklahoma), placebo-controlled study followed patients for a total of 16 weeks to compare rates of recovery for three treatments—cognitive behavioral therapy (CBT), interpersonal therapy (IPT), and imipramine (Elkin et al., 1985; Elkin et al., 1989). The study investigated 239 (560 screened, 250 entered) subjects recruited from psychiatric outpatient services, aged 21–60, who met the RDC for major depressive disorder and had a score of at least 14 on the 17-item Hamilton Depression Rating Scale (HDRS) (Hamilton, 1960). Patients were assessed at entry; at 4, 8, and 12 weeks of treatment; at termination; and then at 6, 12, and 18 months posttreatment (Shea et al., 1992).

Patients were assessed using the HDRS, the Beck Depression Inventory (BDI) (Beck et al., 1961), the Global Assessment Scale (GAS) (Endicott et al., 1976), and the Hopkins Symptom Checklist-90 Total Score (HSCL-90 T) (Derogatis et al., 1973). Follow-up evaluations were done using the LIFE-II, and recovery was defined as a score of 1–2 (no, or minimal depressive symptoms) on the PSR for a minimum of 8 consecutive weeks.

During the acute treatment phase of the study, patients were given a 7- to 14-day drug washout period, then randomly assigned to one of the four treatment conditions (CBT, IPT, imipramine plus clinical management, and placebo plus clinical management). All treatments were 16 weeks in length, with a range of 16–20 one-hour sessions in the psychotherapy groups. The initial pharmacotherapy session was about an hour long, with subsequent sessions of about half an hour. In the follow-up phase (Shea et al., 1992), subjects who recovered during the initial phase of 16 weeks were observed for an additional 18 months. Patients were not specifically treated during this phase— medications were tapered off—and they were encouraged to delay seeking treatment elsewhere.

Of the 239 patients entering treatment, 162 completed the 16-week study; of these, 78 were considered recovered and able to enter the follow-up phase of the study. Relapse was defined as 2 consecutive weeks of symptoms meeting the RDC criteria for major depression, with a PSR score of 5–6.

Medical Outcomes Study (MOS)

The MOS (Wells et al., 1989, 1992) examined patients receiving care in one of three health care systems: large medical group practices and fee-for-service group practices, small groups, and solo practices. There was a representative sample of different specialties, including psychiatry. Five hundred and twenty-three clinicians located in three cities (Los Angeles, Boston, and Chicago) participated, and all patients seen from February through October 1986 were asked to participate. The study focused on five specific diseases: myocardial infarction, congestive heart failure, hypertension, diabetes, and depression.

In studying depression, cases were found through a two-stage process. The first step used a brief depression screen, and those patients exceeding a cutoff score underwent a telephone interview, which included the Diagnostic Interview Schedule (DIS) of the National Institute of Mental Health (Robins et al., 1981). Patients with mania or grief were excluded. *Current depression* was defined as having all the following criteria: (1) a lifetime diagnosis of major depression or dysthymia, (2) an episode of major depression or dysthymia within the last 12 months, and (3) no remission from the most recent major depressive episode (remission was defined as having two or fewer symptoms of depression for at least 8 weeks).

The sample consisted of 12,571 patients in group practices and 9,828 patients in solo practices. Of these, 3,647 were above the cutoff on the depression screen (and thus were eligible for the DIS interview) and 60% of those eligible participated in the study (2,195 patients). Of those completing the DIS, 775 patients had current depressive disorder, and 1,420 had depressive symptoms but no current disorder. Severity of depression was scored using the number of symptoms of depression or dysthymia experienced in the past year and on the five-item version of the Mental Health Inventory (MHI-5) (Stewart et al., 1988a), which was developed for the MOS.

These patients were then assessed 1 and 2 years after the baseline interview, using a modified DIS developed for this study. The response rate at each time point was 74%, with 83% of patients participating in at least one of the follow-up interviews. All patients were over 18, and about half were older than 40. At baseline, patients were classified as having had major depression, dysthymia, both (double depression), or subsyndromal depression.

Yale University Depression Research Unit (YUDRU)

Warner and colleagues (1992) investigated the 2-year course of depression in patients considered to be at high and low risk for depression. The high-risk group was composed of 153 offspring of one or more parents receiving treatment at the YUDRU. Normal controls were taken from a community survey in New Haven that had consisted of four direct interviews; 67 offspring of patients without a history of depression were used. The offspring studied were between the ages of 6 and 23, at the first interview. At the end of 2 years, all families were contacted; 121 offspring of depressed parents and 53 controls were interviewed at the second interview. Assessors were blind to the status of the subject's parents, and assessment items included the SADS. Incident cases were defined as having no evidence of depression at the index interview or in the past, and a first onset of depression between the first and second interview. Recovery was defined as an asymptomatic period of at least 8 weeks. Recurrence of major depressive disorder was defined as an episode of major depression during the year of the baseline interview, followed by a period of remission, then followed by an additional episode of major depression during the 2-year follow-up period. Calculations of episode length included retrospective reports.

Cognitive Therapy and Pharmacotherapy for Depression Study (CPT)

This study (Hollon et al., 1992) was designed as a replication of a study by Rush and colleagues (1977), which found cognitive therapy to be superior to imipramine in the treatment of depression. The earlier study suffered from a number of methodological problems, including the lack of blind ratings, the use of low doses of medication, the lack of plasma monitoring for medication, and the possibility of a site bias (as it was conducted at a center devoted to cognitive behavioral therapy). This study addressed these and other flaws using blind ratings, more typical doses of pharmacotherapy and plasma monitoring, and medication maintenance up through the posttreatment evaluation. The site of the study (two psychiatric facilities in St. Paul, Minnesota) had no particular allegiance to cognitive therapy.

One hundred and seven depressed subjects, who were not psychotic or bipolar, were randomly assigned to receive either cognitive therapy, imipramine, or a combination of the two. In this group, patients met RDC for depression, had HDRS (17-item) scores of $\geq$ 14, and BDI scores of $\geq$ 20. Patients with a history of most other axis I disorders were excluded from the study. The patients studied were generally women (80%), white (91%), about 33 years of age (range 18–62), employed or a houseperson (62% and 13%, respectively), and varied as to marriage status. Almost half had at least some college education, and they were generally lower middle class. Sixty-four percent had recurrent depression, with 37% having three or more episodes in the past; 24% had double depression. Of note is the unusual frequency of suicidal ideation (66%) reported at intake. Also of note is the high rate of attrition in this study: 5% of subjects failed to initiate treatment, and 35% did not complete treatment. Though large, the rates of attrition did not differ across treatment modalities.

The patients were seen in follow-up at 6 and 12 weeks after intake and evaluated with the HDRS, BDI, Raskin Depression Scale (RDS) (Raskin, 1970), GAS, and the Minnesota Multiphasic Personality Inventory (MMPI) (Hathaway and McKinley, 1951), which provides a depression subscale. Thus, four measures of depression were used. Recovery was judged based on the measures, with a cutoff score of 6 for the HDRS and a cutoff score of 9 on the BDI.

Patients who had at least partially responded to acute treatment (evidenced by a BDI $\leq$ 15) were entered into a second 2-year follow-up phase (Evans et al., 1992). Of the 64 treatment "completers," 50 patients were eligible; 44 participated in at least part of the study, and 38 (76% of eligible patients) either completed the 2-year follow-up or relapsed. Half of the patients treated with imipramine during the acute period were continued on imipramine; all other patients were discontinued from medication and cognitive therapy.

Follow-up consisted of monthly mail questionnaires, and 6-month face-to-face evaluations by an independent evaluator. Assessment consisted of the HDRS, BDI, and questions about relapse and participation in treatment. If a subject had a BDI score $\geq$ 16, then he or she was scheduled for a face-to-face "relapse evaluation" (which included a HDRS and a BDI). Relapse was defined as two consecutive BDI scores $\geq$ 16 separated by at least 1 week.

Pittsburgh Study of Maintenance Therapies in Recurrent Depression (PSMTRD)

This study was designed to investigate whether medication (imipramine) provides prophylaxis against recurrence of depression. Patients were followed for 3 (Frank et al., 1990) and then 5 (Kupfer et al., 1992) years of maintenance treatment. The 3-year maintenance trial studied 128 patients between the ages of 21 and 65 who had recurrent depression. *Recurrent depression* was defined here as (1) being currently in a third or higher episode of major depression, with (2) the prior episode not lasting longer than 2.5 years, and (3) a minimum of 10 weeks remission between the prior and index episodes (thus excluding patients with double depression).

Current depression was defined as a HDRS $\geq$ 15 and RDS $\geq$ 7; patients were excluded if they met the criteria for other axis I disorders (except generalized anxiety or panic disorder) or met criteria for antisocial or borderline personality disorder. Potential subjects were then evaluated with the SADS, and those who met RDC criteria for major depressive episode were entered into the study. Of the 230 patients who entered, approximately 80% were women, 56% were married, and 14.3% had bipolar type II disorder.

After a 2-week drug-free washout period, subjects were given a comprehensive evaluation, including sleep electroencephalogram, neuroendocrine studies, and psychosocial measures. All subjects then received a combination of imipramine and IPT until the patient showed a remission (defined as an HDRS $\leq$ 7 and an RDS $\leq$ 5 for 3 consecutive weeks). At the time of remission a second comprehensive evaluation was done. Patients then received combined treatment for 17 weeks, during which the remission had to remain stable. After a third comprehensive evaluation was performed, patients were randomly assigned to one of five maintenance treatments: (1) IPT, (2) IPT plus imipramine at acute treatment doses, (3) IPT plus placebo, (4) imipramine with clinical management alone, and (5) placebo with clinical management. Plasma levels were monitored for the medication groups. They were then continued on the maintenance treatment for 3 years or until they experienced a recurrence of illness. Recurrence was determined by two evaluations during a 7-day period, including an independent clinical evaluation using RDC criteria, HDRS $\geq$ 15, and RDS $\geq$ 7. Patients who met these criteria were further evaluated by a senior psychiatrist (not affiliated with the study and blind to the treatment condition). Of the 218 patients beginning the 3-year maintenance trial, 106 completed it.

An additional phase of this study extended the follow-up beyond the 3-year period to 5 years. Subjects were drawn from the 28 patients who completed the 3 years of maintenance in either of the two active medication groups (imipramine plus IPT or imipramine plus clinical management). These patients were then continued in the same psychotherapy situation as before and randomized to imipramine or placebo (patients assigned to placebo who had been on medication were put on a withdrawal schedule). The definition of illness recurrence and protocol for determining this remained the same as in the first phase of the study. Of the 28 patients eligible from the original study, 20 entered the 2-year extension, making for a much smaller sample size than in the original 3-year study. Their demographic characteristics were similar to the original sample.

THE CHANGE POINTS IN DEPRESSION

Recovery

Depression has usually been characterized as a self-limited disease, with an average duration of 6–9 months. However, newer studies that employ prospective designs suggest that a significant number of patients recover more slowly or do not ever recover fully.

A number of studies over the past two decades have looked at the clinical course of recovery from unipolar depression (Keller and Shapiro, 1981, 1982; Keller et al., 1983ab; Klein et al., 1988; Murphy, 1990; Coryell et al., 1990; Swindle et al., 1989, George et al., 1989; Sargeant et al., 1990). Most have found that severity of depression at baseline and clinical features such as a history of chronicity are predictors of favorable recovery.

Rounsaville and colleagues (1980a) conducted a prospective follow-up of 96 RDC-diagnosed ambulatory subjects with primary major depressive disorder and found that

12% of subjects had not recovered after 16 months of follow-up. Six percent of the subjects had persistent depression despite "adequate treatment."

Kerr and colleagues (1972) followed 126 initially hospitalized patients for 4 years and reported that 6% remained ill for the entire period.

Akiskal and colleagues (1981) examined 137 subjects who had not shown complete recovery from depression after 2 or more years. In this naturalistic study, the authors found that the chronic depressions tended to be low grade and intermittent. They identified four groups among these chronic patients: (1) early onset "dysthymic-type" depression with a family history for affective disorder; (2) subject with personality disorders; (3) subjects with preexisting medical or nonaffective psychiatric disorders, particularly in combination; and (4) patients with incomplete recovery from a late-onset major depressive disorder. The latter group tended to have complicated social, familial, and intrapsychic histories. Factors such as family histories for mood disorders, multiple object losses, comorbid alcohol and sedative dependence, comorbid incapacitating medical disorders, antihypertensive medications, disabled spouses, and marital difficulties characterized this group.

CDS   Recovery was defined as a PSR of 1 to 2, which indicated no to mild symptoms for 8 weeks. It was found that at each interval a significant number of patients were not recovered from the index depressive episode. For example, when the first 133 patients who completed a 2-year follow-up were examined, it was found that of 101 patients who originally had major depressive disorder, 22% of the patients did not recover (Keller and Shapiro, 1982). As the median duration of illness at entry to the study was 1 year, this suggests that much of the patient population had been chronically ill for 3 years.

Factors associated with this slower time to recovery were: longer duration of illness and increased severity of the index episode, a prior history of a nonaffective psychiatric disorder (suggesting that, in those patients, depression might be "secondary"), lower family income, and being married during the index episode (Keller et al., 1984).

At the time of the 5-year follow-up, 88% of 431 patients originally having major depression had recovered (Keller et al., 1992). This prospective evaluation was able to look at probabilities of recovery as a function of time; it was shown that the greatest probability of recovery was early in the course of the episode, with the odds of full recovery decreasing over time. Specifically, 54% of the patients recovered within the first 6 months of the study, and approximately 70% were recovered within 1 year. After the first year the cumulative probability of recovery increased less dramatically: 81% were recovered after 2 years, 87% after 4 years, and 88% after 5 years. Thus, only 18% of the patients still depressed after 1 year recovered by year 5.

At the 5-year follow-up, six factors were found to be significantly associated with poor recovery: long duration of illness before entry into the study, marital status, inpatient hospital status at the time of intake, low family income, the presence of secondary-unipolar subtypes (which include schizophrenia, panic disorder, obsessive compulsive disorder, phobias, schizoaffective and substance use disorders, anorexia, and organic brain syndrome), and admitting research center.

In the CDS, "recovery" implies full remission of all, or all but minimal, symptoms. Thus, many of the patients who did not recover would no longer meet full criteria for depression but rather would be considered "subsyndromal;" only a third of the subjects had major depression for more than half of the time.

Coryell and colleagues (1994) further reported on a 6-year follow-up of the CDS cohort. In this analysis, they studied patients who had recovered from the index episode of depression, and then went on to develop another episode of major depression. The authors then examined the course of the subsequent depressive episode. Thus, they eliminated the methodologic problems inherent in studying an index episode: subjects' recall of the onset of the index episode, particularly if beginning long before the initial interview, may be faulty; and subjects may only present for treatment (or a research study) during particularly severe episodes of depression. By definition, this group was not chronic (i.e., their index episode had remitted) and liable to recurrences of disease. This study was one of the few with sufficient longevity to prospectively observe the episode after the index episode, and follow it long enough to observe recovery.

Of the 605 probands, 431 (71.2%) completed 6 years of follow-up, compared with 589 (71.3%) of 826 controls. In the proband group, 359 had one prospectively observed depressive episode, and 181 had two or more such episodes. This compared with 216 episodes in the control group. Proband and control times to recovery were not significantly different across treatment centers. Perhaps the most interesting result in this study is that both the proband and control group, upon developing an episode of major depression, showed surprisingly similar courses of illness. At 6 months, 55% of the proband group and 57% of the control group had recovered; at 1 year 73% and 69% recovered; by 2 years 83% of the proband and 87% of the control group recovered; and 97% of both groups had recovered by the end of the follow-up period.

TDCRP   During the acute (16-week) phase of the study (Elkin et al., 1989), recovery was measured at the end of the study, and separately analyzed for each of the depression scales. For comparisons of recovery across treatment groups, they relied mainly on the HDRS. Ranges of recovery across treatment groups were 51–57% (compared with 29% in the placebo group) for patients completing treatment, and 40–49% for the 239 patients who entered the study. As defined above, "recovery" really indicates remission of symptoms at the final interview. The subsequent 18-month follow-up study (Shea et al., 1992) was able to provide more data on the stability of remission in the groups. In this phase, recovery was defined as a score of 1–2 (no or minimal depressive symptoms) for a minimum of 8 consecutive weeks on the PSR. They found a lower rate of recovery—only 33% of the total sample had fully recovered. The primary purpose of this study was to compare the effects of different treatments upon recovery rates, which will be discussed more fully later in this chapter.

MOS   In this study, the authors used the term *remission* rather than *recovery*. However, they define it in a manner consistent with definitions of recovery—two or fewer symptoms of depression for 8 weeks or more (Wells et al., 1992); thus, *recovery* will be used here. Patients were grouped by severity: those with few symptoms of major depression (defined using number of symptoms and the MHI-5) had a recovery rate of 40.9% in the first year and 64.7% in the second year, for an overall rate of 58.8% In the more severely depressed group, the recovery rates were 44.7% in the first year and 53.9% in the second, for an overall rate of 64.4%. Rates of depression differed with different types of depression. Subjects with mild double depression had a high likelihood of recovery, whereas double-depressed patients with severe symptomatology had the lowest rate of recovery of any of the groups. Patients with subsyndromal depression at baseline fared the best; however, their rate of major depression during the 2-year period was also high (25%). The effect of treatment was not analyzed. The authors argue that uncontrolled treatment could confound the analysis; for example, more severe patients may be more likely to be in treatment.

YUDRU   Among the offspring of depressed and control parents, 10 cases of major depression were identified as incident cases (Warner et al., 1992). All occurred in the high risk (offspring of depressed parents) group. By the 2-year follow-up, 87% of the depressed cases had recovered. The average time to recovery for the 10 cases was 46 weeks, with a large range (at between 2 and 312 weeks). About 61% recovered within 6 months, 74% after 1 year and 87% after 2 years. Four of the offspring were still depressed beyond 2 years. This study was primarily designed to measure the relative risk posed by a family history of depression, a subject discussed later in the chapter.

CPT   Though the availability of a midtreatment and posttreatment assessment gave some indication of the trend of symptomatology across time, this study defined recovery on symptomatic criteria alone without any time criteria. Thus, the study was measuring response rather than recovery rates.

For patients completing the study, the authors report an overall response rate of 75% using the HDRS (Hollon et al., 1992); for the BDI the rate was 69%. As previously mentioned, there was a high rate of attrition in this study, thus the response rates were lower when calculated for all patients assigned: 52% using the HDRS and 48% using the BDI. No pretreatment variables were found to predict response.

As the study did not exclude suicidal subjects, there was a higher rate of attempted suicide as compared with other research studies. Three patients attempted suicide and two of them died from the attempt. All the attempts were by medication overdose. Two other subjects were withdrawn from the study because of an increased risk of suicide.

Though the authors found no difference between study completers and those who discontinued, the results are limited by the high rate of attrition in the study and the lack of time criteria in the definition of recovery. Though the cutoff scores used are reasonable for symptomatic criteria of recovery, the study does not report the stability of this response across time.

Relapse

The majority of studies on the course of depression have centered on recovery rates; as the change point grows further from the index episode, fewer studies exist. A relatively early study on relapse was by Paykel and colleagues (1976), which concentrated on the characteristics of "relapsers." In this study, 33 subjects with major depression were examined at the time of index episode and several months later at the point of relapse. They found no relationship between the severity of the two episodes, and generally found the relapse episodes to be less severe than the index episodes.

CDS   In 141 of the CDS patients who recovered from the index depressive episode, 22% relapsed within 1 year of follow-up (Keller et al, 1983b). Relapse occurred earlier in patients who had had three or more episodes of major depression. In patients with only one episode of major depression (the index episode), risk factors for shorter time to relapse included older age and a history of a nonaffective psychiatric illness.

A further analysis examined the subsequent depressive episode in patients who relapsed (Keller et al, 1986b). One hundred and one relapsers were followed prospectively. In this group, the likelihood of remaining ill for a year after relapse was 22%. Longer length of the index episode, older age at relapse, and lower family income all predicted prolonged time to recovery from the relapse episode. There was a nonsignificant trend toward longer episodes in patients who were divorced or single. Number of previous episodes, gender, treatment status, RDC subtype of depression, severity of the index episode, and presence of pre-existing dysthymia were not predictive of the length of the relapse episode.

TDCRP In the 18 months of follow-up after active treatment, 20% of the original group (or 24% for whom follow-up data was available) both recovered and remained well. Relapse was defined as having 2 weeks of major depressive disorder level symptoms. Thus, subjects who had a relapse of minor depression were not counted. Relapse rates were 21% at 1 year and 38% by 18 months.

CPT In this group, relapse was defined as two consecutive BDI scores $\geq$ 16 separated by at least 1 week. Using this definition, 27% of the sample met the criterion for relapse during the study. Using more liberal criterion (one elevated BDI), 48% of the subjects relapsed. Fourteen patients sought treatment, although there was no evidence of a relapse.

Thus, a number of studies have reported relapse rates of roughly 20–30% for subjects who recover from a depressive episode. Certain clinical factors (longer length of the index episode) and demographic factors (older age at relapse and lower family income) may predict a risk of relapse. It should be noted that these studies generally used conservative criteria for relapse—as most required 8 weeks of remission for a definition of recovery. Any patient who had a return of depressive symptoms soon after treatment discontinuation was not counted as a relapse. Thus, the relapse rates here are probably lower than those of previous studies using less rigorous criteria.

Recurrence

A number of studies support the view of depression as a lifetime illness. Angst followed a sample of depressed patients in Zurich, Switzerland, in a naturalistic study. Reporting on a 10-year follow-up, he found that only 25% of the patients had a single episode of depression and concluded that from 75–80% of these patients suffered from recurrent depression (Angst, 1992). He examined a number of socioeconomic and demographic variables, including gender, age, race, social class, education, marital status, family history of depression, and having grown up in a "broken home," and found none of these useful in predicting the outcome of depressive episodes.

Likewise, a number of other investigators, including Rounsaville and colleagues (1980b) and Akiskal and colleagues (1980) found that a significant number of depressive episodes are recurrent. Rao and Nammalvar (1977), for example, reported a follow-up of 122 cases of major depression from India. They interviewed 109 of the original 122 cases; interviews took place from 3 to 13 years after the index episode. Of these cases, only 28 had no recurrence. A large number, however, turned out to have a bipolar disorder. They found that an onset of depression before age 40 predisposed an individual to recurrence. Weissman and colleagues (1976), however, reported on a follow-up of 150 women, seen 1 year after completion of outpatient maintenance treatment (either amitriptyline and/or psychotherapy) for depression. In this study, the authors found that only 30% of the patients remained in complete remission, while 60% had recurrences of symptoms and 12% were mildly but chronically symptomatic. A majority (60%) had sought treatment during the year and were receiving some psychotropic medication (Weissman and Kasl, 1976).

PSMTRD   This study investigated the role of medication in the long-term maintenance treatment of depression. Recurrence was evaluated very vigorously, with two evaluations over a 7-day period and confirmation by an independent psychiatrist. The group of 128 patients who completed the first 3 years of the study had a mean survival time of 75.7 weeks (Frank et al., 1990), with a large variance in all groups. Twenty patients were continued for an additional 2-year follow-up. Of these, seven had a recurrence of depression (Kupfer et al., 1992). At both phases of the study, the type of treatment was the major independent variable and, thus, this study will be discussed in more detail later in this chapter.

YUDRU   Although the sample size was small (10 cases of depression out of 174 offspring followed), tentative recurrence rates were calculated from the sample (Warner et al., 1992). Recurrence after the index episode was defined as an asymptomatic period of at least 8 weeks, followed by an additional episode of major depression occurring in the period between initial interview and 2-year follow-up. The 2-year recurrence rate was calculated at 16.1%. A previous diagnosis of dysthymia and problems in social functioning were predictive of recurrence.

Thus, for many, depression is a lifelong illness. Investigators are discovering that significant numbers of patients experience multiple episodes of depression. Others never fully recover from their illness and, instead, stabilize at a level of dysthymia or subsyndromal depression.

PSYCHOSOCIAL OUTCOMES OF DEPRESSION

Though the majority of studies use symptom severity as the primary measure of outcome, some authors have looked at other measures. Some of the most interesting measures are psychosocial outcome measures, such as work performance and social functioning, as they may better reflect the economic burden depression inflicts upon the community.

Some cross-sectional studies have suggested a strong relationship between health status and social functioning. Von Korff and colleagues (1992) looked at a sample of high users of health care services and found that a worse clinical course of depression was associated with more disability days. Kawakami and colleagues (1987) interviewed a group of 60 Japanese workers who returned to work following an episode of major depression. They found that about half of the workers relapsed within 5 years, and that relapse was the best predictor of occupational functioning.

MOS

Wells and colleagues (1989) found that social functioning was worse in patients with current depressive symptomatology. Social functioning was measured using a patient screener (Stewart et al., 1988b) which measured several areas of functioning, including physical, role, and social functioning. The number of days spent in bed were also recorded, as were perceptions of well-being.

When they compared depression with other chronic diseases (hypertension, diabetes, arthritis, gastrointestinal disorders, and lung disorders), they found that depression exerted a greater adverse effect on social and role functioning than the other chronic disorders. Only patients with advanced coronary artery disease had worse functioning on most of the measures. Depression continued to exert an independent effect when it was comorbid with other diseases; the effect was additive.

The relationship between depression and social functioning may go beyond current symptomatology—a number of studies have suggested that social impairment may persist after symptom improvement.

CDS

Coryell and colleagues (1993) reported on a 5-year follow-up study of patients with mood disorders, including 240 unipolar depressed patients. Study subjects were matched with controls and followed-up at 6-month intervals, using the LIFE. First-degree relatives of study subjects were also interviewed to better measure familial functioning. They found that even those study subjects who sustained a 2-year recovery had worse social functioning than controls. This impairment extended into such areas as familial and social relationships, sexual functioning, recreational activities, and overall satisfaction with life. In the proband group, there was a decrease in job status as well as a decrease in income, both of which persisted beyond the relief of symptoms.

Other authors, however, have had mixed results. Mintz and colleagues (1992) reviewed available longitudinal studies of depression that included social functioning in their analysis. They observe that there are a paucity of such studies; however, they summarize findings from 10 different studies (Elkin et al., 1989; Fawcett et al., 1987; Frank et al., 1987; Giller et al., 1988; Glick et al., 1985; Murphy, 1990; Prusoff and Weissman, 1981; Quitkin et al., 1989; Rehm et al., 1987; Rush et al., 1977). They included only patients in the active work force, thus excluding students, housewives, and the disabled. Work performance was measured on the Social Adjustment Scale (Weissman and Bothwell, 1976); the overall incidence of work impairment was about 50%. In each study in which pharmacotherapy was used, work performance improved. This improvement correlated best with symptomatic improvement and length of treatment. One aforementioned study (the TDCRP) compared the occupational outcome of a psychotherapy and placebo group and found comparable outcomes for both groups. However, the placebo appeared to be an active one [described by Elkin and colleagues as "minimal supportive therapy" (Elkin et al., 1989)].

Several of the studies had follow-up data. Patients who relapsed also showed renewed work impairment with symptomatic deterioration in three of the studies (Glick et al., 1985; Murphy, 1990; Rehm et al., 1987).

Mintz pooled data to look for prognostic factors that might predict social functioning; however, none of the baseline demographic, descriptive, or clinical variables were predictive of outcome. Symptomatic outcome and length of treatment remained the only predictive variables.

BIOLOGICAL CORRELATES OF DEPRESSIVE COURSE

Though many physiological measures have been correlated with depression (Ballenger, 1988; Balon, 1989), a number of studies have attempted to extend cross-sectional observations to examine physiological changes during the course of depression. Some examples follow.

Electroencephalogram (EEG) and Sleep Changes

Rieman and Berger (1989) compared the sleep EEG patterns of patients at the time of acute depression and after an average remission of 3 years. They found that upon remission, depressed individuals had improved sleep continuity and a tendency to normalize their rapid eye movement (REM) latency and density. At the time of remission, sleep patterns were comparable to normal controls. The authors suggest that these findings argue against a model of REM abnormalities as a specific trait abnormality among individuals predisposed toward depression. They note, however, that the long symptom-free period may characterize this group as having an unusually low risk of relapse, and it may not be generalizable to all depressed groups.

Though the stability of sleep parameters in depression remains questionable, there is some evidence to suggest that pretreatment sleep abnormalities may predict the course of depression. Giles and colleagues (1989) reported on a group of 25 patients successfully treated for depression and found that patients with a reduced REM latency prior to treatment were more likely to have a relapse or recurrence of depression on follow-up.

Neurochemical and Receptor Markers

Bovier and colleagues (1988) conducted a longitudinal investigation of the erythrocyte membrane transport of tyrosine and tryptophan in a number of mood disorder groups, including 18 bipolar patients, 14 recurrent depressives, and 12 dysthymic patients. Though there were differences in the transport ratios across nosological groups, the predominant findings across all groups was a decreased ratio of tyrosine to tryptophan during acute illness. These changes normalized with improvement in clinical symptoms.

In a similar investigation, Rybakowski and colleagues (1981) studied erythrocyte second-messenger adenosine triphosphatase (ATP-ase) activity in 25 patients with major depression. They found a lowered ATP-ase activity in the acute phase of depression as compared with the remission phase. The remitted depressives did not differ from healthy controls.

Lisansky and colleagues (1984) examined prolactin patterns in 13 patients with melancholia. They determined prolactin levels at 15-minute intervals during the acute illness and after treatment with amitriptyline. Overall, they found greater prolactin levels in recovered patients at most sampling points. Prolactin's relevance to depression may be as an indirect measure of neurotransmitter and receptor activity and, thus, Siever and colleagues' study (1986) is also of interest. Siever and colleagues looked at noradrenergic and serotonergic receptor responsiveness in acutely depressed patients and patients in remission. They used growth hormone response to clonidine as a measure of noradrenergic receptor responsiveness and found blunted responses in both acutely depressed patients and depressed patients in remission. Serotonergic receptor responsiveness was gauged by measuring prolactin response to fenfluramine. In this study, the authors found greater variability with serotonin responsiveness; only a subgroup of depressed patients had a depressed prolactin response. Again, no significant difference was found in the response of acutely depressed and remitted patients. Thus, the role of serotonin in depression is somewhat confusing. Some have suggested that the reason for this is that, while norepinephrine is a measure of depressive "state," serotonin may relate more directly to a depressive "trait" and, thus, not change in response to treatment. Some studies have suggested that, in certain groups of "endogenous" depressives, serotonin turnover remains deficient even after clinical recovery (van Praag, 1977; van Praag and de Hann, 1980). Unfortunately, attempts to use serotonin levels—either through cerebrospinal fluid metabolites or platelet serotonin—as a predictor of clinical course have met with conflicting results (Ballenger, 1988).

Serotonin's role as a "trait" measure remains open to investigation; however, the role of norepinephrine as a "state" measure of depression has good support. For example, in a study by Souetre and colleagues (1986b), the authors investigate 24-hour changes in norepinephrine levels in 12 depressed subjects and 10 normal controls. They found a circadian pattern in the normal subjects; the depressed patients had an abnormal pattern of norepinephrine levels, with amplitude reduction of the pattern and an abnormal phase position. After 3 weeks of treatment and reported recovery from depression, the subjects no longer displayed the circadian abnormalities.

Pickar and colleagues (1978) also investigated norepinephrine, using urinary 3-methoxy-4-hydroxyphenethylene glycol (MHPG), a metabolite of norepinephrine. The authors studied 10 women with primary affective disorders, comparing them with 5 healthy women. In the acute state of disease, the subjects had lower levels of excreted MHPG than controls, a difference that normalized with improvement in the clinical state. Patients with a recurrence of depression continued to excrete lower levels of MHPG than controls.

Postmortem studies have shown relationships between neurotransmitter levels and phase of illness. Both norepinephrine, serotonin, and dopamine have been reported to be lower in postmortem studies of depressed patients, whereas patients in remission tended to have normal levels of all neurotransmitters (Birkmayer and Riederer, 1975).

Endocrine Measures

Abnormalities in thyroid-stimulating hormone (TSH), usually blunting of the TSH response, are frequently reported in association with depression. Loosen and colleagues (1979) conducted a double-blind placebo-controlled comparison of depressed, chronic alcoholics and found that a blunted TSH response persisted into remission despite normalization of other endocrine abnormalities (such as elevated growth hormone and lowered prolactin). This result is contrary to a study by Kirkegaard and Smith (1978) who found that impaired TSH responses normalize during the remission phase. The latter group, however, also reported on a double-blind study of 39 patients in which an abnormal TSH response was predictive of relapse (Krog-Meyer et al., 1984). Souetre and colleagues (1986a) reported on abnormalities in the normal circadian pattern of TSH. They measured TSH levels in 12 depressed subjects and 13 normal controls and found several disturbances in the circadian pattern associated with the depressed groups, including an amplitude reduction and blunted nocturnal secretion of TSH. These measures normalized with recovery from depression.

Thyroid end-hormone abnormalities have also been reported. Kirkegaard and Faber (1981) reported on 80 patients with major depression who had serum levels of thyroxine (T4), 3,3',5-triiodothyronine (T3), 3,3',5-triiodothyronine (rT3), 3,5-diiodothyronine (3,5-T2), 3,3'-diiodothyronine (3,3'-T2), and 3',5'-diiodothyronine (3',5'-T2), drawn before and after treatment with electroconvulsive therapy. During the acutely depressed phase, patients had increased levels of T4, rT3, 3,3'-T2, and 3',5'-T2 compared with recovery levels. Serum concentrations of T3 and 3,5-T2, however, remained constant. This pattern appeared to persist regardless of the presence or absence of TSH response.

Another endocrine measure frequently associated with depression is the dexamethasone suppression test (DST). This effect may relate to serotonin, which seems to help regulate the negative feedback relationship between corticosteroids and corticotropin releasing factor (Nuller and Ostroumova, 1980). Thus, the suppression of corticosteroid release with dexamethasone (a process disrupted in depression) should normalize upon remission of depression. A number of authors have confirmed that this does occur. Nuller and Ostroumova (1980), for example, reported on 52 depressed patients with abnormal baseline DSTs. After successful treatment, the DSTs were comparable to those of normal controls and patients with other mental illnesses.

In the past, some studies have suggested that the DST may have a role in predicting clinical outcome (The APA Task Force on Laboratory Tests in Psychiatry, 1987). In a large meta-analysis, Ribeiro and colleagues (1993) evaluated studies that investigated whether the DST has predictive value in the outcome of depression. They concluded that the pretreatment DST is not of prognostic use. Nonsuppression of cortisol after treatment was, however, associated with a high risk of early relapse. Though this lends some support for the case of DST as a marker of a depressive trait, it is also possible that this group of posttreatment nonsuppressors are still acutely depressed.

Physiologic Measures

Uytdenhoef and colleagues (1984, 1983) looked at cerebral metabolism using regional cerebral blood flow (Xenon 113 method). They found left frontal hypervascularization and a right posterior hypovascularization in patients with major depression, but not in patients with minor depression, bipolar depression, or depression in remission.

Friedman and Meares (1979) studied cortical-evoked potentials in a sample of depressed patients. Twenty-two of these patients were treated with antidepressant medication and 11 with placebo. The authors found a significant difference between visual and auditory-evoked potentials seen during acute depression and recovery, with increased amplitudes evident during the acute period of depression. Interestingly, these evoked potentials were seen both in patients improved on antidepressant medication and patients improved on placebo.

Thus, though the studies above suggest that there are numerous biochemical and physiologic correlates of depressive state, there is neither conclusive evidence for a marker of a depressive trait nor a measure that would be of value in predicting the outcome of a particular depressive episode.

COURSE MODIFIERS

Double Depression

Double depression is the concurrent presence of both dysthymia and major depressive disorder. In this disorder, the episodes of major depression appear to be superimposed upon a more chronic depression (Keller and Shapiro, 1982). By definition, dysthymia and major depression only occur together if the dysthymia precedes the episode of major depression or if there has been remission from major depression for at least 2 months (American Psychiatric Association, 1994). The dysthymia must be of at least 2 years duration before the onset of the major depression. *Minor depression* after a major depressive episode—even when chronic—is considered to be major depression in partial remission. The distinction between episodic major depression and double depression is important in that double depression has a strong influence on the time to recovery, time to relapse or recurrence, and the probability of chronicity. It also influences the severity of the present and of subsequent episodes of affective disorder (Keller et al., 1983a, 1984; Klein et al., 1988).

Double depression is quite common. Rounsaville and colleagues (1980b) examined a sample of 64 depressed patients and found that 66% of them suffered from some form of chronic depression. Akiskal et al. (1980) reported that 55% of a group of depressed patients had *chronic characterological depression* with superimposed major depression. The CDS estimates that 25% of patients who seek treatment with an episode of major depression have a continuous, pre-existing dysthymia and these meet criteria for double depression (Keller and Shapiro, 1982). The Epidemiologic Catchment Area (ECA) Program and comorbidity studies (Kessler et al. 1994; Regier et al., 1988) estimate a population prevalence of dysthymia of approximately 3–4.8%. Since the probability of these patients developing an episode of major depression before recovery from the dysthymia is over 90% (Keller et al., 1995a), it is likely that a high proportion of the population with dysthymia will also meet criteria for double depression.

Several studies have looked at the course of double depression and how it differs from major depression alone. Klein et al. (1988) compared 31 patients with double depression to 50 patients with episodic major depression alone. Both groups were recruited from an outpatient sample of community mental health and university clinic patients. They found that the episodes of major depression were significantly shorter for the double-depression group. However, when the double-depression group was followed over 6 months, they were found to have significantly higher mean levels of depression scores and poorer social and global functioning. Patients in the double-depression group were also more likely to have a history of suicide attempts.

Levitt and colleagues (1991) also compared patients with double depression against patients with major depression alone (41 and 60 patients, respectively). They found that patients with double depression had an earlier age of onset of depression, more episodes of major depression, and higher comorbidity with other disorders, particularly anxiety. The critical variable in this study, however, appeared to be the chronicity of illness. Patients with major depression alone and a history of greater than 6 months of a mood disturbance did not differ from the double-depression group in their course of illness.

MOS Patients with double depression and a high number of initial symptoms had the lowest probability for recovery during the 2 years of this study: The cumulative rate was 40.9% overall in 2 years (compared with 64.4% for subjects with severe major depression alone). The study also noted that patients with double depression had a threefold risk of continued disease when compared with major depression alone (Wells et al., 1992). Unlike the study by Levitt and colleagues (1991), severity of depression and double depression appeared to have an interactive effect; the combination of the two resulted in a worse outcome than severe major depression alone.

CDS   In one analysis of the first 101 patients with major depression to enter the CDS, 26% had an underlying chronic depression (Keller and Shapiro, 1982). In 20 of those patients, the underlying depression met the criteria for chronic depression and 6 patients met criteria for sustained minor depression using the RDC criteria.

A later analysis of 316 patients found 25% of these patients had a pre-existing chronic depression that lasted for more than 2 years (Keller et al., 1983a). There was a tendency for patients with double depression to be female, over 30 years in age, and single; these trends were not statistically significant. Ninety-six percent of the patients had chronic depression for 3 years or more, 73% had it for 5 years or more, and 42% had been ill for over 10 years.

At 1-year follow-up of this group, 88% of the patients with double depression had recovered from the index episode of major depression, whereas only 69% of the patients with major depression alone had recovered in that time. However, the majority of the patients with double depression (58%) did not recover from their underlying chronic minor depression, and they had a higher rate of subsequent relapse into major depression.

On 2-year follow-up (Keller et al., 1983a), the double-depressed subjects continued to recover more rapidly than those with major depression alone. Ninety-seven percent of the patients with double depression had recovered from the index episode of major depression by 2 years, whereas only 79% of the patients with major depression alone had recovered. By the end of the first year, double-depressed subjects still suffering from major depression had an 82% chance of recovery in the second year; subjects still suffering from major depression alone had only a 29% chance of recovery during that time. However, there was again a poor recovery from the underlying chronic depression. Of the subjects with double depression who recovered from their major depressive episode, 58% had not recovered from their underlying dysthymia.

Thus, though a person with double depression recovers more easily from a major depressive episode than a person with major depression alone, recovery is not to a state of "normalcy." It is as if it were easier for the body to return to a state of minor depression than one of "true" health (Keller and Shapiro, 1982). Moreover, relapse is more likely in patients with double depression who recover from the episode of major depression compared to patients with major depression alone who recover. Relapse occurs more frequently with double depression as well. After observing 32 doubly depressed subjects for 2 years of the follow-up period, Keller and colleagues report that 62% went through one entire cycle of recovery and relapse during the period. Only 33% of the 101 with major depression alone went through a similar cycle in that period (Keller et al., 1983a). This likelihood of relapse appears to increase as the length of chronicity increases.

Comorbidity

Comorbid Medical Illness   Some studies suggest that comorbid medical illnesses and psychiatric disorders predispose individuals to a more unfavorable course of depression (Moos, 1990; Shea et al., 1990, Duggan et al., 1990; Andrews et al., 1990). The MOS found an additive effect upon patients functioning when depression and other chronic medical illnesses were combined, suggesting a worse course for the comorbid patients (Wells et al., 1989). There are few longitudinal studies looking at the outcome of depression in medically ill patients, given the difficulty in recruiting such unstable patients. Though it has been suggested that depression in the setting of medical disease (or "secondary" depression) is less responsive to antidepressants than "primary" depression (Reynolds, 1992), this may reflect methodological difficulties in diagnosing depression in a physically ill population.

Personality Disorders   Comorbid personality disorders, or other similar character pathology, are generally thought to have a negative influence on the outcome of depressive disorders. In the past, this view relied more on summed clinical experiences than empirical data. Recent studies, however, have tended to confirm this impression. In a review of the effect of personality disorders on the outcome of treatment, Reich and Green (1991) found several studies that evaluate depressed inpatients (Black et al., 1988; Charney et al. 1981; Pfohl et al., 1984, 1987; Zimmerman et al., 1986) and outpatients (Frank et al., 1987; Pilkonas and Frank, 1988; Reich, 1990) for DSM-III criteria of personality disorder. All the studies reviewed report a poorer outcome and response to treatment in the depressed patients with personality disorders. These studies, however, were generally naturalistic in design, and in most of them the personality disordered patients were more severely depressed than the patients with depression alone. The TDCRP found similar results for imipramine and interpersonal therapy. Depressed patients with personality disorders had worse responses to treatment, although depressed patients with personality disorders seemed to do better in cognitive therapy (Elkin et al., 1989; Shea et al., 1990).

Anxiety Disorders   A number of investigators have demonstrated the frequent co-occurrence of panic disorder and depression (Thompson et al., 1989; Stein et al., 1990). Klein et al. (1988), in a study of patients with dysthymia, found that 56% of patients with early-onset dysthymia also suffered from an accompanying anxiety disorder. Cadoret and colleagues (1980) reported on depressed patients seen in a family practice setting and found a relationship between the presence of somatic complaints, anxiety, and depression. They also reported that the persistence of somatic complaints for over a year of treatment predicted eventual chronicity of the depression.

Coryell and colleagues (1988), in a 2-year follow-up study of 469 patients with major affective disorders, found that depressed patients with panic disorders had been depressed for longer periods of time and had more severe symptoms of depression than depressed patients without panic disorder. At 2-year follow-up, only 59.3% of the depressed patients with panic disorder had recovered from their depression. The depressed patients with panic disorder also reported more impaired psychosocial functioning than those with major depression alone.

Clayton and colleagues (1991) later studied the influence of anxiety upon course of illness. Reporting on 327 CDS subjects with unipolar depression, they developed an anxiety summary score based on six symptoms from the SADS: worrying, panic attacks, somatic anxiety, psychic anxiety, phobic, and obsessive–compulsive features. There was no significant relationship between anxiety scores and sex or gender. They analyzed the 5-year follow-up data for this population and found that depressed patients with higher ratings of anxiety had longer times to recovery (13 weeks versus 26 weeks mean time to recovery in the low- and high-anxiety groups, respectively).

Alcoholism   The comorbid presence of alcoholism exerts a deleterious effect upon the course of major depression. Akiskal and colleagues (1981), looking at 137 subjects who had been depressed for over 2 years, found alcohol and sedative–hypnotic dependence to be among the variables that predicted a chronic course. Mueller and colleagues

(1993), in a review of the epidemiologic data on the subject, characterized the combination of depression and substance abuse as "double trouble," with increased morbidity and poorer prognosis than either disorder alone.

Mueller and colleagues (1994) used the CDS cohort to investigate the relationship between alcohol and the course of depression. They compared 176 subjects having both major depression and alcoholism with 412 subjects having major depression alone. Data for up to 10 years of follow-up was available at the time of this study. Alcoholism status was stratified into three groups: those with current RDC-defined alcoholism, those not currently meeting criteria, and those never meeting criteria for alcoholism. The authors found that subjects who currently suffered from alcoholism were half as likely as the other two groups to recover from their episode of major depression. Alcohol status did not predict recurrence. This relationship between alcohol and depression is all the more disconcerting given the high rates of suicide reported in alcoholics. Beck and Steer (1989) reported on a 5- to 10-year prospective study of suicide attempts and found that alcoholism was the only variable that reliably predicted eventual suicide. Alcoholics in their group had five times the risk for committing suicide than nonalcoholics.

Family History

Familial Alcoholism   The relationship between alcohol and depression may be at the level of inheritance. This hypothesis is supported by studies reporting a relationship between depression in an individual and alcoholism in a relative (Winokur and Coryell, 1991). A number of studies have suggested that patients with such a history have a worse course of depression. Reveley and Reveley (1981) described a group of 18 *secondary depressives* who had a lower rate of recovery than a group of 26 *primary depressives*. The secondary depressives were characterized as having a higher proportion of relatives with alcoholism. This group also had a higher number of suicide attempts than the primary depressives. These findings were seemingly inconsistent with a previous study by VanValkenburg and colleagues (1977), who described a similar group of patients, designating their constellation of symptoms *depressive spectrum disease*. This group was characterized by a history of alcoholism or antisocial personality disorder in a parent. They compared depressive spectrum disease with *pure depressives* who had a history of parental depression. Though the depressive spectrum patients seemed to have poorer psychosocial functioning than their pure counterparts, and were more likely to report a history of depression, they were, nonetheless, more likely to recover from their index episode and not relapse.

These discrepancies may relate to methodological difficulties, particularly in generalizing from a large and diverse population of patients. Kupfer and colleagues (1989a) found the relationship between recurrent depression and familial alcoholism to be most marked when the depressed proband was young (20 or younger); and Winokur and Coryell (1991), in a review of the literature, found that this relationship seemed to apply only to depressed women.

Familial Depression   A family history of depression has long been thought to predispose the offspring to depression (Orvaschel, 1990; Keller et al., 1988; Hammen et al., 1990; Grigoroiu-Serbanescu, 1991; Weissman et al., 1987). In the YUDRU study, the 10 depressed offspring of depressed parents took a longer time to recover from their own episode of depression, with a mean of 54 weeks as compared to 23 weeks in the control group. Multivariate analysis suggested that the variables most predictive of protracted recovery were younger age of onset (younger than 13), exposure to divorce in the family, or exposure to more than one parental episode of depression. Only one previous study had looked at the relationship between parental depression and the course of illness in an offspring (Hammen et al., 1990). That previous study, though using a smaller sample, had results similar to the YUDRU's.

Treatment

Recovery There is a wealth of data supporting the proposition that antidepressants will shorten the length of a depressive episode, and this information forms the core data set justifying the use of antidepressants. As such, this data will be considered separately (Chapter 12). It should be noted, however, that the mere recognition and initiation of treatment does not necessarily lead to improvement in the course, and that many patients recognized as depressed receive inadequate treatment (Weissman and Klerman, 1977).

Ormel and colleagues (1991) examined a cohort of 1,994 patients aged 16–65 seen at general practices in the Netherlands. Of all new patients previously without a psychiatric diagnosis, 38% had scores above the threshold for psychopathology on the General Health Questionnaire (Ormel et al., 1989). Of these patients, 51% met the criteria for some psychiatric disorder. Fifteen patients met the criteria for depression, with a prevalence estimate of 57 per 1,000 new cases. The mean duration of the depressive episode was judged based on a 1-year follow-up, and was reported as 9.8 months. Recognition of the case by the primary physician did not affect the duration of the episode, and the only psychiatric disorder for which recognition improved outcome was anxiety. Though the authors suggest several possible explanations for this, the most likely seems to be inadequate treatment. In this study, only 50% of the depressed patients were recognized as such, and the majority of them were given benzodiazepines as treatment. Only one-quarter of the patients recognized as depressed received antidepressant treatment.

Keller and colleagues reported on an ongoing trial of sertraline and imipramine for the treatment of chronic depression [Keller et al., in press (a)]. *Chronic depression* included both chronic major depression and double depression. Their preliminary report examined the first 212 patients to enter this study. They report that only 26.8% of the subjects (out of 198 patients for whom data was available) ever had an adequate trial of an antidepressant medication (defined as 150 mg/day of imipramine or its equivalent for at least 4 consecutive weeks). This finding is all the more worrisome given the finding that about two-thirds of all patients responded to antidepressant treatment during the 12-week trial.

CDS Keller's findings regarding the inadequacy of treatment for depression—even when recognized—are consistent with earlier reports from the CDS study (Keller et al., 1984). On an analysis of the first 217 depressed subjects to enter the CDS, it was found that most received psychotherapy (67%) or antianxiety medications (55%). Only 34% of the patients received antidepressant medications for 4 consecutive weeks, and of these only 3% received the maximal dose. Subsequent analysis of 338 patients in the CDS found similar results (Keller et al., 1986a).

TDCRP Inadequate treatment can refer both to the type and length of treatment; both of these factors were addressed in the TDCRP. As previously noted, this study compared four treatment conditions (cognitive therapy, interpersonal therapy, imipramine plus clinical management, and placebo plus clinical management) during a 16-week study acute treatment phase. Though there was a high attrition (of 239 patients entered, 162 actually completed the 16-week trial), there was no significant difference in attrition across treatment groups.

Recovery was analyzed both on the HDRS and the BDI. On the HDRS, recovery was defined as a score of 6 or less; using this criterion for the treatment completers, 57% of patients receiving imipramine plus clinical management, 55% of patients receiving interpersonal therapy, 51% of patients receiving cognitive behavioral therapy, and 29% of patients receiving placebo recovered. There was a trend for significance over placebo in the imipramine and interpersonal therapy groups ($P = .02$ and .021, respectively) and no significant difference between cognitive therapy and placebo. The treatments did not differ significantly from each other in outcome. Part of the difficulty in finding a significant difference relates to the high rate of placebo response (a situation relatively common to response studies of depression). This was seen even more dramatically when the BDI was used for comparisons of outcome. Here, using a cutoff score of 9 or less for recovery, 51% of the placebo group responded; though the percentage recovered for the other groups ranged from 65 to 70%, the high placebo response made any differences statistically insignificant.

Severity of illness was an important factor in recovery. Patients who were severely depressed (defined as a GAS less than 50) tended to have lower placebo response. In this subgroup of patients, interpersonal therapy was significantly better than placebo on the HDRS, and imipramine was significantly better than placebo on most measures. Cognitive behavioral therapy was not significantly different from placebo on any measure. Thus, this study lends support to the notion that pharmacotherapy is the most effective treatment in the severely depressed patient.

MOS   Wells and colleagues looked at 634 depressed patients from the MOS cohort to compare the use of antidepressant medications and tranquilizers across different treatment settings (Wells et al., 1994). They found that less than a third of the depressed outpatients were being treated with antidepressants. This finding was true regardless of the specific depressive diagnosis. Patients of psychiatrists were more likely to receive antidepressants. Of these patients, 39% were given subtherapeutic doses of the antidepressant. As with Ormel's study, minor tranquilizers were used more frequently than antidepressants.

Relapse   Thase, in a review of the literature on the treatment of recurrent depression (1990), reported that 50% of "recently improved" patients who were switched from somatotherapy to placebo relapsed, whereas the relapse rate was only 20% in patients maintained on somatotherapy. Coppen and colleagues (1978) reported on 32 patients who had responded to amitriptyline and were continued on this medication for 1 year. Three of these patients were noncompliant with the medication, and they relapsed, as did 5 out of 16 patients on placebo. None of the patients who continued amitriptyline treatment relapsed. Avery and Winokur (1978) reported relapse rates on 519 depressives treated with either ECT or antidepressants (including a subgroup classified as "adequate" antidepressant treatment). They found no difference in relapse rates between the groups.

TDCRP   Shea and colleagues (1992) reported on a naturalistic follow-up of the acute phase of the TDCRP. Patients who completed the first 16 weeks of the study were gradually reduced from any medication they were receiving and seen every sixth month for an 18-month posttreatment follow-up. Patients who relapsed were referred for treatment, and patients who were doing well were encouraged to postpone treatment. Assessment was done with the LIFE-II, and relapse was defined as having 12 consecutive weeks of a LIFE-II score of 5–6 (definite major depressive disorder). A secondary analysis using even more conservative criteria for relapse was also done in which either the above criteria or having received 3 consecutive weeks of treatment in the follow-up period qualified for relapse.

Of the 239 patients originally entering the study, 84% had follow-up data for at least the first 6 months. After 18 months of follow-up, it was found that 33% of the total sample (or 39% of those with follow-up data) met the criteria for recovery. Only 24% of patients entering treatment (or 24% of patients with follow-up data) both recovered and remained well for the entire 18 months. When the more conservative criteria for relapse were used (adding treatment as a criterion), only 19% of the patients with follow-up data both recovered and remained well. There were no statistically significant differences across groups. The conclusion that must be reached from these high rates of relapse is that 16 weeks of any of the studied treatments is not adequate to maintain recovery.

CPT   As previously noted, patients who responded to treatment in the initial phase of this study were continued in a 2-year follow-up to investigate whether imipramine and cognitive therapy have different prophylactic effects (Evans et al., 1992). Half of the patients originally treated with imipramine were continued on imipramine; all others were removed from treatment. They were followed-up monthly (by mail) and every 6 months (in person). The greatest rate of relapse was in the patients treated with imipramine and then discontinued; 50% of this group relapsed. The rates for the other groups were as follows: 32% in the imipramine plus 1 year continuation group, 21% in the cognitive therapy group, and 15% in the combination cognitive and pharmacotherapy group. When the two cognitive therapy conditions were pooled, it was found that they had less than half the rate of relapse than the medication–no continuation group. The medication status of the patients treated with cognitive therapy did not affect this rate. Thus, this study suggests that providing cognitive therapy during the acute treatment period continues to confer some benefit in the posttreatment period, whereas medication confers no benefit once it is discontinued.

Recurrence   The majority of studies available agree that ongoing maintenance medication helps to reduce the risk of depression (Prien and Kupfer, 1986; Frank et al., 1990). The duration for which medication would still confer a benefit is not clear—most controlled studies do not go beyond 3 years in length. Naturalistic studies suggest that even longer periods are beneficial if medication is continued at acute treatment doses (Belsher and Costello, 1988; Keller et al., 1982b).

Peselow and colleagues (1991) studied 217 patients maintained on medication for 5 years with 28 patients discontinued from medication after a 5- to 6-month continuation period. They found the frequency of relapse to be high in both groups, but lower in the ongoing treatment group. For example, the relapse rate at 1 year for the active treatment group was 30%, compared with 51% in the no-treatment group. Fifty percent of the treatment group relapsed by 2 years (versus 74% in the comparison group) and 60% at 3 years (versus 83% in the comparison group).

PSMTRD This study was one of the first maintenance trials to extend the length of the trial beyond 3 years while retaining a placebo-controlled design (Frank et al., 1990; Kupfer et al., 1992). Of the 128 patients beginning the 3-year maintenance trial, 106 completed it. Only four of the patients who dropped out specifically cited medication side effects as the reason for leaving the study. There was a trend for greater attrition from the imipramine groups. The mean survival time for the entire group of 128 patients was 75.7 weeks, with a large variance. The mean survival time for each treatment group, in order of survival, was as follows: IPT plus imipramine, 131 weeks; imipramine with clinical management alone, 124 weeks; IPT, 82 weeks; IPT plus placebo, 74 weeks; placebo with clinical management, 45 weeks.

In the 2-year extension of the study (for a total of 5 years of follow-up) 11 patients received imipramine and 9 received placebo. Six of the active medication group and 7 from the placebo group also received IPT. Of the 20 patients, 12 completed the 5-year maintenance; 7 had a recurrence of depression, and 1 was discontinued because of noncompliance. The active treatment group had a mean survival of 99.4 weeks, versus 54 weeks in the placebo group. Even with the small sample size, the differential hazard of recurrence was highly significant: Only one patient in the medication group had a recurrence (and his blood levels suggested noncompliance), whereas only two-thirds of the placebo group relapsed (Kupfer et al., 1992).

Thus, this study suggests that for patients with recurrent depression, maintenance periods of up to 5 years continue to offer benefit in preventing recurrence. This assertion is somewhat tempered by the small sample size in the 2-year extension of the study. Whether longer, even indefinite treatment maintenance continues to confer such a benefit is a question that awaits further controlled trials.

Even if an episode of depression cannot be prevented, treatment may reduce the severity of the subsequent episode. Kupfer and colleagues (1989b) observed 45 subjects with a history of recurrent depression to see whether early intervention would affect the course of illness. They observed the group through two cycles of illness. The patients were treated with a combination of pharmacotherapy and psychotherapy, which was discontinued after recovery. They found that for both episodes of depression it took a similar time for stabilization—about 11–12 weeks. However, early intervention for the second episode appeared to shorten the overall duration of the episode by 4–5 months.

What type of treatment is most beneficial in preventing recurrence is not clear. Most studies of maintenance have used imipramine, given its status as a "gold standard" antidepressant. Other antidepressants have been studied as well, with results comparable to imipramine (Peselow, 1991). Some studies suggested that nortriptyline lacked prophylactic value (Georgotas et al., 1989). However, when plasma levels are carefully monitored, nortriptyline probably has equal efficacy to other antidepressants (Kragh-Sorensen et al., 1976).

Though fewer studies exist, the newer serotonin reuptake inhibitors appear to have comparable efficacy for preventing relapse and recurrence. Use of most of the newer agents in long-term treatment of depression can now be justified by at least one long-term placebo-controlled study. For example, Montgomery and colleagues (1988) demonstrated a prophylactic effect for fluoxetine after 1 year. In their study, patients successfully treated for major depression during a 6-month open trial of fluoxetine were randomized to receive either fluoxetine (40 mg) or placebo for another year. Of the 220 patients entering, 182 patients actually completed the study. During the 1-year follow-up period, 26% of the fluoxetine-treated patients and 57% of the placebo-treated patients had a relapse of depression. Montgomery and Dunbar (1993) also report a similar 1-year trial of paroxetine, using 135 patients who initially responded to paroxetine during an 8-week trial. They found a 13% relapse rate on the drug compared with a 32% relapse rate on placebo. Doogan and Caillard (1992) treated 480 patients with sertraline for 8 weeks, and then randomized this group to receive either sertraline or placebo. They found a 13% relapse rate during a 44-week trial of sertraline, which compared with a 46% relapse rate on placebo. In each case, the difference in relapse rates between the serotonin reuptake inhibitor group and the placebo group was highly significant.

Lithium is generally not considered to be as effective as antidepressants for the acute treatment of unipolar depression. However, it may be useful in the prophylaxis of depression (Johnson et al., 1987; Fieve et al., 1976), sometimes more so than antidepressants. For example, lithium has been reported to be superior to mianserin (Coppen et al., 1978), imipramine (Quitkin et al., 1978), and maprotiline (Coppen et al., 1976) for maintenance therapy. A number of these studies are flawed by the fact that lithium plasma levels were constantly monitored in these patients, whereas antidepressant plasma levels were often not monitored, or not adjusted in response to plasma levels. Furthermore, the subjects studied in each report had varying levels of psychopathology and periods of euthymia. The significance of such measures of severity was demonstrated by Prien and colleagues (1984), who compared four possible maintenance treatments (lithium carbonate, imipramine, a combination of the two, and placebo). After successful treatment for unipolar depression, 150 subjects were randomized to one of the maintenance groups and studied for 2 years. The authors found that imipramine and combination treatment were more effective than lithium alone for preventing recurrence of illness. Overall, lithium was no better than placebo for maintenance treatment. When treatment severity was considered, however, it was found that lithium was comparable to imipramine for subjects with less severe index episodes. In subjects with more severe episodes, lithium was significantly less effective than imipramine for maintenance therapy.

Maintenance electroconvulsive therapy is another effective option and has a role—at least—in patients unresponsive to medication maintenance (Solomon, 1978; Barton et al., 1973).

Though pharmacotherapy has no benefit following discontinuation (Post, 1959), it is possible that psychotherapy may confer such a benefit. Such a protective effect for psychotherapy has been suggested by a number of naturalistic studies of cognitive therapy (Blackburn et al., 1986; Kovacs et al., 1981; Simons et al., 1986). Naturalistic studies are limited in that they cannot control for the possibility of differential return to treatment; thus controlled studies are needed to better clarify this.

CPT This study, though analyzing relapse, not recurrence, extended its follow-up to two years (Evans et al., 1992). The authors argue that as most of the subjects showed new symptomatology within the first few months, the majority of them were probably relapsing. It is notable, however, that the early relapses tended to occur in the medication-discontinuation group, all of who relapsed within the first 4 months of follow-up. The cognitive therapy group, on the other hand, had a mean survival time of 17.4 months, making it possible that some of these later "relapses" were actually recurrences. As the authors of this study suggest, the question of whether or not cognitive therapy can also prevent recurrence must be answered by subsequent studies that employ longer follow-up periods and larger samples.

- Single episode,
  with antecedent dysthymia

- Single episode,
  without antecedent dysthymia

- Recurrent, with antecedent dysthymia,
  with full interepisode recovery

- Recurrent, with antecedent dysthymia,
  without full interepisode recovery

- Recurrent, without antecedent dysthymia,
  with full interepisode recovery

- Recurrent, without antecedent dysthymia,
  without full interepisode recovery

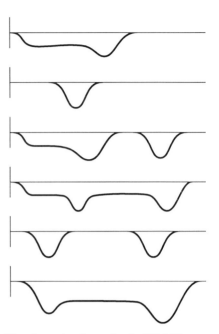

FIGURE 1. Proposed longitudinal course modifiers for major depression in DSM-IV.

Whether preventing relapse or recurrence, it remains unclear what is the crucial ingredient in cognitive therapy that confers a preventive effect. Kavanagh and Wilson (1989), for example, reported that patients with a greater sense of self-efficacy at controlling their mood were less likely to have a recurrence of disease after 1 year. Unfortunately, when they attempted to target this factor in their treatment, the course of depression was not improved.

In summary, treatment appears to be able to affect all aspects of the course of depression. Though the majority of studies have documented the ability of various treatments in enabling an early recovery from depression, a growing number of studies are looking at later aspects of the course. Medications appear to prevent both relapse and recurrence, provided that adequate treatment is continued throughout the course. Certain therapies, such as interpersonal therapies and cognitive therapy, though not necessarily as effective in severe depression, may confer longer lasting benefits in patients who successfully complete them. This preventive effect of psychotherapy may be particularly important, given the potentially large expense of continuing patients on long-term antidepressants and the groups of patients (pregnant mothers, severely ill patients) who may not be able to tolerate an antidepressant.

EPILOGUE: DSM-IV COURSE MODIFIERS

In prior versions of the Diagnostic and Statistical Manual, depression has been classified through cross-sectional assessments of current symptom severity. As the studies reviewed in this chapter suggest, the longitudinal features of depression may better predict prognosis. As such, the Diagnostic and Statistical Manual-IV (American Psychiatric Association, 1994) introduced a system of classification based on the course of the disease. This system will act as a supplement to the previous cross-sectional classification.

This new system is based on three variables: the presence or absence of antecedent dysthymia; single versus recurrent episodes; and, if recurrent, the presence or absence of a full recovery in between episodes. Combining these variables yields six possible groups. These six course patterns are illustrated in Figure 1. In addition, a seventh category—"unspecified"—encompasses those cases that cannot be classified in one of the six categories. In the multicenter DSM-IV Mood Disorders Field Trial, it was found that almost 99% of the 349 subjects with current major depression could be assigned to one of the six groups (Keller et al., 1995b) with fair to good interrater reliability.

Such modifiers, with the greater attention they give to the course of disease, have the potential to enhance our current ideas about the diagnosis, prognosis and treatment of depression. It will be interesting to see the effect of such course modifiers as they make their way from experimental field trials to clinical practice.

REFERENCES

Akiskal HS, King D, Rosenthal TL, Robinson D, Scott-Strauss A (1981): Chronic depression, part I: Clinical and familial characteristics in 137 probands. J Affect Disord 3:297–315.

Akiskal HS, Rosenthal TL, Haykal RF, Lemmi H, Rosenthal RH, Scott-Strauss A (1980): Characterological depression: Clinical and sleep EEG findings from separating "subaffective dysthymias" from "character spectrum disorders." Arch Gen Psychiatry 37:777–783.

American Psychiatric Association (1994): "Diagnostic and Statistical Manual of Mental Disorders" (4th ed). Washington, DC: American Psychiatric Association.

Andrews G, Neilson M, Hunt C, Stewart G, Kilow LG (1990): Diagnosis, personality and the long-term outcome of depression. Br J Psychiatry 157:13–18.

Angst J (1992): How recurrent and predictable is depressive illness? In Montgomery S, Rouillon F (eds): "Long-Term Treatment of Depression." New York: Wiley.

The APA Task Force on Laboratory Tests in Psychiatry (1987): The dexamethasone suppression test: an overview of its current status in psychiatry. Am J Psychiatry 144:1253–1262.

Avery D, Winokur G (1978): Suicide, attempted suicide, and relapse rates in depression. Arch Gen Psychiatry 35:749–753.

Ballenger JC (1988): Biological aspects of depresssion: Implications for clinical practice. In Frances AJ, Hales RE (eds): "Review of Psychiatry," vol. 7. Washington, DC: American Psychiatric Association.

Balon R (1989): Biological predictors of antidepressant treatment outcome. Clin Neuropharmacol 12:195–214.

Barton JL, Mehta S, Snaith RP (1973): The prophylactic value of extra ECT in depressive illness. Acta Psychiatri Scand 49:386–392.

Beck AT, Steer RA (1989): Clinical predictors of eventual suicide: a 5- to 10-year prospective study of suicide attempters. J Affect Disord 17(3):203–209.

Beck AT, Ward CH, Mendelsohn M, Mock J, Erbaugh J (1961): An inventory for measuring depression. Arch Gen Psychiatry 4:561–571.

Belsher G, Costello CG (1988): Relapse after recovery from unipolar depression: A critical review. Psychol Bull 104:84–96.

Birkmayer W, Riederer P (1975): Biochemical post-mortem findings in depressed patients. J Neural Transmission 37(2):95–109.

Black DW, Bell S, Hulbert J, Nasrallah A (1988): The importance of axis II in patients with major depression. J Affect Disord 14:115–122.

Blackburn IM, Eunson KM, Bishop S (1986): A two-year naturalistic follow-up of depressed patients treated with cognitive therapy, pharmacotherapy and a combination of both. J Affect Disord 10:67–75.

Bovier P, Pringuey D, Widmer J, Chiaroni P, Gaillard JM, Dufour H, Tissot R (1988): Joint evolution of erythrocyte membrane transport of tyrosine and tryptophan as a function of the clinical course of depression. Encephale 14(1):19–26.

Cadoret RJ, Widmer RB, North C (1980): Depression in family practice: Long-term prognosis and somatic complaints. J Fam Pract 10:625–629.

Charney DS, Nelson CJ, Quinlan DM (1981): Personality traits and disorder in depression. Am J Psychiatry 138:1601–1604.

Clayton PF, Grove WM, Coryell W, Keller M, Hirschfeld R, Fawcett J (1991): Follow-up and family study of anxious depression. Am J Psychiatry 148:1512–1517.

Coppen A, Ghose K, Rao R, Bailey J, Peet M (1978): Mianserin and lithium in the prophylaxis of depression. Br J Psychiatry 133:206–210.

Coppen A, Montgomery SA, Gupta RK, Bailey JE (1976): A double-blind comparison of lithium carbonate and maprotiline in the prophylaxis of the affective disorders. Br J Psychiatry 128:479–485.

Coryell W, Akiskal HS, Leon AC, Winokur G, Maser JD, Mueller TI, Keller MB (1994): The time course of nonchronic major depressive disorder: Uniformity across episodes and samples. Arch Gen Psychiatry 51:405–410.

Coryell W, Scheftner W, Keller MB, Endicott J, Maser J, Klerman GL (1993): The enduring psychosocial consequences of mania and depression. Am J Psychiatry 150:720–727.

Coryell W, Endicott J, Keller M (1990): Outcome of patients with chronic affective disorder: A five-year follow-up. Am J Psychiatry 147:1627–1633.

Coryell W, Endicott J, Andreasen NC, Keller MB, Clayton PJ, Hirschfeld RMA, Schefner WA, Winokur G (1988): Depression and panic attacks: The significance of overlap as reflected in follow-up and family study data. Am J Psychiatry 145:293–300.

Derogatis LR, Lipman RS, Covi L (1973): SCL-90: An outpatient psychiatric rating scale—preliminary report. Psychopharmacol Bull 9:13–28.

Doogan DP, Caillard V (1992): Sertraline in the prevention of depression. Br J Psychiatry 160:217–222.

Duggan CF, Lee AS, Murray RB (1990): Does personality predict long-term outcome in depression? Br J Psychiatry 157:19–24.

Elkin I, Shea MT, Watkins JT, Imber SD, Sotsky SM, Collins JR, Glass DR, Pilkonis PA, Leber WR, Docherty JP, Fiester SJ, Parloff MB (1989): National Institute of Mental Health Treatment of Depression Collaborative Research Program: general effectiveness of treatments. Arch Gen Psychiatry 46:971–982.

Elkin I, Parloff MB, Hadley SW, Autry JH (1985): NIMH Treatment of Depression Collaborative Research Program: background and research plan. Arch Gen Psychiatry 42:305–316.

Endicott J, Spitzer RL, Fleiss JL, Cohen J (1976): The Global Assessment Scale: a procedure for measuring overall severity of psychiatric disturbance. Arch Gen Psychiatry 33:766–771.

Evans MD, Hollon SD, DeRubeis RJ, Piasecki JM, Grove WM, Garvey MJ, Tuason VB (1992): Differential relapse following cognitive therapy and pharmacotherapy for depression. Arch Gen Psychiatry 49:802–808.

Fawcett J, Clark DC, Aagesen CA, Pisani VD, Tilkin JM, Sellers D, McGuire M, Gibbons RD (1987): A double-blind, placebo controlled trial of lithium carbonate therapy for alcoholism. Arch Gen Psychiatry 44:248–256.

Fieve RR, Kumbaraci T, Dunner DL (1976): Lithium prophylaxis of depression in bipolar I, bipolar II, and unipolar patients. Am J Psychiatry 133:925–929.

Frank E, Prien RF, Jarrett RB, Keller MB, Kupfer DJ, Lavori PW, Rush AJ, Weissman MM (1991): Conceptualization and rationale for consensus definitions of terms in major depressive disorder: remission, recovery, relapse, and recurrence. Arch Gen Psychiatry 48:851–855.

Frank E, Kupfer DJ, Perel JM, Cornes C, Jarrett, DB, Mallinger AG, Thase ME, McEachran AB, Grochocinski VJ (1990): Three-year outcomes for maintenance therapies in recurrent depression. Arch Gen Psychiatry 47:1093–1099.

Frank E, Kupfer DJ, Jacob M, Jarrett D (1987): Personality features and response to acute treatment in recurrent depression. J Pers Disord 1:14–26.

Friedman J, Meares R (1979): The effect of placebo and tricyclic antidepressants on cortical evoked potentials in depressed patients. Biol Psychology 8:291–302.

George LK, Blazer DG, Hughes DC, Fowler B (1989): Social support and the outcome of major depression. Br J Psychiatry 154:478–485.

Georgotas A, McCue RE, Cooper TB (1989): A placebo-controlled comparison of nortriptyline and phenelzine in maintenance therapy of elderly depressed patients. Arch Gen Psychiatry 46:783–786.

Giles DE, Roffwarg HP, Kupfer DJ, Rush AJ, Biggs MM, Etzel BA (1989): Secular trend in unipolar depression: a hypothesis. J Affect Disord 16:71–75.

Giller EG, Bialos D, Riddle MA, Walso MC (1988): MAOI treatment response: Multiaxial assessemnt. J Affect Disord 14:171–175.

Glick ID, Clarkin JF, Spencer JH, Haas G, Lewis AB, Peyser J, DeMane N, Good-Ellis M, Harris E, Lestelle V (1985): A controlled evaluation of inpatient family intervention. I: Preliminary results of the 6-month follow-up. Arch Gen Psychiatry 42:882–886.

Grigoroiu-Serbanescu M, Christodorescu D, Magureanu S, Jipescu I, Totoescu A, Marinescu E, Ardelean V, Popa S (1991): Adolescent offspring of endogenous unipolar depressive parents and or normal parents. J Affect Disord 21:185–198.

Hamilton MA (1960): A rating scale for depression. J Neurol Neurosurg Psychiatry 23:56–62.

Hammen C, Burge D, Burney E, Adrian C (1990): Longitudinal study of diagnoses in children of women with unipolar and bipolar affective disorder. Arch Gen Psychiatry 47:1112–1117.

Hathaway SR, McKinley JC (1951): "The Minnesota Multiphasic Personality Inventory Manual." New York: Psychological Corp.

Hollon SD, DeRubeis RJ, Evans MD, Wiemer MJ, Garvey MJ, Grove WM, Tuason VB (1992): Cognitive therapy and pharmacotherapy for depression: Singly and in combination. Arch Gen Psychiatry 49:774–781.

Johnson J, Weissman MM, Klerman GL (1992): Service utilization and social morbidity associated with depressive symptoms in the community. JAMA 267:1478–1483.

Katz M, Klerman GL (1979): Introduction: Overview of the clinical studies program. Am J Psychiatry 136:49–51.

Kavanagh DJ, Wilson PH (1989): Prediction of outcome with group cognitive therapy for depression. Behavior Res Therapy 27:333–343.

Kawakami N, Kashimura H, Koizumi A (1987): Time course and prognosis of industrial workers with major depression. Sangyo Igaku—Jpn J Ind Health 29:375–383.

Keller MB, Shapiro RW (1982): "Double depression": Superimposition of acute depressive episodes on chronic depressive disorders. Am J Psychiatry 139:438–442.

Keller MB, Shapiro RW (1981): Major depressive disorder: Initial results from a one-year prospective naturalistic follow-up study. J Nerv Ment Dis 169:761–768.

Keller MB, Harrison W, Fawcett JA, Gelenberg A, Hirschfeld RMA, Klein D, Kocsis J, McCullough JP, Rush AJ, Schatzberg A, Thase M (1995a): Treatment of chronic depression with sertraline or imipramine: Preliminary blinded response rates and high rates of undertreatment in the community. Psychopharmcol Bull 31:205–212.

Keller MB, Klein DN, Hirschfeld RMA, Kocsis JH, McCullough JP, Miller I, First MB, Hozler CP, Keitner GI, Marin DB, Shea T (1995b): Results of the DSM-IV Mood Disorder Field Trial. Am J Psychiatry 152:843–849.

Keller MB, Lavori PW, Mueller TI, Endicott J, Coryell W, Hirschfeld RM, Shea T (1992): Time to recovery, chronicity, and levels of psychopathology in major depression: a 5-year prospective follow-up of 431 subjects. Arch Gen Psychiatry 49:809–816.

Keller MB, Beardslee W, Lavori PW, Wunder J, Dorer J, Samuelson H (1988): Course of major depression in nonreferred adolescents: a retrospective study. J Affect Disord 15:235–243.

Keller MB, Lavori PW, Friedman BL, Nielsen E, McDonald-Scott P, Andreasen NC, Endicott J (1987): The Longitudinal Interval Follow-Up Evaluation: A comprehensive method for assessing outcome in prospective longitudinal studies. Arch Gen Psychiatry 44:540–548.

Keller MB, Lavori PW, Klerman GL, Andreasen NC, Endicott NC, Endicott J, Coryell W, Fawcett J, Hirschfeld RMA (1986a): Low levels and lack of predictors of somatotherapy and psychotherapy received by depressed patients. Arch Gen Psychiatry 43:458–466.

Keller MB, Lavori PW, Rice J, Coryell W, Hirschfeld RMA (1986b): The persistent risk of chronicity in recurrent episodes of non-bipolar major depressive disorder: A prospective follow-up. Am J Psychiatry 143:24–28.

Keller MB, Klerman GL, Lavori PW, Coryell W, Endicott J, Taylor J (1984): Long-term outcome of episodes of major depression: clincial and public health significance. JAMA 252:788–792.

Keller MB, Lavori PW, Endicott J, Coryell W, Klerman GL (1983a): "Double depression": two-year follow-up. Am J Psychiatry 140:689–694.

Keller MB, Lavori PW, Lewis CE, Klerman GL (1983b): Predictors of relapse in major depressive disorder. JAMA 250:3299–3304.

Keller MB, Shapiro RW, Lavori PW, Wolfe N (1982a): Recovery in major depressive disorder: Analysis with the life table. Arch Gen Psychiatry 39:905–910.

Keller MB, Shapiro RW, Lavori PW, Wolfe N (1982b): Relapse in major depressive disorder: Analysis with the life table. Arch Gen Psychiatry 39:911–916.

Kerr TA, Roth M, Schapira K, Gurney C (1972): The assessment and prediction of outcome in affective disorders. Br J Psychiatry 121:167–174.

Kessler RC, McGonagle KA, Zhao S, Nelson CB, Hughes M, Eshleman S, Wittchen H-U, Kendler KS (1994): Lifetime and 12-month prevalence of DSM-III-R psychiatric disorders in the United States. Arch Gen Psychiatry 51:8–19.

Kirkegaard C, Faber J (1981): Altered serum levels of thyroxine, triiodothyronines and diiodothyronines in endogenous depression. Acta Endocrinolog 96:199–207.

Kirkegaard C, Smith E (1978): Continuation therapy in endogenous depression controlled by changes in the TRH stimulation test. Psychol Med 8:501–503.

Klein DN, Taylor EB, Harding K, Dickstein S (1988): Double depression and episodic major depression: Demographic, clinical, familial, personality, and socio-environmental characteristics and short-term outcome. Am J Psychiatry 145:1226–1231.

Kovacs M, Rush AJ, Beck AT, Hollon SD (1981): Depressed outpatients treated with cognitive therapy or pharmacology: A 1-year follow-up. Arch Gen Psychiatry 38:33–39.

Kragh-Sorensen, Hansen CE, Baastrup PC, Hvidberg EF (1976): Therapeutic control of plasma concentrations and long-term effect of nortriptyline in recurrent affective disorders. Pharmakopsychiatr Neuro-Psychopharmakol 9:178–182.

Krog-Meyer I, Kirkegaard C, Kijne B, Lumholtz B, Smith E, Lykke-Olesen L, Bjorum N (1984): Prediction of relapse with the TRH test and prophylactic amitriptyline in 39 patients with endogenous depression. Am J Psychiatry 141:945–948.

Kupfer DJ, Frank E, Perel JM, Cornes C, Mallinger AG, Thase ME, McEachran AB, Grochocinski VJ (1992): Five-year outcome for maintenance therapies in recurrent depression. Arch Gen Psychiatry 49:769–773.

Kupfer DJ, Frank E, Carpenter LL, Neiswanger K (1989a): Family history in recurrent depression. J Affect Disord 17:113–119.

Kupfer DJ, Frank E, Perel JM (1989b): The advantage of early treatment intervention in recurrent depression. Arch Gen Psychiatry 46:771–775.

Levitt AJ, Joffe RT, McDonald C (1991): Life course of depressive illness and characteristics of current episode in patients with double depression. J Nerv Ment Dis 179:678–682.

Lisansky J, Fava GA, Buckman MT, Kellner R, Fava M, Zielezny M, Peake GT (1984): Prolactin, amitriptyline, and recovery from depression. Psychopharmacology 84(3):331–335.

Loosen PT, Prange AJ, Jr, Wilson IC (1979): TRH (protirelin) in depressed alcoholic men. Behavioral changes and endocrine responses. Arch Gen Psychiatry 36:540–547.

Mintz J, Mintz LI, Arruda MJ, Hwang SS (1992): Treatments of depression and the functional capacity to work. Arch Gen Psychiatry 49:761–768.

Montgomery SA, Dunbar G (1993): Paroxetine is better than placebo in relapse prevention and the prophylaxis of recurrent depression. Int Clin Psychopharmacol 8:189–195.

Montgomery SA, Dufour H, Brion S, Gailledreau J, Laqueille X, Ferrey G, Moron P, Parant-Lucena N, Singer L, Danion JM, Beuzen JN, Pierredon MA (1988): The prophylactic efficacy of fluoxetine in unipolar depression. Br J Psychiatry (Suppl) 3:69–76.

Moos RH (1990): Depressed outpatients' life contexts, amount of treatment, and treatment outcome. J Nerv Ment Dis 178:105–112.

Mueller TI, Lavori PW, Keller MB, Swartz A, Warshaw M, Hasin D, Coryell W, Endicott J, Rice J, Akiskal H (1994): Prognostic effect of the variable course of alcoholism on the 10-year course of depression. Am J Psychiatry 151:701–706.

Mueller TI, Brown RA, Recupero PR (1993): Depression and substance abuse. RI Medicine 76:409–413.

Murphy, JM (1990): Depression in the community: Findings from the Stirling County Study. Can J Psychiatry 35:390–396.

Nuller JL, Ostroumova MN (1980): Resistance to inhibiting effect of dexamethasone in patients with endogenous depression. Acta Psych Scand 61:169–177.

Ormel J, Koeter MWJ, van den Brink W, van de Willige, G (1991): Recognition, management, and course of anxiety and depression in general practice. Arch Gen Psychiatry 48:700–706.

Ormel J, Koeter MWJ, van den Brink W, Giel R (1989): Concurrent validity of GHQ and PSE as measures of change. Psychol Med 19:1007–1013.

Orvaschel H (1990): Early onset psychiatric disorder in high risk children and increased familial morbidity. J Am Acad Child Adolesc Psychiatry 29:184–188.

Paykel ES, Prusoff BA, Tanner J (1976): Temporal stability of symptom patterns in depression. Br J Psychiatry 128:369–374.

Peselow ED, Dunner DL, Fieve RR, DiFiglia C (1991): The prophylactic efficacy of tricyclic antidepressants—a five year followup. Progress Neuro-Psychopharmacol Biolog Psychiatry 15:71–82.

Pfohl B, Coryell W, Zimmerman M, Stangl D (1987): Prognostic validity of self-report and interview measures of personality disorder in depressed patients. J Clin Psychiatry 48:468–472.

Pfohl B, Stangl D, Zimmerman M (1984): The implications of DSM-III personality disorders for patients with major depression. J Affect Disord 7:309–318.

Pickar D, Sweeney DR, Maas JW, Heninger GR (1978): Primary affective disorder, clinical state change, and MHPG excretion: a longitudinal study. Arch Gen Psychiatry 35:1378–1383.

Pilkonas PA, Frank EL (1988): Personality pathology in recurrent depression: Nature, prevalence and relationship to treatment response. Am J Psychiatry 145:435–441.

Post R (1959): Imipramine in depression. BMJ 2:1252.

Prien RF, Kupfer DJ (1986): Continuation drug therapy for major depressive episodes: How long should it be maintained? Am J Psychiatry 143:18–23.

Prien RF, Carpenter LL, Kupfer DJ (1991): The definition and operational criteria for treatment outcome of major depressive disorder: a review of the current research literature. Arch Gen Psychiatry 48:796–800.

Prien RF, Kupfer DJ, Mansky PA, Small JG, Tuason VB, Voss CB, Johnson WE (1984): Drug therapy in the prevention of recurrences in unipolar and bipolar affective disorders. Arch Gen Psychiatry 41:1096–1104.

Prusoff BA, Weissman MM (1981): Pharmacologic treatment of anxiety in depressed outpatients. In Klein DF, Rabkin J (eds): "Anxiety: New Research and Changing Concepts." New York: Raven Press, pp 341–353.

Quitkin FM, McGrath PJ, Stewart JW, Harrison W, Wager S, Nunes E, Rabkin J, Tricamo E, Klein DF (1989): Phenelzine and imipramine in mood reactive depressives: Further delineation of the syndrome of atypical depression. Arch Gen Psychiatry 46:787–793.

Quitkin F, Rifkin A, Kane J, Ramos-Lorenzi JR, Klein DF (1978): Prophylactic effect of lithium and imipramine in unipolar and bipolar II patients: A preliminary report. Am J Psychiatry 135:570–572.

Rao AV, Nammalvar N (1977): The course and outcome in depressive illness: A follow-up study of 122 cases in Madurai, India. Br J Psychiatry 130:392–396.

Raskin A, Schulterbrandt JG, Reating N, McKeon JJ (1970): Differential response to chlorpromazine, imipramine, and placebo. Arch Gen Psychiatry 23:164–173.

Rehm LP, Kaslow NJ, Rabin AS (1987): Cognitive and behavioral targets in a self-control therapy program for depression. J Consult Clin Psychol 55:60–67.

Reich JH (1990): The effect of DSM-III personality disorders on outcome of tricyclic antidepressant treated nonpsychotic outpatients with major depressive disorder. Psychiatry Res 32:175–181.

Reich JH, Green AI (1991): Effect of personality disorders on outcome of treatment. J Nerv Ment Dis 179:74–82.

Reveley AM, Reveley MA (1981): The distinction of primary and secondary affective disorders: Clinical implications. J Affect Disord 3(3):273–279.

Reynolds CF (1992): Treatment of depression in special populations. J Clin Psychiatry 53 (9, Suppl):45–53.

Ribeiro SCM, Tandon R, Grunhaus L, Greden JF (1993): The DST as predictor of outcome in depression: A meta-analysis. Am J Psychiatry 150:11.

Rieman D, Berger M (1989): EEG sleep in depression and in remission and the REM sleep response to the cholinergic agonist RS 86. Neuropsychopharmacology 2:145–152.

Robins LN, Helzer JE, Croughan J, Ratcliff KS (1981): National Institue of Mental Health Diagnostic Interview Schedule: Its history, characteristics, and validity. Arch Gen Psychiatry 38:381–389.

Rounsaville BJ, Prusoff BA, Padian N (1980a): The course of nonbipolar, primary major depression: A prospective 16-month study of ambulatory patients. J Nerv Ment Dis 168:406–411.

Rounsaville BJ, Shokomskas D, Prusoff BA (1980b): Chronic mood disorders in depressed outpatients: diagnosis and response to pharmacotherapy. J Affect Disord 2:73–88.

Rush AJ, Beck AT, Kovacs M, Hollon AD (1977): Comparative efficacy of cognitive therapy and pharmacotherapy in the treatment of depressed outpatients. Cog Ther Res 1:17–37.

Rybakowski J, Potok E, Strzyzewski W (1981): Erythrocyte membrane adenosine triphosphatase activities in patients with endogenous depression and healthy subjects. Eur J Clin Investig 11:61–64.

Sargeant JK, Bruse ML, Florio LP, Weissman MM (1990): Factors associated with 1-year outcome of major depression in the community. Arch Gen Psychiatry 47:519–526.

Shea MT, Elkin I, Imber SD, Stotsky SM, Watkins JT, Collins JF, Pilkonis PA, Beckham E, Glass DR, Dolan RT, Parloff MB (1992): Course of depressive symptoms over follow-up: Findings from the National Institute of Mental Health Treatment of Depression Collaborative Research Program. Arch Gen Psychiatry 49:782–787.

Shea MT, Pilkonis PA, Beckham E, Collins FJ, Eldin I, Stotsky S, Docherty JF (1990): Personality disorders and treatment outcome in the NIMH Treatment of Depression Collaborative Research Program. Am J Psychiatry 147:711–718.

Siever LJ, Coccaro EF, Benjamin E, Rubinstein K, Davis KL (1986): Adrenergic and serotonergic receptor responsiveness in depression. Ciba Foundation Symposium 123:148–163.

Simons AD, Murphy GE, Levine JL, Wetzel RD (1986): Cognitive therapy and pharmacotherapy for depression: Sustained improvement over 1 year. Arch Gen Psychiatry 43:43–48.

Solomon JG (1978): ECT in the treatment of recurrent psychotic depression. Southern Med J 71:1516–1518.

Souetre E, Salvati E, Pringuey D, Krebs B, Plasse Y, Darcourt G (1986a): The circadian rhythm of plasma thyrotropin in depression and recovery. Chronobiol Internat 3:197–205.

Souetre E, Candito M, Salvati E, Pringuey D, Chambon P, Darcourt G (1986b): 24-hour profile of plasma norepinephrine in affective disorders. Neuropsychobiology 16:1–8.

Stein MB, Tancer ME, Uhde TW (1990): Major depression in patients with panic disorder: Factors associated with course and recurrence. J Affect Disord 19:287–296.

Spitzer RL, Endicott J (1979): "Schedule for Affective Disorders and Schizophrenia" (3rd ed). New York: Biometrics Research Division, New York State Psychiatric Institute.

Spitzer RL, Endicott J, Robins E (1985): "Research Diagnostic Criteria for a Selected Group of Functional Disorders" (2nd ed). New York: Biometrics Research Division, New York State Psychiatric Institute.

Stewart AL, Hays RD, Ware JE, Jr (1988a): The MOS Short-Form General Health Survey: Reliability and validity in a patient population. Med Care 26:724–735.

Stewart JW, Quitkin FM, McGrath PJ, Rabkin JG, Markowitz JS, Tricamo E, Klein DF (1988b): Social functioning in chronic depression: Effect of 6 weeks of antidepressant treatment. Psychiatry Res 25:213–222.

Swindle RW, Cronkite RC, Moos RH (1989): Life stressors, social resources, coping and the 4-year course of unipolar depression. J Abnorm Psychol 98:468–477.

Thase ME (1990): Relapse and recurrence in unipolar major depression: Short-term and long-term approaches. J Clin Psychiatry 51:51–57.

Thompson AH, Bland RC, Helene TO (1989): Relationship and chronology of depression, agoraphobia, and panic disorder in the general population. J Nerve Ment Dis 177:456–463.

Uytdenhoef P, Charles G, Portelange P, Wilmotte J, Mendlewicz J, Jacquy J (1984): Cerebral blood flow and depression. Acta Psychiatrica Belgica 84:93–99.

Uytdenhoef P, Portelange P, Jacquy J, Charles G, Linkowski P, Mendlewicz J (1983): Regional cerebral blood flow and lateralized hemispheric dysfunction in depression. Br J Psychiatry 143:128–132.

van Praag HM. (1977): The Harold E. Himwich Memorial Lecture: Significance of biochemical parameters in the diagnosis, treatment, and prevention of depressive disorders. Biol Psychiatry 12:101–131.

van Praag H, de Hann S (1980): Depression vulnerability and 5-hydroxytryptophan prophylaxis. Psychiatry Res 3:75–83.

VanValkenburg C, Lowry M, Winokur G, Cadoret R (1977): Depression spectrum disease versus pure depressive disease: Clinical, personality, and course differences. J Nerv Ment Disease 165:341–347.

Von Korff M, Ormel J, Katon W, Lin EHB (1992): Disability and depression among high utilizers of health care: A longitudinal analysis. Arch Gen Psychiatry 49:91–100.

Warner V, Weissman MM, Fendrich M, Wickramaratne P, Moreau D (1992): The course of major depression in the offspring of depressed parents: Incidence, recurrence, and recovery. Arch Gen Psychiatry 49:795–801.

Weissman MM, Bothwell S (1976): Assessment of social adjustment by patient self-report. Arch Gen Psychiatry 33:1111–1115.

Weissman MM, Kasl SV (1976): Help-seeking in depressed out-patients following maintenance therapy. Br J Psychiatry 129:252–260.

Weissman M, Klerman G (1977): The chronic depressive in the community: Unrecognized and poorly treated. Copr Psychiatry 18:523–532.

Weissman MM, Gammon GD, John K, Merinkangas KR, Warner V, Prosoff BA, Sholomskas D (1987): Children of depressed parents increased psychopathology and early onset of major depression. Arch Gen Psychiatry 44:847–853.

Weissman MM, Kasl SV, Klerman GL (1976): Follow-up of depressed women after maintenance treatment. Am J Psychiatry 133:757–760.

Wells KB, Katon W, Rogers B, Camp MS (1994): Use of minor tranquilizers and antidepressant medications by depressed outpatients: Results from the Medical Outcomes Study. Am J Psychiatry 151:694–700.

Wells KB, Burnam A, Rogers W, Hays R, Camp P (1992): The course of depression in adult outpatients: Results from the medical outcomes study. Arch Gen Psychiatry 49:788–794.

Wells KB, Stewart A, Hays RD, Burnam A, Rogers W, Daniel M, Berry S, Greenfield S, Ware J (1989): The functioning and well-being of depressed patients—results of the Medical Outcomes Study. JAMA 262:914–919.

Winokur G, Coryell W (1991): Familial alcoholism in primary unipolar major depressive disorder. Am J Psychiatry 148(2):184–188.

Zimmerman M, Coryell W, Pfohl B (1986): ECT response in depressed patients with and without a DSM-III personality disorder. Am J Psychiatry 143:1030–1032.

CHAPTER 12

Treatment of Depression in Adulthood

CAROL R. ESSOM and CHARLES B. NEMEROFF

Department of Psychiatry and Behavioral Sciences, Emory University School of Medicine, Atlanta, GA 30322-4990

INTRODUCTION

The treatment of depression in adults can be challenging as well as highly rewarding. It is challenging because the diagnosis is sometimes unclear and comorbid psychiatric morbidity is common; it is rewarding because most patients respond quite well to therapeutic intervention. A detailed psychiatric history, medical history, and knowledge of current social and work demands is essential both in accurate diagnosis and development of a comprehensive treatment plan. Educating the patient about his or her mood disorder and the treatment options available is also of paramount importance in planning treatment and in ensuring compliance. The patient who is comfortable with the rationale behind the treatment approach chosen is a partner in the choice of treatment and aware of the potentially annoying and often temporary nature of medication side effects and has a better chance of cooperating fully with the clinician during the oftentimes difficult early days of treatment. The options for treatment of major depression include somatic therapy, that is, pharmacologic interventions or electroconvulsive therapy, as well as psychotherapeutic approaches, particularly cognitive and/or behavioral. Nonpharmacological interventions may include sleep deprivation, which has been shown to produce short-term remissions in depression, or phototherapy, which has produced benefits in 5–7 days. This chapter will review the psychopharmacology of depression, as well as to briefly review options to consider in treatment-resistant patients. Depression associated with bipolar disorder and those with psychotic features will not be addressed here.

Given the wide variety of antidepressant agents available today, the clinician should choose one or another medication based on its side effect profile, therapeutic index, the presence of comorbid medical and psychiatric disorders, possible drug–drug interactions, and cost (Table 1). The efficacy of the antidepressants of each of the different classes are comparable, which renders decisions about which particular medication to prescribe most dependent on the other factors listed above.

Mood Disorders Across the Life Span, Edited by Shulman, Tohen, and Kutcher
ISBN 0-471-10477-9   © 1996 Wiley-Liss, Inc.

TABLE 1 Antidepressant Medications

Heterocyclic	Usual Daily Dose (mg/day)	Therapeutic Plasma Level (ng/mL)
Imipramine (IMI)	150–300	>225[a]
Desipramine (DESIP)	50–300	>125
Amitriptyline (AMI)	50–300	>120[a]
Nortriptyline (NOR)	75–150	50–150
Doxepin	100–300	100–250
Trimipramine	100–300	
Protriptyline	15–60	100–200
Maprotiline	100–300	200–400[a]
Amoxapine	200–300	
Clomipramine	150–300	
Selective serotonin reuptake inhibitors		
Fluoxetine	20–80	
Paroxetine	20–50	
Sertraline	50–200	
Fluvoxamine	100–300	
Others		
Bupropion	225–450	
Venlafaxine	75–375	
Trazadone	200–600	
Nefazadone	100–600	

[a] Parent compound and metabolite.

The Agency for Health Care Policy and Research (AHCPR) has issued clinical practice guidelines with the provision that the recommendations made in the guidelines may not be appropriate for use in all circumstances (Depression Guideline Panel, 1993). Another straightforward approach has been proposed for treating major depression and its various subtypes in the form of a treatment algorithm (DeBattista and Schatzberg, 1994).

SELECTIVE SEROTONIN REUPTAKE INHIBITORS

The class of antidepressant medications that is most rapidly growing in terms of number of prescriptions in the United States is the selective serotonin reuptake inhibitors (SSRIs). As their name implies, these drugs inhibit the reuptake of serotonin (5-HT) into the presynaptic nerve terminal in a relatively selective manner. Their selectivity is such that, at the recommended doses, the drugs have minimal effects on the reuptake of norepinephrine (NE) and dopamine (DA). This selectivity, taken together with their very low affinity for the histaminic, α-adrenergic, and muscarinic cholinergic receptors, results in a very favorable side effect profile; it is of particular interest that SSRIs are not associated with significant cardiovascular side effects or electrocardiogram (ECG) changes.

The efficacy, safety profile, and side effect profiles of the four SSRIs currently available in the United States—fluoxetine, sertraline, fluvoxamine, and paroxetine—are all quite similar. Their most common side effects are headache, nausea, nervousness or

TABLE 2   Reported Adverse Effects of SSRIs

Adverse Effect Reported	Fluoxetine (%)	Sertraline (%)	Paroxetine (%)
Nausea	21	26	26
Diarrhea	12	18	12
Sedation or somnolence	2	13	23
Fatigue	4	11	15
Insomnia	14	16	13
Dizziness	6	11	13
Excessive sweating	8	8	11
Anxiety or nervousness	24	6	10
Sexual dysfunction, female	2–3	2	2
Sexual dysfunction, male	2–4	16	10–13

agitation, insomnia, sweating, dizziness, tremor, and dry mouth (Table 2). Fluoxetine use is associated with higher rates of nervousness or agitation, paroxetine with dry mouth and sedation, and sertraline with diarrhea or loose stools. One side effect that is oftentimes troublesome for many patients is sexual dysfunction. Women frequently experience anorgasmia, and men experience delayed ejaculation or frank impotence at higher doses during SSRI treatment. Although no controlled data is available, treatments suggested anecdotally for SSRI-induced sexual dysfunction include: (1) decreasing the SSRI dose or alternatively skipping a single a.m. daily dose; (2) yohimbine, doses needed may range from 2.7 mg prn to 5.4 mg TID; (3) buspirone, 10–20 mg TID; (4) amantadine, 100–200 mg/day (5) cyproheptadine, 4–8 mg/day; and (6) bupropion at low doses, 75–150 mg/day.

As with the antidepressant drugs, there is often a 3- to 5-week delay after initiation of the medication before substantial clinical improvement is noted. The usual dosing schedule is once daily in the morning because of possible activation and accompanied insomnia that may be experienced by the patient. In a small percentage of patients, sedation occurs and the SSRI can then be administered at bedtime. The usual dose of fluoxetine is 20 mg/day. Lower doses (5–10 mg) should be initiated in the elderly, but as much as 80–100 mg/day may be required, albeit infrequently, in some adults. Sertraline is usually initiated at a dose of 50 mg/day, but in our experience patients generally require 100–200 mg/day for optimal response. Paroxetine is usually prescribed initially at 20 mg per day, though some patients may require as much as 50 mg/day (Nemeroff, 1993). Fluvoxamine is approved in the United States only for the treatment of obsessive–compulsive disorder, and therefore will not be discussed in this chapter. However, it is approved for the treatment of depression in several European countries at dosages of 150–250 mg/day. The once-a-day dosing for the SSRIs is optimal for maximizing patient compliance, and their favorable therapeutic index renders these drugs relatively safe after overdose.

In vitro, all of the SSRIs inhibit the activity of various isoenzymes of the hepatic cytochrome P450 system, most notably 2D6, 1A2, and 3A4. Cytochrome P450 2D6 metabolize certain drugs such as secondary amine tricyclic antidepressants (TCAs), warfarin, type 1C antiarrhythmics, certain antipsychotics, and others. This enzyme exhibits genetic polymorphism so that the activity can vary from patient to patient by as much as 10-fold. Therefore, some patients treated with drugs that are substrates for 2D6 and an SSRI will consequently exhibit higher than expected plasma concentrations of the drug metabolized by this isoenzyme. Physicians need to be alert to this possibility when prescribing an SSRI and, for example, desipramine, and to monitor plasma TCA concentrations. In spite of differences in *in vitro* potency between the SSRIs in inhibiting this enzyme, all of these drugs can increase plasma desipramine concentrations *in vivo* (DeVane, 1995).

Inhibition of cytochrome P450 3A4 by sertraline and fluvoxamine can increase plasma alprazolam and triazolam concentrations, as well as concentrations of two common antihistamines, terfenadine and astemizole. Cytochrome P450 1A2 is inhibited by fluoxetine and fluvoxamine, which can elevate plasma theophylline concentrations. We wish to emphasize that physicians have traditionally been aware of drug–drug interactions. When using a polypharmacological approach including SSRIs, psychiatrists need to be aware of these interactions and adjust their dosing accordingly.

The serotonin syndrome—characterized by hypertension, hyperpyrexia, and seizures—occurs when SSRIs and monoamine oxidase inhibitors (MAOIs) are prescribed concomitantly. A washout period of 14 or more days is therefore recommended after the SSRI is discontinued before starting an MAOI. If fluoxetine is the SSRI, 21 days may be a safer interval, given that the half life of fluoxetine is 2–3 days and its active metabolite, norfluoxetine, has a half life of 7–9 days. Although tryptophan is no longer available in the United States, there were reports of the serotonin syndrome after treatment with tryptophan and fluoxetine.

The combination of documented efficacy, safety, and once-daily dosing taken together with a favorable side effect profile has resulted in the view now espoused by many clinicians that SSRIs are the first choice of drugs for patients with major depression.

TRICYCLIC ANTIDEPRESSANTS

The heterocyclic (tricyclic and tetracyclic) antidepressants have been available for more than 30 years and remain in widespread usage despite the availability of newer, more selective drugs with more favorable side effect profiles. As a class, TCAs are thought to act by inhibition of the reuptake of NE and/or 5-HT into presynaptic nerve terminals within the central nervous system (CNS). The differences between the individual heterocyclics are largely their relative potency in inhibiting uptake of 5-HT or NE, as well as differences in their affinity for other receptors that, as it turns out, are responsible for their side effect profile. There is also evidence that other neurotransmitter systems, for example corticotropin-releasing factor (CRF) and signal transduction systems, may be modulated by TCAs and contribute to their clinical efficacy.

Clinicians primarily choose one or another TCA based on their side effect profiles. Amitriptyline and imipramine are the parent compounds of nortriptyline and desipramine, respectively, and the former have a more problematic side effect profile than their metabolites. Patients often complain of the effects produced by the anticholinergic properties of TCAs, including dry mouth, constipation, blurry vision, and urinary retention, and these are frequently the cause of medication discontinuation. Other serious adverse effects of this class of drugs include sedation, orthostatic hypotension, and cardiac conduction delays. Sedation is believed to be largely secondary to the antihistaminic effects of TCAs. Their α_1-adrenergic receptor antagonist properties are responsible for their propensity to cause orthostatic hypotension. The older adult is at higher risk for falls and subsequent hip fracture. Therefore, caution must be exercised when prescribing TCAs in this population. Certain TCAs such as desipramine have also been associated with sudden cardiac death in adolescents; thus, TCAs should be closely monitored in this age group as well. Many clinicians recommend a baseline ECG before initiating a TCA, and repeat ECG monitoring as the TCA dose is increased and certainly if cardiac symptoms occur.

Another side effect of the TCA class of antidepressant medications that is often very disturbing to patients is weight gain. Seizures are rarely encountered as a consequence of TCA use, although this has been a problem with maprotiline, especially when high doses are administered in a single daily dose. Some older adults are more susceptible to confusion or delirium (Livingstone et al., 1983).

Of grave concern is the very low therapeutic index associated with TCA use; in view of the high rate of suicide in depressed patients, TCA use as a first choice is difficult to justify in the fate of the availability of antidepressants that are just as efficacious as TCAs and not lethal in overdose. Indeed TCAs are a major cause of overdose death in the United States.

Tricyclic antidepressant therapy should be initially prescribed in a low dose administered at bedtime. The dose should then be increased every 3–4 days as tolerated. In spite of the common practice of dividing TCA doses into twice or thrice daily doses, this practice makes no sense in terms of the pharmacokinetics of these agents and enhances noncompliance. Therapeutic drug monitoring is available for these medications and is useful for both monitoring compliance and achieving therapeutic plasma levels. Because of the genetic polymorphism of the cytochrome P450 isoenzymes, individuals have varying capacities for metabolizing TCAs; monitoring plasma levels can therefore help optimize dosing for each patient.

TRAZADONE

Trazadone was one of the first antidepressants available that is not lethal when taken in overdose. It is frequently used in conjunction with SSRIs when insomnia remains a significant clinical problem. As an antidepressant, its mechanism of action is probably related to inhibition of serotonin reuptake, as well as 5-HT2 receptor antagonism. It does not have significant anticholinergic properties and does not alter cardiac conduction. It exhibits few drug–drug interactions, the exception being the development of the serotonin syndrome after the combination of trazadone and an MAOI.

Its major side effects are sedation, dizziness, orthostatic hypotension (due to potent α_1-adrenergic receptor antagonism), headache and nausea, and these can best be managed by daily dosing of the drug at bedtime. The usual starting dose is 50–100 mg with increases every 3–4 days as tolerated up to 200–600 mg/day. In men, priapism has occurred in association with the use of trazadone, and some cases have even required surgical intervention.

NEFAZADONE

This recently released antidepressant is a phenylpiperazine compound structurally related to trazadone. It is a weak inhibitor of 5-HT and NE reuptake and it thought to largely act by virtue of its effect as a potent $5\text{-}HT_2$ receptor antagonist.

The side effect profile of nefazadone is rather benign, with no anticholinergic and antihistaminic properties. Adverse effects include headache, nausea, and dizziness (D'Amico et al., 1990). Nefazadone clearly has a better side effect profile when compared to imipramine. Of particular interest are two properties of nefazadone—its reported lack of effect on sexual function and its salutary effects on sleep architecture. Unfortunately, nefazadone must be administered in a twice daily dosing schedule; the therapeutic dose range is 300–600 mg/day (Fontain et al., 1994; D'Amico et al., 1990). There is also evidence that nefazadone is particularly effective in treating the anxiety component of major depression.

BUPROPION

Bupropion is unique in that it is a monocyclic antidepressant. When initially introduced in the United States, it quickly gained a reputation as causing seizures in patients with no previous history of epilepsy. Its subsequent reentry in the field of antidepressants has found it to be as effective as the SSRIs or TCAs and safe when administered in divided doses, with doses not exceeding 450 mg/day. The documented seizure rate in patients with no prior history of seizures is 0.4–4%, depending on the dose (Davidson, 1989). Dosing schedules range from 200 to 300 mg/day in 2 or 3 divided doses. As much as 450 mg/day may be used with caution. A sustained release form of the drug is currently under investigation, which would presumably be associated with a more favorable side effect profile, single-day dosing, and enhanced compliance.

The mechanism of action of bupropion remains obscure, with weak effects on NE, DA, and 5-HT reuptake systems (Wright et al., 1985). Its dopaminergic effects may underlie the unusual side effects of perceptual abnormalities or rare reports of frank psychosis. However, bupropion is clearly better tolerated by patients than TCAs in that it causes less weight gain, is nonsedating, and does not alter the ECG or cause hypotension (Janicak et al., 1993). Bupropion is particularly well tolerated by the older adult due to its lack of anticholinergic side effects and low cardiotoxicity, as well as having no untoward effects on cognitive functioning. Bupropion is not associated with sexual dysfunction in men or women. Adverse effects may include overstimulation or tremor, headache, dry mouth, or nausea as well as the aforementioned propensity for seizures.

Drug–drug interactions are uncommon with bupropion. A standard 2-week washout period after discontinuation of an MAOI is recommended, although few reports exist documenting adverse reactions with this drug combination.

MONOAMINE OXIDASE INHIBITORS

Monoamine oxidase inhibitors were the earliest compounds identified as antidepressants when it was noted that tuberculosis patients in Swiss sanatoriums exhibited mood improvement after treatment with the antitubercular MAOI isoniazid (INH). Monoamine oxidases are enzymes located within the mitochondria that convert biogenic amines such as NE, 5-HT, and DA to their deaminated products. Considerable clinical experience has accrued with this class of antidepressants; new research is focusing on more selective oxidase inhibitors that selectively inhibit the A or B subtypes. MAO-A selectively deaminates NE and 5-HT whereas MAO-B acts selectively on the benzylamines and phenylethylamines. Some biogenic amines like DA, tyramine, and tryptamine are metabolized by MAO-A or B type enzymes. The currently available MAOIs in the United States, phenelzine, tranylcypromine, and isocarboxazide are irreversible enzyme inhibitors and strict dietary restrictions of foods high in tyramine, including aged cheeses, beef liver, chianti wines, and soy sauces are an essential component of the treatment protocol.

The mechanism of action of MAOIs is believed to be a consequence of an increase in intracellular levels of endogenous amines, for example, NE and 5-HT. As is observed with many antidepressants, after chronic treatment a decrease in the number of cerebrocortical β-adrenergic receptors occurs.

Although there are three currently available MAOIs in the United States, isocarboxizide (Marplan) is no longer being manufactured. The other two, phenelzine and tranylcypromine, are prescribed in divided daily doses, usually three times per day. Ideally, when prescribing an MAOI, baseline platelet MAO activity is measured, the patient is treated with a starting dose, and platelet MAO activity is monitored. Optimal treatment response occurs with >80% platelet MAO inhibition (Robinson et al., 1978).

As noted, patients may experience a hypertensive crisis if excess tyramine of sympathomimetic amines, for example, pseudoephedrine, is ingested causing a release of the endogenously stored NE without the enzymatic capability to deaminate and thereby deactivate it available. Cerebrovascular accidents resulting from MAOI hypertensive reactions are rare. More commonly, a rise in blood pressure of approximately 20–30 mmHg occurs, which generally results in a headache, flushing, or sweating. Moderate to severe hypertensive reactions usually require the ingestion of 10–25 mg or more of tyramine. Nevertheless caution should be exercised prior to prescribing MAOIs to suicidal patients or patients with comorbid eating disorders. Above all, patients must not be prescribed meperidine (Demerol) while being treated with an MAOI because that combination can lead to hypertension, hyperpyrexia, seizures, and death. Patients should be advised to notify all of their doctors and family members and perhaps wear a Medic-Alert identification warning of a meperidine (Demerol) allergy. Patients being treated with MAOIs should consult their physician before taking any new medications, even over-the-counter preparations.

MAOIs are particularly effective in so-called atypical depression, characterized by mood responsive to environmental events, overeating, hypersomnia, comorbid anxiety/panic, and reverse diurnal mood variation (i.e., moods are better in the mornings and worse in the evenings). Newer selective MAOIs such as moclobamide now available in Canada and in certain countries in Europe may offer the therapeutic advantages of the nonselective MAOIs, without their troubling side effects and dietary restraints.

VENLAFAXINE

This newly released antidepressant inhibits the reuptake of both 5-HT and NE into presynaptic terminals. It has no significant affinity for muscarinic cholinergic, histaminic, or α_1-adrenergic receptors. Thus it has the advantage of TCAs in inhibiting the reuptake of both NE and 5HT, but none of the disadvantages. Currently, it must be administered in a twice-a-day dose regimen, which is necessary because of its short half life. It is likely that a slow release form will almost certainly be developed. By initially prescribing small doses (25–37.5 mg/day), one can avoid its major side effect, nausea. At daily doses of 300 mg or more, some patients exhibit hypertension. Patients respond to doses as low as 75 mg or as high as 375 mg/day. This drug is of particular interest for several reasons. First, it appears to have little effect on cytochrome P450 2D6, in contrast to the SSRIs. Second, venlafaxine appears to be particularly effective in severe depression, for example, inpatient melancholia, and in treatment refractory depression. Indeed, we have treated patients who failed treatment with electroconvulsive therapy who went on and responded to venlafaxine. In addition, a few reports have suggested that venlafaxine may have an earlier onset of action than other antidepressants, perhaps because it reaches steady state more rapidly than other antidepressants with a longer half-life; further study in this area is urgently needed.

If venlafaxine is administered at an initially low dose and the dose gradually increased to minimize side effects, there is no reason for it not to be a first choice agent in the treatment of depression. Its major drawbacks are the requirement for multiple-day dosing and nausea in patients started on relatively high doses. Clearly it has emerged as the clear second choice over TCAs or MAOIs after SSRI treatment failure.

ELECTROCONVULSIVE THERAPY

Electroconvulsive therapy (ECT) is a highly effective treatment modality for patients suffering major depression. It is strongly indicated for patients with major depression and psychotic features, or who are an acute danger to themselves or others, that is, acutely suicidal or catatonic and unable to care for themselves. For patients who have responded favorably to ECT in the past, this treatment should be considered immediately in those who relapse during antidepressant drug treatment.

Many clinicians prefer to administer complete trials of two or more antidepressant medications before referring a patient for ECT. In severely ill patients or patients with a prior excellent response to ECT, this delay can further prolong patient suffering because the lag time before clinical improvement is often 3–5 weeks with antidepressant medications, but is usually only 2–4 ECT treatments. Preexisting medical conditions may also be a factor in the decision to delay referral for ECT as the fear remains in the lay population of memory loss, myocardial infarction, or stroke as outcomes of ECT. With appropriate medical consultation and judicious administration of medications immediately prior to the treatment, these presumed risks can be minimized.

ECT referrals should occur as early as possible if this treatment is being seriously considered by the clinician and patient. Some medications such as long-acting benzodiazepines or other sedative hypnotics can shorten the seizure duration and therefore adversely effect the efficacy of ECT; these should be discontinued or at least tapered to a minimal dose prior to the first treatment. Lithium can be a cause of dramatic post-ECT confusion and should be discontinued 3–4 days before the first treatment. Theophylline and the SSRIs have been noted to increase seizure duration and should be discontinued prior to ECT. MAOIs and anticonvulsants can shorten the seizure duration and should be discontinued unless the latter has been prescribed for a documented seizure disorder. Patients receiving anticonvulsants as mood stabilizers can have these drugs tapered and discontinued safely prior to the initiation of ECT.

The initial workup of a patient for ECT includes a complete history and physical examination, laboratory studies, an ECG, and an anesthesiology consultation. Many clinicians also prefer a structural brain imaging study [computed tomography (CT) or magnetic resonance imaging (MRI)] as well. This can be helpful in assessing the presence of white matter disease present and aids in the prediction of the likelihood of postictal confusion. There are no absolute contraindications to ECT, but laboratory studies and an ECG can help identify medical conditions that need to be addressed prior to the patient receiving general anesthesia and ECT such as infection, cardiovascular disease, electrolyte abnormalities, hypertension or diabetes.

ECT is administered 2 or 3 days per week for an average course of 6–12 treatments. The patient can then either be continued with ECT as an outpatient, so-called maintenance ECT, or be treated with an antidepressant.

Treatments can be administered unilaterally or bilaterally. the bilateral (bifronto-temporal) positioning of electrodes has been noted to cause more severe cognitive side effects, including disorientation or even a sustained confusional state. Right unilateral treatments produce fewer adverse side effects because the nondominant hemisphere receives the initial stimulus. It is estimated that 70% of left-handed persons have dominance for language functions as do right handers, in the right cerebral hemisphere; 15% of left handers have right-sided dominance and the remaining 15% of the left-handed population have bilateral control of language functions (APA Task Force on ECT, 1990). The level of stimulus intensity must also be modified for each patient, taking into account the patient's age, sex, baseline cognitive status, presence of psychosis, or other medications such as benzodiazepines or anticonvulsants.

COGNITIVE THERAPY

Cognitive therapy (CT) is the process whereby dysfunctional thought patterns, in this case major depression, are modified through verbal and action-oriented procedures. Physicians and patients may choose this therapy alone or in conjunction with pharmacotherapy. Traditionally, CT was believed to exert a greater effect on dysfunctional attitudes, automatic negative thoughts, and irrational beliefs whereas pharmacotherapy has a greater effect on neurovegetative signs or symptoms associated with major depression.

Beck, the founder of CT, believes that a patient can correct his or her emotional disturbance or depression by understanding the misunderstandings he or she has experienced repeatedly in the past (Beck et al., 1979). A patient, after identifying the errors made in the past, is believed capable of rethinking and reassessing surroundings and interpersonal relationships, thereby alleviating himself or herself of the depressive symptoms.

The CT approach utilizes a cooperative partnership between the therapist and patient. Common goals are clearly identified, and the rationale behind each attempted intervention is clearly and completely explained. If homework assignments are incorporated into the treatment plan, a thorough discussion of its requirements, as well as the responsibilities of the therapist and patient is recommended. The patient may have a better chance of working effectively with this program if the concept of self-help is fully understood by the patient to be a core issue in the treatment. A patient's resistance to this approach, after it is initially agreed upon, can be worked through as evidence of the patient's self-defeating tendencies, which may continue to fuel the depressed state. If the patient continues to refuse to complete assigned work, a renegotiation of the treatment goals and overall agenda is indicated.

When described by Beck, CT encompassed an active, directed, time-limited structured treatment course. Over time, CT has come to be a less well defined treatment modality incorporating many therapeutic strategies, interventions, and techniques. Beck maintains that a full knowledge of the theory involved is essential to the effective application of this mode of therapy; therefore, if this is considered to be a part of the treatment strategy, a specially trained clinician should be consulted. Many clinicians today utilize behavioral techniques along with the cognitive approaches espoused by Beck.

TREATMENT-RESISTANT DEPRESSION

Treatment-resistant depression is currently a large, almost catch-all phrase that can refer to a variety of patients from those who exhibit a total lack of response to treatment to those who have only a partial response; it can also include patients with chronic relapsing forms of depression (Hornig-Rohan and Amsterdam, 1994). None of the varied definitions for treatment-resistant depression have been systematically studied. Some of the suggested factors to be included in the definition include duration of illness and length and dose of antidepressant treatment (Fawcett and Kravitz, 1985). A three-level system that takes into account the number and types of treatments for specific subtypes of depressions has been recommended by Schatzberg et al. (1986). Roose et al. (1986) used nonresponse to a single TCA after 4 weeks at an adequate dose as a standard measure. Prien suggests a definition based on lack of response to an MAOI after 4 weeks of an adequate dose (Prien, 1988). Still others have proposed defining treatment-resistant depression as a case of depression that persists for 2 years despite trials of standard drug therapies (Feighner et al., 1985). Amsterdam has defined resistant cases as those failing to respond to five or more adequate treatment trials (Amsterdam and Berwich, 1987, 1989). Joyce and Paykel (1989) have used a <50% reduction in the Hamilton Depression Rating Scale as the definition of a treatment failure.

Implied in the notion of treatment-resistant is that there is a standard understanding of what an adequate treatment trial includes. Most physicians who prescribe antidepressants, and even some psychiatrists, do not routinely increase the dose of antidepressant medications to the generally agreed upon level of 300 mg of imipramine per day or 90 mg/day of phenelzine (Clarly et al., 1990).

Although 300 mg/day is the maximum dose recommended for most TCAs, some patients may require even higher doses. Therapeutic drug monitoring is available for most of the TCAs. The desired therapeutic level of imipramine and desipramine should be at least 150 ng/mL. There is no clearly established upper level of efficacy for imipramine and/or desipramine, but the risk of toxic effects or delirium is increased at levels of 300–400 ng/mL (Livingston et al., 1983; Meador-Woodruff et al., 1988; Preskorn and Simpson, 1982). Assays for detecting the plasma levels of amoxapine, bupropion, doxepin, fluoxetine, maprotiline, protriptyline, trazodone, and trimipramine are available, but no clear therapeutic levels have been determined for them. Knowledge of the patient's plasma level of the prescribed drug is useful in detecting patient noncompliance or poor compliance, a major cause of treatment nonresponse. Therapeutic drug monitoring is also wise in patients who have the potential for a drug–drug interaction, particularly in those patients who are treatment refractory. Patients using medications or drugs that can stimulate the hepatic microsomal enzyme system such as alcohol, anticonvulsants, barbiturates, nicotine, or oral contraceptives should be monitored closely as these drugs can lower plasma concentrations of many antidepressants. Conversely, in patients treated with drugs that have the propensity to inhibit cytochrome P450 2D6, such as SSRIs, together with drugs that are metabolized by the isoenzyme, such as TCAs, plasma levels of the latter are helpful to titrate the TCA dose. In general, we recommend that treatment failure with an agent of one class be followed by a trial with an agent from another class; as noted earlier venlafaxine is a good choice after SSRI treatment failure.

If monotherapy is ineffective, then augmentation with a second agent is recommended. Augmentation generally refers to the process of adding a second or third antidepressant drug to the patients regime but may also include adding a form of psychotherapy. Lithium and thyroid hormones are commonly used as augmenting agents, but TCA–SSRI and SSRI–bupropion combinations have been recommended. In addition, adjunctive administration of psychostimulants, anticonvulsants, and antipsychotics have also been beneficial for some cases of treatment-resistant depression.

The addition of lithium to a poorly or partially responsive antidepressant often occurs in 1–2 weeks and is reported to be as high as 60% (Katona, 1988). The patient needs to be informed of the potential benefits of lithium as well as of its possible side effects, including tremor, weight gain, nausea, diarrhea, and so forth. When lithium carbonate is initiated, the starting dosage is 300 mg twice a day for 2 days followed by an increase to 900 mg/day for 3–4 days, and finally 1,200 mg/day for a 2-week trial period (Schatzberg and Cole, 1991). Plasma lithium levels should be in the 0.8–1.2 mEq/L to optimize its effects.

Thyroid hormones have been used to augment the actions of antidepressants. T_3 has been studied more intensively than T_4 and appears to be more effective. It appears that T_3 is as effective as lithium as an augmenting strategy (Joffe et al., 1993). This approach can be used in patients with normal thyroid function studies and may be a particularly good choice for patients with low normal thyroid function (Nakamura et al., 1990). It is reportedly effective in almost 50% of depressed patients who had not responded to a TCA (Extein and Gold, 1988). Doses of T_3 used were 25–50 μg/day and responses were within 1 week. Clinical trials have also proven thyroid supplementation to be effective in combination with phenelzine or fluoxetine (Joffe, 1988; Crowe et al., 1990).

Multiple studies have evaluated the combinations of TCAs and SSRIs, including clomipramine and fluoxetine (Rosenzweig and Amsterdam, 1992), nortriptyline and fluoxetine, and nortriptyline and sertraline (Seth et al., 1992). They have been found to be useful, provided that TCA plasma levels are monitored.

Boyer and Feighner (1993) studied bupropion and fluoxetine combination therapy in treatment-refractory depression. The patients studied had achieved a partial initial response to either bupropion of fluoxetine alone. When the alternate medication was added, 35% had moderate to marked improvement, 26% had minimal improvement, and 39% could not tolerate the combination. Those who were unable to tolerate the fluoxetine and bupropion combination identified side effects commonly seen with either medication alone such as agitation, headache, anxiety, or insomnia. No seizures or other side effects were reported.

The psychostimulants d-amphetamine, methylphenidate, and pemoline have been used for the treatment of depression. These agents are usually safe in the medically ill, for example, a patient with cancer or poststroke. Of great usefulness is that the response to these agents is very rapid. Patients may improve within hours or days (Woods et al., 1986). The converse is also true, that is, if a patient has an adverse reaction or becomes dysphoric, the response clears rapidly after cessation of the medication. Most patients do not develop tolerance to the antidepressant effects of stimulants. There is no evidence that in the majority of patients, drug abuse of these agents is a significant problem. Magnesium pemoline is classified as a class III drug (the benzodiazepines), and may be an easier choice if prescribing class II drugs (amphetamine or methylphenidate) is restricted by local law. Unfortunately, controlled studies have not demonstrated efficacy of psychostimulant monotherapy in the treatment of depression (Fawcett, 1985). We have utilized psychostimulants as adjuncts to SSRI therapy in treatment-refractory depression with considerable success.

Certain anticonvulsant drugs have been demonstrated to be effective in the treatment of the manic phase of bipolar disorder. Carbamazepine, with its tricyclic structure, has also been found to be effective in bipolar depression in some studies (Cullen et al., 1991; Ballenger, 1988; Post et al., 1986). Placebo-controlled double-blind studies have convincingly demonstrated the efficacy of valproic acid in the treatment of acute mania (Bowden et al., 1994), and most clinicians find it particularly effective in rapid cycling or mixed bipolar states (Calabrese et al., 1992). It appears to lack any efficacy in unipolar depression (McElroy et al., 1988).

Depressed patients with delusions or other psychotic features can be treatment refractory; they should be treated with a combination of an antidepressant and an antipsychotic (Charney and Nelson, 1981; Spiker et al., 1985; Nelson and Bowers, 1978). There is considerable evidence that patients with psychotic depressions do not respond to antidepressant monotherapy. Electroconvulsive therapy is also quite effective in the treatment of psychotic depression. In treatment-refractory patients, a careful search for delusional features is warranted.

In summary, when evaluating a patient who appears to be refractory to antidepressant medications, a careful review of medication trials including type of drug and level of dosage is important. Also useful is a close reevaluation of the patient's medical condition. Is there drug or alcohol use/misuse occurring that needs to be addressed? If so, referral to an addiction specialist or other addictions program would be helpful. Are there other psychosocial factors that are inhibiting the patient's recovery? Individual, marital, or family psychotherapy may be an appropriate addition to the patient's treatment plan as well. Perhaps particular personality traits are interfering with the attainment of the treatment goals. These aspects can be addressed with individual psychotherapy or perhaps a rephrasing of the treatment goals and expectations.

In conclusion, major depression is a disorder that is as treatable as any disorder confronting physicians. With proper evaluation, treatment, and follow-up, restoration to euthymia is an attainable goal in most patients.

REFERENCES

Amsterdam JD, Berwich N (1989): High dose tranylcypromine treatment in refractory depression. Pharmacopsychiatry 22:21–25.

Amsterdam JD, Berwich N (1987): Treatment of refractory depression with combination reserpine and tricyclic antidepressant therapy. J Clin Psychopharmacol 7:238–242.

APA Task Force on Electroconvulsive Therapy (1990): The practice of electroconvulsive therapy: Recommendations for treatment, training and privileging. Washington, DC: American Psychiatric Association.

Ballenger JC (1988): The clinical use of carbamazepine in affective disorders. J Clin Psychiatry 49:13–19.

Beck AT, Rush JA, Shaw BF, Emery G (1979): Cognitive Therapy of Depression. New York: Guilford Press.

Bowden CL, Brugger AM, Swann AC, Calabrese JR, Janicak PG, Petty F, Dilsaver SC, Davis JM, Rush AJ, Small JG, Garza-Trevino ES, Risch SC, Goodnick PJ, Morris DD (1994): Efficacy of divalproex vs lithium and placebo in the treatment of mania. JAMA 271:918–924.

Boyer WF, Feighner JP (1993): The combined use of fluoxetine and bupropion. Abstract NR 746, pg 247. 146th Annual Meeting of the American Psychiatric Association. San Francisco: May 22–27.

Calabrese JR, Markovitz PJ, Kimmel SE, Wagner SC (1992): Spectrum of efficacy of valproate in 78 rapid-cycling bipolar patients. J Clin Psychpharmacol 12:53s–56s.

Charney DS, Nelson JC (1981): Delusional and nondelusional unipolar depression: Further evidence for distinct subtypes. Am J Psychiatry 38:328–333.

Clarly C, Mandos LA, Schweizer E (1990): Results of a brief survey on the prescribing practices for monoamine oxidase inhibitor antidepressants. J Clin Psychiatry 51:226–231.

Crowe D, Collins JP, Rosse RB (1990): Thyroid hormone supplementation of fluoxetine treatment. J Clin Psychopharmacol 10:150–151.

Cullen M, Mitchell P, Brodaty A, Boyce P, Parker G, Hickie I, Wilhelm K (1991): Carbamazepine for treatment-resistant melancholia. J Clin Psychiatry 52:472–476.

D'Amico MF, Roberts DL, Robinson DS, Schwiderski UT, Copp J (1990): Placebo-controlled dose-ranging trial designs in phase II development of nefazadone. Psychopharm Bull 26:147–150.

Davidson J (1989): Seizure and bupropion: A review. J Clin Psychiatry 50:256–261.

DeBattista C, Schatzberg AF (1994): An algorithm for the treatment of major depression and its subtypes. Psychiatric Ann 24:341–347.

Depression Guideline Panel (1993): "Depression in Primary Care: Volume 2 Treatment of Major Depression." Clinical Practice Guidelines, Number 5. Rockville: U.S. Department of Health and Human Services, Public Health Service, Agency for Health Care Policy and Research. AHCPR Publication No. 93-0551.

DeVane CL (1994): Pharmacogenetics and drug metabolism of newer antidepressant agents. J Clin Psychiatry 55:38–45.

Extein IL, Gold MS (1988): Thyroid hormone potentiation of tricyclics. Psychosomatics 29:166–174.

Fawcett N, Kravitz HM (1985): Treatment refractory depression. In Schatzberg AF (ed): "Common Treatment Problems in Depression." Washington, DC: American Psychiatric Press, pp 2–27.

Feighner JP, Herbstein J, Damlouju N (1985): Combined MAOI, TCA and direct stimulant therapy of treatment resistant depression. J Clin Psychiatry 46:206–209.

Fontain R, Ontiveros A, Elie R, Kensler TT, Roberts DL, Kaplita S, Echer JA, Faluda G (1994): A double blind comparison of nefazadone, imipramine, and placebo in major depression. J Clin Psychiatry 55:234–241.

Hornig-Rohan M, Amsterdam JD (1994): Clinical and biological correlates of treatment resistant depression: An overview. Psychiatric Ann 24(5):220–227.

Janicak PG, Davis JM, Preskorn SH, Ayd Jr FJ (1993): Treatment with antidepressants. In "Principles and Practice of Psychopharmacotherapy." Baltimore: Williams & Wilkins. pp 209–288.

Joffe RT (1988): Triiodothyronine potentiation of the antidepressant effects of phenelzine. J Clin Psychiatry 49:409–410.

Joffe RT, Singer W, Levitt AJ, MacDonald C (1993): A placebo-controlled comparison of lithium and triiodothyronine augmentation of tricyclic antidepressants in unipolar refractory depression. Arch Gen Psychiatry 50:387–393.

Joyce PR, Payhel ES (1989): Predictors of drug response in depression. Arch Gen Psychiatry 46:89–99.

Katona CLE (1988): Lithium augmentation in refractory depression. Psychiatr Dev 6:153–171.

Livingston RL, Zuker DK, Isenberg K, Wetzel RD (1983): Tricyclic antidepressants and delirium. J Clin Psychiatry 44:173–175.

McElroy SL, Pope HG Jr, Keck PE Jr, Hudson JE (1988): Treatment of psychiatric disorders with valproate: a series of 73 cases. Cognitive Ther Res 3:81–85.

Meador-Woodruff JH, Mayada A, Wisner-Carlson R, Grunhaus L (1988): Behavior and cognitive toxicity related to elevated plasma tricyclic antidepressant levels. J Clin Psychpharmacol 8:28–32.

Nakamura T, Ushida K, Nomura J (1990): Comparison of thyroid function between responders and nonresponders to thyroid hormone supplementation in refractory depression. 17th CINP Congress Abstracts 1:54.

Nelson CJ, Bowers MB (1978): Delusional unipolar depression: Description and drug responses. Arch Gen Psychiatry 35:1321–1328.

Nemeroff CB (1993): Paroxetine: An overview of the efficacy and safety of a new selective serotonin reuptake inhibitor in the treatment of depression. J Clin Psychopharmacology 13(supp 2):10s–17s.

Post RM, Uhde TN, Roy-Byrne PP, Joffe RT (1986): Antidepressant effects of carbamazepine. Am J Psychiatry 143:29–34.

Preskorn SH, Simpson S (1982): Tricyclic antidepressant induced delirium and plasma drug concentration. J Clin Psychiatry 139:822–823.

Prien RF (1988): Somatic treatment of unipolar depressive disorder. In Frances AJ, Hales RE (eds): "Review of Psychiatry VII." Washington, DC: American Psychiatric Press, pp 213–234.

Robinson DS, Nies A, Pavaris CL, Ives JO (1978): Clinical psychopharmacology of phenelzine: MAOI activity and clinical response. In Lipton MA, Dimascio A, Keltham KS (eds): "Psychopharmacology: A Generation of Progress." New York: Raven Press pp 961–976.

Roose SP, Glassman AH, Walsh BT, Woodring S (1986): Tricyclic nonresponders: Phenomenology and treatment. Am J Psychiatry 143:345–348.

Rosenzweig MH, Amsterdam JD (1992): Clomipramine augmentation in resistant depression. Abstract NR 108, pg 73. 145th Annual Meeting of the American Psychiatric Association. Washington, DC: May 2–7.

Schatzberg AF, Cole JO (eds) (1991): "Manual of Clinical Psychopharmacology," 2nd ed. Washington, DC: American Psychiatric Press, p 271.

Schatzberg AF, Cole JO, Elliot GR (1986): Recent views of treatment-resistant depression. In Halbriech U, Fernberg SS, (eds): "Psychosocial Aspects of Nonresponse to Antidepressant Drugs." Washington, DC: American Psychiatric Press, pp 95–107.

Seth R, Jennings AL, Bendman J, Phillips J, Bergmann K (1992): Combination treatment with noradrenalin and serotonin reuptake inhibitor in resistant depression. Br J Psychiatry 161:562–565.

Spiker DG, Weiss JC, Dealy RS, Griffin SJ, Hanin I, Neil JF, Perel JM, Rossi AJ, Soloff PH (1985): The pharmacological treatment of delusional depression. Am J Psychiatry 142:430–436.

Woods SW, Tesar GE, Murray GB, Cassem NH (1986): Psychostimulant treatment of depressive disorders secondary to medical illness. J Clin Psychiatry 47:12–15.

Wright G, Galloway L, Kim J, Dalton M, Miller L, Stern W (1985): Bupropion in the long term treatment of cyclic mood disorders: Mood stabilizing effects. J Clin Psychiatry 46:22–25.

CHAPTER 13

Clinical Features of Mania in Adulthood

PAUL E. KECK, Jr., SUSAN L. McELROY, GERI F. KMETZ, and KENJI W. SAX

Department of Psychiatry, University of Cincinnati College of Medicine, Cincinnati, OH 45267-0559

CLINICAL DESCRIPTION

History

Emil Kraepelin provided the first modern and detailed descriptions of the phenomenology of mania (Kraepelin, 1921). Kraepelin's landmark contributions to the classification of mood disorders and the various presentations of bipolar disorder have endured and continue to serve as the underpinnings for the nosology of bipolar disorder in DSM-IV (American Psychiatric Press, 1994). However, physicians have recognized mania for over 2,000 years in the historical record. These early accounts are described.

Early Accounts Hippocrates provided not only early descriptions of manic behavior but also hypothesized that mania was a manifestation of a physiological aberration and not the result of spiritual possession (Goodwin and Jamison, 1990). He also placed the origin of manic behavior in the brain. In contrast, Aristotle believed that the seat of pathological mood states was the heart. According to his theory, all humans had black bile circulating within the body and those with a "relative excess" were predisposed to bouts of melancholy. Interestingly, Aristotle linked black bile and melancholic temperament to creative genius in art, music, philosophy, and government. These observations presaged empirical studies from the modern era that identified, an association between bipolar disorder and creativity (Coryell et al., 1989; Andreasen, 1987; Jamison, 1989, 1993; Post, 1994).

Descriptions of an alternation between mania and melancholia date back to the first century B.C. (Goodwin and Jamison, 1990). However, Aretaeus the Cappodacian, a second-century A.D. physician, is cited as the first to speculate that "mania was an end stage to melancholy" (Goodwin and Jamison, 1990). Interestingly, Aretaeus believed that mania originated in the heart, caused elevated brain temperature, and

Mood Disorders Across the Life Span, Edited by Shulman, Tohen, and Kutcher
ISBN 0-471-10477-9 © 1996 Wiley-Liss, Inc.

burned away the brain's "imaginative function" (Goodwin and Jamison, 1990). Other physicians recognized that some individuals with melancholia experienced alternating periods of excitement and that the cyclicity of these alternations was an inherent component of the disease. For example, in 1686, Bonet coined the term, *maniaco-melancholicus,* to describe this cyclic and recurrent course of illness (Winokur, 1991). However, the notion that mania and melancholia could present different phases of the same underlying illness did not appear until the nineteenth century (Goodwin and Jamison, 1990). In summary, early historical descriptions of manic–depressive illness recognized the existence of the pathological states of mania and depression, their biological basis (ascribed to abnormal physiological processes in the brain and/or heart) and the recurrent and often cyclic nature of these mood states.

Kraepelin In the early twentieth century, the German physician Emil Kraepelin (1921) was the first to systematically apply the disease model to the understanding of mood and psychotic disorders by carefully studying illness phenomenology, course, and the role of psychosocial stressors in symptom exacerbation. The application of these techniques culminated in Kraepelin's classification of major psychoses into separate diagnostic categories of manic–depressive illness and dementia praecox (schizophrenia). Kraepelin differentiated manic–depressive illness from dementia praecox by specifying that the former disorder was more likely to be characterized by an episodic course punctuated by intervals of euthymia, a more favorable prognosis, and a strong genetic basis (1921). Kraepelin also recognized that manic–depressive illness was characterized by impairments in three general areas of functioning—mood, cognition and perception, and activity and behavior—and that patients could present with pure manic, depressed, or mixed features in these areas. Kraepelin's descriptions thus incorporated all of the major elements of bipolar disorder recognized at the present time: manic, depressive, and mixed mood states involving disturbances in mood, cognition, and activity; illness cyclicity; a spectrum of severity of illness determined by the severity of acute symptoms and the frequency of recurrence and duration of well-being longitudinally; a genetic predisposition; the influence of psychosocial stressors in contributing to illness recrudescence, but also an element of cycle autonomy.

Classification in Diagnostic and Statistical Manuals of Mental Disorders

The first edition of the *Diagnostic and Statistical Manual of Mental Disorders* (DSM) was published in 1952 and reflected the psychobiologic influence of Adolph Meyer and Blueler's conceptualization of schizophrenia. In the original DSM, mania was classified as an affective reaction and fell under two diagnoses: manic–depressive reaction, manic type (defined as "elation or irritability, with overtalkativeness, flight of ideas, and increased motor activity; transitory, often momentary, episodes of depression may occur") or manic–depressive reaction, other (which included patients with mixed mania, continuous alternation of the two phases, i.e., rapid-cycling, or manic stupor, i.e., catatonia) (American Psychiatric Association, 1952). Duration or severity criteria were not specified, nor was a minimum number of symptoms established. Furthermore, no mention was made of the occurrence of psychotic symptoms, reflecting the overly broad inclusion of patients with psychotic symptoms in the schizophrenic reaction classification.

DSM-II followed in 1968 and differed little from DSM in the diagnostic criteria formulated for mania. In DSM-II, manic–depressive reaction was renamed manic–

depressive illness and was classified as a major affective disorder (affective psychosis). Manic episodes were characterized by "excessive elation, irritability, talkativeness, flight of ideas, and accelerated speech and motor activity" (American Psychiatric Association, 1968). As in DSM, circular (rapid-cycling) and mixed presentations were also described. Minimum symptom, duration, and severity criteria were again undefined. Although grouped under the affective *psychoses,* DSM-II did not discuss the occurrence of psychosis (delusions, hallucinations, formal thought disorder) during manic or mixed episodes.

Based on research conducted during the 1970s, which indicated that reigning concepts of schizophrenia in American psychiatry were overly broad (Carlson and Goodwin, 1973; Abrams and Taylor, 1976; Pope and Lipinski, 1978), the publication of DSM-II in 1980 (American Psychiatric Association, 1980) reflected the recognition that psychotic symptoms were not pathognomic for schizophrenia and, in fact, occurred commonly during mania. In addition, DSM-III divided mood disorders into unipolar (major depression) and bipolar (manic–depressive) disorders. Formal diagnostic criteria were also proposed to define manic, depressive, and mixed mood episodes, although the definition of a mixed episode was ambiguous in its inclusion of both mixed mood states and rapid-cycling (rapidly alternating but not necessarily mixed episodes of mania and depression). Cyclothymia was also categorized as a mood disorder rather than a personality disorder as it had been previously conceptualized.

A number of important modifications in the diagnostic criteria for bipolar disorder were introduced in DSM-IV. First, DSM-IV reinstated the stipulation of a minimum duration of one week (from DSM-III, but not DSM-III-R, American Psychiatric Association, 1987) of a sufficient number of manic symptoms to meet criteria for a manic episode. However, manic symptoms may be of less than one week's duration if hospitalization is necessary. Second, a separate criteria set was defined for a mixed episode. These criteria specify that the symptom criteria for both a manic episode and a major depressive episode are met concurrently nearly every day for at least one week. This provides for an operational but narrow definition of a mixed episode (this issue will be discussed further in this chapter). Third, a separate criteria set is provided for the first time for hypomania. These criteria specify a duration of at least 4 days of mood change (distinct from the usual nondepressed mood) and an unequivocal change in functioning observable by others. In contrast to mania, hypomania is defined as not severe enough to cause marked impairment or to require hospitalization. In conjunction with specific criteria for hypomania, DSM-IV has also introduced bipolar II disorder as a separate diagnosis distinct from bipolar I disorder. Fifth, DSM-IV introduced a number of diagnostic specifiers (e.g., with catatonic features, with postpartum onset, course specifiers, with seasonal pattern, or with rapid-cycling) that reflect the importance of these factors on treatment choice and prognosis. These issue are described in more detail further in this chapter.

Clinical Features

Currently, as defined in DSM-IV, an acute manic episode is a distinct period of abnormally and persistently elevated, expansive, or irritable mood lasting at least one week or necessitating hospitalization (American Psychiatric Association, 1994). In order for this mood disturbance to qualify as a manic episode, three or more of a cluster of symptoms must have persisted to a significant degree (four or more of them if mood is only irritable). These symptoms include: (1) inflated self-esteem or grandiosity; (2) a decreased need for sleep; (3) increased talkativeness or pressured speech; (4) flight of ideas or a sense of racing thoughts; (5) distractibility; (6) psychomotor agitation or an increase in goal-directed activity, either socially, at work or school, or sexually; and (7) excessive involvement in pleasurable activities with a high potential for painful consequence. The mood disturbance cannot be due to a substance (e.g., drug abuse or medication) or general medical condition. In a departure from previous conceptualizations, mania precipitated solely by antidepressant medications is not classified as mania associated with bipolar disorder. The episode must also be severe enough to cause marked occupational impairment or interference with social activities or relationships; alternatively, it must be severe enough to necessitate hospitalization to prevent harm to the patient or others. With these criteria in mind, systematic studies of the clinical features of mania in adults are reviewed below.

Mania is "a complicated, volatile, and fluctuating cauldron of symptoms" (Goodwin and Jamison, 1990). Fortunately, a number of careful descriptive studies have closely examined the mood, behavioral, and cognitive features of the manic state. Pooled data (weighted mean frequency) from studies examining mood type and frequency of mood symptoms during mania indicate that most patients experience depression (72%), irritability (80%), expansiveness (60%), and mood lability (the classic "mood swings" of manic–depressive illness) (69%) as often as euphoria (71%) (Clayton et al., 1965; Winokur et al., 1969; Beigel and Murphy, 1971; Kotin and Goodwin, 1972; Carlson and Goodwin, 1973; Taylor and Abrams, 1973; Winokur and Tsuang, 1975; Abrams and Taylor, 1976; Pope and Lipinski, 1978; Prien et al., 1988; McElroy et al., 1992; summarized in Goodwin and Jamison, 1990). The type and combination of mood symptoms in adult mania are determined, in part, by the degree of severity or stage of mania (Carlson and Goodwin, 1973). In a careful longitudinal analysis of mood changes during mania, Carlson and Goodwin (1973) divided the course of a manic episode into three stages, based primarily on the predominant mood as follows: Stage I, mood is characterized by euphoria; stage II, by irritability, dysphoria, and depression; and stage III, by severe anxiety (often escalating to panic), dysphoria, and delirium. These changes in mood symptoms through stages I–III, as mania escalates, are also often recapitulated in reverse as mania subsides by switching or with treatment. As will be discussed later, the stages of mania involve not only progressive changes in mood symptoms, but also a similar spectrum of alterations in behavior and cognition.

Pooled data (weighted mean frequency) from studies of behavioral disturbances in mania in adults reveal that the most common symptoms, occurring in over 50% of patients, are pressured speech (98%), hyperverbosity (89%), physical hyperactivity (87%), decreased sleep (81%), hypersexuality (57%), and extravagance (55%) (Lange, 1922; Allison and Wilson, 1960; Clayton et al., 1965; Carlson and Goodwin, 1983; Taylor and Abrams, 1973; Abrams and Taylor, 1976; Leff et al., 1976; Loudon et al., 1977; Taylor and Abrams, 1977; Abrams and Taylor, 1981). Less commonly occurring behavioral symptoms included violent or assaultive acts (49%), religiosity (39%), head decoration (34%), public sexual exposure (29%), pronounced regression (28%), catatonia (22%) (thus the provision of this specifier in DSM-IV), and fecal smearing or incontinence (13%).

Historically, mania was thought to be distinguishable from schizophrenia by its lack of thought disorder. Psychotic and nonpsychotic cognitive symptoms are now recognized to be common in mania (Goodwin and Jamison, 1990). Pooled data (weighted mean frequency) from systematic studies, which characterized nonpsychotic cognitive symptoms during mania, found that grandiosity (78%), racing thoughts (71%), and distractibility/poor concentration (71%) were most common (Lundquist, 1945; Clayton et al., 1965; Winokur et al., 1969, Carlson and Goodwin, 1973; Taylor and Abrams, 1973; Abrams and Taylor, 1976; Leff et al., 1976; Loudon et al., 1977, Taylor and Abrams, 1977; Braden and Ho, 1981; summarized in Goodwin and Jamison, 1990). Confusion (25%) during mania was also observed, but less commonly in these studies. The wide variance in the reported frequency of confusion across these studies (ranging from 8 to 53%) is in part attributable to different definitions used to define this symptom. For example, definitions of confusion ranged from "somewhat confused and unable to follow the gist of conversation" to frank disorientation and severe immediate and short-term memory disturbance (Goodwin and Jamison, 1990).

Preliminary evidence also suggests that differences in cognitive functioning may also exist between mixed and pure mania. Deficits in sustained attention as measured by continuous performance testing (CPT) have been consistently found in studies examining cognitive deficits in patients with schizophrenia (Orzack and Kornetsky, 1966; Wohlberg and Kornetsky, 1973; Nuechterlein et al., 1986; Cornblatt et al., 1989). Although CPT has been less extensively applied to patients with bipolar disorder, results from available studies indicate that patients with mania are also significantly impaired on this measure (Nuechterlein et al., 1991; Rund et al., 1992). A recent study comparing CPT between adult patients with pure and mixed mania found that patients with mixed mania exhibited greater overall impairment (Sax et al., 1995). Significant differences were also found in the severity of positive and negative thought disorder, with the pure group having more severe positive formal thought disorder and the mixed group more severe negative formal thought disorder (Sax et al., 1995). Other differences between pure and mixed mania in adults are discussed later in this chapter.

Over 25 studies (summarized in Goodwin and Jamison, 1990) have demonstrated that all forms of psychosis (e.g., delusions, hallucinations, formal thought disorder) can be present during mania. These include, in addition to the classic symptoms of grandiose and religious delusions, mood-incongruent delusions and first-rank Schneiderian symptoms (Pope and Lipinski, 1978). Pooled data from studies reviewed by Goodwin and Jamison (1990) indicate that at least two-thirds of patients with bipolar disorder were reported to have a lifetime history of at least one psychotic symptom, usually during mania. Delusions were three times more likely to be present during mania as hallucinations. Nearly 20% of patients displayed first-rank Schneiderian symptoms (Goodwin and Jamison, 1990). In summary, the nonspecificity of psychotic symptoms across diagnoses of schizophrenia and psychotic mood disorders; the predominance of psychotic symptoms over affective symptoms during state III mania; the high likelihood of therapeutic response to treatment of mania with lithium, valproate, or carbamazepine; and the potential deleterious effects of protracted neuroleptic exposure in patients with mania mistakenly diagnosed with schizophrenia places great importance on carefully searching for evidence of mania in patients presenting for treatment with a first episode of psychosis.

Evidence from several studies has demonstrated an important association between age of onset of bipolar disorder and the presence of psychotic symptoms (Carlson and Strober, 1979; Rosenthal et al., 1980; Rosen et al., 1983). The findings from these studies suggest that bipolar I patients who become ill during adolescence are more likely to present with predominant psychotic symptoms than those patients with a later age of onset. In the study by Rosen and colleagues (1983), less than 20% of adolescent patients and patients with onset in early adulthood (ages 20–29) presented without psychotic symptoms, whereas nearly 40% of adult patients with onset of illness after age 30 presented without psychotic features.

Although not formally recognized by DSM-IV as a symptom of mania, widespread clinical experience suggests that impaired insight and lack of recognition of symptoms of manic behavior is a common symptom of mania in adults. However, the frequency of impaired insight in mania has not been systematically studied. Evidence from studies of treatment compliance with pharmacotherapy (primarily lithium) suggest that poor insight into the recognition of the behavioral manifestations of the illness and the need for treatment are commonly associated with noncompliance and poor outcome (Jamison et al., 1979; O'Connell et al., 1991). In this sense, lack of insight in mania may be one of the most insidious symptoms of the syndrome.

CLASSIFICATION OF MANIA IN ADULTHOOD

Spectrum Versus Dimensional Models

Mania is typically thought of as the antithesis of depression, that is, that mania and depression represent opposite or polar pathophysiologic states along a spectrum separated by a range of normal mood and cognitive and behavioral functioning (euthymia). Evidence for such a model for conceptualizing bipolar disorder includes the identification of classic syndromes of mania (marked by euphoric mood, increased energy, decreased need for sleep, psychomotor agitation, inflated self-esteem, grandiose, religious and other mood-congruent delusions, etc.), which phenomenologically appear to be the opposite of classic syndromes of depression (characterized by depressed mood, diminished energy, inability to sleep or hypersomnia, psychomotor retardation, poor self-esteem, somatic, nihilistic and other mood-congruent delusions, etc.); the bidirectional switch process, either spontaneously or pharmacologically induced, from mania to depression or depression to mania; the temporal or chronological separation of manic and depressive episodes; and different pharmacologic treatments for mania and depression.

However, this spectrum model (mania–euthymia–depression), with different degrees of severity of illness within manic and depressive episodes, does not accommodate the not infrequent occurrence of mixed states or the simultaneous presence of manic and depressive symptoms (McElroy et al., 1992). An alternative or dimensional model, which can account for mixed mania, rests on the hypothesis that mania and depression occur as independent but not necessarily opposite pathophysiologic states that vary in intensity and interaction. Although the range of presentations of mania can usually be classified as bipolar I, bipolar II, and cyclothymia, the presentation of mania in many adult patients may fall in the gray areas between these discretely defined categories. Thus, the concept of dimensions of manic and depressive symptoms presenting within a discrete mood episode may be a useful approach to diagnosis and treatment. Mixed mania will be discussed further in this chapter.

Bipolar I Disorder

For the diagnosis of bipolar I disorder, DSM-IV requires the presence of only one manic episode and no past major depressive episodes, that the manic episode is not better accounted for by schizoaffective disorder, and is not superimposed on schizophrenia, schizophreniform disorder, delusional disorder, or psychotic disorder not otherwise specified (NOS). Specifiers include manic versus mixed (discussed below under Mixed Mania), severity, psychotic, remission, with catatonic features, or with postpartum onset.

To date, no conclusive evidence exists to suggest that unipolar mania is a persistent phenomenon over the course of illness in a subgroup of patients with bipolar I disorder (Goodwin and Jamison, 1990). Studies that carefully examined the phenomenology and course of patients with bipolar disorder reported that patients whose course of illness was marked by manic episodes with no apparent history of depression were rare, typically constituting less than 5% of all patients studied (Leonhard, 1957; Perris, 1966; Angst, 1986; Winokur et al., 1969). Most investigators have found that patients with apparent unipolar mania either had retrospectively undetected mild episodes of depression or had not been followed long enough prospectively to exclude future episodes of depression (Goodwin and Jamison, 1990).

Treatment guidelines for bipolar I (and other forms of the disorder) have recently been published (Hirschfeld et al., 1994). Evidence from double-blind, placebo-controlled studies indicates that three medications—lithium, valproate, and carbamazepine—have efficacy in the treatment of acute mania in adults (Hirschfeld et al., 1994; Keck et al., 1992).

Bipolar II Disorder

The essential feature of bipolar II disorder, according to DSM-IV, is a clinical course characterized by the occurrence of one or more episodes of major depression and at least one hypomanic episode. This definition emphasizes the predominance and severity of depressive episodes, which characterize the course of most patients with bipolar II illness (Goodwin and Jamison, 1990). Interestingly, data from the ongoing genetic linkage study of bipolar I families suggest that bipolar II disorder may be the most common phenotype in both bipolar I and bipolar II families (Simpson et al., 1993). These data support a long held clinical impression that bipolar II disorder may be more common than bipolar I disorder. The underrecognition of bipolar II disorder in research and clinical settings in adult patients may be attributable to difficulties associated with the diagnosis of hypomania. Several reasons may account for this difficulty. First, individuals with bipolar II disorder may not view hypomanic episodes as pathological, although others may be disturbed by the individuals' erratic behavior. Second, since many patients do not find hypomania to be troublesome, they may not seek treatment until experiencing a depressive episode. Third, patients presenting for treatment in the throes of a major depressive episode may not recall or distinguish previous hypomanic episodes from euthymia without collateral information from family members and friends. Thus, the diagnosis of bipolar II disorder requires a high index of suspicion and should especially be considered in a patient with apparent recurrent unipolar depression (Goodwin and Jamison, 1990).

As already described hypomania may often be experienced as very desirable by adult patients. Characteristic features such as elevated energy, enhanced self-confidence, rapid, creative associative thinking, and increased productivity are not unexpectedly experienced as pleasurable. However, low frustration tolerance and irritability are also associated with hypomania and may be less ego-syntonic and identifiable as problems by the patient. Hypomania as it occurs in bipolar II disorder is thought to represent a stable ceiling of the severity of manic symptoms. However, hypomania may also represent a transitional state (approximating stage I mania) from euthymia to frank mania in patients with bipolar I disorder. Hypomania, like mania, can also be characterized by mixed symptoms, which may make it difficult to distinguish diagnostically from agitated depression and the mood instability associated with borderline personality disorder (McElroy et al., 1992).

In contrast to studies of antimanic and mood stabilizing agents in the treatment of bipolar I disorder, there is a paucity of data from controlled studies regarding the pharmacologic treatment of bipolar II disorder. Lithium, valproate, and carbamazepine are frequently used to treat hypomania acutely and to address the overall mood instability in bipolar II disorder. However, these three mood-stabilizing agents are thought to exert less robust antidepressant effects. Since severe major depressive episodes complicated by suicidality frequently pose the most troublesome aspect of the disorder, antidepressants are often indicated in conjunction with mood-stabilizing agents (Hirschfeld et al., 1994).

Mixed Mania in Adults

DSM-IV requires that the criteria for a manic episode and for a major depressive episode (except for duration) are met nearly every day during at least a one-week period for a diagnosis of mixed mania (American Psychiatric Association, 1994). In addition, the mood disturbance must be of sufficient severity to cause marked impairment in occupational functioning or in usual social activities or relationships with others, or to necessitate hospitalization to prevent harm to self or others, or to produce psychotic symptoms. The mixed symptoms cannot be due to the direct physiological effects of a substance (e.g., a drug of abuse, a medication, or other treatment) or a general medical condition. As discussed earlier, the exclusion of a diagnosis of mania or mixed mania precipitated by antidepressant medications, ECT, or light therapy is currently the subject of debate and further research.

Since Kraepelin (1921) first described mixed states of manic–depressive insanity, it has been known that some patients with acute mania or hypomania simultaneously experience prominent depressive symptoms. However, considerable ambiguity has surrounded this condition (McElroy et al., 1992). For example, mixed mania, also called dysphoric mania, has been described as a distinct affective state distinguishable from nondysphoric mania (Kraepelin, 1921; Campbell, 1953; Himmelhoch et al., 1976; Himmelhoch, 1979; Himmelhoch and Garfinkel, 1986; Nunn, 1979; Krishnan et al., 1983; Evans and Nemeroff, 1983; Secunda et al., 1985, 1987; Swann et al., 1986; Keller, 1988; Keller et al., 1986; Prien et al., 1988; Cohen et al., 1988; Post et al., 1989; Tohen et al., 1990; Dell'Osso et al., 1991), as a form of typical mania (Kotin and Goodwin, 1972; Murphy and Beigel, 1974; Loudon et al., 1977); as a stage-related or particularly severe form of mania (Carlson and Goodwin, 1973; Post et al., 1989), and as a transitional state between mania and depression (Kraepelin, 1921; Himmelhoch et al., 1976; Himmelhoch, 1979; Himmelhoch and Garfinkel, 1986; Nunn et al., 1979; Akiskal and Puzantian, 1979; Bunney et al., 1972a,b,c). Much of the ambiguity surrounding mixed mania has been due to the lack of widely accepted, empirically based operational diagnostic criteria for the disorder. As previously mentioned, the criteria for mixed mania in DSM-III-R (American Psychiatric Association, 1987) contributed to this ambiguity by including rapid-cycling as well as mixed manic and depressive symptoms. Since rapid-cycling and mixed states can usually be distinguished clinically (Himmelhoch et al., 1976; Post et al., 1989), the separation of mixed mania, in DSM-IV, from rapid-cycling, which was subsumed under the criteria for mixed mania in DSM-III and DSM-III-R, is an important nosological clarification and improvement.

Historically, mixed mania has been defined in broad, intermediate, or narrow terms: broad—mania or hypomania accompanied by *any* depressive symptom; intermediate—mania or hypomania accompanied by *several* depressive symptoms; and narrow—mania accompanied by full-scale or *syndromal* major depression. The broad definition of mixed mania lacks specificity since, as previously described, many patients with acute mania simultaneously display at least some degree of depressed mood. By requiring the presence of mania and full syndromal criteria for major depression, the DSM-IV definition is narrow. The clinical implications of this narrow definition are of greater specificity of diagnosis but at the cost of diminished sensitivity. In other words, patients with mania or hypomania accompanied by several (but subsyndromal) depressive symptoms, that is, those meeting an intermediate definition of mixed mania, will not meet criteria for mixed mania by DSM-IV. This categorical approach to the diagnosis of mixed mania, defined by DSM-IV in narrow terms, has important treatment implications. First, many studies that have examined the prevalence, demographic features, biological measures, course of illness, pharmacologic treatment response, and outcome of patients with mixed mania have employed intermediate definitions of the disorder (Kotin and Goodwin, 1972; Murphy and Beigel, 1974; Himmelhoch et al., 1976; Nunn, 1979; Krishnan et al., 1983; Secunda et al., 1985, 1987; Keller 1988; Cohen et al., 1988; Post et al., 1989; Tohen et al., 1990). These studies have shown that as compared to patients with pure mania, patients with mixed mania differ in a number of important ways. The overall mean estimated prevalence of mixed mania (defined according to intermediate or narrow criteria) from pooled studies is 31% (McElroy et al., 1992). Thus, mixed mania in adults is not uncommon in clinical settings. First, phenomenologic studies suggest that mixed mania is more likely to be associated with depressive delusions (Strakowski et al., 1992) and suicidality (Jamieson, 1936; Kukopulos et al., 1980; Dilsaver et al., 1994). Second, although most studies reported that patients with mixed and nonmixed mania had similar ages, Himmelhoch and Garfinkel (1986) reported that adolescents with mania frequently presented with mixed symptoms. Third, studies of demographics, course of illness, and family history suggest that, compared with patients with typical mania, mixed-manic patients may be more likely to be female; to have an earlier age of onset and a longer duration of illness; to have higher rates of depression in their early histories and families; and to have protracted episodes, poorer short- and long-term outcome, and a higher likelihood of recurrence. Biological studies suggest that mixed mania may be more frequently associated with postdexamethasone nonsuppression of plasma cortisol than pure mania. Finally, treatment response studies suggest that, compared with pure mania, mixed mania is less likely to respond to lithium but more likely to respond to valproate or carbamazepine (Post et al., 1989; Freeman et al., 1992; McElroy et al., 1992; Bowden et al., 1994).

Recent data regarding the phenomenology of mixed mania suggest that a dimensional (assessing the relative degrees or contributions of manic and depressive symptoms) rather than a categorical (dichotomous mixed versus nonmixed, as represented in DSM-IV) may have substantial clinical relevance (McElroy et al., 1995). In a study of 71 patients with bipolar disorder, manic episodes were defined according to intermediate (McElroy et al., 1992) or narrow (DSM-III-R) criteria as mixed or nonmixed. Twenty-four (34%) patients met DSM-III-R criteria for mixed bipolar disorder; 28 (40%) met intermediate criteria. Compared with nonmixed patients, DSM-III-R mixed patients had significantly more depressive symptoms, were more likely to be female, experienced more prior mixed episodes, displayed higher rates of comorbid obsessive–compulsive disorder, and had longer hospitalizations. When mixed mania was more broadly defined, differences in gender and hospitalization length disappeared. Interestingly, regardless of the definition used, mixed and pure mania were similar on most other variables assessed. In other words, the results of this study suggest that mixed mania overlaps significantly with pure mania, especially when it is defined by a lesser degree of associated depression. This finding, in turn, suggests that dimensional rather than categorical systems describing the degree of associated depression might be more relevant clinically when classifying mania. Rather than classifying mania into pure or mixed dichotomous categories based on the absence or presence of a certain number of degrees of depressive symptoms, therefore, mania might be better subtyped as being associated with a mild, moderate or severe degree of depression. This latter conceptualization might also increase clinical awareness about mixed states in general, and heighten the recognition that affective states are not necessarily polar opposites but, in fact, may frequently overlap (McElroy et al., 1995).

In summary, the presence of prominent depressive symptoms (intermediate definition) or full syndromal depression (narrow or DSM-IV definition) during mania in adults has important prognostic and treatment implications that make it important to distinguish mixed from nonmixed mania.

Rapid-Cycling

Although the recurrent nature of bipolar disorder has been recognized since Kraepelin's description of manic–depressive insanity in the early 1900s, it was not until the early 1970s that the phenomenon of rapid-cycling was clearly defined by Dunner and Fieve (1974). Their description of rapid-cycling emerged from early research attempting to identify factors associated with lithium prophylaxis failure in patients with bipolar disorder. Dunner and Fieve identified a subgroup of patients experiencing four or more affective episodes per year as being disproportionately represented in the prophylaxis-failure group. These investigators coined the term *rapid-cycling* to describe these patients. Since then, other variations in the definition of rapid-cycling have appeared, including a continuous circular course of affective episodes with short cycles (hypomanic or manic episodes alternating with depressive episodes with at least two cycles per year) (Kukopulos et al., 1980), and as rapidly alternating unremitting symptoms without intervening euthymia (Akiskal and Mallya, 1987).

DSM-IV has adopted the original description of Dunner and Fieve in defining rapid-cycling as "the occurrence of four or more mood episodes during the previous 12 months" (American Psychiatric Association, 1994). Furthermore, DSM-IV specifies that these episodes can occur in any combination and order. Except for their more frequent occurrence, the mood episodes that occur during a period of rapid-cycling are no different from those that occur during a nonrapid-cycling interval and must meet both the symptom and duration criteria for a manic, hypomanic, mixed, or major depressive episode. Mood episodes precipitated by a substance or a general medical condition that contribute to a rapid-cycling pattern are excluded according to DSM-IV criteria. However, in contrast to the exclusion of mania induced by antidepressant treatment from the diagnosis of bipolar I disorder, DSM-IV allows for the use of rapid-cycling as a course specifier even if hypomanic or manic episodes are precipitated by antidepressants. The resolution of this apparent contradiction awaits subsequent editions of DSM.

Rapid-cycling is an important clinical phenomenon in adult patients for several reasons. First, it is associated with greater morbidity (Fawcett et al., 1987). Second, rapid-cycling is often difficult to treat pharmacologically. For example, not only do patients with rapid-cycling respond poorly to treatment with lithium, but evidence suggests that other standard treatments for bipolar disorder, especially antidepressants and antipsychotics, may actually induce or exacerbate cycling (Roy-Byrne et al., 1987; Alarcon, 1985; Kukopulos et al., 1980; McElroy and Keck, 1993). On the other hand, preliminary data suggest that patients with rapid-cycling may have a more favorable response to valproate or carbamazepine (McElroy et al., 1988; Calabrese and Delucci, 1990; Post et al., 1987). Third, rapid-cycling presents in a variety of ways and thus may go unrecognized or misdiagnosed. Finally, surveys of clinical populations suggest that rapid-cycling is not uncommon, occurring in 5–20% of adult patients with bipolar disorder (Wehr et al., 1988; Calabrese and Delucci, 1990; McElroy and Keck, 1993). Rapid-cycling is also more common in female patients and may be associated with clinical or subclinical hypothyroidism (McElroy and Keck, 1993). Thus, careful evaluation of a patient's prior course of illness, in particular the number of prior mood episodes for the presence of periods of rapid-cycling, is necessary in adult patients with mania because of the important treatment and prognostic implications of this course specifier.

CONCLUSIONS

The presentation of mania in adults includes symptoms affecting mood, behavior and activity, and cognition and perception. Evolving nosologies of manic–depressive illness have gradually recognized that different mixtures of symptoms across these three domains of human functioning may occur, accounting for manic, mixed, and depressive mood episodes; that bipolar disorder is a recurrent illness and that the frequency of these recurrences may culminate in rapid cycling; that hypomania is a distinct presentation of bipolar illness, may be more common than mania, and corresponds to the diagnosis of bipolar II disorder, now recognized in DSM-IV. These changes in the classification of the type and severity of mood episode and frequency of recurrence have been incorporated in DSM-IV and have important treatment and prognostic implications.

REFERENCES

Abrams R, Taylor MA (1981): The importance of schizophrenic symptoms in the diagnosis of mania. Am J Psychiatry 138:658–661.

Abrams R, Taylor MA (1976): Mania and schizoaffective disorder, manic type: A comparison. Am J Psychiatry 133:1445–1447.

Akiskal HS, Mallya G (1987): Criteria for the "soft" bipolar spectrum: Treatment implications. Psychopharmacol Bull 23:68–73.

Akiskal HS, Puzantian VR (1979): Psychotic forms of depression and mania. Psychiatr Clin North Am 2:419–439.

Alarcon RD (1985): Rapid cycling affective disorders: A clinical review. Compr Psychiatry 26:522–540.

Allison JB, Wilson WP (1960): Sexual behaviors of manic patients: A preliminary report. South Med J 53:870–874.

American Psychiatric Association (1994): "Diagnostic and Statistical Manual of Mental Disorders," 4th ed. Washington, DC: American Psychiatric Press.

American Psychiatric Association (1987): "Diagnostic and Statistical Manual of Mental Disorders," 3rd ed, revised. Washington, DC: American Psychiatric Press.

American Psychiatric Association (1980): "Diagnostic and Statistical Manual of Mental Disorders," 3rd ed. Washington, DC: American Psychiatric Press.

American Psychiatric Association (1968): "Diagnostic and Statistical Manual of Mental Disorders," 2nd ed. Washington, DC: American Psychiatric Press.

American Psychiatric Association (1952): "Diagnostic and Statistical Manual of Mental Disorders." Washington, DC: American Psychiatric Press.

Andreasen NC (1987): Creativity and mental illness: Prevalence rates in writers and their first-degree relatives. Am J Psychiatry 144:1288–1292.

Angst J (1986): The course of affective disorders. Psychopathol 19(Suppl 2):47–52.

Beigel A, Murphy DL (1971): Assessing clinical characteristics of the manic state. Am J Psychiatry 128:688–694.

Bowden CL, Brugger AM, Swann AC, Calabrese JR, Janicak PG, Petty F, Dilsaver SC, Davis JM, Rush AJ, Small JG, Garza-Trevino ES, Risch SG, Goodnick PJ, Morris DD (1994): Efficacy of divalproex vs lithium and placebo in the treatment of mania. JAMA 271:918–924.

Braden W, Ho CK (1981): Racing thoughts in psychiatric inpatients. Arch Gen Psychiatry 38:71–75.

Bunney WE, Murphy DL, Goodwin FK, Borge GF (1972a): The "switch process" in manic–depressive illness. I: A systematic study of sequential behavioral changes. Arch Gen Psychiatry 27:295–302.

Bunney WE, Goodwin FK, Murphy DL, House KM, Gordon EK (1972b): The "switch process" in manic–depressive illness. II: Relationship to catecholamines, REM sleep, and drugs. Arch Gen Psychiatry 27:304–309.

Bunney WE, Goodwin FK, Murphy DL (1972c): The "switch process" in manic–depressive illness. III: Theoretical implications. Arch Gen Psychiatry 27:312–317.

Calabrese JR, Delucci GA (1990): Spectrum of efficacy of valproate in 55 patients with rapid-cycling bipolar disorder. Am J Psychiatry 147:431–434.

Campbell JD (1953): "Manic–Depressive Disease: Clinical and Psychiatric Significance." Philadelphia: JB Lippincott.

Carlson GA, Goodwin FK (1973): The states of mania: A longitudinal analysis of the manic episode. Arch Gen Psychiatry 28:221–228.

Carlson GA, Strober M (1979): Affective disorders in adolescence. Psychiatr Clin North Am 2:511–526.

Clayton PJ, Pitts FN, Jr, Winokur G (1965): Affective disorder: IV. Mania. Compr Psychiatry 6:313–322.

Cohen S, Khan A, Robinson J (1988): Significance of mixed features in acute mania. Compr Psychiatry 29:421–426.

Cornblatt BA, Lenzenweger MF, Erlenmeyer-Kimling L (1989): The continuous performance test, identical pairs version: II. Contrasting attentional profiles in schizophrenic and depressed patients. Psychiatry Res 29:65–85.

Coryell W, Endicott J, Keller M, Andreasen J, Grove W, Hirschfeld RMA, Scheftner W (1989): Bipolar affective disorder and high achievement: A familial association. Am J Psychiatry 146:983–988.

Dell'Osso L, Placidi GF, Nassi R, Freer P, Cassano GB, Akiskal HS (1991): The manic–depressive mixed state: Familial, temperamental and psychopathologic characteristics in 108 female inpatients. Eur Arch Psychiatry Clin Neurosci 240:234–239.

Dilsaver SC, Chen Y-W, Swann AC, Shoaib AM, Krajewski KJ (1994): Suicidality in patients with pure and depressive mania. Am J Psychiatry 151:1312–1315.

Dunner DL, Fieve RR (1974): Clinical factors in lithium carbonate prophylaxis failure. Arch Gen Psychiatry 30:229–233.

Evans DL, Nemeroff CG (1983): The dexamethasone suppression test in mixed bipolar disorder. Am J Psychiatry 140:615–617.

Fawcett J, Scheftner W, Clark D (1987): Clinical predictors of suicide in patients with major affective disorders: A controlled prospective study. Am J Psychiatry 144:35–40.

Freeman TW, Clothier JL, Pazzaglia P, Lesem MD, Swann AC (1992): A double-blind comparison of valproate and lithium in the treatment of acute mania. Am J Psychiatry 149:108–111.

Goodwin FK, Jamison KR (1990): "Manic–Depressive Illness." New York: Oxford University Press.

Himmelhoch JM (1979): Mixed states, manic–depressive illness and the nature of mood. Psychiatr Clin N Am 2:449–459.

Himmelhoch JM, Garfinkel ME (1986): Mixed mania: Diagnosis and treatment. Psychopharmacol Bull 22:613–620.

Himmelhoch JM, Mulla D, Neil JF, Detre TP, Kupfer DJ (1976): Incidence and significance of mixed affective states in a bipolar population. Arch Gen Psychiatry 33:1062–1066.

Hirschfeld RMA, Clayton PJ, Cohen I, Fawcett J, Keck PE, McClellan J, McElroy SL, Post RM, Satloff A (1994): Practice guideline for the treatment of patients with bipolar disorder. Am J Psychiatry 151(Suppl):1–31.

Jamieson GR (1936): Suicide and mental disease: A clinical analysis of one hundred cases. Arch Neurol Psychiatry 36:1–12.

Jamison KR (1993): "Touched with Fire: Manic–Depressive Illness and the Artistic Temperament." New York: Free Press.

Jamison KR (1989): Mood disorders and seasonal patterns in British writers and artists. Psychiatry 52:125–134.

Jamison KR, Gerner RH, Goodwin FK (1979): Patient and physician attitudes toward lithium: Relationship to compliance. Arch Gen Psychiatry 36:866–869.

Keck PE, Jr, McElroy SL, Nemeroff CB (1992): Anticonvulsants in the treatment of bipolar disorder. J Neuropsychiatry Clin Neurosci 4:395–405.

Keller MB (1988): The course of manic–depressive illness. J Clin Psychiatry 49:4–6.

Keller MB, Lavori PW, Coryell W, Andreasen NC, Endicott J, Clayton PJ, Klerman GL, Hirschfeld RMA (1986): Differential outcome of pure manic, mixed/cycling, and pure depressive episodes in patients with bipolar illness. JAMA 255:3138–3142.

Kotin J, Goodwin FK (1972): Depression during mania: Clinical observations and theoretical implications. Am J Psychiatry 129:679–686.

Kraepelin E (1921): "Manic–Depressive Insanity and Paranoia." Edinburgh: E & S Livingstone; reprinted New York: Arno Press, 1976.

Krishman RR, Maltbie AA, Davidson JRT (1983): Abnormal cortisol suppression in bipolar patient with simultaneous manic and depressive symptoms. Am J Psychiatry 140:203–205.

Kukopulos A, Reginaldi D, Laddomadda P (1980): Course of the manic–depressive cycle and changes caused by treatments. Pharmacopsychiatr 13:156–167.

Lange J (1922): "Katatonische Erscheinungen im Rahmen Manischer Erkrankungen." Berlin: Julius Springer.

Leff JP, Fischer M, Bertelsen AC (1976): A cross-national epidemiological study of mania. Br J Psychiatry 129:428–442.

Leonhard K (1957): "The Classification of Endogenous Psychosis." Berlin: Akademie-Verlag.

Loudon JB, Blackburn IM, Ashworth CM (1977): A study of the symptomatology and course of manic illness using a new scale. Psychol Med 7:723–729.

Lundquist G (1945): Prognosis and course in manic–depressive psychoses: A follow-up study of 319 first admissions. Acta Psychiatr Neurol (Suppl 35):1–96.

McElroy SL, Keck PE, Jr (1993): Rapid cycling. In Dunner DL: (ed): "Current Psychiatry Therapy." Philadelphia: WB Saunders.

McElroy SL, Strakowski, SM, Keck PE, Jr, Tugrul KC, West SA, Lonczak HS (1995): Differences and similarities in mixed and pure mania. Compr Psychiatry 36:187–194.

McElroy SL, Keck PE, Jr, Pope HG, Jr, Hudson JI, Faedda GL, Swann AC (1992): Clinical and research implications of the diagnosis of dysphoric or mixed mania or hypomania. Am J Psychiatry 149:1633–1644.

McElroy SL, Keck PE, Jr, Pope HG, Jr, Hudson JI (1988): Treatment of rapid cycling bipolar disorder with sodium valproate. J Clin Psychopharmacol 8:275–279.

Murphy DL, Beigel A (1974): Depression, elation and lithium carbonate responses in manic patient subgroups. Arch Gen Psychiatry 31:643–654.

Nuechterlein KH, Dawson ME, Ventura J, Mikowitz D, Konishi G (1991): Information processing anomalies in the early course of schizophrenia and bipolar disorder. Schizophr Res 5:195–196.

Nuechterlein KH, Edell WS, Norris M, Dawson ME (1986): Attentional vulnerability indicators, thought disorder, and negative symptoms. Schizophr Bull 12:408–426.

Nunn CMH (1979): Mixed affective states and the natural history of manic–depressive psychosis. Br J Psychiatry 134:153–160.

O'Connell RA, Mayo JA, Flatow L, Cuthbertson B, O'Brien BE (1991): Outcome of bipolar disorder on long-term treatment with lithium. Br J Psychiatry 159:123–129.

Orzack MH, Kornetsky C (1966): Attention dysfunction in chronic schizophrenia. Arch Gen Psychiatry 14:323–326.

Perris C (1966): A study of bipolar (manic–depressive) and unipolar recurrent depressive psychoses. Acta Psychiatr Scand 42(Suppl 94):68–82.

Pope HG, Jr, Lipinski JF, Jr (1978): Diagnosis in schizophrenia and manic–depressive illness: A reassessment of the specificity of "schizophrenic" symptoms in light of current research. Arch Gen Psychiatry 35:811–828.

Post F (1994): Creativity and psychopathology: A study of 291 world-famous men. Br J Psychiatry 165:22–34.

Post RM, Rubinow DR, Uhde TW, Roy-Byrne PP, Linnoila M, Rosoff A, Cowdry R (1989): Dysphoric mania: Clinical and biological correlates. Arch Gen Psychiatry 46:353–358.

Post RM, Uhde TW, Roy-Byrne PP (1987): Correlates of antimanic response to carbamazepine. Psychiatry Res 21:71–83.

Prien RF, Himmelhoch JM, Kupfer DJ (1988): Treatment of mixed mania. J Affective Disord 15:9–15.

Rosen LN, Rosenthal NE, Van Dusen PH, Dunner DL, Fieve RR (1983): Age at onset and number of psychotic symptoms in bipolar I and schizoaffective disorder. Am J Psychiatry 140:1523–1524.

Rosenthal NE, Rosenthal LN, Stallone F, Dunner DL, Fieve RR (1980): Toward the validation of RDC schizoaffective disorder. Arch Gen Psychiatry 37:804–810.

Roy-Byrne PP, Jaffe RT, Uhde TW (1987): Approaches to the evaluation and treatment of rapid-cycling affective illness. Br J Psychiatry 145:543–550.

Rund BR, Orbeck AL, Landro JK (1992): Vigilance deficits in schizophrenics and affectively disturbed patients. Acta Psychiatr Scand 86:207–212.

Sax KW, Strakowski SM, McElroy SL, Keck PE, Jr, West SA (1995): Attention and formal thought disorder in mixed and pure mania. Biol Psychiatry 37:420–423.

Secunda SK, Swann A, Katz MM, Koslow SH, Croughan J, Chang S (1987): Diagnosis and treatment of mixed mania. Am J Psychiatry 144:96–98.

Secunda SK, Katz MM, Swann A, Koslow SH, Maas JW, Chuang S, Croughan J (1985): Mania: Diagnosis, state, measurement and prediction of treatment response. J Affect Disord 8:113–121.

Simpson SG, Folstein SE, Meyers DA, McMahon FJ, Brusco DM, DePaulo JR (1993): Bipolar II: The most common bipolar phenotype? Am J Psychiatry 150:901–903.

Strakowski SM, Tohen M, Stoll AL, Faedda GL, Goodwin DC (1992): Comorbidity in mania at first hospitalization. Am J Psychiatry 149:554–556.

Swann AC, Secunda SK, Katz MM, Koslow SH, Maas JW, Chang S, Roins E (1986): Lithium treatment of mania: Clinical characteristics, specificity of symptom change, and outcome. Psychiatry Res 18:127–141.

Taylor MA, Abrams R (1973): The phenomenology of mania: A new look at some old patients. Arch Gen Psychiatry 29:520–522.

Taylor MA, Abrams R (1977): Catatonia: Prevalence and importance in the manic phase of manic–depressive illness. Arch Gen Psychiatry 34:1223–1225.

Tohen M, Waternaux CM, Tsuang MT (1990): Outcome in mania: A 4-year prospective follow-up of 75 patients utilizing survival analysis. Arch Gen Psychiatry 47:1106–1111.

Winokur G (1991): "Mania and Depression. A classification of Syndrome and Disease." Baltimore: Johns Hopkins University Press.

Winokur G, Clayton PJ, Reich T (1969): "Manic Depressive Illness." St. Louis: C. V. Mosby.

Winokur G, Tsuang MT (1975): Elation versus irritability in mania. Compr Psychiatry 16:435–436.

Wohlberg GW, Kornetsky C (1973): Sustained attention in remitted schizophrenics. Arch Gen Psychiatry 28:533–537.

CHAPTER 14

Outcome of Mania in Adults

CARLOS A. ZARATE, Jr. and MAURICIO TOHEN

McLean Hospital, Harvard University, Belmont, MA 20178-9106

NEED FOR PREDICTORS OF RELAPSE AND TREATMENT OUTCOME

The ability to predict the most likely outcome of a psychiatric disorder is an important clinical and public health consideration. The issue of prediction of response to treatment has had a long history in psychiatry. Electroconvulsive therapy and antidepressant treatments in particular attracted many attempts to forecast which approach would have a successful outcome (Hamilton, 1974). Understanding more about the relationship of the course of illness and clinical treatment to patient outcome will help determine which intervention is most likely to lead to a more favorable response. In order to determine what are the clinical, treatment, and biological predictors of response, outcome studies are needed. The importance of outcome studies and their influence on clinical practice and in mental health policy planning has been described in detail elsewhere (Tohen, 1991). Treatment outcome refers to the effect of a specific therapeutic intervention (defined in terms of length of treatment period, therapeutic agent, dose of medication, and schedule of administration) on symptom severity or course of illness. In contrast, illness outcome usually refers to the course and consequences of an illness. Obviously, although treatment outcome and illness outcome and their respective predictors may be interrelated, they are not necessarily identical. The relationships between treatment and course are bi-directional (outcome also causes treatment) and cannot easily be disentangled.

Predicting response to treatment in mania is important for clinical and research purposes. Manic–depressive disorder is by nature a recurring illness. These recurring episodes have a cumulative deteriorative effect on functioning and treatment response (Prien and Gelenberg, 1989; Prien and Potter, 1990). In 1979, the Medical Practice Information Demonstration Project concluded that, without treatment, the average woman with bipolar disorder beginning at age 25 will lose 9.2 years of life, 14.2 years of major life activity, and 11.9 health status years. With optimal treatment the woman will regain 6.5 years of life, 10.2 years of major life activity, and 8.5 health status years (DHEW, 1979). Thus implying that the sooner bipolar patients are diagnosed and

Mood Disorders Across the Life Span, Edited by Shulman, Tohen, and Kutcher
ISBN 0-471-10477-9 © 1996 Wiley-Liss, Inc.

treated, the better the chances of recovery. We will review the predictors of outcome in mania, as well as the predictors of response to treatment with conventional mood stabilizers.

In order to best serve the needs of this clinical population, it is important for clinicians, hospital administrators, and mental health policy planners to develop a clear understanding of the various outcomes of mania in both treated and untreated populations.

In addition, because outcome is most likely to be heterogeneous, it is also critical to identify those factors that predict time to recovery and relapse, and treatment response for various subgroups of manic patients.

NATURAL COURSE OF MANIA

Kraepelin emphasized the importance of longitudinal outcome data in differentiating the major psychoses. By utilizing this approach he was able to classify the major psychoses into three types—dementia praecox, manic–depressive illness, and paranoia. Dementia praecox was referred to as an illness with a deteriorating course in contrast to manic–depressive illness, which was episodic with full recovery between episodes, and described to have a good prognosis (Kraepelin, 1921). However, later studies did not find that a good outcome was always the case (Cassidy et al., 1955; Hastings, 1958; Bratfos and Haug, 1968; Shobe and Brion, 1971; Carlson et al., 1974; Fahndrich and Wirtz, 1987). These differences in findings may be accounted for by differences in the methodology used in the different studies (Zis and Goodwin, 1979). These methodological problems include nonsystematic sampling, loss of patients to follow-up, and the differences in diagnostic criteria and how outcome measures are collected and analyzed (Kraepelin, 1921; Hastings, 1958; Bratfos and Haug, 1968; Shobe and Brion, 1971; Fleiss et al., 1976).

A common methodological problem is the lack of a generally accepted convention for collecting data on course or for defining recovery and relapse. Until recently, most outcome studies used cross-sectional, as opposed to longitudinal, analysis methods. Yet the latter provide higher statistical power and more continuous description of patients over an entire follow-up period. Instruments such as the Life Chart Methodology (Post et al., 1988) and the Longitudinal Interval Follow-up Evaluation (LIFE) have been created to provide a method of supplementing diagnostic and quantitative assessments in the study of the long-term course of affective disorders (Keller et al., 1987), making it easy to determine whether a particular medication worsens or improves the course of the illness. Even more problematic is the fact that most longitudinal studies of mental disorders collect data at a limited number of time points following a subject's entry into a study, and that subsequent analyses are performed at each time point separately. Fleiss et al. (1976) recommended using the life table for analyzing data from longitudinal studies in which the outcome under study occurs randomly.

Another concern with longitudinal studies is that the effects of treatment in outcome are, at times, difficult to disentangle in naturalistic studies. As Keller et al. (1983) noted, treatment as prescribed by clinicians in response to the patient's condition sometimes becomes an outcome in itself. When obtaining information on episodes occurring during the course of illness, severe episodes are usually easy to recognize as patients are frequently rehospitalized. The difficulty is more apparent with episodes of less intensity, or in cases of rapid-cycling. Most classic studies of bipolar patients were done with patients hospitalized for mania and thus do not include the bipolar II subgroup. Also, it is difficult to determine when an episode begins and ends. Similarly, patients who are noncompliant with medications may make the assessment of episodes difficult to determine. An area that has been neglected in longitudinal studies of bipolar disorder is functional recovery and quality of life. Gathering this additional information is important because even though patients are syndromically recovered, they may continue functionally impaired.

Another problem encountered in reviewing the literature on mania has to do with the use of diagnostic terms. In the earlier literature, patients given a diagnosis of manic–depressive illness sometimes included individuals with psychotic depression who had never experienced manic episodes. In addition, diagnoses were most often established on the basis of clinical impression, as opposed to the use of structured diagnostic interviews. Similarly, for many years, there were differences in the diagnostic criteria used by psychiatrists in different parts of the world (Kendell et al., 1974). In the well-known U.S.–U.K. diagnostic study, American psychiatrists, in contrast to their British counterparts, were more likely to diagnose mania as schizophrenia, thus possibly underestimating the true incidence and prevalence of this disorder (Cooper et al., 1972). Nonetheless, it is estimated that 60–80% of the cases of bipolar disorder will present initially with a manic episode. At least 80% of patients who have an initial episode of mania will have a course marked by multiple recurrences of major depressive and manic episodes (Winokur et al., 1969; Gelenberg et al., 1993). Furthermore, between 10 and 15% of unipolar patients will have subsequent episodes that will involve manic or hypomanic symptoms, at which point they are reclassified as having a bipolar disorder.

Kraepelin (1921) observed the majority of 459 manic patients for over 20 years and noted that 208 (45%) had only one attack and only 30% of the sample had three or more attacks. Lundquist (1945) noted that 55% of those who remained diagnostically stable had only one attack. However, most studies in the preneuroleptic era suggest that the majority of patients with manic–depressive illness will have multiple episodes. Zis and Goodwin (1979) reviewed a series of studies and reported high rates of relapse among bipolar patients. Similarly, Rennie (1942) and Stenstedt (1952) found high rates of relapse, with 64 and 86% of bipolars having three or more episodes, respectively. Nearly 60% of the bipolars in Perris (1966) study had six or more episodes, and bipolar patients in Taschev's study (1974) averaged 4.7 episodes. Zis and Goodwin (1979) suggest that methodological differences most likely account for the inconsistencies across studies. Lavori and colleagues (1984) come to similar conclusions.

Kraepelin (1921) reported that the great majority of manic attacks extended over many months, but the range varied considerably, and in some cases the attacks lasted for several years. Wertham (1929) collected the largest series and, among 2,000 cases, the most frequent duration was 4 months. A later study also was in agreement with this finding (Winokur, et al., 1969). The number of episodes in a lifetime have ranged from 1 to more than 30, and the mean number of episodes has been estimated to be around 9 (Clayton, 1981). However, impaired functioning may continue long after symptomatic recovery has taken place (Dion et al., 1988).

In studies of clinical course and outcome, there are methodological issues to consider. In some studies, illness episodes were only considered to have occurred if hospitalization was required. Another source of discrepancy in these outcome studies is related to the duration of observation, which is most evident in the percentage of patients reported to have had a single episode of mania, ranging from 0 to 58% across studies (Zis and Goodwin, 1979).

In exploring the natural course of mania, Angst (1968) conducted a 20-year follow-up of patients with affective disorders at the University Clinic in Zurich, Switzerland. The sample included 95 patients with bipolar disorder who were followed from the onset of their illness. The average length of follow-up was 19 years. In this group of patients, 15% had no relapse after recovering from the initial index episode. Later age of onset was a predictor of higher rate of recurrence. The study also suggested that the number of symptom-free intervals of euthymia seem to decrease with age and with the number of previous episodes. Angst also reported that the duration of euthymic episodes tended to plateau after the fourth episode and usually last 8–12 months. He suggested that early-onset bipolar patients be treated prophylactically until age 65 and that late-onset cases be treated until age 75.

These findings are consistent with more recent studies (Keller et al., 1986; Tohen, 1988; Tohen et al., 1990a,b) that also suggest that bipolar illness is not always a benign, remitting illness, but rather has a variable prognosis ranging from complete recovery to functional incapacitation.

RECOVERY FROM ACUTE MANIA

With a few exceptions (Keller et al., 1986; Tohen et al., 1990a) the definition of recovery across studies has been inconsistent. For example, in some studies, depression following a manic episode is considered to be part of the index episode. In others, it is considered a new episode. Another factor to keep in mind is that the recovery rate cited in a given study depends largely on the length of follow-up and the definition of recovery peculiar to that study. Poort (1945) and Bratfos and Haug (1968) reported relatively high rates of chronicity associated with index episodes (56 and 45%, respectively). Most recent studies (Keller et al., 1986; Tohen et al., 1990a) have used survival analysis methodology (Cox, 1972; Kalbfleish and Prentice, 1980) to study time to recovery and to relapse.

Data provided by the National Institutes of Mental Health (NIMH) Collaborative Study (Keller et al., 1986) suggest that the polarity of the index episode may predict speed of recovery in that patients who presented with mania recovered at a faster rate than patients who presented depressed or in a mixed state. The probability of not recovering for at least 12 months was 7% for the "pure" manic group compared to 32% of the mixed-cycling group. Recovery estimates for bipolar patients presenting with a depressive episode fell between the pure manic and mixed-cycling groups. Keller and colleagues (1986) also pointed out that these differences in recovery rates could be explained by availability of more effective treatments for pure mania than for mixed-cycling episodes. Thus, the median time needed for recovery was 5 weeks in their pure manic group, 9 weeks for the pure depressive group, and 14 weeks for the mixed-cycling group. A history of previous major affective episodes also predicted delayed recovery. These investigators emphasized the importance of preventing a purely depressed or purely manic patient from developing a mixed-cycling condition. Another aspect that up until recently was not considered is the stage of the illness. The vast majority of follow-up studies start the follow-up period following the "index" episode. Recent studies (Tohen et al., 1990a, 1995), however, have reported that outcome will be different in first episode as opposed to multiple-episode cases. Thus, predictors of outcome really differ between first and multiple-episode patients.

PREDICTORS OF COURSE IN MANIA

Another major area of interest in outcome studies of bipolar disorder has been in the prediction of relapse. The literature, however, has been inconsistent and many different predictor variables have been identified. To date, there are no definite predictors of future course in bipolar disorder, although several have been proposed (Secunda et al., 1985). The proposed predictors of relapse in manic patients include low vocational advancement at illness onset (Fahndrich and Wirtz, 1987), poor occupational status prior to index episode (Tohen et al., 1990b), symptoms of depression (Kraepelin 1921; Winokur et al., 1969; Morgan 1972; Fahndrich and Wirtz, 1987), number of previous episodes (Cassidy et al., 1955, Bratfos and Haug, 1968; Tohen et al., 1990a), presentation of mixed affective states (Winokur et al., 1969; Morgan, 1972; Kotin and Goodwin, 1972; Himmelhoch et al., 1976; Nunn, 1979; Keller et al., 1986), comorbidity including a history of alcoholism (Black et al., 1988; Tohen et al., 1990a, 1995), psychotic features during the index manic episode (Winokur et al., 1969; Morgan, 1972; Rosenthal et al., 1979; Rosen et al., 1983; Coryell et al., 1990; Tohen et al., 1990a,b), mood-incongruent psychotic features (Brockington et al., 1983; Tohen et al., 1992), and presence of interepisode symptoms (Goodnick, 1987a,b; Tohen et al., 1990a). Less is known about predictors of recovery. Keller and colleagues (1986) found that by 8 weeks, 61% of the pure manics were recovered, compared with 44% of the pure depressives and 33% of the mixed and cycling patients. Cycling within the index episode predicts a relatively low likelihood of recovery for bipolar I patients (Keller et al., 1986; Coryell et al., 1987). Coryell and colleagues (1990) found that the factors associated with recovery in patients with chronic mania of more than 2 years were less severe illness at intake, lack of psychotic features, good friendship patterns in adolescence, and, most important, a relatively high maximum level of functioning in the 5 years preceding intake.

Presence of comorbidity (Figure 1) illustrates the month-to-month probability of nonrecovery for a group of bipolar manic and mixed patients discharged from McLean Hospital. The sample is divided by the presence or absence of substance use disorder (SUD) comorbidity (Tohen et al., 1995). The figure shows that by 6 months postdischarge, the probability of nonrecovery was 37.5% (3/8) for patients with SUD comorbidity and 11.1% (4/36) for patients without such comorbidity. However, 2 years after the index hospitalization, 12.5% of the patients with SUD comorbidity were not yet recovered, compared to only 2.8% of those without SUD comorbidity. The age of onset appears to influence outcome, early age of onset being associated with a polyepisodic course (Winokur and Kadrmas, 1989). With regard to gender, female sex has been reported to be a robust predictor of rapid-cycling (Coryell et al., 1992). The polarity of index episode suggests that patients with purely manic index episodes recovered at a much faster rate than did those whose index episodes were mixed or cycling.

PSYCHOSOCIAL ADJUSTMENT IN MANIC PATIENTS

Another problem until recent years was that most of the outcome studies in mania focused exclusively on symptomatic recovery. The studies of Winokur et al. (1969)

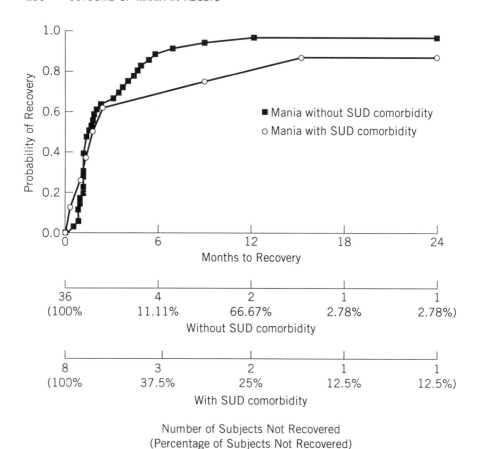

FIGURE 1. Twenty-four month cumulative probability of recovery after first manic episode with and without SUD comorbidity.

and Carlson et al. (1974) both differentiated symptomatic recovery from social recovery and found that symptomatic remission was more frequent than full social recovery (family stability, return to job, etc.). Very little was known about how patients were functioning after the index manic episode. Previous studies of the functioning of patients with manic–depressive illness include Lundquist (1945), who interviewed 103 manic patients up to 30 years after onset of illness and reported 87 (85%) to be "socially recovered." He concluded that (bipolar) manic–depressive illness has a generally good prognosis. Winokur and colleagues (1969) followed 28 bipolar patients for an average of 2 years following hospitalization for a manic episode and found that close to 80% of subjects who suffered from recurrent mania lost their jobs. The literature has been inconsistent in defining the parameters of psychosocial outcome. Indeed, in most studies, outcome assessment consists of applying a combination of psychosocial and relapse/remission variables. Until recently, with the exception of the Iowa 500 study (Tsuang et al., 1979), psychosocial outcome per se has not been clearly operationalized. This 40-year retrospective cohort study used structured diagnostic and outcome instruments and experienced minimal loss of patients to follow-up. Good outcome in residential and occupational adjustment was found in 69 and 67% of patients, respectively. In this regard, data from a McLean Hospital cohort (Tohen, 1988) were quite similar. At the 4-year evaluation, 72% of patients were rated as good in terms of their occupational status, and 80% were rated as good with respect to their residential status.

In another study conducted at McLean Hospital, Dion and colleagues (1988) followed a cohort of 67 patients prospectively for 6 months after discharge and compared their functional outcome to their symptomatic outcome. After 6 months, most were rated symptom-free; however, one-third of the cohort was considered disabled, and only 21% were working at their previous level. Thus, although short-term treatment is effective in symptom amelioration, it does not necessarily lead to rapid restoration of occupational functioning. These data also suggest that in manic patients discharged from an inpatient setting, follow-up treatment should focus on their rehabilitative needs so as to restore previous levels of functioning. The current trend toward shorter hospitalizations means that aftercare planning should address not only symptom amelioration but psychosocial rehabilitation as well.

MORTALITY AND SUICIDE

Excess mortality from natural causes was significant in the first half of the century but now appears rare; however, death from suicide remains a significant problem (Ödegård, 1952; Stenstedt, 1952; Perris, 1966; Bratfos and Haug, 1968; Weeke and Vaeth, 1986; Black et al., 1987). Suicide is a major contributor to mortality in patients with manic–depressive illness. The best approach to determine the proportion of deaths caused by suicide is to study mortality in a cohort comprised of deceased patients. In carrying out such studies, Taschev (1974), in a postmortem study of 122 bipolar patients, found that 27% had committed suicide, whereas Tsuang and colleagues (1979) found that 11% of patients with mania committed suicide. Perris (1966) found that 11% of the deaths in his patients were due to suicide, which is identical to data reported by Tsuang et al. (1979). In the McLean cohort, 4% of subjects committed suicide (Tohen, 1988, Tohen et al., 1990a).

PREDICTORS TO TREATMENT RESPONSE

Many controlled studies have shown that maintenance lithium lessens the frequency and severity of episodes of mania and depression in bipolar patients and helps stabilize mood between episodes (Baastrup et al., 1970; Stallone et al., 1973; Prien et al., 1973, 1974; Prien, 1988; Fieve et al., 1976; Gelenberg, 1989; Goodwin and Jamison, 1990). In addition, a number of studies have compared the prophylactic benefit of lithium compared to placebo (Baastrup et al., 1970; Coppen et al., 1971; Cundall et al., 1972; Prien et al., 1973; Stallone et al., 1973; Bowden et al., 1994). Additional investigations of the efficacy of lithium in the prophylactic treatment of mania comes from the work of Prien and colleagues (1973), who published the only randomized, double-blind study of lithium versus placebo that specified the probability of remaining in remission at different time intervals. In Prien's study, 32% of patients on placebo continued in remission for at least 1 year, 23% remained in remission for 1 year, and 73% of those still being followed were well after 2 years. However, various outcome studies of bipolar patients maintained on lithium have found relapse rates in excess of 20%, despite adequate blood levels of lithium (Prien, 1984; Mander, 1986; Goodnick et al., 1987a). A study by Gelenberg et al. (1989) of outcomes in patients maintained at standard (0.8–1.0 mmol/L) and low-range (0.4–0.6 mmol/L) lithium levels found that although relapse rates were lower among patients maintained at the standard range, these patients were three times more likely to have dropped out of the study because of side effects from lithium compared to the patients maintained on a low range of lithium.

Another important and now well-studied question concerns the use of preventive drug treatment after just one manic episode. Zarin and Pass (1987) reviewed this subject using a Markov model to study the trade-off between costs (exposure to lithium) and benefits (i.e., preventing relapse). Such studies are of utmost importance in evaluating the risk–benefit ratio of all treatment modalities. In addition, long-term lithium treatment also appears to reduce the risk of early mortality for bipolar patients: Without treatment, early mortality is two to three times higher than that of the general population; with treatment, it is not significantly different (Muller-Oerlinghausen et al., 1992). Also, approximately one-fourth of bipolar patients attempt suicide (Weissman et al., 1991). In general, the pharmacotherapy of acute mania is effective; however, 30–40% of manic patients do not respond to, or cannot tolerate, lithium (Dunner et al., 1976; Prien, 1984; Small et al., 1988; Harrow et al., 1990). Some patients may be entirely refractory while others continue to have mild to moderate symptoms. The introduction of valproate and carbamazepine in the treatment of bipolar disorder has been of enormous importance. Thus, predictors of response to each drug must be sought.

What factors predict a positive response to lithium, carbamazepine, and valproate in manic patients? Determining what factors may predict either a favorable or unfavorable response is of enormous importance. Being able to determine which agent should be used in a particular situation will perhaps avoid unnecessary drug trials, perhaps reducing the risk for side effects and possibly treatment resistance. However, even though many studies have been conducted in order to determine correlates or predictors of response, most of these findings are uncontrolled and therefore tentative. Table 1 compares the demographic, clinical, and biological predictors of response to lithium, carbamazepine, and valproate in mania. One of the major methodological weaknesses in research on the prediction of lithium response has been the lack of a definition of lithium response (Grof et al., 1983). Another problem in evaluating predictors of antimanic response is the variability of treatment response in the same patient from one episode to the next (Stokes et al., 1971).

In different studies, age, sex, marital status, race, nationality, family history, age at onset, duration of illness, and presence of psychotic symptoms have not appeared associated with an antimanic response to lithium (Mendlewicz et al., 1973; Hoffman et al., 1974; Petterson, 1977; Prien, 1980; Rybakowski et al., 1980; Taylor and Abrams, 1981; Miller et al., 1991a). In contrast, severity of mania (Prien et al., 1972; Swann et al., 1986), mixed states (Himmelhoch et al., 1976, Himmelhoch and Garfield, 1986; Keller et al., 1986; Prien et al., 1988), predominance of paranoid over elated/grandiose symptoms (Murphy and Biegel, 1974; Winokur, 1984), rapid-cycling (Dunner and Fieve 1974; Post et al., 1987; Abou-Saleh and Coppen, 1986; Goodnick et al., 1987a), duration of manic episode prior to hospitalization (Keller et al., 1986), secondary mania (Krauthammer and Klerman, 1978), "atypical features" (Baastrup and Schou, 1967), and alcohol and drug abuse (Himmelhoch et al., 1976) seemed to be associated with a lack

TABLE 1. Clinical Predictors of Antimanic Response to Lithium, Carbamazepine, and Valproate[a]

Patient Characteristics	Prediction		
	Lithium	Carbamazepine	Valproate
Demographic			
Age	0	0	0
Sex	+/0	0	0
Marital status	0	?	0
Clinical			
Diagnosis	+	?	+
Family history of mood disorder	+	−	0
Positive response of first-degree relatives to lithium therapy	+	?	?
Age of onset	0	?	+
Duration of illness	0	?	0
Severity of mania	−	+	0
Predominance of paranoid over elated/grandiose symptoms	−	?	0
Quality of free interval (remission)	+	?	?
Psychotic symptoms	0	?	0
Soft neurological signs	?	?	0
Psychosensory symptoms	?	0	0
Rapid-cycling	−	+	+
Mania with prominent dysphoria	−	+	+
Poor initial response	−	?	?
Response to other lithium/ antiepileptics	?	?	0
Closed head trauma antedating onset of affective symptoms or secondary mania	−	?	+
History of alcohol or drug abuse	−	?	0
Good functioning between episodes	+	?	?
Patterns of episode related to degree of response (mania–depression)	+	?	?
Neurological abnormalities			
Biological/other			
Brain CT/MRI scan findings	?	?	0
Nonparoxysmal EEG abnormalities	?	0	+
Positive M antigen in blood	+	?	?
Platelet MAO	0	?	?
Erythrocyte lithium concentration	0	?	?
Serum Li, CBZ, VPA concentration	+	?	+
"Abnormal" MMPI profile	−	?	?

[a] + = positive response, − = negative response; 0 = no association; ? = not studied; MAO = monoamine oxidase; Li = lithium; CBZ = carbamazepine; VPA = valproate; MMPI = Minnesota multiphasic personality inventory.

of response. With regard to clinical predictors of prophylactic response to lithium, the data is more scanty, and it is unclear how much of the antimanic predictors may be extrapolated to maintenance treatment (Prien et al., 1974; Grof et al., 1979). It has been suggested that patterns of episodes are related to the degree of lithium prophylaxis. A high proportion (approximately 80%) of patients exhibiting the pattern of mania followed by depression respond to lithium. In contrast, those who demonstrate the pattern of depression followed by mania and a well interval show a substantially reduced response to lithium, on the order of one-fourth to one-third of the patients (Kukopulos et al., 1980; Haag et al., 1987; Grof et al., 1983; Faedda et al., 1991).

Data from double-blind studies suggest that carbamazepine is similar to lithium in the maintenance treatment of bipolar disorder (Okuma et al., 1973, 1981; Placidi et al., 1986; Watkins et al., 1987; Lusznat et al., 1988; Small, 1990). Post and colleagues (1983) cited a number of studies that have found that use of carbamazepine alone, or in combination with other drugs (e.g., lithium), may reduce the frequency of relapse in manic–depressive illness. Carbamazepine has been shown to be effective in the acute and prophylactic treatment of mania both in double-blind and open-label studies (Okuma et al., 1973, 1981; Ballenger and Post, 1980; Stromgren and Boller, 1985; Post, 1988). However, data bearing on predictors of response to treatment with carbamazepine are sparse. In an analysis of clinical characteristics associated with antimanic response to carbamazepine, Post et al. (1987, 1989) found that patients who improved had more severe mania, were more dysphoric, and more frequently exhibited a recent history of rapid-cycling. Also, a negative family history of mood disorder was found to be associated with carbamazepine response.

Only recently was the first large-scale study with both divalproex and lithium conducted that showed they were significantly more effective than placebo in reducing the symptoms of acute mania (Bowden et al., 1994). In the one other placebo-controlled study of divalproex in acute mania, which was limited to patients nonresponsive to, or intolerant of, lithium, Pope et al. (1991) reported a median of 54% improvement in the 17 divalproex-treated patients compared with a median of 5% improvement for the 19 patients treated with placebo. Also, valproate appears to have a role in the maintenance treatment of bipolar disorder (Emrich et al., 1980; Prien and Potter, 1990); however, to date no long-term controlled studies with divalproex have been published. Recently, open-label studies of divalproex administered as maintenance therapy over longer periods have been promising (Calabrese and Delucchi, 1990). Numerous clinical and biological correlates to antimanic response to valproate have been studied and are summarized in Table 1. Age, sex, duration of illness, psychotic symptoms, "soft" neurological signs or symptoms, family history of mood disorder, brain computerized axial tomography, and magnetic resonance imaging have not been associated with an antimanic response to valproate (McElroy et al., 1987, 1991). A diagnosis of bipolar disorder rather than schizoaffective disorder (Emrich et al., 1985; McElroy et al., 1987, 1988a), rapid-cycling (Calabrese and Delucchi, 1990; McElroy et al., 1988a,b), mania with prominent dysphoria (Freeman et al., 1990), nonparoxysmal electroencephalogram (EEG) abnormalities (Stoll et al., 1994), and closed head trauma antedating onset of affective symptoms (Pope et al., 1988) seem to favor valproate response. Less data exists with regards to predictors of prophylactic response to valproate.

Similarly important is to know how different drugs used in the treatment of bipolar disorder may affect the course of illness. Factors reported to increase relapse rates (i.e., rapid-cycling) or precipitate mania include the use of antidepressants, especially tricyclic antidepressants (Prien et al., 1973; Kukopulos et al., 1980; Wehr and Goodwin,

1987; Wehr et al., 1988). Parenthetically, it has been reported that the use of neuroleptics (i.e., to control manic symptoms) accentuates the depression that often follows manic episodes (Kukopulos et al., 1980) and may also affect long-term functioning (Tohen et al., 1990b). If lithium is going to be discontinued in a bipolar patient who had been stable, one needs to keep in mind that the risk of early recurrence of bipolar illness, especially of mania, evidently is increased following discontinuation of lithium use and may exceed that predicted by the course of the untreated disorder (Suppes et al., 1991, 1993). A metanalysis of 14 studies involving 257 patients with bipolar disorder who had been stable on maintenance treatment showed that more than 50% of new episodes of illness occurred within 10 weeks of stopping an average of 30 months of treatment. By survival analysis of 124 cases in which the time to a new episode was known, the computed time to 50% failure of remission was 5.0 months after stopping therapy; the time to 25% recurrence of mania was 5.2 times earlier than for depression (2.7 vs. 14 months). Consideration of the natural history of bipolar disorder suggests that among the patients with bipolar I disorder, an overall 50% recurrence risk by 5 months off lithium treatment, and even more rapid onset of mania, may well exceed the average episode interval in untreated bipolar disorder of perhaps 2 years. If lithium is going to be discontinued, how rapidly should one do so? Faedda and colleagues (1993) reported that the overall risk of a new episode of mania was significantly greater after rapid (<2 weeks) than gradual (2–4 weeks discontinuation). Thus, lithium should probably be tapered off slowly over several months. Finally, it has been suggested that high motor activity determined by wrist-worn actigraphs may be a sensitive marker of subclinical manic tendencies and early relapse following lithium discontinuation (Klein et al., 1992).

Other forms of therapy shown to affect the course of illness include group therapy and family therapy. Group therapy combined with lithium has been reported to decrease rehospitalization more than patients receiving only medications (Davenport et al., 1977; Shakir et al., 1979; Goodwin and Jamison, 1990). Family therapy has been reported to decrease rehospitalization and relapse as well as improve functioning in occupational and social roles (Glick et al., 1985; Miklowitz and Goldstein, 1990; Miller et al. 1991b).

CONCLUSIONS

Further research is needed to provide clinical and biological predictors of response to lithium, valproate, and carbamazepine. The predictors of response to one anticonvulsant is not necessarily predictive of a response to another one (Placidi et al., 1986; McElroy et al., 1988b). Identifying clinical and biological predictors of response is not only important for patient care but also may help elucidate common pathophysiologic mechanisms in bipolar disorder. Being able to predict response to an effective treatment in mania means that we have isolated some variables of central importance and achieved some progress in our understanding of the nature of affective disorders. A successful prediction of treatment response may also be instrumental in adjusting our classification of disorders in a more meaningful, practically useful way.

REFERENCES

Abou-Saleh MT, Coppen A (1986): Who responds to prophylactic lithium? J Affect Disord 10:115–125.

Angst J (1968): The course of affective disorders. Psychopathology 19(Suppl):47–52.

Baastrup PC, Schou M (1967): Lithium as a prophylactic agent: Its effect against recurrent depression and manic–depressive psychosis. Arch Gen Psychiatry 16:162–172.

Baastrup PC, Poulsen JC, Schou M, Thomsen K, Amdisen A (1970): Prophylactic lithium: Double blind discontinuation in manic–depressive and recurrent-depressive disorders. Lancet 2:326–330.

Ballenger JC, Post RM (1980): Carbamazepine in manic–depressive illness: A new treatment. Am J Psychiatry 137:782–790.

Black DW, Winokur G, Hubert J, Nasarallah A (1988): Predictors of immediate response in the treatment of mania: The importance of comorbidity. Biol Psychiatry 24:191–198.

Black D, Winokur G, Hasrallah A (1987): Is death from natural causes still excessive in psychiatric patients? A follow-up of 1593 patients with major affective disorder. J Nerv Men Dis 175:674–680.

Bowden CL, Brugger AM, Swann AC, Calabrese JR, Janicak PG, Petty F, Dilsaver SC, Davis JM, Rush J, Small JG, Garza-Trevino S, Risch C, Goodnick PJ, Morris DD (1994): Efficacy of divalproex vs lithium and placebo in the treatment of mania. JAMA 271:918–924.

Bratfos O, Haug JO (1968): The course of manic–depressive psychosis. Acta Psychiatr Scand 44:89–112.

Brockington IF, Hillier VF, Francis AF, Helzer JE, Wainwright S (1983): Definitions of mania: Concordance and prediction of outcome. Am J Psychiatry 140:435–439.

Calabrese JR, Delucchi GA (1990): Spectrum of efficacy of valproate in 55 patients with rapid-cycling bipolar disorder. Am J Psychiatry 147:431–434.

Carlson GA, Kotin J, Davenport YB, Adland M (1974): Follow-up of 53 bipolar manic–depressive patients. Br J Psychiatry 124:134–139.

Cassidy WL, Flanagan NB, Spellman M, Cohen ME (1955): Clinical observations in manic–depressive disease. JAMA 164:1535–1546.

Clayton PJ (1981): The epidemiology of bipolar affective disorder. Compr Psychiatry 22:32–43.

Cooper JE, Kendell RE, Gurland BJ, Sharpe L, Cooperland JRB, Simon R (1972): Psychiatric Diagnosis in New York and London: A Comparative Study of Mental Admissions. Maudsley Monograph No. 20. London: Oxford University Press.

Coppen A, Noguera R, Bailey J, Burns BH, Swani MS, Hare EH, Gardner R, Maggs R (1971): Prophylactic lithium in affective disorders. Lancet 2:275–279.

Coryell W, Endicott J, Keller M (1992): Rapidly cycling affective disorder. Arch Gen Psychiatry 49:126–131.

Coryell W, Endicott J, Keller M (1990): Outcome of patients with chronic affective disorder: A five-year follow-up. Am J Psychiatry 147:1627–1633.

Coryell W, Andreasen NC, Endicott J, Keller M (1987): The significance of past mania or hypomania in the course and outcome of major depression. Am J Psychiatry 144:309–315.

Cox DR (1972): Regression models and life tables. J Roy Stat Soc Series B 34:187–220.

Cundall RL, Brooks PW, Murray LG (1972): A controlled evaluation of lithium prophylaxis in affective disorders. Psychol Med 2:308–311.

Davenport YB, Ebert MH, Adland ML, Goodwin FK (1977): Couples group therapy as an adjunct lithium maintenance of the manic patient. Am J Orthopsychiatry 47:495–502.

DHEW (1979): Medical Practice Project. A State-of-the Science Report for the Office of the Assistant Secretary for the US Department of Health, Education and Welfare. Baltimore, MD: Policy Research.

Dion GL, Tohen M, Anthony WA, Waternaux CS (1988): Symptoms and functioning of patients with bipolar disorder six months after hospitalization. Hosp Community Psychiatry 39:652–657.

Dunner DL, Fieve RR (1974): Clinical factors in lithium carbonate prophylaxis failure. Arch Gen Psychiatry 30:229–233.

Dunner DL, Fleiss JL, Fieve RR (1976): Lithium carbonate prophylaxis failure. Br J Psychiatry 129:40–44.

Emrich HM, Dose M, von Zerssen D (1985): The use of sodium valproate, carbamazepine, and oxcarbamazepine in patients with affective disorders. J Affect Disord 8:243–250.

Emrich HM, Von Zerssen D, Kissling W, Moller HJ, Windorfer A (1980): Effect of sodium valproate on mania: The GABA-hypothesis of affective disorders. Arch Psychiatr Nervenkr 229:1–16.

Faedda GL, Tondo L, Baldessarini RJ, Suppes T, Tohen M (1993): Outcome after rapidly vs gradual discontinuation of lithium treatment in bipolar disorders. Arch Gen Psychiatry 50:448–455.

Faedda GL, Baldessarini RJ, Tohen M, Strakowski SM, Waternaux C (1991): Episode sequence in bipolar disorder and response to lithium treatment. Am J Psychiatry 148:1237–1239.

Fahndrich E, Wirtz EF (1987): Verlaufspradikotoren affecktiver Psychosen. Schweiz Arch Neurol Psychiatr 138:17–30.

Fieve RR, Kumbarachi T, Dunner DL (1976): Lithium prophylaxis of depression in bipolar I, bipolar II and unipolar patients. Am J Psychiatry 133:925–929.

Fleiss JL, Dunner DL, Stallone F, Fieve RR (1976): The life table. A method for analyzing longitudinal studies. Arch Gen Psychiatry 33:107–112.

Freeman TW, Clothier JL, Pazzaglia P, Lesem MD, Swann AC, Roache A (1990): Valproate in mania: A double-blind study (Abstract No. 393). In "New Research Program and Abstracts," Washington, DC: American Psychiatric Association.

Gelenberg AJ, Kane JM, Keller MB, Lavori P, Rosenbaum JF, Cole K, Lavalle J (1989): Comparison of standard and low serum levels of lithium for maintenance treatment of bipolar disorder. N Engl J Med 321:1489–1493.

Gelenberg AJ, Hopkins HS (1993): Report on efficacy of treatments for bipolar disorder. Psychopharmacology Bull 29:447–456.

Glick ID, Clarkin JF, Spencer JH, Maas GL, Lewis AB, Peyser J, DeMane N, Good-Ellis M, Harris E, Lestelle V (1985): A controlled evaluation of inpatient family intervention: Preliminary results of the six-month follow-up. Arch Gen Psychiatry 42:882–886.

Goodnick PJ, Fieve RR, Schlegel A, Kaufman K (1987a): Interepisode major and subclinical symptoms in affective disorder. Acta Psychiatr Scand 74:597–600.

Goodnick PJ, Fieve RR, Schlegel A, Baxter N (1987b): Predictors of interepisode symptoms and relapse in affective disorder patients treated with lithium carbonate. Am J Psychiatry 144:367–369.

Goodwin FK, Jamison KR (1990): "Manic–Depressive Illness." New York: Oxford University Press.

Grof P, Hux M, Grof E, Arato M (1983): Prediction of response to stabilizing lithium treatment. Pharmacopsychiatria 16:195–200.

Grof P, Lane J, MacCrimmon D, Werstiuk E, Blajchman M, Daigle L, Varma R (1979): Clinical and laboratory correlates of the responses to long-term lithium treatment. In Schou, M, Stromgren, E, eds: "Origin, Prevention and Treatment of Affective Disorders." London: Academic Press, pp 28–40.

Haag H, Heidorn A, Haag M, Greil W (1987): Sequence of affective polarity and lithium response: Preliminary report on Munich sample. Prog Neuropsychopharmacol 11:205–208.

Hamilton M (1974): Prediction of response to ECT in depressive illness. In Angst J (ed): "Classification and Prediction of Outcome of Depression." Symposia Medica Hechst, Schattauer-Verlag, pp 273–288.

Harrow M, Goldberg JF, Grossman LS, Meltzer HY (1990): Outcome in manic disorders: A naturalistic follow-up study. Arch Gen Psychiatry 47:655–671.

Hastings DW (1958): Follow-up results in psychiatric illness. Am J Psychiatry 114:1057–1060.

Himmelhoch JM, Garfinkel ME (1986): Sources of lithium resistance in mixed mania. Psychopharmacol Bull 22:613–620.

Himmelhoch JM, Mulla D, Neil JF, Detre TP, Kupfer DJ (1976): Incidence and significance of mixed affective state in a bipolar population. Arch Gen Psychiatry 33:1062–1066.

Hoffman G, Grünberger J, König P, Presslich O, Wolf R (1974): Die mehrjährige lithium therapie affektiver störungen. Langzeiteffekte und begleiterscheinungen. Psychiatr Clin 7:129–148.

Kalbfleisch JD, Prentice RL (1980): "The Statistical Analysis of Failure Time Data." New York: Wiley.

Keller MB (1988): The course of manic–depressive illness. J Clin Psychiatry 49(11, Suppl):4–6.

Keller MB, Lavori PW, Friedman B, Nielsen E, Endicott J, McDonald-Scott P, Andreasen NC (1987): The longitudinal interval follow-up evaluation (LIFE): A comprehensive method for assessing outcome in prospective longitudinal studies. Arch Gen Psychiatry 44:540–548.

Keller MB, Lavori PW, Coryell W, Andreasen NC, Endicott J, Clayton PJ, Klerman GL, Hirschfeld RMA (1986): Differential outcome of pure manic, mixed cycling, and pure depressive episodes with bipolar illness. JAMA 13:3138–3142.

Keller MB, Lavori PW, Endicott J, Coryell W, Klerman GL (1983): "Double depression": Two year follow-up. Am J Psychiatry 140:689–694.

Kendell RE, Pichot P, Von Cranach M (1974): Diagnostic criteria of English, French, German psychiatrists. Psychol Med 4:187–195.

Klein E, Lavie P, Meiraz R, Sadeh A, Lenox RH (1992): Increased motor activity and recurrent manic episodes: Predictors of rapid relapse in remitted bipolar disorder patients after lithium discontinuation. Biol Psychiatry 31:279–284.

Koting J, Goodwin F (1972): Depression during mania: Clinical observations and theoretical implications. Br J Psychiatry 129:679–686.

Kraepelin E (1921): Manic–depressive insanity and paranoia. Edinburgh: E & S Livingstone.

Krauthammer C, Klerman GL (1978): Secondary mania: Manic syndromes associated with antecedent physical illness or drugs. Arch Gen Psychiatry 35:1333–1339.

Kukopulos A, Reginaldi D, Laddomada P, Floris G, Serra G, Tondo L (1980): Course of manic–depressive cycle and changes caused by treatment. Pharmakopsychiatr Neuropsychopharmakol 13:156–167.

Lavori PW, Keller MB, Klerman GL (1984): Relapse in affective disorders: A reanalysis of the literature using life table methods. J Psychiatr Res 18:13–25.

Lundquist G (1945): Prognosis and course in manic–depressive psychoses. A follow-up study of 319 first admissions. Acta Psychiatrica Neurologica 35(Suppl 1):1–96.

Lusznat RM, Murphy DP, Nunn CMH (1988): Carbamazepine vs. lithium in the treatment and prophylaxis of mania. Br J Psychiatry 153:198–204.

Mander AJ (1986): Clinical prediction of outcome and lithium response in bipolar affective disorder. J Affect Disord 11:35–41.

McElroy SL, Keck PE Jr, Pope HG Jr, Hudson JI, Morris D (1991): Correlates of antimanic response to valproate. Psychopharmacology Bull 27:127–133.

McElroy SL, Keck PE, Jr, Pope HG Jr, Hudson JI (1988a): Treatment of psychiatric disorders with valproate: A series of 73 cases. Psychiatrie Psychobiologie 3:81–85.

McElroy SL, Keck PE Jr, Pope HG Jr, Hudson JI (1988b): Valproate in the treatment of rapid-cycling bipolar disorder. J Clin Psychopharmacol 8:275–279.

McElroy SL, Keck PE Jr, Pope HG Jr (1987): Sodium valproate: Its use in primary psychiatric disorders. J Clin Psychopharmacol 7:16–24.

Mendlewicz J, Fieve RR, Stallone F (1973): Relationship between the effectiveness of lithium therapy and family history. Am J Psychiatry 130:1011–1013.

Miklowitz DJ, Goldstein MJ (1990): Behavioral family treatment for patients with bipolar affective disorder. Behav Modif 4:457–489.

Miller F, Tanenbaum JH, Griffin A, Ritvo E (1991a): Prediction of treatment response in bipolar, manic disorder. J Affect Dis 21:75–77.

Miller IW, Keitner GI, Epstein NB, Bishop DS, Ryan CE (1991b): Families of Bipolar Patients: Dysfunction, Course of Illness, and Pilot Treatment Study. Presented at the meeting of the Association for the Advancement of Behavior Therapy, New York.

Morgan HG (1972): The incidence of depressive symptoms during recovery from hypomania. Br J Psychiatry 120:537–539.

Muller-Oerlinghausen B, Ahrens B, Grof E, Grof P, Lenz G, Schou M, Simhandl C, Thau K, Volk J, Wolf R, Wolf T (1992): The effect of long-term lithium treatment on the mortality of patients with manic–depressive and schizoaffective illness. Acta Psychiatr Scand 86:218–222.

Murphy D, Beigel A (1974): Depression, elation and lithium carbonate responses in manic patient subgroups. Arch Gen Psychiatry 31:643.

Nunn CMH (1979): Mixed affective states and the natural history of manic–depressive psychosis. Br J Psychiatry 134:153–160.

Ödegård Ö (1952): The excess mortality in the insane. Acta Psychiatr Scand 27:353–367.

Okuma T, Inanaga K, Otsuki S, Sarai K, Takahaski R, Hazama H, Mori A, Watanabe M (1981): A preliminary double-blind study of the efficacy of carbamazepine in prophylaxis of manic–depressive illness. Psychopharmacology (Berlin) 73:95–96.

Okuma T, Kishimoto A, Inoue K, Matumoto H, Ogura A, Matsushita T, Nakao T, Ogura C (1973): Anti-manic and prophylactic effects of carbamazepine on manic–depressive psychosis. Folia Psychiatr Neurol Jap 27:283–297.

Perris C (1966): The course of depressive psychoses. Acta Psychiatr Scand 44:238–248.

Petterson U (1977): Manic–depressive illness: A clinical, social and genetic study. Acta Psychiatr Scand (Suppl 269):1–93.

Placidi GF, Lenzi A, Lazzerini F, Cassano GB, Akiskal HS (1986): The comparative efficacy and safety of carbamazepine versus lithium: A randomized, double-blind 3-year trial in 83 patients. J Clin Psychiatry 47:490–494.

Poort R (1945): Catamnestic investigation on manic–depressive psychoses with special reference to the prognosis. Acta Psychiatr Neurol 20:59–74.

Pope HG Jr, McElroy SL, Keck PE Jr, Hudson JI (1991): Valproate in the treatment of acute mania: A placebo-controlled study. Arch Gen Psychiatry 48:62–68.

Pope HG Jr, McElroy SL, Satlin A, Keck PE Jr, Hudson JI, Kalish R (1988): Head injury, bipolar disorder, and response to valproate. Compr Psychiatry 29:34–38.

Post RM (1988): Effectiveness of carbamazepine in the treatment of bipolar affective disorder. In McElroy SL, Pope HG (eds): "Use of Anticonvulsants in Psychiatry." Clifton, NJ: Oxford Health Care, pp 25–41.

Post RM, Rubinow DR, Uhde TW, Roy-Byrne PP, Linnoila M, Rosoff A, Cowdry R (1989): Dysphoric mania. Arch Gen Psychiatry 46:353–358.

Post RM, Roy-Byrne PP, Uhde TW (1988): Graphic representation of the life course of illness in patients with affective disorder. Am J Psychiatry 145:844–848.

Post RM, Uhde TW, Roy-Byrne PP, Joffe RT (1987): Correlates of antimanic response to carbamazepine. Psychiatry Res 21:71–83.

Post RM, Uhde TW, Ballenger JC (1983): Prophylactic efficacy of carbamazepine in manic–depressive illness. Am J Psychiatry 140:1602–1604.

Prien RF (1988): Maintenance treatment of depressive and manic states. In Georgotas A, Cancro R (eds): "Depression and Mania." New York: Elsevier Science Publishing.

Prien RF (1984): NIH report: Five-center study clarifies use of lithium, imipramine for recurrent affective disorders. Hosp Community Psychiatry 35:1097–1098.

Prien RF (1980): Predicting lithium responders and nonresponders: Illness indicators. In Johnson FN (ed): "Handbook of Lithium Therapy." Lancaster, England: MTP Press, pp 133–136.

Prien RF, Gelenberg AJ (1989): Alternatives to lithium for preventive treatment of bipolar disorder. Am J Psychiatry 146:840–848.

Prien RF, Potter WZ (1990): NIMH workshop report on treatment of bipolar disorder. Psychopharmacol Bull 26:409–427.

Prien RF, Himmelhoch JM, Kupfer DJ (1988): Treatment of mixed mania. J Affect Disord 15:9–15.

Prien RF, Caffey EM, Klett CJ (1974): Factors associated with lithium responses in the prophylactic treatment of bipolar manic–depressive illness. Arch Gen Psychiatry 31:189–192.

Prien RF, Caffey EM, Klett CJ (1973): Prophylactic efficacy of lithium carbonate in manic–depressive illness: Report of the Veterans Administration and National Institute of Mental Health Collaborative Study Group. Arch Gen Psychiatry 28:337–341.

Prien RF, Caffey EM Jr, Klett CJ (1972): Comparison of lithium carbonate and chlorpromazine in the treatment of mania. Arch Gen Psychiatry 26:146–153.

Rennie T (1942): Prognosis in manic–depressive psychoses. Am J Psychiatry 98:801–814.

Rosen LN, Rosenthal NE, Dunner DL, Fieve RR (1983): Social outcome compared in psychotic and nonpsychotic bipolar I patients: J Nerv Men Dis 171:272–275.

Rosenthal NE, Rosenthal LN, Stallone F (1979): Psychosis as a predictor of response to lithium maintenance treatment in bipolar affective disorder. J Affect Disord 1:237–245.

Rybakowski J, Chtopocka-Wozniak M, Kapelski Z, Strzyzewski W (1980): The prophylactic efficacy of lithium against mania and depressive recurrences in bipolar patients. Int Pharmacopsychiatry 15:86–90.

Secunda SK, Katz MM, Swann AC, Koslow SH, Maas JW, Chang S, Croughan J (1985): Mania: Diagnosis, state measurement and prediction of treatment response. J Affect Disord 8:113–121.

Shakir SA, Volkmar FR, Bacon S, Pfferbaum A (1979): Group psychotherapy as an adjunct to lithium maintenance. Am J Psychiatry 136:455–456.

Shobe FO, Brion P (1971): Long term prognosis in manic-depressive illness. Arch Gen Psychiatry 24:334–337.

Small JG (1990): Anticonvulsants in affective disorders. Psychopharmacol Bull 26:25–36.

Small JC, Klapper MH, Kellams JJ, Miller MJ, Milstein V, Sharpley PH, Small IF (1988): Electroconvulsive therapy compared with lithium in the management of manic states. Arch Gen Psychiatry 45:727–732.

Stallone F, Shelley E, Mendlewicz J (1973): The use of lithium in affective disorders: III. A double-blind study of prophylaxis in bipolar illness. Am J Psychiatry 130:1006–1010.

Stenstedt Å (1952): A study in manic–depressive psychosis. Acta Psychiatr Scand (Suppl 79):1–111.

Stokes PE, Shamoian CA, Stoll PM, Patton MJ (1971): Efficacy of lithium as acute treatment of manic–depressive illness. Lancet 1:1319–1325.

Stoll AL, Banov M, Kolbrenner M, Mayer PV, Tohen M, Strakowski SM, Castillo J, Suppes T, Cohen BM (1994): Neurologic factors predict a favorable valproate response in bipolar and schizoaffective disorders. J Clin Psychopharmacol 14:311–313.

Stromgren LS, Boller S (1985): Carbamazepine in treatment and prophylaxis of manic–depressive disorder. Psychiatr Dev 4:349–367.

Suppes T, Baldessarini RJ, Faedda GL, Tondo L, Tohen M (1993): Discontinuing maintenance treatment in bipolar manic–depression: Risks and implications. Harvard Rev Psychiatry 1:131–144.

Suppes T, Baldessarini RJ, Faedda GL, Tohen M (1991): Risk of recurrence following discontinuation of lithium treatment in bipolar disorder. Arch Gen Psychiatry 48:1082–1088.

Swann AC, Secunda SK, Katz MM, Koslow SH, Maas JW, Chang S, Robins E (1986): Lithium treatment of mania: Clinical characteristics, specificity of symptom change, and outcome. Psychiatr Res 18:127–141.

Taschev T (1974): The course and prognosis of depression on the basis of 652 patients deceased. In Angst J (ed): "Classification and Prediction of Outcome of Depression." New York: FK Schattauer Verlag.

Taylor M, Abrams R (1981): Prediction of treatment response in mania. Arch Gen Psychiatry 38:800–803.

Tohen M (1991): Course and treatment outcome in patients with mania. In Mirin SM, Gossett JT, Grub MT (eds): "Psychiatric Treatment Advances in Outcome Research." Washington, DC, American Psychiatric Press.

Tohen M (1988): Outcome in bipolar disorder. Ph.D. Dissertation, Harvard University, Cambridge, MA.

Tohen M, Zarate CA Jr, Turvey C, Centorrino F, Hegarty J (1995): The McLean First-episode Mania Project. 148th Ann Meeting Am Psychiatric Assoc, Miami.

Tohen M, Tsuang MT, Goodwin DC (1992): Prediction of outcome in mania by mood-congruent or mood-incongruent psychotic features. Am J Psychiatry 149:1580–1584.

Tohen M, Waternaux CM, Tsuang MT, Hunt AT (1990a): Four-year follow-up of twenty-four first episode manic patients. J Affect Disord 19:79–86.

Tohen M, Waternaux CM, Tsuang MT (1990b): Outcome in mania. A 4-year prospective follow-up of 75 patients utilizing survival analysis. Arch Gen Psychiatry 47:1106–1111.

Tsuang MT, Woolson RF, Fleming JA (1979): Long term outcome of major psychosis: I. Schizophrenia and affective disorders compared with psychiatrically symptom-free surgical conditions. Arch Gen Psychiatry 36:1295–1301.

Watkins SE, Callender K, Thoma DR, Tidmarsh SF, Shaw DM (1987): The effect of carbamazepine and lithium on remission from affective illness. Br J Psychiatry 150:180–182.

Weeke A, Vaeth M (1986): Excess mortality of bipolar and unipolar manic–depressive patients. J Affect Disord 11:227–234.

Wehr TA, Goodwin FK (1987): Can antidepressants cause mania and worsen the course of affective illness? Am J Psychiatry 144:1403–1411.

Wehr TA, Sack DA, Rosenthal NE, Cowdry RW (1988): Rapid cycling affective disorder: Contributing factors and treatment responses in 51 cases. Am J Psychiatry 145:179–184.

Weissman MM, Bruce ML, Leaf PJ, Florio LP, Holzer C (1991): Affective disorders. In Robins LN, Regier DA (eds): "Psychiatric Disorders in America: The Epidemiologic Catchment Area Study." New York: Free Press, pp 53–80.

Wertham FI (1929): A group of benign chronic psychoses: Prolonged manic excitements. Am J Psychiatry 9:17–78.

Winokur G (1984): Psychosis in bipolar and unipolar affective illness with special reference to schizo-affective disorder. Br J Psychiatry 145:236–242.

Winokur G, Kadrmas A (1989): A polyepisodic course in bipolar illness: Possible clinical relationships. Compr Psychiatry 30:121–127.

Winokur G, Clayton PJ, Reich T (1969): "Manic–Depressive Illness." St. Louis: CV Mosby.

Zarin DA, Pass TM (1987): Lithium and the single episode. Medical Care 25(Suppl):76–84.

Zis AP, Goodwin FK (1979): Major affective disorder as a recurrent illness: A critical review. Arch Gen Psychiatry 36:835–839.

CHAPTER 15

Pharmacological Treatment of Bipolar Disorder Throughout the Life Cycle

ROSS J. BALDESSARINI, LEONARDO TONDO, TRISHA SUPPES, GIANNI L. FAEDDA, and MAURICIO TOHEN

McLean Hospital, Harvard University, 115 Mill Street, Belmont, MA 02178 (R.J.B., M.T.); Department of Psychiatry, University of Cagliari and Lucio Bini Center for Mood Disorders bp1Research, Cagliari, Sardinia, Italy (L.T.); Department of Psychiatry, Southwestern Medical Center, University of Texas, Dallas, TX 75235 (T.S.); Department of Psychiatry, Albert Einstein College of Medicine, Bronx, NY 10461 (G.L.F.)

The modes of mania are infinite in species, but one alone in genus. If the disease . . . should be seen as relapsing, there will be need of greater remedies . . . Dotage, commencing with old age never intermits, but accompanies the patient until death, while mania intermits, and with care ceases altogether . . . There may be an imperfect intermission, if it . . . is not thoroughly cured by medicine . . . In those periods of life with which much heat and blood are associated, persons are most given to mania, namely, those about puberty, young men, and such as possess general vigour.

—Aretaeus of Cappadocia, ca. 150 AD (Adams, 1856)

INTRODUCTION

Bipolar manic–depressive disorders (type I with mania and type II with hypomania) are major psychiatric syndromes, recognized increasingly commonly over a broad range of the human life-cycle. They present many clinical challenges and therapeutic opportunities that are rapidly advancing (Goodwin and Jamison, 1990). The original concept of manic–depressive insanity included cases of recurrent episodes of depression as well as persons manifesting both mania and depression (Kraepelin, 1921). In the middle of this century, a greater distinction was made between bipolar and unipolar types of manic–depressive disorders (Kleist, 1953; Leonhard, 1957). Currently, in most international conceptualizations, manic–depressive illness includes both bipolar and unipolar major affective disorders, though American psychiatrists tend to treat them

Mood Disorders Across the Life Span, Edited by Shulman, Tohen, and Kutcher
ISBN 0-471-10477-9   © 1996 Wiley-Liss, Inc.

as separate entities (Perris, 1982; Goodwin and Jamison, 1990). The prevalence of bipolar I manic–depressive illness is at least 1% in the general population; lifetime risk approaches 2%, but the total risk of manic–depressive illness is several times higher if bipolar II disorder is added, and exceeds 10% if severe recurrent major depression is included (Kessler et al., 1994). Bipolar and unipolar major affective disorders lead to high rates of intermittent or sustained, and often severe, disability and excess mortality from suicide (Goodwin and Jamison, 1990; Tohen 1991).

In addition to their clinical importance as a source of excess mortality and morbidity, the major mood disorders lead to reduced productivity and represent an extraordinary economic burden on society. Mental disorders and dementia together account for perhaps $260 billion in direct and indirect costs annually in the United States, or about 2.5 times more than cancer and 60% more than cardiovascular diseases. Of this amount, perhaps $30–50 billion per year are accounted for by major affective disorders alone (Greenberg et al., 1993; Rice and Miller, 1994).

Major affective disorders have become increasingly prevalent in psychiatric hospitals in recent decades, rising from about 12% of discharge diagnoses in the early 1970s to over 40% in the 1990s, as the diagnosis of schizophrenia has become much less common (Stoll et al., 1993). Factors contributing to this diagnostic shift probably include improved differential assessment of psychotic disorders, innovations in treatment of mood disorders, and a greater economic impact of chronic psychotic disorders. Even though they are very common medical conditions, major affective disorders are frequently undiagnosed or misdiagnosed and are inadequately treated in the great majority of cases (Goodwin and Jamison, 1990; McCombs et al., 1990; Katon et al., 1992).

Bipolar mood disorders have relatively consistent clinical features, tend to run in families, have high concordance rates in identical twins, and manifest a relatively unique pattern of treatment responses. These and other psychobiological characteristics strongly suggest that they approach the status of a discrete disease rather than a nonspecific syndrome, at least in young adults. Accordingly, hopes for clarification of the genetics, pathophysiology, and etiology of bipolar manic–depressive illness are now unprecedentedly high among investigators, as is reflected in other chapters in this volume. Moreover, their responsiveness to available treatments and relatively favorable course under treatment make them particularly appealing disorders for studies in experimental therapeutics. Adequately treated patients often retain substantial levels of vocational and social functioning and self-sufficiency. Despite these compelling features, there are many gaps in current knowledge of the bipolar manic–depressive disorders, particularly regarding treatment in the pediatric and geriatric age groups.

Most of the available research on experimental therapeutics and clinical pharmacology in bipolar disorders has been conducted in relatively young adult patients, with interest in these syndromes among pediatric and geriatric populations still emerging (Shulman, 1993; Faedda et al., 1995). Indeed, until recently bipolar disorders were considered rare, if even possible, in prepubertal children, though they have been observed rather commonly among adolescents: about one quarter of cases of mania have been first diagnosed in persons below age 20 (Faedda et al., 1995). However, in this young age group, diagnosis is complicated by the need to differentiate bipolar disorders from other affective, psychotic, developmental, neurological, or behavioral syndromes (Carlson et al., 1994; Faedda et al. 1995). In geriatric populations the assessment of new cases of mania is complicated by their emergence secondary to degenerative or other brain disorders (Krauthammer and Klerman, 1978; Shulman, 1993). In both preadolescent and geriatric groups controlled experimental therapeutic studies of mania remain rare (Goodwin and Jamison, 1990; Nemeroff and Schatzberg, 1995). Moreover, the study of bipolar depression has been excluded from most studies of antidepressant therapies in all age groups (Zornberg and Pope, 1993; Baldessarini, 1985, 1996).

TREATMENT WITH LITHIUM SALTS

Lithium salts are relatively specific for the treatment of mania and can improve and stabilize the fundamental mood changes in the disorder (Goodwin and Jamison, 1990; Abou-Saleh, 1992). The first modern report of the antimanic effects of lithium carbonate by John Cade in Melbourne, Australia, in 1949 marked the beginning of the contemporary era of psychopharmacology (Cade, 1949; Johnson, 1984; Baldessarini, 1985).

Early recognition of the antimanic action of lithium salts is sometimes ascribed to nineteenth-century neuropsychiatric physicians in the United States, who used bromide salts as sedatives to control psychotic agitation of various kinds. These physicians believed that lithium bromide might be a superior sedative to other bromide salts (Mitchell, 1870). More specifically, William Hammond initially reported that lithium bromide was superior to other bromides in mania, but he later seemed to doubt this impression (Hammond, 1871, 1883; Yeragani and Gershon, 1986). The modern rediscovery by Cade of the utility of lithium as an antimanic agent was evidently based on his observations of possibly toxic central depressant actions of lithium in laboratory animals (Cade, 1949, 1978). Cade's laboratory studies followed erroneous concepts of nineteenth-century medicine, which included use of lithium salts to dissolve renal calculi and urate deposits in gout, and even considered mania a manifestation of cerebral inflammatory disease possibly related to gout (Ure, 1843; Garrod, 1876; Johnson, 1984).

Cade's observations of beneficial effects of lithium carbonate in mania were extended by European psychiatric investigators after 1950 (Schou et al., 1954; Schou, 1957; Amdisen 1984; Johnson, 1984; Vestergaard, 1992). In American medicine, the psychiatric application of lithium was met with skepticism arising largely from the uncontrolled substitution of lithium compounds for table salt by infirm persons, which resulted in severe intoxication and some deaths and the withdrawal of lithium salts from clinical use (Talbott, 1950). In the late nineteenth and early twentieth centuries, the United States Pharmacopoeia accepted several lithium salts for the treatment of gout, including the carbonate, citrate, and others, and the bromide salt was accepted as a sedative (Wood and LaWall, 1926). The Food and Drug Administration (FDA) did not accept lithium as a psychotropic agent in the United States until 1970, and then only for acute mania in adults. Even now, FDA-approved indications are for mania and prevention of "recurrences" in manic–depressive disorder with mania (bipolar I disorder) in persons above age 12; bipolar and unipolar types of depression are not addressed (Sifton, 1995). However, other respected scientific authorities acknowledge the growing clinical and research support for broader indications for lithium salts, including potentiation of the effects of antidepressants and prevention of recurring depressive and schizoaffective disorders as well as short-term and preventive treatment for both mania and depression in bipolar disorders (Goodwin and Jamison, 1990; Bennett, 1993; Keck et al., 1994).

Lithium salts are currently available in the United States in various commercial formulations (the standard carbonates Eskalith and Lithonate, carbonate in the controlled-release forms Eskalith-CR and Lithobid, the citrate Cibalith, and generic forms of both salts; several other salts are used outside of the United States). Most unit doses are set to provide 8.1 mEq of lithium ion: for example, with 300 mg of the dibasic carbonate (molecular weight = 73.9, with 2 Eq/mol) or one teaspoonful (5 ml) of the tribasic citrate (typically prepared in a dilithium form, of molecular weight = 137, with 2 Eq/mol).

Owing to the relative specificity of lithium therapy for manic–depressive disorders, the neuropharmacology of lithium has attracted interest for leads to the development of innovative antimanic or mood-stabilizing treatments and for clues to the pathophysiology of the idiopathic major mood disorders. However, these hopes have not yet been realized. While much has been learned about the safe and effective application of lithium in manic–depressive disorders, no innovative treatments have been based on the pharmacology of lithium and, indeed, the clinically relevant pharmacodynamic mechanisms of lithium in bipolar disorders remain uncertain. Lithium ion can inhibit neuronal release of brain catecholamines but may also increase synaptic availability of serotonin, at pharmacologically relevant concentrations (Katz and Kopin, 1969; Baldessarini and Vogt, 1988). It also has complex interactions with molecular processes that carry out neurotransmitter and hormone functions. These activities of lithium ion include inhibiting effects mediated by adenylyl cyclase or its associated regulatory G-proteins, inhibiting inositol monophosphatase in the phosphatidylinositol pathway, and altering the function of protein kinases—all of which are crucial in *second-messenger* pathways for intercellular signaling (Avissar and Schreiber, 1992; Jope and Williams, 1994; Manji and Lenox, 1994; Manji et al., 1995). Some of these *receptor–effector* interactions probably contribute to side effects of lithium, including interference with the actions of thyrotropin on the thyroid gland and also with the actions of antidiuretic hormone on the distal nephron. The possible contribution of these interactions to antimanic or mood-stabilizing effects of lithium, however, remains obscure. Compounds that may act as selective inhibitors of inositol phosphatase in brain tissue have been developed, but their clinical potential as lithiumlike agents remains untested (Leysen and Pinder, 1994).

Lithium is an effective monotherapy for mania in adults, and more limited information suggests similar efficacy in pediatric populations, with relatively variable outcomes as also have been encountered in geriatric mania (Table 1). Lithium has outperformed chlorpromazine in some studies of mania in young adults (Prien et al., 1972; Takahashi et al., 1975), though neuroleptic agents and potent sedatives are also effective and act more rapidly against manic agitation (Johnson et al., 1971; Goodwin and Zis, 1979; Garfinkel et al., 1980). The onset of antimanic actions of lithium is slow—typically, 5–10 days. For this reason, and because of the limited margin of safety (therapeutic index) of lithium, many acutely manic, poorly cooperative, and metabolically unstable patients are not treated immediately or primarily with lithium in acute mania (Johnson, 1980; Baldessarini, 1985, 1996a,b; Goodwin and Jamison, 1990; Jefferson and Greist, 1994; Price and Heninger, 1994). Instead, they are treated temporarily with an antipsychotic agent or a sedative, often a high-potency benzodiazepine such as lorazepam or clonazepam (Baldessarini, 1996a,b). Aggressive early dosing with the anticonvulsant valproate may also induce rapid improvement in mania (McElroy et al., 1993). Lithium salts can be safely added in gradually increasing doses as acute manic agitation is brought under control with sedative or antipsychotic agents.

TABLE 1 Trials of Lithium in Acute Mania vs. Age[a]

Age Group	Trials (n)	Years	Subjects (N)	Response Rate (%)	Variance (CV %)
Pediatric	15	1968–1994	203	83.3 ± 24.2	29.1
Adult	7	1954–1972	162	65.4 ± 5.6	8.6
Geriatric	4	1970–1984	134	70.1 ± 17.3	24.7

[a]Pediatric studies employed lithium as the primary antimanic agent; a few permitted supplementation with a neuroleptic. The cases include some adolescents, and diagnostic methods varied from unspecified clinical criteria to use of standard contemporary methods, including RDC and DSM-III criteria. Only four of the 15 trials (33 subjects) involved controlled designs, and the variance between trials (CV, or SD/mean) is high. Data are reanalyzed from Faedda et al. (1995) and references therein.

Adult data are reanalyzed after Goodwin and Zis (1979) and Goodwin and Jamison (1990), and references therein. Three studies used placebo-crossover designs, and four compared lithium to a neuroleptic (usually chlorpromazine). Placebo response is not quantified in two studies, and remarkably high (39–40%) in two others (Stokes et al., 1971; Bowden et al., 1994). The results for neuroleptic alone were surprisingly poor (19.7 ± 0.8% responding in four trials), even though neuroleptics out-performed lithium, at least with respect to nonspecific agitation and hyperactivity in several trials (Johnson et al., 1971; Prien et al., 1972; Shopsin et al., 1975; Takahashi et al., 1975; Garfinkel et al., 1990).

Geriatric data are reanalyzed after four representative reports (van der Velde, 1970; Himmelhoch et al., 1980; Shulman and Post, 1980; Schaffer and Garvey, 1984), none rigorously controlled. Variance (CV) between trials is higher than in the adult and pediatric studies, though the number of studies is small. All mean ± SD response rates are weighted by N subjects per study.

LONG-TERM MAINTENANCE TREATMENT WITH LITHIUM SALTS

Lithium is particularly useful for continuation treatment in the months following clinical recovery from an acute episode of mania or depression in bipolar disorders, to reduce the high risk of early relapse. However, its most important current application is in long-term maintenance treatment, to reduce the risk or severity of future recurrences of mania or bipolar depression in cases with severe or multiple episodes (Johnson, 1980; Goodwin and Jamison, 1990; Jefferson and Greist, 1994; Jefferson and Sen, 1994; Price and Heninger, 1994). The long-term efficacy of lithium monotherapy in bipolar disorders is substantial but hardly complete. Failure rates, as measured by the recurrence of a major affective episode, are typically 20–40% within 2 or 3 years of follow-up, and many adult bipolar disorder patients treated with lithium experience only partial reductions of the severity of recurring episodes (Gelenberg et al., 1989; Vestergaard, 1992; Jefferson and Greist, 1994). Such rates of failure or of unsatisfactory mood stabilization, as a measure of effectiveness of lithium maintenance treatment, are higher in uncontrolled clinical samples, probably owing largely to inconsistent adherence to prescribed treatment (Schou, 1993; Guscott and Taylor, 1994). Nevertheless, the long-term general efficacy of lithium in recurring adult bipolar manic–depressive disorders is well substantiated. There have been at least 15 controlled studies reported since 1970 that compared maintenance treatments of mainly bipolar manic–depressive patients. They indicate that the mean risk of recurrent major affective episodes of either polarity was nearly sixfold lower with lithium than with an inactive placebo, as determined by averaging the ratio of recurrence risks with the alternative treatments for each trial (Table 2).

Relatively unsatisfactory responses to lithium tend to be more common in patients who present with agitated, dysphoric mixed bipolar syndromes, with mania secondary to coarse brain disease, with comorbid substance abuse, and with a rapid-cycling course

TABLE 2   Summary: Controlled Trials of Lithium Against Manic and Depressive Recurrences[a]

Trials (n)	Years	Subjects (N)	Recurrence Rate (%)		Mean Protection Ratio
			Placebo	Lithium	
15	1970–1994	879	81.1 ± 7.1	33.3 ± 3.2	5.66 ± 0.67

[a]Data are reanalyzed after Baldessarini (1985) and Goodwin and Jamison (1990), and references cited therein. The average duration of studies was about 2 years. Computed values are weighted (by N subjects per study) means ± SD from individual studies (assuming a value of 1% as a minimum on lithium to avoid dividing by zero when computing the mean ± SD protection ratio, or proportion relapsing on placebo/lithium); the unweighted mean protection ratio is 9.79-fold, and the ratio of the means is 2.44. Early European studies probably include some patients with unipolar as well as bipolar manic–depressive disorders.

involving four or more major mood disturbances per year (Goodwin and Jamison, 1990; Suppes et al., 1993). In addition, patients presenting with depression before switching to mania may do less well during lithium maintenance treatment than those who present first with mania (Kukopulos et al., 1980; Faedda et al., 1991). Optimal indications for long-term maintenance treatment with lithium or other putative mood-stabilizing agents, and the long-term impact of delaying such treatment remain unclear, and the timing and duration of treatment remain matters of clinical judgment (Zarin and Pass, 1987; Jefferson and Greist, 1994).

Lithium maintenance treatment may be somewhat more effective against manic than depressive phases in adult bipolar disorders, though this point also remains unresolved (Goodwin and Jamison, 1990; Jefferson and Greist, 1994). In contrast to a 6-fold reduction of manic recurrences, the average reduction of risk of bipolar I or II depression by lithium compared to a placebo was less than 4-fold among 10 studies, and only 3.5-fold in 7 studies yielding relatively high rates of depression with a placebo (Table 3). Some of this difference may reflect a greater risk of early recurrence of mania (62%) over depression (37%) after treatment was interrupted to initiate a placebo phase of follow-up (Table 3), as is discussed in the next section (Suppes et al., 1991, 1993). Interestingly, the absolute mean recurrence risk during maintenance treatment with lithium was about the same for depression as for mania (19%) thus confounding the interpretation of the ratios just cited (Table 3).

Use of an antidepressant without lithium or another mood-stabilizing agent in bipolar disorder may induce an excess of mania or an unstable course with rapid-cycling. Though this phenomenon is commonly encountered and widely accepted clinically (Bunney et al., 1977; Kukopulos et al., 1983; Jefferson and Greist, 1994), research to quantify the antidepressant-associated versus spontaneous risk of manic or unstable mood remains limited and inconsistent (Lewis and Winokur, 1982; Prien et al., 1984; Baldessarini, 1985, 1996; Wehr and Goodwin, 1987; Goodwin and Jamison, 1990). It is also not clear whether the apparent risk differs appreciably between classes of antidepressants. There is some evidence that the short-acting and relatively mild stimulantlike antidepressant, bupropion, perhaps monoamine oxidase (MAO) inhibitors and some serotonin reuptake inhibitor (SRI) antidepressants, may carry somewhat less risk of inducing mania than tricylic-type antidepressants (Goodwin and Jamison, 1990; Sachs et al., 1994; Stoll et al., 1994). However, this impression is not secure, and the risk of stimulants, mixed norepinephrine- and serotonin-potentiating agents, and the newer reversible MAO inhibitors compared to other antidepressants is unclear

TABLE 3   Efficacy of Lithium Against Bipolar Mania vs. Depression[a]

Trials (n)	Years	Subjects (N)	Recurrence Rate (%)		Mean Protection Ratio
			Placebo	Lithium	
Mania					
7	1970–1994	702	61.6 ± 12.4	19.3 ± 3.4	5.72 ± 0.95
Depression					
10	1970–1994	766	36.9 ± 3.1	19.4 ± 1.9	3.87 ± 0.50

[a]Data are reanalyzed after Baldessarini (1985, 1996) and Goodwin and Jamison (1990), and references cited therein. The duration of studies averaged about 1.5 years. Computed values are weighted (by N subjects per study) means ± SD from individual studies (protection ratios ± SD, or the proportion relapsing on placebo/lithium, are computed assuming a value of 1% as a minimum on lithium to avoid dividing by zero). The mean protection ratio is 1.5-fold greater for mania ($t = 3.5, p < 0.005$). The protective effect of lithium against mania as the ratio of weighted means is 3.19; for depression (including three studies of bipolar II disorder), the ratio of means is 1.90. While the apparent protection against mania was thus 1.48 to 1.68 times greater than against bipolar depression, note that the mean risk of depression on placebo was 1.67 times lower than for mania, and that the overall mean risks of mania and depression on lithium are virtually identical. If only studies ($n = 7$) with ≥40% risk of bipolar I or II depression during placebo maintenance are considered, the apparent depression-sparing efficacy ratio of lithium vs. placebo averaged only 3.53 ± 0.65, with weighted mean recurrence risks of 51.1 ± 3.4% with placebo vs. 34.1 ± 2.4% with lithium (1.50-fold ratio of weighted means; $t = 11, p < 0.001$).

(Potter et al., 1982; Fogelson et al., 1992). In addition, electroconvulsive therapy (ECT) may carry a particularly low risk of inducing mania or rapid mood cycling, though the interpretation of this proposal in view of the efficacy of ECT for mania as well as depression is not clear (Kukopulos et al., 1980; Mukherhjee et al., 1994).

The optimally safe and effective clinical management of bipolar depression remains unsatisfactory and under-investigated (Zornberg and Pope, 1993; Baldessarini, 1996). Improved treatment of bipolar depression is a matter of both public health concern, since it accounts for a large proportion of morbidity and disability in bipolar disorders, and of great urgency since it is the most common mental state associated with an extraordinarily high long-term risk of suicide, approaching 15% of cases (Goodwin and Jamison 1990; Tondo et al., 1996). Lithium may enhance responses to antidepressants in nonbipolar depression, including cases of apparent antidepressant unresponsiveness or tolerance (Austin et al., 1991; Souza and Goodwin, 1991; Zornberg and Pope, 1993; Jefferson and Greist, 1994; Baldessarini, 1996). Despite their wide clinical acceptance, applications of lithium in conditions other than acute mania or prevention of recurrences of mania and depression in bipolar I disorder, and perhaps depression in bipolar II disorder, can be considered quasi-investigational (Sifton, 1995).

DOSING OF LITHIUM

Decades of clinical experience indicate that "trough" levels (daily minimum serum or plasma concentrations of lithium at about 12 hours after the last dose) between 0.5 and 1.5 mEq/L cover or exceed the therapeutic range, and concentrations of about 0.6–1.0 mEq/L (usually attained by daily doses ranging from 600 to 1,200 mg, or sometimes at 300–2,400 mg) are widely accepted as effective and tolerable for long-term use in medically healthy adults (Baldessarini, 1985; Jefferson and Greist, 1994).

Routine monitoring of blood concentrations of lithium ion was introduced mainly to provide protection from overdosing with this potentially highly toxic agent. Lithium has an unusually limited margin of safety or therapeutic index, as reflected in a ratio of only about 3 or 4 between nominally therapeutic to potentially intoxicating levels. Serum concentrations below 0.6 mEq/L are less effective. Levels above 1.0 mEq/L probably provide limited additional benefit but increase side effects. Therefore, they are usually reserved for acute mania, and perhaps a rapid-cycling course or otherwise treatment-resistant cases (Amdisen, 1980). In addition, dosing with lithium needs to be more cautious in the elderly owing mainly to poor tolerability and age-related loss of efficiency in eliminating lithium (Nilsson and Axelsson, 1989).

Preliminary observations with nuclear magnetic spectroscopy indicate that levels of lithium in human brain tissue are closely correlated with plasma concentrations, and average about 60% of clinically assayed serum levels at about 12 hours after the last daily dose (Plenge et al., 1994; Baldessarini, 1996b). This technique has also shown that peak brain concentrations of lithium lag only slightly behind those in serum and that the rate of elimination of this cation from human brain tissue is about 75% slower than from plasma. The plasma half-life of lithium in humans averages about 16–22 hours in medically healthy young adult patients but can vary widely between subjects from perhaps 12 to 120 hours. Half-life may increase with years of continuous use and can rise to 30–40 hours above age 60 (Lehman and Merten, 1974; Amdisen, 1980; Vestergaard and Schou, 1984; Nilsson and Axelsson, 1989). Given that its clearance from the brain is appreciably slower than from blood, it is conceivable that lithium may accumulate in brain tissue, perhaps contributing to the risk of cerebral intoxication, especially in the elderly. However, even relatively slow removal from brain tissue may not be sufficient to provide adequate prophylaxis by dosing with lithium every other day (Jensen et al., 1995).

There have been few well-controlled, prospective, randomized, long-term dose–effect studies with lithium, and dose–effect information concerning most other proposed mood-stabilizing agents is even more limited (Baldessarini, 1996a,b). Most investigations of lithium dosage have involved reassignment of previously stabilized bipolar manic–depressive and unipolar depressive patients to lower plasma concentrations of lithium. An early study failed to detect significant differences in recurrence risk over a year after random assignment of unipolar and bipolar manic–depressive patients to plasma lithium levels in a highly restricted range averaging 0.5, 0.6, or 0.7 mEq/L (Jerram and McDonald, 1978). There also was little difference in results of a 1-year trial with manic and depressed patients randomly reassigned to reduced plasma lithium levels between 0.5 and 0.7 mEq/L (Coppen et al., 1983). A third similar study found a clear difference in recurrence risk in manic and depressed patients followed for a year at reassigned serum lithium concentrations averaging 0.6 or 0.3 mEq/L, with a 3.75-fold higher recurrence rate with the lower dose: 61.5 versus 16.4% (Hullin, 1980). Moreover, in a blind crossover trial there were five times more recurrences of bipolar episodes in patients reassigned abruptly to relatively low versus high plasma levels of lithium for 6-month periods: 34.5 versus 6.9% at 0.5 versus 1.0 mEq/L (Waters et al., 1982). A well-designed study used prospective double-blind follow-up for 2 years after random assignment of newly recovering bipolar disorder patients to one of several lithium blood levels ranging from 0.35 to 0.85 mEq/L, following initial stabilization by lithium (Maj et al., 1986). There was a progressive gain of benefit (fewer days ill per year) as the blood level rose from about 0.4 to 0.7 mEq/L, with little further gain at higher levels. Side effects, as indicated by the severity of polyuria and tremor increased to parallel gains in benefit but appeared to continue to rise with blood levels above 0.7 mEq/L. These studies suggest that circulating lithium levels of 0.6–0.8 mEq/L are adequate and tolerable for many patients, that lower levels probably provide inferior efficacy, and that higher levels may offer little additional gain in mood stabilization, while probably increasing side effects.

A recent controlled study of lithium dosing in bipolar disorder patients raises a potentially important point about both the design and interpretation of long-term therapeutic trials (Gelenberg et al., 1989). It involved rapidly reassigned outpatients previously stabilized on lithium, to serum concentrations averaging either 0.5 or 0.8 mEq/L in up to 3 years of double-blind follow-up. The results indicated a threefold higher crude risk of a recurrence of mania or depression with lower lithium levels (38 vs. 13%). However, interpretation of these findings may be complicated by the association of a disproportionate risk among those changed rapidly from a relatively high to a low serum concentration. This effect does not seem to represent a confounding of lithium dose with severity or frequency of previous illness, but it does appear to be consistent with a phenomenon of excess risk associated with withdrawal of lithium (Rosenbaum et al., 1992; Suppes et al., 1993). A comparable effect may obtain in another similarly designed study (Waters et al., 1982).

A final question pertaining to lithium dosing is whether it is advantageous and safe to dose with an entire daily dose of lithium at one time for both convenience and better compliance with prescribed long-term treatment. Based on both animal experimentation and inconsistent clinical data, it has been suggested that dosing with ordinary lithium carbonate once daily to increase the ratio of peak-to-trough plasma concentrations of lithium may reduce renal side effects, particularly polyuria and nocturia, and perhaps other subjective side effects (Hetmar et al., 1991). In six clinical studies involving a total of 316 patients, the mean difference in 24-hour urine volume at once-daily versus divided daily dosing of lithium (at a similar mean serum level of 0.8 mEq/L) was small [ca. 8%: 2.26 ± 0.03 vs. 2.45 ± 0.03 liters ($\pm$SD); Baldessarini, unpublished]. Given this evidence of limited protection from polyuria, the limited risk of irreversible nephrotoxicity, and the narrow margin of safety, once-daily dosing of lithium cannot be recommended as a routine practice, though it may be feasible in selected patients who find the approach tolerable, and has even been used safely at moderate doses in elderly manic patients.

RISKS OF DISCONTINUING LITHIUM

Many patients and physicians are reluctant to continue maintenance mood-stabilizing regimens indefinitely, even after several major episodic recurrences. Frequent reasons for stopping lithium include prolonged periods of doing well, intolerance of side effects, or pregnancy. However, discontinuing lithium, and perhaps even sharply reducing the dose, appears to be associated with a high risk of early recurrence (Small et al., 1971; Wilkinson, 1979; Lapierre et al., 1980; Klein et al., 1981; Waters et al., 1982; Suppes et al., 1991, 1993; Rosenbaum et al., 1992; Faedda et al., 1993). Rates of 50% within 5 months were observed, even in 124 bipolar I disorder patients who had been euthymic for several years on lithium maintenance treatment (Suppes et al., 1991). The risk of a recurrence of mania was about three times that for depression in bipolar I cases within the first 12 months after interrupting lithium therapy (60 vs. 22%); a 25% risk was attained in 2.7 months for mania and 14.0 months for depression (Suppes et al.,

1991). Risk of recurrence of depression in bipolar II patients within 1 year of rapid withdrawal from previously successful maintenance with lithium monotherapy was 45% in 12 months, or more than twice that of bipolar I patients but similar to their risk for mania (Table 4; Faedda et al., 1993; Suppes et al., 1993). The polarity of the first recurring episode after stopping treatment may be predictable: it was the same as the first lifetime episode of mania or depression in more than 80% of cases in one series (Faedda et al., 1993).

There is some anecdotal evidence that a minority of bipolar disorders patients may become relatively treatment resistant following interruption of successful lithium maintenance therapy (Post et al., 1992, 1993; Bauer, 1994; Maj et al., 1995). However, the frequency of such an effect, its relationship to discontinued treatment, and its clinical implications remain uncertain.

These early recurrence risks following discontinuation of lithium appear to be much higher than predicted from knowledge of the natural history of untreated manic–depressive disorders, and assuming that reasons for stopping treatment in the preceding studies did not include subtle prodromal hypomanic denial of illness or depressive discouragement with treatment (Faedda et al., 1993; Suppes et al., 1993). Spontaneous cycling in untreated bipolar disorders averages about one episode per year over many years of follow-up, though the interval may be longer early in the life history and decrease with progression of the illness (Zis and Goodwin, 1979; Roy-Byrne et al., 1985; Angst, 1986). Support for the view that recurrence risk shortly following removal of lithium maintenance is excessive arises from considering the experience of a small series of bipolar I patients with well-documented histories (Suppes et al., 1991, 1993). Their shortest time between major affective episodes prior to lithium maintenance treatment averaged 11.6 ± 6.3 months. After interrupting lithium treatment that had been successful for an average of 3.6 years, the interval to a new episode of acute illness was only 1.78 ± 2.10 months, or nearly sevenfold less than the shortest spontaneous interval.

In addition to recurrences of major affective episodes, the risk of suicidal behavior may increase after interruption of lithium maintenance treatment, even when the

TABLE 4   One-year Recurrence Risk after Abrupt vs. Gradual Discontinuation of Lithium in Bipolar Disorders[a]

| | Recurrence Rate (%) | | |
	Abrupt	Gradual	Risk Ratio
Bipolar-I			
Mania	47.8	20.0	2.4
Depression	30.4	0.0	>30
All episodes	78.3	20.0	3.9
Bipolar-II			
Depression	45.5	20.0	2.3
All Cases			
Any recurrence	67.6	20.0	3.4

[a]Data are adapted from Faedda et al. (1993) and Suppes et al. (1993); $N = 38$ bipolar I and 26 bipolar II cases discontinued from 3.6 years of successful lithium monotherapy, usually electively and not in an impending episode, over 1–14 (abrupt) vs. 15–30 (gradual) days. In addition, the overall latency to 25% risk of a new episode after stopping lithium was 8 months after abrupt, and 37 months after gradual discontinuation of lithium (a highly significant 4.6-fold difference).

treatment has had an unsatisfactory effect on mood (Müller-Oerlinghausen et al., 1992; Suppes et al., 1993). The risk of life-threatening (parasuicidal) or fatal suicidal behaviors in bipolar I or II patients following discontinuation of lithium maintenance treatment that had lasted for nearly 6 years was compared with the risk found before and during lithium maintenance treatment. The risk within 12 months after stopping lithium was not only more than 10 times greater than during lithium treatment but also severalfold greater than the risk of suicidal behaviors prior to initiating lithium maintenance therapy. There was some predictability of these dangerous behaviors, since nearly all instances of self-injury or suicide (92%) were associated with recurrences of bipolar depression or less common dysphoric mixed-mood states (Baldessarini et al., 1996; Tondo et al., 1996).

There is preliminary evidence that slowing the rate of discontinuing lithium may reduce the risk of early recurrences in bipolar disorders, and that a similar effect may accompany the discontinuation of other maintenance psychotropic treatments (Suppes et al., 1993; Baldessarini and Viguera, 1995; Viguera et al., 1996). Thus, following discontinuation over 2–4 weeks versus shorter periods, the risk of mania within 1 year was reduced by 2.4-fold (48 vs. 20%), and the risk of bipolar I depression was reduced from 29% to nil, while that in bipolar II disorder fell by more than twofold (45 vs. 20%; Table 4; Faedda et al., 1993; Suppes et al., 1993). It is not known whether suicidal risk is decreased by gradual discontinuation of lithium or whether other antimanic or alternative mood-stabilizing agents also might protect against excessive risk of illness following rapid discontinuation of lithium. However, since suicidal behavior was strongly associated with recurrence of depression, it is reasonable and prudent to expect a reduction of suicidal risk with slowed discontinuation of maintenance treatment if it does lower risk of early recurrence of mood disorder.

In addition to the clear clinical significance of the effects of abruptly interrupting maintenance treatment with lithium and other psychotropic agents, there may also be some implications concerning the ethics, organization, cost, and interpretation of experimental therapeutic protocols designed to test continuation or maintenance treatments. The great majority of reported studies of this kind involve a period of active treatment of acute illness followed by varying periods of stabilization prior to randomly assigning patients to contrasting treatment options. Most commonly, these options include continuation of active drug at full or reduced dose versus blind assignment to an inactive placebo. The findings just summarized, and others, strongly suggest that such interventions may lead to unnaturally increased contrasts between continued and interrupted treatment. That is, stopping maintenance treatment is evidently not identical to no treatment at all but instead may carry iatrogenic-pharmacologic risks above those associated with the natural history of untreated illness (Suppes et al., 1994; Baldessarini and Viguera, 1995; Baldessarini et al., 1996; Viguera et al., 1996). The implications and the management of this potentially confounding phenomenon require further critical evaluation. One plausible but inconveniently prolonged means of limiting excess risk of early recurrences may be to provide at least several months of stabilization followed by gradual reduction or withdrawal of medication, perhaps over another month or more, as a prelude to reassigning treatment and further follow-up (Prien and Kupfer, 1986; Faedda et al., 1993; Suppes et al., 1993).

Finally, even if the apparent association of treatment discontinuation and early recurrence of bipolar illness is confounded by risk factors such as a severe past history or the subtle emergence of prodromal mood changes, the predictive power of the association would still be important for management of clinical care and research protocols.

SIDE EFFECTS OF LITHIUM

Characteristic side effects of lithium include frequent initial polyuria and thirst in up to half of patients starting lithium treatment (Goodwin and Jamison, 1990). Noticeably sustained elevation of 24-hour urine volume has been reported in perhaps 20% of patients after prolonged lithium treatment. Less often, severe and persistent, but reversible nephrogenic diabetes insipidus arises during maintenance treatment in association with elevated circulating levels of antidiuretic hormone and unresponsiveness to exogenous synthetic antidiuretic peptides (Boton et al., 1987). Very high 24-hour urine volumes (5 liters or more) have been associated with elevated risk of histopathological changes in renal biopsies indicative of chronic granulomatous inflammation with anatomical distortion of the nephrons (Rafaelsen et al., 1979; Boton et al., 1987). Nevertheless, irreversible renal insufficiency due to lithium treatment is rare and is sensitively and simply detected by quarterly monitoring of serum creatinine concentration (Hetmar et al., 1991; Povlsen et al., 1992; Gitlin, 1993; Walker, 1993).

In less than 10% of cases, lithium leads to benign, diffuse, and reversible enlargement of the thyroid. Elevated circulating levels of thyrotropin are a sensitive early indication of potential thyroid dysfunction found in perhaps 15–20% of patients on long-term lithium treatment, but clinically symptomatic or even chemical hypothyroidism is not common (Lazarus, 1986; Jefferson and Greist, 1994). On the other hand, even moderate decreases in thyroid hormone levels sometimes are associated with poor clinical response to lithium treatment, including persisting depression (Goodwin and Jamison, 1990).

Subtle cognitive or motor impairment, including resting tremor and impaired manual dexterity or handwriting, as well as weight gain or skin disorders (acne, worsening of psoriasis, mild alopecia) are common clinical problems that often lead to refusal of lithium (Gitlin et al., 1989). Though cognitive impairment is not easily verified clinically, it can be documented by careful neuropsychological assessment (Kocsis et al., 1993). Varying degrees of mental confusion or delirium can occur even when trough plasma concentrations are in the nominally therapeutic range, particularly in elderly or neurologically impaired patients.

In the past, there was some concern that lithium may interact with certain neuroleptic agents, particularly haloperidol, to produce severe and irreversible central neurotoxicity (Cohen and Cohen, 1974). Evidence for a specific neurotoxic interaction of lithium with haloperidol or other neuroleptics is unconvincing and many patients have been treated safely with such combinations (Baastrup et al., 1976; Jefferson and Greist, 1980). Nevertheless, sporadic case reports suggestive of such an interaction still arise, and warnings concerning it remain in place in pharmaceutical information statements (Sifton, 1995). It is prudent to apply particularly close clinical monitoring, and special caution in elderly or demented patients, when lithium is combined with antipsychotics, benzodiazepines, or other central depressants, and also antidepressants including MAO inhibitors and other serotonin-potentiating agents. Moreover, overdoses of lithium and occasional reactions to neuroleptics alone can induce severe, persistent, or even fatal neurotoxic states. Sometimes those following severe overdoses of lithium alone resemble the *neuroleptic malignant syndrome* with varying combinations of catatonia, elevated serum creatine kinase, fever, confusion, stupor, and unstable vital signs with some fatalities (Talbott, 1950; Pearlman, 1986; Rosebush et al., 1989; Sternbach, 1991; Rosenburg and Green, 1989). Elements of the so-called serotonin syndrome may also arise with acute overdoses of lithium marked by restlessness, myoclonus, hyperreflexia, rigidity, elevated serum creatine kinase, seizures, fever, sweating, shivering, and tremor. This reaction is commonly associated with combinations of an SRI antidepressant with an MAO inhibitor, and possibly related catastrophic toxic interactions also occur between MAO inhibitors and phenylpiperidine analgesics (especially meperidine) or a tricyclic antidepressant (Sternbach, 1991; Nierenberg and Semprebon, 1993).

Other interactions of drugs with lithium include elevations of plasma concentrations of lithium to toxic levels with diuretics (particularly thiazides), nonsteroidal anti-inflammatory agents including indomethacin and perhaps aspirin and ibuprofen, the antiprotozoal agent metronidazole, and angiotensin-converting enzyme (ACE) inhibitors, including captopril (Johnson, 1986; Sifton, 1994). In addition, calcium channel blockers such as verapamil can interact with lithium to induce a severe neurotoxic state of uncertain mechanism.

A greatly elevated risk of major fetal cardiovascular malformations was suspected in the use of lithium during the first trimester of pregnancy, particularly of Ebstein's tricuspid valve malformations with variable septal defects. The proposed association, based mainly on reports to an international lithium registry (Warkany, 1988; Cohen et al., 1994), has been interpreted as a basis for avoiding pregnancy or terminating lithium treatment during or before pregnancy. However, the teratogenic risk of lithium probably has been exaggerated. Recent controlled epidemiological evidence suggests that the risk of Ebstein's malformation may rise from a spontaneous base rate of about 1/20,000 live births to perhaps one in several thousand (Warkany 1988; Cohen et al., 1994). This risk needs to be balanced against the substantial risk of a major recurrence of bipolar disorder itself, particularly within the several months after rapid removal of lithium (Suppes et al., 1993; Cohen et al., 1994).

The long-term efficacy of most alternatives to lithium is not well studied, and switching to an alternative form of pharmacological management during pregnancy may not be safe, as is discussed in the next section. For example, the antimanic anticonvulsants valproate and carbamazepine probably have even greater teratogenic risks than lithium (Robert and Guibaud, 1982; Rosa, 1991). While these antimanic anticonvulsants are not safe during pregnancy, cautious use of neuroleptics or antidepressants in low doses can be used when necessary; ECT is also considered safe and effective for both mania or depression during pregnancy (Remick and Maurice, 1988; Black et al., 1987; Schnur et al., 1992).

ALTERNATIVE ANTIMANIC OR MOOD-STABILIZING TREATMENTS

Lithium salts remain the cornerstone of rational long-term medical management of bipolar disorder patients. Nevertheless, adjuncts or alternatives are needed in view of the frequently incomplete efficacy of lithium, its variable acceptability to patients due to social stigma or to its substantial side effects, and potentially severe neurotoxicity with an overdose. The use of several alternatives has been reported in both controlled and uncontrolled applications in acute mania, and also in largely uncontrolled or only partially controlled long-term clinical trials (Prien and Gelenberg, 1989; Goodwin and Jamison, 1990; Chou, 1991; Vanelle et al., 1994; Delgado and Gelenberg, 1996).

Innovative options in common clinical use include treatment with antimanic anticonvulsant agents useful in temporal lobe or *psychomotor* epilepsy as well as other types of seizure disorders. Despite the widening clinical psychiatric application of anticonvulsants and additional drugs licensed for conditions other than bipolar disorders, the research evidence supporting these therapeutic alternatives remains very limited (Prien and Gelenberg, 1989; Chou, 1991; Delgado and Gelenberg, 1996; Table 5). Available options include the long-term use of neuroleptics, atypical antipsychotic agents, anticonvulsants, potent sedatives, or antihypertensive drugs as possible mood-stabilizing agents. Most of these agents appear to be effective in acute mania but their long-term mood-stabilizing effects and their efficacy in bipolar depression remain poorly established.

There is a tendency to add these drugs to lithium (*polypharmacy*) in response to the commonly encountered imperfect responsiveness of many cases of bipolar illness to lithium monotherapy. Despite the understandable inclination to try various plausible options for treatment-unresponsive patients, the efficacy and safety of most combination treatments in bipolar disorders lack systematic assessment. In addition, it is not clear whether *intermittent* application of antidepressants or neuroleptics may instead contribute to long-term instability of mood.

Carbamazepine

Carbamazepine (Tegretol) is one of the most frequently prescribed of all anticonvulsants internationally. This tricyclic iminostilbene, like other structurally dissimilar anti-

---

TABLE 5   Possible Treatment Alternatives to Lithium in Bipolar Disorder

- Anticonvulsants
    Carbamazepine: effective acutely and probably long-term; lowers levels of other drugs; may be teratogenic.
    Valproate: effective acutely and probably long-term; limited drug-interactions; risk of spina bifida and liver damage.
- Antipsychotic agents
    Typical neuroleptics: effective acutely; commonly used long-term or intermittently despite limited research; elevated tardive dyskinesia risk.
    Atypical antipsychotics: only clozapine evaluated, in limited uncontrolled trials.
- Sedative-anxiolytics
    Clonazepam: effective short-term, possibly useful intermittent adjunct; untested long-term.
    Lorazepam: effective short-term, may have less intoxication risk, possibly useful intermittent adjunct; untested long-term.
- Antihypertension agents
    Calcium antagonists: some evidence of limited antimanic activity of verapamil; can raise lithium levels.
    Clonidine: limited antimanic effect with rapid tolerance.
    Angiotensin-converting enzyme (ACE) inhibitors: little evidence of efficacy; neurotoxic with lithium.
- Miscellaneous
    Thyroid hormone: may stabilize rapid-cycling or limit anergic depression.
    L-Tryptophan: possible mildly antimanic, limited research; impure samples toxic; can be toxic with serotonin reuptake inhibitors.

convulsants, is believed to interfere with the membrane transport of sodium and perhaps other cations, and shows cross tolerance (loss of similar pharmacological actions with repeated exposure to either agent) with valproate, suggesting that both agents share some actions. Like lithium, carbamazepine may also have an antagonistic effect against neuronal release of norepinephrine. Despite its superficial structural resemblance to imipramine, carbamazepine has little pharmacological similarity to the tricyclic antidepressants and, specifically, has little or no interaction with monoamine transporters. Carbamazepine undergoes a complex metabolism and has an elimination half-life averaging about 15 hours (Kravitz and Fawcett, 1987; Post et al., 1992). This mood-altering anticonvulsant is widely used for the treatment of manic–depressive disorders at blood concentrations of 6–12 μg/mL (25–50 μM; molecular weight = 236), commonly achieved at daily doses of 400–1,200 mg. Such drug doses and serum concentrations follow those employed in epilepsy, though dose–effect relationships have not been tested systematically in psychiatric patients.

Carbamazepine has been used relatively extensively in the treatment of mania or other acute excited psychotic states and also for the prevention of recurrences in manic–depressive disorders (Ballenger and Post, 1980; Klein et al., 1984). It is effective in acute mania, even for patients who may have responded poorly to lithium (Klein et al., 1984; Emrich et al., 1985; Post et al., 1987; Small et al., 1991). Its prophylactic efficacy has received support from uncontrolled case experience (Kravitz and Fawcett, 1987), a few long-term comparisons with lithium (Table 6), and at least one placebo-controlled trial carried out for one year (Okuma et al., 1981). Several of the controlled studies are limited in size and duration of follow-up; about half include patients with various diagnoses in addition to bipolar disorders, and their control of exposure to other treatments is incomplete (Prien and Gelenberg, 1989; Baldessarini, 1996b).

There is some largely anecdotal evidence that carbamazepine may be effective in severely ill patients who respond poorly to lithium, including those with prominent psychotic or mixed agitated–dysphoric episodes of bipolar or schizoaffective illnesses, or rapidly cycling bipolar disorders (Strömgren and Boller, 1985; Post et al., 1990). In addition, carbamazepine, like lithium, may have useful protective effects against both depression and mania in manic–depressive disorders (Schaffer et al., 1985; Post et al., 1986). It has been associated with mood-elevating effects and even the induction of mania in a few cases (Post et al., 1986; Faedda et al., 1995). Despite its widespread empirical application, the long-term efficacy of carbamazepine as a monotherapy may

TABLE 6 Carbamazepine Maintenance Therapy in Adult Major Mood Disorders[a]

Trials		Subjects	Dropouts	Duration	Failure Rate (%)	
(n)	Years	(N)	(%)	(mo)	Carbamazepine	Lithium
7	1984–1992	382	28.9 ± 1.9	23.5 ± 4.6	45.5 ± 4.6	44.1 ± 4.1

[a]Data are mean ± SD values from seven trials; four involved unipolar and psychotic, as well as bipolar patients; many were also given neuroleptic, antidepressant, or other medications, as well as varying doses of carbamazepine. Failures represent a major recurrence during follow-up. Data are adapted from Baldessarini (1996) and Goodwin and Jamison (1990), and references cited therein. In addition to these comparisons with lithium and to several open or retrospective trials, Ballenger and Post (1980) carried out a blinded crossover trial of several weeks between carbamazepine and placebo in six patients with major affective or schizoaffective disorders allowing other treatments, with favorable results in 50% of cases during the anticonvulsant phase. Also, Okuma et al. (1981) compared the drug with placebo in 24 bipolar patients followed (25% dropped-out) under double-blind conditions for 12 months, with 30 and 56% failure rates with carbamazepine and placebo, respectively.

be limited: loss of effectiveness (tolerance, as well as falling blood levels) may emerge, and its acceptability by patients does not seem to represent a consistent improvement over lithium (Prien and Gelenberg, 1989; Post et al., 1990; Chou, 1991; Small et al., 1991; Denikoff et al., 1994; Price and Heninger, 1994).

Relatively common side effects of carbamazepine include excessive sedation, confusion, nausea, rashes, and blood dyscrasias including mild leukopenia, and very rare agranulocytosis or aplastic anemia in fewer than 1/100,000 cases (Zajecka, 1993; Tohen et al., 1995a). A further similarity to tricyclic antidepressants is that carbamazepine also has some potential to depress cardiac condition (Kasarskis et al., 1992; Labrecque et al., 1992). In addition, carbamazepine increases its own metabolism and interacts significantly with many other drugs (Callahan et al., 1993; Goff and Baldessarini, 1993; Zajecka, 1993; Anderson and Graves, 1994; Delgado and Gelenberg, 1996). Such interactions can reduce circulating concentrations of antidepressants, neuroleptics, anticoagulants, and contraceptive steroids, by inducing their hepatic oxidative metabolism; in turn, some SRI antidepressants and perhaps verapamil and valproic acid can increase circulating concentrations of unbound carbamazepine, and valproate can increase production of a potentially toxic metabolite carbamazepine-epoxide. Carbamazepine has also induced hypertensive or other toxic reactions when mixed with an MAO inhibitor. Carbamazepine may be teratogenic and has been associated with a fetal alcohol-like dysmorphic syndrome in the newborn, and somewhat increased risk of spina bifida and developmental delay (Rosa, 1991).

Valproate

Another commonly used anticonvulsant, valproic acid or sodium valproate (dipropylacetic acid) is also employed in the treatment of bipolar disorder as an adjunct or alternative to lithium (Pope et al., 1991; Emrich and Wolf, 1992; McElroy et al, 1992; Joffe, 1993; Balfour and Bryson, 1994; Bowden et al., 1994). It has also been used in combination with carbamazepine and clozapine (Kando et al., 1994; Centorrino et al., 1994; Tohen et al., 1994a). This branched-chain fatty acid is proposed to act as an agonist of the brain's key inhibitory neurotransmitter γ-aminobutyric acid (GABA), and it also shares with other anticonvulsants some ability to inhibit the neuronal membrane transport of sodium and other cations. Valproate is available as valproic acid itself (Depakene), its possibly better-tolerated enteric-coated monosodium salt divalproex sodium (Depakote, prepared as a mixture with valproic acid in equal parts), and the amide derivative valpromide (dipropylacetamide, not available in the United States). Valproate has a short plasma elimination half-life of about 12 hours and complex metabolism, which may include potentially hepatotoxic oxidized products (Balfour and Bryson, 1994).

Valproate has been convincingly demonstrated to be effective in acute mania in doses producing plasma concentrations of 50–100 μg/mL (300–700 μM; molecular weight = 143), usually attained at daily doses of 750–2,000 mg, as are employed in the treatment of epilepsy (Table 7). If side effects are tolerated, rapidly administered "loading" doses of valproate (ca. 20 mg/kg body wt.) aimed at providing similar plasma concentrations may have a particularly rapid antimanic action like that of neuroleptics or potent sedatives (McElroy et al., 1993). Valproate is increasingly employed for maintenance treatment in major or psychotic affective disorders, particularly in patients who are intolerant or unresponsive to lithium. Nevertheless, its long-term prophylactic efficacy as a monotherapy against recurrences of bipolar episodes, to date, has been evaluated

TABLE 7   Controlled Trials of Valproate in Adult Mania[a]

Trials (n)	Years	Subjects (N)	Response Rate (%)		
			Valproate	Standard	Placebo
4	1985–1994	217	59.6	58.0	39.0

[a]Data are from Emrich et al. (1985), Pope et al. (1991), Freeman et al. (1992), and Bowden et al. (1994). All studies used lithium as the standard treatment except that Emrich used carbamazepine and its analog, oxcarbamazepine. The remarkably high placebo response rate was found by Bowden et al. (1994).

only in uncontrolled trials, which have provided encouraging observations (Calabrese et al., 1993; Schaff et al, 1993; Balfour and Bryson, 1994; Calabrese and Woyshville, 1994). Controlled long-term trials are in progress, and it remains to be clarified specifically whether valproate benefits recurrences of bipolar depression as well as mania.

Valproate can induce nausea, vomiting, and other gastrointestinal symptoms, headache, excessive sedation, tremor, rashes, hair loss, and usually benign abnormalities of liver function tests in perhaps a third of cases (Zajecka, 1993). There have also been rare (1/10,000 to 1/50,000 cases) instances of lethal hepatic toxicity associated with valproate monotherapy (Dreifuss et al., 1987). The risk appears to be particularly elevated in children under age 10 receiving multiple anticonvulsants and may fall with adolescence (Rettie et al., 1987). Interactions with hepatic oxidase-inducing anticonvulsants such as carbamazepine or phenytoin may facilitate the conversion of valproate to hepatotoxic metabolites (Rettie et al., 1987; Balfour and Bryson, 1994), although the combination has been used with apparent safety in small numbers of bipolar disorder patients (Tohen et al., 1994a). Valproate, like lithium, carbamazepine, neuroleptics, and tricyclic antidepressants, is associated with weight gain during its long-term use. Valproate has also been associated with an excess of several fetal malformations, including minor anomalies and cardiac malformations, and also a high risk of spina bifida of more than 1% of newborns of epileptic mothers (Robert and Guibaud, 1982; Thisted and Ebbesen, 1993). In contrast to carbamazepine, valproate has been associated with a very low incidence of blood dyscrasias (Tohen et al., 1995a).

Unlike most older anticonvulsants, valproate does not induce the metabolic clearance of other agents and, in contrast to carbamazepine, by competing for hepatic oxidative pathways, may even raise serum levels of some other drugs moderately (Anderson and Graves, 1994; Balfour and Bryson, 1994; Centorrino et al., 1994). Overall, valproate may be somewhat better tolerated than carbamazepine and perhaps lithium by many bipolar disorder patients, including those in the pediatric and geriatric age groups (Tohen, 1995). More controlled comparisons are needed to test these impressions as well as to compare the efficacy of alternative agents with that of lithium in both short- and long-term treatment of manic–depressive disorders, with particular consideration of risks of side effects, loss of effectiveness over time, risk of relapse after withdrawal, and loss of refractoriness to resumed treatment.

Antipsychotic Agents

Neuroleptic agents have useful adjunctive actions in the short-term management of manic patients, and this has been a commonly accepted application since the 1950s (Baldessarini, 1985), and in one recent study, a majority of hospitalized manic patients were receiving a neuroleptic at discharge (Tohen et al., 1990). However, evidence for their long-term mood-stabilizing efficacy in manic–depressive disorders is meager (Kielholz et al., 1979; Ahlfors et al., 1991; White et al., 1993), and mood disorders may carry an increased risk of neuroleptic-induced tardive dyskinesias (Baldessarini, 1988; Kane and Jeste, 1992). These considerations suggest an unfavorable risk–benefit ratio. Nevertheless, long-term exposure of bipolar patients to neuroleptic agents is very common and typically *intermittent* (Tohen et al., 1990; Sernyak and Woods, 1993). The implications for mood stability or risk of tardive dyskinesia of such exposure are unknown (Casey, 1987).

The highly effective antipsychotic agent clozapine carries an atypically low risk of inducing acute extrapyramidal neurological side effects and a very low risk of inducing tardive dyskinesia (Baldessarini and Frankenburg, 1991) and has demonstrated acute antimanic effects (Mueller and Heipertz, 1977; Green et al., 1995). It also has growing clinical applications for long-term management of otherwise treatment-resistant bipolar or schizoaffective disorder patients, though controlled studies are lacking (Suppes et al., 1992, 1994; Keck et al., 1994; Banov et al., 1994; Frankenburg and Zanarini, 1994; Zarate et al., 1995a,b). Risperidone and other new antipsychotic agents may have mood-altering or other useful effects in bipolar disorders and possibly reduced risk of neurological side effects at low doses, but have not yet been systematically evaluated in bipolar disorder (Meltzer, 1992; Chouinard et al., 1993; Marder and Meibach, 1994; Baldessarini, 1996). Nevertheless, it appears to have an antimanic effect (Tohen et al., 1995b), and a mood-elevating action of risperidone has been associated with a paradoxical induction of mania in a few cases (Dwight et al., 1994).

Miscellaneous Treatments

Sedatives, particularly potent benzodiazepines with anticonvulsant effects, including clonazepam (Klonopin) and lorazepam (Ativan) can provide clinically useful sedative effects in acute mania and may even be antimanic. For this indication they are commonly employed in combination with neuroleptics or lithium in adult patients (Modell et al., 1985; Chouinard, 1987). Their safety and tolerability at the extremes of the age range of bipolar disorder are not secure: Young patients may abuse these agents, seeking their disinhibiting or intoxicating effects; geriatric patients are at increased risk for severe intoxication or falls and fractures during aggressive treatment with benzodiazepines or other central depressants (Ray et al., 1987). The prophylactic efficacy of benzodiazepines is virtually untested in bipolar disorder. Their long-term use might lead to tolerance, dependence, and risk of withdrawal reactions, particularly in patients who are unreliable in adhering to medication prescriptions (Chouinard, 1987; Colwell and Lopez, 1987; Prien and Gelenberg, 1989).

Other agents have very limited experimental or clinical support for their efficacy in bipolar disorder (Prien and Gelenberg, 1989; Chou, 1991; Hopkins and Gelenberg, 1994; Leysen and Pinder, 1994; Baldessarini, 1996a,b). Examples include antihypertensive drugs, some of which can interact unfavorably or even dangerously with lithium, as already discussed. The α_2-adrenergic autoreceptor agonist clonidine can exert a short-lived sedative-antimanic effect, which may undergo rapid tolerance (Jouvent et al., 1980). Among calcium channel blockers, verapamil has suggestive evidence of antimanic activity, but its long-term utility and safety, particularly when combined with other mood-stabilizing agents, are unproved (Baron and Gitlin, 1987; Prien and Gelenberg, 1989; Dubovsky, 1993; Dubovsky and Buzan, 1995). Other similar drugs, including diltiazem and nifedipine, are even less well evaluated as treatments for bipolar disorders (Prien and Gelenberg, 1989; Dubovsky, 1993).

Supplemental addition of vigorous thyroid hormone therapy (in supraphysiologic daily doses of thyroxin, T_4, of up to 0.5 mg) may help to stabilize some rapidly cycling bipolar patients, though the degree of effectiveness and the safety of this approach remain unclear (Stancer and Persad, 1982; Bauer and Whybrow, 1990; Baumgartner et al., 1994). Adding smaller doses of thyroid hormones in the treatment of bipolar disorder patients may reduce time spent in anergic-depressive states (Stein and Avni, 1988).

Electroconvulsive therapy remains a powerful intervention in both mania and severe depression, as well as having paradoxical anticonvulsant activity (Fink, 1979; Black et al., 1988; Schnur et al., 1992; Mukherjee et al., 1994). After a prolonged period of little progress in the treatment of epilepsy, a series of novel anticonvulsant agents are entering clinical application or trials, and some may eventually be applied to the treatment of bipolar disorders. They include eterobarb, fosphenytoin, gabapentin, lamotrigine, levetiracetam, loreclezole, oxcarbamazepine, piracetam, remacemide, stiripentol, tiagabine, topiramate, vigabatrin, zonisamide, and others. For now, however, their potential for psychiatric applications remains untested (Vajda, 1992; Patsalos and Duncan, 1994). Gabapentin (Neurontin) and lamotrigine (Lamictal) have recently become available for general use and have been tried clinically with encouraging anecdotal results and good tolerability in occasional bipolar disorder patients; they require formal assessment of their potential for psychiatric applications.

Finally, it is important to add that nonpharmacological aspects of the treatment of bipolar patients remain important. Cost-effective psychological treatments can support or increase the effectiveness of pharmacological treatments in bipolar disorder (Glick et al., 1985; Hopkins and Gelenberg, 1994).

TREATMENT OF PEDIATRIC AND GERIATRIC BIPOLAR DISORDERS

The treatment of bipolar disorders is not well evaluated at the extremes of the age spectrum, in prepubertal and geriatric patients. This situation reflects an evidently widespread clinical impression that primary bipolar manic–depressive disorders are rare or difficult to diagnose in these age groups (Goodwin and Jamison, 1990). Nevertheless, the onset of mania in adolescence is commonly recognized and various forms of major mood disorders are being found increasingly often in adolescents and children (Klerman et al., 1985; Goodwin and Jamison, 1990; Faedda et al., 1995; Carlson, in press; Wozniak et al., in press). In addition, both newly diagnosed manic–depressive syndromes and bipolar illnesses continuing from earlier life have been described in geriatric populations (Kraepelin, 1921; Angst, 1986; Shulman and Post, 1980; Stone, 1989; Shulman, 1993). Well-controlled studies of the treatment of mania and of bipolar depression are almost nonexistent in both groups, though there is growing clinical evidence that both adolescents and elderly manic patients, and perhaps children, may respond to treatments found effective in adult bipolar disorders (DeLong and Aldershof, 1987; Strober et al., 1990; Shulman, 1993; Faedda et al., 1995). Many aspects of pediatric and geriatric manic–depressive disorders are considered in other chapters of this volume.

Pediatric Bipolar Disorders

Until recently, the preadolescent onset of primary major affective disorders, and particularly bipolar disorders, was considered rare. Many developmental theorists even doubted their possibility before puberty (Anthony and Scott, 1960; Lefkowitz and Burton, 1978; Kron et al., 1982; Carlson, 1983; Akiskal et al., 1985; Kovacs, 1989; Biederman, 1994; Faedda et al., 1995). Epidemiological studies of the onset of bipolar disorders have identified the ages of 15–45 as the time of greatest likelihood, with about a quarter to a third of cases known or suspected to have begun prior to the age of 21 (Goodwin and Jamison, 1990). However, only a small minority (well below 1%) have been considered to begin before puberty (Kraepelin, 1921; Goodwin and Jamison, 1990; Faedda et al., 1995; Wozniak et al., 1995).

A major factor in this low rate of early recognition of bipolar disorders in children may be the lack of clarity of early manifestations and their possible dissimilarity from stereotyped clinical descriptions, which are heavily biased toward adult manic and bipolar depressive syndromes. There is a strong impression, for example, that bipolar disorders often present in children as mixed dysphoric agitated states, irritability, anger, suspiciousness, and interpersonal distress that may or may not be episodic, and are unlikely to show clear alternations between mania and depression (Biederman, 1994; Faedda et al., 1995; Wozniak et al., 1995). In addition, differentiation of bipolar disorder in childhood from other conditions, sometimes present at the same time, can be difficult. There is a particularly strongly suspected relationship between attention-deficit hyperactivity disorder and bipolar disorder, but other conditions to be differentiated include a broad range of affective, behavioral, psychotic, attentional, neuropsychiatric, and substance-abuse related disorders of childhood or adolescence (Weller et al., 1986b; DeLong and Aldershof, 1987; Geller et al., 1993; Biederman, 1994; Carlson et al., 1994; Carlson, 1995; Wozniak et al., 1995). The possible comorbidity of such disorders with bipolar disorders further complicates diagnosis in children and adolescents. Misdiagnosis may account for at least a twofold underestimate of the incidence of mania in childhood (Weller et al., 1986b). Perhaps a fifth of the 2–5% of depressed children later manifest bipolarity of mood disorder before adulthood (Anderson et al., 1987; Kashani et al., 1987; Kovacs, 1989) and some depressed children are found to be bipolar when they become manic or experience rapidly fluctuating mood or behavior during treatment with an antidepressant. Bipolarity might contribute to the generally poor record of success of antidepressant treatment of pediatric depressions (Jensen et al., 1992; Geller et al., 1993; Biederman, 1994; Faedda et al., 1995). These several factors have contributed to a lack of extensive research on bipolar disorders in children and adolescents. It remains for future research to improve early recognition and to evaluate the optimal treatment of these conditions in young patients.

There has been some effort to evaluate the efficacy of lithium in pediatric manic–depressive populations. Most of this work has involved adolescents in whom mania is often readily recognized by its syndromal similarity to adult mania (Youngerman and Canino, 1978; Carlson, 1983, 1995; Campbell et al., 1984; Younes et al., 1986; DeLong and Aldershof, 1987; Veranka et al., 1988; Strober et al., 1990; Faedda et al., 1995). Most of the available research, however, is variable in both quality and quantity. Thus, among 15 studies of lithium therapy in pediatric mania through 1994 only four involved controlled designs, and these four accounted for only 16.3% of the 203 total subjects reported to date (Table 1). Despite the need for caution indicated by the largely anecdotal nature of these clinical findings, they suggest rates of response to lithium that compare well with the adult samples reviewed above, with an average of over 80% responding favorably (Table 1). It should be noted that although lithium currently is not specifically approved by the FDA for use in children below age 12 years (Sifton,

1995) and its long-term consequences are not well evaluated, it is nevertheless fairly widely used in patients in this age group.

In addition to these short-term evaluations of lithium in mania, 10 studies have followed a total of 222 patients considered to have pediatric-onset mania for an average of 8.4 ± 7.3 years (Faedda et al., 1995). Three of the studies were reported between 1921 and 1961, and 5 between 1977 and 1993. The weighted average proportion with a favorable outcome in the earlier era was $27.2 \pm 25.2\%$, and later $74.8 \pm 13.1\%$ ($p < 0.05$). Interpretation of this marked improvement is limited by a lack of controlled treatment and by a confounding difference in time at risk, in that earlier studies involved longer follow-up (15.8 ± 8.0 in 44 cases vs. 3.00 ± 0.74 years in 103 cases). Thus, these observations do not conclusively favor an effect of improved treatment that usually included lithium in recent decades.

Most clinical applications of lithium in pediatric patients have sought similar plasma concentrations as those found to be effective and safe in adult manic–depressive disorders, although dose–response relationships have been investigated only in adults. Experience with antidepressants and other drugs indicates that their metabolic clearance in children is much faster than in adults. Accordingly, doses per kilogram of body weight required to attain blood drug concentrations considered to be therapeutic are usually higher than in adults (Wilens et al., 1992). This relationship may include lithium salts. In a small group of children aged 6–12 (18–24 kg body weight), an average daily dose of lithium carbonate of 28.2 ± 0.2 mg/kg (ca 600 mg/day) was required to provide serum concentrations of lithium averaging 0.8–1.0 mEq/L (Weller et al., 1986a). This dose is nearly twice those typically required in young adults (ca 900–1,200 mg in persons weighing 60–70 kg, or about 12–20 mg/kg).

The ability to predict responsiveness to lithium or other treatments in pediatric bipolar disorders also remains underdeveloped. It has been suggested that very early onset age, presence of prominent psychotic features, mixed dysphoric mood states, rapid-cycling, or even a tendency toward chronic instability of mood, comorbidity with attentional, behavioral, or substance abuse disorders all may predict a reduced likelihood of response, as well as uneven compliance with recommended treatment (Ryan et al., 1987; Ryan and Puig-Antich, 1987; Strober et al., 1988; Carlson et al., 1994; Faedda et al., 1995; Carlson, 1995). Many of these features are associated with poor response in adult bipolar disorder patients (Goodwin and Jamison, 1990; Baldessarini, 1996). The apparently common presence of psychotic features in many bipolar children and adolescents, in particular, may complicate treatment or limit responsiveness to lithium (Ryan et al., 1987; Ryan and Puig-Antich, 1987; Jensen et al., 1992; Faedda et al., 1995). In general, the poor responsiveness of pediatric depressive disorders to pharmacological treatment remains noteworthy but unexplained, and its potential generalization to pediatric bipolar disorders is unknown (Ryan and Puig-Antich, 1987; Kovacs, 1989).

Studies of therapeutic alternatives to lithium in pediatric bipolar disorders are extremely limited. Carbamazepine has been used in some children and adolescents with a variety of affective, behavioral, or neuropsychiatric disorders, but controlled studies of bipolar disorder are lacking (Evans et al., 1987). This drug may not only be antimanic but also antidepressant, as has been reported in adult patients, and may even induce mania or excitement in children (Pleak et al., 1988; Post et al., 1986). Information about the adverse effects of carbamazepine derives from a large clinical experience with this anticonvulsant in the treatment of pediatric epileptic patients. A review of side effects in 220 such children below the age of 16 indicated that the risks were similar to those found in adult epileptic or bipolar patients treated with this agent (Pellock, 1987). They included excessive sedation (43%), vertigo or ataxia (26%), other evidence of mild central nervous system (CNS) intoxication (tremor, slurring, diplopia, movement disorder, often related to blood concentrations of the drug) or headache (16%), nausea and vomiting or other gastrointestinal complaints (9%), and rashes or other skin reactions (5%). Valproate appears to be a promising and generally well-tolerated alternative to lithium, at least in small numbers of adolescent bipolar disorder patients (Papatheodorou et al., 1996). Studies of long-term neuroleptic treatment of pediatric bipolar disorders are surprisingly absent from the literature, though many cases are probably included among children misdiagnosed with schizophrenia or other psychotic disorders (Carlson, 1983; Carlson et al., 1994; Faedda et al., 1995). Pediatric experience with other agents used in adult bipolar disorders appears only in rare anecdotes (Faedda et al., 1995).

The overall effectiveness and potential risks of early intervention in definite or probable bipolar disorders in young patients, particularly in prepubertal children, remain uncertain. Effective early intervention should reduce long-term morbidity and dysfunction and impaired learning and social development, too, but these hopeful possibilities have not been systematically investigated. In addition, differential specification of long-term risks that may be involved in exposure to lithium or other mood-altering agents started in childhood and continued over many years, remains to be defined. Regarding lithium in particular, some concerns arise about its influence on thyroid and parathyroid function or growth and maturation of bone, and also its potential for subtle impairment of cognitive functions at crucial stages of development. The experience with treating epileptic children with anticonvulsants may provide useful guidance. In addition to these specifically medical issues, there are long-held professional and public attitudes leading to skepticism concerning the long-term medication of children that can impede efforts to address these questions (Biederman, 1994).

Overall, definition of the optimal treatment of bipolar disorder in children remains a major task for contemporary pediatric psychiatry. Children present special and urgent challenges in light of the sometimes devastating and potentially lifelong impact of severe affective and psychotic illness of early onset (Kovacs, 1989). The tendency toward psychotic and mixed mood states, a chronic course of illness, and high frequency of comorbid conditions or substance abuse in pediatric bipolar disorders further complicate clinical management and increase the likelihood of exposure of children and adolescents to complex treatments with undefined long-term toxic or developmental consequences. In short, there are many uncertainties as to whether, how, and when to intervene with a comprehensive program of mood-stabilizing pharmacological treatment, psychological treatment, rehabilitation, and family support so as to obtain optimal long-term results in this age group.

Geriatric Bipolar Disorders

Many cases of bipolar disorder starting in adolescence or early adult years persist into old age. While some cases may become less active or symptomatically severe with advancing age, many continue or even become more frequently recurrent or virtually chronic (Zis and Goodwin, 1979; Angst, 1986). Relatively few new cases of bipolar manic–depressive illness are first diagnosed in the geriatric population, but many others are probably undiagnosed or misdiagnosed. Epidemiological studies have found that only 1–3% of cases of bipolar disorder begin at ages above 60, and even some of these may be based on misinformation concerning early history (Goodwin and Jamison, 1990). Some cases of late-onset mania have occurred many years after depressive illness in earlier life (Shulman and Post, 1890; Broadhead and Jacoby, 1990). Of bipolar patients diagnosed with mania after age 60, approximately 42% were known to have had mania or depression earlier and about a third had only depressions at younger ages (Stone, 1989; Broadhead and Jacoby, 1990). These findings suggest that the presence or absence of bipolarity in major mood disorders may not always be diagnosed with certainty in young adults. Bipolar syndromes are not rare in geropsychiatric populations and undoubtedly are diagnosed more often when there is a high level of suspicion of their presence. They may account for more than 10% of geriatric affective disorders (Post, 1992), and according to one study first episodes of bipolar disorder, they accounted for 5% of admissions to a typical geropsychiatric unit (Yassa et al., 1988).

The syndrome of geriatric mania is highly heterogeneous (Stone, 1989; Broadhead and Jacoby, 1990; Post, 1992; Young, 1992; Young and Klerman, 1992; Shulman, 1993; Tohen et al., 1994b). Elderly manic patients can be less dramatically excited than younger patients, often manifest admixed depression with agitation, are commonly delusional, may respond unsatisfactorily to treatment, and often follow an unfavorable course. They also have relatively high rates of comorbid neurological and general medical disorders, typically are exposed to complex medication regimens, and encounter high mortality rates due to cardiovascular or other serious medical illnesses. Such medical problems, in turn, often limit the vigor of pharmacological treatment of geriatric mood disorders (Black et al., 1988; Broadhead and Jacoby, 1990; Young, 1992; Shulman, 1993; Tohen et al., 1994b).

Among cases of mania of geriatric onset, a high but unknown proportion are probably not examples of primary bipolar disorder of late onset. Many toxic, metabolic, and degenerative neuropsychiatric conditions that are common in old age present with manic or depressive features (secondary mood disorders) and require diligent differential assessment (Krauthammer and Klerman, 1978; Shulman and Post, 1980; Summers, 1983; Casey and Fitzgerald, 1988; Wright and Silove, 1988; Stone, 1989; Young, 1992; Young and Klerman, 1992; Shulman, 1993). The opposite diagnostic problem can also arise because elderly persons with sustained bipolar illness may closely resemble patients with Alzheimer's disease or other forms of dementia (Casey and Fitzgerald, 1988; Shukla et al., 1988; Wright and Silove, 1988).

There also is a diagnostic problem in distinguishing the diagnoses of middle-aged or older patients who present with a mixture of chronic psychotic and affective symptoms, many of whom may be considered cases of schizophrenia or schizoaffective disorder if an adequate past history and family history are not available to assist in diagnosis (Goodwin and Jamison, 1990). This may be a particular problem in patients with any major affective disorder of late onset; many of these patients have admixed psychotic features and a poor prognosis, with a relatively chronic course (Zis and Goodwin 1979; Shulman, 1993).

The treatment of bipolar disorder in the elderly has included approaches used in younger adults, possibly with more frequent use of ECT, which may be used in response to the tendency toward chronicity, admixture of depression or psychotic agitation with mania, or due to side effects and sometimes poor responses to pharmacological treatments (Fink, 1979). The presence of psychotic features or persisting agitation also contribute to mixing antipsychotic agents with mood-altering treatments in elderly bipolar disorder patients. Presumably, such combinations carry a greater risk of side effects or delirium than in younger adults (Sargenti et al., 1988).

Despite the availability of a substantial literature on the treatment of geriatric mania, there are very few reports with quantitative characterizations of treatment efficacy, and no well-controlled treatment trials (Foster and Rosenthal, 1980; Young and Klerman, 1992; Shulman, 1993). Four representative uncontrolled studies provide data on short-term responses to lithium in acute mania in patients over age 60. The average results are strikingly similar to those found in adult and pediatric mania, though responses were much more variable than in studies of younger patients (Table 1). There are no data from well-controlled, long-term studies of lithium or other agents in geriatric bipolar disorders. Nevertheless, favorable initial responses are reported to have been followed by sustained beneficial effects of lithium for months or years of follow-up in some manic–depressive patients in this age group (van der Velde, 1970; Abou-Saleh and Coppen, 1983).

Whether responsiveness to lithium consistently decreases with advancing age is an unresolved question. Some observers find little evidence of a loss of short-term anti-manic response to lithium with advanced age (Young and Falk, 1989), while others have suggested such a trend as a clinical impression (Hewick et al., 1977; Murray et al., 1983). Still other investigators find compelling evidence that the average proportion of bipolar patients benefiting from lithium treatment fell strikingly with advancing age. For example, in a clinical case series, van der Velde (1970) found that only a third of 12 manic patients over age 60 responded well, compared to 81.0% of 63 younger patients; with long-term follow-up over 3 years, the response rates were only 8.3% in the elderly subjects but 52.4% in the younger adults. In the same study, lithium appeared to have especially poor long-term benefit in geriatric bipolar depression. In contrast, Abou-Saleh and Coppen (1983) found similar morbidity scores (duration of mania or depression times severity) in an uncontrolled long-term follow-up of 47 mainly depressed manic–depressive patients aged 60 as in 101 younger subjects.

A serious confounding factor in evaluating the efficacy of lithium in geriatric manic–depressive illness is that while some elderly patients tolerate the treatment and benefit from it others are severely intoxicated and, overall, worsened from a neuropsychiatric perspective. Many studies are consistent in reporting neurotoxic effects of lithium in elderly patients, even at doses and blood lithium concentrations (ca 0.8–1.0 mEq/L) that are tolerated by younger patients, and in some cases even at levels below 0.75 mEq/L. Typical manifestations include confusion or delirium and worsening of Parkinsonism or oral-facial dyskinesias (van der Velde, 1971; Strayhorn and Nash, 1977; Roose et al., 1979; Himmelhoch et al., 1980; Smith and Helms, 1982; Chacko et al., 1987; Shukla et al., 1988; Post, 1992). Such risks of cerebral intoxication probably rise in direct proportion to dose or blood concentrations of lithium (Chacko et al., 1987). In contrast, the nature and risks of minor side effects (such as early thirst, polyuria, or nocturia) are probably similar to those in younger patients, and evidence of an unusually high risk of renal or thyroid impairment with lithium in the elderly is lacking (Murray et al., 1983; Foster and Rosenthal, 1980; Broadhead and Jacoby, 1990; Young and Klerman, 1992; Shulman, 1993).

Neurotoxic effects in the elderly may directly limit benefits in some patients, but intolerance to lithium also limits doses that can be given safely to elderly and infirm patients, probably with a corresponding loss of benefit. In general, bipolar disorder patients with complex illnesses that include comorbidity with other psychiatric disorders or severe medical or neurological disorders may respond less well to lithium and receive less vigorous mood-stabilizing treatment than those with simpler conditions (Black et al., 1988). Patients with schizoaffective, other psychotic, or dementing conditions may also respond less well than those with primary manic–depressive syndromes (Johnson et al., 1971; Young and Klerman, 1992; Shulman, 1993).

Elderly patients are at least moderately less able to clear lithium as efficiently as children or young adults (Vestergaard and Schou, 1984; Hardy et al., 1987; Shulman et al., 1987). Consequently, they require or tolerate relatively lower doses than younger patients. Doses of lithium salts in patients above age 65 are typically about half those given to younger adults. The decrease in lithium clearance in the aged, presumably due to the effects of aging on renal and cardiovascular function, no doubt contributes importantly to a tendency to obtain similar blood concentrations at perhaps 30% lower daily doses (Hewick et al., 1977; Smith and Helms, 1982). In addition, poor tolerability in the elderly limits dosing and blood levels even further (Hewick et al., 1977; Schaffer and Garvey, 1984; Chacko et al., 1987; Shulman et al., 1987; Mirchandani and Young, 1993). Accordingly, typical daily doses of lithium carbonate per kilogram of body weight average less than half those tolerated by younger adults (commonly from 150–300 up to 600–900 mg, or about 5–10 mg/kg in the elderly), with serum concentrations above 0.75 mEq/L likely to carry substantial risks of cerebral intoxication in many elderly persons.

Studies of the effects of agents other than lithium in geriatric bipolar disorders are extremely few and limited in content. Neuroleptic agents are commonly employed in the treatment of mania, depressive, paranoid, and organic psychotic disorders that are common in the geriatric population, with very limited formal study of their efficacy or safety in psychotic disorders and virtually none in bipolar disorders. The elderly are at high risk of neuroleptic-induced or worsened Parkinsonism and tardive dyskinesia (Smith and Baldessarini, 1980; Baldessarini, 1985, 1996). These risks are probably greater with neuroleptics of high potency, while lower-potency agents carry relatively high risks of inducing hypotension, confusion or delirium, as has been reported recently to be a frequent limitation of otherwise useful treatment with clozapine in elderly psychotic patients (Frankenburg and Kalunian, 1994). There are only scattered case reports on the use of the antihypertensive agent verapamil or the anticonvulsants carbamazepine or valproate to treat elderly manic patients, and valproate may be a somewhat better tolerated anticonvulsant in the elderly (McFarland et al., 1990; Shulman, 1993).

It is not certain whether the elderly are at increased risk of intoxication by specific drug combinations. Any agent with the potential to induce confusion or extrapyramidal effects can be expected to have an increased risk of doing so when combined with lithium in the psychogeriatric population. Thus, combining lithium with neuroleptics of either low or high potency, with tricyclic antidepressants or with benzodiazepines should be considered particularly risky in this age group. In addition, there is some evidence that the combination of ECT with lithium may increase risk of delirium (Mandel et al., 1980; Rudorfer and Linnoila, 1986). Unsteadiness and confusion due to psychotropic drugs of all types are major contributors to the risks of falling, with related injuries and potentially incapacitating hip fractures (Ray et al., 1987).

CONCLUSIONS

The preceding overview of the contemporary state of therapeutics for bipolar disorder throughout the life cycle indicates that lithium is an effective and acceptably safe and tolerable form of pharmacological treatment for most adult patients. Its relatively slow onset limits its application as a sole or primary therapy for acute mania, in which adjunctive treatment with a neuroleptic or potent benzodiazepine is commonly provided for what may be largely nonspecific sedative effects. Despite these useful short-term applications, the long-term mood-stabilizing efficacy of neuroleptic or sedative agents remains unproved.

The most important contemporary use of lithium treatment is to prevent early relapses within perhaps 6–12 months following recovery from acute mania or bipolar depression and also for longer-term maintenance treatment, which is indicated in cases of demonstrated severity and recurrence risk. Maintenance treatment can prevent or modify the risk of later recurring episodes of mania or bipolar depression, which are highly probable, at an average lifetime risk of about one per year. Benefits for mania appear to be superior to those for bipolar depression, with both lithium and other antimanic agents. Lithium may also contribute a mood-stabilizing effect in many cases of apparently nonbipolar depression, and can probably enhance the efficacy of antidepressants. However, the efficacy of lithium in all these applications is limited, and at least partial failure can be expected in up to half of adult patients within several years.

The optimally safe and effective treatment for recurrent bipolar depression remains to be defined and is surprisingly poorly studied. Sustained or overly aggressive use of most antidepressants, particularly in the absence of lithium, almost certainly carries increased risk of agitation or mania and may contribute to greater long-term mood instability or briefer euthymic intervals. Since many bipolar disorder patients suffer greatly from depression and are disabled by it, and since the risk of suicide in bipolar disorder is highest during depression, improved treatment of bipolar depression at all ages should be viewed as a major public health issue and therapeutic challenge.

Effective and safe doses of lithium salts provide serum concentrations in the range of 0.6 to 1.0 mEq/L for long-term treatment of adult and pediatric patients. Only somewhat lower concentrations are likely to be tolerated by geriatric bipolar disorder patients, even though they may be theoretically less effective. Dosing with standard lithium preparations once daily is sometimes feasible and may facilitate compliance but appears to provide only marginal gains in reducing polyuria and nocturia and probably carries increased risk of cerebral intoxication, particularly in elderly or infirm patients. Long-term dosing with lithium reportedly can sometimes be reduced to every other day without loss of efficacy.

Recent evidence strongly suggests that interruption of maintenance treatment with lithium and perhaps other psychotropic agents, particularly abruptly, carries a markedly increased risk of a major recurrence of illness within several months. Risk of mania exceeds that for depression in bipolar I cases, but the risk of depression in bipolar II cases is similar to that of mania in bipolar I disorder. Moreover, risk of suicidal behaviors also increases sharply, but predictably, in association with recurrence of depression or dysphoria. Slow discontinuation of lithium probably reduces the excessive early risk of a major recurrence. Safe and effective alternatives that can replace lithium when it is removed due to side effects or pregnancy remain to be discovered. Indications for interrupting lithium maintenance treatment need to be balanced against the high risk of recurrences of potentially disruptive or even life-threatening major affective illness, especially in the months following interruption.

The imperfect prophylactic effectiveness of lithium in bipolar disorders, and the limits to its acceptability by many patients, strongly encourage the search for alternative treatments. Substantial research is accumulating to support an antimanic action of certain anticonvulsants, notably carbamazepine and valproate. Carbamazepine may also have some mood-elevating activity, but the efficacy of virtually all proposed antimanic or putative mood-stabilizing agents against recurrences of depression may be more limited than efficacy against mania. Even though research evidence for the long-term benefits of carbamazepine is stronger than for all alternatives to lithium, its acceptance by doctors and patients for the long-term treatment of bipolar disorders is limited. It causes sometimes poorly tolerated side effects and also complex interactions with other drugs, including neuroleptics and antidepressants, typically leading to a decrease of their circulating concentrations and a loss of efficacy. Valproate, an effective antimanic agent, appears to be somewhat better tolerated, even with aggressive early dosing, and controlled studies of its prophylactic efficacy in bipolar disorders are in progress. Both anticonvulsants appear to carry excess risks of fetal teratogenic effects in excess of those of lithium, and including spina bifida and perhaps developmental delays.

Typical neuroleptic agents lack substantial research support for a mood-stabilizing action and probably carry an excess risk of tardive dyskinesia in mood disorders. Specific risks of their commonly intermittent use for bipolar disorder patients are not clear but might include mood instability and dyskinesia. The atypical antipsychotic agent clozapine has little risk of tardive dyskinesia. Despite its tendency to induce excessive sedation, weight gain (common to virtually all known mood-stabilizing treatments) and seizures and also potentially life-threatening leukopenia, clozapine has growing support in cases of affective psychotic disorders unresponsive to other treatments. Risperidone may have both antimanic and mood-elevating effects, but its place in the treatment of bipolar disorders requires further study. Support for the benefits of other mood-stabilizing alternatives, such as antihypertensive calcium channel blockers and ACE inhibitors, remains largely anecdotal and unconvincing, and some of these drugs can interact dangerously with lithium.

Mania is not uncommon in adolescents and is no longer considered rare in childhood, though its early recognition and differentiation from other childhood psychiatric disorders present formidable diagnostic challenges. In addition, mania's common comorbidity with other behavioral and substance-abuse disorders in adolescents and its frequent psychotic and dysphoric features in pediatric cases complicate treatment, encourage polypharmacy, and may limit both adherence and response to treatment. The limited available evidence strongly suggests that responses to lithium and perhaps valproate in adolescent and some preadolescent bipolar patients may be similar to those in adults. Nevertheless, the disappointing performance of antidepressants in controlled trials in childhood depression suggests a need for circumspect assessment of diagnosis and treatment of pediatric bipolar manic–depression and encourages controlled long-term studies in this age group. The hope of preventing developmental and long-term disability, comorbidity, developmental delay, and suicide strongly encourages more interest in early recognition and intervention in pediatric bipolar disorders.

Bipolar disorders are also not rare in geriatric psychiatric populations, though new cases starting after age 65 are relatively uncommon. Many cases represent secondary manic or depressive syndromes associated with coarse brain disease, effects of systemic illnesses, or neurotoxic reactions to medical treatments. Formal research on the differential assessment, active treatment, and outcome of potentially reversible manic–depressive syndromes of the elderly is strikingly limited. The elderly often poorly tolerate lithium and other antimanic or antidepressant drugs; this complication frequently limits efforts to treat geriatric manic–depressive disorders. Nevertheless, there is some evidence that elderly bipolar disorder patients who can tolerate lithium and perhaps valproate may respond well in short- and longer-term treatment.

ACKNOWLEDGMENTS

Supported, in part, by USPHS (NIMH) grants MH-31154, MH-47372 a NARSAD investigator award, and an award from the Bruce J Anderson Foundation and the McLean Private Donors Neuropharmacology Research Fund. Mr. Corby Kummer provided valuable editorial advice.

REFERENCES

Abou-Saleh MT (1992): Lithium. In Paykel ES (ed): "Handbook of Affective Disorders." Edinburgh: Churchill Livingstone, pp 369–385.

Abou-Saleh MT, Coppen A (1983): The prognosis of depression in old age: The case for lithium therapy. Br J Psychiatry 143:527–528.

Adams F (ed) (1856): "The Extant Works of Aretaeus, the Cappadocian." London: Sydenham Society.

Ahlfors UG, Baastrup PC, Dencker SJ, Elgen K, Lingjærde O, Pedersen V, Schou M, Aaskoven O (1991): Flupenthixol decanoate in recurrent manic–depressive illness. Acta Psychiatr Scand 64:226–237.

Akiskal HS, Downs J, Jordan P, Watson S, Daugherty D, Pruitt DB (1985): Affective disorders in referred children and younger siblings of manic–depressives: Mode of onset and prospective course. Arch Gen Psychiatry 42:996–1003.

Amdisen A (1984): Lithium treatment of mania and depression over one hundred years. In Corsini GU (ed): "Current Trends in Lithium and Rubidium Therapy." Lancaster, UK: MTP Press, pp 11–26.

Amdisen A (1980): Monitoring lithium dose levels: Clinical aspects of serum lithium estimation. In Johnson FN (ed): "Handbook of Lithium Therapy." Baltimore: University Park Press, pp 179–195.

Anderson GD, Graves NM (1994): Drug interactions with antiepileptic agents: Prevention and management. CNS Drugs 2:268–279.

Anderson JC, Williams S, McGee R, Silva PA (1987): DSM-III disorders in preadolescent children: Prevalence in a large sample from the general population. Arch Gen Psychiatry 44:69–76.

Angst J (1986): The course of affective disorders. Psychopathology 19(Suppl 2):47–52.

Anthony EJ, Scott P (1960): Manic–depressive psychosis in childhood. J Child Psychol Psychiatry 1:53–72.

Aronson TA, Shulka S, Hirschowitz J (1989): Clonazepam treatment of five lithium-refractory patients with bipolar disorder. Am J Psychiatry 146:77–80.

Austin MPV, Souza FGM, Goodwin GM (1991): Lithium augmentation in antidepressant-resistant patients: A quantitative analysis. Br J Psychiatry 159:510–514.

Avissar S, Schreiber G (1992): Interaction of antibipolar and antidepressant treatments with receptor-coupled G proteins. Pharmacopsychiatry 25:44–50.

Baastrup PC, Hollnagel P, Sorensen R, Schou M (1976): Adverse reactions in treatment with lithium carbonate and haloperidol. JAMA 236:2645–2646.

Baldessarini RJ (1996a): Drugs and the treatment of psychiatric disorders: Antimanic and antidepressant agents. In Harden W, Rudin W, Molinoff PB, Rall T (eds): "Goodman and Gilman's The Pharmacologic Basis of Therapeutics," 9th ed. New York: McGraw-Hill Press, pp 431–459.

Baldessarini RJ (1996b): Antimanic and mood-stabilizing agents. In "Chemotherapy in Psychiatry: Principles and Practice," 3rd ed. Cambridge, MA: Harvard University Press (in press).

Baldessarini RJ (1988): A summary of current knowledge of tardive dyskinesia. L'Encephale (Paris) 14:363–368.

Baldessarini RJ (1985): Lithium salts and antimanic agents. In "Chemotherapy in Psychiatry: Principles and Practice, 2nd ed. Cambridge, MA: Harvard University Press, pp 93–129.

Baldessarini RJ, Frankenburg FR (1991): Clozapine—a novel antipsychotic agent. N Engl J Med 324:746–754.

Baldessarini RJ, Suppes T, Tondo L (1996): Lithium withdrawal in bipolar disorder: Implications for clinical practice and experimental therapeutics research. Am J Therapeutics 4: (in press).

Baldessarini RJ, Viguera AC (1995): Neuroleptic withdrawal in schizophrenic patients. Arch Gen Psychiatry 52:189–192.

Baldessarini RJ, Vogt M (1988): Release of [³H]-dopamine and analogous monoamines from rat striatal tissue. Cell Mol Neurobiology 8:205–216.

Balfour JA, Bryson HM (1994): Valproic acid: A review of its pharmacology and therapeutic potential in indications other than epilepsy. CNS Drugs 2:144–173.

Ballenger JC, Post RM (1980): Carbamazepine in manic–depressive illness: A new treatment. Am J Psychiatry 137:782–790.

Banov MD, Zarate CA Jr, Tohen M, Scialabba D, Wines JD Jr, Kolbrener M, Kim J-W, Cole JO (1994): Clozapine therapy in refractory affective disorders: Polarity predicts response in long-term follow-up. J Clin Psychiatry 55:295–300.

Baron BM, Gitlin MJ (1987): Verapamil in treatment-resistant mania: An open trial. J Clin Psychopharmacol 7:101–103.

Bauer MS (1994): Refractoriness induced by lithium discontinuation despite adequate serum lithium levels (letter). Am J Psychiatry 151:1522.

Bauer ME, Whybrow PC (1990): Rapid cycling bipolar affective disorder. II. Treatment of refractory rapid-cycling with high-dose levothyroxine: A preliminary study. Arch Gen Psychiatry 47:427–440.

Baumgartner A, Bauer M, Hellveg R (1994): Treatment of intractable non-rapid cycling bipolar affective disorder with high-dose thyroxin: An open clinical trial. Neuropsychopharmacology 10:183–189.

Bennett DR (ed) (1993): Drugs used in mood disorders. In "Drug Evaluation Annual 1993 (DE 1993)." Chicago: American Medical Association, pp 277–306.

Biederman J (1994): Recent developments in child and adolescent psychiatry and psychopharmacology. Curr Affect Illness 13(11):5–13.

Black DW, Winokur G, Bell S, Nasrallah A, Hulbert J (1988): Complicated mania. Arch Gen Psychiatry 45:232–236.

Black DW, Winokur G, Nasrallah A (1987): Treatment of mania: A naturalistic study of ECT vs. lithium in 438 patients. J Clin Psychiatry 48:132–139.

Boton R, Gaviria M, Battle DC (1987): Prevalence, pathogenesis, and treatment of renal dysfunction associated with chronic lithium therapy. Am J Kidney Dis 10:329–345.

Bowden CL, Brugger AM, Swann AC, Calabrese JR, Janicak PG, Petty F, Dilsaver SC, Davis JM, Rush AJ, Small JG, Garza-Treviño ES, Risch C, Goodnick PJ, Morris DD (1994): Efficacy of divalproex vs. lithium and placebo in the treatment of mania. JAMA 271:918–924.

Broadhead J, Jacoby R (1990): Mania in old age: A first prospective study. Int J Geriatr Psychiatry 5:215–222.

Bunney WE Jr, Wehr TR, Gillin JC, Post RM, Goodwin FK, van Kammen DP (1977): The switch process in manic–depressive psychosis. Ann Int Med 87:319–335.

Cade JFJ (1978): Lithium—past, present and future. In Johnson FN, Johnson S (eds): "Lithium in Medical Practice." Baltimore: University Park Press, pp 5–16.

Cade JFJ (1949): Lithium salts in the treatment of psychotic excitement. Med J Austral 36:349–352.

Calabrese JR, Woyshville MJ (1994): Diagnosis and treatment of rapid-cycling bipolar disorder. Directions Psychiatry 14(16):1–8.

Calabrese JR, Woyshville MJ, Kimmel SE, Rapport DJ (1993): Predictors of valproate response in bipolar rapid cycling. J Clin Psychopharmacol 13:280–283.

Callahan AM, Fava M, Rosenbaum JF (1993): Drug interactions in psychopharmacology. Psychiatr Clin No Am 16:647–671.

Campbell M, Perry R, Green WH (1984): Use of lithium in children and adolescents. Psychosomatics 25:95–106.

Carlson GA (1995): Bipolar affective disorder in children and adolescents: Commentary. J Am Acad Child Adolesc Psychiatry 34:750–753.

Carlson GA (1983): Bipolar affective disorders in childhood and adolescence. In Cantwell DP, Carlson GA (ed): "Affective Disorders in Childhood and Adolescence: An Update." New York: Spectrum Publications, pp 61–83.

Carlson GA, Fennig S, Bromet EJ (1994): The confusion between bipolar disorder and schizophrenia in youth: Where does it stand in the 1990s? J Am Acad Child Adolesc Psychiatry 33:453–460.

Casey DE (1987): Tardive dyskinesia. In Meltzer HY (ed): "Psychopharmacology: The Third Generation of Progress." New York: Raven Press, pp 1411–1419.

Casey DA, Fitzgerald BA (1988): Mania and pseudodementia. J Clin Psychiatry 49:73–74.

Centorrino F, Baldessarini RJ, Kando J, Frankenburg FR, Volpicelli SA, Puopolo R, Flood JG (1994): Serum concentrations of clozapine and its major metabolites: Effects of cotreatment with fluoxetine or valproate. Am J Psychiatry 151:123–125.

Chacko RC, Marsh BJ, Marmion J, Sworkin R, Telschow R (1987): Lithium side effects in elderly bipolar outpatients. Hillside J Clin Psychiatry 9:79–88.

Chou J C-Y (1991): Recent advances in treatment of acute mania. J Clin Psychopharmacol 11:3–21.

Chouinard G (1987): Clonazepam in acute and maintenance treatment of bipolar affective disorder. J Clin Psychiatry 48(Suppl 10):29–37.

Chouinard G, Jones B, Remington G, Bloom D, Addington D, MacEwan GW, Labelle A, Beauclair L, Arnott W (1993): A Canadian multicenter placebo-controlled study of fixed doses of risperidone and haloperidol in the treatment of chronic schizophrenic patients. J Clin Psychopharmacol 13:25–40.

Cohen WJ, Cohen NH (1974): Lithium carbonate, haloperidol and irreversible brain damage. JAMA 230:1283–1287.

Cohen LS, Friedman JM, Jefferson JW, Johnson EM, Weiner ML (1994): A re-evaluation of risk of in utero exposure to lithium. JAMA 271:146–150.

Colwell BL, Lopez JR (1987): Clonazepam in mania. Drug Intell Clin Pharm 21:794–795.

Coppen A, Abou-Saleh MT, Wood KM, Milln P, Bailey J, Wood K (1983): Decreasing lithium dosage reduces morbidity and side-effects during prophylaxis. J Affect Disord 5:353–362.

Delgado PL, Gelenberg AJ (1996): Antidepressant and antimanic medications. In Gabbard GO (ed): "Treatment of Psychiatric Disorders: The DSM-IV Edition." Washington: American Psychiatric Press.

DeLong GR, Aldershof A (1987): Long-term experience with lithium treatment in childhood: Correlation with clinical diagnosis. J Am Acad Child Adolesc Psychiatry 26:389–394.

Denikoff KD, Meglathery SB, Post RM, Tandeciarz SI (1994): Efficacy of carbamazepine compared with other agents: A clinical practice survey. J Clin Psychiatry 55:70–76.

Dreifuss FE, Santilli N, Langer DH, Sweeney KP, Moline KA, Menander KB (1987): Valproic acid hepatic fatalities: A retrospective review. Neurology 37:379–385.

Dubovsky SL (1993): Calcium antagonists in manic–depressive illness. Neuropsychobiology 27:184–192.

Dubovsky SL, Buzan R (1995): The role of calcium channel bockers in the treatment of psychiatric disorders. CNS Drugs 4:47–57.

Dwight MM, Keck PE Jr, Stanton SP, Strakowski SM, McElroy SL (1994): Antidepressant activity and mania associated with risperidone treatment of schizoaffective disorder. Lancet 344:554–555.

Emrich HM, Wolf R (1992): Valproate treatment of mania. Prog Neuropsychopharmacol Biol Psychiatry 16:691–701.

Emrich HM, Dose M, von Zerssen D (1985): The use of sodium valproate, carbamazepine and oxcarbamazepine in patients with affective disorders. J Affect Disord 8:243–250.

Evans RW, Clay TH, Gualtieri ST (1987): Carbamazepine in pediatric psychiatry. J Am Acad Child Adolesc Psychiatry 26:2–8.

Faedda GL, Baldessarini RJ, Suppes T, Tondo L, Becker I, Lipschitz DS (1995): Pediatric-onset bipolar disorder: A literature review. Harvard Rev Psychiatry 3:171–195.

Faedda GL, Tondo L, Baldessarini RJ, Suppes T, Tohen M (1993): Outcome after rapid vs. gradual discontinuation of lithium treatment in bipolar mood disorders. Arch Gen psychiatry 50:448–455.

Faedda GL, Baldessarini RJ, Tohen M, Strakowski SM, Waternaux C (1991): Episode sequence in bipolar disorder and response to lithium treatment. Am J Psychiatry 148:1237–1239.

Fink M (1979): "Convulsive Therapy: Theory and Practice." New York: Raven Press.

Fogelson DL, Bystritsky A, Pasnau R (1992): Bupropion in the treatment of bipolar disorders: The same old story? J Clin Psychiatry 53:443–446.

Foster JR, Rosenthal JS (1980): Lithium treatment in the elderly. In Johnson FN (ed): "Handbook of Lithium Therapy." Baltimore: University Park Press, pp 414–420.

Frankenburg FR, Kalunian D (1994): Clozapine in the elderly. J Geriatr Psychiatry Neurol 7:131–134.

Frankenburg FR, Zanarini M (1994): Uses of clozapine in nonschizophrenic patients. Harvard Rev Psychiatry 2:142–150.

Freeman TW, Clotheir JL, Pazzaglia P, Lesem MD, Swann AC (1992): A double-blind comparison of valproate and lithium in the treatment of acute mania. Am J Psychiatry 149:108–111.

Garkinkel PE, Stancer HC, Persad E (1980): A comparison of haloperidol, lithium carbonate, and their combination in the treatment of mania. J Affect Disord 2:279–288.

Garrod AB (1876): "A Treatise on Gout and Rheumatic Gout (Rheumatoid Arthritis)." London: Longmans, Green.

Gelenberg AJ, Kane JM, Keller MB, Lavori PW, Rosenbaum JF, Cole K, Lavelle J (1989): Comparison of standard and low serum levels of lithium for maintenance treatment of bipolar disorder. N Engl J Med 321:1489–1493.

Geller B, Fox LW, Fletcher M (1993): Effect of tricyclic antidepressants on switching to mania and on the onset of bipolarity in depressed 6- to 12-year olds. J Am Acad Child Adolesc Psychiatry 32:43–50.

Gitlin MJ (1993): Lithium-induced renal insufficiency. J Clin Psychopharmacol 13:276–279.

Gitlin MJ, Cochran SD, Jamison KR (1989): Maintenance lithium treatment: Side effects and compliance. J Clin Psychiatry 50:127–131.

Glick ID, Clarkin JF, Spencer JH, Maas GL, Lewis AB, Peyser J, DeMane N, Good-Ellis M, Harris E, Lestelle V (1985): A controlled evaluation of inpatient family intervention. Arch Gen Psychiatry 42:882–886.

Goff D, Baldessarini RJ (1993): Interactions of drugs with antipsychotic agents. J Clin Psychopharmacol 13:57–67.

Goodwin FK, Jamison KR (1990): "Manic–Depressive Illness." New York: Oxford University Press.

Goodwin FK, Zis AP (1979): Lithium in the treatment of mania: Comparisons with neuroleptics. Arch Gen Psychiatry 36:840–844.

Green A, Tohen M, Banov M, Pate J, Schatzberg A, Cole JO (1995): Clozapine in the treatment of acute mania (unpublished).

Greenberg PE, Stiglin LE, Finkelstein SN, Berndt ER (1993): The economic burden of depression in 1990. J Clin Psychiatry 54:405–418.

Guscott R, Taylor L (1994): Lithium prophylaxis in recurrent affective illness: Efficacy, effectiveness, and efficiency. Br J Psychiatry 164:741–746.

Hammond WA (1883): The treatment of insanity. In "A Treatise on Insanity." New York: Appleton pp 718–756.

Hammond WA (1871): The treatment of insanity. In "A Treatise on Diseases of the Nervous System." New York: Appleton pp 325–384.

Hardy BG, Shulman KI, Mackenzie SE, Kutcher SP, Silverberg JD (1987): Pharmacokinetics of lithium in the elderly. J Clin Psychopharmacol 7:153–158.

Hetmar O, Povlsen UJ, Ladefoged J, Bolweg TG (1991): Lithium: Long-term effects on the kidney, a prospective follow-up study ten years after kidney biopsy. Br J Psychiatry 158:53–58.

Hewick DS, Newbury P, Hopwood S, Naylor G, Moody J (1977): Age as a factor affecting lithium therapy. Br J Clin Pharmacol 4:201–205.

Himmelhoch JM, Neil JF, May SJ, Fuchs CZ, Licata SM (1980): Age, dementia, dyskinesias, and lithium response. Am J Psychiatry 137:941–945.

Hopkins HS, Gelenberg AJ (1994): Treatment of bipolar disorder: How far have we come? Psychopharmacol Bull 30:27–38.

Hullin RP (1980): Minimum lithium levels for effective prophylaxis. In Johnson FN (ed): "Handbook of Lithium Therapy." Baltimore: University Park Press, pp 243–247.

Jefferson JW, Greist JH (1994): Lithium in psychiatry: A review. CNS Drugs 1:448–464.

Jefferson JW, Greist JH (1980): Haloperidol and lithium: Their combined use and the issue of their compatibility. In Ayd FJ (ed): "Haloperidol Update: 1958–1980." Baltimore: Ayd Medical Communications, pp 73–82.

Jefferson JW, Sen D (1994): Manic–depressive disorder and lithium over the decades: The very educational case of Mrs. L. J Clin Psychiatry 55:340–343.

Jensen PS, Ryan ND, Prien R (1992): Psychopharmacology of child and adolescent major depression: Present status and future. J Child Adolesc Psychopharmacol 2:31–45.

Jensen HV, Plenge P, Mellerup ET, Davidsen K, Toftegaard L, Aggernæs H, Bjørum N (1995): Lithium prophylaxis of manic–depressive disorders: Daily lithium dosing schedule vs. every other day. Acta Psychiatr Scand 92:69–74.

Jerram TC, McDonald R (1978): Plasma lithium control with particular reference to minimum effective levels. In Johnson FN, Johnson S (eds): "Lithium in Medical Practice." Baltimore: University Park Press, pp 407–413.

Joffe RT (1993): Valproate in bipolar disorder: The Canadian perspective. Can J Psychiatry 38(Suppl 2):S45–S50.

Johnson FN (ed) (1986): "Lithium Combination Treatment." Basel: Karger Verlag.

Johnson FN (1984): "The History of Lithium Therapy." London: MacMillan Press.

Johnson FN (1980): "Handbook of Lithium Therapy." Baltimore: University Park Press.

Johnson G, Gershon S, Burdock EI, Floyd A, Hekimian L (1971): Comparative effects of lithium and chlorpromazine in the treatment of acute manic states. Br J Psychiatry 119:267–276.

Jope RS, Williams MB (1994): Lithium and brain signal transduction systems. Biochem Pharmacol 47:429–441.

Jouvent R, Lecrubier Y, Peuch AJ, Simon P, Widlocher D (1980): Antimanic effect of clonidine. Am J Psychiatry 137:1275–1276.

Kando JC, Tohen M, Castillo-Ruiz J, Centorrino F (1994): Concurrent use of clozapine and valproate in affective and psychotic disorders. J Clin Psychiatry 55:255–257.

Kane JM, Jeste DV (eds) (1992): "Tardive Dyskinesia: A Task Force Report of the American Psychiatric Association." Washington, DC: American Psychiatric Association.

Kasarskis EJ, Kuo CJ, Berger R, Nelson KR (1992): Carbamazepine induced cardiac dysfunction: Characterization of two distinct syndromes. Arch Int Med 152:186–191.

Kashani JH, Carlson GA, Beck NC, Hoeper EW, Corcoran CM, McAlister JA, Fallahi C, Rosenberg TK, Reid JC (1987): Depression, depressive symptoms, and depressed mood among a community sample of adolescents. Am J Psychiatry 144:931–934.

Katon W, von Korff M, Lin E, Bush T, Ormel J (1992): Adequacy and duration of antidepressant treatment in primary care. Medical Care 30:67–76.

Katz RI, Kopin IJ (1969): Release of norepinephrine-³H and serotonin-³H evoked from brain slices by electrical field stimulation—Calcium dependency and the effects of lithium, ouabain, and tetrodotoxin. Biochem Pharmacol 18:1935–1939.

Keck PE Jr, McElroy SL, Strakowski SM, West SA (1994): Pharmacologic treatment of schizoaffective disorder. Psychopharmacology 114:529–538.

Kessler RC, McGonigle KA, Zhao S, Nelson CB, Hughes M, Eshleman S, Wittchen H-U, Kendler KS (1994): Lifetime and 12-month prevalence of DSM-III-R psychiatric disorders in the United States: Results from the national comorbidity study. Arch Gen Psychiatry 51:8–19.

Kielholz P, Terzani S, Pöldinger W (1979): The long-term treatment of periodical and cyclic depressions with flupenthixol decanoate. Int Pharmacopsychiatry 14:305–309.

Klein E, Bental E, Lerer B, Belmaker RH (1984): Carbamazepine and haloperidol vs. placebo and haloperidol in excited psychoses. Arch Gen Psychiatry 41:165–170.

Klein HE, Broucek B, Greil W (1981): Lithium withdrawal triggers psychotic states. Br J Psychiatry 139:255–264.

Kleist K (1953): Die Gleiderung der neuropsychischen Erkrankungen. Monatschr Psychiatr Neurol 125:526–554.

Klerman GL, Lavori P, Rice J, Reich T, Endicott J, Andreasen NC, Keller MB, Hirschfeld R (1985): Birth-cohort trends in rates of major depressive disorder among relatives of patients with affective disorder. Arch Gen Psychiatry 42:689–693.

Kocsis JH, Shaw ED, Stokes PE, Wilner P, Elliot AS, Sikes C, Myers B, Manevitz A, Parides M (1993): Neuropsychologic effects of lithium discontinuation. J Clin Psychopharmacol 13:268–276.

Kovacs M (1989): Affective disorders in children and adolescents. Am Psychologist 44:209–215.

Kraepelin E (1921): "Manic–Depressive Insanity and Paranoia" (Barclay RM, translator; Robertson GM, ed). Edinburgh: E & S Livingstone.

Krauthammer C, Klerman GL (1978): Secondary mania: Manic syndromes associated with antecedent physical illness or drugs. Arch Gen Psychiatry 35:1333–1339.

Kravitz HM, Fawcett J (1987): Carbamazepine in the treatment of affective disorders. Med Sci Res 15:1–8.

Kron L, Decina P, Kestenbaum CJ, Farber S, Gargan M, Fieve R (1982): The offspring of bipolar manic–depressives: Clinical features. In Feinstein SC, Looney JG, Schwartzbert AZ (eds): "Adolescent Psychiatry," Vol 10. Chicago: University of Chicago Press, pp 273–291.

Kukopulos A, Caliari B, Tundo A, Minnai G, Floris G, Reginaldi G, Tondo L (1983): Rapid cyclers, temperament, and antidepressants. Compr Psychiatry 24:249–258.

Kukopulos A, Reginaldi D, Laddomada P, Floris G, Serra G, Tondo L (1980): Course of the manic–depressive cycle and changes caused by treatments. Neuropsychopharmakologie 13:156–167.

Labrecque J, Coté MA, Vincent P (1992): Carbamazepine-induced atrioventricular block. Am J Psychiatry 149:572–573.

Lazarus JH (1986): "Endocrine and Metabolic Effects of Lithium." New York: Plenum Press.

Lapierre YD, Gagnon A, Kokkinidis L (1980): Rapid recurrence of mania following lithium withdrawal. Biol Psychiatry 15:859–864.

Lefkowitz MM, Burton N (1978): Childhood depression: A critique of the concept. Psychol Bull 85:716–726.

Lehman K, Merten X (1974): Die Elimination von Lithium in Abhängigkeit vom Lebensalter bei Gesunden und Niereninsufizienten. Int J Clin Pharmacol Ther Toxicol 10:292–298.

Leonhard K (1957): "Aufteilung der Endogene Psychosen." Berlin: Academie Verlag.

Lewis JL, Winokur G (1982): The induction of mania: A natural history study with controls. Arch Gen Psychiatry 39:303–306.

Leysen D, Pinder RM (1994): Toward third generation antidepressants. Ann Reports Med Chem 29:1–12.

Maj M, Pirozzi R, Magliano L (1995): Nonresponse to reinstituted lithium prophylaxis in previously responsive bipolar patients: Prevalence and predictors. Am J Psychiatry 152:1810–1811.

Maj M, Starace F, Nolfe G, Kemali G (1986): Minimum plasma lithium levels required for effective prophylaxis in DSM-III bipolar disorder. A prospective study. Pharmacopsychiatry 19:420–423.

Mandel MR, Madsen J, Miller AL, Baldessarini RJ (1980): Intoxication associated with lithium and ECT. Am J Psychiatry 137:1107–1109.

Manji HK, Lenox RH (1994): Long-term actions of lithium: A role for transcriptional and post-transcriptional factors regulated by protein kinase C. Synapse 16:11–28.

Manji HK, Potter WZ, Lenox RH (1995): Signal transduction pathways: Molecular targets for lithium's actions. Arch Gen Psychiatry 42:431–543.

Marder SR, Meibach RC (1994): Risperidone in the treatment of schizophrenia. Am J Psychiatry 151:825–835.

McCombs JS, Nichol MB, Stimmel GL, Sclar DA, Beasley CM Jr, Gross LS (1990): The cost of antidepressant drug therapy failure: A study of antidepressant use patterns in a Medicaid population. J Clin Psychiatry 51(Suppl 6):60–69.

McElroy SL, Keck PE Jr, Bennett JA (1993): Valproate as a loading treatment in acute mania. Neuropsychobiology 27:146–149.

McElroy SL, Keck PE Jr, Pope HG Jr, Hudson JI (1992): Valproate in the treatment of bipolar disorder: Literature review and clinical guidelines. J Clin Psychopharmacol 12(Suppl 3):42S–52S.

McFarland BH, Miler MR, Straumfjord AA (1990): Valproate use in the older manic patient. J Clin Psychiatry 51:479–481.

Meltzer HY (ed) (1992): "Novel Antipsychotic Drugs." Raven Press, New York.

Mirchandani IC, Young RC (1993): Management of mania in the elderly: An update. Ann Clin Psychiatry 5:67–77.

Mitchell SW (1870): On the use of bromide of lithium. Am J Med Sci 60:443–445.

Modell JG, Lenox RH, Weiner S (1985): Inpatient clinical trial of lorazepam for the management of manic agitation. J Clin Psychopharmacol 5:109–113.

Mukherjee S, Sackheim HA, Schnur DB (1994): Electroconvulsive therapy of acute manic episodes: A review of 50 years' experience. Am J Psychiatry 151:169–176.

Müller-Oerlinghausen B, Müser-Causemann B. Volk J (1992): Suicides and parasuicides in a high-risk patient group on and off lithium long-term medication. J Affect Disord 25:261–270.

Mueller P, Heipertz R (1977): Zur behandlung manischer Psychosen mit Clozapin. Fortschr Neurol Psychiatrie 45:420–424.

Murray N, Hopwood S, Balfour SJK, Ogston S, Hewick DS (1983): The influence of age on lithium efficacy and side-effects in out-patients. Psychol Med 13:53–60.

Nemeroff CB, Schatzberg AF (eds) (1995): "Textbook of Psychopharmacology." Washington, DC: American Psychiatric Press.

Nierenberg DW, Semprebon M (1993): The central nervous system serotonin syndrome. Clin Pharmacol Ther 53:85–88.

Nilsson A, Axelsson R (1989): On the elimination half-life of lithium in long-term treatment of patients with affective disorders. Human Psychopharmacol 4:247–257.

Okuma T, Inanaga K, Otsuki S, Sarai K, Takahashi R, Hazama H, Mori A, Watanabe S (1981): A preliminary double-blind study on the efficacy of carbamazepine in prophylaxis of manic–depressive illness. Psychopharmacology 73:95–96.

Papatheodorou G, Kutcher SP, Katic M (1996): The efficacy and safety of divalproex sodium in the treatment of acute mania in adolescents and young adults: An open clinical trial (in press).

Patsalos PN, Duncan JS (1994): New antiepileptic drugs: A review of their current status and clinical potential. CNS Drugs 2:40–77.

Pearlman CA (1986): Neuroleptic malignant syndrome: A review of the literature. J Clin Psychopharmacology 6:257–273.

Pellock JM (1987): Carbamazepine side effects in children and adults. Epilepsia 28(Suppl 3):64S–70S.

Perris C (1982): The distinction between bipolar and unipolar affective disorders. In Paykel ES (ed): "Handbook of Affective Disorders." New York: Guilford Press, pp 45–58.

Pleak RR, Birmaher B, Gavrilescu A, Abichandani C, Williams DT (1988): Mania and neuropsychiatric excitation following carbamazepine. J Am Acad Child Adolesc Psychiatry 27:500–503.

Plenge P, Stensgaard A, Jensen HV, Thomsen C, Mellerup ET, Henricksen O (1994): 24-Hour lithium concentration in human brain studies by Li-7 magnetic resonance spectroscopy. Biol Psychiatry 36:511–516.

Pope HG Jr, McElroy SL, Keck PE, Hudson HI (1991): Valproate in the treatment of mania. Arch Gen Psychiatry 48:62–68.

Post F (1992): Affective disorders in old age. In Paykel ES (ed): "Handbook of Affective Disorders." New York: Guilford Press, pp 393–402.

Post RM, Leverich GS, Altshuler LL, Mikalauskas K (1992): Lithium-discontinuation-induced refractoriness: Preliminary observations. Am J Psychiatry 149:1727–1729.

Post RM, Leverich GS, Pazzaglia PJ, Mikalauskas K, Denocoff K (1993): Lithium tolerance and discontinuation as pathways to refractoriness. In Birch NJ, Padgham C, Hughes MS (eds): "Lithium in Medicine and Biology." Carnforth, UK: Marius Press, pp 71–84.

Post RM, Weiss SRB, Chuang D-M (1992): Mechanisms of action of anticonvulsants in affective disorders: Comparisons with lithium. J Clin Psychopharmacol 12(Suppl 1):23S–35S.

Post Rm, Leverich GS, Rosoff AS, Altshuler LL (1990): Carbamazepine prophylaxis in refractory affective disorders: A focus on long-term follow-up. J Clin Psychopharmacol 10:318–327.

Post RM, Uhde TW, Roy-Byrne PP, Joffe RT (1987): Correlates of antimanic responses to carbamazepine. Psychiatry Res 21:71–83.

Post RM, Uhde TW, Roy-Byrne PP, Joffe RT (1986): Antidepressant effects of carbamazepine. Am J Psychiatry 143:29–34.

Potter WZ, Murphy DL, Wehr TA, Linnoila M, Goodwin FK (1982): Clorgyline: A new treatment for patients with refractory rapid-cycling disorder. Arch Gen Psychiatry 39:505–510.

Povlsen UJ, Hetmar O, Ladefoged J, Bolwig TG (1992): Kidney functioning during lithium treatment: A prospective study of patients treated with lithium for up to ten years. Acta Psychiatr Scand 85:56–60, 1992.

Price LH, Heninger GR (1994): Lithium in the treatment of mood disorders. N Engl J Med 331:591–597.

Prien FR, Gelenberg AJ (1989): Alternatives to lithium for preventive treatment of bipolar disorder. Am J Psychiatry 146:840–848.

Prien RF, Kupfer DJ (1986): Continuation drug therapy for major depressive episodes: How long should it be maintained? Am J Psychiatry 143:18–23.

Prien RF, Kupfer DJ, Mansky PA, Small JG, Tuason VB, Voss CB, Johnson WE (1984): Drug therapy in the prevention of recurrences in unipolar and bipolar affective disorders. Arch Gen Psychiatry 41:1096–1104.

Prien RF, Caffey EM Jr, Klett CJ (1972): Comparison of lithium carbonate and chlorpromazine in the treatment of mania. Arch Gen Psychiatry 26:1436–1453.

Rafaelsen OJ, Bolwig TG, Ladefoged J, Bruc C (1979): Kidney function and morphology in long-term treatment. In Cooper TB, Gershon S, Kline N, Schou M (eds): "Lithium: Controversies and Unresolved Issues." Amsterdam: Excerpta Medica, pp 578–583.

Ray WA, Griffin MR, Schaffner W, Baugh DK, Melton LJ III (1987): Psychotropic drug use and the risk of hip fracture. N Engl J Med 316:363–369.

Remick RA, Maurice WL (1988): ECT in pregnancy. Am J Psychiatry 135:761–762.

Rettie AE, Rettenmeier AW, Howald WN, Baillie TA (1987): Cytochrome P-450 catalyzed formation of D^4-VPA, a toxic metabolite of valproic acid. Science 235:890–893.

Rice DP, Miller LS (1994): The economic burden of depression and other affective disorders. In McCombs JS (ed): "The Economics of Depression." Proceedings of a National Managed Health Care Congress, New York: Philips, Gianettino and Meredith, pp 8–11.

Robert E, Guibaud P (1982): Maternal valproic acid and congenital neural tube defects. Lancet 2:937.

Roose SP, Bone S, Haidorfer C, Dunner DL (1979): Lithium treatment in older patients. Am J Psychiatry 136:843–844.

Rosa FW (1991): Spina bifida in infants of women treated with carbamazepine in pregnancy. N Engl J Med 324:674–677.

Rosebush P, Stewart TD, Gelenberg AJ (1989): Twenty neuroleptic rechallenges after neuroleptic malignant syndrome in 15 patients. J Clin Psychiatry 50:295–298.

Rosenbaum JF, Sachs GS, Lafer B, Kane JM, Keller MB, Gelenberg AJ (1992): High rates of relapse in bipolar patients abruptly changed from standard to low plasma lithium levels in a double-blind, controlled trial. "Proceedings of the Annual Meeting of the New Clinical Drug Evaluations Unit (NCDEU)." Boca Raton, FL: US National Institute of Mental Health (NIMH).

Rosenburg MR, Green, M (1989): Neuroleptic malignant syndrome: Review of response to therapy. Arch Intern Med 149:1927–1931.

Roy-Byrne PP, Post RM, Uhde TW, Porcu T, Davis D (1985): The longitudinal course of affective illness. Acta Psychiatr Scand 71(Suppl 317):1–34.

Rudorfer MV, Linnoila M (1986): Electroconvulsive therapy. In Johnson FN (ed): "Lithium Combination Treatment." Basel: Karger Verlag, pp 164–178.

Ryan ND, Puig-Antich J (1987): Pharmacological treatment of adolescent psychiatric disorders. J Adolesc Health Care 8:137–142.

Ryan ND, Puig-Antich J, Ambrosini P, Rabinovich H, Robinson D, Nelson B, Iyengar Twomey J (1987): The clinical picture of major depression in children and adolescents. Arch Gen Psychiatry 44:854–861.

Sachs GS, Lafer B, Stoll AL, Banov M, Thibault AB, Tohen M, Rosenbaum JF (1994): A double-blind trial of bupropion vs. desipramine for bipolar depression. J Clin Psychiatry 55:391–393.

Sargenti CJ, Rizos AL, Jeste DV (1988): Psychotropic drug interactions in the patient with late-onset psychosis and mood disorder. Psychiatr Clin No Am 11:235–252.

Schaff MR, Fawcett J, Zejecka JM (1993): Divalproex sodium in the treatment of refractory affective disorders. J Clin Psychiatry 54:380–384.

Schaffer CB, Garvey MJ (1984): Use of lithium in acutely manic elderly patients. Clin Gerontologist 3:58–60.

Schaffer CB, Mungas D, Rockwell E (1985): Successful treatment of psychotic depression with carbamazepine. J Clin Psychopharmacol 5:233–235.

Schnur DB, Mukherjee S, Sackheim HA, Lee C, Roth SD (1992): Symptomatic predictors of ECT response in medication-nonresponsive manic patients. J Clin Psychiatry 53:63–66.

Schou M (1993): Lithium prophylaxis: About "naturalistic" or "clinical practice" studies. Lithium 4:77–81.

Schou M (1957): Biology and pharmacology of the lithium ion. Pharmacol Rev 9:17–58.

Schou M, Juel-Nielsen N, Strömgren E Voldby H (1954): The treatment of manic psychoses by the administration of lithium salts. J Neurol Neurosurg Psychiatry 17:250–260.

Sernyak MJ, Woods SW (1993): Chronic neuroleptic use in manic–depressive illness. Psychopharmacol Bull 29:375–381.

Shopsin B, Gershon S, Thompson H, Collins P (1975): Psychoactive drugs in mania: A controlled comparison of lithium carbonate, chlorpromazine, and haloperidol. Arch Gen Psychiatry 32:34–42.

Shukla WS, Cook BL, Hoff AL, Aronson TA (1988): Failure to detect organic factors in mania. J Affect Disord 15:17–20.

Shulman KI (1993): Mania in the elderly. Intl Rev Psychiatry 5:445–453.

Shulman KI, Post F (1980): Bipolar affective disorder in old age. Br J Psychiatry 136:26–32.

Shulman KI, Mackenzie S, Hardy B (1987): The clinical use of lithium carbonate in old age: A review. Prog Neuropsychopharmacol Biol Psychiatry 11:159–164.

Sifton DW (ed) (1995): "Physician's Desk Reference (PDR)," 49th ed. Montvale, NJ: Medical Economics Data Production.

Small JG, Klapper MH, Milstein V, Kellams JJ, Miller MJ, Marhenki JD, Small IF (1991): Carbamazepine compared with lithium in the treatment of mania. Arch Gen Psychiatry 48:915–921.

Small JG, Small IF, Moore DF (1971): Experimental withdrawal of lithium in recovered manic–depressive patients: A report of five cases. Am J Psychiatry 127:1555–1558.

Smith JM, Baldessarini RJ (1980): Changes in prevalence, severity, and recovery in tardive dyskinesia with age. Arch Gen Psychiatry 37:1368–1373.

Smith RE, Helms PM (1982): Adverse effects of lithium therapy in the acutely ill elderly patient. J Clin Psychiatry 43:94–99.

Souza FGM, Goodwin GM (1991): Lithium treatment and prophylaxis in unipolar depression: A meta-analysis. Br J Psychiatry 158:666–675.

Stancer HC, Persad E (1982): Treatment of intractable rapid-cycling manic–depressive disorder with levothyroxine. Arch Gen Psychiatry 39:311–312.

Stein D, Avni J (1988): Thyroid hormones in the treatment of affective disorders. Acta Psychiatr Scand 77:623–636.

Sternbach H (1991): The serotonin syndrome. Am J Psychiatry 148:705–713.

Stokes PE, Shamoian CA, Stoll PM, Patton MJ (1971): Efficacy of lithium as acute treatment of manic–depressive disease. Lancet 1:1319–1325.

Stoll AL, Mayer PV, Kolbrener M, Goldstein E, Suplit B, Lucier J, Cohen BM, Tohen M (1994): Antidepressant-associated mania: A controlled comparison with spontaneous mania. Am J Psychiatry 151:1642–1645.

Stoll AL, Tohen M, Baldessarini RJ, Goodwin DC, Stein S, Katz S, Geenens D, Swinson RP, Goethe JW, McGlashan T (1993): Shifts in diagnostic frequencies of schizophrenia and major affective disorders at six North American psychiatric hospitals, 1972–1988. Am J Psychiatry 150:1668–1673.

Stone K (1989): Mania in the elderly. Br J Psychiatry 155:220–224.

Strayhorn JM, Nash JL (1977): Severe neurotoxicity despite "therapeutic" serum lithium levels. Dis Nerv Syst 38:107–111.

Strober M, Morrell W, Lampert C, Burroughs J (1990): Relapse following discontinuation of lithium maintenance therapy in adolescents with bipolar I illness: A naturalistic study. Am J Psychiatry 147:457–461.

Strober M, Morrell W, Burroughs J, Lampert C, Danforth H, Freeman R (1988): A family study of bipolar I disorder in adolescence: Early onset of symptoms linked to increased familial loading and lithium resistance. J Affect Disord 15:255–268.

Strömgren LS, Boller S (1985): Carbamazepine in treatment and prophylaxis of manic–depressive disorder. Psychiatric Develop 4:349–367.

Summers WK (1983): Mania with onset in the eighth decade: Two cases and a review. J Clin Psychiatry 44;141–143.

Suppes T, Phillips KA, Judd CR (1994): Clozapine treatment of nonpsychotic rapid cycling bipolar disorder: A report of three cases. Biol Psychiatry 36:338–340.

Suppes T, Baldessarini RJ, Faedda GL, Tondo L, Tohen M (1993): Discontinuing maintenance treatment in bipolar manic–depression: Risks and implications. Harvard Rev Psychiatry 1:131–144.

Suppes T, McElroy SL, Gilbert J, Dessain EC, Cole JO (1992): Clozapine in the treatment of dysphoric mania. Biol Psychiatry 32:270–280.

Suppes T, Baldessarini RJ, Faedda GL, Tohen M (1991): Risk of recurrence following discontinuation of lithium treatment in bipolar disorder. Arch Gen Psychiatry 48:1082–1088.

Takahashi R, Sakuma A, Itoh K, Itoh H, Kurihara M (1975): Comparison of efficacy of lithium carbonate and chlorpromazine in mania. Arch Gen Psychiatry 32:1310–1318.

Talbott JH (1950): Use of lithium salts as a substitute for sodium chloride. Arch Int Med 85:1–10.

Thisted E, Ebbessen F (1993): Malformations, withdrawal manifestations, and hypoglycæmia after exposure to valproate in utero. Arch Dis Childhood 69:288–291.

Tohen M (1995): Adverse effect profile and safety of divalproex (unpublished).

Tohen M (1991): Course and treatment outcome in patients with mania. In Mirin SM, Gosett JT, Grob MT (eds): "Psychiatric Treatment: Advances in Outcome Research." Washington, DC: American Psychiatric Press, pp 127–142.

Tohen M, Castillo-Ruiz J, Baldessarini RJ, Kando KC, Zarate CA (1995a): Blood dyscrasias with carbamazepine and valproate: A pharmacoepidemiological study of 2,228 cases at risk. Am J Psychiatry 152:413–418.

Tohen M, Zarate CZ, Centorrino F, Hegarty JM, Froerch M, Zarate SB (1995b): Risperidone in the treatment of mania (unpublished)

Tohen M, Castillo-Ruiz J, Pope HG Jr, Herbstein J (1994a): Concomitant use of valproate and carbamazepine in bipolar and schizoaffective disorders. J Clin Psychopharmacol 14:67–70.

Tohen M, Shulman KI, Satlin A (1994b): First-episode mania in late life. Am J Psychiatry 151:130–132.

Tohen M, Waternaux CM, Tsuang MT (1990): Outcome in mania: A four-year prospective study of 75 patients utilizing survival analysis. Arch Gen Psychiatry 47;1106–1111.

Tondo L, Baldessarini RJ, Floris G, Silvetti F, Rudas N (1996): Lithium maintenance treatment reduces risk of suicidal behavior in bipolar disorder patients. In Gallicchio VS, Birch NJ, (eds.) "Lithium: Biochemical and Clinical Advances." New Haven: Science Park Press, 1996, in press.

Ure A (1843): Observations and researches upon a new solvent for stone in the bladder. Pharmaceut J 8:71–74.

Vajda FJE (1992): New anticonvulsants. Curr Opinion Neurol Neurosurg 5:519–525.

van der Velde CD (1971): Toxicity of lithium carbonate in elderly patients. Am J Psychiatry 127:115–117.

van der Velde CD (1970): Effectiveness of lithium carbonate in the treatment of manic–depressive illness. Am J Psychiatry 127:345–351.

Vanelle JM, Leigh TH, Lôo H, Priest RG (1994): Resistance to lithium: What alternatives exist? Human Psychopharmacol 9:321–327.

Veranka TM, Weller RA, Weller EB, Fristad MA (1988): Lithium treatment of manic episodes with psychotic features in prepubertal children. Am J Psychiatry 145:1557–1559.

Vestergaard P (1992): Treatment and prevention of mania: A Scandinavian perspective. Neuropsychopharmacology 7:249–259.

Vestergaard P, Schou M (1984): The effect of age on lithium dosage requirements. Pharmacopsychiatry 17:199–201.

Viguera AC, Baldessarini RJ, Hegarty JM, Van Kammen D, Tohen M (1996): Risk of discontinuing maintenance medication in schizophrenia. Arch Gen Psychiatry.

Walker RG (1993): Lithium nephrotoxicity. Kidney Intl 44(Suppl 42):93S–98S.

Warkany J (1988): Teratogen update: Lithium. Teratology 38:593–596.

Waters B, Lapierre Y, Gagnon A, Cahudhry R, Tremblay A, Sarantidis D, Gray R (1982): Determination of the optimal concentration of lithium for the prophylaxis of manic–depressive disorder. Biol Psychiatry 17:1323–1329.

Wehr TA, Goodwin FK (1987): Can antidepressants cause mania and worsen the course of affective illness? Am J Psychiatry 144:1403–1411.

Weller EB, Weller RA, Fristad MA (1986a): Lithium dosage guide for prepubertal children: A preliminary report. J Am Acad Child Adolesc Psychiatry 25:92–95.

Weller EB, Weller RA, Rucker SG, Fristad MA (1986b): Mania in prepubertal children: Has it been underdiagnosed? J Affect Disord 11:151–154.

White E, Cheung P, Silverstone T (1993): Depot antipsychotics in bipolar affective disorder. Int Clin Psychopharmacol 8:119–122.

Wilens TE, Biederman J, Baldessarini RJ, Puopolo P, Flood JG (1992): Developmental changes in serum concentrations of desipramine and 2-hydroxydesipramine during treatment with desipramine. J Am Acad Child Adolesc Psychiatry 31:691–698.

Wilkinson DG (1979): Difficulty in stopping lithium prophylaxis. Br Med J 1:235–236.

Wood HC Jr, LaWall CH (1926): "The Pharmacopoeia of the United States of America," 21st ed. Philadelphia: JB Lippincott CO, pp 658–662.

Wozniak J, Biederman J, Kieley K, Ablon JS, Faraone SV, Mundy E, Mennin D (1995): Mania-like symptoms suggestive of childhood-onset bipolar disorder in clinically referred children. J Am Acad Child Adolesc Psychiatry 34:867–876.

Wright JM, Silove D (1988): Pseudodementia in schizophrenia and mania. Austral N Z J Psychiatry 22:109–114.

Yassa R, Nair NPV, Iskandar H (1988): Late-onset bipolar disorder. Psychiatr Clin No Am 11:117–131.

Yeragani VK, Gershon S (1986): Hammond and lithium: Historical update. Biol Psychiatry 21:1101–1109.

Younes RP, DeLong GR, Neiman G, Rosner B (1986): Manic-depressive illness in children: Treatment with lithium carbonate. J Child Neurology 1:364–368.

Young RC (1992): Geriatric mania. Clinics Geriatric Med 8:387–399.

Young RC, Falk JR (1989): Age, manic psychopathology and treatment response. Int J Geriatr Psychiatry 4:73–78.

Young RC, Klerman GL (1992): Mania in late life: Focus on age at onset. Am J Psychiatry 149:867–876.

Youngerman J, Canino IA (1978): Lithium carbonate use in children and adolescents. Arch Gen Psychiatry 35:216–224.

Zajecka JM (1993): Pharmacology, pharmacokinetics, and safety issues of mood stabilizing agents. Psychiatr Ann 23:79–85.

Zarate CA, Tohen M, Baldessarini RJ (1995a): Clozapine therapy in severe mood disorders. J Clin Psychiatry 56:411–417.

Zarate CA, Tohen M, Banov MD, Weiss MC, Cole JO (1995b): Is clozapine a mood-stabilizer? J Clin Psychiatry 56:108–112.

Zarin DA, Pass TM (1987): Lithium and the single episode: When to begin long-term prophylaxis for bipolar disorder. Medical Care 25(Suppl 12):S76–S84.

Zis AP, Goodwin FK (1979): Major affective disorder as recurrent illness. Arch Gen Psychiatry 36:835–839.

Zornberg GL, Pope HG Jr (1993): Treatment of depression in bipolar disorders: New directions for research. J Clin Psychopharmacol 13:397–408.

PART IV

OLD AGE

CHAPTER 16

Clinical Features and Pathogenesis of Depression in Old Age

NATHAN HERRMANN

Department of Psychiatry, Sunnybrook Health Science Centre, Toronto, Ontario, Canada
M4N 3M5

Mrs. S., an 83-year-old woman, presents with complaints of headache, nausea, constipation, and a burning sensation all over her body. She has been a healthy woman with no contributing medical history. She denies feeling depressed though admits to significant worry about the possibility of a medical illness. On further examination there is evidence of recent onset of sleep difficulties with early morning awakening as well as decreased appetite and a 10-lb weight loss over one month.

Mr. R. is a 76-year-old gentleman who was treated 20 years earlier for a major affective disorder with ECT. He presents complaining of memory problems and inability to function. On examination he admits that he is terrified of developing Alzheimer's disease and as a result has been feeling depressed and anxious. He is anhedonic, passively suicidal, has lost his appetite, and complains of significant initial insomnia. On cognitive assessment there is some memory and concentration impairment and he scores 24/30 on the Mini Mental State Examination.

Mrs. T. is a 68-year-old woman with a history of recurrent depressive illness. She presents in an extremely agitated state after refusing to eat and drink for 24 hours. There is a history of increasing depression and social withdrawal for approximately 2 weeks. On examination she is desperate and pleads for help. She admits she has not been eating as a punishment for her sins. She refuses the offer of admission because she believes that she cannot pay for her hospital care and proceeds to describe in detail what are clearly delusions of poverty.

INTRODUCTION

These three presentations, examples of somatization and hypochondriasis, pseudodementia, and psychosis with agitation, have long been considered among the hallmarks of depression in old age. Numerous clinical reviews have focused on the atypical

Mood Disorders Across the Life Span, Edited by Shulman, Tohen, and Kutcher
ISBN 0-471-10477-9 © 1996 Wiley-Liss, Inc.

presentation of depression in the elderly including pseudodementia, pain syndromes, masked depression (depressive equivalents), somatization, importuning, and psychosis (see, e.g., McCullough, 1991; Goldfarb, 1967; Shamoian, 1985; Finlayson and Martin, 1982). A more recent review concluded that depression in late life can present as a disorder of behavior including the accentuation of premorbid personality traits, shoplifting, late-onset alcohol abuse, and the new onset of complaints of loneliness (Baldwin, 1991). Some reviews have suggested that these atypical presentations occur just as frequently as the more typical classic symptoms of the DSM Major Depressive Episode (McCullough, 1991).

But how common are these atypical presentations? Have research studies shown that the presentation of depression in late life differs significantly from younger populations? If differences in presentation do exist, does this suggest that depression in late life may have a different cause than depression that occurs earlier in the life cycle? This chapter will attempt to review some of the studies that have examined the phenomenology and etiological correlates of late-life depression with an aim to answer some of these questions.

Prior to a review of the studies on late-life depression it is important to consider some of the methodological problems associated with this work. Geriatric psychiatry is still a relatively young subspecialty, and as a result there are relatively few studies addressing these issues. Many of these studies are hampered by small sample sizes or have relied on mixed-age populations with an average age that is much lower than typically seen by a geriatric clinician. The diagnostic criteria such as DSM-III-R and DSM-IV tend to describe a relatively homogeneous illness, thereby possibly ruling out a diagnosis of depression in someone with an atypical presentation. It would therefore not be surprising that studies that utilize such criteria would find few differences between younger and older populations. This problem may be compounded by the tendency of elderly people to minimize feelings of sadness (Georgotas, 1983) or deny feelings of depression either in an attempt to present better and healthier or because of lack of awareness (Raskin, 1979; Salzman and Shader, 1979). Many studies have also excluded patients with significant medical illnesses or cognitive impairment, two very common comorbid features seen in depressed elderly. Numerous studies suffer from a referral filter bias and rely largely on inpatient populations, with much fewer studies having been done on outpatients. Even the relatively rare epidemiological studies on depression in late life contain serious flaws. For example, a well-described criticism of the important Epidemiological Catchment Area study (Myers, et al., 1984) is that it may have seriously underestimated the prevalence of depression in late life by not surveying elderly patients in long-term care facilities (Snowdon, 1990). Finally, another concern often raised is the validity of using rating scales that were designed for use in young and middle-age populations for examining depression in the elderly. This concern, which presupposes that there are significant differences between these two populations, has received support from a number of authors who believe that use of the popular Hamilton Depression Rating Scale might be problematic because of the heavy weighting toward somatic symptoms (Thompson et al., 1988). It should be pointed out, however, that studies often show high correlations between a variety of rating scales and instruments designed specifically for the elderly, such as the Geriatric Depression Scale (Koenig and Blazer, 1992; Yesavage et al., 1983).

CLINICAL FEATURES OF DEPRESSION IN LATE LIFE

Hypochondriasis and Somatic Complaints

According to a recent review by Reifler (1994), geriatric psychiatrists generally regard medically unexplained somatic complaints as equivalent to depressed mood in elderly patients being examined for depression. This view, however, may be based on relatively little empirical data. Gurland (1976) found the only difference between older and younger depressives was an increase in hypochondriacal symptoms in the former. Similarly, Brown et al. (1984) found that older patients and those with late-onset depressive illnesses had more hypochondriacal complaints. These studies, however, did not assess for actual physical illness, which might account for symptoms such as anorexia, weight loss, psychomotor retardation, and poor energy even in the absence of a clinical depressive illness. In contrast, Blazer et al. (1987a), comparing a young and elderly inpatient psychiatric population, as well as Musetti et al. (1989), comparing a large outpatient population of young and older depressives, found that there were no differences in somatization and hypochondirasis. Looking at this issue with a different sample, Koenig et al. (1993), studying depression in young and older medically ill patients, found the frequency of somatic complaints the same in both depressed groups. They also found the large number of somatic complaints in the elderly group as a whole was due primarily to more severe physical illness in that group rather than the depression per se. It is possible that the clinical impression of the importance of hypochondriasis in late-life depression is based on the tendency of geriatric psychiatrists to see older people who fit the description of the "frail elderly" with mutliple pathologies of both medical and psychiatric illnesses (Baldwin, 1991).

Psychosis

The association of psychotic symptoms and late-life depression is another good example of a feature that shows little agreement from study to study. Some studies show the prevalence of psychosis increases with age (Meyers et al., 1984; Brodaty et al., 1991), and prevalence increases with later age of onset (Meyers et al., 1984; Meyers and Greenberg, 1986). Other studies show no association with age or age of onset (Nelson and Bowers, 1978; Glassman and Roose, 1981; Charney & Nelson, 1981; Nelson et al., 1989; Herrmann et al., 1989), and one study even shows a trend for psychosis to decrease with age (Musetti et al., 1989). Part of the variability of these studies may be due to differences in sample populations. With regard to psychosis it is likely that in-patient groups will have a higher prevalence of these symptoms compared to a sample of outpatients. Caine et al. (1994) suggest that another possible confounder is the fact that younger, psychotic, depressed patients who may appear as unipolar depressives at the time of the study may subsequently develop manic episodes in the context of a bipolar illness, an event that would be likely less common in an older sample. It is also possible that some of the psychotic depressives in certain samples may have unrecognized subtle neurodegenerative disorders and other organic causes that might make psychosis more likely.

Pseudodementia

Pseudodementia (a.k.a. the dementia syndrome of depression, depressive pseudodementia) has attracted a tremendous amount of attention among geriatric psychiatrists and invited considerable controversy. Kiloh (1961) described 10 cases of a syndrome in which patients presented with cognitive impairment presumed to be caused by *functional* illness that was nonprogressive and could be reversed with adequate treatment. While Kiloh did not limit the description to the elderly or the diagnosis of depression, by the time the term became popularized with descriptions by Wells (1979) and Caine (1981), the syndrome became a major focus for geriatric psychiatrists. For a young subspecialty searching to identify itself, its assessment provided an area of specific expertise not shared by other psychiatrists who rarely saw demented patients. It also provided an antidote for some of the therapeutic nihilism associated with the care of dementia patients; these studies seemed to suggest that substantial numbers of patients with *dementia* were not progressive and untreatable but with appropriate investigation and treatment the condition was, in fact, reversible.

According to Post (1982), the characteristic presentation of the patient with pseudodementia includes the vociferous chief complaint of memory and cognitive difficulties, an abrupt "datable" onset, short duration, and a previous personal or family history of depression. On examination, these patients respond to cognitive testing with "I don't know" responses, there is marked variability in performance (often dependent on motivation), and deficits in remote and recent memory that present as being equally impaired.

Because there are no generally agreed-upon diagnostic criteria for this syndrome, its true prevalence is not known. While a number of studies suggest that between 10 and 20% of depressed elderly patients have significant cognitive deficits (Reynolds et al., 1988), it is not known how many of these fit the description mentioned previously. The prevalence will also clearly vary depending on whether samples were obtained through a psychiatric department or a dementia clinic. For example, Rabins (1981) found pseudodementia in 4% of patients evaluated for dementia on neurology and other medical services. A review of the literature on clinical features suggests that the elapsed time between onset and the seeking of medical help is usually shorter, there is more previous personal and family history of depression, and more severe depressive symptoms. The use of "I don't know" responses and the frequency of memory complaints, however, have not proven to be reliable factors that distinguish pseudodementia from depression with dementia (Emery and Oxman, 1992).

If nonprogression and reversibility are a hallmark of the syndrome, it is essential to review the studies on outcome. Unfortunately, there are only a few studies, and all suffer from the problems described previously. Pearlson et al. (1989) and Rabins et al. (1984) in 2-year follow-up studies show little progression to dementia, while other studies have shown high rates of progression (Kral, 1983; Kral and Emery, 1989; Reding et al., 1985). In the only controlled study using survival analysis, Alexopoulos et al. (1993) found 42% of patients with depression and reversible dementia had developed irreversible dementia on 33-month follow-up. Survival analysis demonstrated that this group had a 4.69 times higher chance of developing irreversible dementia than patients with depression alone. The authors conclude that their results are similar to a clinical study by Kral and Emery (1989) that showed an 89% rate of development of irreversible dementia at 8-year follow-up.

The conflicting results have led some authors to question the utility of the pseudodementia syndrome (Shraberg, 1978; Reifler, 1982). Reifler has argued forcibly that the term should be abandoned. He is concerned that the term potentially leads clinicians to consider dementia and depression as mutually exclusive pathological processes. Furthermore, pseudodementia may be used diagnostically rather than descriptively.

Emery and Oxman (1992), however, have suggested that depression and dementia be viewed on a continuum that includes major depression without dementia, depressive dementia (pseudodementia), degenerative dementia without depression, depression of degenerative dementia, and the independent co-occurrence of degenerative dementia and depression.

From a clinical perspective, one can conclude that there does appear to be a group of patients with major depression who also present with features described as pseudodementia and whose cognitive impairment will reverse with adequate therapy for depression. This small group includes a large proportion of patients who, if followed long enough, will progress to an irreversible dementing illness. These is also a much larger group of patients, however, with bona fide irreversible dementing illness who have significant depressive symptoms. The DSM-IV has recognized this group by allowing clinicians to make the diagnosis of dementia with depressed mood. The clinician's responsibility is to attempt to treat both these groups aggressively and subsequently reassess on follow-up in order to help determine prognosis. In the future, however, the distinction may become more important as specific therapies for dementia as well as dementia with depression are elucidated.

PATHOGENESIS

There are a number of methodological problems with the studies on the etiological correlates of depression in late life. Because most of the studies are correlational in design, it is important to remember causation cannot be inferred. Many studies lack normal controls for the significant number of changes that occur as a result of aging alone. While all studies choose age as a variable, the more promising variable across a number of studies appears to be age of onset. Unfortunately, in the absence of longitudinal studies, the determination of age of onset in the elderly by patient or informant may have questionable reliability. Some studies have failed to report their criteria for determination of age of onset (e.g., Buysse et al., 1988; Nelson et al., 1989) or utilized rather arbitrary criteria. Other studies have used specific diagnostic instruments such as the Schedule for Affective Disorders and Schizophrenia, life-term version (Meyers et al., 1984) or age of first hospitalization (Herrmann et al., 1989). In a study by Steingart and Herrmann (1991), age of onset was assessed by determining the age of symptom onset, the age the patient first saw a health care professional about his or her symptoms, and the age of first hospitalization. In that study, all three variables were highly correlated, and using any one of the three did not change the direction of the study findings. Unfortunately, none of these methods address the reliability of recall of depressive episodes in the elderly. Farrer et al. (1989) studied a large sample of patients with major depression in order to determine the reliability of self-reported age of onset. Reliability for the sample as a whole was good, but individuals in the oldest birth cohort (80–89 years) were significantly less reliable than individuals in other cohorts. Lyness et al. (1994a) have raised other conceptual concerns. Older patients with recurrent, early-onset depression may be a poorer comparison group for late-onset depressives because of "scarring" or alterations of phenomenology, psychosocial correlates, or underlying brain pathobiology, as a result of illness severity and chronicity. While research with this group assumes homogeneity over time, it is possible that recurrent episodes may have different causes at different ages. Despite these concerns, the authors remain optimistic that age of onset will prove a useful research tool. From a clinical standpoint, the age of onset clearly raises important questions: Why would an otherwise healthy 80-year-old with no family or personal history of depression suddenly develop this illness in late life? What follows is a review of the psychosocial and biological correlates of late-life depression.

Psychosocial Correlates

Psychosocial correlates include a myriad of factors such as demographics, early life events, later life events, social integration, social suupports, and personality factors. With such a multiplicity of factors, it is not surprising that many researchers have focused on the interaction of these factors rather than individual effects (see, e.g., George, 1994). Some of these factors are difficult to characterize as either psychosocial or biological. For example, medical illness such as stroke can be an important psychological precipitant (e.g., a form of narcissistic injury; dealing psychologically with disability), a social precipitant (e.g., forced retirement; barrier to social integration), or a biological precipitant (e.g., direct effect of vascular injury to neurotransmitter systems). As a result, medical factors will be discussed separately.

Similar to younger populations, most studies have shown that a preponderance of females suffer from depression in late life compared to males. For example, the Epidemiological Catchment Area (ECA) study (Weissman et al., 1988) reported prevalence rates of 0.1–0.8% in males and 0.6–1.0% in females for major depressive disorder in the population over 65 years of age. A more recent Australian community sample, which included long-term care facilities, unlike the ECA study, found major depressive disorder in 0.4% of men and 1.5% of women over the age of 70 (Henderson et al., 1993). Blazer et al. (1987b), however, found that differences in rates of depression between sexes in older age groups become progressively smaller and may disappear.

Few studies have looked specifically at the effects of early life events such as poverty, abuse, parental separation, divorce, or death on depression in the elderly. Studies examining the effects of early parental loss have shown robust findings in younger populations (e.g., Brown and Harris, 1978). Such factors would continue to operate in late life, according to such theorists as Bolby (1973), who suggest that expectations based on attachment developed in infancy persist relatively unchanged throughout the rest of life. While methodological problems abound with the retrospective collection of data on parents (Halverson, 1988), findings in the elderly have been inconsistent. Murphy (1982) found there were no differences with respect to early parental loss in a group of elderly depressives compared to normal controls. In a large community sample of elderly, the quality of maternal or paternal care was not associated with higher depression scores (Andersson and Stevens, 1993). While not looking specifically at depression, Krause (1993) examined the effect of early parental loss on feelings of personal control in a large community sample of elderly. In this study, early parental loss may have been associated with decreased feeling of control; however, this was because it interfered with education, which resulted in a subsequent decrease in financial security later in life.

Some of the later life events that have been examined include occupation, income, and marital status. Low socioeconomic status and low occupational attainment have been associated with increased risk of depression in the elderly (Blazer et al., 1985). Murphy (1982) found that depression was higher in the working class, likely secondary to more severe life events and poor physical health rather than social class per se. Part of the problem with these studies includes the fact that most people's incomes decrease after retirement and the effect of their previous jobs may wane over time (George, 1994). A number of studies have shown that social support is inversely related to depression in the elderly (Holahan and Holahan, 1987; Lewinsohn et al., 1991), and the risk of depression is lower for married, elderly adults compared to nonmarried elderly adults (Blazer et al., 1985). This literature, however, contains multiple methodological issues that necessitate a review of the number, structure, and composition of individuals available for social support, as well as the type, quantity, quality, and the subject's perception of support (George, 1994). For example, Murphy (1982) found that the degree of intimacy is not a factor, except for those having no confiding relationship at all, in which case the risk of depression is significantly higher.

Studies have shown that depression in late life is frequently preceded by stress and serious life events (George, 1994), though some studies have found inconsistent results (Lewinsohn et al., 1991). Murphy (1982) demonstrated that depressive elderly patients had more severe life events in the preceding year, including bereavement and life-threatening illness in close relatives. Despite the methodological concerns with the caregiver literature (Barer and Johnson, 1990), studies have consistently shown that caregivers of demented patients, and in particular elderly spouses, have very high rates of depression (Gallagher et al., 1989; Cohen and Eisdorfer, 1988). Of all life stresses, spousal bereavement is often considered the one most likely to result in significant psychopathology (Holmes and Rahe, 1967). Spousal bereavement was shown to be an important risk factor for major depression in the ECA study (Weissman et al., 1991). Numerous studies have documented the high prevalence of major depression associated with grief (Futterman et al., 1990; Zisook and Shuchter, 1991). Furthermore, research has indicated that bereavement with depression has similar risk factors to other forms of depression (Harlow et al., 1991; Nuss and Zubenko, 1992), as well as similar sleep correlates (Reynolds et al., 1992). While a number of studies have shown that elderly widows and widowers may actually suffer less depression than younger groups, when added to the other losses that commonly occur in late life, bereavement may contribute to a substantial proportion of the psychopathology in this age group (Parkes, 1992).

With respect to psychosocial correlates, a recent review concluded that, on the whole, these factors appear to be less powerful predictors of depression in late life than they are in young adulthood and middle age. It is possible that specific factors have not yet been identified, that the elderly may not be as sensitive to social context, or that the illness is actually different in late life (George, 1994). This suggests that a closer examination of medical comorbidity and biological factors is required.

Genetic Factors

Of all the etiological correlates in late-life depression, family history has proven to be the most consistent factor. Many studies have replicated the findings that probands with late-onset depression had significantly fewer relatives with depression than probands with early onset (Stenstedt, 1959; Hopkinson, 1964; Mendlewicz, 1976; Baron et al., 1981). In a more recent study, Bland et al. (1986) found the relationship more complicated. The lowest risk in relatives (3.4%) was associated with probands who have late-onset depression and a single episode. The highest risk (17.4%) was for families of probands with recurrent early-onset depression. These authors also found that the two factors (onset age and number of episodes) acted independently of one another.

Some of the criticisms of the genetic studies include the fact that many studies do not actually use elderly probands or age-matched normal controls. In an attempt to deal with these criticisms, Maier et al. (1991) reported their results, utilizing a family study method of 91 probands between 60 and 70 years of age and age-matched general population controls. Results confirmed the previous findings, including those of Bland et al. (1986), but also noted the families of late-onset probands were still at higher risk for developing depression than controls (9.7 vs. 5.6%). From a clinical perspective, family history remains an important factor as other studies have found a positive family history of depression in up to a third of patients with late-onset depression (Baldwin, 1990). Taken together with the previous psychosocial factors, it is important to emphasize the following question: If psychosocial factors and genetic factors play a small role in the genesis of late-onset depression, what does cause this disorder?

Physical Illness

The relationship between physical illness and depression in late life has been recognized since the dawn of the specialty of psychogeriatrics. In 1956, Roth and Kay studied a large group of elderly patients. While physical illness and sensory impairment were common in the group as a whole (62% of men, 51% of women), there was significantly more illness in the group with late onset. While reluctant to attribute an etiological role, they concluded that "in cases of late onset, physical illness played a part in overpowering defenses against breakdown that had proven effective during the greater part of life" (p. 147). As described earlier, the role of physical illness is extremely complicated and as yet remains unclear. Hypotheses concerning the relationship between depression and physical illness include: (1) the relationship is coincidental in view of the significant prevalence of each in late life; (2) there is a direct biological link, that is, physical illness produces depression, via a direct or indirect affect on brain structure and/or function; (3) depressive illness directly or indirectly leads to physical illness; and (4) physical illness and depression interact, each influencing the course of the other (Eastwood and Corbin, 1986).

Studies examining the relationship between medical illness and depression in late life can be roughly divided into two categories: those which examine a large group of depressed elderly to determine the type and amount of medical illness and those that examine certain medical disorders, for example, stroke or Parkinson's disease, to determine prevalence and severity of depression. Numerous studies of depressed, elderly patients have shown correlations between medical illness and depression, though the number and types of medical illnesses are highly variable (Murphy, 1982; Palinkas et al., 1990; Kennedy et al., 1989; Wesner and Winokur, 1988). Medical illness also likely interacts with other factors; in a large community sample of elderly, depression onset was significantly associated with poorer physical health and social support, which played both additive and interactive roles (Phifer and Murrell, 1986). Questioning the role of illness specificity, in a large screening study in elderly primary care patients, Callahan et al. (1994) found only the diagnosis of hemorrhoids was significantly associated with high scores on a depression rating scale. Similarly, several studies have suggested that it is the disability caused by the medical illness that is the most important factor, rather than a specific medical diagnosis (Kennedy et al., 1990; Aneshensel et al., 1984). Examining the effects of chronic medical disability and age on depression, Turner and Beiser (1990) found that while the physically disabled are twice as likely as nondisabled to receive a lifetime diagnosis of depression and three times more likely to report an occurrence in the 6 months preceding the interview, this relationship was not observed in the elderly sample. They hypothesized that the meaning, implication, and impact of physical disability vary with age. Since some forms of disability might be considered "normal" in the elderly and physical disability is less likely to interfere with life goals and satisfaction at this stage, this might constitute less of a risk for a major depression. This theory is based on the premise that medical disability represents a psychosocial stress that, as documented previously, seems to play a smaller role in late-life depression. It does not account for what may be direct effects of certain medical illnesses nor the biological consequences of aging and the associated interactions with affective illness. It is also possible that acute medical illness in the elderly plays a more important role than chronic illness in the precipitation of depression.

While much of the support is anecdotal and correlational, there are a number of specific medical conditions that may "cause" depression and are common in late life. Examples include cancer (e.g., pancreas, lung, brain tumors), endocrine disorders (e.g., hypothyroidism, hyperthyroidism, Cushings disease, hypercalcemia), nutritional disorders (e.g., B_{12} deficiency, folic acid deficiency), infections (e.g., syphilis), and medications (e.g., steroids, beta-blockers, alpha-methyldopa, reserpine, L-dopa) (see e.g., Ouslander, 1982). Previous research has also suggested a relationship between hearing loss and depression (Mahapatra, 1974; Eastwood et al., 1985). Alexopoulos (1990), for example, has found hearing loss was more frequent in geriatric patients with late-onset compared to early-onset depression. The specific medical illnesses that have received the most attention, however, are neurological.

Because the neuroanatomical and physiological features of neurological illnesses are well documented, the relationship between depression and disorders, such as Wilson's disease (Dening and Berrios, 1989), Huntington's disease (Jensen et al., 1993), multiple sclerosis (Joffe et al., 1987), Alzheimer's disease (Wragg and Jeste, 1989), and Parkinson's disease (Sano et al., 1989) has important heuristic value. For example, patients with Parkinson's disease and depression may have greater frontal lobe dysfunction and more impairment in dopaminergic and noradrenergic systems than nondepressed patients (Cummings, 1992). In a positron emission tomography (PET) study of Huntington's disease patients, Mayberg et al. (1992) found significant hypometabolism in the orbital-frontal and inferior prefrontal cortices in the depressed Huntington's disease patients. In a neuropathological study of depression in Alzheimer's disease, Zubenko and Moossy (1988) suggest that depression is associated with degeneration of the locus ceruleus and substantia nigra. Once again, it is important to note that not all studies have found the rates of depression to be increased in many of these disorders when compared to other equally disabling, non-neurological conditions (see, e.g., Hantz et al., 1994).

The best studied neurological condition associated with depression is stroke, with estimates of 30–50% of patients developing depression following a cerebral vascular accident (Starkstein and Robinson, 1989). Important correlates of this condition include the relationship between increased frequency and severity of depression in patients with left-hemisphere lesions and those closer to the anterior pole (Robinson et al., 1984; Eastwood et al., 1989). While depression can occur with cortical or subcortical lesions (Starkstein et al., 1987), another study examining a group of stroke patients with lesions restricted to the basal ganglia and thalamus found a significant frequency of depression with basal ganglia lesions, but no depression in the group with thalamic lesions (Starkstein et al., 1988). These findings combined with laboratory investigations have led to the suggestion that depression following lesions in the frontal cortex or basal ganglia may result from more severe depletion of norepinephrine or serotonin, while the relationship between depression and laterality is due to the lack of compensatory upregulation of serotonin receptors in left-hemisphere lesions but not in right-sided lesions (Robinson and Starkstein, 1990). As impressive and influential as this literature has been, a number of recent, large, well-designed studies have failed to confirm the higher prevalence of depression in stroke patients or the relationship with left-sided lesions (House et al., 1990, 1991; Sharpe et al., 1990, 1994).

Despite the inconsistencies, taken together, the findings of depression in neurological illness suggest the syndrome may be caused by involvement of multiple neurotransmitter systems, including norepinephrine, dopamine, and serotonin, as well as brain regions, such as the basal ganglia and frontal lobes. According to Cummings (1993), an important principle of neuropsychiatry posits a contingent, but not obligatory, relationship between anatomy and behavioral syndromes. Based on this principle, certain lesions may increase a patient's vulnerability to depression, but the occurrence of the syndrome may also require psychosocial or environmental factors. To what, if any, extent these mechanisms apply to the etiology of late-life depression in the absence of any medical illness is unknown.

Biological Correlates

The biological correlates of aging and depression have received a lot of attention in the past decade. In an early study, searching for a biological marker, Cawley et al. (1973) studied barbiturate tolerance in elderly patients. Compared with early-onset depressives, patients with late-onset depression had lower thresholds for sleep and sedation, findings that were similar to a control group of patients with significant cerebral pathology. More recently, findings, including hyperactivity and dysregulation of the hypothalamic–pituitary–adrenal axis, blunted thyrotropin response to thyrotropin-releasing hormone, changes in monoamine metabolites, platelet alpha-2-adrenoreceptor binding, and topographical electroencephograph (EEG) changes have been noted (Veith and Raskind, 1988; Schneider, 1992; Alexopoulos, 1994). Unfortunately, many of these studies have shown conflicting results. Limitations in this area of research include almost exclusive reliance on cross-sectional studies, examination of characteristics that typically discriminate depressed from nondepressed, without addressing age effects, and use of markers that are not sufficiently sensitive and specific (Schneider, 1992). For example, many studies of younger depressed populations have found reductions in platelet ^{3}H-imipramine binding, a marker for serotonin innervation in the brain (Langer et al., 1987). While several studies have also demonstrated similar reductions in depressed elderly compared to normal age-matched controls (Nemeroff et al., 1988; Schneider et al., 1988; Suranyi-Cadotte et al., 1985), others have failed to replicate this finding (Georgotas et al., 1987), and only one study has examined for age effects (Nemeroff et al., 1988). In terms of lack of specificity, low platelet ^{3}H-imipramine binding has also been found in anorexia nervosa, obsessive–compulsive disorder, panic disorder, and enuresis (Langer et al., 1987).

One marker that has been studied more carefully in the elderly is platelet monoamine oxidase (MAO) activity. Platelet MAO activity increases significantly with aging (Bridge et al., 1985) and further increases in the presence of Alzheimer's disease (Adolffson et al., 1980). Alexopoulos et al. (1984) have observed that early-onset depression was associated with low MAO activity in a group of elderly female inpatients compared to those with late-onset depression. This group has also demonstrated (Alexopoulos et al., 1987) that elderly patients with depression and reversible dementia had higher platelet MAO activity than depressed patients without dementia. In summary, while a search for a biological marker for depression in late life seems promising, studies, thus far, have been inconsistent.

Neuropsychological Impairment

While the disorder of depression has proven a fertile ground for neuropsychological studies, many studies have serious methodological limitations, and the results have often been conflicting. Some of the methodological concerns include failure to do pre- and postdepression assessments (thus enabling the researchers to answer the "state versus trait" question), dealing with medication effects, and failure to account for premorbid IQ and severity of clinical symptoms. A recent review, however, concluded that some of the more consistent findings in depressed patients of all ages include impairment in verbal fluency, visuospatial ability, visuomotor speed, visual memory, and motor performance (Brumback, 1993).

Fewer studies have focused on an exclusively older age group, which may lead to significantly different results. For example, in a prospective study of inpatients, Bulbena and Berrios (1993) demonstrated significant impairment in attention, memory, visuospatial function, and reaction time, which varied significantly with age and age of onset of depression. On follow-up, there were no differences found compared to normal controls, except for visuospatial ability, which still showed significant improvement compared with the depressed phase. In a frequently quoted study, Abas et al. (1990) compared elderly depressives to normal elderly controls and dementia patients during the depressed phase and during recovery. They found that 70% of the depressives showed impairment on tests of visual memory and measures of latency. Following recovery, 37% still showed impairment on visual memory and learning tests. One of the possible explanations for the differences in these results includes the former study's average patient age was 50 (SD = 16) while the latter's was 70 (SD = 6.1). This discrepancy, which suggests a separate age effect, receives support from a number of other studies. Lyness et al. (1994b) compared a group of younger and older depressed patients and found no differences on verbal memory or verbal fluency. These investigators did find an effect of age alone on visuospatial tests and a combined effect of age and depression on visuomotor scanning. These results led them to hypothesize that the depression may reflect frontal and subcortical dysfunction while aging results in right-hemisphere impairment. Further complicating the relationship between aging, depression, and cognition is a study by Deptula et al. (1993), examining the effect of mood on memory function in normal young and elderly volunteers. In this study, only the elderly volunteers exhibited significant correlations between their performance on verbal recall and their ratings of depression and anxiety (i.e., higher levels of depression and anxiety were associated with poorer memory).

Examining an exclusively elderly population, Steingart and Herrmann (1991) found that performance on the Mini Mental Status Examination was significantly negatively correlated with age of depression onset in a group of depressed elderly day hospital attenders. Focusing specifically on memory deficits, some authors have found poor performance on explicit memory tests in elderly depressives compared with normal controls (Gianotti and Marra, 1994; Hart et al., 1987) while others have failed to confirm these results (Niederehe, 1986; O'Hara et al., 1986). In one of the few studies of language function in elderly depressives, Emery and Breslau (1989) found greater impairment in several tests, including word fluency compared to age-matched normal controls.

In summary, while the results have not always been consistent, it appears that elderly depressives are more vulnerable to cognitive impairment from both the effects of the depressive illness as well as the effects of aging and brain pathology as described later. Future studies should, therefore, utilize both normal age-matched controls as well as young depressed controls matched for education and premorbid IQ.

Neuroimaging Correlates

In an early computed tomography (CT) study of elderly depressives, Jacoby and Levy (1980) found only 1 of 16 cases of early-onset depressives had enlarged lateral ventricles, compared with 8 of 25 late-onset depressives ($p < 0.06$). Subsequently, this finding has been replicated by others (Rossi et al., 1987; Shima et al., 1984), including a recent study that found the ventricular enlargement in late-onset depressives to be similar to Alzheimer's disease patients (Alexopoulos et al., 1992). A number of studies have utilized magnetic resonance imaging (MRI) to examine the prevalence of white matter and other lesions in elderly depressives. Coffey et al. (1988, 1989, 1990) found the majority of late-onset depressives had subcortical and periventricular white matter lesions, as well as the most severe lesions. While some studies have confirmed these findings (Krishnan, et al., 1988), other studies have not (Churchill et al., 1991; Zubenko et al., 1990). Krishnan et al. (1993) found elderly depressives had smaller caudate nuclei and putaminal complexes and more subcortical hyperintensities compared to normal controls, findings that were even more pronounced in late-onset depressives. A recent study by Miller et al. (1994), however, found no differences in white matter and subcortical lesions in a group of elderly depressives, Alzheimer's disease, and age-matched controls, when all subjects were selected for freedom from major vascular risk factors, such as hypertension. Age, however, was correlated with white matter lesions in both Alzheimer's disease and depression. In a striking study by Fujikawa et al. (1993), silent cerebral infarctions (single lesions greater than 20 mm or at least four lesions greater than 5 mm) were found in 65.9% of early-onset elderly depressives, compared with 93.7% of late-onset cases. These authors have somewhat boldly suggested that this entity might be designated as *prestroke depression* because of the association with increased risk of further symptomatic ischemic stroke.

The structural neuroimaging literature suffers from significant methodological limitations (Baldwin, 1993). Volumetric changes and white matter lesions can occur in both aging and cardiovascular disease (Krishnan et al., 1993). While these changes might cause depression, depression might cause the structural changes, or the changes may be due to secondary effects, such as the treatment of depression with antidepressants that cause hypotensive episodes. The clinical significance of white matter lesions is unclear and there are as yet no uniform criteria for evaluating these lesions (Baldwin, 1993). Finally, many of these studies have relied on inpatient populations and severe depressive illness, which may not reflect a representative sample.

Despite the significant potential of functional neuroimaging utilizing PET and single photon emission tomography (SPECT), very few studies have been done in the elderly, possibly because of the difficulty in recruiting elderly depressives into scanning studies (Kumar, 1993). Sackeim et al. (1990) used ^{133}Xe-inhalation scans to compare a mixed-age group of subjects with major depression in normal controls. Depressed subjects had marked reduction in global flow and deficits in selective areas of the frontal, temporal, and parietal regions. Flow reduction was also correlated with the severity of depression, age, and length of depressive episode. Kumar et al. (1993) found significant reductions in resting regional glucose metabolism with PET in neocortical, subcortical, and paralimbic regions in a group of elderly depressives, who were similar to age-matched Alzheimer's disease patients.

One of the possible confounding variables in the studies on neuroimaging, biological correlates, and neuropsychology is the inclusion of a group of patients within the depressed subjects who have early neurodegenerative disorders. A study by Weiner et al. (1994) found depression preceded the onset of dementia by several years in 44% of the depressed Alzheimer's disease patients in this study. Whether this represents a confounding variable in late-life depression or only one aspect of the true heterogeneous nature of this late-life illness will be discussed next. This last finding, however, may have marked clinical significance. If it becomes clearly established that late-life depression is a harbinger for dementing illness in certain cases, the syndrome may serve as a marker or early-warning sign, allowing for earlier interventions and treatments, possibly before irreversible deterioration of neurotransmitter systems or pathological changes are caused by the dementia.

CONCLUSIONS

In view of the serious methodological problems and inconsistencies described in the studies of late-life depression, one must cautiously summarize, synthesize, and hypothesize about this entity. It appears, however, that depression in the elderly, while not more prevalent than in younger populations, may present with more atypical presentations, more psychosis, and more cognitive impairment. Comorbid medical conditions probably play important direct and indirect roles in these disorders, while family history and psychosocial factors appear less important than in younger depressives. Emerging biological and neuroimaging correlates suggest an important, if not crucial, role for organic factors in the genesis of this disorder. According to one neurobiological theory of depression (Cummings, 1993), mood, affect, anhedonia, cognition, and vegetative features might all be associated with different but interrelated neurotransmitter systems and neuroanatomical sites. Thus aging, with its associated comorbid medical conditions, might variably affect some of these systems and structures, sparing others, and lead to a heterogeneous presentation.

A common theme in this review has been that the most consistent findings of these studies are the inconsistencies between the studies. While methodological limitations can always be raised to account for the differences, it appears more likely that these inconsistencies represent further support for the hypothesis that late-life depression is a very heterogeneous disorder with multiple etiologies. At one end of the spectrum are elderly patients with recurrent illnesses that begin in early life who have strong family histories, significant psychosocial factors, and obvious adverse life-event precipitants. At the other end of the spectrum are patients with single episodes, occurring for the first time in late life, who have no family histories, unremarkable psychosocial factors, and obvious neuropsychological impairments and abnormal neuroimaging findings. While the former's illness will likely follow a similar course to that in earlier life, the latter's may progress to reveal a bona fide neurological disorder, such as dementia. In the middle of the spectrum is a group that has mixed features of both extremes.

While this hypothesis may not please the late-life depression researcher searching for a unitary or comprehensive etiological theory, clinicians are likely to be less concerned. Regardless of etiology, depression in late life appears to respond to similar therapeutic interventions, whether it is early onset, late onset, associated with bereavement, stroke, Parkinson's disease, or other medical illness. Clinicians should, therefore, treat the illness appropriately, deal with comorbid factors, and then be prepared to follow these patients with a healthy degree of concern regarding ultimate prognosis.

REFERENCES

Abas MA, Sahakian BJ, Levy R (1990): Neuropsychological deficits and CT scan changes in elderly depressives. Psychol Med 20:507–520.

Adolffson R, Gottfries CG, Orland L, et al. (1980): Increased activity of brain and platelet monoamine oxidase in dementia of Alzheimer type. Life Sci 27:1029–1034.

Alexopoulos GS (1994): Biological correlates of late-life depression. In Schneider LS, Reynolds CF, Lebowitz BD (eds): "Diagnosis and Treatment of Depression in Late Life." Washington, DC: APA Press, pp 101–116.

Alexopoulos GS (1990): Clinical and biological findings in late-onset depression. In Tasman A, Goldfinger SM, et al (eds): "American Psychiatric Press Review of Psychiatry," Vol. 9. Washington DC: APA Press, pp 249–262.

Alexopoulos GS, Meyers BS, Young RC, Mattis S, Kakuma T (1993): The course of geriatric depression with "reversible dementia": a controlled study. Am J Psychiatry 150:1693–1699.

Alexopoulos GS, Young RC, Shindledecker RD (1992): Brain computed tomography findings in geriatric depression and primary degenerative dementia. Biol Psychiatry 31:591–599.

Alexopoulos GS, Lieberman KW, Young RC, et al. (1987): Platelet MAO activity in geriatric patients with depression and dementia. Am J Psychiatry 144:1480–1483.

Alexopoulos GS, Lieberman KW, Young RC (1984): Platelet MAO activity and age at onset of depression in elderly depressed women. Am J Psychiatry 141:1276–1278.

Andersson L, Stevens N (1993): Associations between early experiences with parents and well-being in old age. J Gerontology 48:P109–P116.

Aneshensel CS, Frerichs RR, Huba GJ (1984): Depression and physical illness: A multiwave, nonrecursive causal model. J Health Soc Behav 25:350–371.

Baldwin RC (1993): Late life depression and structural brain changes: A review of recent magnetic resonance imaging research. Int J Geriatr Psychiatry 8:115–123.

Baldwin RC (1991): Depressive illness. In Jacoby R, Oppenheimer C (eds): "Psychiatry in the Elderly." Oxford: Oxford University Press, pp 676–719.

Baldwin R (1990): Age of onset of depression in the elderly. Br J Psychiatry 156:445–446.

Barer BM, Johnson CL (1990): A critique of the caregiver literature. Gerontologist 30:26–29.

Baron M, Mendlewicz J, Klotz J (1981): Age-of-onset and genetic transmission in affective disorders. Acta Psychiatr Scand 64:373–380.

Bland RC, Newman SC, Orn H (1986): Recurrent and nonrecurrent depression: A family study. Arch Gen Psychiatry 43:1085–1089.

Blazer D, Bachar JR, Hughes DC (1987a): Major depression with melancholia: A comparison of middle-aged and elderly adults. J Am Geriatr Soc 35:927–932.

Blazer DG, Hughes DC, George LK (1987b): The epidemiology of depression in an elderly community population. Gerontologist 27:281–287.

Blazer DG, George LK, Landerman R, Pennybacker M, Melville ML, Woodbury M, Mantan KG, Jordan K, Locke B (1985): Psychiatric disorders: A rural/urban comparison. Arch Gen Psychiatry 42:651–656.

Bolby J (1973). "Attachment and Loss: Volume 2. Separation: Anxiety and Anger." New York: Basic Books.

Bridge TP, Soldo BJ, Phelps BH, et al. (1985): Platelet monoamine oxidase activity: Demographic characteristics contribute to enzyme activity variability. J Gerontol 40:23–28.

Brodaty H, Peters K, Boyce P, Hickie I, Parker G, Mitchell P, Wilhelm K (1991): Age and depression. J Affect Disord 23:137–149.

Brown GW, Harris T (1978): "Social Origins of Depression: A Study of Psychiatric Disorder in Women." London: Tavistock.

Brown RP, Sweeney J, Loutsch E, Kocsis J, Frances A (1984): Involutional melancholia revisited. Am J Psychiatry 141:24–28.

Brumback RA (1993): Is depression a neurologic disease? Neurol Clin 11:79–104.

Bulbena A, Berrios GE (1993): Cognitive function in the affective disorders: A prospective study. Psychopathology 26:6–12.

Buysse DJ, Reynolds CF, Houck PR, Stack I, Kupfer DJ (1988): Age of illness onset and sleep EEG variables in elderly depressives. Biol Psychiatry 24:355–359.

Caine ED (1981): Pseudodementia. Arch Gen Psychiatry 38:1359–1364.

Caine ED, Lyness JM, King DA, Connors L (1994): Clinical and etiological heterogeneity of mood disorders in elderly patients. In Schneider LS, Reynolds CF, Lebowitz BD, Friedhoff AJ (eds): "Diagnosis and Treatment of Depression in Late Life." Washington DC: American Psychiatric Press, pp 23–53.

Callahan CM, Hendrie HC, Dittus RS, Brater DC, Hui SL, Tierney WM (1994): Depression in the late life: The use of clinical characteristics to focus screening efforts. J Gerontol 49:M9–M14.

Cawley RH, Post F, Whitehead A (1973): Barbiturate tolerance and psychosocial functioning in elderly depressed patients. Psychol Med 3:39–52.

Charney DS, Nelson JC (1981): Delusional and nondelusional unipolar depression: Further evidence for distinct subtypes. Am J Psychiatry 138:328–333.

Churchill CM, Priolo CV, Nemeroff CB, Krishnan KRR, Breitner JCS (1991): Occult subcortical magnetic resonance findings in elderly depressives. Int J Geriatr Psychiatry 6:213–216.

Coffey CE, Figiel GS, Djang WT, Weiner RD (1990): Subcortical hyperintensity on magnetic resonance imaging: A comparison of normal and depressed elderly subjects. Am J Psychiatry 147:187–189.

Coffey CE, Figiel GS, Djang WT, Saunders WB, Weiner RD (1989): White matter hyperintensity on magnetic resonance imaging: Clinical and neuroanatomic correlates in the depressed elderly. J Neuropsychiatry 1:135–143.

Coffey CE, Figiel GS, Djang WT, Cress M, Saunders WB, Weiner RD (1988): Leukoencephalopathy in elderly depressed patients referred for ECT. Biol Psychiatry 24:143–161.

Cohen D, Eisdorfer C (1988): Depression in family members caring for a relative with Alzheimer's disease. J Am Geriatr Soc 36:885–889.

Cummings JL (1993): The neuroanatomy of depression. J Clin Psychiatry 54(11 Suppl):14–20.

Cummings JL (1992): Depression and Parkinson's disease: A review. Am J Psychiatry 149:443–454.

Dening TR, Berrios GE (1989): Wilson's disease: A prospective study of psychopathology in 31 cases. Br J Psychiatry 155:206–213.

Deptula D, Singh R, Pomara N (1993): Aging, emotional states, and memory. Am J Psychiatry 150:429–434.

Eastwood MR, Corbin SL (1986): The relationship between physical illness and depression in old age. In Murphy E (ed): "Affective Disorders in the Elderly." Edinburgh: Churchill Livingstone, pp 177–186.

Eastwood MR, Rifat SL, Nobbs H, Ruderman J (1989): Mood disorder following cerebrovascular accident. Br J Psychiatry 154:195–200.

Eastwood MR, Corbin SL, Reed M, Nobbs H, Kedward HB (1985): Acquired hearing loss and psychiatric illness: An estimate of prevalence and co-morbidity in a geriatric setting. Br J Psychiatry 147:552–556.

Emery OB, Breslau LD (1989): Language deficits in depression: Comparisons with SDAT and normal aging. J Gerontol 44:M85–M92.

Emery VO, Oxman TE (1992): Update on the dementia spectrum of depression. Am J Psychiatry 149:305–317.

Farrer LA, Florio LP, Bruce ML, Leaf PJ, Weissman MM (1989): Reliability of self-reported age at onset of major depression. J Psychiatr Res 23:35–47.

Finlayson RE, Martin LM (1982): Recognition and management of depression in the elderly. Mayo Clinic Proceedings 57:115–120.

Fujikawa T, Yamawaki S, Touhouda Y (1993): Incidence of silent cerebral infarction in patients with major depression. Stroke 24:1631–1634.

Futterman A, Gallagher D, Thompson LW (1990): Retrospective assessment of marital adjustment and depression during the first two years of spousal bereavement. Psychol Aging 5:277–283.

Gallagher D, Rose J, Rivera P, Lovett S, Thompson LW (1989): Prevalence of depression in family caregivers. Gerontologist 4:449–456.

George LK (1994): Social factors and depression in late life. In Schneider LS, Reynolds CF, Lebowitz BD, Friedhoff AJ (eds): "Diagnosis and Treatment of Depression in Late Life." Washington DC: American Psychiatric Press, pp 131–153.

Georgotas A (1983): Affective disorders in the elderly: Diagnostic and research considerations. Age Aging 12:1–10.

Georgotas A, Schweitzer J, McCue RE, et al. (1987): Clinical and treatment effects on ^{3}H-clonidine and ^{3}H-imipramine binding in elderly depressed patients. Life Sci 40:2137–2143.

Gianotti G, Marra C (1994): Some aspects of memory disorders clearly distinguish dementia of the Alzheimer's type from depressive pseudo-dementia. J Clin Exp Neuropsychol 16:65–78.

Glassman AB, Roose SP (1981): Delusional depression: A distinct clinical entity? Arch Gen Psychiatry 38:424–427.

Goldfarb AI (1967): Masked depression in the old. Am J Psychotherapy 21:791–803.

Gurland BJ (1976): The comparative frequency of depression in various adult age groups. Gerontology 31:283–292.

Halverson CF (1988): Remembering your parents: Reflections on the retrospective method. J Personality 56:435–449.

Hantz P, Caradoc-Davies G, Caradoc-Davies T, Weatherall M, Dixon G (1994): Depression in Parkinson's disease. Am J Psychiatry 151:1010–1014.

Harlow SD, Goldberg EL, Comstock GW (1991): A longitudinal study of risk factors for depressive symptomatology in elderly widowed and married women. Am J Epidemiology 134:526–538.

Hart RP, Keventus JA, Taylor JR, Harkins SW (1987): Rate of forgetting in dementia and depression. J Consult Clin Psychology 55:101–105.

Henderson AS, Jorm AF, Mackinnon A, Christensen H, Scott LR, Korten AE, Doyle C (1993): The prevalence of depressive disorders and the distribution of depressive symptoms in later life: A survey using draft ICD 10 and DSM IIIR. Psychol Med 23:719–729.

Herrmann N, Lieff SJ, Silberfeld M (1989): The effect of age of onset on depression in the elderly. J Geriatr Psychiatry Neurol 2:182–187.

Holahan CK, Holahan CJ (1987): Self-efficacy, social support, and depression in aging: A longitudinal analysis. J Gerontology 42:65–68.

Holmes, T, Rahe R (1967): The social readjustment rating scale. J Psychosomatic Res 11:213–218.

Hopkinson G (1964): A genetic study of affective illness in patients over 50. Br J Psychiatry 110:244–254.

House A, Dennis M, Mogridge L, Warlow C, Hawton K, Jones L (1991): Mood disorders in the year after first stroke. Br J Psychiatry 158:83–92.

House A, Dennis M, Warlow C, Hawton K, Molyneux A (1990): Mood disorders after stroke and their relation to lesion location: A CT scan study. Brain 113:1113–1129.

Jacoby RJ, Levy R (1980): Computed tomography in the elderly. 3: Affective disorder. Br J Psychiatry 136:270–275.

Jensen P, Sorensen SA, Fenger K, Bolwig TG (1993): A study of psychiatric morbidity in patients with Huntington's disease, their relatives, and controls. Br J Psychiatry 163:790–797.

Joffe RT, Lippert GP, Gray TA, et al. (1987): Mood disorder and multiple sclerosis. Arch Neurol 44:376–378.

Kennedy GJ, Kelman HR, Thomas C, Wisniewski W, Metz H, Bijur PE (1989): Hierarchy of characteristics associated with depressive symptoms in an urban elderly sample. Am J Psychiatry 146:220–225.

Kennedy GJ, Kelman HR, Thomas CJ (1990): The emergence of depressive symptoms in late life: The importance of declining health and increasing disability. J Commum Health 15:93–103.

Kiloh LG (1961): Pseudo-dementia. Acta Psychiatric Scand 37:336–351.

Koenig HG, Blazer DG (1992): Mood disorders and suicide. In Birren JE, Sloane RB, Cohen GD (eds): "Handbook of Mental Health and Aging." San Diego: Academic Press, pp 379–407.

Koenig HG, Cohen HJ, Blazer DG, Krishnan KRR, Sibert TE (1993): Profile of depressive symptoms in younger and older medical inpatients with major depression. J Am Geriatr Soc 41:1169–1176.

Kral VA (1983): The relationship between senile dementia (Alzheimer Type) and depression. Can J Psychiatry 28:304–306.

Kral V, Emery O (1989): Long term follow-up of depressive pseudodementia. Can J Psychiatry 34:445–447.

Krause N (1993): Early parental loss and personal control in later life. J Gerontology 48:P117–P126.

Krishnan KRR, McDonald WM, Doraiswamy PM, Tupler LA, Husain M, Boyko DB, Figiel GS, Ellinwood EH (1993): Neuroanatomical substrates of depression in the elderly. Eur Arch Psychiatry Clin Neurosci 243:41–46.

Krishnan KRR, Goli V, Ellinwood EH, France RD, Blazer DG, Nehmeroff CB (1988): Leukoencephalopathy in patients diagnosed as major depressive. Biol Psychiatry 23:519–522.

Kumar A (1993): Functional brain imaging in late-life depression and dementia. J Clin Psychiatry 54(suppl):21–25.

Kumar A, Newburg A, Alavi A, et al. (1993): Regional cerebral glucose metabolism in late life depression and Alzheimer's disease: A preliminary PET study. Proc Natl Acad Sci USA 90:7019–7023.

Langer SZ, Galzin AM, Poirier MF, et al. (1987): Association of ^{3}H-imipramine and ^{3}H-paroxetine binding with the 5HT transporter in brain and platelets: Reference to studies in depression. J Receptor Res 7:499–521.

Lewinsohn PM, Rohde P, Fischer SA, Seeley JR (1991): Age and depression: Unique and shared effects. Psychology Aging 6:247–260.

Lyness JM, Pearson JL, Lebowitz BD, Kupfer DJ (1994a): Age at onset of late-life depression. Am J Geriatr Psychiatry 2:4–8.

Lyness SA, Eaton EM, Schneider LS (1994b): Cognitive performance in older middle-aged depressed outpatients and controls. J Gerontol 49:P129–P136.

Mahapatra SB (1974): Deafness and mental health: Psychiatric and psychosomatic illness in the deaf. Acta Psychiatr Scand 50:596–611.

Maier W, Lichtermann D, Minges J, Heun R, Hallmayer J, Klingler T (1991): Unipolar depression in the aged: Determinants of familial aggregation. J Affect Disord 23:53–61.

Mayberg HS, Starkstein SE, Peyser CE, et al. (1992): Paralimbic frontal lobe hypometabolism in depression associated with Huntingdon's disease. Neurology 42:1791–1797.

McCullough PK (1991): Geriatric depression: Atypical presentations, hidden meanings. Geriatrics 46:72–76.

Mendlewicz J (1976): The age factor in depressive illness: Some genetic considerations. J Gerontol 31:300–303.

Meyers BS, Greenberg R (1986): Late-life delusional depression. J Affect Disord 11:133–137.

Meyers BS, Kalayam B, Mei-Tal V (1984): Late-onset delusional depression: A distinct clinical entity? J Clin Psychiatry 45:347–349.

Miller D, Kumar A, Yousem D, Gottlieb GL (1994): MRI high-intensity signals in late-life depression and Alzheimer's disease: a comparison of subjects without major vascular risk factors. Am J Geriatr Psychiatry 1:257–258.

Murphy E (1982): Social origins of depression in old age. Br J Psychiatry 141:135–142.

Musetti L, Perugi G, Soriani A, Ross VM, Cassano GB, Akiskal HS (1989): Depression before and after age 65: A re-examination. Br J Psychiatry 155:330–336.

Myers JK, Weissman MM, Tischler GL, Holzer CE, Leaf PJ, Orvaschel H, Anthony JC, Boyrd JH, Burke JD, Kramer M, Stoltzman R (1984): Six month prevalence of psychiatric disorders in three communities. Arch Gen Psychiatry 41:959–967.

Nelson JC, Bowers MB (1978): Delusional unipolar depression: Description and drug response. Arch Gen Psychiatry 35:1321–1328.

Nelson JC, Conwell Y, Kim K, Mazure C (1989): Age at onset in late-life delusional depression. Am J Psychiatry 146:785–786.

Nemeroff CB, Knight DL, Krishnan KRK, et al. (1988): Marked reduction in the number of platelet ^{3}H-imipramine binding sites in geriatric depression. Arch Gen Psychiatry 45:919–923.

Niederehe G (1986): Depression and memory impairment in the aged. In Poon LW (ed): "Clinical Memory Assessment of Older Adults." Washington DC: American Psychological Association, pp 226–237.

Nuss WS, Zubenko GS (1992): Correlates of persistent depressive symptoms in widows. Am J Psychiatry 149:346–351.

O'Hara MW, Hinrichs JV, Kohout FJ, Wallace RB, Lemke JH (1986): Memory complaint and memory performance in the depressed elderly. Psychol Aging 1:208–214.

Ouslander JG (1982): Physical illness and depression in the elderly. J Am Geriatr Soc 30:593–599.

Palinkas LA, Wingard DL, Barrett-Conner E (1990): Chronic illness and depressive symptoms in the elderly: A population-based study. J Clin Epidemiol 43:1131–1141.

Parkes CM (1992): Bereavement and mental health in the elderly. Rev Clin Gerontol 2:45–51.

Pearlson GD, Rabins PV, Kim WS, Speedie LJ, Moberg PJ, Burns A, Bascom MJ (1989): Structural brain CT changes and cognitive deficits in elderly depressives with and without reversible dementia ("pseudodementia") Psychol Med 19:573–584.

Phifer JF, Murrell SA (1986): Etiologic factors in the onset of depressive symptoms in older adults. J Abnormal Psychol 95:282–291.

Post F (1982): Functional disorders. In Levy R, Post F (eds): "The Psychiatry of Late Life." Oxford: Blackworth, pp 176–221.

Rabins PV (1981): The prevalence of reversible dementia in a psychiatric hospital. Hosp Community Psychiatry 32:490–492.

Rabins PV, Merchant A, Nestadt G (1984): Criteria for diagnosing reversible dementia caused by depression: Validation by 2-year follow-up. Br J Psychiatry 144:488–492.

Raskin A (1979): Signs and symptoms of psychopathology in the elderly. In Raskin A, Jarvik L (eds): "Psychiatric Symptoms and Cognitive Loss in the Elderly." Washington, DC: Hemisphere, pp 3–18.

Reding M, Haycox J, Blass J (1985): Depression in patients referred to a dementia clinic. Arch Neurol 42:894–896.

Reifler BV (1994): Depression: diagnosis and comorbidity. In Schneider LS, Reynolds CF, Lebowitz BD, Friedhoff AJ (eds): "Diagnosis and Treatment of Depression in Late Life." Washington DC: American Psychiatric Press, pp 55–60.

Reifler BV (1982): Arguments for abandoning the term pseudodementia. J Am Geriatr Soc 30:665–668.

Reynolds CF, Hoch CC, Buysse DJ, Houck PR, Schlernitzauer M, Frank E, Mazumoar S, Kupfer DJ (1992): Electroencephalographic sleep in spousal bereavement and bereavement-related depression of late life. Biol Psychiatry 31:69–82.

Reynolds CF, Hoch CC, Kupfer DJ, Buysse DJ, Houck PR, Stack JA, Campbell DW (1988): Bedside differentiation of depressive pseudodementia from dementia. Am J Psychiatry 145:1099–1103.

Robinson RG, Starkstein SE (1990): Current research in affective disorders following stroke. J Neuropsychiatry Clin Neurosci 2:1–4.

Robinson RG, Kubos KL, Starr LB, Rao K, Price TR (1984): Mood disorders in stroke patients: Importance of location of lesion. Brain 107:81–93.

Rossi A, Stratta P, Petruzzi C, et al. (1987): A computerized tomographic study in DSM-III affective disorders. J Affect Disord 12:259–262.

Roth M, Kay DWK (1956): Affective disorder arising in the senium. II. Physical disability as an aetiological factor. J Mental Sci 102:141–150.

Sackeim HA, Prohovnik I, Moeller JR, Brown PR, Apter S, Prudic J, Devanand DP, Mukherjec S (1990): Regional cerebral bloodflow in mood disorders. 1: Comparison of major depressives and normal controls at rest. Arch Gen Psychiatry 47:60–70.

Salzman C, Shader RI (1979): Clinical evaluation of depression in the elderly. In Raskin A, Jarvik L (eds): "Psychiatric Symptoms and Cognitive Loss in the Elderly." Washington DC: Hemisphere, pp 39–72.

Sano M, Stern Y, Williams J, Cote L, Rosenstein R, Mayeux R (1989): Coexisting dementia and depression in Parkinson's disease. Arch Neurol 46:1284–1286.

Schneider LS (1992): Psychobiologic features of geriatric affective disorder. Clin Geriatr Med 8:253–265.

Schneider LS, Severson J, Chui HC, et al. (1988): ^{3}H-imipramine binding and MAO activity in Alzheimer's patients with agitation and delusions. Psychiatry Res 25:311–322.

Shamoian CA (1985): Assessing depression in the elderly patient. Hosp Comm Psychiatry 36:338–339.

Sharpe M, Hawton K, Seagroatt V, Bamford J, House A, Molyneux A, Sandercock P, Warlow C (1994): Depressive disorders in long-term survivors of stroke: Associations with demographic and social factors, functional status, and brain lesion volume. Br J Psychiatry 164:380–386.

Sharpe M, Hawton K, House A, Molyneux A, Sandercock P, Bamford J, Warlow C (1990): Mood disorders in long-term survivors of stroke: Associations with brain lesion location and volume. Psychol Med 20:815–828.

Shima S, Shikano T, Kitamura T, et al. (1984): Depression and ventricular enlargement. Acta Psychiatr Scand 70:274–277.

Shraberg D (1978): The myth of pseudodementia: Depression and the aging brain. Am J Psychiatry 135:601–603.

Snowdon J (1990): The prevalence of depression in old age. Int J Geriatric Psychiatry 5:141–144.

Starkstein SE, Robinson RG (1989): Affective disorders and cerebral vascular disease. Br J Psychiatry 154:170–182.

Starkstein SE, Robinson RG, Berthier ML, Parikh RM, Price TR (1988): Differential mood changes following basal ganglia versus thalamic lesions. Arch Neurol 45:725–730.

Starkstein SE, Robinson RG, Price TR (1987): Comparison of cortical and subcortical lesions in the production of poststroke mood disorders. Brain 110:1045–1059.

Steingart A, Herrmann N (1991): Major depressive disorder in the elderly: The relationship between age of onset and cognitive impairment. Int J Geriatr Psychiatry 6:593–598.

Stenstedt A (1959): Involutional melancholia. Acta Psychiatr Scand (suppl 127).

Suranyi-Cadotte BE, Gauthier S, Lafaille F, et al. (1985): Platelet ^{3}H-imipramine binding distinguishes depression from Alzheimer dementia. Life Sci 37:2305–2311.

Thompson LW, Futerman A, Gallagher D (1988): Assessment of late-life depression. Psychopharmacol Bull 24:577–586.

Turner RJ, Beiser M (1990): Major depression and depressive symptomatology among the physically disabled: assessing the role of chronic stress. J Nerv Ment Dis 178:343–350.

Veith RC, Raskind MA (1988): The neurobiology of aging: Does it predispose to depression? Neurobiol Aging 9:101–117.

Weiner ME, Edland SD, Luszczynska H (1994); Prevalence and incidence of major depression in Alzheimer's disease. Am J Psychiatry 151:1006–1009.

Weissman MM, Livington BM, Leaf PJ, Florio LP, Holzer C (1991): Affective disorders. In Robins LN, Regier DA (eds): Psychiatric Disorders in America: The Epidemiologic Catchment Area Study. New York: Free Press.

Weissman MM, Leaf PJ, Tischler GL, Blazer DG, Karno M, Bruce ML, Florio LP (1988): Affective disorders in five United States communities. Psychol Med 18:141–153.

Wells CE (1979): Pseudodementia. Am J Psychiatry 136:895–900.

Wesner RB, Winokur G (1988): An archival study of depression before and after age 55. J Geriatr Psychiatry Neurol 1:220–225.

Wragg RE, Jeste DV (1989): Overview of depression and psychosis in Alzheimer's disease. Am J Psychiatry 146:577–587.

Yesavage JA, Brink TL, Rose TL, Lum O, Huang V, Adey M, Leirer VO (1983): Development and validation of a geriatric depression screening scale: A preliminary report. J Psychiat Res 17:37–49.

Zisook S, Shuchter SR (1991): Depression through the first year after the death of a spouse. Am J Psychiatry 148:1346–1352.

Zubenko GS, Moossy J (1988): Major depression in primary dementia: clinical and neuropathologic correlates. Arch Neurol 45:1182–1186.

Zubenko GS, Sullivan P, Nelson JP, Belle SH, Huff J, Wolf GL (1990): Brain imaging abnormalities in mental disorders of late life. Arch Neurol 47:1107–1111.

CHAPTER 17

Major Depression in Old Age: Outcome Studies

MARTIN G. COLE

Department of Psychiatry, St. Mary's Hospital, Montreal, Quebec, Canada H3T 1M5

INTRODUCTION

Traditional views of the prognosis of depression are usually traced to Kraepelin (1987) who stated that the prognosis of manic–depressive insanity was favorable for the individual episode but that repeated episodes or even eventual intractable illness could occur. In Kraepelin's series of 440 cases with depression alone, 58% had one episode only, 29% had two episodes, and 13% had three or more episodes. Significantly, less than 11% of his cases were over the age of 60 and less than 2% were over the age of 70.

Prognostic studies of depression in the elderly have since been published. Unfortunately, there are many reported variations in outcome. Thus, the purpose of this chapter is to determine the outcome of major depression in the elderly by reviewing systematically and critically all recent original reports. This review process, modified from Oxman and Guyatt (1988), involved systematic selection of studies, assessment of their validity, and examination of their results.

SELECTION OF ORIGINAL STUDIES

Systematic selection of original studies involved three steps: first, three computer databases (Medline, Psychological Abstracts, and Mental Health Abstracts) were searched for all relevant articles published for the time period January, 1980, to May, 1994, using the keywords "prognosis," "depression," and "elderly." Second, the bibliographies of the retrieved articles were searched for additional references. Finally, all the articles collected were screened to meet the following inclusion criteria: original study, published in English or French after 1950, sample of at least 20 patients, inclusion of patients over age 60 only, mean follow-up period of at least one year, and description or classification of patients' mental state during the follow-up period. This selection process yielded 16 hospital-based (Kay et al., 1955; Post, 1962, 1972; Gordon, 1981;

Mood Disorders Across the Life Span, Edited by Shulman, Tohen, and Kutcher
ISBN 0-471-10477-9 © 1996 Wiley-Liss, Inc.

Murphy, 1983; Cole, 1983, 1985; Baldwin and Jolley, 1986; Godber et al., 1987; Magni et al., 1988; Agbayewa, 1990; Meats et al., 1991; Burvill et al., 1991; Hinrichsen, 1992; Baldwin et al., 1993; Brodaty et al., 1993) and 5 community-based (Ben-Arie et al., 1990; O'Connor et al., 1990; Kivela et al., 1991; Copeland et al., 1992; Forsell et al., 1994) studies involving 1,487 and 249 patients, respectively (Tables 1 and 2).

Different diagnostic criteria for major depression were used to enroll subjects in the 21 studies: in one (Kay et al., 1955) the criteria of Roth (1955) were used, in two (Post, 1962, 1972) those of "depressive symptoms," in one (Ben-Arie et al., 1990) the Present State Exam criteria (Wing et al., 1974), in eight (Gordon, 1981; Murphy, 1983; Cole, 1983, 1985; Baldwin and Jolley, 1986; Godber et al., 1987; Meats et al., 1991; Hinrichsen, 1992) the Feighner research diagnostic criteria (Feighner et al., 1972), in seven (Magni et al., 1988; Agbayewa, 1990; O'Connor et al., 1990; Burvill et al., 1991; Baldwin et al., 1993; Brodaty et al., 1993; Forsell et al., 1994) the DSM-III criteria (American Psychiatric Association, 1980), and in two (Baldwin et al., 1993; Forsell et al., 1994) the DSM-III-R criteria (American Psychiatric Association, 1987). Furthermore, many studies enrolled subjects with several depressive subtypes (e.g., unipolar depression and atypical depression). Because there is no solid evidence of a relation between diagnostic criteria or depressive subtypes and the course of depressive illness in the elderly, the presence of particular diagnostic criteria or particular depressive subtypes was not considered an inclusion criteria for the review.

ASSESSMENT OF VALIDITY

To determine the validity of the studies, the methods and design of each study was assessed using the criteria described by the Department of Clinical Epidemiology and Biostatistics, McMaster University (1981) (Tables 3 and 4). These criteria include formation of an inception cohort, description of referral pattern, completion of follow-up, development and use of objective outcome criteria, blind outcome assessment, and adjustment for extraneous prognostic factors.

Hospital-Based Studies

Formation of an Inception Cohort Depression in elderly patients should be identified at an early and uniform point in its course so that patients who recover completely or die are included with those who relapse or whose depression persists. Patients with multiple relapses or chronic depression have multiple chances of being included in the study and make the prognosis of depression appear worse than it really is. Ideally, only elderly experiencing a first lifetime episode of depression or at least a first episode of depression in old age should be included.

Fifteen of the 16 studies did not meet this criterion. The inception cohort was formed of consecutive referrals, consecutive admissions, or consecutive discharges, and one study (Godber et al., 1987) included only referred cases treated with electroconvulsive therapy. Consequently, in these 15 studies the inception episode represented the first lifetime episode of depression in 27–65% of cases, and in one study (Baldwin and Jolley, 1986) the first episode in old age in 79% of cases. Murphy's study (1983) was the exception: Subjects aged over 65 years were included only if the inception episode represented the first one after age 60 so that all of the study patients were experiencing a first episode of depression in old age.

TABLE 1 Results of Original Hospital-Based Outcome Studies of Depression in the Elderly

Reference	Number of Patients	Age (and Mean) (yr)	Sex (No. of Patients) Female	Sex (No. of Patients) Male	Population	Length Follow-up (and Mean) (mo.)	Outcome and Percent of Patients
Kay et al. (1955)	175	≥60 (68)	117	58	Inpatients	9–27 (20.5)	Well 38, relapse 18, ill 29, died 15
Post (1962)	100[a]	≥60	53	47	Inpatients	72	Lasting recovery 31, relapse with recovery 28, symptoms or relapse 23, ill 17
Post (1972)	92	≥60	—	—	Inpatients	36	Lasting recovery 26, relapse with recovery 37, symptoms or relapse 25, continuously ill 12
Gordon (1981)	74	≥65	57	17	Inpatients	12	Symptoms free 64, relapse 15[b]
Murphy (1983)	124	65–89	88	36	Inpatients Outpatients	12	Well 35, relapse 19, continuously ill 29, dementia 3, died 14
Cole (1983)	38	65–88 (70)	28	10	Inpatients	7–31 (18)	Completely well 41, tolerably well 25, ill 22, died 12
Cole (1985)	60	65–92 (71)	38	22	Outpatients	24–63 (48)	Completely well 18, tolerably well 52, ill 30
Baldwin et al. (1986)	100	65–88 (74)	79	21	Inpatients	12	Well 58, relapse 15, residual symptoms or continuously ill 18, died 8
Godber et al. (1987)	163	≥65 (76)	120	43	Inpatients	42–104	Lasting recovery 22, relapse with recovery 39, depressive invalidism 32, continuously ill 7
Magni et al. (1988)	64	68–92	45	19	Outpatients	36	No relapse 33, relapse with good recovery 28, relapse with poor recovery 34, other 5
Agbayewa (1990)	29	≥65 (75)	17	12	Medical Day Hospital	12	Well 31, ill 69
Meats et al. (1991)	56	65–89 (75)	43	13	Inpatients	12	Well 50, relapse 19, continuously ill 12, died 19
Burvill et al. (1991)	103	60–93 (71)	66	37	Inpatients	12	Well 68, relapse 13, continuously ill 3, died 16
Hinrichsen (1992)	150	≥60 (71)	105	45	Inpatients	12	Well 47, relapse 18, invalidism 13, continuously ill 11, died 11
Baldwin et al. (1993)	98	70–84 (76)	73	25	Inpatients	12	Well 29, relapse 11, continuously ill 23, other 34, died 3
Brodaty et al. (1993)	61	≥60 (69)	46	15	Outpatients	12	Well 42, continuously ill 18, improved 21, died 19
						45	Well 25, relapse 20, continuously ill 15, residual symptoms 38, died 2
							Well 34, relapse 23, continuously ill 7, residual symptoms, 20, died 16

[a] Includes 19 patients with dementia.
[b] Information on remaining patients was unavailable.

TABLE 2 Results of Original Community-Based Outcome Studies of Depression in the Elderly

Reference	Number of Patients	Age (and Mean) (yr)	Sex (No. of Patients)		Length of Follow-up (and Mean) (mo.)	Outcome and Percent of Patients
			Female	Male		
Ben-Arie et al. (1990)	23	≥65	17	6	42	Well 32, relapse 27 continuously ill 14, other 18, died 9
O'Connor et al. (1990)	27	≥75	—	—	12	Well 22, continuously ill 44, other 4, died 30
Kivela et al. (1991)	42	60–94 (70)	17	13	12	Well 46, relapse 12, continuously ill 14, other 14, died 14
Copeland et al. (1992)	123	≥65	91	32	36	Well 23, continuously ill 31, other 23, died 23
Forsell et al. (1994)	34	≥75	—	—	36	Well 6, continuously ill 36, other 18, died 40.

TABLE 3 Validity of Hospital-Based Studies with Respect to Meeting (+) or not Meeting (−) Validity Criteria

Reference	Formation of Inception Cohort	Description of Referral Pattern	Completion of Follow-up	Development and Use of Objective Outcome Criteria	Blind Outcome Assessment	Adjustment for Extraneous Prognostic Factors
Kay et al. (1955)	−	−	+	−	−	+/−
Post (1962)	−	−	+	−	−	+/−
Post (1972)	−	−	+	−	−	+/−
Gordon (1981)	−	−	+	−	−	−
Murphy (1983)	+	+/−	+	−	−	+/−
Cole (1983)	−	−	+	−	−	+
Cole (1985)	−	−	+	+/−	−	+/−
Baldwin and Jolley (1986)	−	−	+	−	−	+/−
Godber et al. (1987)	−	+/−	+	−	−	−
Magni et al. (1988)	−	−	−	−	−	+/−
Agbayewa (1990)	−	+/−	+	−	−	+/−
Meats et al. (1991)	−	−	+	−	−	+/−
Burvill et al. (1991)	−	−	+	+	−	+/−
Hinrichsen (1992)	−	−	+	+	−	+/−
Baldwin et al. (1993)	+/−	−	+	+	−	+
Brodaty et al. (1993)	−	+/−	+	+/−	−	+/−

365

TABLE 4 Validity of Community-Based Studies with Respect to Meeting (+) or not Meeting (−) Validity Criteria

Reference	Formation of Inception Cohort	Description of Referral Pattern	Completion of Follow-up	Development and use of Objective Outcome Criteria	Blind Outcome Assessment	Adjustment for Extraneous Prognostic Factors
Ben-Arie et al. (1990)	+	+	+	+	−	−
O'Connor et al. (1990)	+	+	+	+	−	+/−
Kivela et al. (1991)	+	+	+	−	−	+/−
Copeland et al. (1992)	+	+	+	+	+	+/−
Forsell et al. (1994)	+	+	+	+	−	+/−

Description of Referral Pattern The pathways by which patients enter a study should be described. Three types of sample bias can distort prognostic studies of depression: centripedal bias, in which experts are referred problem cases; popularity bias, in which experts preferentially follow interesting cases; and finally, referral filter bias, in which secondary or tertiary care services receive cases different from those in the general population.

None of the 16 studies described adequately the referral patterns or potential sample biases. Three (Murphy, 1983; Agbayewa, 1990; Brodaty et al., 1993) provided some information about referral pattern; one (Godber et al., 1987) described the catchment area but not the referral pattern to the service. Notably, all the studies involving psychogeriatric services excluded the large number of depressed patients who grow old within adult psychiatric services.

Completion of Follow-up All members of the inception cohort should be accounted for at the end of follow-up period. The McMaster group proposed that a loss of more than 20% of the study cohort is unsatisfactory.

Accordingly, follow-up was completed satisfactorily in all but two studies (Magni et al., 1988; Agbayewa, 1990) in which at least 32 and 45%, respectively, of the inception cohorts were lost to follow-up.

Development and Use of Objective Outcome Criteria Prognostic outcomes should be stated in explicit and objective terms to enable readers to relate the results to their own practice. As well, there should be reassurance that the outcome criteria were applied in a reliable and consistent manner.

Although all of the studies reported outcomes in one of two–eight categories ranging from "completely well" to "chronically ill," only three (Hinrichsen, 1992; Baldwin et al., 1993; Brodaty et al., 1993) specified criteria for assignment to these categories. Moreover, in all studies it was impossible to distinguish cases with few and brief relapses from cases with frequent and prolonged relapses. One study (Cole, 1985) attempted to address this quantitative issue by calculating the percent of time well during the follow-up period. Finally, there was no evidence (i.e., calculation of agreement between raters on category assignment) in any of the studies that cases were assigned to outcome categories in a reliable and consistent manner.

Blind Outcome Assessment Outcome should be assessed by clinicians who are blind to potentially important prognostic events. Judgments about outcome can be dramatically influenced by knowledge of previous clinical features or expectations about the course of depression. In this respect, the outcome assessment was not blind in any of the studies.

Adjustment for Extraneous Prognostic Factors To determine the prognosis of depression in the elderly, interference from other factors (e.g., disability, physical illness, cognitive impairment, premorbid personality, social factors, and treatments) that might affect the prognosis should be eliminated or at least accounted for.

None of the investigators eliminated the influence of disability on prognosis. In one study (Cole, 1983) the influence of both physical illness and definite cognitive impairment was eliminated. In 13 studies (Kay et al., 1955, Post, 1962, 1972; Murphy, 1983; Cole, 1985; Baldwin and Jolley, 1986; Magni et al., 1988; Agbayewa, 1990; Meats et al., 1991; Burvill et al., 1991; Hinrichsen, 1992, Baldwin et al., 1993, Brodaty et al., 1993), the influences of disability, physical illness, and cognitive impairment were examined but not eliminated. Kay et al. (1955) used psychometric tests to assign patients with depression to categories of mixed, doubtful, or no organicity and determined the prognosis independently in the three groups; Post (1962) assigned patients to no, doubtful, or definite cognitive impairment and determined outcome. Two studies (Agbayewa, 1990; Baldwin et al., 1993) examined outcome in patients with no or definite cognitive impairments. Three studies (Murphy, 1983; Cole, 1985; Baldwin and Jolley, 1986) excluded patients with definite cognitive impairment. Five studies (Murphy, 1983; Brodaty et al., 1993; Meats et al., 1991; Burvill et al., 1991; Hinrichsen, 1992) examined the relation of physical health to prognosis. Two studies (Post, 1962, 1972) examined the influence of disabling physical illness. One study (Baldwin and Jolley, 1986) examined the relation of initial health problems and further health changes to prognosis. One study (Cole, 1985) considered the influence of minor organic signs and moderate physical disability on prognosis. Finally, one study (Magni et al., 1988) considered the influence of physical and central nervous system (CNS) diseases on course and outcome.

In nine studies (Post, 1962; Murphy, 1983; Cole, 1983, 1985; Baldwin and Jolley, 1986; Magni et al., 1988; Burvill et al., 1991; Hinrichsen, 1992; Baldwin et al., 1993), the effect of social factors on prognosis were considered but not eliminated or accounted for. The social factors included marital status, living circumstances (i.e., household composition), social class, income, property ownership, employment, activities, number of social contacts, precipitating severe life events (e.g., loss of loved one, personal illness), intervening severe life events, major social difficulties (e.g., housing, finances, children), and the presence of an intimate confiding relationship. Four reports (Post, 1962, 1972; Burvill et al., 1991; Brodaty et al., 1993) examined the relation of premorbid personality to course of illness.

In all but two studies (Kay et al., 1955; Agbayewa, 1990) the types of treatments received by the study subjects as a group were described briefly. No study controlled for treatments or related treatments to prognosis.

Community-Based Studies

The methods and designs of the community-based studies were generally better than the hospital-based studies although the sample sizes were small.

As to adjustment for extraneous prognostic factors, one study (Kivela et al., 1991) excluded those with cognitive impairment and examined the influence of physical illness but not disability on outcome; one study (Copeland et al., 1992) considered the influence of cognitive impairment (pseudodementia); two studies (O'Connor et al., 1990; Forsell et al., 1994) considered the influence of dementia. None of the studies examined premorbid personality. One study (Kivela et al., 1991) examined the relation of social factors (education, occupation, marital status, hobbies, visiting contact, social participation, living alone, intimacy of relationships, stress factors) to outcome. Three studies (Ben-Arie et al., 1990; Copeland et al., 1992; Forsell et al., 1994) determined the frequency of antidepressive treatments.

RESULTS

Hospital-Based Studies

Assessment of the validity of the 16 hospital-based studies revealed serious and multiple methodological flaws in all (Table 1). Consequently, their results are questionable.

Not even one study was methodologically sound enough to serve as a benchmark in evaluating the results of the others.

Despite the questionable validity, the results were examined. Sample size ranged from 29 to 175 patients. The patients' ages were 60–93 years; 12 studies reported the mean age (68–76 years). Fifteen studies reported gender; 21–47% of patients were men. Only inpatients were included in 11 studies, only outpatients were included in 2 studies; both were included in 2 studies, and day hosptial patients in 1 study. The length of follow-up was 6–104 (mean 26.3) months.

The studies were separated into two groups according to length of follow-up. The first group included 12 studies (Kay et al., 1955; Gordon, 1981; Murphy, 1983; Cole, 1983; Baldwin and Jolley, 1986; Magni et al., 1988; Agbayewa, 1990; Meats et al., 1991; Burvill et al., 1991; Hinrichsen, 1992; Baldwin et al., 1993; Brodaty et al., 1993) with a mean follow-up of less than 24 months; the second included 6 studies (Post, 1962, 1972; Cole, 1985; Baldwin and Jolley, 1986; Godber et al., 1987; Brodaty et al., 1993) with a mean follow-up of more than 24 months. The studies by Baldwin and Jolley (1986) and Brodaty et al. (1993) presented both 12-month and 4-year follow-up data and were included in both groups. The mean follow-up period for the first group was 13.2 months and for the second 51.8 months.

The prognostic outcomes are in Table 1. Only three outcome categories were consistent across most of the studies: well, relapse with recovery, and continuously ill. The other outcomes (e.g., dead, relapsed, lost to follow-up, unknown, other) were categorized as other in this analysis. The ranges of outcomes and combined prognostic outcomes in the two follow-up groups are given in Table 5.

The investigators attempted to identify prognostic factors although definition and measurement of these factors varied from one study to the next. Poor prognosis was associated with cognitive impairment in three studies (Kay et al., 1955; Post 1962; Magni et al., 1988) but not in three others (Agbayewa, 1990; Burvill et al., 1991; Baldwin et al., 1993), with physical illness in six (Post, 1962, 1972; Murphy, 1983; Cole, 1985; Baldwin and Jolley, 1986; Meats et al., 1991) but not in four others (Magni et al., 1988; Burvill et al., 1991; Brodaty et al., 1993; Hinrichsen, 1992), with onset of first depressive episode before 60 years of age in three studies (Kay et al., 1955; Cole, 1983; Brodaty, et al., 1993) but not in four others (Post, 1962, 1972; Bruvill et al., 1991; Hinrichsen, 1992), with advanced patient age in two studies (Post, 1962; Murphy, 1983) but not in three others (Cole, 1983, 1985; Baldwin and Jolley, 1986), and with severity of depressive symptoms in four studies (Post, 1962; Murphy, 1983; Baldwin and Jolley,

TABLE 5 **Results and Combined Results of Hospital-Based Studies by Length of Follow-up**

	Length of Follow-up: Percent of Patients			
	<24 months		>24 months	
Prognosis Category	Results	Combined Results (n = 1,059)	Results	Combined Results (n = 576)
Well	25–64	41.5	18–34	28.1
Relapse with recovery	11–25	15.8	23–52	33.1
Continuously ill	3–69	21.9	7–30	9.5
Other	8–40	20.8	23–39	29.3

1986; Baldwin et al., 1993) but not in five others (Post, 1972; Agbayewa, 1990; Meats et al., 1991; Hinrichsen, 1992; Brodaty et al., 1993). Finally, previous episodes were identified as a poor prognostic factor in two studies (Meats et al., 1991; Brodaty, et al., 1993) but not in one other (Hinrichsen, 1992).

Seven (Post, 1962; Murphy, 1983; Cole, 1983, 1985; Baldwin and Jolley, 1986; Magni et al., 1988; Hinrichsen, 1992) of the nine studies that considered the influence of social factors on prognosis reported that marital status and living circumstances were not related to course, but one study (Baldwin et al., 1993) reported that those living alone had a poorer outcome. Post (1962) examined employment and number of social contacts, changes in living circumstances, income, and activities and concluded that favorable social circumstances at the time of admission or favorable social changes were linked with good clinical outcomes in only a few instances. Property ownership was related to good outcome in one study (Murphy, 1983); severe intervening life events were related to poor outcome in two studies (Murphy, 1983; Baldwin et al., 1993), but good outcome was reported in one study (Burvill et al., 1991); social class, major social difficulties, and the presence of an intimate confiding relationship were not related to outcome (Murphy, 1983).

As for premorbid personality, Post (1962) reported that extroversion was associated with a better outcome but anxious–obsessional–hypochondriacal or cyclothymic traits and poor sexual adjustment were not. Abnormal personality traits were related to poor outcome in one study (Brodaty et al., 1993) but not in two others (Post, 1972; Burvill et al., 1991).

The treatments described and the proportion of patients with a favorable outcome in each of the studies are given in Table 6.

Community-Based Studies

The results were as follows. Sample size ranged from 23 to 123 subjects. The subjects' ages were 60–94 years; two studies reported the mean age (70 and 73 years). Three studies reported gender: 26–31% of patients were men. The length of follow-up was 12–42 (mean 27.6) months. The prognostic outcomes are given in Table 2.

The reports were separated into two groups according to length of follow-up. Two studies (O'Connor et al., 1990; Kivela et al., 1991) had a follow-up of less than 24 months (the mean was 12 months); three studies (Ben-Arie et al., 1990; Copeland et al., 1992; Forsell et al., 1994) had a follow-up of more than 24 months (the mean was 38 months). Only two outcome categories were consistent across these studies: well and continuously ill. The other outcomes (relapse with recovery, other, dead) were categorized as other. The ranges of outcomes and combined prognostic outcomes are given in Table 7.

As for prognostic factors, one study (Kivela et al., 1991) reported that physical illness and social factors were not related to outcome; two studies (O'Connor et al., 1990; Forsell et al., 1994) reported that patients with dementia were less likely than patients without dementia to be depressed at follow-up. Among the three studies that determined the frequency of psychiatric treatment only 4% (Copeland et al., 1992), 9% (Ben-Arie et al., 1990) and 33% (Forsell et al., 1994), respectively, of subjects received antidepressive therapy despite the fact that most were in regular contact with family physicians. Furthermore, only two patients were referred to a psychiatrist (Forsell et al., 1994).

TABLE 6 Treatments of Depression and Proportion of Patients with Favorable Outcome

Reference	Treatment and Percent of Patients	Favorable Outcome, Percent of Patients
Kay et al. (1955)	Not described	56
Post (1962)	Electroconvulsive therapy (ECT) 51.9, routine 46.9, psychotropic drugs 1.2	59
Post (1972)	Psychotropic drugs 80.5, ECT 17.4, routine 2.1	63
Gordon (1981)	Combined medical milieu and behavior therapies with psychotropic drugs, and ECT (in 5% of cases); aftercare as indicated	64
Murphy (1983)	ECT 16[a]	35–54
Cole (1983)	Tricyclics alone 55, tricyclics or monoamine oxidase inhibitors with or without neuroleptics, lithium, ECT, or sleep deprivation 45	66
Cole (1985)	Antidepressants and psychotherapy 100, maintenance antidepressants 51	70
Baldwin and Jolley (1986)	Nine ECT sessions on average plus psychotropic drugs 48, antidepressants alone 45,[a] all received aftercare: maintenance antidepressants 38, antidepressants as needed 19, little medication 43	58–73[b] 61[c]
Godber et al. (1987)	ECT and antidepressants in most cases	61
Magni et al. (1988)	Tricyclics with or without anxiolytics, neuroleptics or lithium in all cases	31
Agbayewa (1990)	Not described	69
Meats et al. (1991)	Neuroleptics 75, anxiolytics 21, antidepressants 86, ECT 29	81
Burvill et al. (1991)	ECT 38[a]	65
Hinrichsen	Antidepressants, ECT	40
Baldwin et al. (1993)	Antidepressants 70	63
Brodaty et al. (1993)	Antidepressants 90, ECT 38, psychosocial 51, family therapy 33, individual psychotherapy 25	45[b] 67[c]

[a] No treatment was specified for remaining patients.
[b] After follow-up of 12 months.
[c] After follow-up of 42–104 months.

DISCUSSION

This review had a number of limitations in the selection, assessment of validity, and examination of results of the studies. A search strategy involving different databases in other languages using different keywords and time periods might have resulted in a different set of articles. Furthermore, different inclusion criteria might have been used and the consistency with which the bibliographies were reviewed and inclusion criteria applied might have been quantified. Finally, the degree of publication bias

TABLE 7 Results and Combined Results of Community-based Studies by Length of Follow-up

	Length of Follow-up: Percent of Patients			
	<24 months		>24 months	
Prognosis Category	Results	Combined Results (n = 69)	Results	Combined Results (n = 180)
Well	22–46	37	20–32	22
Relapse with recovery	—	—	—	—
Continuously ill	14–44	26	14–31	25
Other	34–40	37	27–59	53

(tendency to publish reports with "significant" findings) might have been assessed, but this type of bias probably had little influence on the publication of studies of prognosis.

With respect to the validity assessment, the criteria were arguably too rigorous for these studies. For example, description of referral patterns and blind outcome assessment might have been unnecessary. On the other hand, the criteria were arguably not rigorous enough and could have included additional items concerning explicit diagnostic criteria, minimum severity of depression for inclusion, prospective collection of data, minimum length of follow-up, and definition of the follow-up interval (i.e., Does the interval begin on admission to the study or on discharge from hospital or at the end of active treatment?). In addition, the criteria could have described a method of classifying patients who die during follow-up—whether they should be mixed into outcome categories with the living (according to prognosis until the time of death) or be placed in separate categories. Interestingly, Godber et al. (1987) classified groups of living and dead subjects separately into depression outcome categories and found very similar results in the two groups.

Some of the criteria may have been met by other types of information. For example, the absence of a description of referral pattern in the hospital-based studies may have been offset by a detailed description of the patient population (i.e., quality and quantity of depressive symptoms, cognitive impairment, physical illness, functional disability etc.), but such descriptions were often not reported.

Ideally, the validity should have been assessed by at least one other reviewer, each of us blind to the other's decision, and the extent of the agreement should have been recorded. In this review, the validity was assessed only by me; however, the assessment criteria were relatively simple and did not require considerable judgment in their application. Some of the validity criteria were not met because information presented in the reports was inadequate: This information (e.g., description of referral patterns) might have been available from authors of the reports but they were not contacted.

The examination of the results was complicated by the questionable validity of many of the studies, the differences in lengths of follow-up and outcome categories from one study to the next and the small number of community-based studies. Combining the results was controversial, but given the gross similarities in study designs, populations, and some outcome categories among the hospital-based and community-based studies, it seemed reasonable.

The percentage of patients in each of the four outcome categories of the hospital-based studies (Table 5) was varied. For example, in the group whose follow-up was

24 months or less, 25–64% of the patients remained well. Although these variations can probably be attributed mostly to differences in three basic study components (population, intervention, outcome measures), none of these components was described well enough to enable comparison, contrast, or explanation of the variations.

The combined results of the hospital-based studies were more useful. In comparing the short- and long-term follow-up groups, the proportion of subjects in the well category declined by 13.4% and the percent of cases in the relapse with recovery group increased by 17.3%. It seems that, in both the short-term and the long-term follow-up groups, approximately 60% of the patients remained well or had relapses with recovery. Given that most of the inception cohorts included subjects with multiple previous depressive episodes, that most referrals were to secondary or tertiary rather than primary-care services, and that extraneous and negative prognostic factors (i.e., cognitive impairment, physical illness, severity of depression) were not eliminated in most of the studies, this estimate of 60% probably underestimates the true proportion with a favorable prognosis.

For the same reasons the proportion of subjects in the continuously ill category in the short-term follow-up group is probably an overestimate. In the long-term follow-up group it is impossible to know whether the proportion in this category declined because the patients had recovered or because some had been placed in the other category. Notably, Brodaty et al. (1993) reported that 36% of their subjects so classified at 12-month follow-up were reclassified in better outcome categories at 46 months. Whatever the explanation, the large percentage of continuously ill subjects in the short-term follow-up group represents considerable morbidity. These patients should probably be involved in independent investigations to determine the factors that cause and those factors that sustain chronic mood disorder in the elderly.

Physical illness, severity of depressive symptoms, and cognitive impairment were frequently associated with poor prognosis although not consistently so. The social factors (excluding severe intervening life events) were not associated with prognosis. However, more reliable, valid, and responsive measures of all prognostic factors are needed to enable more sophisticated analyses of the relation between prognostic factors and the course of major depression.

The relationship of treatments to prognosis is unclear. None of the hospital-based studies examined this, and the comparison of treatments and outcomes was difficult because the treatments were poorly described, the outcome categories dissimilar, and the follow-up periods unequal. Nonetheless, when the outcomes of the hospital-based studies (Table 6) conducted over the past 40 years are compared, there is no evidence that the new treatments introduced during this period (e.g., antidepressant drugs and expanded psychogeriatric services) have appreciably changed the prognosis. However, compliance with follow-up and treatment, which can be poor (Cole, 1985), was not documented in most of the reports; poor compliance rather than inefficacious treatments may account for the apparent lack of improvement in prognosis over time.

There was considerable variation in the proportions of patients in each of the three outcome categories of the community-based studies. For example in the short-term, 22–46% of the patients remained well, 14–44% were continuously ill, and 34–40% were in the other category. Admittedly, this variation may be explained by the small numbers of subjects in most of the studies.

The combined results of the community-based studies showed a reduction of 15% in the proportion of subjects remaining well in the long-term and an increase of 16%

in the other category, most of whom had died. The proportion remaining continuously ill was remarkably constant (25–26%).

Inasmuch as comparisons of the combined results of the hospital-based and community-based studies are possible, the short-term outcomes are similar (Tables 5 and 7). The long-term outcomes, however, are different: The percentage of subjects remaining well is similar (22 vs. 28%), but the percentage of continuously ill subjects is greater in the community-based studies (25 vs. 9.5%). Given that few subjects in the community received any antidepressive treatments, these results suggest that the principal benefit of treatment may not be the short-term response but the prevention of the morbidity and mortality associated with chronic depression. Clearly, there is a need for programs to improve the detection and management of major depression among the elderly in the community, an opinion that echoes the conclusions of a recent consensus conference (NIH Concensus Development Panel, 1992).

Interestingly, Kivela et al. (1991, 1993) reported the 1- and 5-year outcomes of 199 community subjects with dysthymic disorder (DSM-111 criteria, American Psychiatric Associations, 1980). After 1 year 40% were well, 42% were continuously ill, and 18% were in the other category; after 5 years, 36% were well, 26% were continuously ill, and 38% were in the other category. Apparently, more community subjects with dysthymic disorder recovered than did subjects with major depression; similar proportions remained continuously ill. At the least, these results suggest that we should reexamine our classification of these two disorders in the elderly.

CONCLUSIONS AND RECOMMENDATIONS

To date, there are 16 hospital-based and 5 community-based studies of the outcome of depression in old age in the English and French language literature. In the short-term the results of the hospital- and community-based studies are similar: 37–41% of subjects were well and 22–26% were continuously ill. In the long term only 22–28% of subjects remained well, many had relapses with recovery, and up to one-quarter were continuously ill. The worst outcome was among community subjects, most of whom were continuously ill or had died.

To advance knowledge future studies should pay attention to methods and design:

1. Adequate numbers of depressed elderly subjects should be selected from community samples. If cases are selected from hospital or clinic populations, referral patterns should be described in detail.
2. The subjects should be assigned to categories on the basis of previous history of depression (e.g., none or one previous episode versus two or more previous episodes).
3. The selection criteria should include explicit diagnostic criteria and minimum severity of depression criteria.
4. Important characteristics of the cases and possible prognostic factors (e.g., depressive symptoms, physical illness, disability, cognition, premorbid personality, social factors) should be described using valid and reliable measures.
5. The minimum follow-up period for all cases should be 2 years. The follow-up interval should begin on entry to the study.

6. Descriptions of depression outcome categories should be specific and clearly independent of one another. If possible, the proportion of time cases are well during the follow-up period should be calculated.
7. The outcome assessments should be blind.
8. All treatments should be recorded in detail and related to course of illness and outcome.
9. The subjects could be further categorized on the basis of the presence or absence of severe physical illness (or disability) and cognitive impairment. The prognosis of each category could be reported independently.
10. All phases of the study (e.g., selection of subjects, diagnosis, use of outcome measures, and categorization of outcomes) should have demonstrated reliability.

REFERENCES

Agbayewa MO (1990): Outcome of depression in a geriatric medical day hospital following psychiatric consultation. Int J Geriatr Psychiatry 5:33–39.

American Psychiatric Association (1987): "Diagnostic and Statistical Manual of Mental Disorders," 3rd ed, revised. Washington, DC: American Psychiatric Press.

American Psychiatric Association (1980): "Diagnostic and Statistical Manual of Mental Disorders," 3rd ed. Washington, DC: American Psychiatric Press.

Baldwin R, Jolley D (1986): The prognosis of depession in old age. Br J Psychiatry 149:574–583.

Baldwin RC, Benbow SM, Mariott A, Tomenson B (1993): Depression in old age: A reconsideration of cerebral disease in relation to outcome. Br J Psychiatry 163:82–90.

Ben-Arie O, Welman M, Teggin AF (1990): The depressed elderly living in the community: A follow-up study. Br J Psychiatry 157:425–427.

Brodaty H, Harris L, Peters K, Wilhelm K, Hickie L, Boyce P, Mitchell P, Parker G, Eyers K (1993): Prognosis of depression in the elderly: A comparison with younger patients. Br J Psychiatry 163:589–596.

Burvill PW, Hall WD, Stampfer HG, Emmerson JP (1991): The prognosis of depression in old age. Br J Psychiatry 158:64–71.

Cole MG (1985): The course of elderly depressed outpatients. Can J Psychiatry 30:217–220.

Cole MG (1983): Age, age of onset and course of primary depressive illness in the elderly. Can J Psychiatry 28:102–104.

Copeland JR, Davidson PA, Dewey ME, Gilmore C, Larkin B, McWillim C, Saunders P, Scott A, Sherma V, Sullivan C (1992): Alzheimer's disease, other dementias, depression and pseudodementia: Prevalence, incidence and three-year outcome in Liverpool. Br J Psychiatry 161:230–239.

Department of Clinical Epidemiology and Biostatistics, McMaster University (1981): How to read clinical journals: III. To learn the clinical course and prognosis of disease. Can Med Assoc J 124:869–872.

Feighner J, Robbins E, Guze S, et al. (1972): Diagnostic criteria for use in psychiatric research. Arch Ger Psychiatry 26:57–63.

Forsell E, Jorm AF, Winblad B (1994): Outcome of depression in demented and non-demented elderly: Observations from a three-year follow-up in a community-based study. Int J Geriatr Psychiatry 9:5–10.

Godber C, Rosenwinge H, Wilkinson D, Smithies J (1987): Depression in old age: Prognosis after ECT. Int J Ger Psychiatry 2:19–24.

Gordon WF (1981): Elderly depressives: Treatment and follow-up. Can J Psychiatry 26:110–113.

Hinrichsen GA (1992): Recovery and relapse from major depressive disorder in the elderly. Am J Psychiatry 149:1575–1579.

Kay D, Roth M, Hopkins B (1955): Affective disorders in the senium: Their association with organic cerebral degeneration. J Ment Sci 101:302–316.

Kivela SL, Kongats-Saviaro P, Pahkala E, Kesti E, Laippala P (1993): Five year prognosis of dysthymic disorder in old age. Int J Geriatr Psychiatry 8:939–947.

Kivela SL, Pahkala K, Laippala P (1991): A one-year prognosis of dysthymic disorder and major depression in old age. Int J Geriatr Psychiatry 6:81–87.

Kraepelin E (1987): "Manic Depressive Insanity and Paranoia," reprint edition. Salem, NH: Ayer Co.

Magni G, Palazzolo O, Bianchin G (1988): The course of depression in elderly outpatients. Can J Psychiatry 33:21–24.

Meats P, Timol M, Jolley D (1991): Prognosis of depression in the elderly. Br J Psychiatry 159:659–663.

Murphy E (1983): The prognosis of depression in old age. Br J Psychiatry 142:111–119.

NIH Consensus Development Panel on Depression in Late Life (1992): Diagnosis and treatment of depression in late life. JAMA 268:1018–1024.

O'Connor DW, Politt PA, Roth M (1990): Co-existing depression and dementia in a community survey of the elderly. Int Psychogeriatr 2:45–53.

Oxman A, Guyatt G (1988): Guidelines for reading literature reviews. Can Med Assoc J 138:697–703.

Post F (1972): The management and nature of depressive illness in late life: A follow-through study. Br J Psychiatry 121:393–404.

Post F (1962): "The Significance of Affective Symptoms in Old Age," Mandsley Monographs 10. London: Oxford University Press.

Roth M (1955): The natural history of mental disorder in old age. J Ment Sci 101:281–301.

Wing PK, Cooper JE, Sartorius N (1974): The Measurement and Classification of Psychiatric Symptoms. London: Cambridge University Press.

CHAPTER 18

Treatment of Depression in the Elderly

ALASTAIR J. FLINT

Departments of Psychiatry, The Toronto Hospital and The Queen Elizabeth Hospital, Toronto, Ontario, Canada, M5G 2C4

INTRODUCTION

Factors associated with aging can affect the management of depression in several important ways. First, changes in pharmacokinetics and pharmacodynamics increase the older person's sensitivity to the effects of medications. These changes are often magnified by the presence of chronic medical conditions. Second, age-related disorders such as cardiac arrhythmias, postural hypotension, prostatic hypertrophy, and cognitive impairment can be adversely affected by antidepressant medications. Third, elderly people take more prescribed and over-the-counter medications than younger individuals and, as a result, are at increased risk of drug interactions, incorrect use of medications, and noncompliance. Forgetfulness, sensory impairment, social isolation, and financial hardship can also interfere with compliance with somatic and psychosocial treatments. Finally, in addition to the biological changes of aging, there are psychological and social issues specific to the elderly that may influence the type of treatment used. For these reasons, there are advantages to considering the treatment of geriatric depression separately from that for young and middle-aged adults.

The goals of treatment include symptom reduction, minimizing the risk of relapse and recurrence, enhancing quality of life, maintaining independent functioning, improving physical health, reducing mortality from medical causes and suicide, and decreasing health care costs (NIH Consensus Development Panel, 1992). Most treatment data relate to the use of pharmacotherapy and electroconvulsive therapy (ECT) in the physically well elderly patient. There is a paucity of information with respect to psychosocial therapies and the treatment of depression in older persons with concomitant active medical problems. It should be kept in mind that the elderly are a heterogeneous population and that there may be profound biological and psychosocial differences between the "young-old" and the "old-old." Also, biological age does not necessarily correlate with chronological age. However, research on the treatment of depression in old age has seldom taken into account this variability, and very little work has focused on the frail elderly.

Mood Disorders Across the Life Span, Edited by Shulman, Tohen, and Kutcher
ISBN 0-471-10477-9 © 1996 Wiley-Liss, Inc.

Taking these limitations into account, this chapter discusses the role of pharmacotherapy, psychotherapy, and ECT in the management of geriatric unipolar depression. It also focuses on the treatment of depression associated with certain medical and neurological conditions that tend to be specific to late life. Recent advances in treatment are emphasized.

PHARMACOTHERAPY

A review of 25 double-blind antidepressant drug studies conducted in patients aged 55 years and older found that all medications were superior to placebo and of comparable therapeutic efficacy (Gerson et al., 1988). Similarly, a recent meta-analysis of controlled trials comparing tricyclic antidepressants (TCAs) and selective serotonin reuptake inhibitors (SSRIs) found that both classes of drugs had comparable efficacy in the treatment of geriatric depression (Mittmann et al., 1995). Therefore, the choice of antidepressant medication in the elderly is based on the side-effect profile and the potential for drug interactions (Gerson et al., 1988).

Tricyclic Antidepressants

Secondary amine TCAs, such as nortriptyline and desipramine, have fewer anticholinergic, sedative, and hypotensive effects than the tertiary amine compounds and, therefore, tend to be the preferred choice of tricyclic in the elderly (Preskorn and Burke, 1992). Most research on the use of secondary amine TCAs in old age has focused on nortriptyline. One of the best designed antidepressant studies in the elderly compared nortriptyline, phenelzine, and placebo (Georgotas et al., 1986). Both drugs were associated with a 60% remission rate compared with 13% for placebo. Anticholinergic side effects were more common in the nortriptyline group but only 8% of this group terminated treatment because of adverse effects. Similarly, Miller et al. (1991) found that only 7% of 35 elderly outpatients treated with nortriptyline over a 30-week period discontinued treatment because of side effects.

The TCAs potential for producing cardiovascular effects, in particular orthostatic hypotension and cardiac arrhythmias, is of particular concern in the elderly. Hypotension can lead to falls, which have been associated with hip fractures, cerebrovascular accidents, and myocardial ischemia (Halper and Mann, 1988). However, in both medically healthy patients and patients with congestive heart failure, nortriptyline is associated with significantly less orthostatic hypotension than other tricyclic antidepressants (Roose et al., 1986; Roose and Dalack, 1992). It was previously thought that therapeutic doses of TCAs could impair ventricular function. However, controlled studies, using radionuclide scan measurements of ventricular emptying, have found no evidence to support this, even in patients with diminished ejection fractions (Halper and Mann, 1988). All tricyclics, including nortriptyline, have a quinidinelike effect on the heart and, as a result, no TCA is safe in patients with bundle branch block (Roose et al., 1987; Roose and Dalack, 1992).

Studies evaluating nortriptyline's effect on cognitive performance have yielded conflicting results. Georgotas et al. (1989b) found that treatment with nortriptyline, at plasma levels of 50–180 ng/mL, did not affect elderly patients' performance on cognitive tasks. Young et al. (1991) evaluated the effects of a fixed dose of 75 mg/day of nortriptyline on patients' cognitive performance. Higher nortriptyline plasma levels were associated with worse immediate free recall but no change in recognition memory or digit span. Meyers et al. (1991) also found that, in recovered elderly depressives, nortriptyline impaired immediate free recall but did not affect delayed recall. Therefore, these studies suggest that selected aspects of memory can be affected by nortriptyline.

The results of these studies indicate that nortriptyline is effective and well tolerated by many elderly patients and, in particular, has significantly less potential for causing orthostatic hypotension compared to tertiary amine TCAs. It should be noted that trials of new antidepressant medications nearly always use a tertiary amine tricyclic as the comparison drug. In the elderly, such a comparison is more likely to favor the newer drug in terms of side effects. In this age group it would be far more appropriate to use a secondary amine drug as the gold standard.

Although secondary amine TCAs are preferred in the elderly, tertiary amine drugs can still be useful in certain situations. A recent report described five cases of elderly women with depressive illness and obsessional features who were successfully and safely treated with clomipramine after failing to respond to other antidepressants (Kunik et al., 1994). Plasma clomipramine levels were carefully monitored and a therapeutic steady state was reached at doses lower than that reported for nongeriatric patients.

Nearly all the adverse effects associated with TCAs are concentration dependent (Preskorn, 1993). Because of altered pharmacokinetics, TCAs have a relatively narrow therapeutic index in old age (Preskorn, 1993). For a given dose there is wide interindividual variation in plasma levels. Also, older individuals are likely to take multiple medications, and the plasma levels of TCAs can be altered by drugs that interfere with their metabolism (Preskorn, 1993). As a result, monitoring plasma TCA levels in the elderly patient can be particularly helpful in order to maximize clinical response and minimize adverse effects. Therapeutic drug monitoring can also be used to monitor patient compliance. Although there has been controversy about the predictive value of plasma tricyclic levels, there is now a consensus that there is a curvilinear relationship between plasma levels of nortriptyline and its therapeutic effect, with clinical response most likely to occur in the range of 50–150 ng/mL (Rockwell et al, 1988). Desipramine appears to have a sigmoidal response curve, although it is not clear whether the threshold concentration of therapeutic response is the same in the elderly as for younger adults (Rockwell et al., 1988). An area worthy of further investigation is the relationship of TCA hydroxymetabolites to therapeutic response and side effects in elderly patients.

Monoamine Oxidase Inhibitors

In all age groups, monoamine oxidase inhibitors (MAOIs) have probably been underutilized because of concerns about their potential for producing hypertensive crises and the resulting need for dietary and drug restrictions. However, brain monoamine oxidase levels increase with age (Robinson et al., 1971) and, for this reason, MAOIs may be particularly advantageous in the elderly. In recent years the dietary restrictions have been reviewed and modified, and as a result they are now less onerous (Shulman et al., 1989).

The only rigorously designed double-blind placebo-controlled study of MAOIs in the elderly found that phenelzine, given at an average dose of 54 mg/day was as efficacious as nortriptyline and superior to placebo (Georgotas et al., 1986). Somewhat surprisingly, phenelzine produced no more orthostatic hypotension than nortriptyline. In this trial, there were very few anticholinergic side effects and there were no cases of hypertensive crisis. Clinical experience has long indicated that MAOIs may be particularly useful in treating depression that has failed to respond to other antidepressant medications. Controlled trials in nongeriatric patients have reported a 60–80% response rate to phenelzine and tranylcypromine in patients whose depression has not improved with TCAs (Thase et al., 1992; McGrath et al., 1993). Although there have been no similar controlled trials in the elderly, open studies have described patients responding to MAOIs when they have failed to respond to TCAs or ECT (Georgotas et al., 1983a,b).

Reversible inhibitors of monoamine oxidase A (RIMAs) may be better tolerated than first-generation MAOIs. In younger patients, moclobemide has been found to be as effective as older MAOIs and TCAs and superior to placebo (Priest, 1990; Norman et al., 1992), although one recent study found it to be less effective than clomipramine (Danish University Antidepressant Group, 1993). In the elderly, moclobemide has been found to have equal efficacy to mianserin and maprotiline (DeVanna et al., 1990), but we still do not know how well it compares to other MAOIs and TCAs.

Side effects of RIMAs include nausea, headache, and insomnia. They do not cause the hypotension, edema, weight gain, and sexual dysfunction associated with first-generation MAOIs and do not have anticholinergic effects or cardiotoxicity (Priest, 1990). Unlike the first-generation compounds, moclobemide has not caused fatalities when taken in overdose at doses of 900–2000 mg (Moll and Hetzel, 1990). Another significant advantage of RIMAs is they do not have a tyramine pressor effect with diets containing less than 100 mg of tyramine per day, and therefore there is no need for dietary restrictions as long as tyramine-containing foods are taken in moderation (Norman et al., 1992). This is a particular advantage in the elderly who, because of forgetfulness, may not otherwise be compliant with dietary and drug restrictions. The results of single-dose and multiple-dose studies suggest that the pharmacokinetics of moclobemide are not significantly different between older and younger patients (Stoeckel et al., 1990). Thus RIMAs offer advantages in terms of side effects and tolerability in elderly patients, although their efficacy in this population needs to be better established.

Selective Serotonin Reuptake Inhibitors

In controlled trials, SSRIs have been found to have the same efficacy as TCAs in treating depression in old age (Wakelin, 1986; Feighner et al., 1988; Altamura et al., 1989; Cohn et al., 1990; Ashford and Rahman, 1990). SSRIs have been shown to be effective for the treatment of depression that has failed to respond to TCAs (Beasley et al., 1990; Grimsley and Jann, 1992), although these studies were not specific to the elderly.

SSRIs selectively inhibit neuronal serotonin reuptake and have minimal affinity for muscarinic, histaminergic, noradrenergic, and dopaminergic receptors (Grimsley and Jann, 1992). Therefore, they do not have the anticholinergic, hypotensive, and cardiac effects associated with TCAs. In the elderly, a particular attraction of the SSRIs is their apparent lack of cardiac toxicity. However, it should be noted that studies examining the cardiovascular properties of these drugs have been in physically healthy patients, and the results cannot be automatically extrapolated to depressed patients with cardiovascular disease or the medically ill or frail elderly. In contrast to TCAs and first-generation MAOIs, SSRIs are well tolerated in overdose and no deaths have been reported with an overdose of an SSRI alone (Cooper, 1988).

The side effects of SSRIs result from excessive blockade of peripheral and central serotonin reuptake and tend to be dose related (Rickels and Schweizer, 1990; Preskorn, 1993). Adverse effects include gastrointestinal upset (nausea, vomiting, and loose stools), central nervous system dysfunction (insomnia, sedation, nervousness, restlessness, tremor, and headaches) and sexual dysfunction (decreased libido, anorgasmia, and delayed orgasm). The syndrome of inappropriate secretion of antidiuretic hormone and Parkinsonism have also been associated with the use of SSRIs in the elderly (Cohen et al., 1990; Chouinard and Sultan, 1992).

The SSRIs are a structurally heterogeneous group of drugs, and this is reflected in differences in their pharmacokinetics (De Vane, 1992). Fluoxetine has an elimination half-life of 70 hours and its pharmacologically active metabolite, norfluoxetine, has a half-life of 330 hours (Rickels and Schweizer, 1990). Therefore, there is a delay of several weeks before steady-state plasma concentrations are reached and a lengthy washout period when the drug is stopped. Because of this, 5 weeks need to elapse following the discontinuation of fluoxetine before an MAOI can be started (Preskorn and Burke, 1992). This can be a particular limitation in the management of some depressed patients. In contrast, fluvoxamine, paroxetine, and sertraline have elimination half-lives of 15, 21, and 26 hours, respectively, and they do not have pharmacologically active metabolites (De Vane, 1992; Grimsley and Jann, 1992). Aging increases the half-lives and steady-state plasma concentrations of fluoxetine, paroxetine, and, to a lesser extent, sertraline and this has implications for dosing of these drugs in the elderly (Murdoch and McTavish, 1992; Preskorn, 1993). It should be noted that most pharmacokinetic studies of SSRIs in the elderly have been on physically healthy volunteers, and studies in elderly patients who are depressed, medically ill, or very old need to be carried out.

The SSRIs are eliminated by hepatic metabolism and all competitively inhibit cytochrome P450 IID6, an hepatic isoenzyme involved in the oxidative metabolism of TCAs, benzodiazepines, neuroleptics, anticonvulsants, type 1c antiarrhythmics, and a number of other drugs (Crewe et al., 1991; Grimsley and Jann, 1992; Preskorn, 1993). Plasma levels of these drugs will be increased when they are administered concurrently with SSRIs, especially paroxetine and fluoxetine, which are the most potent inhibitors of P450 IID6, or within 6 weeks of discontinuing fluoxetine. The potential for these drug interactions is particularly important in elderly patients, who take more medications than younger individuals. Case reports and a double-blind study have demonstrated that fluoxetine can cause a 2- to 10-fold increase in TCA plasma levels, an effect that persists for several weeks after fluoxetine's discontinuation (Preskorn and Burke, 1992). Therefore, one has to be cautious when switching from fluoxetine to a TCA in the elderly because of the risk of TCA toxicity. In this situation, the TCA should be started at a lower than normal dose, titrated more slowly, and plasma levels should be carefully monitored.

Unlike the TCAs, the SSRIs have a flat dose–response curve (Preskorn, 1993). Therefore, for most patients, increasing the dose beyond the minimum effective dose does not lead to additional efficacy but does cause more side effects. There have been no published studies determining the minimum effective dose of SSRIs in the elderly, and at the current time data from mixed-age populations is used to guide dosing in the elderly. Because of age-related differences in pharmacokinetics, the starting dose for many elderly patients, especially those who are frail or physically debilitated, may need to be lower than that used for younger adults, with subsequent dose adjustments based on tolerance and clinical response.

Plasma SSRI levels have not been found to be helpful in determining optimum dose (Schatzberg, 1991; Preskorn, 1993). However, some recent work has suggested that high levels of norfluoxetine may inhibit the therapeutic response to fluoxetine (Montgomery et al., 1990; Tyrer et al., 1990), and this may explain why some patients unresponsive to high doses of fluoxetine have been found to respond to lower doses (Schatzberg, 1991). This finding has potential implications for the use of this drug in the elderly and requires further study in this age group.

Other Antidepressants

Trazadone inhibits serotonin reuptake but, along with its major metabolite, also blocks serotonin receptors (Georgotas et al., 1982). It has a short elimination half-life (3–9 hours), which necessitates multiple daily dosing to achieve therapeutic plasma levels (Georgotas et al., 1982). This may increase the risk of noncompliance among elderly patients who may forget to take the required number of doses. This medication is free of anticholinergic adverse effects, but it frequently produces sedation and orthostatic hypotension, with the risk of falls (Georgotas et al., 1982; Rudorfer and Potter, 1989). Although it was previously believed that trazadone was free of cardiotoxicity, it is now known that it can cause arrhythmias in patients with preexisting cardiac disease (Halper and Mann, 1988). Priapism is an infrequent but serious side effect that has been reported only rarely in older men (Preskorn, 1993).

Bupropion is a unicyclic aminoketone. Its mechanism of action is not known. It has no significant effect on the uptake of serotonin or noradrenaline or on MAO activity (Preskorn, 1993). It does have weak dopamine reuptake blocking properties, but it is not clear whether this action accounts for its antidepressant effect. Its advantages for older patients is that it does not have a significant effect on the cardiovascular system and does not cause sedation or cognitive impairment (Rudorfer and Potter, 1989; Preskorn 1993). However, it also has several disadvantages in the elderly (Preskorn, 1993). It has a short half-life requiring multiple daily dosing and, therefore, an increased risk of noncompliance. Second, it has a narrow therapeutic index and large interindividual variations in its metabolism. Third, it has three active metabolites with half-lives that are significantly longer than the parent drug and that accumulate with repeated dosing. High plasma concentrations of these metabolites may contribute to side effects that include agitation, headaches, dizziness, tremor, insomnia, anorexia, nausea, and rarely seizures. Buproprion's narrow therapeutic index and its potential for toxicity suggest that therapeutic drug monitoring would be particularly helpful in the elderly (Preskorn, 1993). However, to date, there has not been enough study of plasma monitoring of buproprion to make this approach clinically useful. Because buproprion lowers the seizure threshold to a greater extent than TCAs, MAOIs, or SSRIs, it is not recommended for use in elderly patients with a history of seizure disorder (Rudorfer and Potter, 1989; Preskorn and Burke, 1992).

Augmentation Strategies

Augmentation (potentiation) strategies have been proposed as one way of improving the rate of response in depressed patients who do not have remission with a therapeutic trial of antidepressant medication. Lithium has been the most frequently studied adjunctive agent. Four published double-blind placebo-controlled trials in the general adult population have demonstrated the efficacy of lithium augmentation (Heninger et al., 1983; Cournoyer et al., 1984; Schopf et al., 1989; Joffe et al., 1993). However, there have been no controlled trials of lithium potentiation that are specific to the elderly. Case reports (which tend to report successes rather than failures) and retrospective case series quote high rates of response in the elderly, but the results of systematic prospective trials are less striking (Flint, 1995). Zimmer et al. (1991) and Flint and Rifat (1994) reported rates of complete response of 20 and 23%, respectively, less than half the rate reported for most open and placebo-controlled studies in mixed-age populations. Also, a number of reports indicate that elderly people may be more vulnerable to side effects with lithium augmentation (Flint, 1995). In several trials, 50% of patients developed significant side effects, and lithium was prematurely discontinued in one-quarter of cases. Thus, although the data are far from conclusive, there is some indication that lithium potentiation may be less efficacious and less well tolerated in the elderly. There is also an anecdotal literature, based entirely on case reports, of the successful use of triiodothyronine, stimulants, carbamazepine, valproate, and TCA–SSRI combinations as augmentation strategies in the elderly (Flint, 1995).

In addition to the need for studies to establish the efficacy and safety of different potentiation techniques in old age, there is also a need to determine whether one augmentation strategy is more useful than another, whether patient characteristics predict response to one strategy over another, and the optimal duration of augmentation once response has occurred.

Duration of Treatment with Antidepressant Medication

In their double-blind, placebo-controlled comparison of nortriptyline and phenelzine, Georgotas et al. (1986) found that the majority of elderly depressed patients did not show significant improvement until the fifth week of treatment. Patients who had not responded to the 7-week trial of antidepressant medication were given an additional 2 weeks of treatment. Nearly half of these patients had remission of their depression during this extended period, with phenelzine-treated patients benefiting the most (Georgotas and McCue, 1989). In this study, therapeutic blood levels of nortriptyline were reached by the end of the first week of treatment and the phenelzine group achieved greater than 70% platelet MAO inhibition by the end of the second week. Thus, the delayed response could not be accounted for by an inappropriately slow titration of dose. These findings suggest that, in the elderly, TCAs and MAOIs should be continued for at least 6–8 weeks before a decision is made about their efficacy. There are no data relating to the optimal duration of acute treatment with SSRIs in the elderly. However, in a group of younger patients treated with fluoxetine, Schweizer et al. (1990) found that over half the group did not respond until weeks 4–8 of treatment.

In recent years, there has been a growing awareness of the importance of continuation and maintenance treatment in the management of depression. Continuation treatment is designed to prevent relapse or the reemergence of symptoms of the index episode of depression. Maintenance therapy, on the other hand, aims to prevent future episodes of depression once there has been complete recovery from the index episode. The mean duration of an untreated episode of depression in late life may be much longer than the 6 months commonly quoted for younger adults (Flint, 1992). Therefore, attempting to distinguish between continuation and maintenance phases of treatment in the elderly may be somewhat arbitrary.

In mixed-age populations, it is now well established that when antidepressant medication is continued at full dosage for at least 4 months after remission of depressive symptoms the rate of relapse is approximately 20%, compared to 50% for patients treated with placebo (Prien and Kupfer, 1986). In a double-blind continuation study in the elderly, Georgotas et al. (1988) found similar rates of response, with only 16.7% of patients treated with nortriptyline and 20% of patients treated with phenelzine relapsing during 4–8 months of continuation treatment.

There have been only two published placebo-controlled trials of maintenance treatment in the elderly. Georgotas et al. (1989a) found that with one year of maintenance treatment, 65.2% of patients treated with placebo had a further episode of depression compared with only 13.3% of those taking phenelzine. However, the recurrence rate on nortriptyline was nearly that of placebo, a finding for which there was no obvious explanation. In contrast, Reynolds et al. (1988) reported an 81.5% survival rate for elderly patients treated with maintenance nortriptyline over an 18-month period. The Old Age Depression Interest Group (OADIG) (1993) study found that dothiepin, prescribed over a 2-year period, reduced the risk of recurrence 2½ times compared to placebo. It should be noted that, unlike trials of maintenance antidepressant treatment in younger individuals that select patients at high risk of recurrence (Frank et al., 1990), the studies of Georgotas et al. (1989a) and OADIG (1993) did not select patients on the basis of previous recurrence. The OADIG study found that patients with a first episode of depression had the same risk of recurrence as those who had previous episodes (Jacoby, 1993), a finding that is consistent with other research data (Flint, 1992). It is also important to note that these studies maintained patients on a full dose of antidepressant medication. The efficacy of this approach, as opposed to tapering to a lower maintenance dose, is supported by data from younger patients (Frank et al., 1993).

Thus, there is increasing evidence that the majority of elderly people with major depression require at least 2 years of full-dose antidepressant treatment, irrespective of whether they are experiencing a first or recurrent episode of depression. There is a need for more research in the elderly to better determine predictors of recurrence and the comparative efficacy of different types of antidepressants as maintenance treatment.

PSYCHOTHERAPY

There has been very little systematic study of psychotherapy as a treatment for geriatric depression. In a study by Sloane et al. (1985), 55 medically stable outpatients, with a mean age of 64 years, suffering from major depression of moderate severity were randomly assigned to receive nortriptyline, placebo, or weekly interpersonal therapy. Following 6 weeks of treatment all groups had shown a statistically significant reduction in mean Hamilton Depression Rating Scale (HDRS) scores from baseline, although improvement was only modest and a number of patients in each group remained depressed. The poor response to nortriptyline in this study may have been due to a slow titration of dose, with many patients not reaching therapeutic steady-state plasma levels until after the fourth week of treatment. By the end of 16 weeks of treatment medication and psychotherapy groups had shown further gains with a mean reduction of HDRS scores from baseline of 58 and 64%, respectively (Schneider et al., 1986).

In an uncontrolled open trial, Gallagher and Thompson (1983) compared the efficacy of cognitive, behavioral, and dynamic psychotherapies, administered for 16 sessions over 12 weeks, in 30 outpatient volunteers (mean age 68 years) with Research Diagnostic Criteria (RDC) defined endogenous and nonendogenous depression. In the nonendogenous group, 80% of patients had remission of their depression following psycho-therapy and 58% remained free of depressive symptoms at 12-month follow-up. However, only 33% of patients with endogenous depression had remission posttreat-ment and 13% had maintained remission at 12 months. In a subsequent randomized controlled study, the same investigators compared the effectiveness of these three types of psychotherapy in the treatment of 91 outpatients aged 60 years and older (Thompson, et al., 1987). Patients met RDC for major depression and had a minimum HDRS score of 14. Outcome measures were administered by independent evaluators but were not blind. After 16–20 psychotherapy sessions, given over 4 months, 52% of the treatment group attained remission by the end of therapy and another 18% showed significant improvement. The control group, who were on a 6-week waiting list for therapy, showed no improvement. All three treatment modalities were found to be equally effective, which raises the issue of whether nonspecific factors, such as having a relationship with an understanding and helpful therapist, were more important than differences in philosophy and technique. Following the termination of therapy, patients were then followed up for 2 years (Gallagher-Thompson et al., 1990). Of the group whose depression had resolved with psychotherapy, 53% remained in remission for the first year and 49% were in remission for the second year. Thus, approximately 50% of this group had relapses or recurrences over the 2-year period.

These studies show that in young-old, physically healthy outpatients, brief psycho-therapy leads to a rate of improvement in nonendogenous major depression that is comparable to that achieved with antidepressant medication. However, the rate of relapse and recurrence in the follow-up studies of Gallagher and Thompson (1983) and Gallagher-Thompson et al. (1990) is higher than that reported for patients treated with maintenance phenelzine (Georgotas et al., 1989a), dothiepin (Old Age Depression Interest Group, 1993), or nortriptyline (Reynolds et al., 1988). Therefore, in elderly patients with major depression, especially with endogenous features, a brief course of psychotherapy is not as effective as ongoing pharmacotherapy in maintaining remission. There have been no published studies directly comparing maintenance psychotherapy with maintenance pharmacotherapy in the treatment of elderly depressed patients, although in younger patients monthly interpersonal therapy was found to be only half as effective as imipramine in maintaining remission over 3 years and a combination of the TCA and psychotherapy was no more effective than medication alone (Frank et al., 1990).

COMBINED PHARMACOTHERAPY AND PSYCHOTHERAPY

It has been hypothesized that a combination of pharmacotherapy and psychotherapy may be more effective than monotherapy in the treatment of depression. To date there have been no controlled trials of combined therapy in the acute, continuation, or maintenance phases of the treatment of depression in old age. However, in an uncontrolled open study Reynolds et al. (1992) treated depressed patients aged 60 years and older with nortriptyline and interpersonal therapy for a median interval of 9 weeks of acute and 16 weeks of continuation treatment. By the end of the continuation period, 78.7% had full remission and an additional 4.9% were partial responders. In an earlier uncontrolled study, the same research group reported that, when treated with nortriptyline alone, 76.9% of patients had remission of the acute episode but at 6-month follow-up only 52% of patients were in remission with most of the remainder having HDRS scores in the range of 11–17 (Reynolds et al., 1988). However, as previously noted, Georgotas et al. (1988) found that 80% of patients treated with 16 weeks of continuation nortriptyline remained well. Thus, from these data, it is unclear whether a combination of antidepressant medication and psychotherapy is more effective than antidepressant medication alone in the acute and continuation phases of treatment. Reynolds and colleagues (1992) hypothesized that combining psychotherapy and pharmacotherapy would reduce the dropout rate. However, the 19.2% rate of attrition in their study was somewhat higher than that reported by Georgotas et al. (1986, 1988) and Miller et al. (1991) for acute and continuation treatment with nortriptyline alone.

ELECTROCONVULSIVE THERAPY

Acute Treatment

Electroconvulsive therapy has well-documented efficacy and safety as a treatment for depression in older adults. Mulsant et al. (1991) recently reviewed 15 studies, conducted between 1980 and 1989, of ECT in elderly depressed patients. Good response was reported in a mean of 66% of patients (range 51–100%), poor response in 17% (range 0–37%), with the remainder having intermediate outcome. Six percent of patients had significant medical complications and 11% had significant confusion and delirium.

Predictors of favorable response to ECT in geriatric depression include psychosis, endogenous features, and psychomotor change, especially retardation (Benbow, 1989). Many psychiatrists consider ECT to be a first-line treatment for psychotic depression (Gaspar and Samarasinghe, 1982; Clinical Research Centre, Division of Psychiatry, 1984; Finlay-Jones and Parker, 1993). Psychotic depression has a poor response to antidepressants alone, but 70–80% of patients will respond to a combination of an antipsychotic and antidepressant medication (Dubovsky and Thomas, 1992). There have been no published trials directly comparing the efficacy and safety of combined drug treatment and ECT in psychotic depression. Because of the similar suggested efficacy rates, such a trial would require a sample size of at least 300 subjects in order to have a 90% chance of finding a significant result (Spiker et al., 1985). However, a recent meta-analysis of studies involving patients of mixed age groups found a trend for ECT to be superior to combination drug treatment (Parker et al., 1992). Also, a number of elderly patients are unable to tolerate the side effects of full-dose combined antidepressant–antipsychotic medication, although the availability of newer medications such as SSRIs and selective dopamine blockers may improve the tolerability and safety of this treatment approach.

Other indications for ECT as a first-line treatment include refusal of food and fluid, high risk of suicide, catatonia, a good previous response to ECT, and patient choice. Electroconvulsive therapy is also indicated when there has been a failure to respond to antidepressant medication or when there has been failure to tolerate or comply with medication. However, patients who have not responded to a therapeutic trial of antidepressant medication have a lower rate of response to ECT compared to individuals who have had inadequate or no pharmacotherapy (Prudic et al., 1990).

There are no absolute contraindications to ECT, although a number of conditions can increase the risk of using this treatment [American Psychiatric Association (APA), 1990]. Each patient needs to be assessed on an individual basis in terms of the relative risks and benefits of using ECT compared with alternate or no treatment (APA, 1990). A number of case reports and case series have described the successful use of ECT in depressed patients with cardiac disease, cardiac pacemakers, aortic aneurysm, cerebral aneurysm, chronic subdural hematoma, stroke, severe osteoporosis, and multiple myeloma (Abrams, 1991; Weller and Kornhuber, 1992).

Over the years there has been controversy about the relative efficacy of bilateral versus unilateral electrode placement. Studies in the elderly have yielded conflicting results with some showing bilateral treatment to be superior to unilateral treatment and others showing that both treatments have equal efficacy (Benbow, 1989). At the time these studies were performed it was assumed that as long as a generalized seizure, exceeding a minimum duration, was induced at each session the patient was receiving optimal treatment. However, recent research has demonstrated that although a generalized seizure is necessary, it is not in itself sufficient to ensure therapeutic response (Sackheim et al., 1991). Also, seizure duration alone does not serve as a marker of adequacy of treatment (Sackheim et al., 1991). It has now been established that the degree to which the electrical dose exceeds the individual patient's seizure threshold is critical in determining efficacy, speed of response, and cognitive side effects (Sackheim et al., 1991). Also, it is now recognized that there is marked variability with respect to seizure threshold, and this is related to patient characteristics (seizure threshold is higher in men and in the elderly) and treatment factors, in particular electrode placement (Sackheim et al., 1991).

In a recent double-blind study, 96 depressed patients with a mean age of 57 years were randomly allocated to one of the following four ECT treatments: high-dose unilateral, high-dose bilateral, low-dose unilateral, or low-dose bilateral (Sackheim et al., 1993). Low electrical dose was just above each patient's seizure threshold and high dose was 2.5 times the threshold. Increasing energy in the unilateral group increased the rate of response (17% for low-energy group, 43% for the high-energy group) but not to the same level as with bilateral treatment (63% for the high-energy group and 65% for the low-energy group). Patients who failed to respond to the experimental treatment were subsequently switched to high-dose bilateral treatment. Eighty percent of those who failed to respond to low-dose unilateral placement subsequently responded to the bilateral treatment. Regardless of electrode placement, high-dose treatment resulted in a more rapid response. Electrode placement had a greater effect on cognitive function than did dosage. Unilateral treatment was associated with less postictal disorientation and less severe retrograde amnesia 1 week posttreatment, but 2 months after treatment there was no difference in cognitive performance between the groups.

The findings of this rigorously designed study have several implications:

1. It is no longer tenable to give all patients the same dose of electricity. To maximize efficacy and minimize side effects electrical dosage needs to be adjusted to the individual patient based on his or her seizure threshold. Seizure threshold can be determined on the basis of algorithms, by electrical dose titration, or a combination of these methods.
2. Low-dose unilateral treatment has poor efficacy and should not be used.
3. Although bilateral treatment has greater efficacy than high-dose unilateral, it also produces more cognitive side effects, and therefore its use needs to be tempered by the patient's vulnerability to memory impairment. In patients who

have dementia or are predisposed to developing cognitive impairment (e.g., through preexisting stroke or Parkinson's disease), it is probably wise to start with high-dose unilateral ECT, but if there is no improvement after four to five treatments then the treatment should be switched to bilateral placement (Fink, 1990).

Fink (1990) has recommended that bilateral placement should be the treatment of choice in patients who are severely agitated, delusional, suicidal, or stuporous, patients with concomitant medical conditions whose high-risk status mandates the fewest possible anaesthetic inductions, and individuals who have previously responded to bilateral but not unilateral treatment. A recent meta-analysis found bilateral ECT to be superior to unilateral ECT in the treatment of psychotic depression (Parker et al., 1992).

Continuation and Maintenance Treatment

A number of older studies demonstrated that, if patients were treated with antidepressant medication following ECT, the rate of depressive relapse could be reduced from 50 to 20% (Seager and Bird 1962; Imlah et al., 1965; Kay et al., 1970). However, in these predominantly British studies ECT was often the first-line treatment. Recent research has shown that, despite maintenance antidepressants, patients who have failed to respond to an adequate trial of antidepressant medication prior to ECT have a much higher rate of relapse compared to patients who received inadequate or no pharmacotherapy before ECT (Spiker et al., 1985; Sackheim et al., 1990). These findings suggest that if patients have failed a particular class of antidepressant treatment prior to ECT, a different class of medication should be used for continuation treatment.

Maintenance ECT has been used in patients who have responded to ECT but subsequently had relapse or recurrence on pharmacotherapy (Monroe, 1991). Other proposed indications for maintenance ECT include medication intolerance or noncompliance and patient preference (Monroe, 1991). Controlled trials of maintenance ECT support its efficacy in geriatric patients (Monroe, 1991). Patients who persevere with maintenance ECT have been shown to suffer fewer relapses than patients who give up the treatment (Monroe, 1991). The appropriate frequency of treatments and the duration of maintenance ECT have not yet been determined although case reports have described its use for up to 6 years in elderly patients (Thienhaus et al., 1990; Dubin et al., 1992). Godber et al. (1987) followed up 163 elderly depressed patients 3 years after they had received ECT. Despite maintenance pharmacotherapy in the majority of patients, 66% of patients had had one or more relapses or recurrences during the 3 years, but 80% of these episodes took place in the first 18 months of the follow-up period. Therefore, it may be that most elderly patients in need of maintenance ECT require treatment for at least 2 years, if not longer. There is no evidence that prolonged ECT, administered under standard conditions, leads to brain damage (Devanand et al., 1994).

No study has attempted to look at response to maintenance ECT according to depression subtype. Patients with psychotic depression are particularly susceptible to relapse, although there is some evidence from mixed-age populations that continuing an antidepressant–antipsychotic combination following remission reduces this risk (Dubovsky and Thomas, 1992). However, this approach increases the elderly person's vulnerability to side effects and puts them at high risk of developing tardive dyskinesia. Maintenance ECT may reduce the rate of relapse and recurrence in psychotic depression with fewer long-term risks and therefore may be the treatment of choice for this condition. However, like so many other issues relating to maintenance ECT, this strategy awaits further study.

TREATMENT OF DEPRESSION IN SPECIAL POPULATIONS

There is a small amount of literature on the treatment of depression in elderly patients with dementia, other neurological disorders, medical illness, and the very frail and institutionalized elderly. Virtually all data pertains to pharmacological management and ECT. Brief psychotherapy may be particularly applicable to elderly patients who cannot tolerate antidepressant medications because of coexistent medical conditions or in whom illness-associated disability is a significant contributor to the depression. However, there appears to have been no attempt to systematically evaluate the efficacy of psychotherapy in these elderly populations.

Alzheimer's Disease

Several studies have found that approximately 20% of patients with Alzheimer's disease also meet criteria for major depression. In an uncontrolled retrospective chart review, Reifler et al. (1986) found that 85% of subjects with Alzheimer's disease and DSM-III major depression showed clear evidence of improvement in mood, vegetative signs, and activities of daily living after treatment with a tricyclic antidepressant. In the only double-blind placebo control trial of treatment of depression complicating Alzheimer's disease, Reifler et al. (1989) reported that outpatients with mild to moderate levels of depression showed a significant improvement in depression scores with both imipramine and placebo. Patients in both treatment conditions received substantial personal attention over the 8-week study period, suggesting that supportive psychotherapy and psychosocial stimulation may have an important role in the management of depression in dementia. Patients treated with imipramine showed greater cognitive decline than those treated with placebo, probably due to the anticholinergic effects of the TCAs.

Compared to TCAs, SSRIs should have less tendency to aggravate cognitive impairment in patients with Alzheimer's disease and other dementias (Mattila et al., 1988). Sertraline does not adversely affect cognitive performance in healthy elderly volunteers (Mattila et al., 1988; Hindmarch et al., 1990). However, there have been no trials directly comparing the efficacy and side effects of these two classes of drugs in patients with dementia and depression.

Because MAO levels increase in Alzheimer's disease (Gottfries, 1985), MAOIs may have a valuable role in the treatment of depression in this disorder. There have been several case reports describing the efficacy and safety of phenelzine and tranylcypromine in patients with dementia and depression (Jenike, 1985), but the first-generation MAOIs should only be used in demented patients when dietary and drug restrictions can be carefully monitored. RIMAs are safer and allow for increased flexibility of prescribing in these patients. In an open study, moclobemide, administered at doses of 150–225 mg/day, was found to improve depression in a small number of outpatients with senile dementia (Postma and Vranesic, 1985). Moclobemide has been found to antagonize scopolamine-induced cognitive impairment in healthy volunteers (Wesnes et al., 1990), and therefore this medication may have a unique role in improving both depressive and cognitive symptoms in patients with Alzheimer's disease.

Electroconvulsive therapy has been found to be an effective treatment for depression complicating degenerative and vascular dementias. In a recent review of cases, Price and McAllister (1989) found that depressive symptoms improved in 73% of patients and cognition improved in 29%, whereas 21% had cognitive side effects. Mulsant et al. (1991) and Nelson and Rosenberg (1991) also found that patients with organic mental disorders experienced the same rate of improvement in depression as nondemented patients but had more interictal confusion. Some studies have found that patients with caudate hyperintensities on magnetic resonance imaging of the brain have an increased risk of developing interictal delirium with ECT (Figiel et al., 1989).

Medical Illness and Neurological Disorders

Major depression occurs in 12–45% of hospitalized medical inpatients, and several studies have demonstrated a poor prognosis for physical illnesses complicated by untreated depression (Koenig and Breitner, 1990). However, there had been few controlled studies of antidepressant medications in this population. Koenig et al. (1989) attempted to study nortriptyline in a group of medical inpatients but had to prematurely discontinue the trial because of a lack of recruitment of subjects. Medical illness and/or medical contraindications to TCAs prevented 80% of eligible patients from participating in or completing the study. Lakshmanan et al. (1986) found that doxepin, administered at 10–20 mg/day for 3 weeks led to a statistically significant improvement in HDRS, but not Geriatric Depression Rating Scale, scores in 24 elderly depressed patients on a medical rehabilitation ward. However, the medication group still had a mean HDRS score of 15 at the end of the 3 weeks, suggesting significant residual depression in a number of subjects. A longer trial and/or a higher dose of doxepin may have led to more clincially meaningful results but also may have caused more side effects.

Lipsey et al. (1984) evaluated the efficacy of nortriptyline in a placebo-controlled trial of 34 inpatients with poststroke depression. Patients treated with nortriptyline showed significantly greater improvement of depression than those on placebo, but 3 of 17 patients on the TCA developed delirium. A recent 6-week double-blind trial compared the SSRI citalopram with placebo in the treatment of 66 patients (mean age 67 years) with poststroke depression (Andersen et al., 1994). Sixty percent of the citalopram group, but only 28% of patients taking placebo, responded to treatment, a statistically significant difference. One half of the patients who entered the study 2–6 weeks after suffering the stroke recovered independently of the treatment given. This indicates a high rate of spontaneous recovery of depression in the early phase of stroke. In contrast, recovery was infrequent in placebo-treated patients whose depression started 7 weeks or more after the stroke. Side effects of citalopram were mild and usually transient, and in particular it did not cause sedation, confusion, or cardiovascular events. This research indicates that SSRIs may be as efficacious but better tolerated than TCAs in the treatment of poststroke depression.

In a recent review of depression complicating Parkinson's disease, Cummings (1992) identified four double-blind controlled trials demonstrating the efficacy of imipramine, nortriptyline, desipramine, and buproprion in the treatment of depression complicating Parkinson's disease. Fifty to sixty percent of patients treated with the tricyclics responded, whereas only 42% of patients treated with buproprion improved. Interestingly, in three of the trials, the antidepressant medication also led to an improvement in symptoms of Parkinson's disease. Since SSRIs do not cause cognitive impairment or postural hypotension, they have potential advantages over the TCAs in the treatment of depression complicating Parkinson's disease. However, SSRIs can cause extrapyramidal symptoms through their effect on serotonin input and dopamine cell firing in the substantia nigra (Baldwin et al., 1991), and at least one case report has described an exacerbation of Parkinson's disease with fluoxetine (Chouinard and Sultan, 1992). Thus, the role of SSRIs in managing these patients needs further evaluation.

Electroconvulsive therapy has also been shown to be effective in the treatment of depression and Parkinson's disease (Rasmussen and Abrams, 1991). In most cases, both the mood and motor symptoms improve and the motor response usually precedes the mood response. However, the improvement in the motor abnormalities of Parkinson's disease usually lasts only several weeks but is occasionally more prolonged (Rasmussen and Abrams, 1991).

The Frail Patient

Despite the fact that major depression is common in nursing home populations and contributes to increased mortality, it is generally unrecognized and undertreated (Heston et al., 1992; Rovner, 1993). Katz et al. (1990) performed a 7-week double-blind study of nortriptyline and placebo in a frail group of elderly patients with the mean age of 84 years living in a nursing home. Patients were treated with a mean nortriptyline dose of 65 mg/day, which produced a mean plasma level of 76 ng/mL. Fifty-eight percent of the medication group responded compared with only 9% of patients treated with placebo. However, adverse events necessitated early termination of treatment in 33% of patients, highlighting the increased vulnerability of very old patients to TCA side effects. In these frail patients, newer drugs such as SSRIs and RIMAs may be safer and better tolerated, although comparative data in this population are not yet available.

SUMMARY AND CONCLUSION

Most research on the treatment of depression in old age has focused on patients who are less than 80 years old and who are not medically ill. In these individuals, an adequate trial of an appropriately selected antidepressant medication leads to a rate of response that is comparable to that found in younger adults. However, it is unclear whether patients with concurrent medical illness respond as well to pharmacotherapy. Virtually all studies of antidepressant treatment in the medically ill or frail elderly used tricyclic antidepressants that, in these patients, were associated with a high rate of adverse effects. Preliminary data suggest that newer antidepressants such as SSRIs may be better tolerated in these populations. Electroconvulsive therapy has documented efficacy and safety in the depressed elderly, including patients with coexistent medical illness, neurological disorder, or dementia. However, despite a number of well-documented indications for its use, ECT still tends to be underutilized and viewed as a treatment of last resort.

Increasing emphasis is being placed on the long-term management of depression. For most elderly people depression is a recurrent condition, and they require long-term treatment if they are to remain well. To date, TCAs and first-generation MAOIs have been shown to be effective in reducing relapse and recurrence in the elderly. Further research is needed to determine predictors of recurrence in old age and the long-term efficacy and safety of SSRIs and RIMAs. There is also a need to further evaluate the role of maintenance ECT in patients who have had recurrences despite maintenance pharmacotherapy and in patients with psychotic depression.

Cognitive, interpersonal, and dynamic psychotherapies have been shown to be effective in the acute treatment of nonendogenous geriatric depression. Brief psychotherapy has not been shown to be as effective as ongoing pharmacotherapy in the prevention of relapse or recurrence, although no study has evaluated the efficacy, safety, and cost effectiveness of maintenance psychotherapy in old age. To date, psychotherapy studies have recruited subjects who are relatively young, physically healthy, cognitively intact, and able to attend regularly as outpatients. It remains to be seen whether findings from these studies can be generalized to the older, frailer patient more typically encountered in geriatric practice. In addition to cognitive and interpersonal therapies, there is also a need to study the role of other psychosocial interventions, such as psychoeducation, supportive therapy, and social case work, which, in clinical practice, are frequently combined with medication in the management of the elderly depressed patient.

REFERENCES

Abrams R (1991): Electroconvulsive therapy in the medically compromised patient. Psychiatr Clin North Am 14(4):871–885.

Altamura AC, De Novellis F, Guercetti G, Invernizzi G, Percudani M, Montgomery SA (1989): Fluoxetine compared with amitriptyline in elderly depression: A controlled clinical trial. Int J Clin Pharmacol Res 9:391–396.

American Psychiatric Association (1990): "The Practice of Electroconvulsive Therapy: Recommendations for Treatment, Training and Privileging." Washington, DC: American Psychiatric Press.

Andersen G, Vestergaard L, Lauritzen L (1994): Effective treatment of poststroke depression with the selective serotonin reuptake inhibitor citalopram. Stroke 25(6):1099–1104.

Ashford JJ, Rahman K (1990): Fluvoxamine versus dothiepin: A double-blind study in elderly depressed patients. J Psychopharmacol 4:299.

Baldwin D, Fineberg N, Montgomery S (1991): Fluoxetine, fluvoxamine and extrapyramidal tract disorders. Int Clin Psychopharmacol 6(1):51–58.

Beasley CM, Sayler ME, Cunningham GE, Weiss AM, Masica DN (1990): Fluoxetine in tricyclic refractory major depressive disorder. J Affect Disord 20:193–200.

Benbow SM (1989): The role of electroconvulsive therapy in the treatment of depressive illness in old age. Br J Psychiatry 155:147–152.

Chouinard G, Sultan S (1992): A case of Parkinson's disease exacerbated by fluoxetine. Hum Psychopharmacol Clin Exp 7:63–66.

Clinical Research Centre, Division of Psychiatry (1984): The Northwick Park ECT trial: Predictors of response to real and simulated ECT. Br J Psychiatry 144:227–237.

Cohen BJ, Mahelsky M, Adler L (1990): More cases of SIADH with fluoxetine. Am J Psychiatry 147(7):948–949.

Cohn CK, Shrivastava R, Mendels J, Cohn JB, Fabre LF, Glaghorn JL, Dessain EC, Itil TM, Lautin A (1990): Double-blind, multicenter comparison of sertraline and amitriptyline in elderly depressed patients. J Clin Psychiatry 51:(12, suppl B):28–33.

Cooper GL (1988): The safety of fluoxetine—an update. Br J Psychiatry 153 (suppl 3):77–86.

Cournoyer G, DeMontigny C, Ouellette J, LeBlanc G, Langlois R, Elie R (1984). Lithium addition in tricyclic-resistant unipolar depression: A placebo-controlled study. Abstracts of Collegium Internationale Neuropsychopharmacologicum, Florence, Italy, p 179.

Crewe HK, Lennard MS, Tucker GT, Wood FR, Haddock RE (1991): The effect of paroxetine and other specific 5-HT reuptake inhibitors on cytochrome P45011D6 activity in human liver microsomes. Br J Clin Pharmacol 32:658P–659P.

Cummings JL (1992): Depression and Parkinson's disease: A review. Am J Psychiatry 149:443–454.

Danish University Antidepressant Group (1993): Moclobemide: A reversible MAO-A-inhibitor showing weaker antidepressant effect than clomipramine in a controlled multicenter study. J Affect Disord 28:105–116.

Devanand DP, Dwork AJ, Hutchinson ER, Bolwig TG, Sackeim HA (1994): Does ECT alter brain structure? Am J Psychiatry 151:957–970.

De Vane CL (1992): Pharmacokinetics of the selective serotonin reuptake inhibitors. J Clin Psychiatry 53(2, suppl):13–20.

De Vanna M, Kummer J, Agnoli A, Gentili P, Lorizio A, Anand R (1990): Moclobemide compared with second-generation antidepressants in elderly people. Acta Psychiatr Scand 82(suppl 360):64–66.

Dubin WR, Jaffe R, Roemer R, Siegel L, Shoyer B, Venditti ML (1992): The efficacy and safety of maintenance ECT in geriatric patients. J Am Geriatr Soc 40(7):706–709.

Dubovsky SL, Thomas M (1992): Psychotic depression: Advances in conceptualization and treatment. Hosp Community Psychiatry 43(12):1189–1198.

Feighner JP, Boyer WF, Meredith CH, Hendrickson G (1988): An overview of fluoxetine in geriatric depression. Br J Psychiatry 153(suppl 3):105–108.

Figiel GS, Coffey CE, Weiner RD (1989): Brain magnetic resonance imaging in elderly depressed patients receiving electrovulsive therapy. Convulsive Therapy 5:26–34.

Fink M (1990): Electrode placement: A clincian's guide. Convulsive Therapy 6(4):263–265.

Finlay-Jones R, Parker G (1993): A consensus conference on psychotic depression. Aust NZ J Psychiatry 27:581–589.

Flint AJ (1995): Augmentation strategies in geriatric depression. Int J Geriatric Psychiatry 10:137–146.

Flint AJ, Rifat SL (1994): A prospective study of lithium augmentation in antidepressant-resistant geriatric depression. J Clin Psychopharmacol 14(5):353–356.

Flint AJ (1992): The optimum duration of antidepressant treatment in the elderly. Int J Geriatric Psychiatry 7:617–619.

Frank E, Kupfer DJ, Perel JM, Cornes C, Mallinger AG, Thase ME, McEachran AB, Grochocinski VJ (1993): Comparison of full-dose versus half-dose pharmacotherapy in the maintenance treatment of recurrent depression. J Affect Disord 27:139–145.

Frank E, Kupfer DJ, Perel JM, Cornes C, Jarrett DB, Mallinger AG, Thase ME, McEachran AB, Grochocinski VJ (1990): Three-year outcomes for maintenance therapies in recurrent depression. Arch Gen Psychiatry 47:1093–1099.

Gallagher DE, Thompson LW (1983): Effectiveness of psychotherapy for both endogenous and nonendogenous depression in older adult outpatients. J Gerontol 38(6):707–712.

Gallagher-Thompson D, Hanley-Peterson P, Thompson, LW (1990): Maintenance of gains versus relapse following brief psychotherapy for depression. J Consult Clin Psychol 58(3):371–374.

Gaspar D, Samarasinghe LA (1982): ECT in psychogeriatric practice—a study of risk factors, indications and outcome. Compr Psychiatry 23:170–175.

Georgotas A, McCue RE (1989): The additional benefit of extending an antidepressant trial past seven weeks in the depressed elderly. Int J Geriatric Psychiatry 4:191–195.

Georgotas A, McCue RE, Cooper TB (1989a): A placebo-controlled comparison of nortriptyline and phenelzine in maintenance therapy of elderly depressed patients. Arch Gen Psychiatry 46:783–786.

Georgotas A, McCue RE, Reisberg B, Ferris SH, Nagachandran N, Chang I, Mir P (1989b): The effects of mood changes and antidepressants on the cognitive capacity of elderly depressed patients. Int Psychogeriatr 1(2):135–143.

Georgotas A, McCue RE, Cooper TB, Nagachandran N, Chang I (1988): How effective and safe is continuation therapy in elderly depressed patients? Arch Gen Psychiatry 45:929–932.

Georgotas A, McCue RE, Hapworth W, Friedman E, Kim OM, Welkowitz J, Chang I, Cooper TB (1986): Comparative efficacy and safety of MAOIs versus TCAs in treating depression in the elderly. Biol Psychiatry 21:1155–1166.

Georgotas A, Friedman E, McCarthy M, Mann J, Krakowski M, Siegel R, Ferris S (1983a): Resistant geriatric depressions and therapeutic response to monoamine oxidase inhibitors. Biol Psychiatry 18(2):195–205.

Georgotas A, Kim OM, Hapworth W, Bow AD, Friedman E (1983b): Monoamine oxidase inhibitors and affective disorders in the elderly. Psychopharmacol Bull 19:662–665.

Georgotas A, Thomas L, Forsell TL, Mann JJ, Kim M, Gershon S (1982): Trazodone hydrochloride: A wide spectrum antidepressant with a unique pharmacological profile. A review of its neurochemical effects, pharmacology, clinical efficacy, and toxicology. Pharmacotherapy 2:255–264.

Gerson SC, Plotkin DA, Jarvik LF (1988): Antidepressant drug studies, 1964 to 1986: Empirical evidence for aging patients. J Clin Psychopharmacol 8(5):311–322.

Godber C, Rosenvinge H, Wilkinson D, Smithies J (1987): Depression in old age: Prognosis after ECT. Int J Geriatric Psychiatry 2:19–24.

Gottfries CG (1985): Alzheimer's disease and senile dementia: Biochemical characteristics and aspects of treatment. Psychopharmacology 86:245–252.

Grimsley SR, Jann MW (1992): Paroxetine, sertraline and fluvoxamine: New selective serotonin reuptake inhibitors. Clin Pharm 11:930–957.

Halper JP, Mann JJ (1988): Cardiovascular effects of antidepressant medications. Br J Psychiatry 153(suppl 3):87–98.

Heninger GR, Charney DS, Sternberg DE (1983): Lithium carbonate augmentation of antidepressant treatment: An effective prescription for treatment-refractory depression. Arch Gen Psychiatry 40:1335–1342.

Heston LL, Garrard J, Makris L, Kane RL, Cooper S, Dunham T, Zelterman D (1992): Inadequate treatment of depressed nursing home elderly. J Am Geriatr Soc 40:1117–1122.

Hindmarch I, Shillingford J, Shillingford C (1990): The effects of sertraline on psychomotor performance in elderly volunteers. J Clin Psychiatry 51 (12 suppl B):34–36.

Imlah NW, Ryan E, Harrington JA (1965): The influence of antidepressant drugs on the response to electroconvulsive therapy and on subsequent relapse rates. Neuropsychopharmacology 4:438–442.

Jacoby R (1993): Longterm antidepressant treatment in the elderly. Br J Psychiatry 163:551.

Jenike MA (1985): Monoamine oxidase inhibitors as treatment for depressed patients with primary degenerative dementia (Alzheimer's disease). Am J Psychiatry 142(6):763–764.

Joffe RT, Singer W, Levitt AJ, MacDonald C (1993): A placebo-controlled comparison of lithium and triiodothyronine augmentation of tricyclic antidepressants in unipolar refractory depression. Arch Gen Psychiatry 50:387–393.

Katz IR, Simpson GM, Curlick SM, Parmalee PA, Muhly C (1990): Pharmacologic treatment of major depression for elderly patients in residential care settings. J Clin Psychiatry 51 (7 suppl):41–47.

Kay DWK, Thomas F, Garside RF (1970): A seven-month double-blind trial of amitriptyline and diazepam in ECT-treated depressed patients. Br J Psychiatry 117:667–671.

Koenig HG, Breitner JCS (1990): Use of antidepressants in medically ill older patients. Psychosomatics 31:22–32.

Koenig HG, Goli V, Shelp F, Kudler HS, Cohen HJ, Meador KJ, Blazer DG (1989): Antidepressant use in elderly medical inpatients: Lessons from an attempted clinical trial. J Gen Intern Med 4(6):498–505.

Kunik ME, Pollock BG, Perel JM, Altieri L (1994): Clomipramine in the elderly: Tolerance and plasma levels. J Geriatr Psychiatry Neurol 7:139–143.

Lakshmanan M, Mion LC, Frengley JD (1986): Effective low dose tricyclic antidepressant treatment for depressed geriatric rehabilitation patients. A double-blind study. J Am Geriatr Soc 34:421–426.

Lipsey JR, Robinson RG, Pearlson GD, Rao K, Price TR (1984): Nortriptyline treatment of post-stroke depression: A double-blind study. Lancet 1:297–300.

Mattila MJ, Saarialho-Kere U, Mattila M (1988): Acute effects of sertraline, amitriptyline, and placebo on the psychomotor performance of healthy subjects over 50 years of age. J Clin Psychiatry 49(8 suppl):52–58.

McGrath PJ, Stewart JW, Nunes EV, Ocepek-Welikson K, Rabkin JG, Quitkin FM, Klein DF (1993): A double-blind crossover trial of imipramine and phenelzine for outpatients with treatment-refractory depression. Am J Psychiatyr 150(1):118–123.

Meyers BS, Mattis S, Gabriele M, Kakuma T (1991): Effects of nortriptyline on memory self-assessment and performance in recovered elderly depressives. Psychopharmacol Bull 27(3):295–299.

Miller MD, Pollock BG, Rifai AH, Paradis C, Perel JM, George C, Stack JA, Reynolds CF (1991): Longitudinal analysis of nortriptyline side effects in elderly depressed patients. J Geriatr Psychiatry Neurol 4:226–230.

Mittmann N, Shear NH, Einarson TR, Naranjo CA (1995): Are selective serotonin reuptake inhibitors superior to tricyclic antidepressants in the elderly? Clin Pharmacology Therapeutics 57(2):139.

Moll E, Hetzel W (1990): Moclobemide safety in depressed patients. Acta Psychiatr Scand 360(suppl):69–70.

Monroe RR (1991): Maintenance electroconvulsive therapy. Psychiatr Clin North Am 14(4):947–960.

Montgomery SA, Baldwin D, Shah A, Green M, Fineberg N, Montgomery D (1990): Plasma-level response relationships with fluoxetine and zimelidine. Clin Neuropharmacol 13(1 suppl):S71–S75.

Mulsant BH, Rosen J, Thornton JE, Zubenko GS (1991): A prospective naturalistic study of electroconvulsive therapy in later-life depression. J Geriatr Psychiatry Neurol 4:3–13.

Murdoch D, McTavish D (1992): Sertraline. A review of its pharmacodynamic and pharmacokinetic properties, and therapeutic potential in depression and obsessive compulsive disorder. Drugs 44(4):604–624.

Nelson JP, Rosenberg DR (1991): ECT treatment of demented elderly patients with major depression: A retrospective study of efficacy and safety. Convulsive Therapy 7(3):157–165.

NIH Consensus Development Panel (1992): Diagnosis and treatment of depression in late life. JAMA 268:1018–1024.

Norman TR, Judd FK, Burrows GD (1992): New pharmacological approaches to the management of depression: From theory to clinical practice. Austr NZ J Psychiatry 26:73–81.

Old Age Depression Interest Group (1993): How long should the elderly take antidepressants? A double-blind placebo-controlled study of continuation/prophylaxis therapy with dothiepin. Br J Psychiatry 162:175–182.

Parker G, Roy K, Hadzi-Pavlovic D, Pedic F (1992): Psychotic (delusional) depression: A meta-analysis of physical treatments. J Affect Disord 24:17–24.

Postma JU, Vranesic D (1985): Moclobemide in the treatment of depression in demented geriatric patients. Acta Therapeutica 11(2):1–4.

Preskorn SH (1993): Recent pharmacologic advances in antidepressant therapy for the elderly. Am J Medicine 94(suppl 5A):2S–12S.

Preskorn S, Burke M (1992): Somatic therapy for major depressive disorder: Selection of an antidepressant. J Clin Psychiatry 53(9, suppl):1–14.

Price TR, McAllister TW (1989): Safety and efficacy of ECT in depressed patients with dementia: A review of clinical experience. Convulsive Therapy 5:61–74.

Prien RF, Kupfer DJ (1986): Continuation drug therapy for major depressive episodes: How long should it be maintained? Am J Psychiatry 143:18–23.

Priest RG (1990): Moclobemide and the reversible inhibitors of monoamine oxidase antidepressants. Acta Psychiatr Scand (suppl 360):39–41.

Prudic J, Sackeim HA, Devanand DP (1990): Medication resistance and clinical response to electroconvulsive therapy. Psychiatry Res 31:287–296.

Rasmussen K, Abrams R (1991): Treatment of Parkinson's disease with electroconvulsive therapy. Psychiatr Clin North Am 14(4):925–933.

Reifler BV, Teri L, Raskind M, Keith R, Barnes R, White E, McLean P (1989): Double-blind trial of imipramine in Alzheimer's disease patients with and without depression. Am J Psychiatry 146(1):45–49.

Reifler BV, Larson E, Teri L, Poulsen M (1986): Dementia of Alzheimer's type and depression. J Am Geriatr Soc 34:855–859.

Reynolds CF, Frank E, Perel JM, Imber SD, Cornes C, Morycz RK, Mazumdar S, Miller MD, Pollock BG, Rifai AH, Stack JA, George CJ, Houck PR, Kupfer DJ (1992): Combined pharmacotherapy and psychotherapy in the acute and continuation treatment of elderly patients with recurrent major depression: A preliminary report. Am J Psychiatry 149(12):1687–1692.

Reynolds CF, Perel JM, Frank E, Imber S, Thornton J, Morycz RK, Cornes C, Kupfer DJ (1988): Open-trial maintenance pharmacotherapy in late-life depression: Survival analysis. Psychiatry Res 27:225–231.

Rickels K, Schweizer E (1990): Clinical overview of serotonin reuptake inhibitors. J Clin Psychiatry 51(12, suppl B):9–12.

Robinson DS, Davis JM, Nies A, Ravaris CL, Sylvester D (1971): Relationship of sex and aging to monoamine oxidase activity of human brain, plasma and platelets. Arch Gen Psychiatry 24:536–539.

Rockwell E, Lam RW, Zisook S (1988): Antidepressant drug studies in the elderly. Psychiatr Clin North Am 11(1):215–233.

Roose SP, Dalack GW (1992): Treating the depressed patient with cardiovascular problems. J Clin Psychiatry 53(9 suppl):25–31.

Roose SP, Glassman AH, Giardina EGV, Walsh BT, Woodring S, Bigger JT (1987): Tricyclic antidepressants in depressed patients with cardiac conduction disease. Arch Gen Psychiatry 44:273–275.

Roose SP, Glassman AH, Giardina EGV, Johnson LL, Walsh BT, Woodring S, Bigger JT (1986): Nortriptyline in depressed patients with left ventricular impairment. JAMA 256:3253–3257.

Rovner BW (1993): Depression and increased risk of mortality in the nursing home patient. Am J Medicine 94(suppl 5A):19S–22S.

Rudorfer MV, Potter WZ (1989): Antidepressants. A comparative review of the clinical pharmacology and therapeutic use of the "newer" versus the "older" drugs. Drugs 37:713–738.

Sackeim HA, Prudic J, Devanand DP, Kiersky JE, Fitzsimons L, Moody BJ, McElhiney MC, Coleman EA, Stettembrino JM (1993): Effects of stimulus intensity and electrode placement on the efficacy and cognitive effects of electrovconvulsive therapy. N Eng J Med 328(12):839–846.

Sackeim HA, Devanand DP, Prudic J (1991): Stimulus intensity, seizure threshold and seizure duration: Impact on the efficacy and safety of electroconvulsive therapy. Psychiatr Clin North Am 14(4):803–843.

Sackeim HA, Prudic J, Devanand DP, Decina P, Kerr B, Malitz S (1990): The impact of medication resistance and continuation pharmacotherapy on relapse following response to electroconvulsive therapy in major depression. J Clin Psychopharmacol 10:96–104.

Schatzberg AF (1991): Dosing strategies for antidepressant agents. J Clin Psychiatry 52(5 suppl):14–20.

Schneider LS, Sloane RB, Staples FR, Bender M (1986): Pretreatment orthostatic hypotension as a predictor of response to nortriptyline in geriatric depression. J Clin Psychopharmacol 6(3):172–176.

Schopf J, Baumann P, Lemarchand T, Ray M (1989): Treatment of endogenous depressions resistant to tricyclic antidepressants or related drugs by lithium addition: Results of a placebo-controlled double-blind study. Pharmacopsychiatry 22:183–187.

Schweizer E, Rickels K, Amsterdam JD, Fox I, Puzzuoli G, Weise C (1990): What constitutes an adequate antidepessant trial for fluoxetine? J Clin Psychiatry 51(1):8–11.

Seager CP, Bird RL (1962): Imipramine with electrical treatment in depression—a controlled trial. J Ment Sci 108:704–707.

Shulman KI, Walker SE, MacKenzie S, Knowles S (1989): Dietary restriction, tyramine, and the use of monoamine oxidase inhibitors. J Clin Psychopharmacol 9(6):397–402.

Sloane RB, Staples FR, Schneider LS (1985): Interpersonal therapy versus nortriptyline for depression in the elderly. In Burrows GD, Norman TR, Dennerstein L (eds): "Clinical and Pharmacological Studies in Psychiatric Disorders." London: John Libbey and Co, pp 344–346.

Spiker DG, Weiss JC, Dealy RS, Griffin SJ, Hanin L, Neil JF, Perel JM, Rossi AJ, Soloff PH (1985): The pharmacological treatment of delusional depression. Am J Psychiatry 142:430–435.

Stoeckel K, Pfefen JP, Mayersohn M, Schoerlin MP, Andressen C, Onnhaus EE, Frey F, Guentert TW (1990): Absorption and disposition of moclobemide in patients with advanced age or reduced liver or kidney function. Acta Psychiatr Scand 82(suppl 360):94–97.

Thase ME, Mallinger AG, McKnight D, Himmelhoch JM (1992): Treatment of imipramine-resistant recurrent depression, IV: A double-blind crossover study of tranylcypromine for anergic bipolar depression. Am J Psychiatry 149(2):195–198.

Thienhaus OJ, Margletta S, Bennett JA (1990): A study of the clinical efficacy of maintenance ECT. J Clin Psychiatry 51(4):141–144.

Thompson LW, Gallagher D, Breckenridge JS (1987): Comparative effectiveness of psychotherapies for depressed elders. J Consult Clin Psychol 55(3):385–390.

Tyrer SP, Marshall EP, Griffiths HW (1990): The relationship between response to fluoxetine, plasma drug levels, imipramine binding to platelet membranes and whole-blood 5-HT. Neuropsychopharmacol Biol Psychiatry 14:797–805.

Wakelin JS (1986): Fluvoxamine in the treatment of the older depressed patient: Double-blind, placebo-controlled data. Int Clin Psychopharmacol 1:221–230.

Weller M, Kornhuber J (1992): Electroconvulsive therapy in a geriatric patient with multiple bone fractures and generalized plasmocytoma. Pharmacopsychiat 25:278–280.

Wesnes K, Anand R, Lorscheid T (1990): Potential of moclobemide to improve cerebral insufficiency identified using a scopolamine model of aging and dementia. Acta Psychiatr Scand 82 (suppl 360):71–72.

Young RC, Mattis S, Alexopoulso GS, Meyers BS, Schindledecker RD, Dhar AK (1991): Verbal memory and plasma drug concentrations in elderly depressives treated with nortriptyline. Psychopharmacol Bull 27(3):291–294.

Zimmer B, Rosen J, Thornton JE, Perel JM, Reynolds CF (1991): Adjunctive lithium carbonate in nortriptyline-resistant elderly depressed patients. J Clin Psychopharmacol 11:254–256.

CHAPTER 19

Mania in Old Age

KELLY L. DUNN and PETER V. RABINS

Department of Psychiatry, Sheppard and Enoch Pratt Hospital, Baltimore, MD 21204 (K.L.D.);
The Johns Hopkins University, Baltimore, MD 21287-7279 (P.V.R.)

OVERVIEW, PREVALENCE AND ONSET

Clinical studies suggest that mania (bipolar disorder, manic phase) is a common cause of severe psychopathology in the elderly, accounting for 4.6–18.5% of psychiatric hospitalizations of the elderly (Yassa et al., 1988; Moak, 1990; Post, 1965; Glasser and Rabins, 1984). Prevalence studies in the community, on the other hand, suggest that mania is rare. In the Epidemiologic Catchment Area (ECA) study of more than 20,000 Americans, the lifetime and one-year prevalence rates in persons 65 years of age and older were 0.1% (Weissman et al., 1991). This compares to lifetime rates of 1.1% in 18–29 year olds, 1.4% in 30–45 year olds, and 0.3% in 45–64 year olds (Weissman et al., 1991). Whether this decreasing prevalence is due to an increasing incidence rate in younger cohorts, a lower likelihood of the elderly to report symptoms or a higher mortality rate that decreases the number of persons with bipolar disorder living to old age is unclear. Little is known about the treated prevalence of late-life bipolar illness in outpatient settings or about the prevalence of bipolar II disorder in the elderly.

Because few studies are longitudinal, questions about changes in symptomatology over time and outcome are difficult to answer with certainty. Furthermore, some of the available data is contradictory. This chapter will review published reports that address the clinical presentation and course of mania in the elderly and its purported etiologies. It will adopt the common practice of comparing early-onset and late-onset disease although definitions of "early" and "late" vary widely.

One caveat in reviewing this subject is that the exact dating of age of onset of mood disorder is difficult, especially retrospectively. In the several studies that have examined age of onset and sequence of symptom development, the evidence suggests that the majority of late-life bipolar disorder patients first experienced a depressive syndrome. For example, Snowden (1991) found that 54% of elderly individuals with a first manic episode had had three or more depressive attacks prior to the mania. Glasser and Rabins (1984) found the mean age of onset of affective illness to be 43.7 years and the mean age of the first manic episode to be 51.1 years in a retrospective study.

Mood Disorders Across the Life Span, Edited by Shulman, Tohen, and Kutcher
ISBN 0-471-10477-9   © 1996 Wiley-Liss, Inc.

They stated that the first presentation was usually a depression, a conclusion partially supported by other studies. Shulman and Post (1980) reported that 62.7% of patients experienced a depressive syndrome preceding the index manic episode by 10 years while Stone (1989) reported that 30% of the elderly patients with a first episode of mania in late life had had a prior depressive episode. Yassa et al. (1988) found that 60% of elderly manics experienced a depression 1–26 years prior to the manic episode while Broadhead and Jacoby (1990) found an interval of 9.6 years between index depressive and manic episodes. Most of these studies excluded patients with late-onset manic episodes triggered by treatment for depression [i.e., medications, electroconvulsive therapy (ECT)], a widely recognized phenomenon. Clearly then, many patients with late-onset mania have bipolar disorder that began with an "earlier" onset of depression.

ETIOLOGY

Many studies of bipolar illness indicate a familial or genetic diathesis in the development of the illness. Several studies have reported a more frequent family history for affective illness in families of elderly patients with early-onset bipolar disease (Weissman et al., 1991; Shulman and Post, 1980; Stone, 1989). However, the studies of Glasser and Rabins (1984) and Carlson et al. (1977) found no difference in the rate of a positive family history between early- and late-onset cases, but they used a priori age cutoffs of 60 and 45, respectively. Dhingra and Rabins (1991), in reanalyzing the Glasser and Rabins data (1984), did find that age of onset is correlated within families, suggesting that family studies of late-onset bipolar disorder will need to correct for the lower likelihood that elderly relatives live through the age of risk (Chase et al., 1983).

Krauthammer and Klerman (1978) use the term *secondary mania* to refer to mania with an identifiable cause. They identified brain disease, medications, and remote effects of systemic illness as identifiable etiologies of mania. Several studies demonstrate that secondary mania is more likely in late-onset cases than early-onset disease. Shulman et al. (1992) found that 36% of elderly manics had brain disease as opposed to 8% of elderly depressives. Stone (1989) reported that 24% of elderly manics had brain disease and typically these patients had a later age of onset. Tohen et al. (1994) found that 71% of elderly manic patients with late-onset manic disorder had brain disease. Broadhead and Jacoby (1990) reported that 20% of manic patients had the onset of mania within close proximity to an episode of cerebral disease while Berrios and Bakshi (1991) found that older manic patients score higher on the Hachinski scale, an indicator of high risk for cerebrovascular disease. Thus, familial disorder is more common in the young while nongenetic etiologies such as brain injury and substance abuse (Slavney et al., 1977) occur more in older individuals, but genetic and nongenetic factors play a role at all ages. In general, though, the etiology of mood disorder appears to be more heterogeneous in late-onset cases. The role of genetic (or at least familial) factors as predisposing and modifying agents needs further study.

It is common for individuals who develop secondary mania to first experience depression following their insult (Starkstein et al., 1987, 1988, 1990; Miller et al., 1992). Several studies have found that 25–50% of the individuals who develop symptomatic mania have a positive family history of mood disorder (Starkstein et al., 1987, 1988, 1991; Robinson et al., 1988), suggesting a genetic or familial predisposition. However,

Jorge et al. (1993) did not find that family history was a risk for developing secondary mania.

Almost any insult to the central nervous system (CNS) places an individual at risk of developing a mood disorder, including mania. Studies have documented new onset of mania following closed head injury, tumor, tumor resection, stroke, and CNS infection in patients of all ages (Starkstein, 1987, 1988, 1990, 1991; Miller et al., 1992; Robinson et al., 1988; Jorge et al., 1993; Clark and Davison, 1987; Robinson and Starkstein, 1989; Bogousslavsky et al., 1988). However, there is growing data to support the role of specific brain lesions. Injury of the right hemisphere, particularly to the head of the caudate, thalamus, and limbic-frontal connections, appear to have more specific linkages (Starkstein, 1987, 1988, 1990, 1991; Miller et al., 1992; Robinson et al., 1988; Jorge et al., 1993; Robinson and Starkstein, 1989; Bogousslavsky et al., 1988). Specific disorders associated with secondary mania include brain vascular disease, multiple sclerosis (MS), and Alzheimer's disease (AD). Burns et al. (1990) reported that 3.5% of patients with Alzheimer's disease developed manic symptoms. In the elderly the most common CNS etiology may be cerebral vascular disease. For example, McDonald et al. (1991) found that subjects with late-onset mania had prevalent subcortical hyperintensities, most often in the middle third of brain parenchyma. They also reported that 25% of the patients had a positive family history for affective disorder. Joffe et al. (1987) noted that the frequency of bipolar illness in patients with MS was 13 times greater than in the general population. However, this was a sample primarily of young individuals.

Secondary mania can be precipitated by many medications, particularly drugs used to treat depression. Other causes of drug-induced mania include streoids, bromides, and L-dopa. There are also case reports of hydralazine, yohimbine, metrizamide, thyroxine, amantadine, captopril, baclofen, procanamide, phenytoin, and beclomethasone spray inducing mania in elderly patients (Stewart, 1992; Rice et al., 1988; Phelan, 1989; Patten et al., 1989, 1991; Kwentus et al., 1984; Hubain et al., 1982; Gajula, and Berlin, 1993). Withdrawal from baclofen and benzodiazepines has also been reported to induce secondary mania (Rigby et al., 1989; Arnold et al., 1980) as has thyroid replacement therapy for hypothyroidism (Josephson and Mackenzie, 1980).

Case reports linking new onset mania to systemic illness primarily describe older patients. Vitamin B_{12} deficiency (Goggans, 1984), small-cell lung carcinoma with ectopic adrenocorticotropic hormone (ACTH) production (Collins and Oakley-Browne, 1988) and polycythemia-induced mania (although the patient also had previously suffered small bilateral parietal infarcts) (Chawla and Lindesay, 1993) have been linked to bipolar disorder. As these are single case reports, the linkage with onset of mania must be considered tentative.

Several studies have explored the relationship between stressful life events and the onset of mania (Ambelas, 1987). In a group of subjects with a wide range of ages, Ambelas found that patients with negative life events preceding an episode of mania tended to be older (48.1 vs. 28 years). Yassa et al. (1988) reported precipitating stressors in 70% of elderly manic patients. Walter-Ryan reported a case of new onset mania in an 81-year-old man with "a severe precipitating stress of choosing between a high-risk surgical procedure or imminent death" (Walter-Ryan, 1983). Unfortunately, these studies lack adequate controls. This is particularly important in the area of life events since the elderly may experience more adverse life events than the young. Thus, it is unclear whether there is a direct link between stressors and the onset of late-life bipolar disorder.

The psychodynamic etiology of mania and hypomania, proposed by Abraham (1953) and Lewin (1950), was not specific for the older population. They hypothesized that mania was a defense against depression and deprivation, and a consequence of a fusion of the ego with the superego. The hypothesis remains untested.

CLINICAL PRESENTATION

Mania is diagnosed more commonly in females than males [the ratio is approximately 1.5 : 1 (Yassa et al., 1988; Glasser and Rabins, 1984)], but it is not clear whether this is explained by the greater longevity of women.

The clinical impression that the symptomatology of late-life mania is often attenuated and less severe than in the young (Stater and Roth, 1977) has been confirmed by several studies. Young and Falk (1989) reported lower Young Mania Rating Scale scores in the elderly on three subscales: the increased activity–energy subscale, the language–thought disorder subscale, and the sexual interest subscale. Likewise, Broadhead and Jacoby (1990) found that young patients had more severe Modified Mania Rating Scale scores and were more likely to be preoccupied with religious concerns. However, they also found that the rates of "positive symptoms" was similar between older and younger patients. In retrospective chart reviews, Glasser and Rabins (1984) and Yassa et al. (1988) found that sleeplessness, hyperactivity, and grandiose delusions were similar across the age span.

Several studies have examined variation in symptomatology by age of onset. In general, the presentation does not vary by age of onset (Glasser and Rabins, 1984), but Broadhead and Jacoby (1990) noted late-onset patients scored higher on the Blackburn Scale items for happiness and cheerfulness.

Mania can present with hallucinations and delusions. Tohen et al. (1994) found that 43% of late-onset cases experienced one or both during mania. Young et al. (1983) and Broadhead and Jacoby (1990) report no differences in the presence or quality of hallucinations and delusions between younger and older patients. Several studies have found no association between delusions and late-age onset of mania (Broadhead and Jacoby, 1990; Rosen et al., 1983). Mania can also present with a chief complaint of destructive behavior. Petrie et al. (1982) reviewed the diagnosis of patients admitted to a psychogeriatric unit because of episodes of violence. Nine percent of "aggressive" patients were manic and 16% of "violent" patients were manic.

Dysphoria and mixed affective states can occur during episodes of mania. Post (1965) believed this was more likely in the older patient based on his clinical experience. However, Broadhead and Jacoby (1990) found no differences between old and young manics in the prevalence of depressive and mixed features. They also found no difference between elderly patients with early onset and late onset.

Cognitive slowing and impairment, so-called pseudodementia, are known to accompany affective disorders. Depression is best known (Rabins and Pearlson, 1994), but there is growing recognition of an association between this phenomenon and mania. Broadhead and Jacoby (1990) found older patients performed more poorly on tests of cognition than did younger manic patients, with 32% of the elderly manics scoring in the demented range of the Kendrick Battery. Berrios and Bakshi (1991) reported that older manics, in comparison to depressed individuals and controls were more likely to be cognitively and psychosocially impaired, confused, and behaviorally disordered.

This reversible cognitive impairment of mania may presage a permanent dementing illness, and some data suggest that older age of onset is associated with greater likelihood of developing permanent cognitive impairment. Stone (1989) found that 60% of the elderly manic patients with "cerebral organic impairment" and impaired memory had a later age of onset of mania than those without impaired memory. This may be explained by the higher rate of secondary mania in this group of patients with brain disease. Dhingra and Rabins (1991) and Shulman et al. (1992) reported higher than expected rates of dementia in bipolar subjects on long-term follow-up.

CLINICAL COURSE AND PROGNOSIS

Data on the course of mania or bipolar illness in the elderly is sparse. Carlson et al. (1977) examined the course of a mixed-age manic patient population of patients and reported that the mean episode frequency per year did not differ by age. Likewise, Angst (1987) and Winokur (1975) found few differences in disease course between early- and late-onset patients in retrospective studies. In contrast, however, Eagles and Whalley (1985) found that the number of hospitalizations for mania increases with age.

In 1955 Roth reported a poor outcome for elderly patients over the age of 65 with mania. At 2-year follow-up 65% of the elderly manic patients remained hospitalized, a far worse prognosis for the elderly depressed patients. Subsequent studies suggest that the prognosis has improved (Yassa et al., 1988). For example, Glasser and Rabins (1984) reported a much improved prognosis in 1984, noting that the average length of hospital stay was 23.4 days and that 78.6% of the patients were discharged to home. Stone (1989) reported that only 8% of elderly manic patients remained hospitalized at a 6-month follow-up. Nonetheless, Young and Falk (1989) found that older patients responded less quickly and tended to have higher Young Mania Scale scores after 2 weeks of treatment than younger patients. In addition they found older age to correlate with longer hospitalization. Likewise Berrios and Bakshi (1991) found that elderly manic patients had a worse outcome and poorer response to treatment than depressed patients or controls.

Relapse rates are high in late-life mania. Stone (1989) noted a readmission rate of 51.7% in her study of elderly manic patients, Shulman and Post (1980) reported that 75.7% of their patients experienced relapses following the index episode, and Dhingra and Rabins (1991) found a 32% relapse rate over a 5- to 7-year follow-up period. Direct comparisons with young patient samples are needed to determine if these rates are higher than early-life cases because the few studies to date reach different conclusions. One problem in comparing studies is that they vary by number of years of follow-up and by age groups being compared.

Similar variation is present in studies comparing early- and late-onset patients. Dhingra and Rabins (1991) found no difference in relapse rates while Stone (1989) found higher readmission rates for early-onset patients. Conversely, Shulman et al. (1992) reported increased rates of rehospitalization for later-onset manics.

Cognitive dysfunction appears to be another complication of mania in the elderly. Dhingra and Rabins (1991) found that 32% of elderly manics had Mini-Mental State Exam (MMSE) scores below 24 (i.e., the cutoff for cognitive impairment) at 5- to 7-year follow-up. Twenty percent of the patients were so cognitively and functionally impaired that they required nursing home placement. Shulman et al. (1992) reported similar results. In a study with a shorter follow-up period, Charron et al. (1991) reported no evidence of dementia after 2.5 years. As noted above, the reported associations between mania and cognitive impairment in most other studies has been in the midst of the manic episode.

CONCLUSION

There is growing evidence that bipolar illness in the elderly is a heterogenous entity. With increasing age a wider range of factors contribute to etiology, clinical presentation, and outcome. Prospective studies are needed to better understand this illness in the elderly. Questions remain about specific effects that the environment has on presentation and course and about the contributions of changes attributable to normal aging and pathological aging.

REFERENCES

Abraham K (1979): Trans. Bryan D, Strachey A. In "Selected Papers of Karl Abraham." New York: Brunner Mazel.

Ambelas A (1987): Life events and mania: A special relationship? Br J Psychiatry 150:235–240.

Angst J (1987): The course of affective disorders. Intenational Commemerative Symposium— World Health Organization and World Psychiatric Association: Latest findings on the aetiology and therapy of depression (1986, Basel, Switzerland). Psychopathology 19:47–52.

Arnold ES, Rudd SM, Kirshner H (1980): Manic psychosis following rapid withdrawal from Baclofen. Am J Psychiatry 137:1466–1467.

Berrios GE, Bakshi N (1991): Manic and depressive symptoms in the elderly: Their relationships to treatment outcome, cognition and motor symptoms. Psychopathology 24:31–38.

Bogousslavsky J, Ferrazzini M, Regli F, Assal G, Tanabe H, Delaloye-Bischof A (1988): Manic delirium and frontal-like syndrome with paramedian infarction of the right thalamus. J Neurol, Neurosurg Psychiatry 51:116–119.

Broadhead J, Jacoby R (1990): Mania in old age: A first prospective study. Int J Ger Psychiatry 5:215–220.

Burns A, Jacoby R, Levy R (1990): Psychiatric phenomena in Alzheimer's disease. III: Disorder of mood. Br J Psychiatry 157:81–86.

Carlson GA, Davenport YB, Jamison K (1977): A comparison of outcome in adolescent and late-onset bipolar manic–depressive illness. Am J Psychiatry, 134:919–922.

Charron M, Fortin L, Paquette I (1991): De novo mania among elderly people. Acta Psychiatr Scandinav 84:503–507.

Chase GA, Folstein MF, Breitner JCS, Beaty TH, Self SG (1983): The use of life tables and survival analysis in testing genetic hypotheses, with an application to Alzheimer's disease. Am J Epidemiology 117:590–597.

Chawla M, Lindesay J (1993): Polycythaemia, delirium, and mania. Br J Psychiatry 162:833–835.

Clark AF, Davison K (1987): Mania following head injury: A report of two cases and a review of the literature. Br J Psychiatry 150:841–844.

Collins C, Oakley-Browne M (1988): Mania associated with small cell carcinoma of the lung. Australian New Zeal J Psychiatry 22:207–209.

Dhingra U, Rabins PV (1991): Mania in the elderly: A 5-7 year follow-up. J Am Geriatr Soc 39:581–583.

Eagles JM, Whalley LJ (1985): Ageing and affective disorders: The age at first onset of affective disorders in Scotland, 1969–1978. Br J Psychiatry 147:180–187.

Gajula RP, Berlin RM (1993): Letter: Captopril-induced mania. Am J Psychiatry 150:1429–1430.

Glasser M, Rabins P (1984): Mania in the elderly. Age & Ageing 13:210–213.

Goggans FC (1984): A case of mania secondary to vitamin B_{12} deficiency. Am J Psychiatry 141:300–301.

Hubain PP, Sobolski J, Mendlewicz J (1982): Cimetidine-induced mania. Neuropsychobiology 8:223–224.

Joffe RT, Lippert GP, Gray TA, Sawa G, Horrath Z (1987): Mood disorder and multiple sclerosis. Arch Neurol 44:376–378.

Jorge RE, Robinson RG, Starkstein SE, Arndt SV, Forrester AW, Geisler FH (1993): Secondary mania following traumatic brain injury. Am J Psychiatry 150:916–921.

Josephson AM, Mackenzie TB (1980): Thyroid-induced mania in hypothyroid patients. Br J Psychiatry 137:222–228.

Krauthammer C, Klerman GL (1978): Secondary mania: Manic syndromes associated with antecedent illness or drugs. Arch Gen Psychiatry 35:1333–1339.

Kwentus JA, Silverman JJ, Sprague M (1984): Manic syndrome after metrizamide myelography. Am J Psychiatry 141:700–702.

Lewin BD (1950): "The Psychoanalysis of Elation." New York: Norton.

McDonald WM, Krishnan KRR, Doraiswamy PM, Blazer DG (1991): Occurrence of subcortical hyperintensities in elderly subjects with mania. Psychiatry Res Neuroimaging 40:211–220.

Miller LS, Garde IB, Moses JA, Jr, Zipursky RB, Kravitz K, Faustman WO (1992): Letter: Head injury and mood disturbance. J Clin Psychiatry 53:171–172.

Moak GS (1990): Characteristics of demented and non-demented geriatric admissions to a state hospital. Hosp Comm Psychiatry 41:799–801.

Patten SB, Brager N, Sanders S (1991): Letter: Manic symptoms associated with the use of Captopril. Can J Psychiatry 36:314–315.

Patten SB, Klein GM, Lussier C, Sawa R (1989): Organic mania induced by phenytoin: A case report. Can J Psychiatry 34:827–828.

Petrie WM, Lawson EC, Hollender MH (1982): Violence in geriatric patients. JAMA 248:443–444.

Phelan ML (1989) Letter: Beclomethasone mania. Br J Psychiatry 155:871–872.

Post F (1965): "The Clinical Psychiatry of Late Life." New York: Pergamon Press, pp 79–82.

Rabins PV, Pearlson GD (1994): Depression induced cognitive impairment. In Burns A, Levy R, (eds): Dementia. London: Chapman & Hall Medical, pp 667–679.

Rice H, Haltzman S, Tucek C (1988): Letter: Mania associated with procainamide. Am J Psychiatry 145:129–130.

Rigby J, Harvey M, Davies DR (1989): Mania precipitated by benzodiazepine withdrawal. Acta Psychiatr Scandinav 79:406–407.

Robinson RG, Starkstein SE (1989): Mood disorders following stroke: New findings and future directions. J Geriatr Psychiatry 22:1–15.

Robinson RG, Boston JD, Starkstein SE, Price TR (1988): Comparison of mania and depression after brain injury: Causal factors. Am J Psychiatry 145:172–178.

Rosen LN, Rosenthal NE, Van Dusen PH, Dunner DL, Fieve RR (1983): Age at onset and number of psychotic symptoms in bipolar I and schizoaffective disorder. Am J Psychiatry 140:1523–1524.

Roth M (1955): The natural history of mental disorder in old age. J Mental Sci 101:281–301.

Shulman K, Post F (1980): Bipolar affective disorder in old age. Br J Psychiatry 136:26–32.

Shulman KI, Tohen M, Satlin A, Mallya G, Kalunian D (1992): Mania compared with unipolar depression in old age. Am J Psychiatry 149:341–345.

Slater E, Roth M (1977): In Mayer-Gross W, Slater E (eds): "Clinical Psychiatry," 3rd ed. London: Bailliere, Tindall and Cassell, pp 571–572, 600.

Slavney PR, Rich GB, Pearlson GD, McHugh PR (1977): Phencyclidine abuse and symptomatic mania. Biol Psychiatry 12:697–700.

Snowden J (1991): A retrospective case-note study of bipolar disorder in old age. Br. J Psychiatry 158:485–490.

Starkstein SE, Fedoroff P, Berthier ML, Robinson RG (1991): Manic–depressive and pure manic states after brain lesions. Biological Psychiatry 29:149–158.

Starkstein SE, Mayberg HS, Berthier ML, Fedoroff P, Price TR, Dannals RF, Wagner HN, Liguarda R, Robinson RG (1990): Mania after brain injury: Neuroradiologic and metabolic findings. Ann Neurol 27:652–659.

Starkstein SE, Boston JD, Robinson RG (1988): Mechanisms of mania after brain injury; 12 case reports and review of the literature. J Nerv Mental Disease 176:87–100.

Starkstein SE, Pearlson GD, Boston J, Robinson RG (1987): Mania after brain injury: A controlled study of causative factors. Arch Neurol 44:1069–1073.

Stewart JJ (1992): Letter: A case of mania associated with high-dose baclofen therapy. J Clin Psychopharmacol 12:215–217.

Stone K (1989): Mania in the elderly. Br J Psychiatry 155:220–224.

Tohen M, Shulman KI, Satlin A (1994): First-episode mania in late life. Am J Psychiatry 151:130–132.

Walter-Ryan WG (1983): Letter: Mania with onset in the ninth decade. J Clin Psychiatry 44:430–431.

Weissman MM, Bruce ML, Leak PJ, Florio LP, Holzer C III (1990): Affective disorders. In Robins LN, Regier, DA (eds): "Psychiatric Disorders in America: The Epidemiologic Catchment Area Study." New York: Free Press, pp 53–80.5.

Winokur G (1975): The Iowa 500: Heterogeneity and course in manic–depressive illness (bipolar). Comp Psychiatry 16:125–131.

Yassa R, Nair V, Nastase C, Camille Y, Belzile L (1988): Prevalence of bipolar disorder in a psychogeriatric population. J Affect Disord 14:197–201.

Young RC, Falk JR (1989): Age, manic psychopathology and treatment response. Int J Geriatr Psychiatry 4:73–78.

Young RL, Schreiber MT, Nysewander RW (1983): Psychotic mania. Biol Psychiatry 18:1167–1173.

CHAPTER 20

Outcome Studies of Mania in Old Age

KENNETH I. SHULMAN and MAURICIO TOHEN

Department of Psychiatry, Sunnybrook Health Science Centre, University of Toronto, Toronto, Canada, M4N 3M5 (K.I.S.); McLean Hospital, Harvard University, Belmont, MA 02178-9106 (M.T.)

INTRODUCTION

Data on outcome of mania in the elderly is still very limited and comes essentially from two retrospective cohort studies (Dhingra and Rabins, 1991; Shulman et al., 1992b). Both studies followed patients for approximately the same period of time subsequent to the index admission; that is, 5–7 years and 3–10 years, respectively, averaging approximately 6 years of follow-up. A naturalistic cross-sectional study by Berrios and Bhakshi (1991) provides limited data on outcome that was rated in a "global" fashion by clinicians following the index admission. Dhingra and Rabins (1991) monitored outcome in terms of mortality, rehospitalization, and also attempted to reassess mood state and cognitive function. In contrast, Shulman et al. (1992b) monitored only mortality rates and rehospitalization.

DHINGRA AND RABINS (1991)

Dhingra and Rabins (1991) were able to trace 38 of 42 hospitalized elderly manic patients after a 5- to 7-year follow-up. They determined that 13 out of 38 (34%) died while the outcome was unknown in 4 of the 42 patients. If we assume that all 4, who were untraced, had died at follow-up, then the mortality rate becomes 40% in this sample after an average 6-year follow-up. No comparison groups were used.

Of the 38 patients they were able to trace, 25 agreed to be interviewed and examined. On assessment of mood state, 18 out of 25 (72%) were considered euthymic while 4 out of 25 (16%) were clinically depressed, and 3 out of 25 (12%) were either hypomanic or manic at the time of follow-up. Relapse requiring hospitalization occurred in 8 out of 25 patients who were interviewed. On assessment of cognitive function, 32% had a Mini-Mental State score of less than 24, indicating significant cognitive impairment. Of those interviewed, 5 out of 25 (20%) were living in nursing homes. Thus of the 42

Mood Disorders Across the Life Span, Edited by Shulman, Tohen, and Kutcher
ISBN 0-471-10477-9 © 1996 Wiley-Liss, Inc.

original patients, they were able to determine that 20 out of 42 (48%) were still living in the community. No differences in mortality rates or prevalence of dementia was elicited by differential age of onset, and the authors felt that mania is not an early manifestation of dementia reinforcing the conclusion of other authors (Shulman and Post, 1980). Compared to Sir Martin Roth's classic study in 1955, Dhingra and Rabins concluded that the prognosis for mania in old age had improved. In Roth's original study, only 35% of the sample were still living outside the hospital after only a 2-year follow-up.

SHULMAN ET AL. (1992b)

Shulman et al. (1992b) followed 50 elderly manic inpatients consecutively admitted to the McLean Hospital and compared them to a group of age- and sex-matched patients with unipolar depression. Mortality rates were compared by survival analysis (Figure 1), and it was clear that there was an increased mortality for elderly manics compared to depressives after controlling for age, sex, previous episodes, and even neurological disorders. At the end of an average 6-year follow-up (range 3–10 years), 25 out of the 50 (50%) of the manic patients were dead compared to only 10 of 50 (20%) of the depressives. Using survival analysis, the authors determined that after 10 years of follow-up, the probability of remaining alive for the depressive group was 75% compared to only 30% for the manic group. Even after surviving for 5 years, the manic group's probability of remaining alive for an additional 5 years was 54% compared

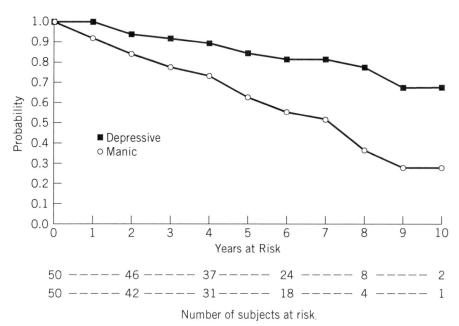

FIGURE 1. Mortality rates for elderly manics compared to depressives. Figure used with permission of the American Journal of Psychiatry.

to a significantly higher 82% for depressives. No attempt was made in the study to characterize the cause of death except for suicide. However, none of the manic patients were determined to have suicided at follow-up compared to only one of the elderly depressives.

Permanent institutionalization occurred earlier and also more frequently in depressives (37%) compared to elderly manics (30%). This suggests that the elderly depressives may have suffered from more chronic and less fatal conditions. Rehospitalization and psychiatric units occurred in 46% of the elderly manics compared to the 32% found in the Dhingra and Rabins study (1991). Neurological disorders were significantly associated with subsequent psychiatric hospitalizations but interestingly did not influence mortality rates.

Tohen et al. (1994) using the original sample of elderly manics, examined the outcome of a subgroup of 14 elderly manic patients whose first episode of mania occurred after age 65. During the follow-up period (3–10 years), 5 of these 14 patients relapsed, all with a manic episode. Furthermore, 4 out of 14 patients were institutionalized in nursing homes while 9 out of 14 required subsequent medical hospitalizations. Being male was a significant predictor of mortality at follow-up. Five out of 6 men (83.3%) died compared to only 1 out of 8 women (12.5%). A neurological disorder was associated with 5 of the 6 patients who died during follow-up. Compared to the multiple-episode group of manics, first episode manics in late life did not show a statistically significant difference in outcome.

BERRIOS AND BAKSHI (1991)

Berrios and Bhakshi (1991) recorded a clinical rating of bad outcome in each of their three patient groups, which included 31 depressives, 19 manic patients, and 20 without an affective illness. In their study, 13 out of 19 manic patients were rated as having a bad outcome (68%). This was significantly higher than the depressives who were rated as having a bad outcome in 17 out of 31 cases (54%) and in 4 out of the 20 (20%) of patients without affective illness on their inpatient psychogeriatric unit. While these are coarse measures, they do contribute to the clinical impression that manic symptoms and syndromes in old age do carry a relatively poor prognosis.

DISCUSSION

While data is still limited, it would appear that there is reasonable evidence to conclude that mania in old age carries with it significant morbidity and mortality even when compared to age- and sex-matched elderly depressives who themselves have been shown to have high rates of recurrence, morbidity, and mortality (Jacoby and Levy, 1980; Murphy, 1983; Katona, 1994). The association with a heterogenous group of neurological disorders (Shulman et al., 1992b), especially cerebrovascular disease, is a likely cause of both the high morbidity and mortality. Late-onset mania carries a lower but still significant familial predisposition, but it also carries a very high prevalence of neurological disorders and a poor outcome, especially in males.

Information on outcome comes exclusively from retrospective cohort or brief prospective studies. It is now necessary to turn to larger sample prospective studies that can identify variables that may predict outcome in this vulnerable population. In light of the treated prevalence of eight elderly manic patients per year on a typical psychogeriatric inpatient unit (Shulman et al., 1992a), it will be necessary to conduct multicenter studies in order to gain sufficient statistical power or meaningful data.

As funding for health services becomes tied to severity and outcome indicators, this type of information becomes increasingly important to providers and purchasers of health care. The burden of mania and depressive disorders on our health care system is increasingly evident and requires more careful characterization.

REFERENCES

Berrios GE, Bakshi N (1991): Manic and depressive symptoms in the elderly: Their relationships to treatment outcome, cognition and motor symptoms. Psychopathology 24:31–38.

Dhingra U, Rabins PV (1991): Mania in the elderly: a 5–7 year follow-up. JAGS 39:581–583.

Jacoby RJ, Levy R (1980) Computed tomography in the elderly. 3. Affective disorder. Br J Psychiatry 136:270–275.

Katona CLE (1994): "Depression in Old Age." New York: Wiley.

Murphy E (1983): The prognosis of depression in old age. Br J Psychiatry 42:111–119.

Roth M (1955): The natural history of mental disorder in old age. J Ment Sci 101:281–301.

Shulman KI, Post F (1980): Bipolar disorder in old age. Br J Psychiatry 136:26–32.

Shulman KI, Tohen M, Satlin A (1992a): Mania revisited. In Arie A (ed): "Recent Advances in Psychogeriatrics." London: Churchill Livingstone, pp 71–79.

Shulman KI, Tohen M, Satlin A, Mallya G, Kalunian D (1992b): Mania compared to unipolar depression in old age. Am J Psychiatry 149(3):341–345.

Tohen M, Shulman KI, Satlin A (1994): First-episode mania in late life. Am J Psychiatry 151(1):130–132.

CHAPTER 21

Treatment of Geriatric Mania

ROBERT C. YOUNG

The New York Hospital and Cornell Institute of Geriatric Psychiatry, Westchester Division, White Plains, NY 10605

INTRODUCTION

Manic syndromes comprise 5–10% of geriatric patients presenting for treatment of affective disorders (Yassa et al., 1988). Therefore, with continuing growth of the geriatric population clinicians are faced increasingly often with such patients. Their management has been ، relatively neglected area of investigation, however. Much of the limited available literature is in the form of case reports or case studies, and few studies have been designed to answer pharmacodynamic questions. Nevertheless, this chapter will review broad principles of treatment, discuss available data, and emphasize areas most in need of future study.

The management of mania in the elderly is in many ways similar to that in younger patients. For example, the same somatic treatments can be effective in elderly as in younger patients. Efforts are similarly directed at acute suppression of symptoms, at continuation of treatment to prevent immediate relapse, and at long-term maintenance.

Differences in emphasis between geriatric and younger patients include the necessity of excluding mood disorder due to medical conditions as well as substance-induced mood disorders in geriatric patients, especially those with first episodes or late age at onset of illness (Young and Klerman, 1992). Weighing of risks and benefits of treatments, essential in all patients, is also highlighted in geriatric patients.

GENERAL ACUTE MANAGEMENT CONSIDERATIONS

Assessment

History Documentation of both course of psychiatric illness and its prior treatment are fundamental to management. The differential diagnosis of geriatric patients with manic syndromes includes bipolar disorder, delusional disorder, schizoaffective disor-

Mood Disorders Across the Life Span, Edited by Shulman, Tohen, and Kutcherᶜ
ISBN 0-471-10477-9   © 1996 Wiley-Liss, Inc.

der, mood disorder due to medical condition, substance-induced mood disorder, dementia, and delirium. Clarification of diagnosis will rest on history.

History of medical conditions, their treatment, and their chronology relative to the manic syndrome will identify potential etiologic factors. It will also inform selection of psychotropic agents and highlight side effects of particular concern in the individual patients. Sources of information will necessarily include family, other caregivers, and medical records.

Information regarding course of psychiatric illness assists in setting priorities as regards evaluation for "organic" factors in manic patients. In mixed-age patients, onset of manic episode for the first time after age 40 is associated with medical and neurologic illnesses and drug treatments (Krauthammer and Klerman, 1978), which may be addressed in an effort to reduce psychopathology. In geriatric manic patients, medical disorders or neurologic comorbidity are frequently noted (Shulman and Post, 1980; Stone, 1989).

Knowledge of previous treatment efforts and associated response directs selection of drug treatments. When possible treatment history will include both identification of drugs used, their dose and duration, as well as information concerning drug plasma levels; this information will permit judgments concerning adequacy of previous therapeutic trials. If available, treatment history concerning family members may also suggest anticipated response in the patient.

Examination   Thorough physical and neurologic examinations and a mental status examination are essential in the geriatric manic patient. These, again, assist in consideration of potential etiologic factors and in identification of comorbidity, which will be relevant to psychiatric management.

Mental status examination in the geriatric manic patient prior to treatment includes assessment of psychotic features, level of consciousness, and cognitive performance, in addition to affective state. Pretreatment cognitive performance provides information regarding possible associated dementia or reversible dementia and an index against which to monitor for adverse changes associated with treatment.

Laboratory Tests   Routine evaluation prior to treatment of geriatric manic patients will include laboratory tests directed at differential diagnosis and assessment of comorbid conditions. Factors relevant to specific psychotropic treatments are also assessed, as outlined later in conjunction with each agent described.

Treatment Setting

Manic states can be treated in various settings, but hospitalization is often optimal. Judgment as to whether hospitalization is necessary reflects multiple factors, including overall severity and duration, the patient's physical condition, and the level of available supervision and enforcement of compliance in the existing setting. Hospitalization can provide an opportunity for rapid examination and laboratory assessment, staff expertise in use and evaluation of treatments, restriction of socially damaging behavior, and support of the patient's physical needs.

Environmental, Behavioral, and Interpersonal Aspects of Management

These play a critical role in the acute management of geriatric manic patients. Flexible limitation of environmental/social stimulation through scheduled room restriction can be therapeutic. Interpersonal interactions should have a firm and directive style. Effective communication among staff avoids the "splitting" that can be common with manic patients. When agitation is severe, periods of monitored seclusion may be helpful. Physical restraint is used if necessary.

Effective use of such modalities will allow the most avoidance of, or conservative dosing with, adjunctive medications. This in turn will reduce the toxicities associated with their use.

ACUTE PHARMACOTHERAPY

General Considerations

Available modalities include lithium salts, anticonvulsants, and other agents, and adjunctive psychotropics. Selection of agents is, again, directed by current assessment, prior treatment history, and consideration of comorbid medical conditions. In general, use of multiple drug classes simultaneously should be avoided in favor of monotherapy if clinically feasible. Use of prn (as needed) medications should be minimized in favor of frequent assessment of behavior and changes in standing orders. Multiple divided doses should be avoided when appropriate, as this is frequently not pharmacokinetically rational and is costly in terms of staff time.

Lithium Salts

Lithium salts have been first-line agents for treatment of acute mania in the geriatric age group. The literature concerning their use in the elderly, while limited, is more extensive than that for other agents.

Therapeutic Efficacy Response to lithium in acute mania has not been contrasted with placebo in geriatric patients; in part this reflects ethical concerns. Response to lithium has also not been contrasted in the elderly with response to other drugs.

Available systematic studies have been primarily retrospective analyses (Glasser and Rabins, 1984; Himmelhoch et al., 1980; Stone, 1989); some have included demented patients (Himmelhoch et al., 1980). Treatment studies in mixed-age populations have generally not examined age effects (Shopsin et al., 1975; Stokes et al., 1971; Taylor and Abrams, 1981; Secunda et al., 1985; Swann et al., 1987; Bowden et al., 1994); a naturalistic study that did suggest a weak negative age effect on response did not include many elderly patients (Young and Falk, 1989).

Guidelines for Practice

Pretreatment Assessment A baseline electrocardiogram (ECG) is included to assess sinus node function, because use of lithium salts may be associated with sick sinus syndrome (Roose et al., 1979). This complication might be encountered particularly in older patients with coronary artery disease that has already compromised the sinus node.

Baseline evaluation also includes renal function tests. Serum creatinine is not a sensitive index of renal function. Creatinine clearance can be approximated from age, body weight, and serum creatinine (Friedman et al., 1989) in those patients with renal insufficiency who require careful monitoring and for whom collection of 24-hour urine is not feasible.

Assessment of thyroid status, including thyroid-stimulating hormone (TSH), is especially important in the elderly. Diminished thyroid reserve accompanies aging (Sawin et al., 1985), and lithium antagonizes thyroid gland function.

Dosing   The pharmacokinetics of lithium in the elderly have been studied by Hardy et al. (1987). A number of age-associated factors influence distribution and elimination in this population; these include physiologic changes, diseases, and drugs. Decreased proportion of body water with age influences the distribution of lithium, which is hydrophilic. Decreased volume of distribution may contribute to higher plasma concentrations. Decreases in glomerular filtration rate and renal blood flow can occur with age. Because lithium is renally eliminated, reduction of renal function is associated with decreased lithium clearance and prolongation of its elimination half-life.

Lower lithium doses, by 30–60%, may therefore be required to achieve equivalent plasma lithium levels in elderly compared with younger patients. Changes in doses need to be made more slowly, as steady-state concentrations are reached more slowly (Liptzin, 1984). A conservative approach would be to start with 75–150 mg/day, usually in a single dose (Shulman et al., 1987; Jefferson and Griest, 1979). Alternate day or less frequent dosing can also be used. Jensen et al. (1990) have suggested that using a single nightly dose or 150% of the daily dose every other night reduces side effects and improves compliance without decreasing effectiveness.

The pharmacokinetics of lithium in the elderly can be further influenced by concomitant diseases. Extra caution is required in treating patients who have cardiac disease (Shulman et al., 1987), as this can further decrease renal function. In the presence of renal disease, careful monitoring of plasma lithium levels is required, and lower doses are generally required compared with doses required for elderly patients without renal disease (Jefferson and Griest, 1979; Van der Velde, 1971). Despite persistent controversy, there is no clear evidence that lithium causes or accelerates the course of renal failure in the vast majority of patients (Meyers and Kalayam, 1989). However, a small minority of patients treated with lithium have been identified who develop impaired renal concentrating ability (de Paulo et al., 1981) and/or diminished glomerular function that may progress to insufficiency (Gitlin, 1993).

The pharmacokinetics of lithium can be altered by other drugs (Shulman et al., 1987; Jefferson et al., 1981; Goodwin and Jamison, 1990). Thiazide diuretics block reabsorption of sodium in the distal tubule, leading to increased proximal reabsorption of both sodium and lithium and an increase in lithium plasma levels by 33% or more. Furosemide, a loop diuretic, has no significant effect on plasma lithium levels (Crabtree et al., 1991). Amiloride, a potassium-sparing diuretic, has less of this effect than thiazides.

Nonsteroidal antiinflammatory drugs are commonly used by elderly patients. Some of these agents diminish renal clearance of lithium by nearly 50% (Jefferson et al., 1981). Availability of over-the-counter forms of these agents emphasizes the need to instruct elderly patients and caregivers not to begin any new medication without prior discussion.

A few cases of elevated lithium levels in association with use of angiotensin-converting enzyme (ACE) inhibitors have been reported. A study of lithium combined with enalapril in 10 healthy young volunteers failed to find an effect of the ACE inhibitor, although one subject did have a 31% increased lithium level (Das Gupta et al., 1992). Clinicians are advised to monitor lithium levels carefully when an ACE inhibitor is added to a patient's regimen.

Lithium pharmacodynamics, that is, the relationship between specific plasma concentrations and therapeutic or toxic responses, is not well understood in the elderly, despite clinical lore suggesting "increased sensitivity." As regards acute efficacy, case reports (Schaffer and Garvey, 1984) have suggested response in geriatric manics at lower levels (e.g., 0.4–0.8 mEq/L) than are optimal in mixed-age adults. However, a recent study of naturalistic treatment suggested better response to higher lithium levels in both younger and geriatric patients (Young et al., 1992).

Toxicity   The adverse effects of lithium can involve many organ systems. Many toxic effects of lithium are probably both concentration and time dependent, but since these issues are not well understood in the elderly, this discussion will approach toxic effects based on the treatment context in which they are reported.

Increased vulnerability to lithium toxicity on the basis of age per se has been suggested (Van der Velde, 1971; Strayhorn and Nash, 1977). This has not been adequately tested. In most studies that have compared older and younger patients, lithium levels have not been comparable in the two groups; thus, pharmacokinetic factors confound the examination of pharmacodynamic differences (Mirchandani and Young, 1993). Smith and Helms (1982) did compare elderly and young adults treated with comparable lithium levels. They noted no difference in total side effects, but there was an excess of serious side effects in the elderly patients.

Medical and neurologic illness may predispose elderly patients to lithium toxicity. Concomitant medications may do the same.

Central Nervous System Effects   Delirium can occur during lithium treatment. Elderly patients, especially those with neurologic illness including extrapyramidal disease, can develop delirium at lithium levels at or below the usual therapeutic range for younger patients (Schaffer and Garvey, 1984; Strayhorn and Nash, 1977). Foster et al. (1990) have suggested that elevated erythrocyte lithium levels might predict neurotoxicity in elderly patients, but point out the need for systematic studies. Combined treatment with neuroleptics even at low doses may be another risk factor for neurotoxicity in the elderly (Liptzin, 1984; Miller et al., 1986).

Delirium and other neurologic sequelae, such as cerebellar dysfunction, can last for weeks after lithium levels are undetectable in elderly patients (Schou, 1984; de Paulo et al., 1982; Nambudiri et al., 1991; Hansen and Amdisen, 1978). Electroencephalographic changes can persist longer than clinical effects (de Paulo et al., 1982).

There is scant literature concerning lithium and cognitive function in nondelirious elderly patients. Lithium may adversely affect cognitive performance in mixed-age patients (Shaw et al., 1985) and normal controls (Judd et al., 1977); however, the literature is conflicting (Jefferson et al., 1987a). The potential effects of mood state itself on cognitive performance need to be taken into account. In demented elderly patients without affective disorder, cognitive performance is not improved or can be worsened by lithium treatment (Kelwala et al., 1984). Systematic studies of effects of lithium on cognition in geriatric manic patients with and without dementia are needed.

Lithium-induced tremor is dependent on dose and concentration. In elderly patients, tremor may occur more often than in younger patients at equivalent plasma concentrations (Murray et al., 1983). Lithium can worsen preexisting Parkinson's disease in geriatric psychiatric patients. Extrapyramidal side effects can also occur *de novo* in elderly patients treated with lithium (Jefferson, 1983).

Endocrine Effects Lithium can suppress thyroid function and elevation in TSH levels is then noted (Vestergaard, 1983). Although subclinical hypothyroidism is associated with increased age, it is not clear whether there is an increased vulnerability to effects of lithium on thyroid function in the elderly.

Gastrointestinal Effects Liptzin (1984) has suggested that gastric irritation associated with lithium treatment is more often a problem in the elderly. Systematic evidence for this is lacking.

Cardiovascular Effects In mixed-age patients, the effects of lithium on cardiac function and ECG include dose-dependent T-wave flattening or inversion, sinus node dysfunction, lengthening of PR interval, and ventricular arrhythmias (Jefferson et al., 1987b; Csernansky and Hollister, 1985). Bushey et al. (1963) reported that 3 of 12 elderly nursing home patients chronically treated with lithium had significant sinus bradycardia; it is difficult to interpret these findings, however. Preexisting sinus node disease may increase the risk of sinus node dysfunction associated with lithium treatment (Roose et al., 1979); drugs used to treat cardiovascular disease, such as digitalis and beta blockers, may also increase this risk. It is prudent therefore not only to obtain baseline ECG in older adults before prescribing lithium but also to monitor the ECG and pulse during treatment.

Renal Effects Lithium can reduce tubular concentrating ability (Lazarus, 1986). Reversible, nephrogenic diabetes insipidus may compound age-related decline in renal concentrating ability. In elderly patients with other urologic dysfunction this may lead to incontinence.

Other Effects The possibility of lithium-associated acceleration of lenticular opacification was raised by a report by Makeeva et al. (1975) who noted such changes in 3 of 7 elderly patients. A causal relationship cannot be established based on such case report material, however.

Other Clinical Situations Neurologic status, including extrapyramidal syndromes and dementia, but not age, predicted delayed and/or poor treatment response, including lithium-induced neurotoxicity in the report of Himmelhoch and associates (1980); lithium levels were not specified. Black et al. (1988) reported that "complicated" manias, that is, those with coexisting nonaffective psychiatric illness or with serious medical illness, had poorer immediate response to lithium. Shukla and colleagues (1987) also reported that mixed-age patients with "secondary manias" had a relatively poor acute lithium response.

Anticonvulsants

Valproate and carbamazepine have been used as alternatives for treatment of mania in young adults. The efficacy of valproate in acute mania has recently been demonstrated (Bowden et al., 1994; Pope et al., 1991). The literature concerning clonazepam monotherapy in manic patients is very limited. Anticonvulsants have been used most often in patients with poor tolerance of, or failure to respond to, lithium salts or contraindication to lithium.

Therapeutic Efficacy   There are no placebo-controlled studies of the efficacy of anticonvulsant drugs in geriatric mania. A case report literature suggests that valproate as adjunctive treatment or as monotherapy can be helpful in geriatric manic patients (McFarland et al., 1990; Gnam and Flint, 1993). The literature concerning carbamazepine in the elderly is also limited to case reports (Kellner and Neher, 1991, Schneier and Kahn, 1990). There are apparently no reports concerning clonazepam treatment in the elderly.

Guidelines for Practice

Pretreatment Assessment   Patients treated with carbamazepine or valproic acid should undergo baseline hematologic assessment and liver function tests. In patients being considered for carbamazepine treatment, an ECG should be obtained.

Dosing   Optimal dosing with these agents has not been established in geriatric patients. Relationships between carbamazepine and valproate plasma concentrations and antimanic response are not well delineated in any age group. Active metabolites of these compounds are generated.

Valproate has a shorter half-life than carbamazepine and multiple daily dosing is necessary. Valproate is highly bound to albumin, and protein binding is dose dependent. Higher free fraction of valproate with age has been reported, but its clinical significance is not known (Rimmer and Richens, 1985).

Clinicians need to be alert to the potential for drug–drug interaction associated with anticonvulsant use. Valproate can inhibit hepatic enzymes and thereby decrease metabolism of some concomitantly administered drugs. Carbamazepine on the other hand induces hepatic enzyme activity and thereby can increase metabolism of other drugs.

Toxicity   Valproate can be well tolerated in the elderly. Sedative and anticholinergic effects are relatively weak. Minimal cognitive toxicity on neuropsychological testing was reported by Craig and Tallis (1994) in a series of geriatric patients with seizure disorder. Inhibition of platelet production and function can occur. Hepatic enzyme elevations, usually of mild degree, can be noted. Valproate has also been well tolerated in a small case report literature in demented elderly.

Carbamazepine can cause sedation, confusion, ataxia, and sialorrhea. Direct comparisons of carbamazepine with valproate are needed to assess whether carbamazepine is less well tolerated in the elderly, as has been suggested. Central nervous system side effects are generally dose dependent and occur particularly at concentrations above 9 μg/mL (Schneier and Khan, 1990). It also has quinidine-like properties, and prolongation of cardiac conduction time can occur in the therapeutic context; therefore, an ECG should be repeated during treatment. Hepatic enzyme elevations can occur, usually small and transient. In view of the possibility of agranulocytosis, complete blood count should be monitored; slight reduction in leukocyte count occurs frequently.

The toxicity profile of clonazepam is that of benzodiazepines. No literature dealing with clonazepam toxicity in the elderly has been available.

Other Clinical Situations   Mazure et al. (1992) reported that adjunctive use of valproate can be helpful in patients with organic mental syndromes and behavioral disorders; valproate concentrations were below the anticonvulsant range. Mellow et al. (1993) noted that valproate produced sustained improvement in 2 of 4 demented patients who were agitated and aggressive.

Gleason and Schneider (1990) reported that hostility and irritability were improved in an open study of carbamazepine in probable Alzheimer patients. However, Chambers et al. (1982) reported a placebo-controlled trial in 19 patients with dementia and noted toxicity but no benefit.

Adjunctive Medication

Neuroleptics   Neuroleptic medications continue to have a role as pharmacologie adjuncts in initial management of acute mania. They have not been studied systematically in this context in the elderly. In this age group, concerns regarding toxicity include sedation, orthostatic hypotension, adverse cognitive effects, peripheral anticholinergic side effects, acute extrapyramidal reactions, and tardive dyskinesia. As low a dosage should be used as possible. Neuroleptics should be viewed as temporary measures; tapering of dosage and discontinuation prior to discharge should be attempted. Selection of low-dose, high-potency neuroleptics such as haloperidol will minimize anticholinergic and hypotensive effects, but extrapyramidal toxicity can be expected.

Recently, new neuroleptic agents have been introduced that may have differing toxicity profiles. Risperidone is an atypical agent with serotonergic as well as dopaminergic receptor antagonist properties. It may have lower propensity for extrapyramidal side effects and anticholinergic effects than typical neuroleptics. There is little data available concerning risperidone use in the elderly. Clozapine also has a relatively low propensity for extrapyramidal side effects and can be useful in neuroleptic refractory patients (Bajulaiye and Addonizio, 1992; Ball, 1992; Oberholzer et al., 1992; Salzman et al., 1995; Frankenburg and Kalunian, 1994). However, it has potent anticholinergic properties, and lethargy, sedation, respiratory distress, and leukopenia have been noted despite low dosages in the elderly; agranulocytosis is a risk. Thus, while risperidone and clozapine each have potential advantages, their efficacy, dosing requirements, and relative risks await systematic assessment in the elderly.

Benzodiazepines   Benzodiazepines including lorazepam and clonazepam have both been reported to be useful in younger manic patients; nevertheless, high dropout rates in recent studies of acute mania (Bowden et al., 1994; Pope et al., 1991) suggest limited efficacy. They have not been studied systematically in elderly manic patients. In the elderly, the clinician must be vigilant for sedation, ataxia, cognitive toxicity, and paradoxical disinhibition. Use of long-acting agents with active metabolites should be avoided.

Other Agents

Calcium Channel Blockers   Calcium channel blockers such as verapamil have received limited study as antimanic agents (Aldenhoff et al., 1986). Dubovsky et al. (1986) have reported on a small number of manic patients with dementia in whom verapamil was effective and well tolerated. Special concerns regarding verapamil in elderly patients, particularly those with cardiovascular disease, include potential associated hypotension, bradycardia, and intracardiac conduction prolongation; the latter may be potentiated if verapamil is given in combination with lithium.

ACUTE ELECTROCONVULSIVE THERAPY

Electroconvulsive therapy (ECT) has a clear role in treatment of mixed-age manic patients (Mukherjee et al., 1994). It can reduce length of hospitalization, and it can be life-saving in patients who are poorly tolerant of psychotropic medications and/or have severe psychopathology.

Therapeutic Efficacy Efficacy of ECT in geriatric mania has not received specific study.

Guidelines for Practice

Pretreatment Assessment Physical and neurologic examination and laboratory data should be reviewed when considering ECT to weigh risks and identify special considerations for anethesia and monitoring. Patients with intracranial mass lesions or unstable cardiovascular states are at highest risk.

Dosing There are contradictory reports concerning electrode placement and efficacy of ECT in mania (Mukherjee et al., 1994). It has been suggested that, pending further evidence, bilateral electrode placement is recommended. Cognitive side effects in the elderly can be managed by reducing frequency of treatments; if necessary, unilateral electrode placement can be utilized.

Concurrent lithium with ECT can increase severity of post-ECT confusion, memory loss, delirium, and can prolong seizures (Alexopoulos et al., 1989; El-Mallabh, 1988; Penney et al., 1990; Abrams, 1988). Abrams (1988) has pointed out that lithium treatment concurrent with ECT can prolong muscular blockade of succinyl choline. Thus, the risks of continuing lithium during ECT in the elderly are significant, and benefits have not been established.

Toxicity The safety of ECT in geriatric patients with major depression has been discussed in the case report literature already cited.

Other Clinical Situations Coexisting dementia syndrome is not a contraindication to ECT in geriatric patients. Clinicians must be alert to possible increased ECT-associated confusion.

CONTINUATION AND MAINTENANCE TREATMENT

General Considerations

Continuation treatment means its extension immediately following resolution of the acute episode to prevent relapse. *Maintenance* treatment refers to more prolonged efforts directed at prevention of recurrence. This distinction is not generally made, however, in the available literature concerning elderly manic patients. There is a great need for studies of continuation and maintenance treatment of mania in the elderly because of possible increasing vulnerability to relapse/recurrence in late-onset illness (Angst et al., 1973) and because of potential complexity associated with comorbidity in the elderly.

Lithium Salts

Therapeutic Efficacy   A number of outpatient investigations have been available but have design limitations confounding interpretation (Mirchandani and Young, 1993). A report by Hewick et al. (1977) is difficult to interpret due to lack of comparable plasma lithium levels in the geriatric and young patient groups. Abou-Saleh and Coppen (1983) noted no difference in affective morbidity over an average of 5 years in elderly compared to younger patients maintained on similar, relatively high lithium levels. Murray et al. (1983) noted some increase in manic psychopathology, but not hospitalizations, in older compared with younger patients in a mixed-age sample that was followed prospectively at equivalent, moderate lithium levels. Stone (1989) found, retrospectively, no difference in hospital readmissions among those geriatric patients who had been treated with lithium and those who were not, but interpretation is limited by the naturalistic design.

Guidelines for Practice

Dosing   Optimum plasma concentrations for lithium continuation or maintenance treatment have not been defined through prospective investigation. Foster and Rosenthal (1980), based on clinical experience, recommended levels of 0.4–0.7 mEq/L for maintenance treatment. Shulman et al. (1987) similarly recommended maintaining levels at approximately 0.5 mEq/L and using a single bedtime dose to reduce nephrotoxicity.

When a decision is made to discontinue lithium, the dose should probably be tapered gradually. Experience in mixed-age patients suggests that abrupt discontinuation may adversely affect outcome (Suppes et al., 1991). There should, of course, be close subsequent clinical monitoring in the elderly patient.

Toxicity   Toxicity in the context of continuation and maintenance treatment has received only preliminary, generally retrospective study in this population. Roose et al. (1979) reported more cardiac sinus node dysfunction and hypothyroidism in elderly compared with younger bipolar patients on comparable moderate lithium levels. In the study of Murray et al. (1983) tremor was more frequent in older patients, but polydipsia and polyuria were unrelated to age. Stone (1989) noted greater than expected toxicity with lithium in the elderly. Chacko et al. (1987) interviewed 19 elderly patients on lithium prophylaxis and reported that gastrointestinal side effects and neurotoxicity were the most frequently encountered problems; these were not significantly bothersome to the patients, however.

Again, clinicians need to be alert to any change in physical health, diet, or medication regimen in geriatric patients. Dosage adjustment may be necessary in these circumstances. Patients and caregivers should be educated regarding these issues in advance.

Laboratory monitoring of geriatric patients maintained on lithium salts should include twice yearly monitoring of renal and thyroid function (Lazarus, 1986; Young and Meyers, 1991). Changes in function have not been assessed in the elderly, however.

As discussed above, the impact of long-term lithium on renal function in mixed-age patients remains controversial (de Paulo et al., 1981; Schou, 1989).

Other Clinical Situations   The implications of comorbid dementia syndromes for continuation and maintenance treatment in elderly manic patients remains to be assessed.

The management of depressive episodes in geriatric bipolar disorders is beyond the scope of this discussion.

Anticonvulsants

The literature concerning anticonvulsants in geriatric patients has not addressed continuation or maintenance treatment. These are priorities for clinical investigation.

Adjunctive Medication

A recent report in mixed-age adults highlights the frequent continuation of neuroleptic use after manic episodes (Sernyak et al., 1994). In geriatric patients the need to minimize long-term use of neuroleptics owing to risks of tardive dyskinesia are apparent. The long-term risks of benzodiazepine use, including tolerance and dependence, also argue strongly for tapering and discontinuation as soon as possible.

Electroconvulsive Therapy

In geriatric manic patients who respond to acute ECT, continuation therapy with a mood stabilizer is generally indicated. Selection of agent will involve review of prior treatment history.

In some cases consideration can be given to ECT in the continuation and maintenance therapy of manic geriatric patients. Yet there has been no data available on the basis of which to make such decisions, in contrast to an emerging case report literature concerning geriatric major depression.

Nonsomatic Treatment Modalities

Psychotherapy   In the long-term management of geriatric patients with recent manic episode, clinical experience suggests that individual or group psychotherapy in the broadest sense can serve important functions. Discussion of the nature of the disorder can be especially necessary in cases with recent onset compared to recurrent cases. Compliance with medication can be enhanced by the patients' understanding of rationale and potential toxicity, and development of an alliance in reporting on symptoms and side effects, and in decision making. The significance of life events as regards the etiology and course of late-life mania needs study (Young and Klerman, 1992); the same is true of differences in personality traits. Psychotherapeutic management can be provided by the psychiatrist and by other disciplines.

Social Structure   Daily rhythms are often irregular in bipolar patients (Halberg, 1968). Recently, investigators have called for studies of the impact of treatment focused on regularizing daily routine in an effort to reduce recurrence of psychopathology

(Ehlers et al., 1988). While ongoing studies are focused on young adults, these issues are equally relevant to geriatric patients.

Family and Caregivers Involvement of family and other caregivers in management is at least as important in geriatric patients as in younger patients. When patients have concomitant cognitive impairment or dementia such involvement becomes crucial; their education concerning the nature of the disorder and its treatment becomes essential to compliance with management. Family and other caregivers are also sources of observational data used in assessing therapeutic effects and drug toxicity.

ACKNOWLEDGMENTS

This work was supported by MH42522, MH001192, and MH49762.

REFERENCES

Abou-Saleh MT, Coppen A (1983): Prognosis of depression in old age: The case for lithium therapy. Br J Psychiatry 143:527–528.

Abrams R (1988): "Electro Convulsive Therapy." New York: Oxford Press.

Aldenhoff JB, Schlegel S, Heuser I, Wetzel H (1986): Antimanic effects of the calcium antagonist D600: A double-blind placebo controlled study. Proceedings of 15th Collegium Internationale Neuro-Psychopharmacologicum Congress.

Alexopoulos GS, Young RC, Abrams RC (1989): ECT in the high-risk geriatric patient. Convul Ther 5:75–87.

Angst J, Baastrup P, Grof P, Hippius H, Poldinger W, Weis P (1973): The course of monopolar and bipolar depression and bipolar psychosis. Psychiat Neurol Neurochir 76:489–500.

Bajulaiye R, Addonizio G (1992): Clozapine in the treatment of psychosis in an 82 year old woman with tardive dyskinesia. J Clin Psychopharmacol 12(5):364–365.

Ball CJ (1992): The use of clozapine in older people. Int J Geriatr Psychiatry 7(9):689–692.

Black DW, Winokur G, Bell S, Nasrallah A, Hulbert J (1988): Complicated mania. Arch Gen Psychiatry 45(3):232–236.

Bowden CL, Brugger AM, Swann AC, Calabrese JR, Janicak PG, Petty F, Dilsaver SC, Dovis JH, Rush AJ, Small JG (1994): Efficacy of Divalproex vs lithium and placebo in the treatment of mania. JAMA 271(12):918–923.

Bushey M, Rotberg V, Bowers MB (1963): Lithium treatment in a very elderly nursing home population. Compr Psychiatry 24:392–396.

Chacko RC, Marsh BJ, Marmion J, Dworkin RJ, Telschow R (1987): Lithium side effects in elderly bipolar outpatients. Hillside J Clin Psychiatry 9(1):79–88.

Chambers CA, Bain J, Rosbottom R, Ballinger BR, Mclaren S (1982): Carbamazepine in senile dementia and overactivity: A placebo controlled double blind trial. IRCS Med Sci 10:505–506.

Crabtree BL, Mack JE, Johnson CD, Amyx BC (1991): Comparison of hydrochlorthiazide and furosemide on lithium disposition. Am J Psychiatry 148:1060–1063.

Craig I, Tallis R (1994): Impact of valproate and phenytoin on cognitive function in elderly patients: Results of a single-blind randomized comparative study. Epilepsia 35(2):381–390.

Csernansky JG, Hollister LE (1985): Using lithium in patients with cardiac and renal disease. Hospital Formulary 20:726–735.

Das Gupta K, Jefferson JW, Kobak KA, Greist JH (1992): The effect of enalapril on serum lithium levels in healthy men. J Clin Psychiatry 53:398–400.

de Paulo JR, Folstein MF, Correa EI (1982): The course of delirium due to lithium intoxication. J Clin Psychiatry 43:447–449.

de Paulo JR, Correa EI, Sapir DG (1981): Renal glomerular function and longterm lithium therapy. Am J Psychiatry 138:3.

Dubovsky SL, Franks RD, Allen S, Murphy J (1986): Calcium antagonists in mania. Psychiatry Res 18:309–320.

Ehlers CL, Frank E, Kupfer DJ (1988): Social zeitgebers and biological rhythms. Arch Gen Psychiatry 45:948–952.

El-Mallabh RS (1988): Complications of concurrent lithium and electroconvulsive therapy: A review of clinical material and theoretical considerations. Biol Psychiatry 23:595–601.

Foster JR, Rosenthal JS (1980): Lithium treatment of the elderly. In Johnson FN (ed): "Handbook of Lithium Therapy." Lancaster, England: MTP Press, pp 414–420.

Foster JR, Silver M, Boksay IJ (1990): Lithium in the elderly: A review with special focus on the use of intraerythrocyte (RBC) levels in detecting serious impending neurotoxicity. Int J Ger Psychiatry 5(1):1–7.

Frankenburg FR, Kalunian D (1994): Clozapine in the elderly. J Ger Psychiatry Neurol 7:129–132.

Friedman JR, Norman DC, Yoshikawa TT (1989): Correlation of estimated renal function parameters versus 24-hour creatinine clearance in ambulatory elderly. J Am Ger Soc 37:145–149.

Gitlin MJ (1993): Lithium-induced renal insufficiency. J Clin Psychopharm 132(4)276–279.

Glasser M, Rabins P (1984): Mania in the elderly. Age Aging 13:210–213.

Gleason RP, Schneider LS (1990): Carbamazepine treatment of agitation in Alzheimer's outpatients refractory to neuroleptics. J Clin Psychiatry 51(3):115–118.

Gnam W, Flint AJ (1993): New onset rapid cycling bipolar disorder in an 87 year old woman. Can J Psychiatry 38(5):324–326.

Goodwin FK, Jamison KR (1990): "Manic–Depressive Illness." New York: Oxford University Press, pp 603–629.

Halberg G (1968): Physiologic considerations underlying rhythmometry with special reference to emotional illness. In De Ajuriaguerra J (ed): "Cycles Biologiques et Psychiatrie." Symposium Bel-Air III. Geneva: Masson et Cie, pp 73–126.

Hansen HE, Amdisen A (1978): Lithium intoxication (report of 23 cases and review of 100 cases from the literature). QJ Med (New Series XLVII) 186:123–144.

Hardy BG, Shulman KI, Mackenzie SE, Kutcher SP, Silverberg JD (1987): Pharmacokinetics of lithium in the elderly. J Clin Psychopharmacol 17:153–158.

Hewick DS, Newburg P, Hopwood S, Naylor G, Moody J (1977): Age as a factor affecting lithium therapy. Br J Clin Pharmacol 4:201–205.

Himmelhoch JM, Neil JF, May SJ, Fuchs SZ, Licata SM (1980): Age, dementia, dyskinesias, and lithium response. Am J Psychiatry 137:941–945.

Jefferson JW (1983): Lithium and affective disorder in the elderly. Compr Psychiatry 24:166–178.

Jefferson JW, Griest JH (1979): Lithium and the kidney. In David JM, Greenblatt D (eds): "Psychopharmacology Update." New York: Grune and Stratton, pp 81–104.

Jefferson JW, Greist JH, Ackerman DL, Carroll JA (1987a): Cardiovascular effects. In "Lithium Encyclopedia for Clinical Practice." Washington DC: American Psychiatric Press, pp 171–179.

Jefferson JW, Greist JH, Ackerman DL, Carroll JA 1987b): "Lithium Encyclopedia for Clinical Practice," 2nd ed. Washington, DC: American Psychiatric Press.

Jefferson JW, Griest JH, Baudhuin M: Lithium (1981): Interactions with other drugs. J Clin Psychopharmacol 1:124–131.

Jensen HV, Olaffson K, Bille A, Anderson J, Mellerup E, Plenge P (1990): Lithium every second day: A new treatment regimen? Lithium 1:55–58.

Judd LL, Hubbard B, Janowsky DS, Huey LY, Takahashi KI (1977): The effect of lithium carbonate on the cognitive functions of normal subjects. Arch Gen Psychiatry 34:355–357.

Kellner MB, Neher F (1991): A first episode of mania after age 80: A case report. Can J Psychiatry 36:607–608.

Kelwala S, Pomara N, Stanley M, Sitaram N, Gershon S (1984): Lithium-induced accentuation of extrapyramidal symptoms in individuals with Alzheimer's disease. J Clin Psychiatry 45:342–344.

Krauthammer C, Klerman G (1978): Secondary mania. Arch Gen Psychiatry 35(11):1333–1339.

Lazarus JH (1986): "Endocrine and Metabolic Effects of Lithium." New York: Plenum.

Liptzin B (1984): Treatment of mania. In Salzman C (ed): "Clinical Geriatric Psychopharmacology." New York: McGraw-Hill, pp 116–131.

Makeeva VL, Gol'davskah IL, Pozdnyakova SL (1975): Somatic changes and side effects from the use of lithium salts in the prevention of affective disorders. Soviet Neurology Psychiatry 7:42–53.

Mazure CM, Druss BG, Cellar JS (1992): Valproate treatment of older psychotic patients with organic mental syndromes and behavioral dyscontrol. J Am Ger Soc 40(9):914–916.

McFarland BH, Miller MR, Straumfjord AA (1990): Valproate use in the older manic patient. J Clin Psychiatry 51(11):479–481.

Mellow AM, Solano-Lopez C, Davis S (1993): Sodium valproate in the treatment of behavioral disturbance in dementia. J Ger Psychiatry Neurol 6(4):205–209.

Meyers B, Kalayam B (1989): Update in geriatric psychopharmacology. Adv Psychosom Med 19:114–137.

Miller F, Menninger J, Whitchup SM (1986): Lithium-neuroleptic neurotoxicity in the elderly bipolar patient. J Clin Psychopharmacol 6:176–178.

Mirchandani I, Young RC (1993): Management of mania in the elderly: An update. Ann Clin Psychiatry 5(1):67–77.

Mukherjee S, Sackeim HA, Schnur DB (1994): Electroconvulsive therapy of acute manic episodes: A review of 50 years' experience. Am J Psychiatry 151(2):169–176.

Murray N, Hopwood S, Balfour DJK, Ogston S, Hewick DS (1983): Influence of age on lithium efficacy and side effects in outpatients. Psychol Med 13:53–60.

Nambudiri DE, Meyers BS, Young RC (1991): Delayed recovery from lithium neurotoxicity. J Ger Psychiat Neurol 4:40–43.

Oberholzer AF, Hendricksen C, Monsch AU, Heierli B, Stahelin HB (1992): Safety and effectiveness of low-dose clozapine in psychogeriatric patients: A preliminary study. Int Psychogeriatrics 4(2):187–195.

Penney JF, Dinwiddie S, Zorumski CF, Wetzel RD (1990): Concurrent and close temporal administration of lithium and ECT. Convul Ther 6:139–145.

Pope HG Jr, McElroy SL, Keck PE Jr, Hudson JI (1991): Valproate in the treatment of acute mania: A placebo-controlled study. Arch Gen Psychiatry 48:62–68.

Rimmer EM, Richens A (1985): An update on sodium valproate. Pharmacotherapy 5(3):171–184.

Roose SP, Bone S, Haidofer C, Dunner DL, Fieve RR (1979): Lithium treatment in older patients. Am J Psychiatry 136(6):843–844.

Salzman C, Vaccaro B, Lieff J, Weiner A (1995): Clozapine in elderly patients with psychosis and behavioral disruption. Am J Ger Psychiatry 3:26–33.

Sawin CT, Castelli WP, Hershman JM, McNamara P, Bacharach P (1985): The aging thyroid: Thyroid deficiency in the Framingham study. Arch Interm Med 145:1386.

Schaffer CB, Garvey MJ (1984): Use of lithium in acutely manic elderly patients. Clin Gerontologist 3:58.

Schneier HA, Khan D (1990): Selective response to carbamazepine in a case of organic mood disorder. J Clin Psychiatry 51(11):485.

Schou M (1989): Lithium prophylaxis: Myths and realities. Am J Psychiatry 146(5):573–576.

Schou M (1984): Long-lasting neurological sequelae after lithium intoxication. Acta Psychiatr Scand 70:594–602.

Secunda SK, Katz MM, Swann A, Koslow SH, Maas JW, Chuang S, Croughan J (1985): Mania: Diagnosis, state measurement, prediction of treatment response. J Affect Disord 8:113–121.

Sernyak MJ, Griffin RA, Johnson RM, Pearsall HR, Wexler BE, Woods SW (1994): Neuroleptic exposure following inpatient treatment of acute mania with lithium and neuroleptic. Am J Psychiatry 151(1):133–135.

Shaw ED, Mann JJ, Stokes PE, Manevitz AZA (1985): Neuropsychological effects of lithium. New Research Abstracts, Annual Meeting, American Psychiatric Association, pp 76, 130.

Shopsin B, Gershon S, Thompson H, Collins P (1975): Psychoactive drugs in mania. Arch Gen Psychiatry 32:34–42.

Shukla S, Hoff A, Aaronson T, Cook BL, Jandorf L (1987): Treatment outcome in organic mania. New Research Program, Annual Meeting, American Psychiatric Association. pg 91, 134.

Shulman K, Post F (1980): Bipolar affective disorders in old age. Br J Psychiatry 136:26–32.

Shulman KI, Mackenzie S, Hardy B (1987): The clinical use of lithium carbonate in old age: A review. Biol Psychiatry 11:159–164.

Smith RE, Helms PM (1982): Adverse effects of lithium therapy in the acutely ill elderly patient. J Clin Psychiatry 43:3.

Stokes PE, Stoll PM, Shamoian CA, Patton MJ (1971): Efficacy of lithium as acute treatment of manic–depressive illness. Lancet 1:1319–1325.

Stone K (1989): Mania in the elderly. Br J Psychiatry 155:220–224.

Strayhorn JM, Nash JL (1977): Severe neurotoxicity despite "therapeutic" serum lithium levels. Dis Nerv Syst 38:107–111.

Suppes T, Baldessarini RJ, Faedda GL, Tohen M (1991): Risk of recurrence following discontinuation of lithium treatment in bipolar disorder. Arch Gen Psychiatry 48:1082–1088.

Swann AC, Koslow SH, Katz MM, Maas JW, Javaid J, Secunda SK, Robins E (1987): Lithium carbonate treatment of mania. Arch Gen Psychiatry 44:345–354.

Taylor MA, Abrams R (1981): Prediction of treatment response in mania. Arch Gen Psychiatry 38:800–803.

Van der Velde CD (1971): Toxicity of lithium carbonate in elderly patients. Am J Psychiatry 127:1075–1077.

Vestergaard P (1983): Clinically important side effects of long term lithium treatment: A review. Acta Psychiatr Scand (Suppl) 67:11–36.

Yassa R, Nair NPV, Iskandar H (1988): Late onset bipolar disorder in psychosis and depression in the elderly. Psychiat Clin No Am 11(1):117–131.

Young RC, Falk JR (1989): Age, manic psychopathology and treatment response. Int J Ger Psychiatry 4:73–78.

Young RC, Klerman GL: Mania in late life (1992): Focus on age at onset. Am J Psychiatry 149:867–876.

Young RC, Meyers BS (1991): Psychopharmacology. In Sadovoy J, Lazarus LW, Jarvik LF (eds): "Comprehensive Review of Geriatric Psychiatry." Washington DC: American Psychiatric Press, pp 453–457.

Young RC, Mattis S, Kalayam B, Tsuboyama G, Alexopoulos GS (1992): Cognitive dysfunction in geriatric mania. Abstracts, Annual Meeting, American Association for Geriatric Psychiatry, p 14.